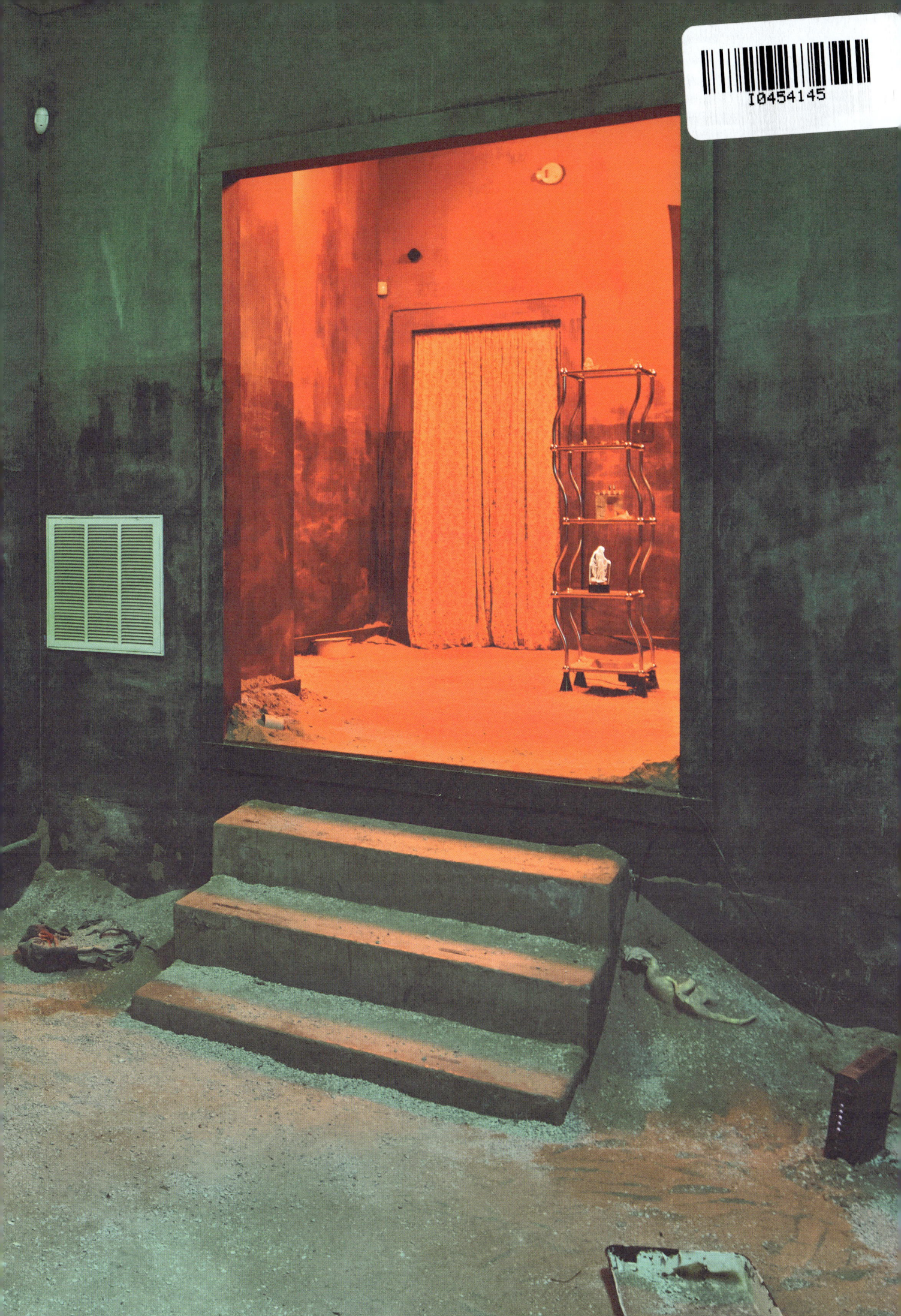

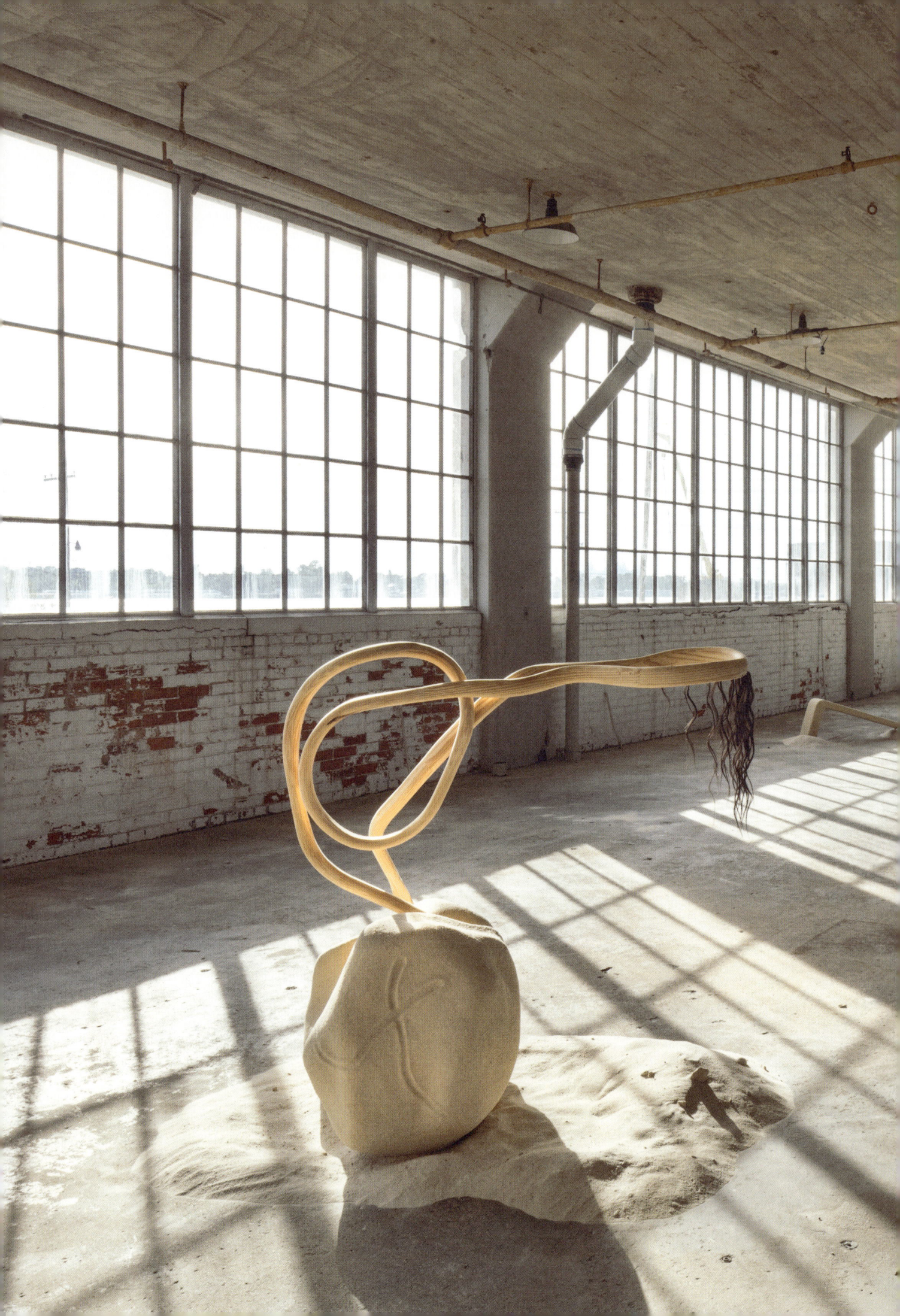

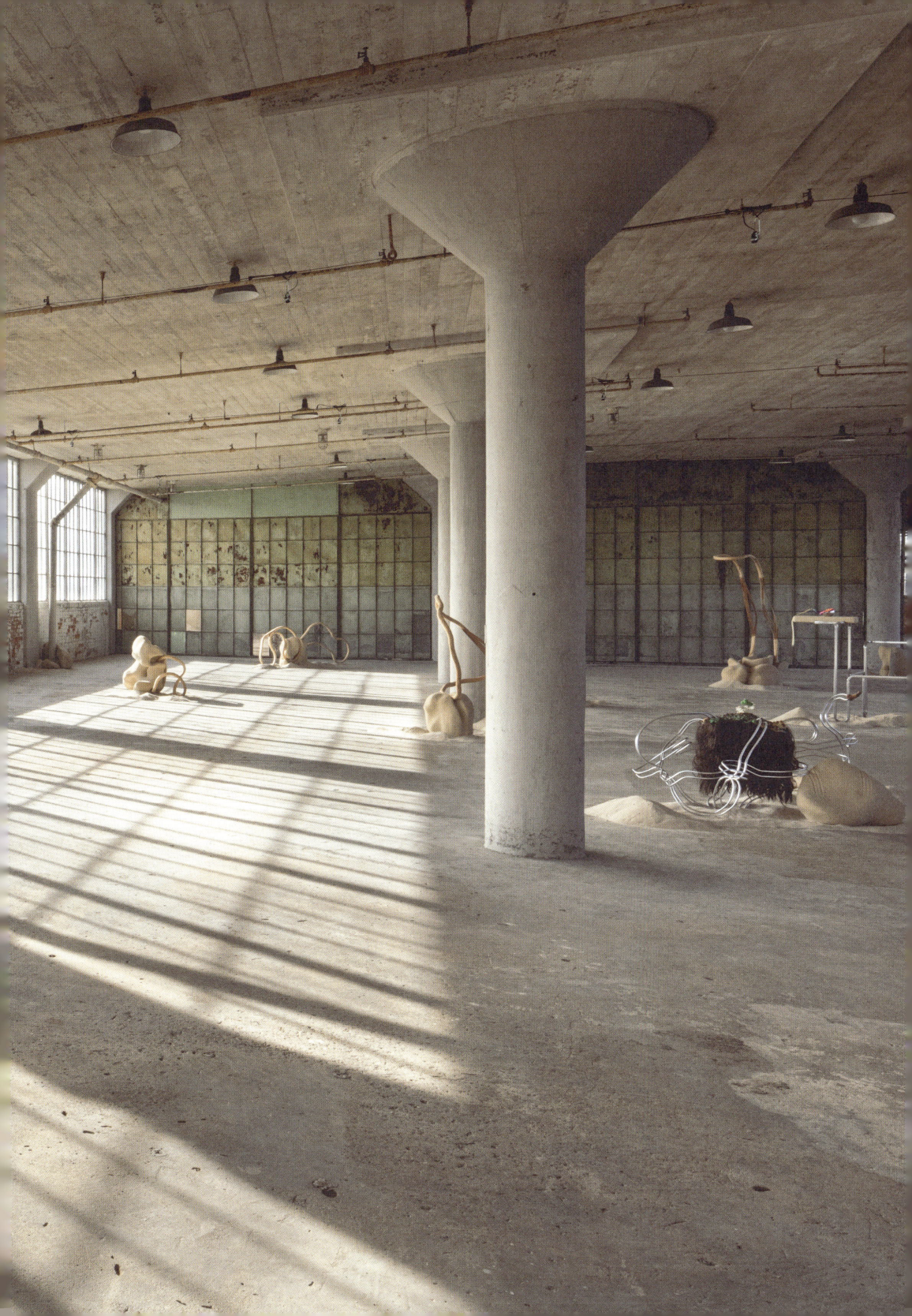

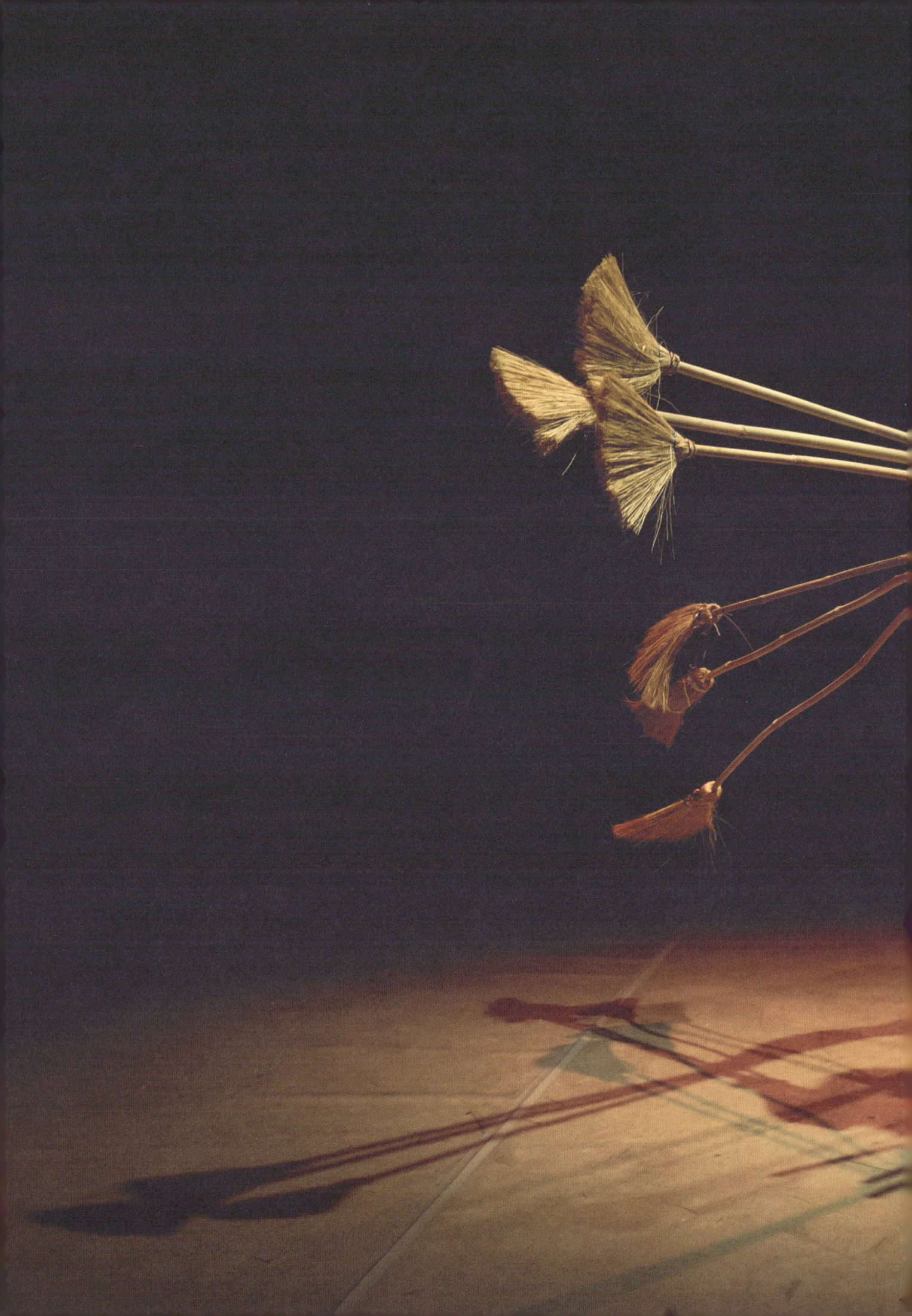

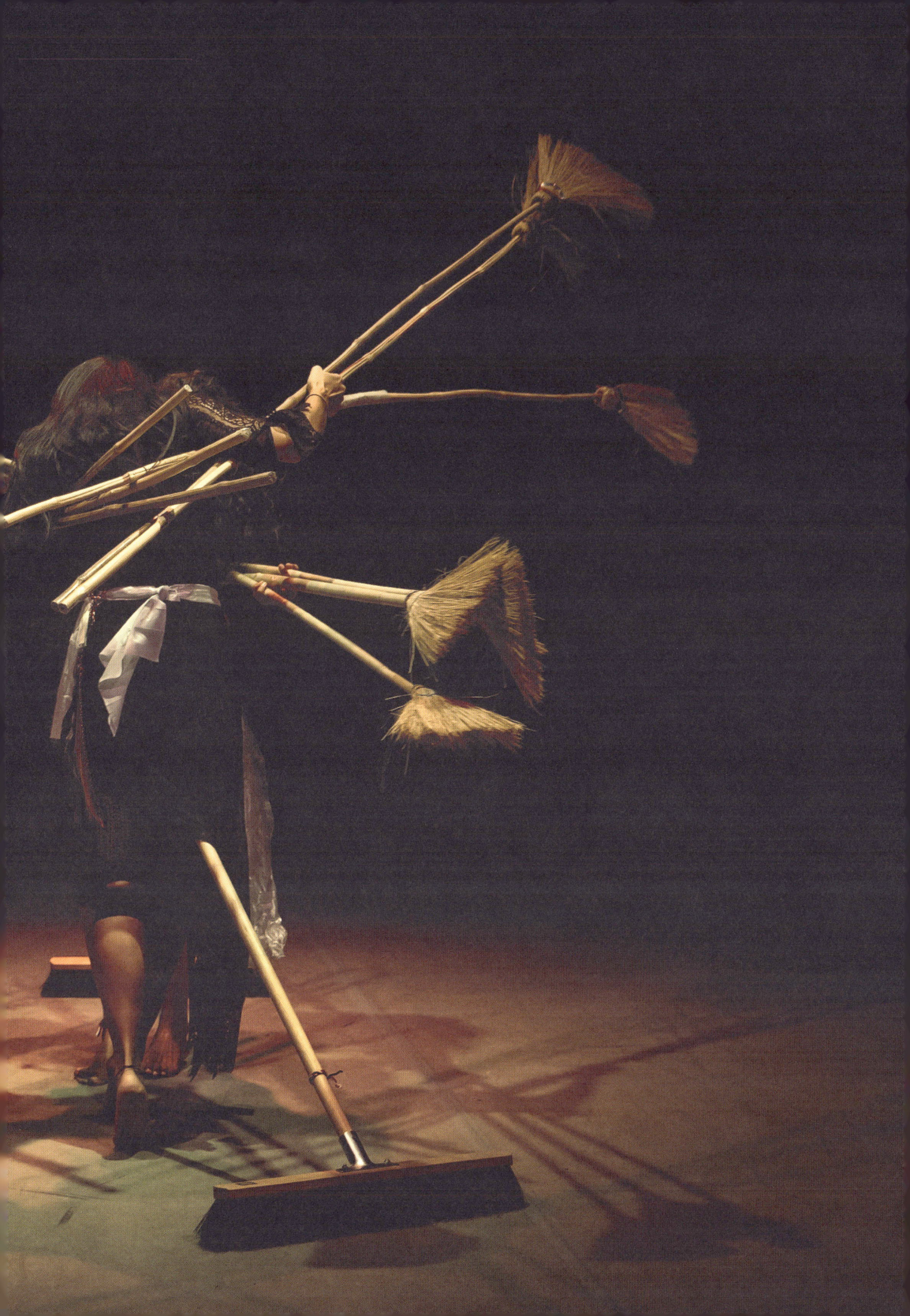

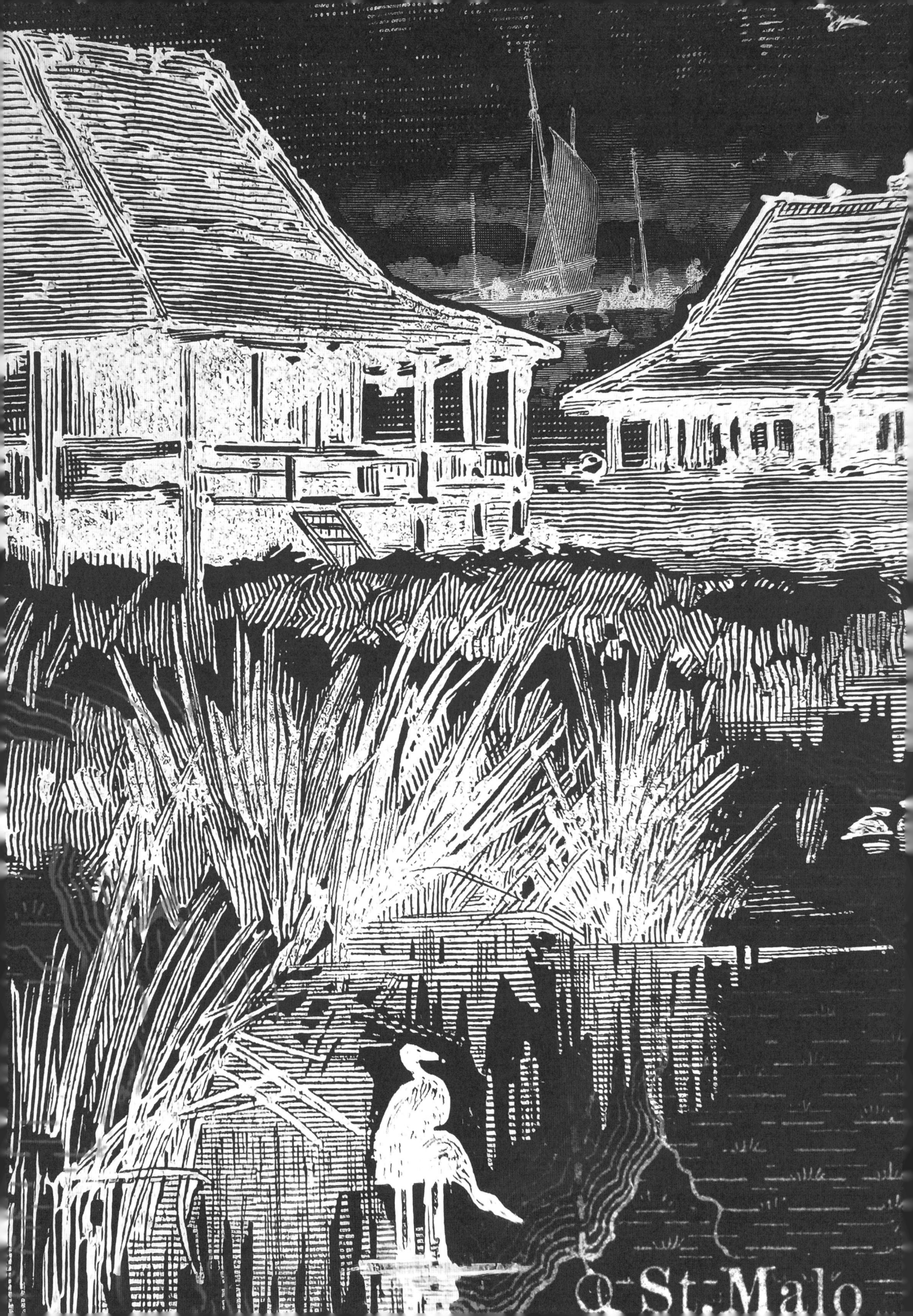

The Future Is Present, The Harbinger Is Home
Prospect.6, New Orleans

The Future→ Is↓ Present The Harbinger◄ Is⊙ Home

Susan Brennan Co-Artistic Directors
Miranda Lash and Ebony G. Patterson

P.6
New Orleans

Letter from the Board Chair

Every three years, Prospect invites a group of talented artists from around the globe to experience New Orleans and create work inspired by the unique culture and complex history of this 300-year-old port city. Together with visionary curators they bring new art to an old city. Against the odds, Prospect's commitment to present a triennial exhibition in New Orleans, largely free of charge to the public, has not changed since Prospect.1 debuted in 2008 in the aftermath of Hurricane Katrina.

Co-Artistic Directors Miranda Lash and Ebony G. Patterson (who is the first artist to hold the position and a Prospect alumna artist) present their powerful exhibition *The Future Is Present, The Harbinger Is Home* with sensitivity and grace. The Board of Trustees of Prospect is deeply honored to present this exhibition.

Christopher J. Alfieri
President & Chairperson

Director's Foreword

Dear Prospect visitors and community,

It's my pleasure to convey something that amazes me every time I say or write it: Prospect is the longest-running citywide exhibition of its kind in North America.

However, while we revere New Orleans for its rhythms and traditions, this is a city that is evolving and changing. Our triennial was meant to reflect this change, but also to resist it, especially where change risked leaving behind the best things about the city—the things that make it look, feel, sound, and act like no other American city.

I hope visitors of multiple Prospect exhibitions will notice that this P.6 catalogue itself is one of the major changes represented by this Prospect cycle. Not only are we working with Monacelli, an imprint of the venerable publisher Phaidon, for the first time, we are also using installation images from the exhibition for the first time since the Prospect.2 catalogue was released. We hope that this catalogue will not only help to remember the experience, but will inform, challenge, and inspire future artists, thinkers, and citizens.

With an effort so vast, the thanking process can be endless. The Susan Brennan Artistic Directors of P.6, Miranda Lash and Ebony G. Patterson, have my eternal thanks for their intellectual rigor and ability to inspire. Thank you to the fifty-one P.6 artists for their best work. There is so much hidden labor in creating something of this magnitude: the installers, fabricators, editors, designers, registrar, and many others who helped keep the heartbeat of Prospect. Thank you to Prospect's board, who has seen it all and yet still looks to evolve and refine an organization founded in 2007. Thank you to the Prospectors, our loyal members and advocates. Thank you to our venues and institutional partners.

But mostly, thank you to Prospect's staff. The work of building a triennial is both wonderful and terribly complex, and the following staff members have been willing and strong-spirited, even when the work was hardest: Emily Alesandrini, LB Barfield, Kalea Cook, Caroline Cox, Tarah Douglas, Erin Foster, Denise Frazier, Taylor Holloway, Nora Kovacs, Andrew Rebatta, and Ana Clara Silva.

Regardless of whether you're a resident of New Orleans or a visitor, I expect you discovered something via this edition of Prospect. An artist, a venue, a shaded spot near the river, an old bar that's new to you. The experience of Prospect is an opportunity to slow down and appreciate, or rediscover, New Orleans. Of course, Prospect is about the art and always will be; but its primary protagonist is the city itself. So take your time, enjoy it, and see it through the eyes of the artists.

Nick Stillman
Executive Director

New Bulbancha

Maurice Carlos Ruffin

All water on our planet is connected, whether it rains from clouds or bubbles up from the tide. Our cities—Cairo, London, Tokyo, Paris, Dakar, and New York—sit on rivers, bays, and oceans. Water makes our existence possible. Our architecture, agriculture, and art only thrive because of the life-giving substance that flows around us. In North America, waters converge from tributaries and cut due south. Those waters are called the Mississippi River. They converge in New Orleans.

But the waters aren't calm. Flooding and hurricanes are becoming more frequent and destructive. It's almost as though the Earth is speaking to us. She may be saying, "If my children won't treat me well, then I will show my displeasure by inundating their civilization."

In mythology, Arcadia is the place where the natural ideal lives. The most beautiful birds. The most lush forests. Flowers that brilliantly bloom in the night. There's something of the Arcardian in this project called Prospect.6.

New Orleans is a beloved city, but it is fragile. The wetlands that surround New Orleans wax and wane, thrive and shrink, by the rhythm of our choices. Despite the looming threat of loss, New Orleans has never lost track of the power to gather in celebration. As long as there is enough dry land—or even if all the buildings sit on stilts—this city will party. Prospect.6 is one of the flowers of the city.

I had a vision for the future of New Orleans. We have learned how to live with the land. The waters of the Mississippi River, Gulf of Mexico, and many lakes are clean. There are no dead zones where aquatic life cannot breathe. We build our habitats out of the kind of sustainable materials meant for this subtropical climate. Less steel and concrete, more bamboo and other organic materials. We use foliage to protect our homes and gathering places from the heat. No AC necessary. In other words, in the future, we return to the practices employed by the Native Americans of the past who called the city Bulbancha. Those were the people who cultivated a healthy civilization, a civilization that produced unique clothing, music, and, yes, art.

In New Orleans, we party to leave the worst of the past behind and embrace the best of the future. The shaking of hips to the bamboula rhythm, the singing of Mardi Gras classics, the twerking, eating, drinking, kissing, and telling. Our raucous spirit is undefeated.

We are a city where art flourishes. Where artists from around the world plant the seeds of their art, which sprout from the landscape like wildflowers. We don't have to imagine a civilization that loves and respects the human spirit of expression—because New Orleans embodies this spirit.

There was a terrible past where many monuments to racism looked down on the city. But some of those statues have been yanked down. And new monuments arise every day, from streets renamed for musicians and educators like Allen Toussaint and Norman C. Francis to those monuments that will be raised by our descendents. Prospect.6 contains the spirit of revolution. It is a braying, temporary party designed to pay homage to the city while knocking down barriers to expression.

New Orleans faces pressures from climate change. Powerful storms are more frequent, as is flooding. But if the post-Katrina era has taught us anything—the era in which Prospect began—it's that we will persist.

As part of the Global South, New Orleans is in the global majority. In this age of reckoning, these communities are reclaiming the right to tell their own stories.

New Orleans is the kindred of all lovers of humanity. Rain falls. Water rises. Rivers run. We persist in our visions, the visions from which art is made. The visions from which celebrations arise. If you haven't heard, celebration is an art. Prospect.6 is both of these.

As the exhibitions blossom across the landscape of the city, take heed of the beauty and power of these visions, of the possibilities that New Orleans embodies. Come and celebrate, the New Bulbancha.

Harbinger, Harbor, and Home: New Orleans Reveals Our Shared Future

Miranda Lash

"What you are learning, we have already known."[1]

What does it mean to live in the future, or to ruminate on what the future holds? For the sixth iteration of Prospect my Co-Artistic Director Ebony G. Patterson and I invite you to consider New Orleans as a city situated in the future, where the world's recent learnings have long been known, and where questions around survival, continuance, and joy are being asked in advance of other places.

Holding the future is a responsibility. We associate the word *harbinger* with a certain heaviness, a coming threat. Peeling back the layers of this word, however, we find its warm core: a host; a haven; harbor; a harborer. The archaic definition of harbinger is one who goes ahead to make lodging for others; the scout who creates a shelter, a safe space. New Orleans is often referred to as a place of danger and uncertainty. Nevertheless, we offer this proposal: If safety and home can be found and made here, it will pave the way for understanding how safety and home can be found and made in other places.

Situating New Orleans within the language of futurity upends how most narratives around this city are built, which frame it largely in relation to the past. People come to this place to witness history crystallized within the city's architecture, cuisine, music, and traditions. For Prospect.6 we posit New Orleans as a globally relevant point of departure for examining our collective future as it relates to climate change, legacies of colonialism, and definitions of belonging and home.

We owe a debt to Afrofuturist writers such as Octavia Butler for giving us tools to contemplate the future in a place where some experts doubt its continued existence in one hundred years. We also owe much to the historians and culture bearers of New Orleans for sharing their rich understanding of the layers of soil upon which we tread. The past is undeniably present here. Like the humid air, it permeates every institution and is felt immediately upon arrival. Knowledge is power, however, and in many ways this deep awareness of history provides a springboard for New Orleanians to move forward. The New Orleans tourism economy (which contributes nearly forty percent of the city's operating budget) plays a complex role in preserving this past and in fostering the idea that New Orleans is impervious to change.[2] Yet whereas tourism thrives on projecting a consistent and authentic experience of culture, we seek to present New Orleans as a place of shift and constant re-negotiation. We strive to honor the city's legacies, while fostering greater inclusion around who can be considered New Orleanian and what New Orleans can be.

All cities are in a state of flux, which leads to another point we wish to emphasize in P.6: the non-uniqueness of New Orleans, or rather, the ways in which New Orleans resembles other places in the US and beyond. Neither of us would deny the specificity of this city's blending of African, Creole, Caribbean, Latinx, and Asian cultures, or the foundational role New Orleans has played in American music, or the glorious feelings of liberation and sanctuary that many have experienced here. Rather, this point re-situates the systemic issues this city faces as something that is familiar in other cities and countries, specifically those that have been experiencing the immediate effects of climate change and long histories of colonialism for many decades. New Orleans is often positioned within a language of exceptionalism with phrases like "There's no place like it." We argue that in many ways, New Orleans reflects how *most* of the world lives.

New Orleans is often referred to as the "northernmost city of the Caribbean" or the "Gateway to Latin America." This orientation, while useful, maintains a US-centric perspective that positions New Orleans as a singular node facing southwards. We suggest instead adopting a multidirectional stance that orients issues in New Orleans within the context of the "global majority," a term used to refer to people of Indigenous, African, Asian, Latin American, and multi-heritage descent, who constitute at least eighty percent of the global population and who live in both hemispheres, not exclusively within the Global South.[3] In doing so we seek to redefine New Orleans as a "global majority" city rather than as a "majority minority" city (a term used by the US Census Bureau to describe US cities largely comprised of people of color).

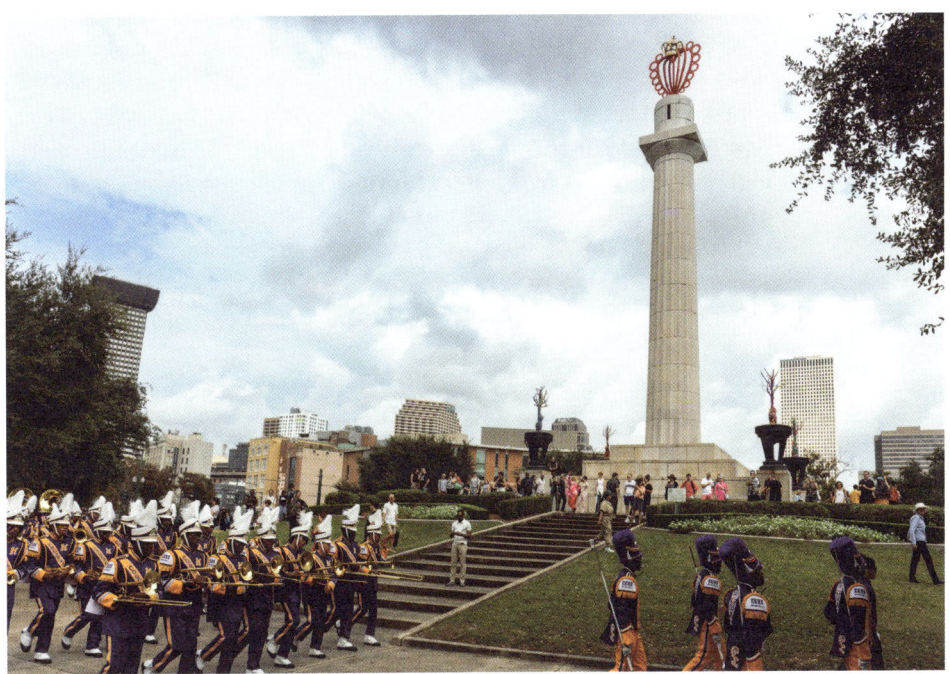

Edna Karr High School Marching Band performs in
Love Burst, an activation for the unveiling of Raúl de Nieves's
*The Sacred Heart of Hours and the Trees of Yesterdays,
Today, and Tomorrow*, 2024. Harmony Circle, October 31, 2024

It's important to reflect on the founding of Prospect in 2007 to explore how the role of a global convening of artists in New Orleans has shifted since then. During the post-Hurricane Katrina period, the justification for Prospect was framed around what New Orleans could uniquely offer a global audience, and what this audience could bring to a city still struggling in the wake of destruction. By inviting thousands of visitors to traverse New Orleans in the pursuit of art, Prospect offered economic revitalization, fresh ideas, and positive press. Many New Orleanians were still living in recovery mode, and pushing back against arguments from urban planners, scientists, and politicians that the city should not be rebuilt according to its previous footprint.[4] In response, the city leaned heavily into a marketing strategy that promoted New Orleans's culture as a jewel of such rareness that America would lose the very essence of its identity if this city were to fade away.[5] New Orleans was positioned as our country's cultural Rosetta Stone; the key to understanding all that is horrific and also redeemable about being American. Prospect joined a chorus of organizations advocating for the incomparable value of New Orleans's culture, even as the city underwent profound shifts.

New Orleans's evolution since Katrina has provoked existential debates around preserving the city's character, while simultaneously drawing this region into global conversations around climate adaptation and racial equity. Recovery efforts by myriad philanthropic foundations, nonprofit organizations, and volunteers—running concurrent to Prospect—enabled some of its citizens to rebuild, with conspicuously higher success in predominantly White neighborhoods. Over the past nineteen years gentrification has progressed rapidly in New Orleans, making it increasingly difficult for poorer residents and artists to remain.[6] The city's population is smaller, still majority Black (although proportionally less so), and has become more White, Hispanic, and multi-racial.[7] Politically, while New Orleans remains a stronghold for the Democratic party, the state of Louisiana has swung markedly further to the right, with ultra-conservative legislation making national headlines in 2024.[8] Due to upstream drought conditions, the Mississippi River is now an imperiled source of drinking water.[9]

Notably, Hurricane Katrina, while cataclysmic, is no longer thought of as a disaster on a scale that could not reoccur in New Orleans, or happen elsewhere. Over the last twenty years cities across the US, from Florida to New York, also experienced devastating hurricanes. Colorado (where I reside), Canada, California, and Oregon suffered massive, record-breaking forest fires, and the overall surface temperature of the Earth continues to increase, with 2024 being our planet's warmest year so far.[10] New Orleanians were chided in 2005 for choosing to stay in a place threatened by climate disaster. In 2024, many, if not most, Americans are willing to acknowledge the possibility of a major storm, drought, heat wave, fire, or flood impacting where they live. The possibility of a climate disaster is no longer thought of as an automatic reason to leave a place, because what places would be left? As wealthier countries and cities absorb the realities of climate change and painful reckonings with the past, New Orleanians have been living in this mode for quite some time.

Ebony and I were early in our careers when Dan Cameron launched Prospect in 2007. Ebony was a practicing artist and a professor at the University of Kentucky, while I was the first curator of modern and contemporary art at the New Orleans Museum of Art—a venue for the triennial—when Prospect.I opened. We both recognized the problematic

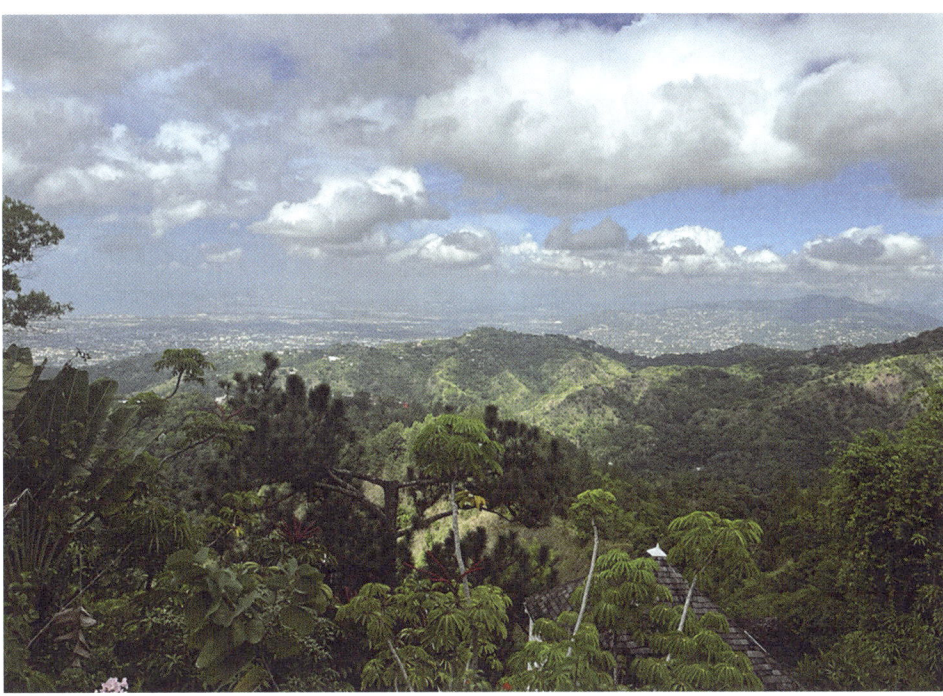

aspects of a project of this scale, and asked: "Who is served? Who is excluded? What is ignored, or worse, disrespected through the process?" Nevertheless, we were moved by the ambition of Prospect's goals, and the assertion embedded within Prospect that New Orleans and places like it are capable and deserving of such an endeavor. Since then, we have each spent over a decade tracking the successes and failures of presenting contemporary art in regions outside the art world's centers. I worked for fourteen years in the American South (in Texas, Louisiana, and Kentucky). Ebony spent twelve years dividing her time between Jamaica and Kentucky (she currently works in Kingston and Chicago). Long before we knew each other, we understood that creative opportunities can play an outsized role in how these regions are judged.

I laid eyes on Ebony's resplendent artworks for the first time in 2014, when she was an exhibiting artist in Prospect.3. In 2016, we were both appointed to artistic director Trevor Schoonmaker's curatorial council for Prospect.4, and we each recommended lists of artists, drawing from Louisiana and the Caribbean respectively. When we signed on as artistic directors for Prospect.6 in 2022, we arrived brimming with ideas for this platform, which over the years had become so significant to the South and the Caribbean. Ebony is Prospect's first artistic director who is a full-time practicing artist, and the first AD born outside the US. I am the first AD to have spent years working in New Orleans prior to engaging with Prospect, though I bring an insider/outsider perspective, as I did not grow up in New Orleans—I was raised in a bilingual Mexican-American household in Los Angeles.

We began our planning conversations not in New Orleans but in Kingston, Jamaica, looking at New Orleans literally and figuratively from a distance. Decamping to the Blue Mountains, we discussed what Kingston and New Orleans have in common: two predominantly Black cities with tourism-based economies, layered and interlinked legacies from colonialism and slavery, high vulnerability to hurricanes, renowned music, extreme income disparity, and stereotypes of either disaster/failure or festivity/licentiousness. We looked at histories of migration flowing in and out of these places and drew maps of the world, charting the communities that passed through New Orleans over the centuries. Our feelings about what is precious to us within our beloved places often had us circling back to the concept of home: What is home for each of us? Where is home? Who is home? Home speaks to our attachments to people, to places, and yearnings for belonging, familiarity, and security. Rather than cast aside these emotions as too sentimental or personal for art-historical use, we leaned into the idea of home as the linchpin that straddles both individual stories and the macroeconomic and political forces causing displacement and instability in our world. We encouraged each other to read treatises on the idea of home that were influential to us. Ebony recommended Jamaica Kincaid's text on Antigua, *A Small Place* (1988), as a comparative window onto the Caribbean. I found myself quoting Sarah Broom's *The Yellow House* (2019) as justification for why we circled around an idea of home that was untethered to specific buildings or houses. We see this tension between attachments to home—however one defines it—and global climate change as one of the defining issues of our foreseeable future.

Home is pivotal to New Orleanian identity, perhaps even more so because this home has been threatened and besieged. Thinking expansively about what home is (beyond a physical location) feels appropriate during a time when climate change, war, and economic necessity are driving millions around the world away from their homes to seek shelter, safety, and income elsewhere.[11] Leaving does not end one's relationship to home. Staying in New Orleans still requires finding creative solutions to keep one's home intact. When home is the harbinger—when home already signals towards its future, or next phase—it collapses living in the present with planning ahead. For artists working in Louisiana, this might mean making art in a studio where the drywall is not replaced all the way down to the floor, in case the room floods again. Yet even in these scenarios, the goal is not just to survive or be resilient. In these homes, residents still desire spaces for vibrance and connection, regardless of what the future holds.

In building our artist list for P.6, we looked to regions tied to New Orleans through histories of voluntary or forced migration (the Caribbean, North and South America, Southeast Asia, and Africa) as well as artists living in Louisiana or who were raised there. We built our curatorial advisory committee with corresponding expertise, calling upon the talents of Ron Bechet, Zoe Butt, Raphael Fonseca, Tumelo Mosaka, Krista Thompson, and Dyani White Hawk. We looked at artists across a wide range of stages in their careers and targeted those whom we felt had consistently shown growth, evolution, and risk-taking, regardless of market success. We made the difficult decision early on to avoid selecting artists who had already shown in Prospect, and prioritized presenting new and different voices to the New Orleans audience. In 2022 we visited documenta fifteen in Kassel, Germany, curated by ruangrupa. While acknowledging this exhibition's controversies, we respected ruangrupa's intentionality of prioritizing artists' practices, and creating opportunities for discussion between and amongst artists. In building our own artist list we often asked ourselves, "How does this engagement with Prospect grow or support the artist's overall practice? How can we foster conversations between artists in this process, either by utilizing existing networks, or creating new ones?" In considering artists with decades-long, established careers, we looked specifically for those whose works have inspired other artists. Internally we referred to these artists (including Mel Chin, Christopher Cozier, and Joan Jonas) as our "fountains," because their work has nourished so many others.

After selection, we encouraged artists to signal towards the future in their artwork and advance new ideas and unexpected directions. Forty three of the fifty one artists in P.6 produced new artworks. Five of the artists who presented existing works (Eisa Jocson, Venuri Perera, Brendan Fernandes, Yee I-Lann, and Kelley-Ann Lindo) have not previously shown these works in the US. Rather than require that artists specifically respond to New Orleans, we selected artists whose practices already resonated with the city and our proposed themes. Some artists elected to make site-specific work, while others brought forward topics from their own communities. We also made a concerted effort to acknowledge more recent immigrant populations in New Orleans from Latin America and Vietnam, recognizing that they too have played a central role in the continuing reshaping of the city.

Having both lived in places typically left off art-world travel routes, it was important for us to travel to multiple locations that were less likely to be visited by our colleagues, and where we knew that the in-person experience would provide an invaluable supplement to our learnings. Ebony met with artists in Barbados, Guadeloupe, and Trinidad. In 2023 we traveled together to Suriname to witness the multifaceted work being done by Marcel Pinas in Moengo. Through his Kibii Foundation, Pinas has founded an international artist residency and public sculpture program, the Contemporary Art Museum Moengo (CAMM) and the Moengo Festival (a popular recurring festival for music, performance, and art), all for the benefit of his beloved Maroon community. We toured his Tembe Art Studio aided only by natural light—the Surinamese government had cut the electricity and damaged sections of the roof as a rebuke of Pinas's efforts. We also visited Pinas's Moiwana Monument and other sculptures by Pinas that incorporate the Afaka script of the Ndyuka language, forms which resurfaced in Pinas's installation for Prospect.6.

In 2024 Ebony and I traveled together to Vietnam, where, with the invaluable guidance of Tuấn Andrew Nguyễn, we met with artists and toured the Mekong Delta and demilitarized zone. In Ho Chi Minh City we met Arlette Quỳnh-Anh Trần at her home and studio where she bases her artistic and curatorial practice. In Hanoi we learned about the Nhà Sàn Collective's model for collaboration from Tuan Mami, who

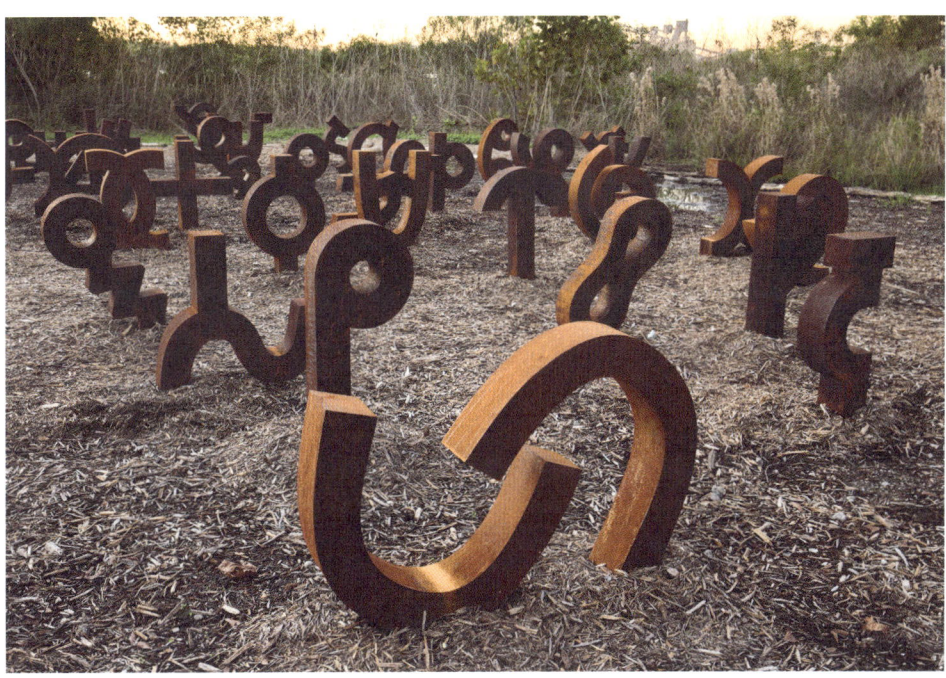

Marcel Pinas, *AFAKA BUKU*, 2024 (detail). The Batture

was at the time hosting a residency for emerging artists within his own studio. Both Suriname and Vietnam provided incredible lenses onto art-making communities upheld by mutual support amongst artists. They are an inspiring tribute to how art can be made despite the menace of government censorship and limited resources. After years of isolation and restricted interactions during the COVID pandemic, it felt moving to be able to drink tea together, share food, breathe the same air, and hear the same sounds without a digital interface.

We regard New Orleanians as Prospect's first audience. In keeping with Prospect's tradition of being a multi-venue presentation, the sites for P.6 are spread throughout different neighborhoods and routes. Our selection of sites celebrates the hard work of local nonprofit arts institutions, while offering moments of surprise and discovery within the city. The sites include beloved gathering places as well as locations whose loaded histories demand careful acknowledgement. In some cases, the sites contain a complete re-imagining beyond the shadow of White supremacy. In our collaborations within the city and other regions, we celebrate the creative communities who manifest a sense of possibility.

"Until the lion has his historian, the hunter will always be a hero."[11]

The artists in P.6 approach history with a desire for investigation, critique, and revision. They are keenly aware of history's power and its ability to influence our understanding of present-day systems. P.6 artists have long been familiar with questioning established narratives. They seek a conceptual and literal deconstruction and an opportunity to participate in this next crucial phase of refilling voids with new narratives. It has now been at least eight years since a wave of Confederate memorials and name designations started coming down around the United States. Streets, universities, and buildings have been renamed around the country (and the world). In New Orleans, Jefferson Davis Parkway became Norman C. Francis Parkway; Robert E. Lee Boulevard now honors Allen Toussaint. As a nation, we are pivoting into a complicated period of redetermining what should be honored and how remembrances should be made. Through their work, these artists disseminate knowledge and assert new worlds, where the "lions" tell their histories and assert their role in shaping the future. The following section of this essay provides an overview of their artworks' themes, which cover a range of social, economic, and ecological concerns.

At the New Orleans African American Museum in Tremé, where Bayou Road is called Governor Nicholls Street, a large, striking red structure asserts itself from behind a courtyard of live oak trees. The Meilleur-Goldthwaite House, a Creole manse built for the keeper of the New Orleans jail c. 1828, was wrapped in fabric by Joiri Minaya, creating the artwork *Fleurs de liberation: an ecology of resistance* (*Cloaking of the Meilleur-Goldthwaite House*) (2024). Since 2019 Minaya has been covering colonial monuments and statues in brilliantly colored fabrics as part of her *Cloaking* series. These fabrics are adorned with what she calls "plants of resistance": flora that reflects Indigenous forms of healing and poison. *Fleurs* widens Minaya's practice from cloaking statues of specific individuals to taking on the architecture of the city itself, and the histories embedded within the buildings' structures. Her artwork's presence on Bayou Road, the oldest surviving street in New Orleans, connects to the Indigenous origins of this land when it was known as Bulbancha, "the place of many tongues." This ancient portage route connected the waterways of Bayou Saint John and the Mississippi River, and was used by the tribes who resided upon this land, including the Atakapa, Caddo, Choctaw, Houma, Natchez, and Tunica.

Ongoing legacies of colonialism appear throughout P.6, as artists look to the past and specific histories from their regions to draw implications for the future. In his sculptural work, *1,001,532 CE* (2023–2024), Blas Isasi imagines a "sci-fi, Andean, post-human reenactment" of the fateful encounter between Spanish conquistador Francisco Pizarro and Inca leader Atahualpa, which ultimately led to the fall of the Inca Empire. Drawing upon the highland Andean tradition of reenacting this event, Isasi created a retelling of this battle one million years after its occurrence with sculptural references to silver and steel (an allusion to wealth and weaponry), sand (reminiscent of the desert landscape), and the twisted forms of the Peruvian carob tree. Stephanie Syjuco, meanwhile, looks to an aftereffect of Spanish colonialism through her investigation of the now-vanished village of St. Malo, Louisiana. In the early nineteenth

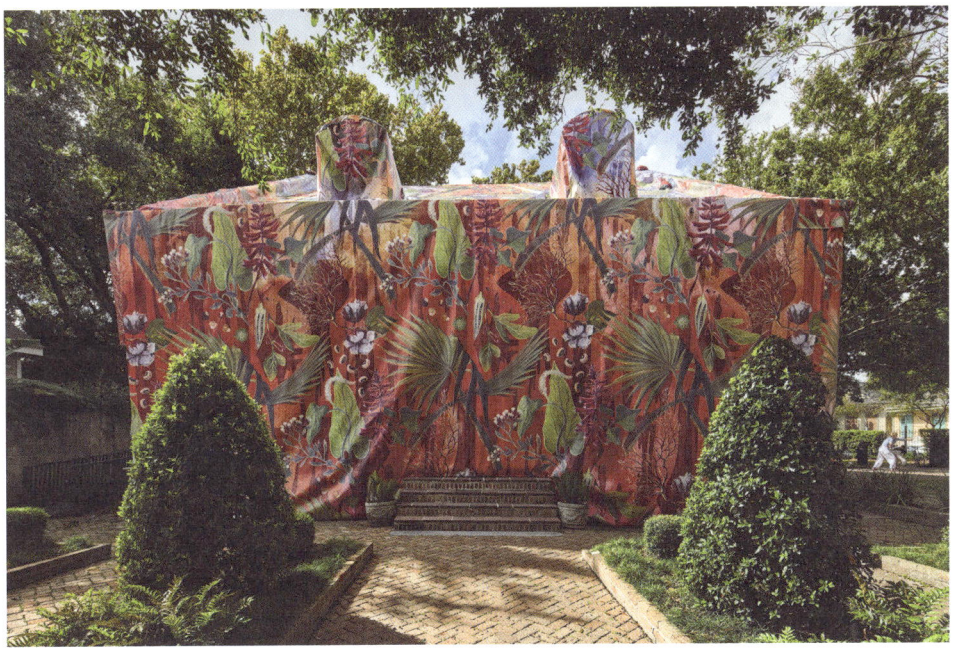

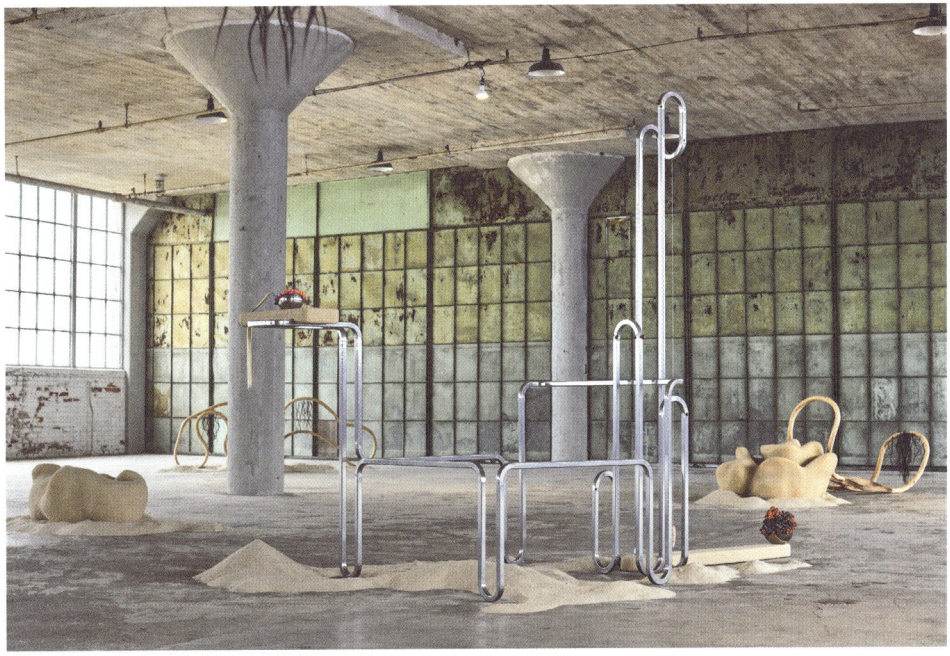

Top: Joiri Minaya, *Fleurs de liberation: an ecology of resistance (Cloaking of the Meilleur-Goldthwaite House)*, 2024.
New Orleans African American Museum

Above: Blas Isasi, *1,001,532 CE*, 2023–2024 (detail).
Ford Motor Plant

century, "Manilamen"—Filipino sailors and escapees from the Spanish Manila galleon trade—established this fishing village on a site previously settled by Indigenous people and Maroons. St. Malo is known as the first permanent Filipino community in the US, and possibly the country's first Asian-American community. Syjuco resuscitates the memory of St. Malo through ephemeral images of the village that are wheat-pasted on buildings around the city. These ghostly reminders of the site are meant to vanish over time, just as St. Malo's former land is slipping away due to coastal erosion.

In New Orleans, histories of colonialism are intertwined with histories of enslavement. Slavery was introduced to Louisiana by the French, who enslaved Indigenous people as early as 1706. By 1710 the French began importing enslaved Africans to the region, a practice continued by the Spanish and the Americans into the nineteenth century. After the US government banned the importation of slaves in 1807–'08, a robust domestic trade of slaves continued until Louisiana fell to Union army control during the Civil War in 1864. For her P.6 project, Abigail DeVille focuses on the period from 1808 to 1864, when slaves were brought to New Orleans from places like Baltimore and Virginia. Using slave ship manifests—the lists that detailed the human cargo—the sounds coming from her human-sized sculptures are inspired by the names of the roughly 130,000 men, women, and children who arrived in New Orleans to be sold. Acknowledging the pervasive effect of the slave market on the New Orleans economy, the sculptures *Carbon* and the sound installation *The heart knows its own bitterness (Manifest)* (2024) were presented in multiple outdoor locations throughout the city. At the Ford Motor Plant, Jeannette Ehlers installed a replica of an antique hoist located in Copenhagen's West India Warehouse. This warehouse housed the Danish West India Company, the chartered company responsible for the trade of goods and the enslaved in the Danish West Indies. Long braids of brown and black hair flow from *Hoist and the Unseen: Journeys Through Tempests in Times of Hunger* (2024), in tribute to the Black individuals whose unpaid labor built New Orleans and the economies of the Caribbean. These voluminous braids, signifiers of Black bodies, were created during Ehlers's braiding workshops for Black women.

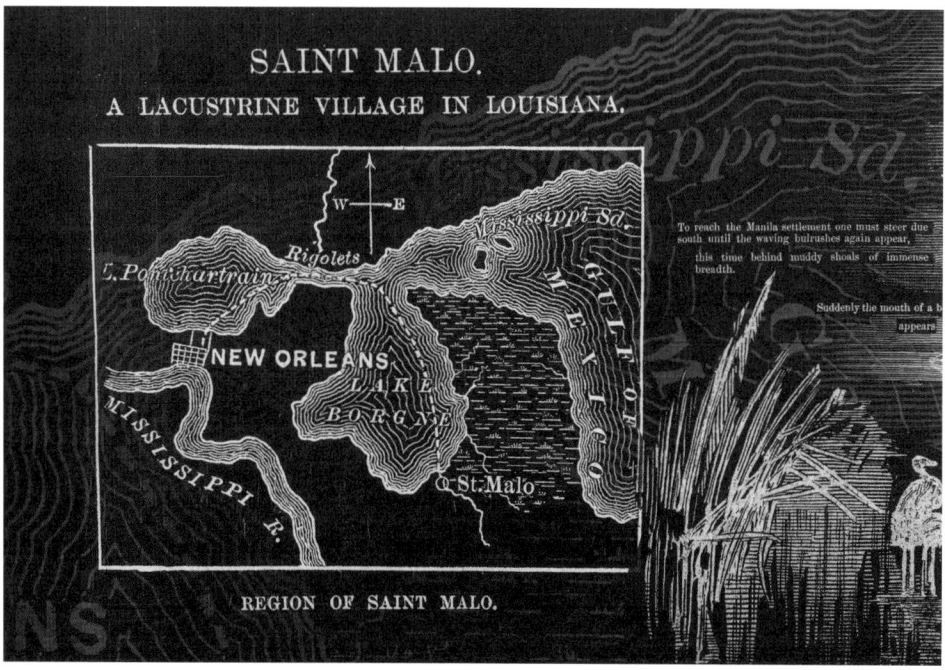

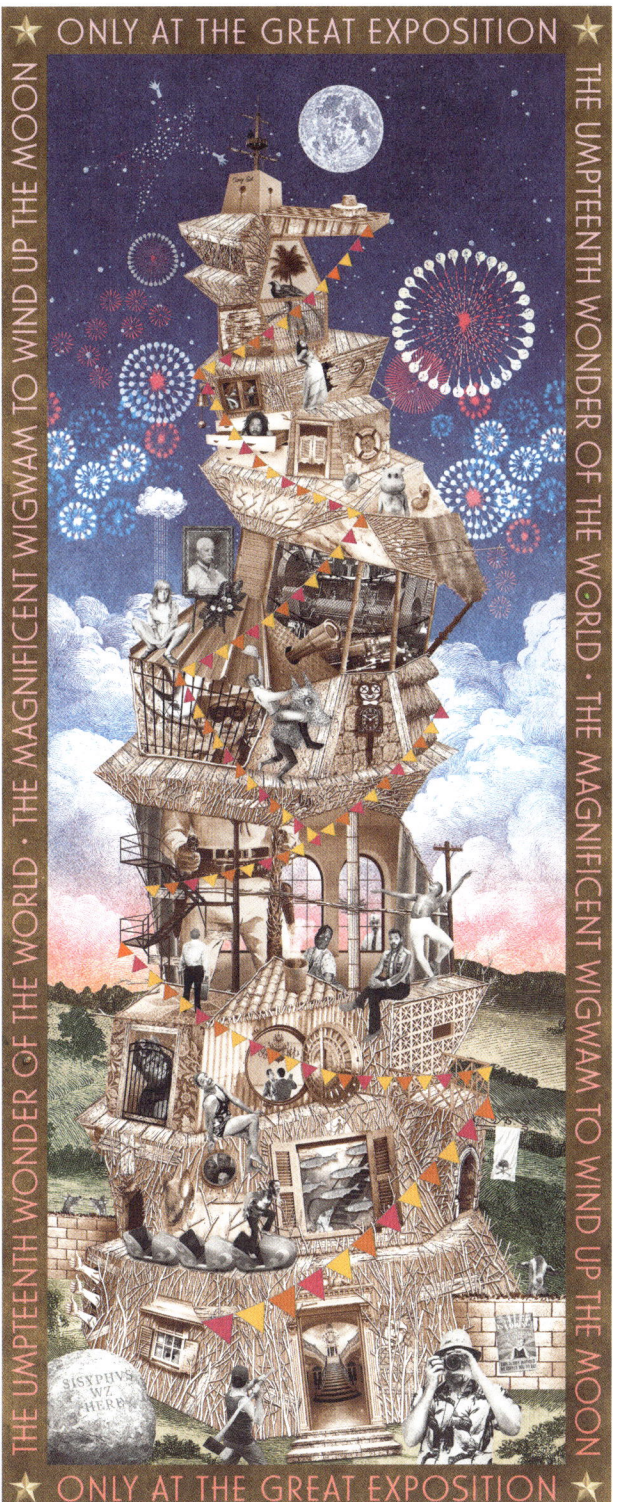

From architecture to domestically scaled furniture, P.6's artists interrogate historic forms, with the aim of revealing and reassessing their origins and purposes. In his sculpture, Brian Jungen (Dane-Zaa) sourced an eighteenth-century French refectory table from Baton Rouge and shot it full of arrows with feathers from birds from throughout the Americas. Inspired by the strong sense of ceremony and regalia that he encountered in New Orleans, his bold and colorful "attack" on a Louisianian colonial structure projects a sense of Indigenous authority and self-defense. Christopher Cozier, meanwhile, investigates the role of bleachers, a tool used in both New Orleans and Trinidad during Carnival season. Acknowledging the intersecting variables of privilege, power, and shared experience involved in watching public spectacles and events, Cozier has installed colonial-style wooden feet into the base of a mobile bleacher. Installed at The Batture, Cozier's installation *it has already been decided*...(2024) invites viewers to contemplate the course of empire as they watch marine vessels travel along the Mississippi River.

Artists Ewan Atkinson, Arturo Kameya, and Clarissa Tossin's contributions to P.6 explore the echoes of colonization in contemporary societies and governments. For over a decade Atkinson has created an intricate and vast archive in what he calls *The Neighbourhood Project*. Replete with satirical characters, marketing slogans, and tales of dysfunction, "the neighborhood" does not represent any specific place, yet it offers glimpses into every tourism-driven economy within the former British Empire, including Atkinson's home of Barbados. For Prospect he curated an exhibition of plans for *The Great Exposition* (a celebration self-reflexively akin to a world's fair, or a triennial) that alas never occurred, having imploded under the weight of its own ambitions. Arturo Kameya, meanwhile, takes on stories of corruption, catastrophe, and inequity from Lima, Peru. He created an otherworldly environment where mashups from popular culture co-exist with ghostly allusions to the burdens carried by the Peruvian people: the debts the Peruvian state owes to its citizens, and the growing crisis of international debt owed by the world's poorest countries to richer nations. Clarissa Tossin's *We are stardust* (2024), an installation of translucent starred

Ewan Atkinson, *The Magnificent Wigwam to Wind up The Moon*, 2024 from *Stories from the Neighbourhood: The Great Exposition*, 2015-2024

flags (loosely based on flags from different nations) is inspired by current and planned enterprises led by international governments and private companies to explore and colonize the Moon, Mars, and the Earth's atmosphere. Her flags and accompanying weavings provoke the question of whether nationalism will become amplified or irrelevant as humans and corporations adapt the playbook of colonization from centuries past to lay claim to new celestial territories.

The story of how power operates in society in many ways can be told through who performs the most difficult, least compensated labors. Louisiana consistently ranks as one of the poorest states in the US: Over eighteen percent of the state's population was recorded as living below the poverty line in 2022.[13] Like many other oil-rich regions of the world, the high output of natural resources from Louisiana has had relatively little effect on the average income of its inhabitants. Stories of labor surface in several P.6 artists' presentations.

In his monumental sculpture, Mel Chin's *Pool of Light* (2024–2025) pays homage to the female secretarial pools who supported white-collar offices during the twentieth century. Using a bevy of mid-century office chairs, Chin created "a chandelier from the cathedrals of capital, illuminating all those who labored 9 to 5 and sprung from those chairs to a boss's beckon."[14] In their performance piece *Magic Maids* (2022–2024) collaborators Eisa Jocson and Venuri Perera also honor female laborers, in this case migrant workers who come from their home countries of the Philippines and Sri Lanka to perform domestic work in wealthier Western countries. Pacing the room with brooms swinging between their legs, they connect histories of European witch hunts with contemporary stories of violence and exploitation against domestic workers.

Maia Ruth Lee has for years addressed the topic of migration and rootlessness through her *Bondage Baggage* series: bundles wrapped in netting reminiscent of how Lee saw packages wrapped at the airport in her childhood home of Kathmandu, Nepal. For P.6 she created an endlessly looping conveyor belt of bundles whose circulation evokes the transitory nature of migrants on their journeys. Kelley-Ann Lindo poignantly addresses the strain of family separations due to labor migration with *Send Love Inna Barrel* (2017–ongoing). *Send Love* is inspired by "barrel children" in the Caribbean: children whose parents work abroad and receive goods from their parents shipped in barrels. Members of the public were invited to sit on opposite ends of Lindo's 32-foot-long barrel and were instructed to communicate with each other. Their words reverberating within the barrel offer a form of intimacy when physical togetherness is not possible.

Through these sculptures and performances, the artists commemorate the unsung workers who support different industries and the effect of labor migration (people migrating outside their home countries in search of work) on both individuals and their families. These artists humanize the people behind the output, acknowledging work that is often unseen or underrecognized.

With every summer ushering in a new hurricane season, New Orleanians are accustomed to planning due to climate change, as every approaching hurricane brings the possibility of relocation. In recent years the city has faced the threat of increasingly severe hurricanes due to rising ocean temperatures, increased flooding due to insufficient drainage infrastructure, and, in 2023, an endangered fresh water supply through the incursion of a saltwater "wedge" from the Gulf of Mexico into the Mississippi River. Multiple artists in P.6 address the power of nature as well as its fragile ecosystems; some offer a critique of the energy industry

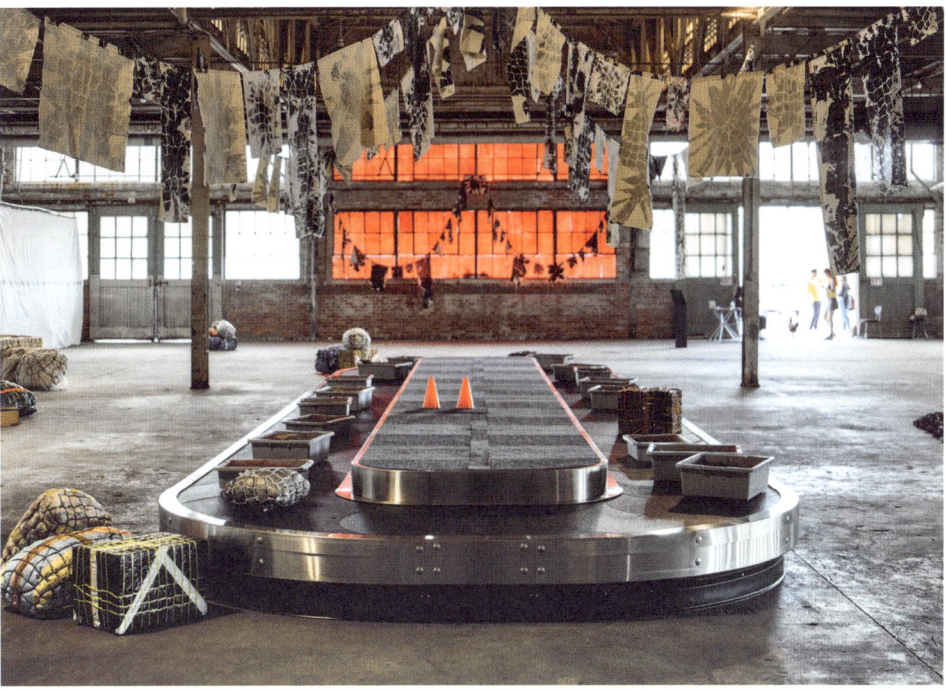

and its impact on our environment. Others articulate a sense of connection with the natural world, seeking a more harmonious relationship between humanity and other species. In many of these works, species and places meld into one another: bodies become birds, towers become trees, men meld with cypresses, coastlines from different regions blur into one another. This intertwining speaks to our interconnectedness with nature, regardless of whether we are acting as a friend or foe to our environment.

Deborah Jack's six-channel video weaves together footage of coastlines and waters in Louisiana, St. Maarten, and Maine, making visible how the character of the water and plant life along these edges of land have changed due to dramatic events such as hurricanes and human interventions. Fascinated by the idea of collapse, her video includes an investigation into Louisiana's Lake Peigneur, a water formation accidentally created by the implosion of an underground salt mine due to improper oil drilling. In contrast to this dramatic debacle, she also includes footage of Neptune Pass, an example of the Mississippi River naturally rebuilding land from its sediment. Building upon this type of push and pull between humans and nature, Hannah Chalew creates an environment out of living plants, various scents, and sugarcane paper mixed with plastic detritus in *Orphan Well Gamma Garden* (2024). As an artist and environmental activist, Chalew investigates the impact of the oil and gas industry and its pipelines on the landscape and people in Louisiana. In her P.6 installation, pipes and plants twist into each other, knotting together in a watery world where growth and waste coexist. Eddie Rodolfo Aparicio also touches upon the energy industry through his research into the enormous electrical towers in New Orleans and his hometown of Los Angeles. For his new sculpture he transformed the shape of these electrical towers into organic, totem-like structures inspired by ceiba trees and his grandmother's handmade dolls from El Salvador. The utilitarian shape of these towers is made unruly and bulging in appearance, stuffed with silk floss from ceiba tree pods and wrapped with items of clothing that have been hand-stitched together. For Aparicio, the tropical ceiba trees offer a metaphor for the migrants who have come from Central

Maia Ruth Lee, *The Conveyor*, 2024 (detail). Ford Motor Plant

America to Los Angeles, leaving behind a humid climate for the semi-arid environment of Southern California.

This blending between human and tree appears also in Didier William's *Gesture to Home* (2024), a series of paintings and sculptures at the Historic New Orleans Collection. His muscular figures emerge from the trunks and knees of cypress trees. Fascinated by the layered historical connections between Louisiana and Haiti, William researched the cypress trees of Louisiana's Atchafalaya Basin and the history of Haitians coming to New Orleans after the Haitian Revolution. His painted "groundscapes," as he calls them, convey the idea that the land holds a "muscle memory" of bloodshed and loss embedded within trees' roots.

Whereas some artists in P.6 consider the shared home of our planet, others focus locally on what home means within the context of neighborhoods and residences in New Orleans. In Brooke Pickett's paintings, there is a subtle allusion to the home as a precarious shelter. After acquiring still lifes of objects from the domestic realm, such as quilts, toys, and cleaning supplies, Pickett transformed these compositions into semi-abstract paintings with an off-kilter sense of balance, as if the viewer or the objects were on the verge of toppling. Her paintings are grand in scale and aspiration, unapologetically arguing for the centrality of the home and its daily exchanges in shaping our identity. For years Abdi Farah has made art inspired by high school football teams in New Orleans and the fragile heroism of their players. His series of figurative sculptures and tear-away banners delve into the glory and vulnerability of these young men and the crusade-like language of battle, divine might, and redemption used around Louisiana football fields. L. Kasimu Harris's photographic series *Vanishing Black Bars & Lounges* (2018–ongoing) pays tribute to Black-owned bars as irreplicable and endangered spaces. In New Orleans these bars play a pivotal role as gathering places for Mardi Gras Indians

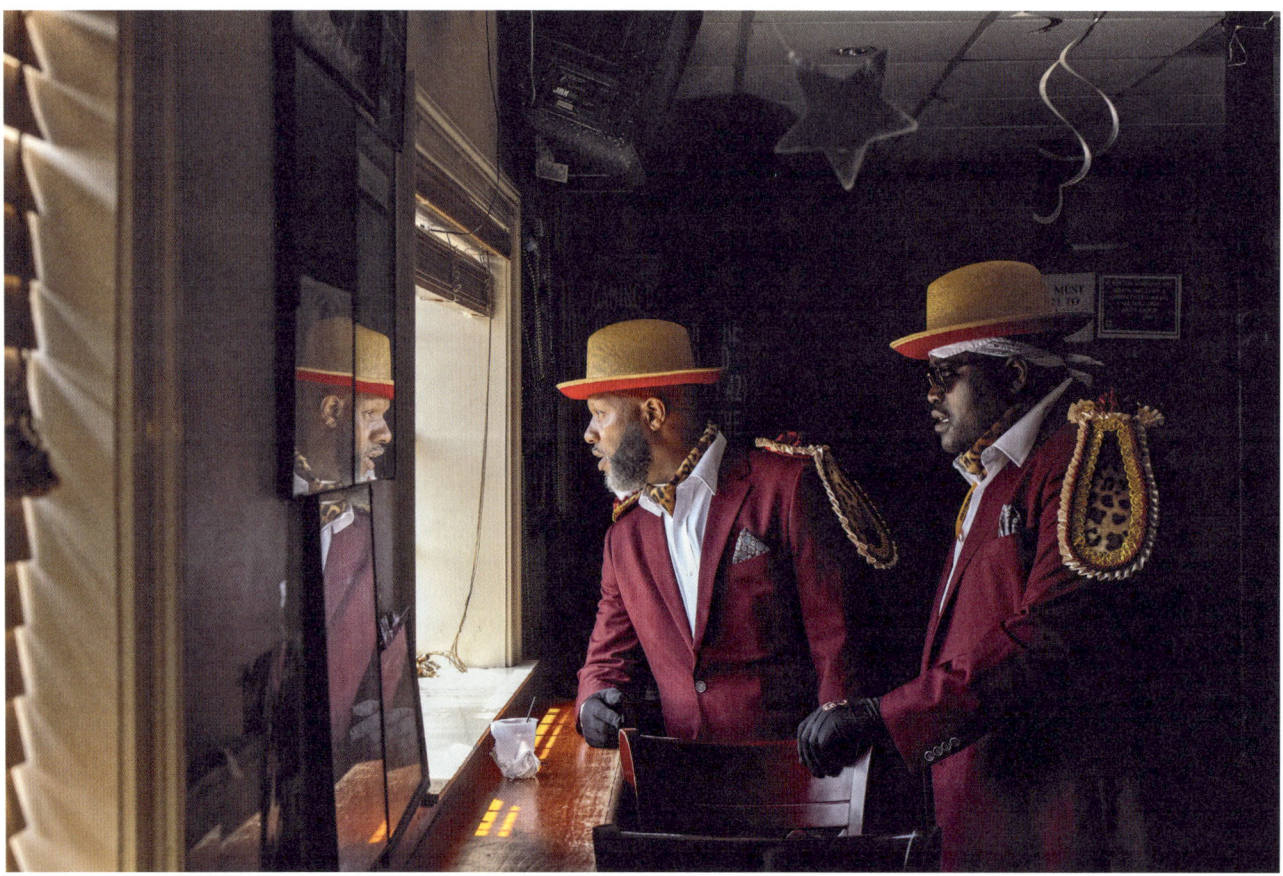

L. Kasimu Harris, *They Out There, Baby Myron Thibodeaux Sr. & Jarvis Lewis of the Zulu Go Getters Bertha's Place Bar & Restaurant, New Orleans*, 2022, from the series *Vanishing Black Bars & Lounges*, 2018–ongoing

and as stops along the routes of second-line parades. Gentrification, particularly since Hurricane Katrina, has chipped away at Black ownership and patronage of these spaces, inspiring Harris to document their ambiance and clientele. Harris's photographs at Sweet Lorraine's Jazz Club feature moments from bars around New Orleans in conversation with images from Black-owned bars in other cities around the US.

Ruth Owens also addresses precarity and Black culture in New Orleans in her multichannel video *Black Delight, An Ecopoem* (2024). Moving from the periods of sunrise, midday, sunset, and midnight, she juxtaposes footage of Black family celebrations with the striking landscape of the Louisiana wetlands. Humans and nature are shown together, underscoring our shared fate and potential for profound beauty. Ashley Teamer looks to New Orleans's musical roots and tambourine traditions as inspiration for her outdoor sculpture. Stretching skyward, the dynamic leaves of Teamer's tree are playable instruments, designed to emanate sound through wind or human intervention. Sited in Lemann Park, just off Claiborne Avenue, her sculpture pays homage to the generations of second-lines and parades that have rolled down Claiborne, a key corridor in the Tremé neighborhood. Teamer's tree also conjures the memory of the long boulevard of oaks that once existed, before the construction of the Interstate 10 highway overpass laid waste to hundreds of trees and buildings along this street.

The continuance of music and community-building on Claiborne Avenue is one of countless examples of New Orleanian adaptation and rebuilding. This iteration of Prospect celebrates the Vietnamese community of New Orleans, acknowledging that 2025 coincides with a landmark year: the fiftieth anniversary of the fall of Saigon in Vietnam, the airlift of thousands of Vietnamese immigrants to New Orleans, and the establishment of Little Saigon in New Orleans East. New Orleans-based artist Christian Việt Đinh honors this anniversary with an installation entitled *Trường Ca Mười Ngàn Năm (A Song of 10,000 Years)* (2024). Đinh evokes the idea of ten thousand horses, an auspicious number that represents the future, longevity, and eternity. He reminds us also that horses are an American symbol, tied to the idea of cowboys and rugged individuals. By marrying Vietnamese and American references, he celebrates a community that was thrice exiled, in three consecutive generations: fleeing first from North to South Vietnam to escape Communist persecution in 1957; relocating to New Orleans from Vietnam in 1975; and displacement due to Katrina in 2005. Tuấn Andrew Nguyễn's film, *Amongst the Disquiet* (2024), made in collaboration with filmmaker Marion Hoàng Ngọc Hill and musician Thảo Nguyễn (performing as THAO), speaks to the ties that bind within a multigenerational Vietnamese family based in New Orleans. Through interwoven vignettes told through dialogue and songs, the film winds through the challenges, longings, and affections between family members, both living and dead. The film probes: What makes a home when home is left behind? Where is home when loved ones are gone? Does home live within us? Or where we bury our dead? The idea of building a sense of home and belonging is also underscored in Tuan Mami's performance and installation *Seeding the Future* (2024). Part of his ongoing project, *Vietnamese Immigrating Garden*, Mami uses plants as a metaphor for migration, acknowledging that many immigrants bring seeds from their home countries to their new residences. For *Seeding the Future* Mami collaborated with the VIET (Vietnamese Initiatives in Economic Training) Community Resource Center and a community of elders in New Orleans East. Once a week Vietnamese elders went to the

Xavier University of Louisiana Art Gallery and taught visitors how to make "seed balls" by embedding individual seeds in small orbs of soft clay. This simple activity offers an opportunity for visitors to exchange stories with the elders around gardening, cuisine, and all aspects of life. The piece fosters a sense of connection amongst New Orleanians who might otherwise never meet and honors the knowledge held by this first-generation Vietnamese American community.

For some artists, creating a space of safety and inclusion is part of their signaling towards the future, and their projects involve the creation of harbors, or spaces of radical welcome. P.6 adds a chapter to the ongoing evolution of Harmony Circle with the installation of Raúl de Nieves's *The Sacred Heart of Hours and the Trees of Yesterdays, Today, and Tomorrow* (2024). Perhaps no public art space has generated more controversy in New Orleans during the past decade than this traffic roundabout that was known as Lee Circle from 1884 to 2017. Atop the sixty-foot-tall granite column that once held a bronze statue of Confederate general Robert E. Lee, de Nieves placed a vivid red heart encircled by a metal ribbon evoking divine light, topped with a crown. The heart (a universal symbol for love) is a call for compassion and inclusion, in a style loosely evocative of the Catholic Sacred Heart of Jesus seen throughout Mexico (de Nieves is from Michoacán). In the four urns surrounding the

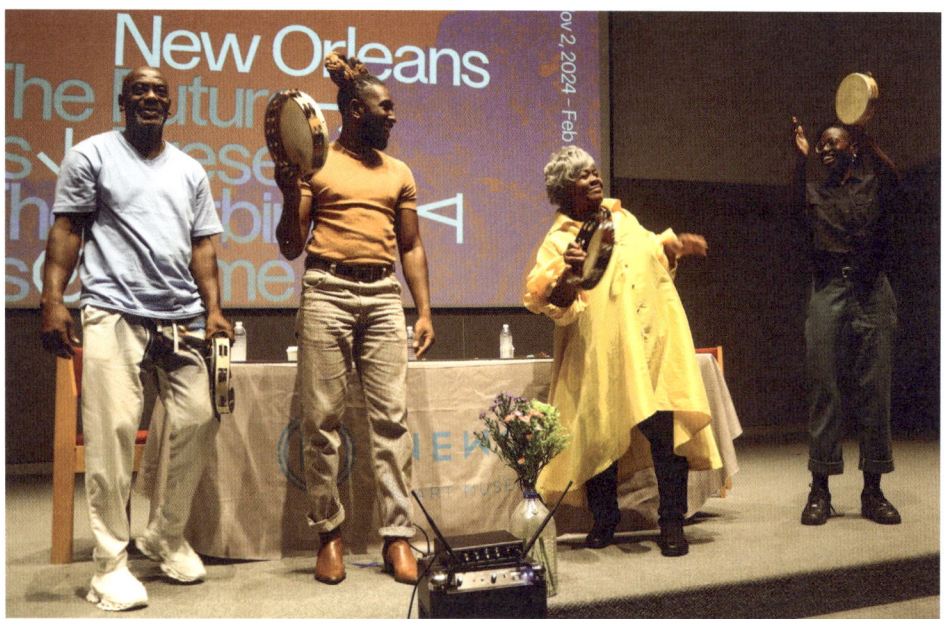

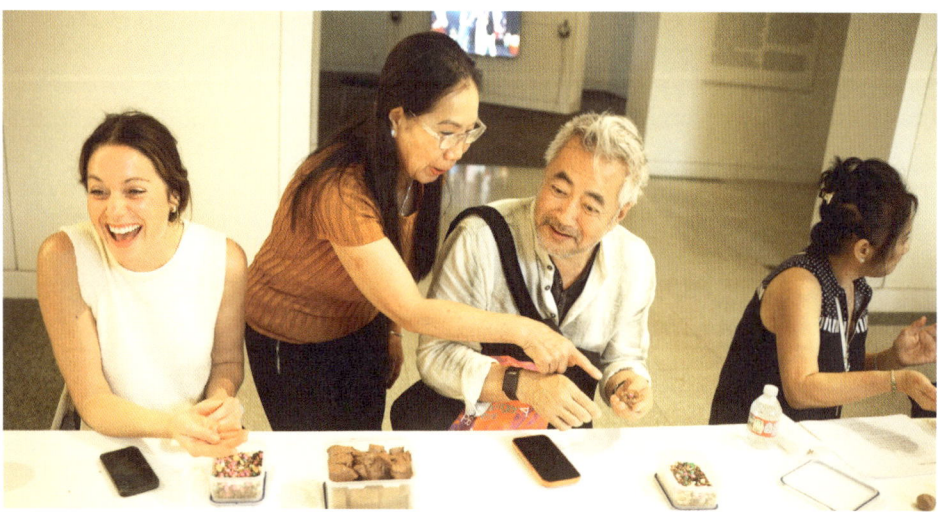

Top: *Tambourine Cypher Part I*, artist talk and performance. L to R: Aaron Washington, Gladney, Rosalie Washington, and Ashley Teamer. Tulane University, Freeman Auditorium, November 3, 2024

Above: *Seeding the Future,* performance by Tuan Mami. L to R: Amanda Sroka, Lan Vu, Akio Tagawa, and Hoa Tran. Xavier University of Louisiana Art Gallery, November 1, 2024

column, de Nieves has installed metal trees intended to channel the vibrance and joy of New Orleanian celebrations. The boldness of this temporary display expresses a desire to reset the narrative of Harmony Circle in a manner that strikingly departs from its tenure as Lee Circle. De Nieves's piece instead welcomes all and points to the relevance of the city's Latinx immigrants and queer communities. Through this gesture of revision, *The Sacred Heart* indicates the inevitability of change, as this site will certainly have more chapters in its future.

In this volume, New Orleans author Maurice Carlos Ruffin's essay leans into the idealism associated with pulling together voices from disparate places with the aim of signaling ambition from a place often disregarded. Looking towards the future in New Orleans is an exercise in hope. We hope that the hurricanes will be merciful and that the levees will hold. We hope that city, state, and federal institutions will take the measures necessary to bolster the city's infrastructure. In the meantime, New Orleans'ss advocates work tirelessly to shore up the gaps where governmental support is lacking. In the future, we anticipate that the New Orleans diaspora will grow, as home insurance companies depart the city and the cost of remaining and rebuilding within the city increases. Nevertheless, for as long as Prospect exists, it will continue to assert that the creativity emanating from this region matters. The last artwork I will mention is Jeffrey Meris's *Our Moons Shine, For All the Worlds to See* (2024), a light sculpture with a simple yet powerful message. From the shores of the Mississippi River in Algiers, near land that once housed a plantation's slave holding pens, Meris has erected a search light that beams out in Morse code the phrase "I am a possibility." From the coastline in the Bahamas, a twin search light from a water tower beams out in Morse code: "I am a promise." These two phrases, culled from a children's gospel hymn, form a call and response across the Caribbean about the potentiality within (and between) these regions and their inhabitants.

As Ebony and I walked through the rainy streets of Ho Chi Minh City and Hanoi in January 2024, the bright red and gold decorations marking Tết—the Vietnamese New Year—offered a prelude of what lay ahead for P.6, and how this endeavor would end. In 2025, P.6 concluded in February, concurrently with Tết. We ended this project by acknowledging a fresh year, and we began P.6 by marking endings and passings. For the first time since Prospect.I, this triennial's opening weekend straddles Halloween, All Saints' Day, and el Día de los Muertos (Day of the Dead). As Prospect's first triennial since May 2023, when the World Health Organization and the US Center for Disease Control declared the end of COVID's pandemic era, we remember the lives lost over the past three years not only to disease, but also to war and genocide. No one who participated in building P.6, including its incredible staff, escaped personal loss and trauma in recent years. We convened in New Orleans at a time of major global political upheaval. We opened on the eve of a US presidential election, with the specter of a growing far right leering from other countries and from within the US. Nevertheless, we continue to believe that places like New Orleans, the harbingers, hold the right to celebrate each day of continuance.

We treasure each opportunity to build anew, and to signal another beginning.

1   Willie Birch in conversation with the author and Ebony G. Patterson, New Orleans, January 25, 2023.

2   Rich Collins, "Tourism is Economic Development," *Biz New Orleans*, November 1, 2023, accessed on June 26, 2024, https://bizneworleans.com/tourism-is-economic-development/

3   While definitions of the "global majority" vary, this term is gaining in popularity over referring to people of color as "minorities." See Nadine White, "What is 'Global majority' and why is it replacing 'BAME'?" *The Independent*, May 17, 2024, accessed on June 26, 2024, https://www.independent.co.uk/news/uk/home-news/global-majority-bame-explained-national-trust-b2546898.html

4   Richard Campanella has written numerous articles on the "footprint debate" of New Orleans, see for example: "The Great Footprint Debate, Updated," *The New Orleans Times-Picayune*, May 31, 2015.

5   "How is it possible that the justification given for saving New Orleans and southeastern Louisiana was not that it's a major metropolitan area, home to 1.3 million people, or the nation's busiest port system, or perhaps the key nodal point in North America's oil and gas infrastructure? . . . . Whether sinful or soulful, post-Katrina New Orleans was to live and die by the sword of exceptionalism, by how those in power assessed the value—not least in monetary terms—of its culture." Thomas Jessen Adams, Sue Mobley, and Matt Sakakeeny, "What Lies Beyond Histories of Exceptionalism and Cultures of Authenticity," *In Remaking New Orleans*, Durham: Duke University Press, 2019, 2.

6   See for example: Charisse Gibson, "'They became white neighborhoods almost overnight'—Katrina supercharged N.O. gentrification," *WWL Louisiana*, November 22, 2023, accessed July 9, 2024, https://www.wwltv.com/article/news/local/orleans/follow-the-line-gentrification-of-new-orleans/289-ebc89d9a-2921-459d-92ec-3e15b1d37df8

7   2020 US Census data. See also Allison Plyer, "Changing New Orleans Neighborhoods," *The Data Center*, September 14, 2021, https://www.datacenterresearch.org/reports_analysis/changing-new-orleans-neighborhoods/

8   Rick Rojas, David W. Chen and Elizabeth Dias, "Louisiana's Ten Commandments Law Signals a Broader Christian Agenda," *The New York Times*, June 21, 2024.

9   Roby Chavez, "Why the saltwater wedge climbing up the Mississippi River is a wake-up call to the region," *PBS News*, October 13, 2023, accessed on June 27, 2024, https://www.pbs.org/newshour/nation/why-salt-water-is-threatening-drinking-water-in-new-orleans-and-what-officials-are-doing-about-it

10   "Annual 2024 Global Climate Report." *National Centers for Environmental Information*, accessed on January 21, 2025, https://www.ncei.noaa.gov/access/monitoring/monthly-report/global/202413

11   117.3 million people worldwide were forcibly displaced in 2023. "Figures at a glance," UNHCR, accessed July 9, 2024, https://www.unhcr.org/about-unhcr/who-we-are/figures-glance

12   This quote appears in Jeannette Ehlers's artwork *Until the Lion*, 2021. The artist found this phrase in a dungeon in Fort Prinzenstein in Keta, Ghana, used by the Danish for the transatlantic slave trade.

13   US Census, American Community Survey, accessed on June 28, 2024, https://data.census.gov/all?q=poverty%20rate,%20louisiana

14   Email correspondence with the artist, via studio assistant Emma Ross Sermons, May 10, 2024.

Startlement

Ada Limón

It is a forgotten pleasure, the pleasure
      of the unexpected blue-bellied lizard

skittering off his sun spot rock, the flicker
      of an unknown bird by the bus stop.

To think, perhaps, we are not distinguishable
      and therefore no loneliness can exist here.

Species to species in the same blue air, smoke—
      wing flutter buzzing, a car horn coming.

So many unknown languages, to think we have
      only honored this strange human tongue.

If you sit by the riverside, you see a culmination
      of all things upstream. We know now,

we were never at the circle's center, instead
      all around us something is living or trying to live.

The world says, What we are becoming, we are
      becoming together.

The world says, One type of dream has ended
      and another has just begun.

The world says, Once we were separate,
      and now we must move in unison.

"Startlement" by Ada Limón was composed as the opening to
NCA5, the National Climate Assessment.

Shannon Alonzo

b. 1988, St. Joseph, Trinidad and Tobago; lives in St. Joseph, Trinidad and Tobago

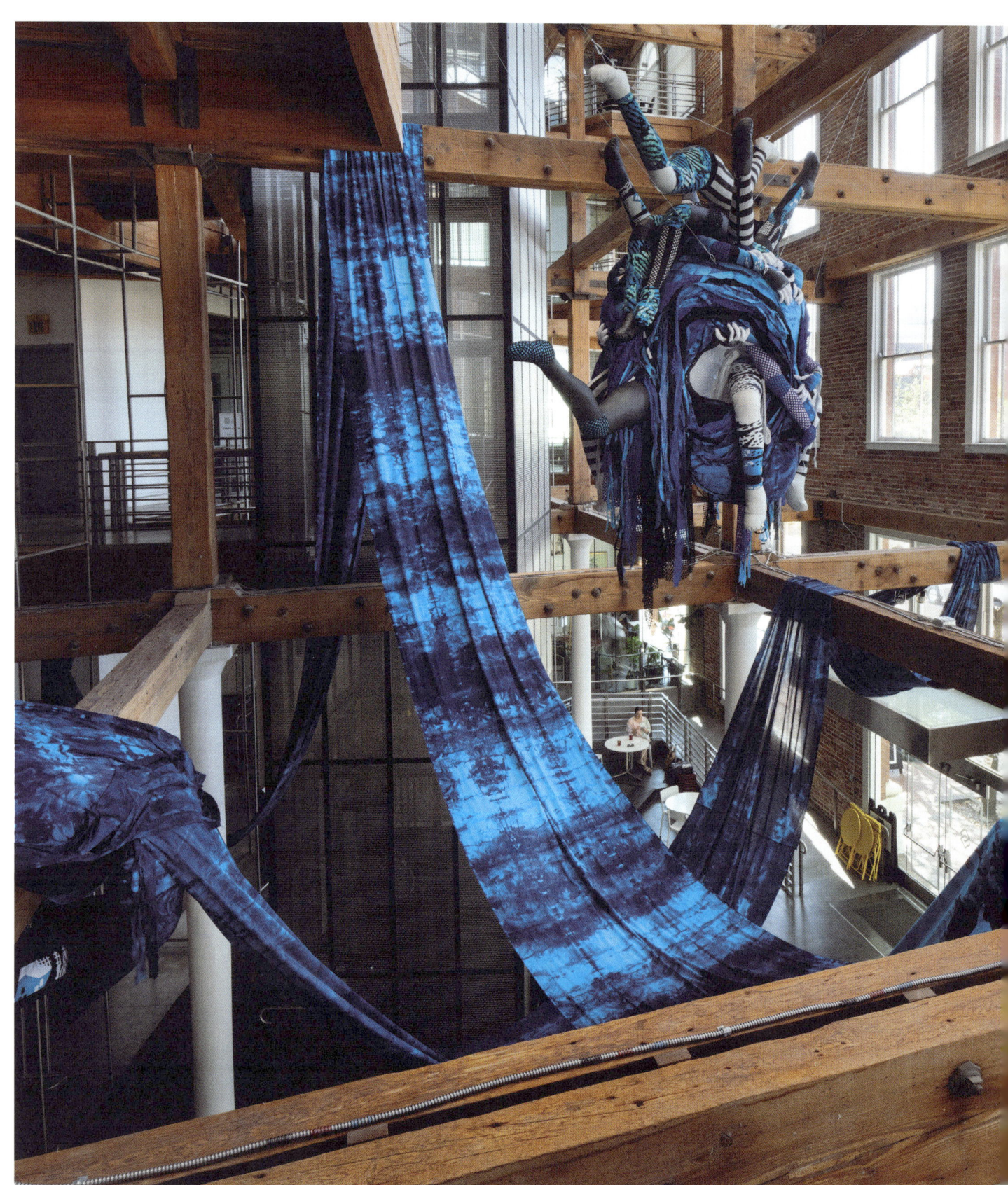

Three Whistles and a Howl, 2024

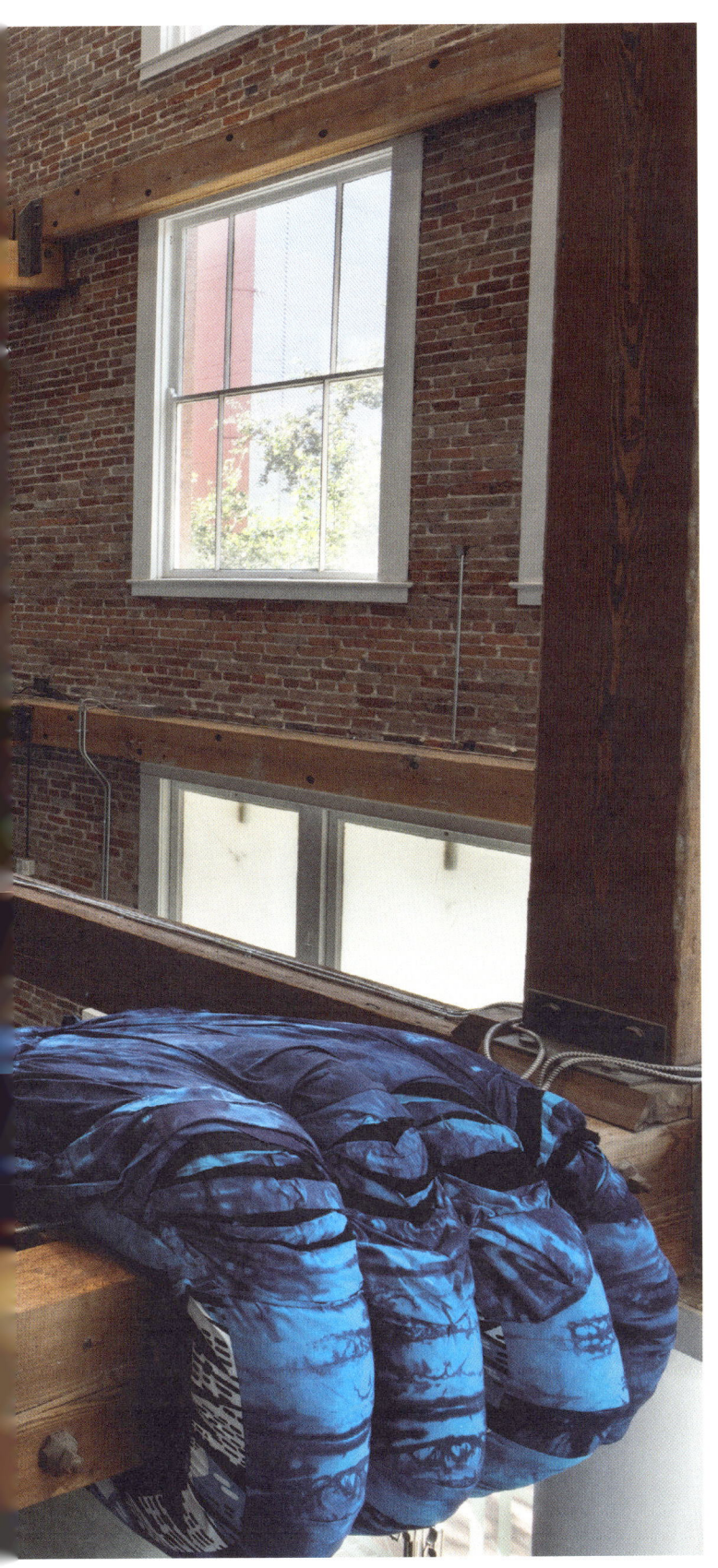

Drawing on her experience as a costume and set designer, Shannon Alonzo threads knots of limbs through masks, mangroves, and sugarcane stalks, in works comprising mural drawings, installation art, and sculpture (much of it sewn and soft). Combined, these elements present fragments of carnival histories and images of collectivity among individuals. Alonzo reveals the Trinidad Carnival, more than mere revelry, to be a stage where bands of performers reprise liberatory events of the past while simultaneously rehearsing for the sake of the future. Continuing the carnival means these events are never truly past. Likewise, the subterranean movement toward liberation predates legally recognized emancipation and has continued unabated since the African encounter with the New World.

After enslaved Africans in Trinidad were emancipated in 1838, once private performances lampooning the upper classes began to take place in public. Music, theatre, dances, parades, and masquerade (*mas*) practices—which appropriated European carnival practices—were developed and performed by organized mas "bands," much like the krewes of Mardi Gras. Collectively, the rituals were named *canboulay*, or *cannes brûlées*, because reenactments of sugarcane fires, or "burnt cane," were customary.

These performances demonstrated a key ambivalence found in the lives of enslaved Trinidadians. On one hand, fire was part of normal harvesting practices, so reenactments

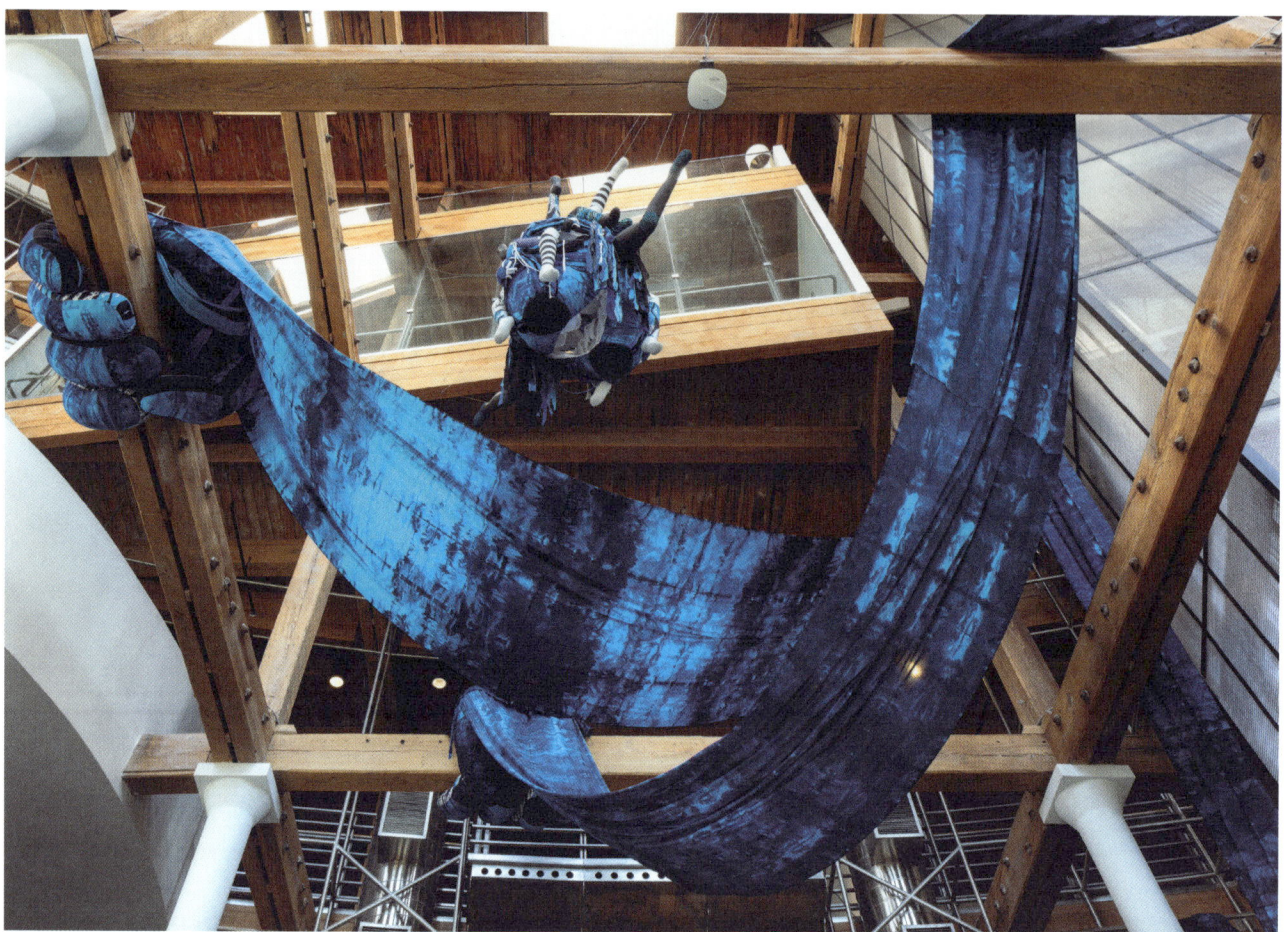

shared real stories of toil and growth; on the other, sometimes enslaved people burned the cane out of rebellion, which meant that canboulay performances also imagined liberation. At the same time, Trinidad's upper classes ceded their carnival practices to the Africans, whom they considered vulgar, and in response, the Africans ratcheted up the violence and sexuality in their festivities.[1] All told, the performance of canboulay instantiated what J.D. Elder called "a duel between the European moral codes and the African canons of freedom."[2] That duel continues anew at Carnival each year and anywhere Black liberation is the goal.

For Prospect.6, Alonzo presents a sculptural installation in the atrium of Contemporary Arts Center, New Orleans: a massive Blue Devil, an homage to bands from the village of Paramin in Trinidad who created their own version of the mas character *Jab Molassie* ("molasses devil"). Now more family friendly, the Blue Devils can still be found at Carnival spitting fire (their trademark) and scaring children. Alonzo's installation, *Three Whistles and a Howl* (2024), features two giant face masks made

of hand-dyed blue cloth, behind which a knot of legs and arms can be seen, with two legs coming out of the eye-holes, and at least two more forming horns. Here the masks form a disguise for individuals, and the legs, indicating both the dances of canboulay and the presence of multiple bodies, form a whole. Each leg, too, is itself a collage: They wear different stockings, so the mask becomes a complex patchwork of different fabrics. In *Three Whistles and a Howl*, Alonzo reminds us that there's a place for everyone, as well as difference, in the collective. Between festivals, perhaps, or wherever subterranean activity aims at liberation, the task seems to be manifold: to find our places, to get organized, to build toward collectivity.

by Terence Washington

1   Milla Cozart Riggio, "Introduction: Theorizing Carnival," in *Carnival: Culture in Action: The Trinidad Experience*. Worlds of Performance, ed. Milla Cozart Riggio (New York: Routledge, 2004), 41–42.
2   J.D. Elder, "Cannes Brûlées," in *Carnival: Culture in Action: The Trinidad Experience*, 49.

Three Whistles and a Howl, 2024 (view from below)

Shannon Alonzo

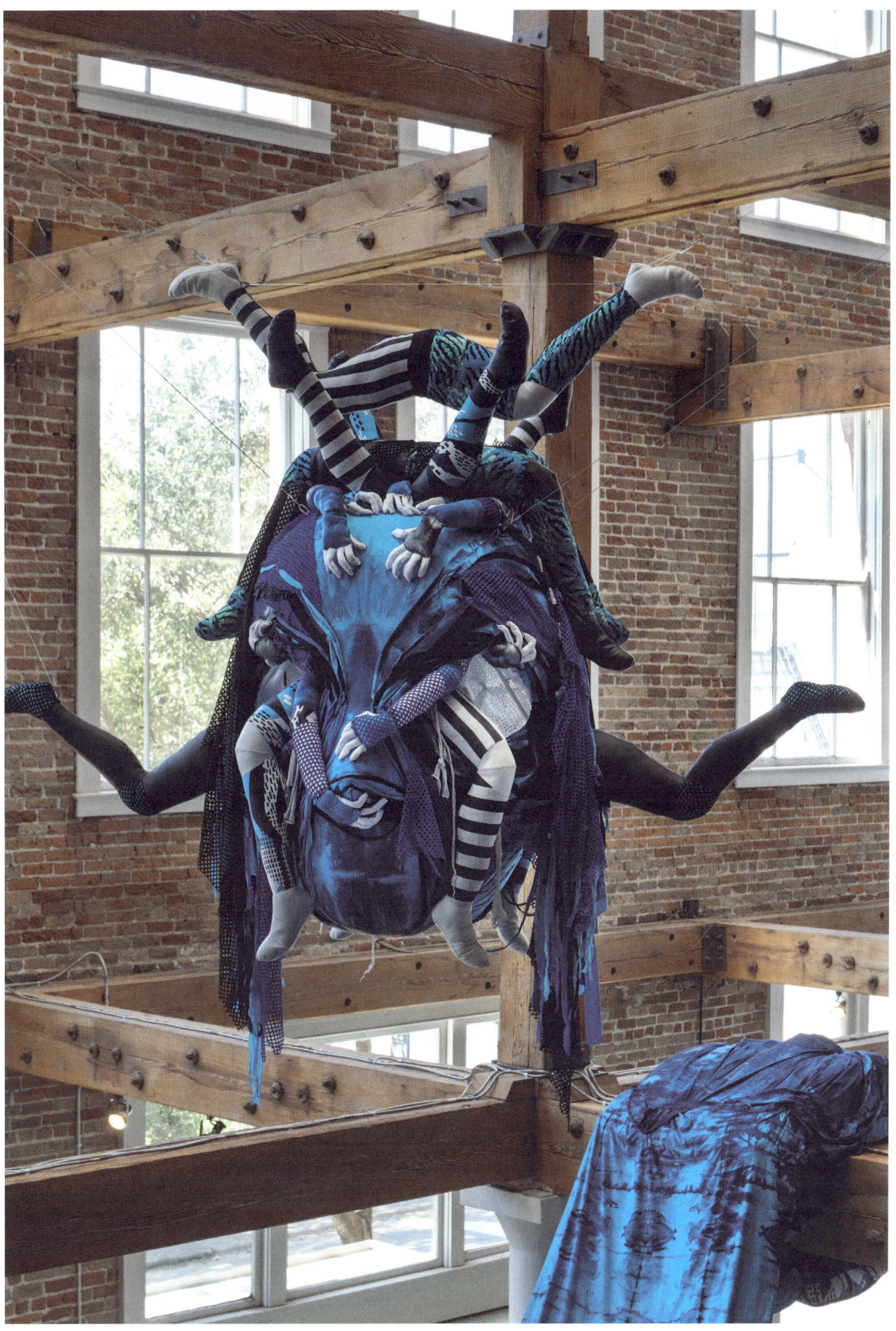

Three Whistles and a Howl, 2024 (detail)

Eddie Rodolfo Aparicio maintains an intimate relationship with trees and the environments they exist in. In MacArthur Park, a cornerstone of Los Angeles's Salvadoran community, a ficus tree's invasive roots raze the adjacent concrete sidewalk, illustrating the power of what lives underground. Like the many waves of people who arrived in the city following exile or escaping violence (including Aparicio's own family from El Salvador), the tree's roots mirror these circumstances: growing quickly, despite the oppression of a system that does not understand their needs—or their power. This is a United Statesian logic of confinement, orchestrated by design, with all its uneven, often violent, transnational flows.

For years Aparicio has created latex-based artworks from these ficus trees. He applies a layer of liquid latex—the fluids found in the rubber tree—onto the bark of one of the ficus trees growing along the LA sidewalk. Aparicio's latex skins are left on the bark for months, and then are slowly and carefully peeled, revealing layers of intimate, interspecies information. The resulting skins feel like ghosts from a specific moment in time—many of the trees he's casted have been cut down. They contain echoes of widespread deforestation, overlapping layers of extraction and accumulation.

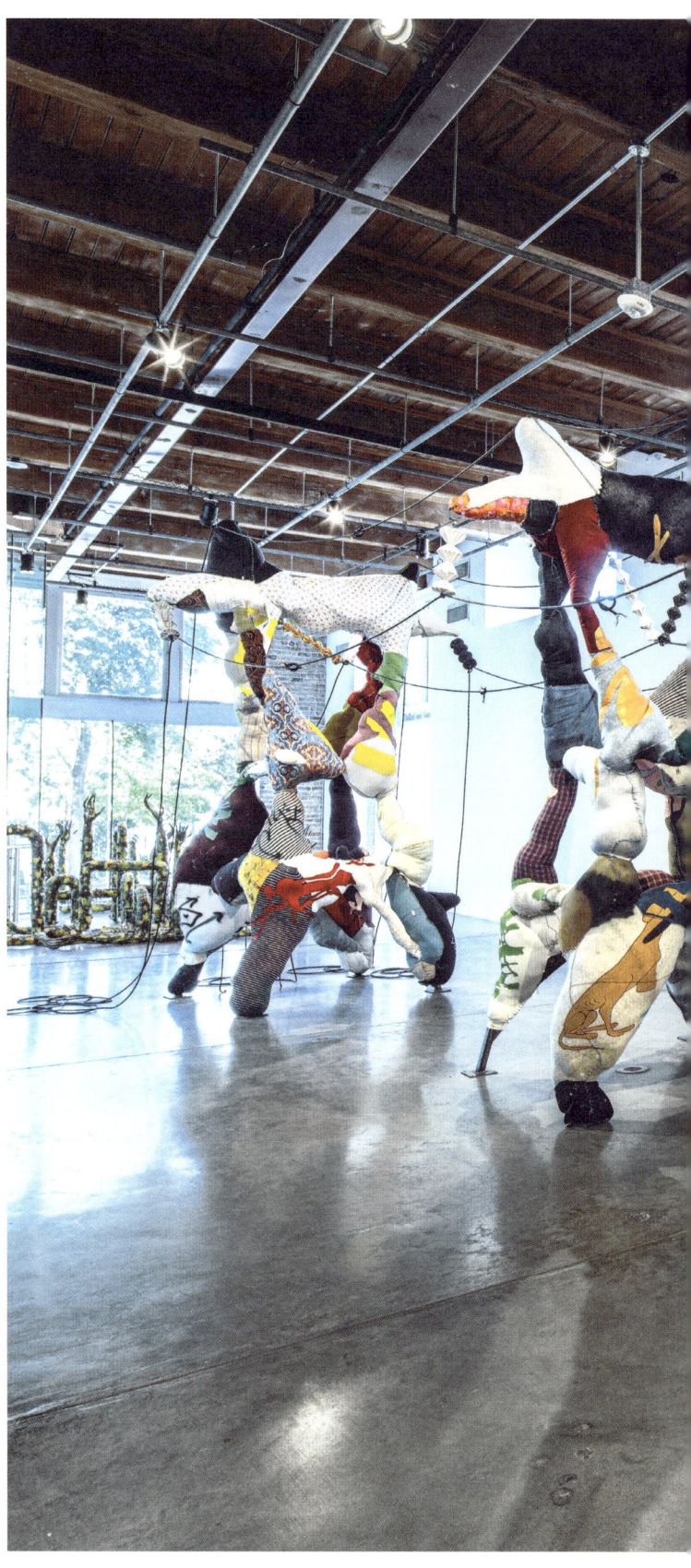

Installation view, L to R: *Muñecas de transmisión (Bridge City/ Whitnall Hwy) (Green)*, 2024; *Muñecas de transmisión (Bridge City/Whitnall Hwy) (Blue)*, 2024; *Muñecas de transmisión (Bridge City/Whitnall Hwy) (Orange)*, 2024

Eddie Rodolfo Aparicio

b. 1990, Los Angeles, CA; lives in Los Angeles, CA

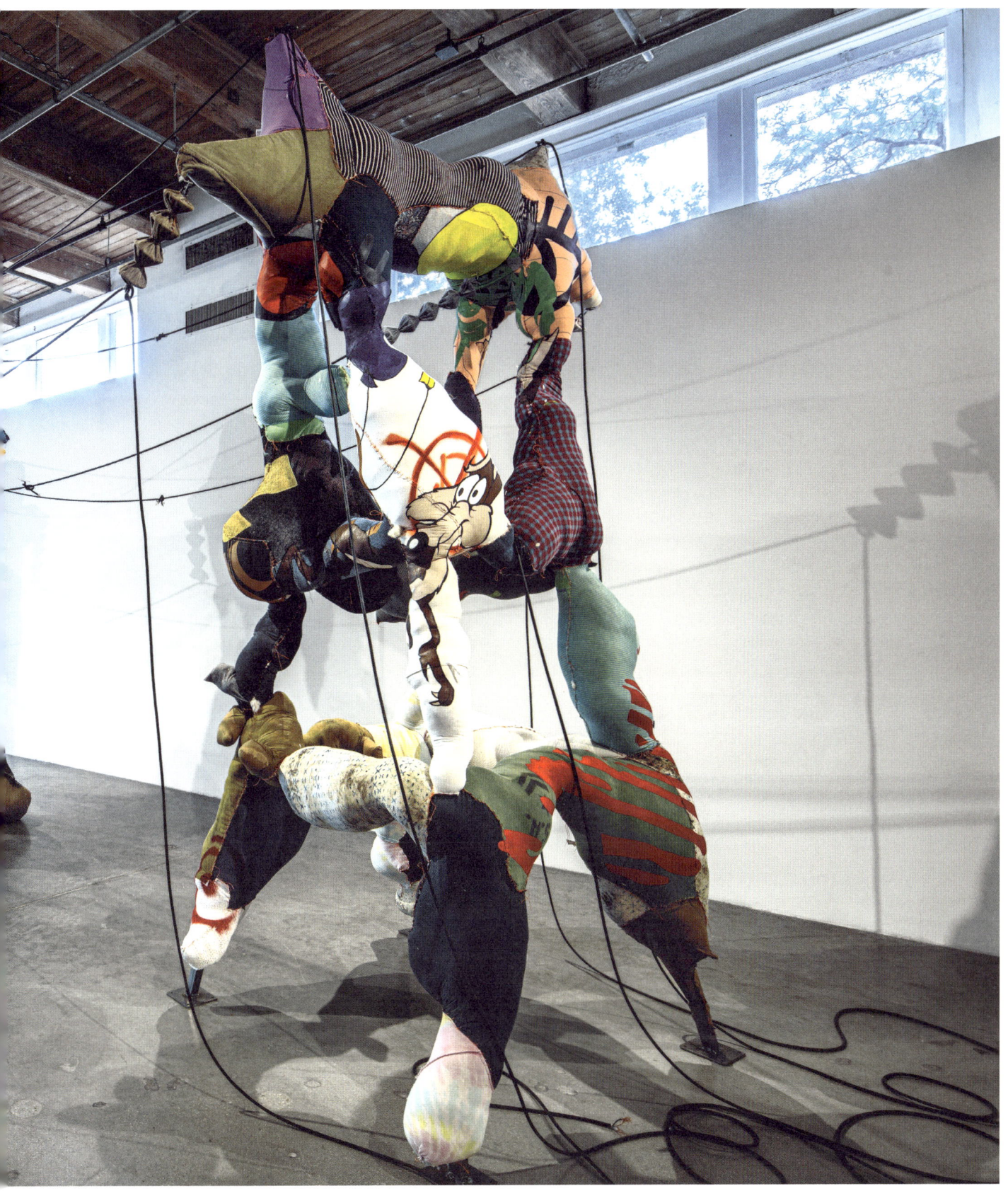

Although Aparicio's arboreal engagement is mostly through the urban landscape of Los Angeles, where the artist was born, raised, and currently lives, he also considers the ceiba tree, which is native to the subtropical Americas. For Prospect.6, Aparicio incorporates kapok from ceiba trees into oversized stuffed dolls, which are adapted into the form of twelve-foot-tall electrical transmission towers. Using a stitching tradition called *diente de lobo* that Aparicio learned from his grandmother, the artist transforms the shape of electrical towers into hand-stitched dolls using the tree's abundant kapok as stuffing—a soft, silky fiber pulled from ceiba fruits, a lightweight material easily dispersed by birds and wind that distributes its seed widely.

These infrastructural bodies, electrical transmission towers, abound in Los Angeles, powering the grid that provides the city's millions of residents with electricity. In each of Aparicio's sculptures, the towers encased in fabric made from various found textiles are assembled like interlocking limbs and clasped hands. Made of kapok, the "dolls" in this context also express humanity's collective potential for movement and change, reflecting our most expansive capacities. When paired with this intelligent plant material, Aparicio's towering lattice structures also embody the unsung histories of migrant labor that have vitalized both LA and New Orleans for decades. In these separate but linked power grids across the country, extractive and exploitative systems are at play, underscoring infrastructure that is designed minimally (yet optimized for maximum efficiency). No matter where it exists, infrastructure imposes onto the landscape and is generative for capital.

Aparicio's works, however, celebrate personalized and communal tactics of survival and ingenuity that have been passed down intergenerationally. Arguing against logics of containment and alienation, Aparicio's work instead points to culture's capacity to relentlessly change, modeled by networks of interspecies reciprocity.

by Alex Santana

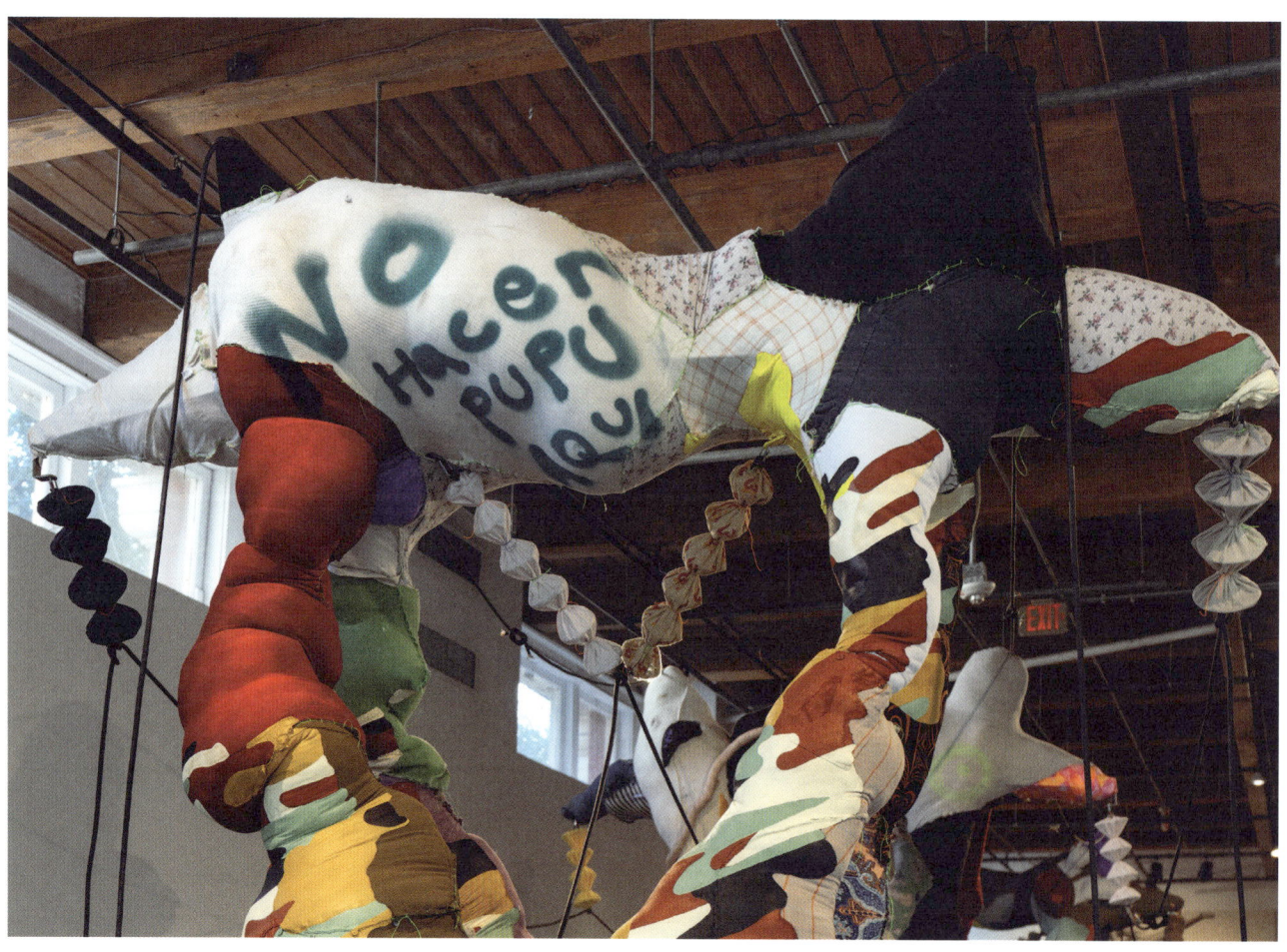

Muñecas de transmisión (Bridge City/Whitnall Hwy) (Green),
2024 (detail)

Ewan Atkinson

b. 1975, Barbados; lives in Barbados

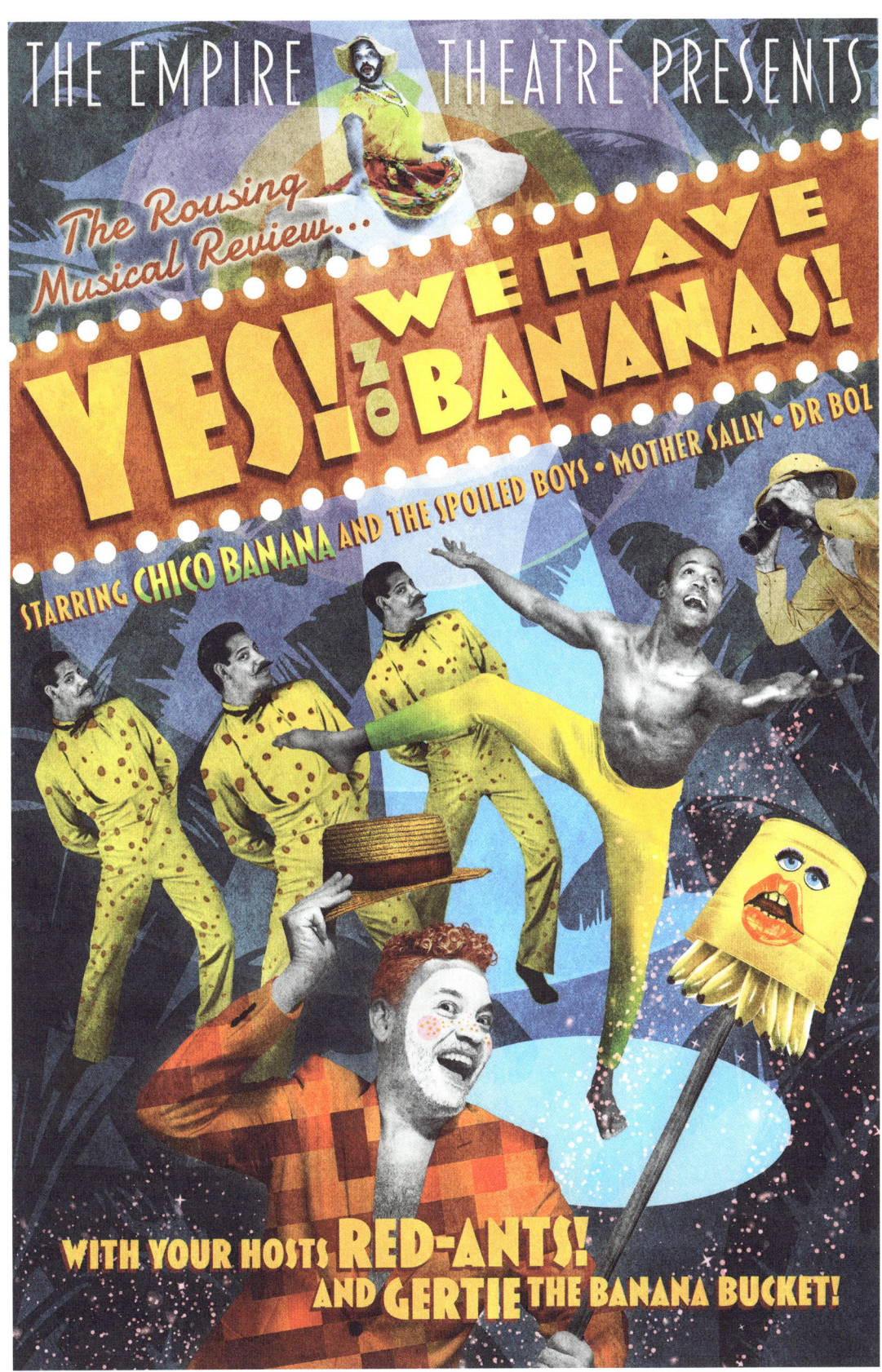

Yes, We Have No Bananas, 2024, from *Stories from
the Neighbourhood: The Great Exposition*, 2015-2024

For Ewan Atkinson's latest iteration of his project *The Neighbourhood* for Prospect.6, titled *The Great Exposition* (2015–2024), the multidisciplinary Barbadian artist welcomes a new host of imagined characters, this time sending them to a fictional version of a world's fair. Board games, digitally altered illustrations from historic books of fairy tales, posters, a vinyl record, and a valentine are just some of the absurdist ephemera that populate the exhibits in the *Exposition*'s various pavilions. Within Atkinson's larger archipelagic worldbuilding, he uses nonlinear storytelling that has expanded since *The Neighbourhood*'s 2006 inception.[1] While the "artifacts" in this iteration reference the bygone Great Expositions—complete with a proverbial 19th-century patina—Atkinson continues his through lines of satire, flirtations with reality, and penetrating critique, all with queer whimsy.

The Neighbourhood parodies Atkinson's own real-world experiences living in Barbados, working in the contemporary art world, and studying distinct Creole traditions dispersed across the Caribbean islands, as well as histories of racial stratification. His characters embody these humorous reckonings, such as the anthrozoologist Dr. Tobias Boz, who makes his return this time gracing a record album as an odalisque and offering his latest scholarship. The album is a spoof of animal field recordings, and the publication of a book of photo-collaged images of "stray dog" genitalia, which, in reality, are dick pics sent (with consent) to Atkinson by previous boyfriends and friends.

The Spinster Sisters stare out confidently from a framed photo-collage as if plucked from a familial shelf; they hold various accoutrements, from a teddy bear to a garden hose and accordion. The trio references Barbadian women who sold "sailor's valentines" to men for their lovers at home. Atkinson's half-dog, half-mongoose Dogoose is a hybrid creature who applies for asylum and journeys through the bureaucratic hoops of post-colonial immigration—documented in photo-collages of a *Ladybird*-like book—only to lose his magical smile. And The Magic Metal Mule(atto), a rabbit-like automaton replacing his counterpart The Magic Mule—created by the artist using AI manipulations—reads fortunes and projects the dawn of technology's co-optation of leisure and perhaps the future writ large. Each of Atkinson's characters bear the artist's own face, revealing his role-play as persona, archivist, and unreliable narrator.[2]

Dr. Tobias Boz, The Spinster Sisters, The Dogoose, and The Metal Magic Mule(latto) seem to speak back from their static artifact forms—thus unmooring the ethnographic foundations of expositions, the histories of which are mired in colonial knowledge productions through discovery, tourism, and ultimately, exploitation. Trafficking in the contrivance of national stereotyping and othering, world's fair-like tactics persist in global contemporary art biennials. Atkinson acknowledges this haunting colonialism in his "queer surrealisms" by upending their hierarchical logics and unveiling the farce of objectivity—this time through the tiny addition of a newspaper clipping announcing this particular world fair's apparent failure.[3]

by Laurel V. McLaughlin

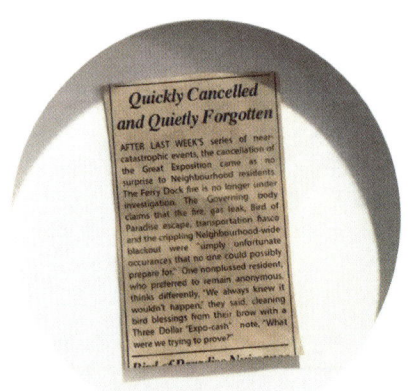

1   I reference Tatiana Flores and Michelle A. Stephen's understanding of the archipelago as a rhizomatic descriptor for the Caribbean islands' entanglement between and among one another, as well as within networks of the mainland, resisting their historical characterization as fragmented and heterogeneous in "Relational Undercurrents: Toward an Archipelagic Model of Insular Caribbean Art," *Relational Undercurrents: Contemporary Art of the Caribbean Archipelago*, ed. Tatiana Flores and Michelle A. Stephens (Long Beach, CA: Museum of Latin American Art, 2017), 15.

2   Author conversation with the artist, July 19, 2024.

3   For more on the queer strategies of storytelling in Atkinson's work, see Jafari S. Allen, "A Queer Decipherment of Select Pages from the Fieldnotes of Dr. Tobias Boz, Anthropologist," *CQV: Caribbean Queer Visualities* (New York, NY: Small Axe, Inc. 2016), 134.

Sight Unseen No.109 (Filler), 2024, from Stories from the Neighbourhood: The Great Exposition, 2015-2024

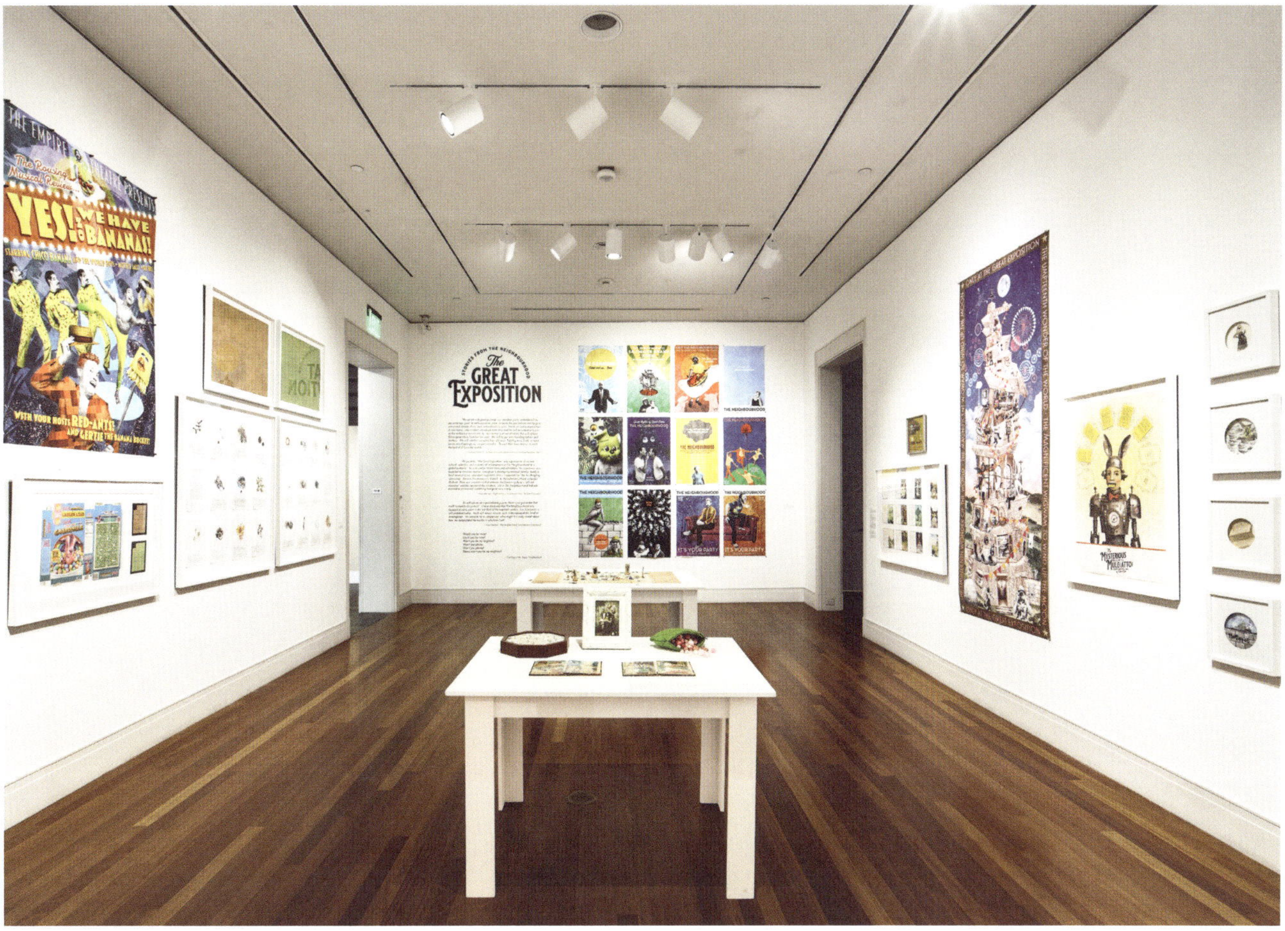

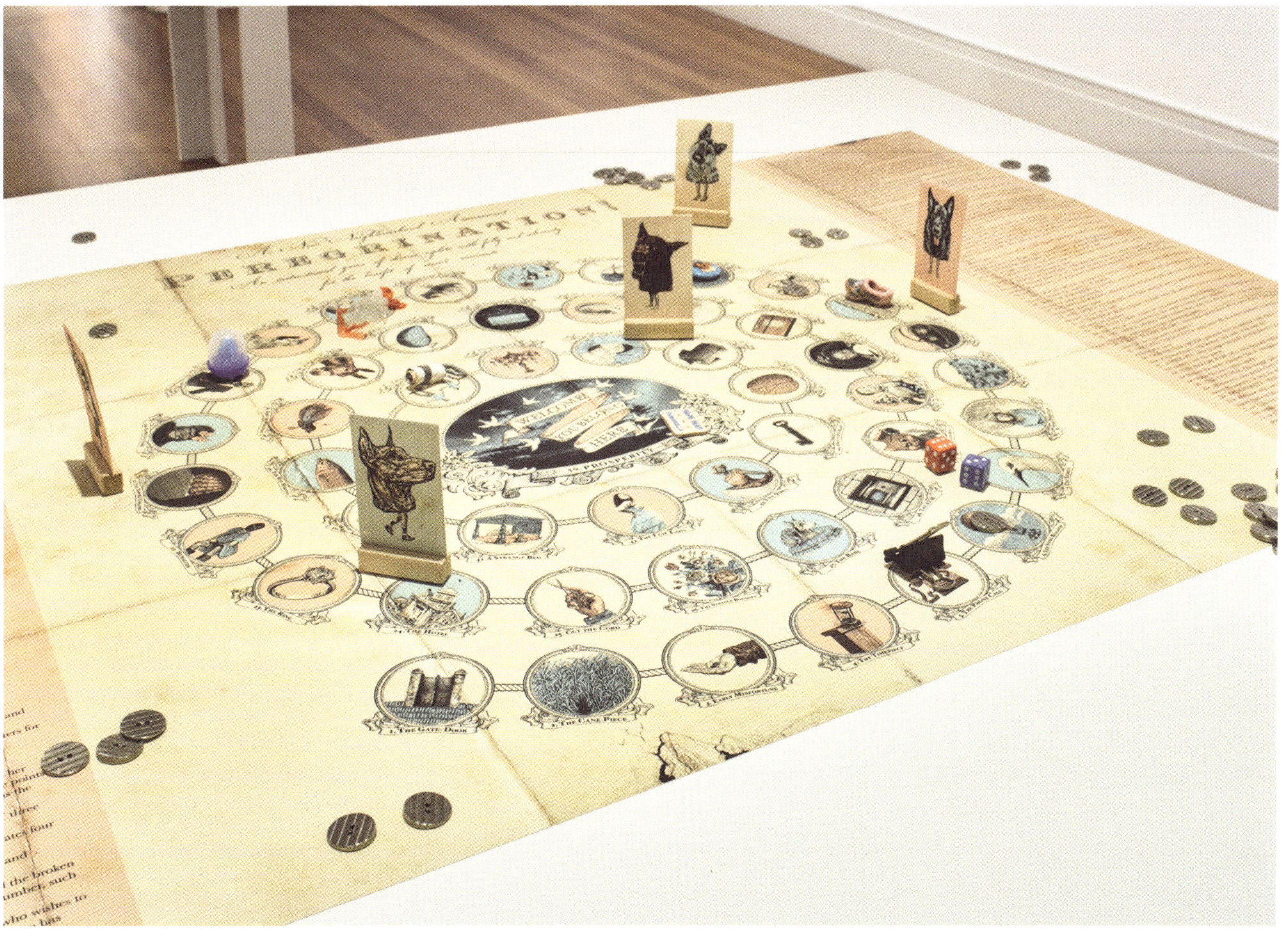

Top: *Stories from the Neighbourhood: The Great Exposition*, 2015–2024

Above: *Peregrination, a Playable Reproduction*, 2018, from *Stories from the Neighbourhood: The Great Exposition*, 2015–2024

Teresa Baker

b. 1985, Watford City, ND; lives in Los Angeles, CA

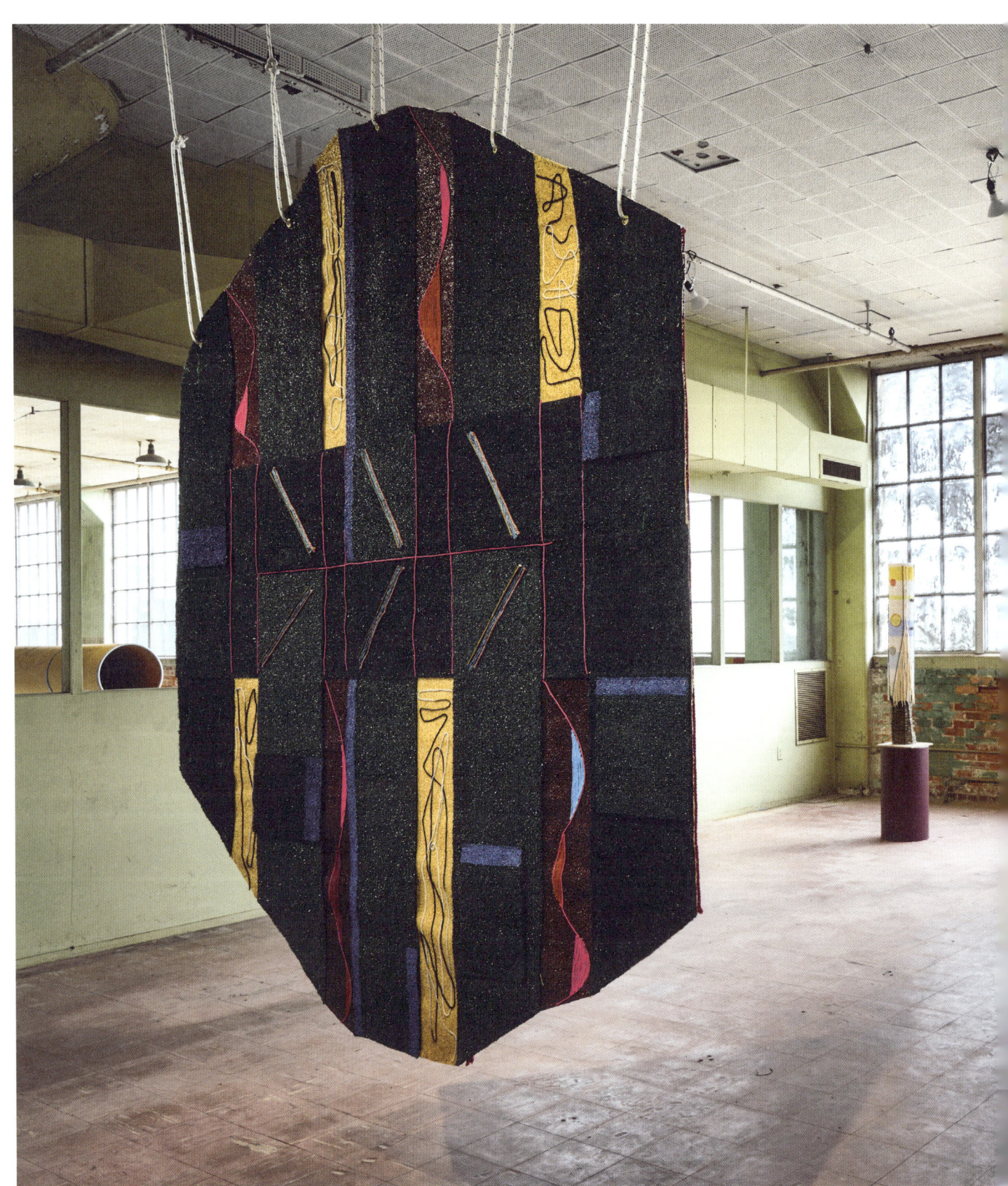

L to R: *Tracing the Dirt*, 2024, *Beacon I*, 2024, *Beacon 3*, 2024, and *Beacon 2*, 2024

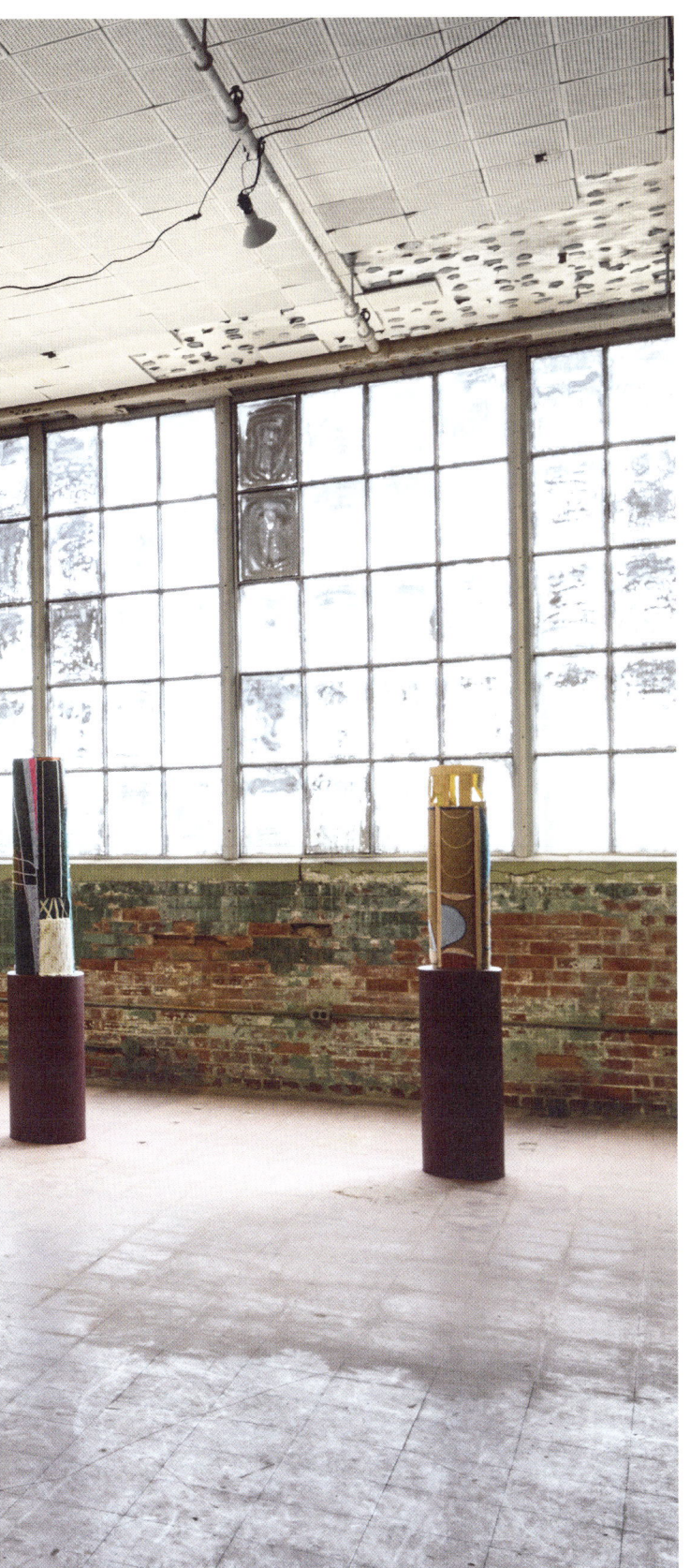

Born in the Northern Plains of North Dakota, Teresa Baker grew up with a profound connection to the land, which has deep-seated significance within her Mandan and Hidatsa tribal communities. Baker's abstract works reference landscapes and topographies, and capture the memories and sensations of her earliest life experiences. Her works speak to the materiality of land: dirt, trees, the animals that graze on it, but also the way it produces belonging and freedom, both physical and spiritual.

For Prospect.6, Baker's forms animate the center of a room at the defunct Ford Motor Plant in playful and fluid ways. The enclosed space allows visitors to encounter her artworks in an intimate, almost mystical environment, akin to the Rothko Chapel. The space is populated by three sculptural works from her *Beacons* series (2024), as well as *Tracing the Dirt* (2024), a suspended object that embraces the liminality of genres between painting, sculpture, and textile. With these works, Baker continues a nearly decade-long use of AstroTurf.[1] After Hurricane Harvey hit the Gulf Coast, Baker, who lived in Beaumont, Texas, at the time, stumbled on the material at Home Depot. The brightly colored artificial grass is an unexpectedly antithetical proxy for the sprawling grasslands of the Northern Plains, however, its crunchy texture and visual exuberance aptly speaks to a form of resilience and adaptability.

Tracing the Dirt's tapestry-like surface is first encountered from its verdant green face, which is intersected by blue color blocks and dyed yarn that fluidly directs the eye. Baker manipulates the surface through intuitive processes, layering paint, yarn, willow

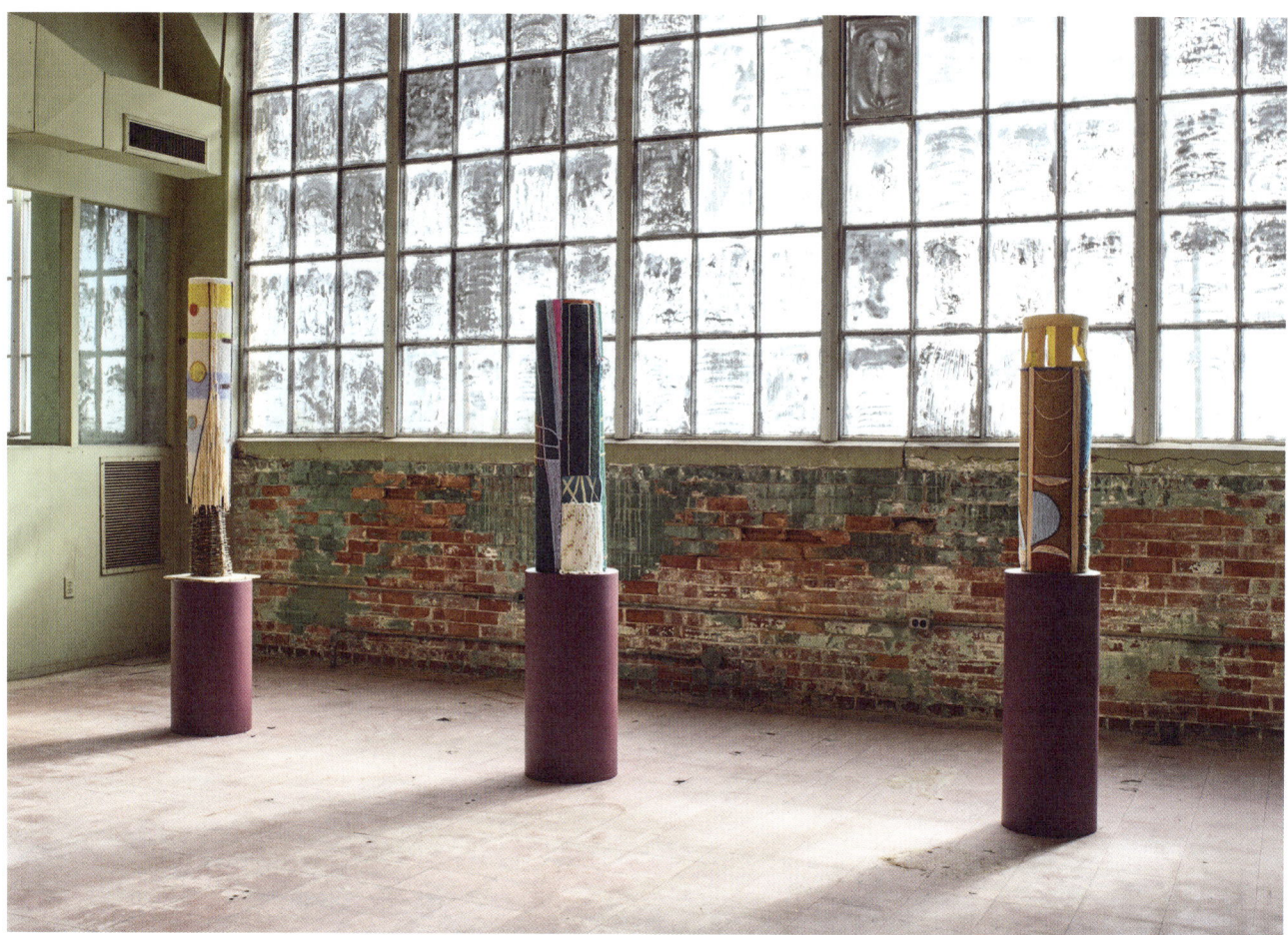

branches, and sections of AstroTurf in some areas, and in others, cutting away at the turf, adding dimensionality. The work's verso appears faded to the tan-brown color of dead grass. The color choice nods to prairie lands, and the drought-ridden landscape of Baker's current home in Los Angeles. Here, the surface is punctuated by thin willow branches and gestural marks drawn with thread. The work's title recalls a childhood pastime of tracing in the dirt, a meditative action, and indicates land's ability to hold memory.

Beacon 1, *2*, and *3* stand like sentinels in a row, positioned in dialogue with the room's window, which faces the banks of the Mississippi River. Cutouts in buckskin-covered cardboard and gaps between woven willow branches channel and filter sunlight, enacting their implied function as lighthouses guiding one's return to land. Baker is interested in the malleability of purpose and meaning of each material and formal choice. Willow, for example, is laden with cultural significance for the Mandan and Hidatsa, holding practical (basket-making and dwelling construction) and spiritual/ceremonial functions at once.

Baker draws connections between the multivalent qualities of culture, history, memory, spirituality, and notions of home. Her forms fuse synthetic and natural materials, breaking from the structural and material boundaries of a traditional rectangular canvas. Baker leaves room for the material and forms to take on narratives through association and personal connection. For the artist, home is associated not only with a specific place, but with the experience of comfort and lack of inhibition. As threats to (home)lands persist, Baker's works act as guides or maps for how to locate and sustain our own sense of freedom in the world.

by Leilani Lynch

1   The siting of Baker's artworks in the Ford Motor Plant is coincidentally apt. In 1962, the Ford Foundation, still affiliated with Ford Motor Company at the time, commissioned Monsanto to research and fabricate a synthetic material for play and exercise, called ChemGrass, eventually renamed AstroTurf. https://astroturf.com/astroturf-the-story-behind-the-product-that-revolutionized-sports-surfaces/

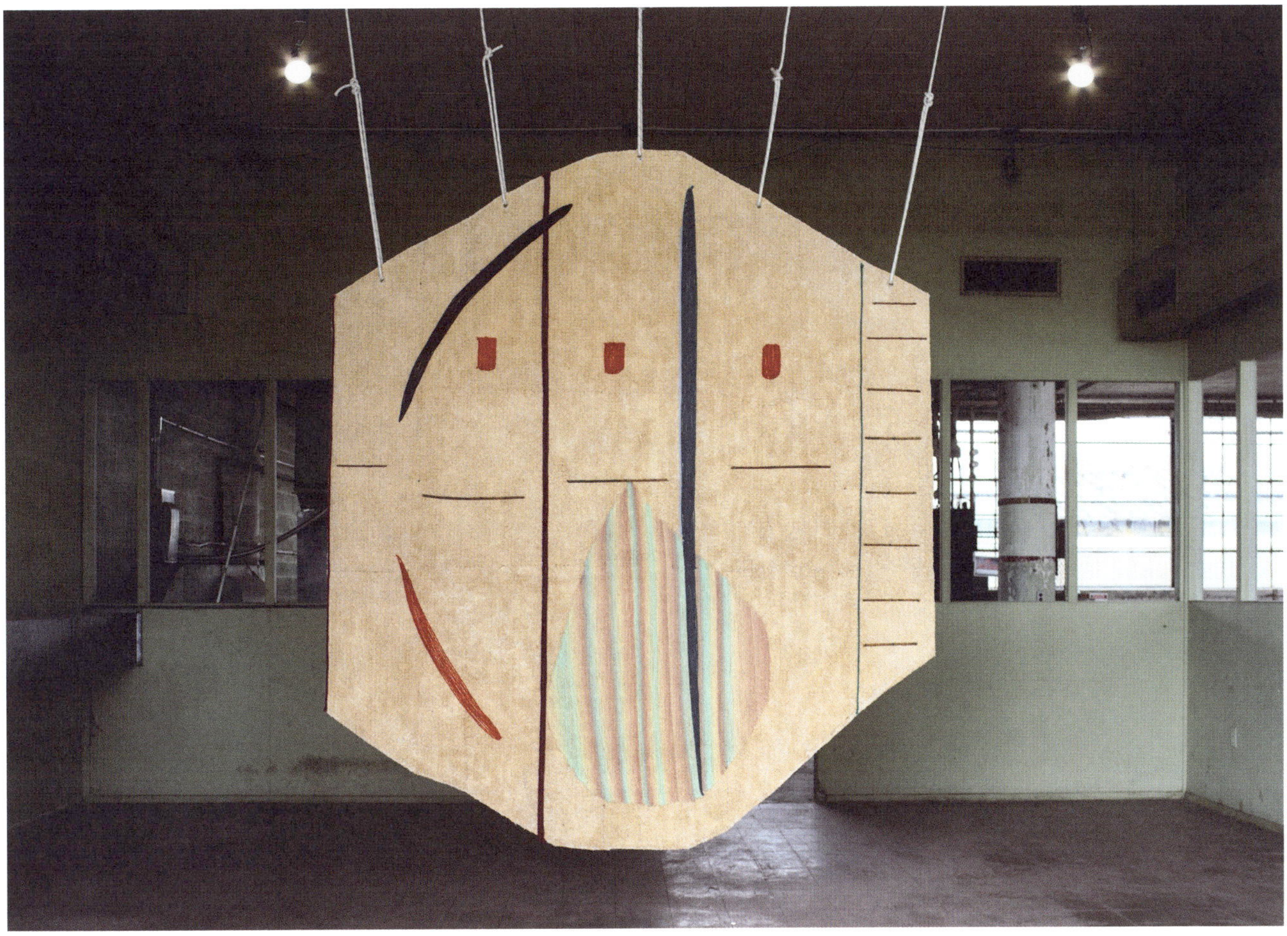

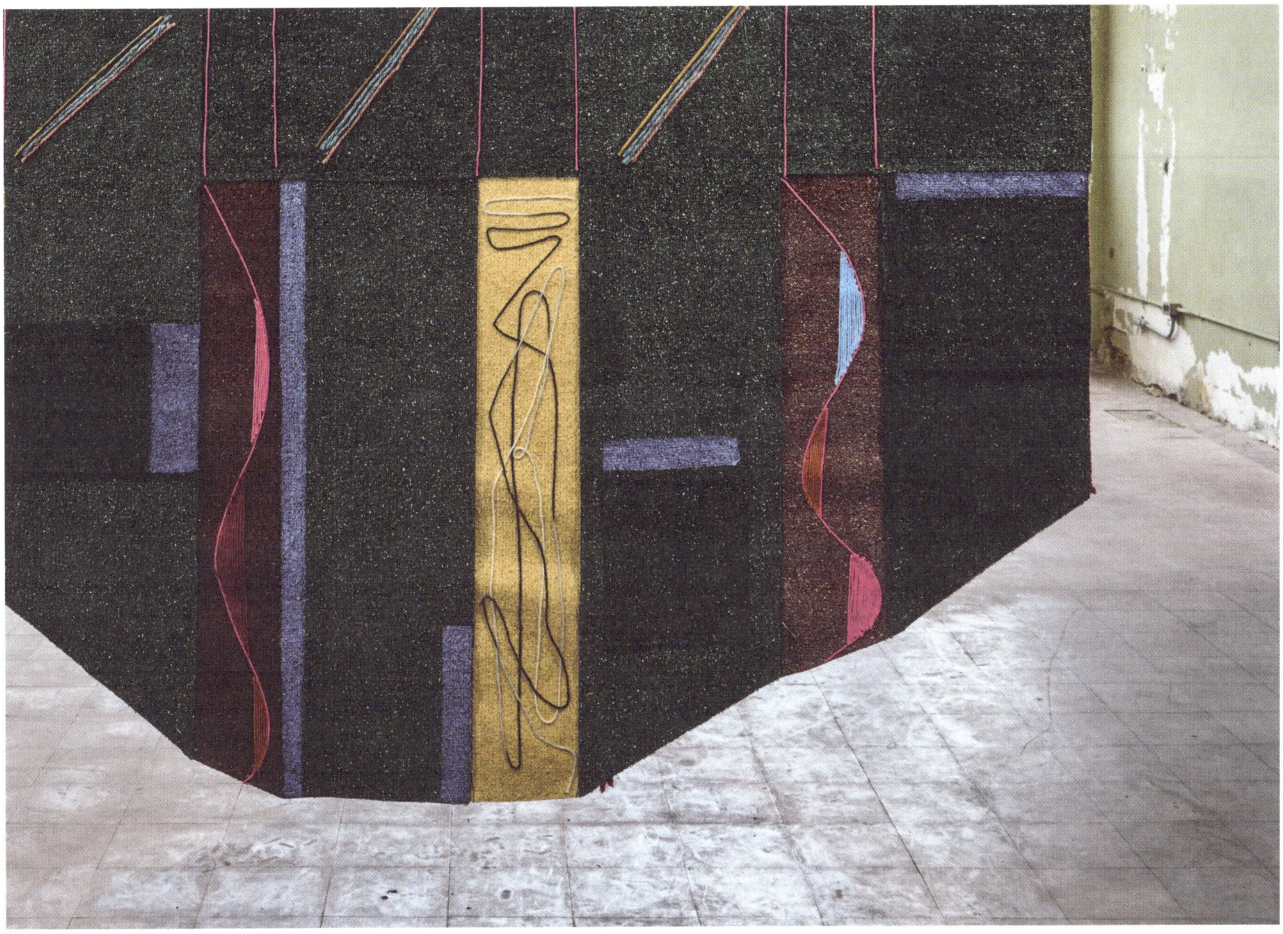

Top: *Tracing the Dirt*, 2024

Above: *Tracing the Dirt*, 2024 (detail)

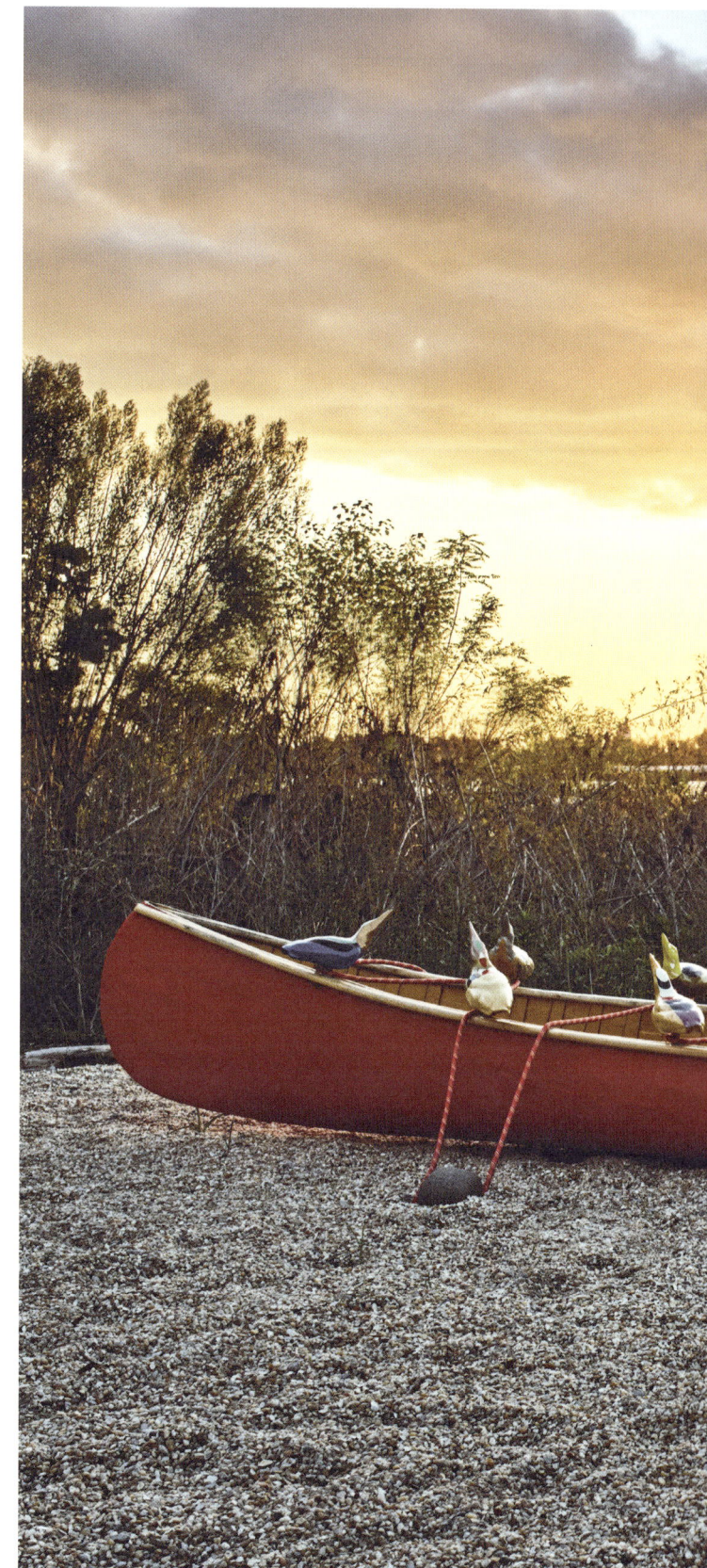

Andrea Carlson's two new artworks for Prospect.6 lean more heavily into the depiction of an object that is often viewed as a Native signifier: the canoe. In these two new sculptural installations, Carlson explores the interconnectedness of communities from the north, like the Ojibwe, to those located in the New Orleans area, including but not exclusive to the Chitimacha, Atakapa, and Choctaw, as well as other Indigenous peoples. She does this by contemplating the historic trade routes of the Mississippi River and the vehicles used to move goods and people along this waterway.

These two works address the future mourning of New Orleans. As climate disruption becomes an ever-increasing reality, those islands, people, and cultures lying in low places are more susceptible to erasure—a painful state of being known all too well by Indigenous people across the world. In her two works, Carlson pays homage to an important artistic influence, Jaune Quick-to-See Smith, who has several pieces that begin with the words "Trade Canoe," including *Trade Canoe for Don Quixote* (2004), *Trade Canoe: Making Medicine* (2018), and *Trade Canoe for the North Pole* (2017). The latter, perhaps, is the most connected to Carlson's two installations.

Trade Canoe for Earthdivers to Come, 2024

Andrea Carlson

b. 1979, USA; lives in Grand Marais, MN

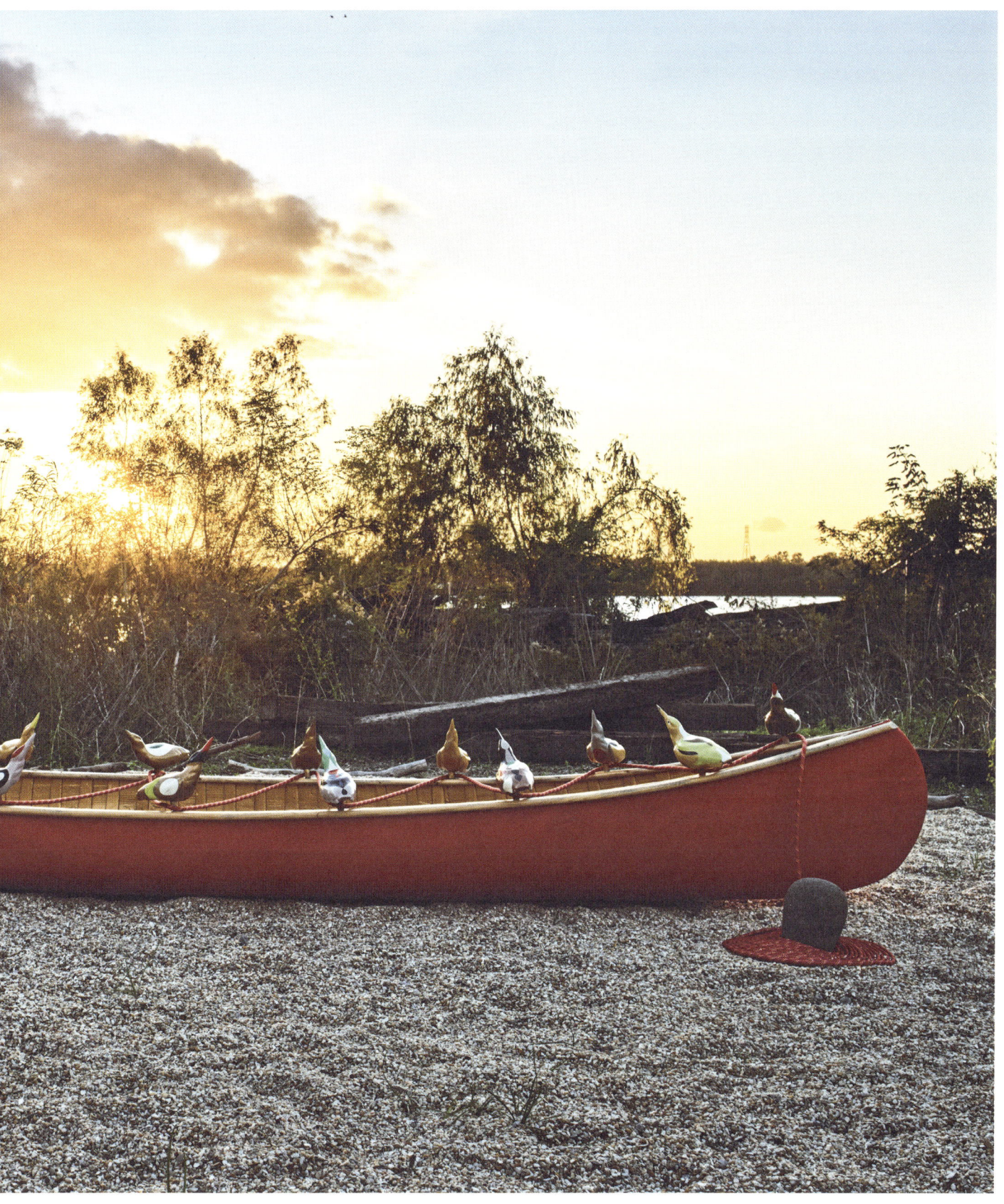

Trade Canoe for the North Pole, according to the Whitney Museum of American Art, "is populated with images of palm trees, buffalo, and rubber ducks . . . which ominously remind viewers of the effects of people's actions in transforming the environment and increasing global warming."[1] Both of Carlson's works—the outdoor piece entitled *Trade Canoe for Earthdivers to Come*, and the indoor work *Trade Canoe for Recollection*—signal Jaune Quick-to-See-Smith as an artistic predecessor, but Carlson brings her own meaning and nuance to the conversation. With their size, and especially with the outdoor canoe's bright red color, the works become something that people have to reckon with, move aside for, and navigate around. They cannot be easily ignored by viewers, in the same way that Indigenous people can be ignored when placed out of sight, or a painting can be passed by without interrupting a stride.

Additionally, in *Trade Canoe for Earthdivers to Come*, Carlson also acknowledges that there will be a rebuilding after the losses caused by climate change, but that some things will be forever lost. This work relates to the Anishinaabe recreation story that tells of Earthdivers who lost their lives trying to rebuild the world after the great flood. The indoor work, *Trade Canoe for Recollection*, is flanked by multiple paintings of Ojibwe assumption sashes. These sashes were also traditionally meant for carrying items when wrapped around the body. When shown together, the artist asks us to contemplate what vehicles or tools we will use to remember, to mourn, to carry, or to anchor ourselves as we move into the murky future.

by Dakota Hoska

1   Whitney Museum of American Art, Teacher Guide: Jaune Quick-to-See Smith: Memory Map, https://whitney.org/education/schools-educators/k-12/teaching-materials/teacher-guides/jaune-quick-to-see-smith/moving-messages, accessed on August 21, 2024.

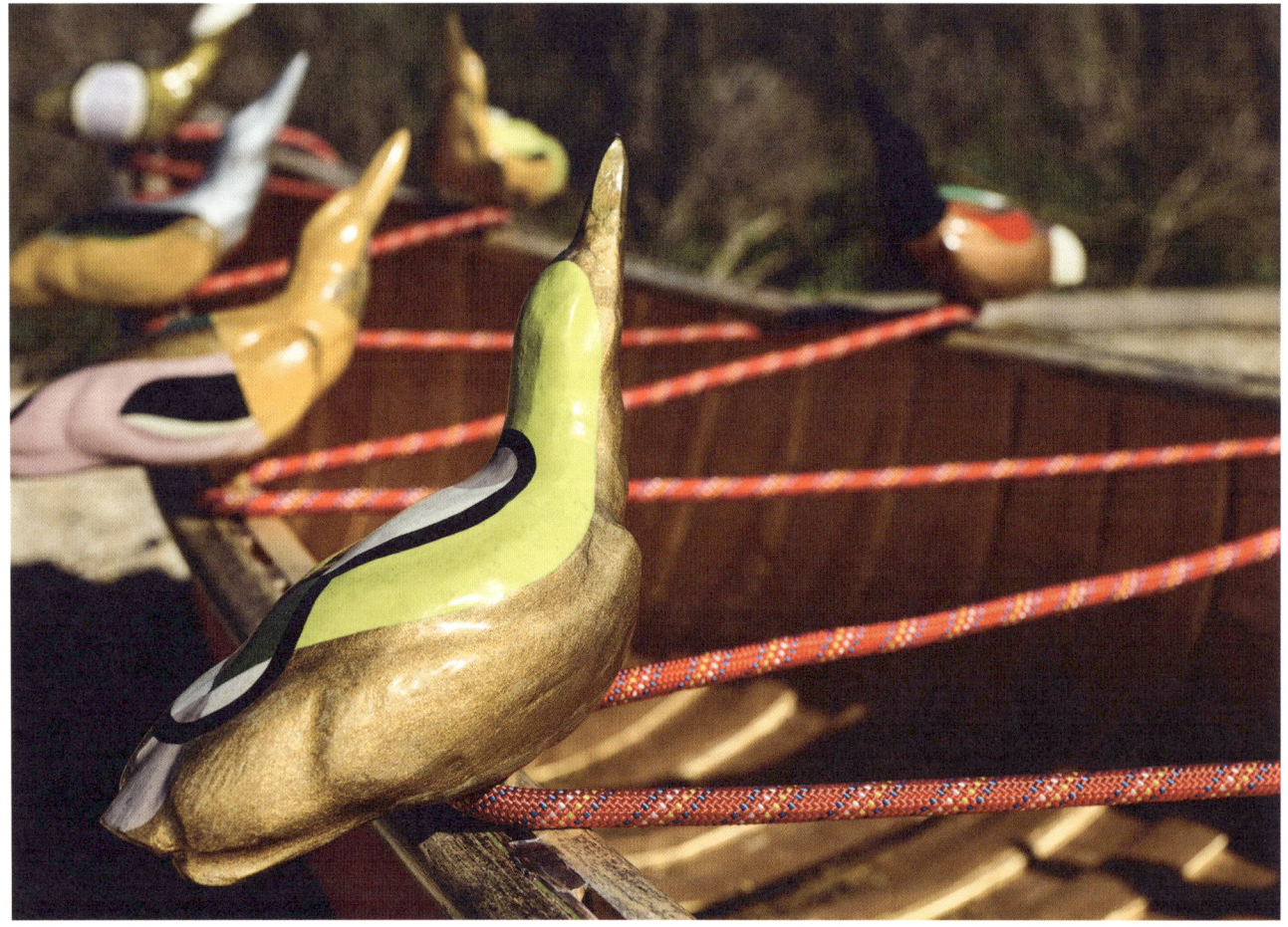

Trade Canoe for Earthdivers to Come, 2024 (detail)

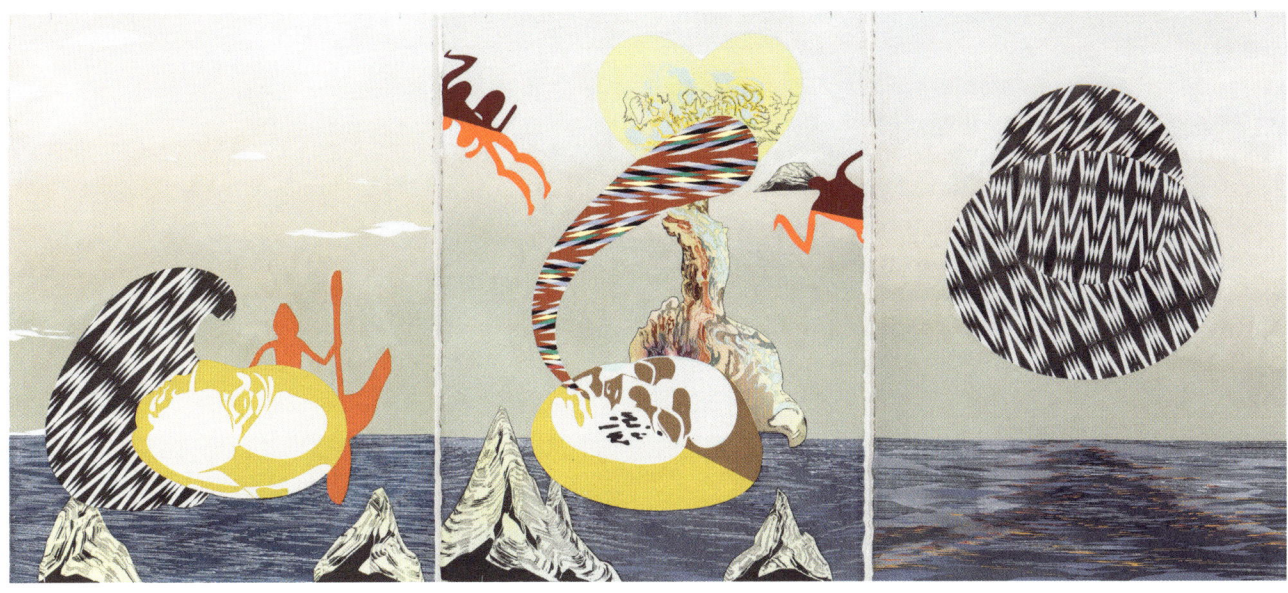

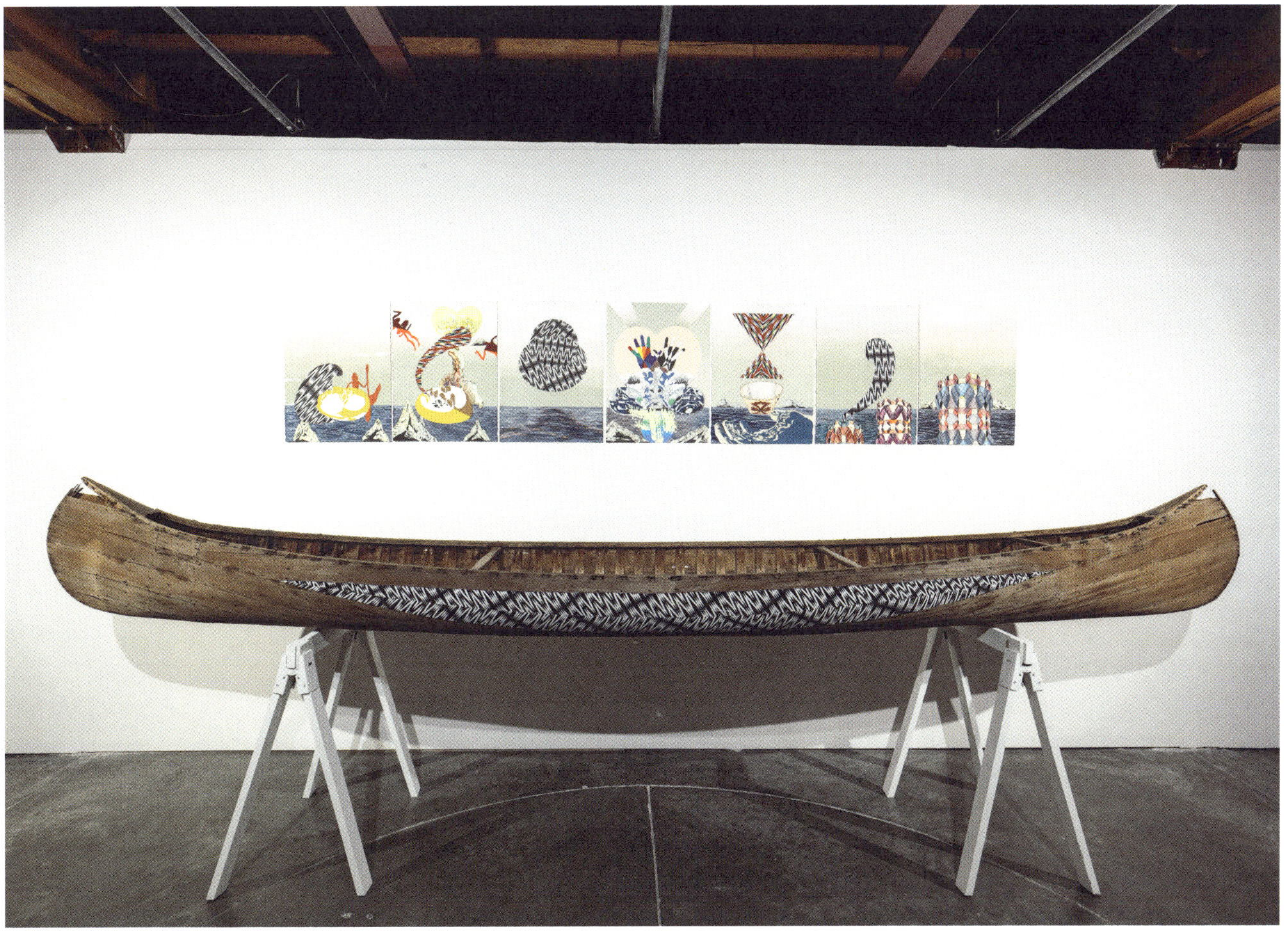

Top: *Trade Canoe for Recollection*, 2024 (detail)   Above: *Trade Canoe for Recollection*, 2024

Hannah Chalew

b. 1986, Baltimore, MD; lives in New Orleans, LA

Hannah Chalew's *Orphan Well Gamma Garden* (2024) is a prophetic warning, a materialized vision for a speculative future where ecologies reengineer remnants of the petrochemical industry into conduits for life beyond humans. For her installation, Chalew salvaged an oil wellhead—a machine part that once propelled the extraction of fossil fuels from the wetlands of New Orleans—from a junkyard. At the Contemporary Art Center, this wellhead has been repurposed as a fountain that supports living plants, as well as sculpted ones made from materials that speak to the longer histories of the wetlands' exploitation.

The New Orleans-based artist and master naturalist looks to the wetlands because climate change's causes and effects are most visibly entangled there. Oil wells populate the Mississippi River Delta, intermingling with cypress trees in swamps and churning beneath the Gulf Stream. Dredging accelerates erosion in these delicate landscapes, while refining emits greenhouse gases that contribute to the intensity and frequency of hurricanes. In Chalew's vision for the afterlife of infrastructure, wetland plants embrace their anatomical resemblance to refinery pipes by overtaking and merging with defunct, industrially scaled equipment. Entwined, the formal rhyme between the networks of pipes and root systems of trees suggests mutation.

The title of Chalew's installation points to two particular phenomena that plague Louisiana's wetlands. First, when no longer financially viable, wells are abandoned instead of dismantled. The wellhead at the center of Chalew's installation is one such orphaned object. Often, abandoned equipment left in the environment leaches toxins. When the toxins are radioactive, the wetlands become unofficial gamma gardens, the second phenomenon to which Chalew's title refers. These atomic-era experiments irradiated plants in order to

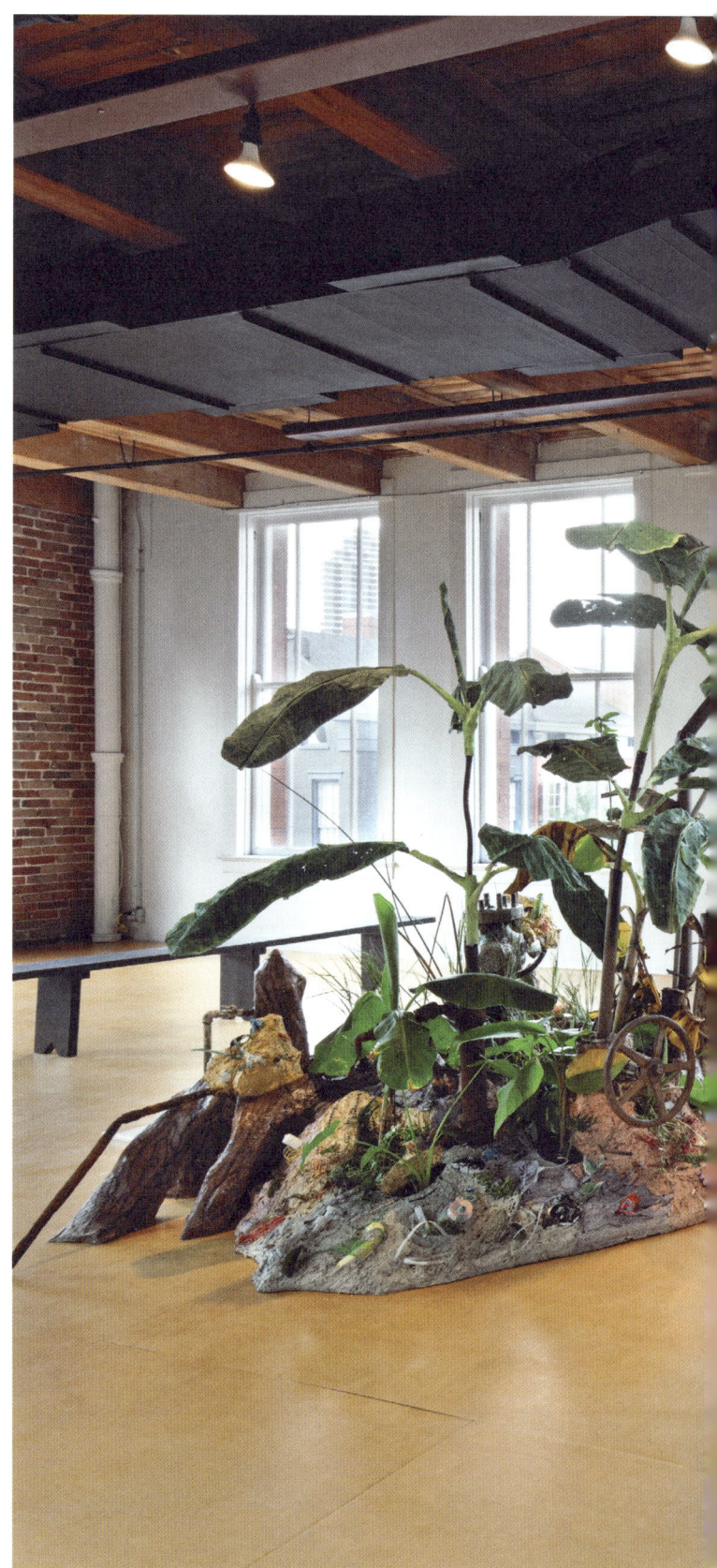

Orphan Well Gamma Garden, 2024

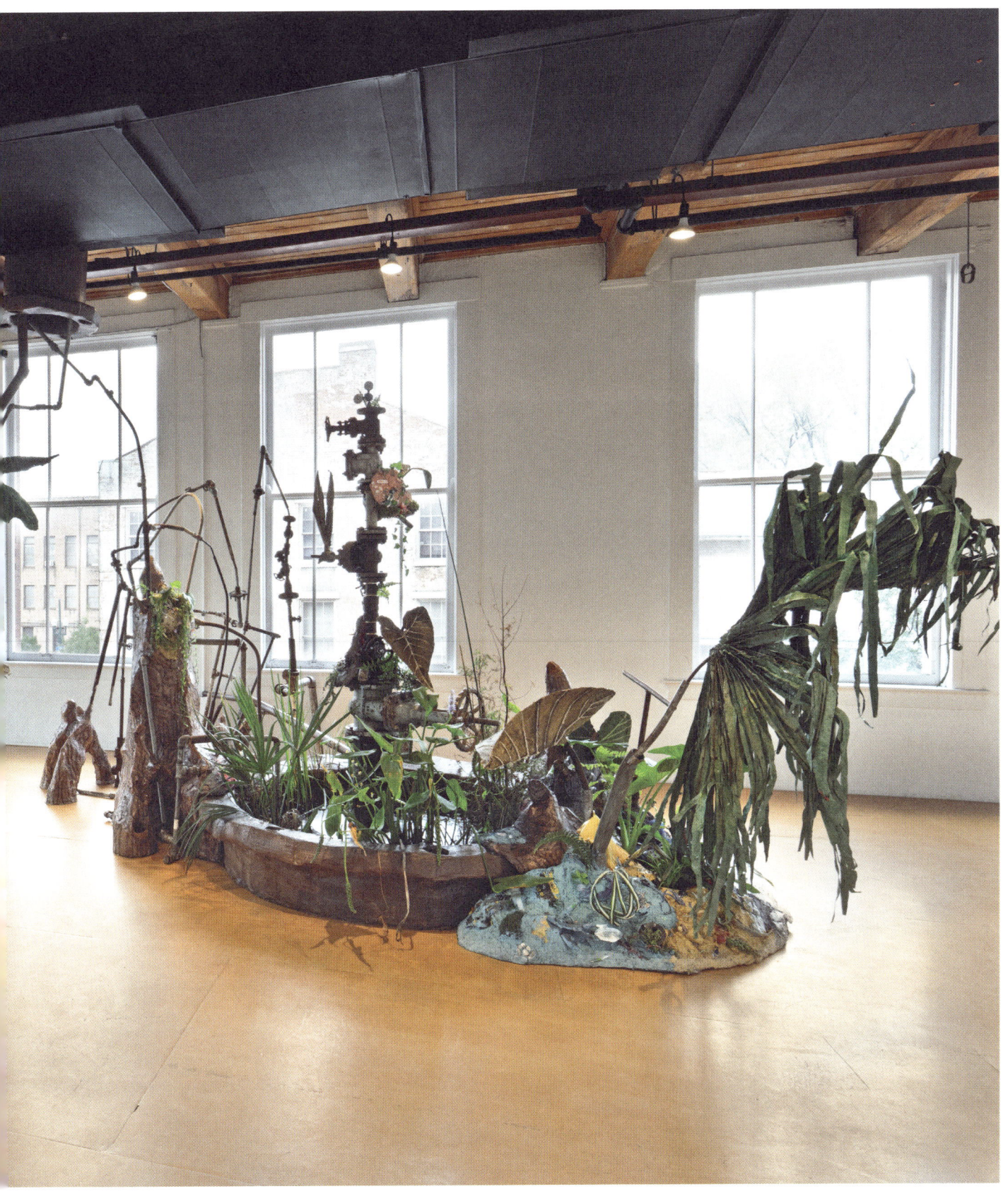

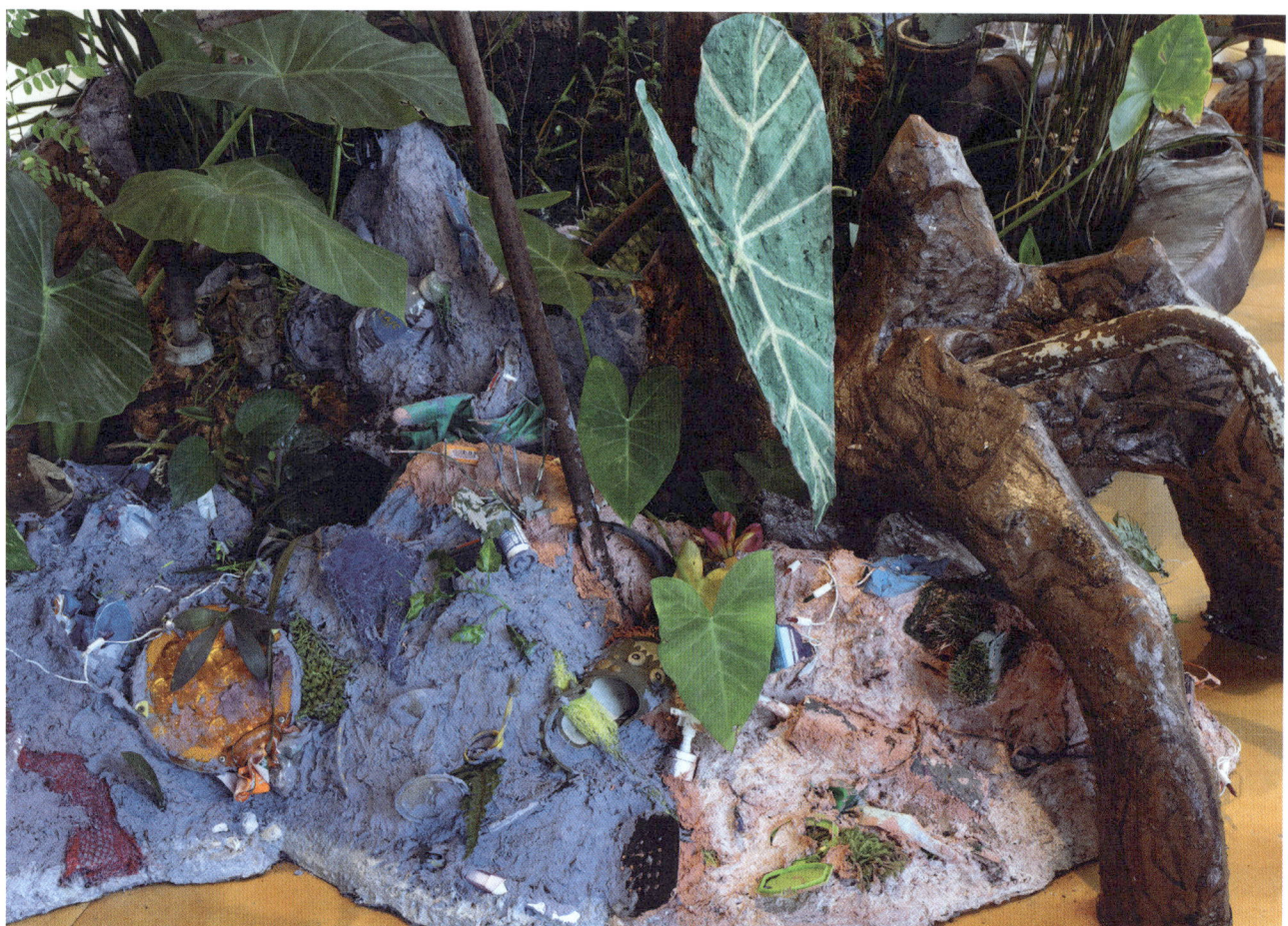

produce mutations that benefitted humans, such as larger, sweeter fruit with longer shelf lives and more abundant crops. In Chalew's post-human gamma garden, the wetland plants mutate to enhance their resilience against the historical conditions of exploitation by humans.

The development of Louisiana's wetlands began in the nineteenth century, when the burgeoning petrochemical industry deemed wetlands to be wastelands. The exploitation of the environment was concurrent with the exploitation of people. Over time, sugarcane plantations became petrochemical refineries. To show how Louisiana's dual legacies of enslavement and extraction extend into our present, Chalew intervenes in the papermaking process with history-laden materials. The constructed plants in her installation are crafted from "plasticane," a material Chalew engineers by mixing shredded plastic with bagasse, the fibrous remains left after the sweetness is extruded from sugarcane. The smell of sugar lingers around *Orphan Well Gamma Garden*: The artist-created fragrance, *Fertile Rot*, introduces the sweet, fermented scent of oakmoss that conjures the decay of a swamp's off-gassing.

The artist works to update our perceptions of nature with sensory information about the wetlands' exploitation.

Chalew's zero-waste and fossil fuel-free philosophy extends beyond sourcing materials from salvage yards. *Orphan Well Gamma Garden* is powered by a reciprocal community carbon offset project called Maktub Forêt, a restoration effort in the coastal wetland forest near the Mississippi River's mouth. The living plants in her installation will find a home there after the exhibition closes. Chalew also finds car-free ways to travel and refuses to participate in "artwashing," the dispersion of money into art institutions that offer oil and gas companies tax breaks and accolades. From the plantation to the refinery to the museum, Chalew's investigations of the ecological and economic footprint of the petrochemical industry ask us to consider what remains as society increasingly moves away from fossil fuels.

by Risa Puleo

Orphan Well Gamma Garden, 2024 (detail)

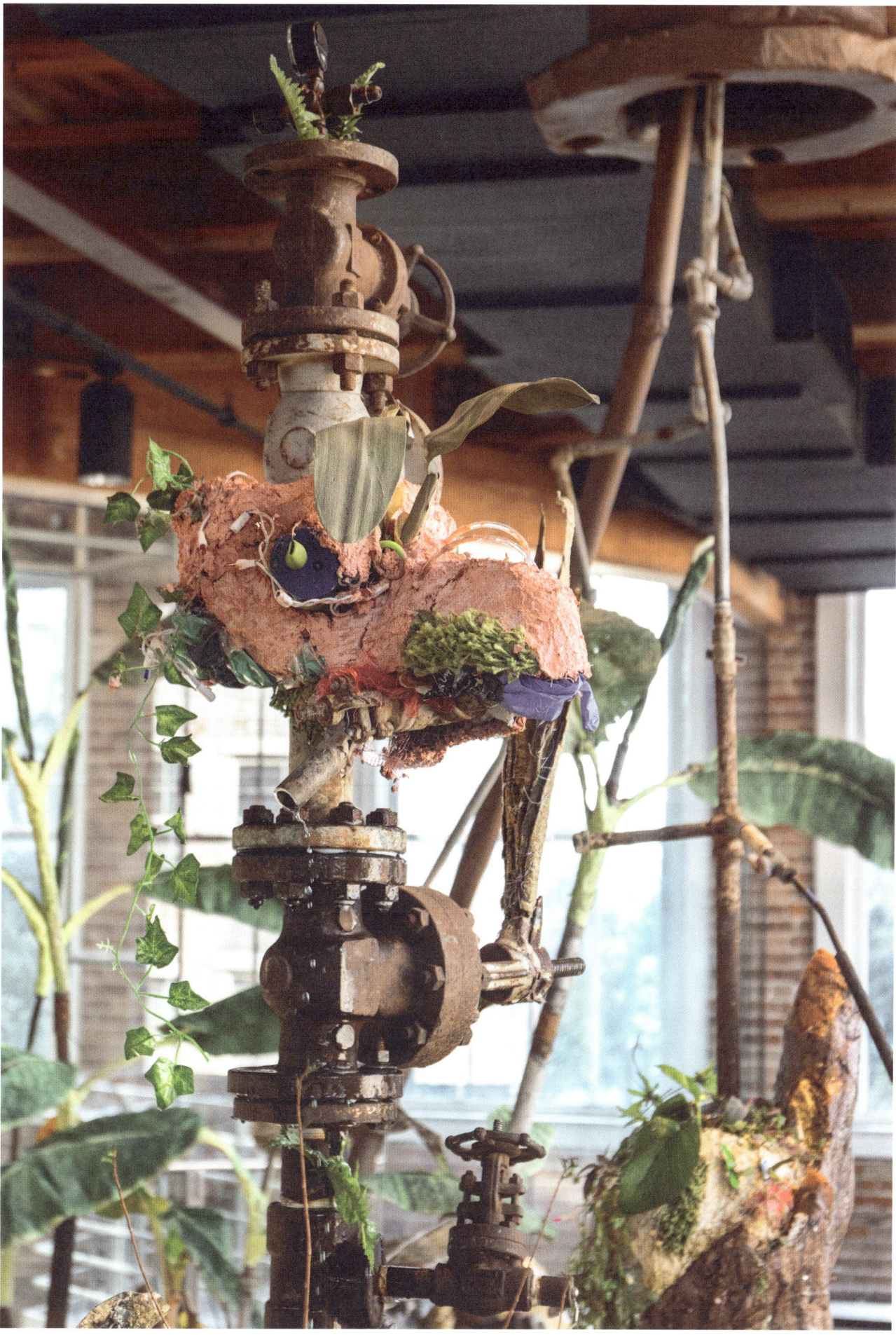

Orphan Well Gamma Garden, 2024 (detail)

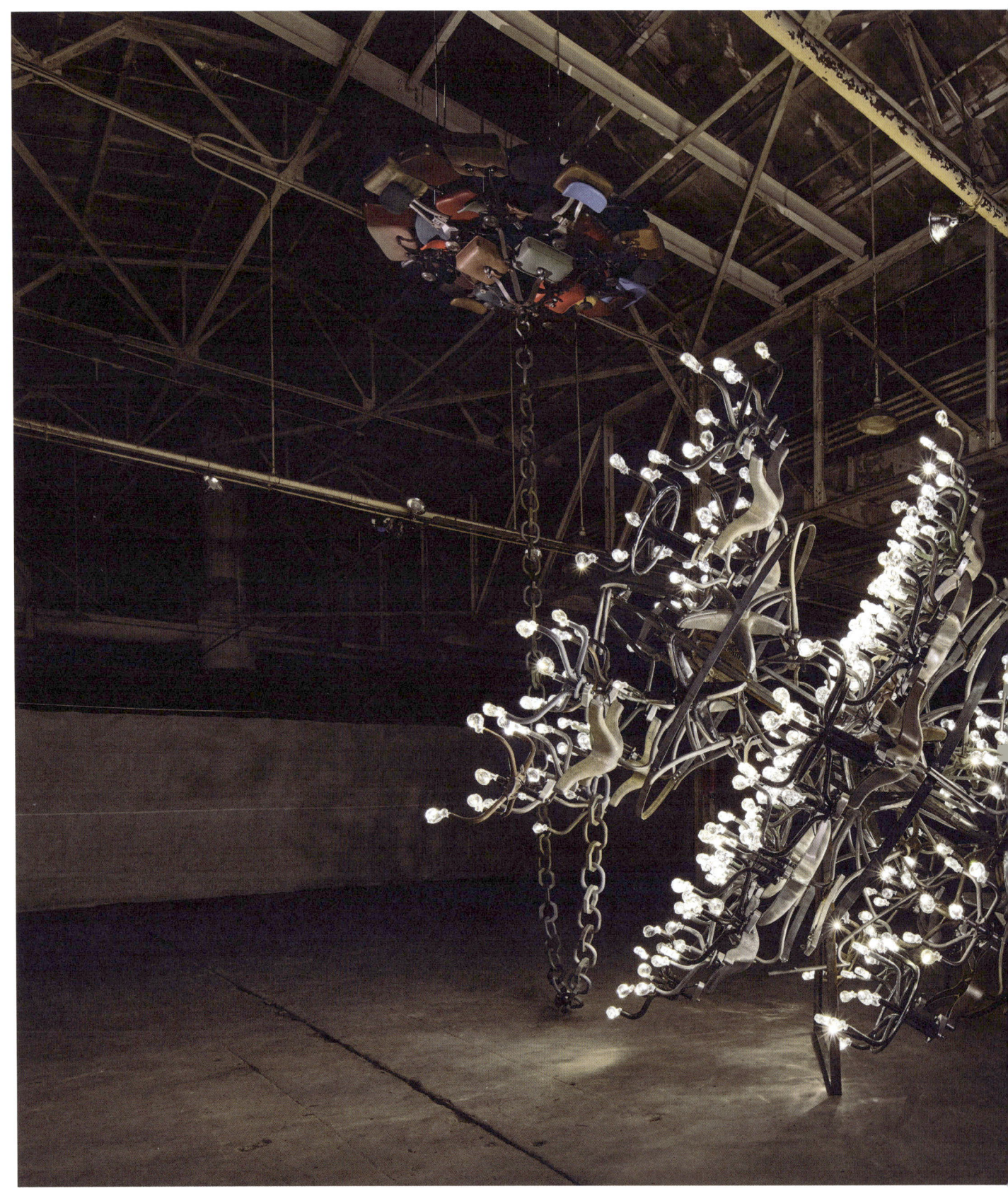

Pool of Light, 2024–2025

Mel Chin

b. 1951, Houston, TX; lives in Egypt Township, NC

The future of work once looked incredibly bright. In 1961, the editors of the trade magazine *Today's Secretary* predicted that within fifty years, secretaries would be free to take months off from work, their jobs made easier by the "electronic computer." Technological advancements and modernist design had already transformed the nature of secretarial work. Typewriters had become progressively faster and less physically taxing on their users, and by 1959, Xerox machines eliminated the need for carbon copies. Major corporate offices, outfitted with sleek desks and chairs drawn from the International Style, championed by the likes of Le Corbusier, Charles and Ray Eames, and Eero Saarinen, kept apace with these changes to bolster a booming postwar economy. When IBM introduced its first word processing computer in 1966, it caused a stir among secretaries. Would their labor, hard earned and still unequally compensated, be replaced with a new technological development that promised efficiency, accuracy, speed? What could a future in which labor is valued and adequately honored look like?

With *Pool of Light* (2024–2025), his commissioned installation for Prospect.6, Mel Chin refracts the question of labor and its value through an examination of mid-century modern design and its cultural cache. Today, well-preserved examples of such design fetch high prices, far above their originally intended affordability. Over the last several years, Chin has been sourcing mid-century modernist office chairs in a panoply of materials. He selects these objects not only to serve as examples of a certain ethos of design, but as objects that bear the traces of human use—their scuff marks and dings reveal the residue of lives overshadowed by the clattering engine of American capitalism. Disassembled to their constituent parts of legs, backs, and seats, the office chairs have been remilled, recast, and rearranged to form a chandelier, strung on a chain. Here then, Chin declares, is your object of desire, but stripped of its glittering lustrousness, its fetishistic claim to cultural dominance.

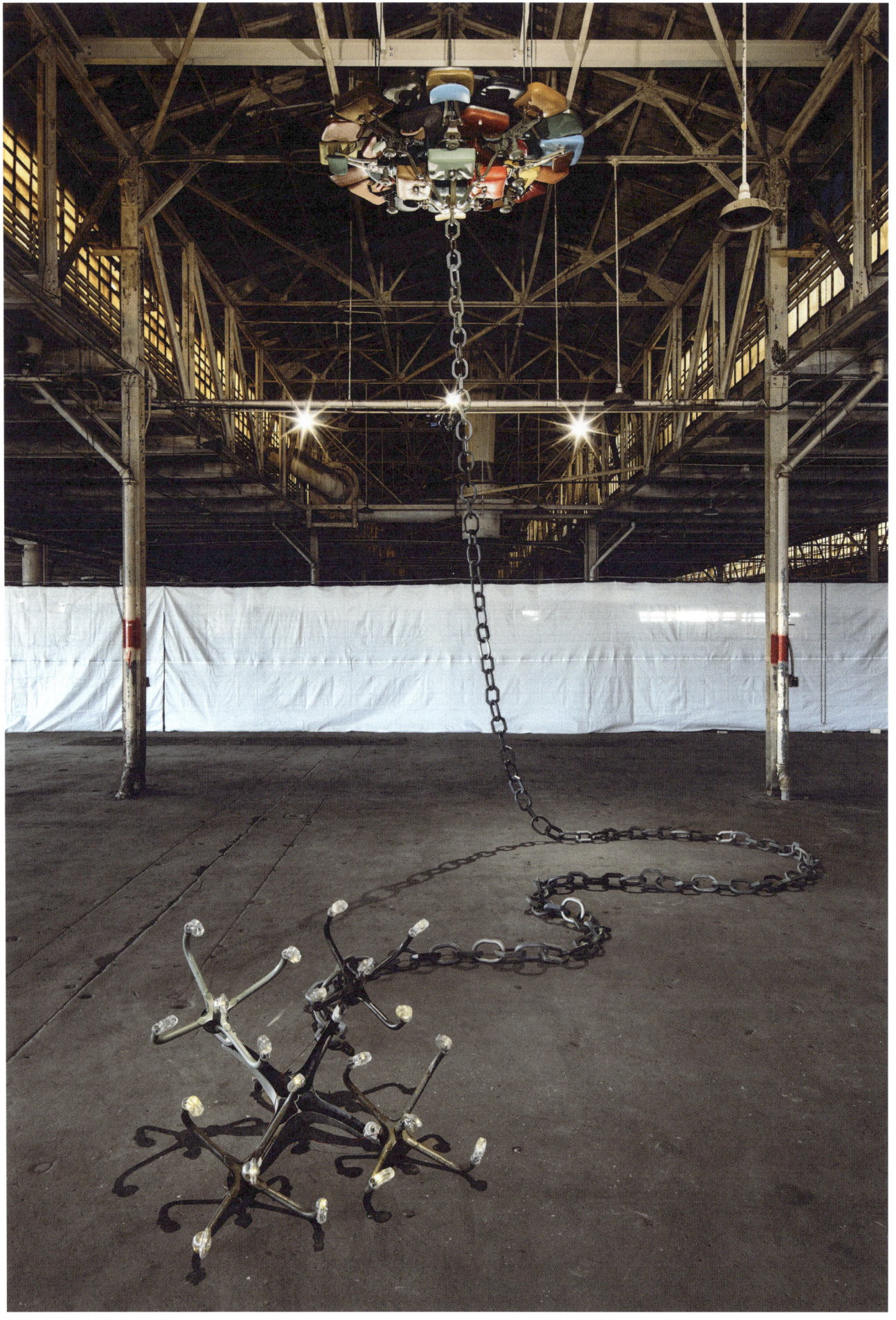

Pool of Light, 2024–2025 (work in progress)

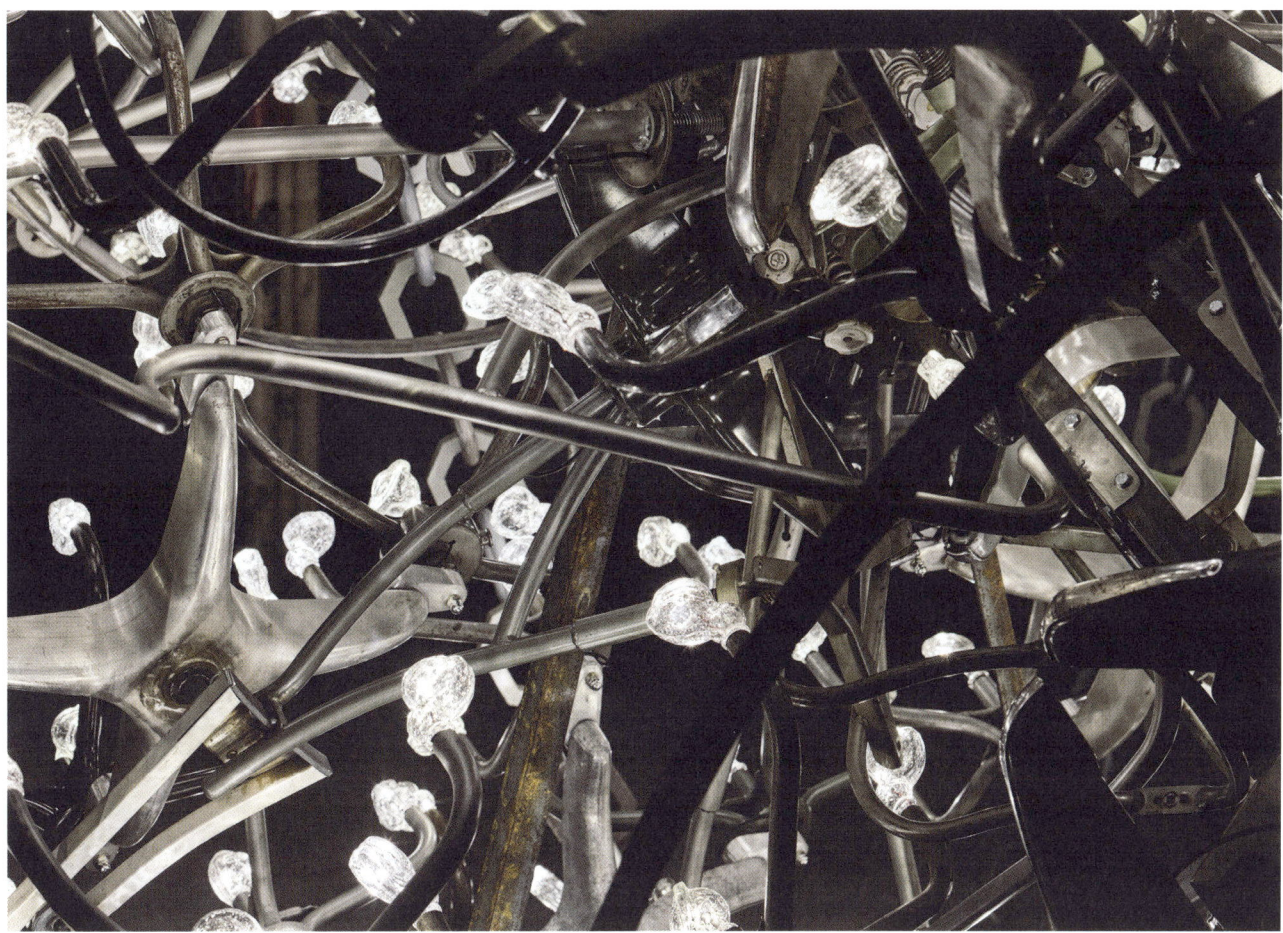

One might wonder how the work fits into Chin's conceptual practice, rooted, as it is, in the examination of ecological, cultural, and social critique, frequently categorized with activist art of the last three decades. Many of his projects have involved direct relationships with specific sites, communities, and groups of individuals. He has enlisted children and their families in post-Katrina New Orleans to draw awareness to childhood lead poisoning in their area by designing their own hundred-dollar bills; he's worked with scientists to model gardens filled with pollution-removing plants; teamed up with software engineers to design games that take inspiration from rugs made by nomadic peoples threatened with the loss of their livelihoods.

Pool of Light is indeed no less rooted in history: The work was inspired by a woman named Pat Fender, who for decades worked among other secretaries in a secretary pool, the years of her labor accumulated in her office chair, which she gifted to Chin. Fender is but one of many hard-working individuals whose labor was placed in service to the American Dream, long mythologized as the engine of US economic dominance.

In the decades of the Cold War, that dream took on newly reinvigorated political dimensions, as US-made cultural products and manufactured goods were weaponized as buffers against a nebulous communist threat. Mid-century modernist design, now well-established in the market and historical canon, promised a better way of living. Looking up at Chin's chandelier, you might imagine those beleaguered workers in their well-designed seats, pausing for a moment to look up toward the light of a tomorrow yet to come.

by Tausif Noor

* On September 26, 2024 Hurricane Helene brought widespread destruction and devastation to multiple regions in the southeastern United States, including the area surrounding Egypt Township, NC, where Chin's studio is located. This artwork was presented as a work in progress, honoring those affected by climate disasters, and the ongoing ripple of the pool's labor across generations. The completed work was presented during Prospect.6's closing weekend.

Bethany Collins

b. 1984, Montgomery, AL; lives in Chicago, IL

The Aeneid: 1981 / 2007, 2024 (detail)

The *Aeneid*. *Moby-Dick*. "The Star-Spangled Banner." "Auld Lang Syne." These great literary texts—Roman epic, antebellum novel, national anthem, Scottish folk song—offer meaning in worlds thrown into crises. For Bethany Collins, these works are fallible, yet coded with hope. The artist proves her thesis by revealing and unrevealing their language, meddling with their sensory forms (touch, sight, sound) to confront how we absorb, how we see, how we hear them. Or, don't. She turns to erasure: wielding tools that are digital (sound engineering), analog (paper, paint), and pedestrian (a Black Magic eraser to excise miles of sentences by hand).

In *The Aeneid* suite (2022–present), Collins compares several translations of Virgil's epic, excerpting passages where Aeneas is lost at sea. She refuses the white page, prints the words onto dark midnight-blue papers, and hangs them on walls painted an inky blue-black. Black space frames the Roman story. Deploying a Black Magic eraser like a shadow weapon ghosting the page, Collins rubs away the passages. An eraser disappears something by rubbing it, in order to correct it. Collins presents us with a paradox: How can we make things right by disappearing them?

In the aftermath of this painstaking labor, Collins leaves legible one sentence, from two translations of the *Aeneid*:

> "Cast from our course, we wander in the dark." (1697)

> "Slammed off our course, we groped through blinding waves." (2021)

One tosses us into passivity—*we* are aimless, lost in the abyss. The other is more violent— deprived of agency, yet *we* feel our way through. Notice in both, all the words but *we* are transmutable. Yet, texts are not unchangeable. They shift as tectonic plates do: slowly towards rupture. The *Aeneid* has seen over a hundred translations. The Constitution has been amended several times, though its first words, *We the People*, remain unchanged in this grand experiment called the United States. When Collins's work opens in New Orleans on the eve of an unprecedented election, which course/ experiment will *We the People* be slammed into?

Because of centuries of erasure—stories mistold, histories unwritten, silences in the archives, voices discarded—Audre Lorde told us, "the master's tools will not dismantle the master's house." But Collins, provocateur of contradictions, exploits erasure as a tool to both disappear and repair.

Collins places the *Aeneid* in conversation with texts that point to a sense of landlessness. In *Moby Dick, Vol. 3* (2024), she erases its passages with a blue eraser, but leaves the word "sea" untouched. Wearing away the paper's cotton fibers becomes symbolic. From the eraser's detritus, its discarded castaways, Collins erects a monument anew. In *The Patriot's Banner* (2024) soundwork, when the 1858 abolitionist version of "The Star-Spangled Banner" is sung, we ironically can't hear the words imploring us to *hear* the looming violence of the Civil War. Collins engineers the lyrics towards illegibility until they reverberate like crashing waves. In the performance *Civil Dusk* (2024), two voices battle each other to render several versions of "Auld Lang Syne." At first, they are out of synchronicity. When Collins orchestrates their alignment for a fleeting moment of sonic clarity, we encounter the 1917 version, in which WWI soldiers sang of the horrors of war, "We're here, because we're here." When we find ourselves yet again, like Aeneas, groping through darkness, Collins leans on the ambiguity of the soldier's version. Do they sing of hope or futility? Are *we (still) here*? Or, are *we here (again)*?

Poet Rosamond S. King was right to warn us, "Do not trust the eraser." In the masterful hands of Collins, erasure is mark-making, erasure is annotation, erasure is reconciliation, erasure is unsilencing.

by Grace Aneiza Ali

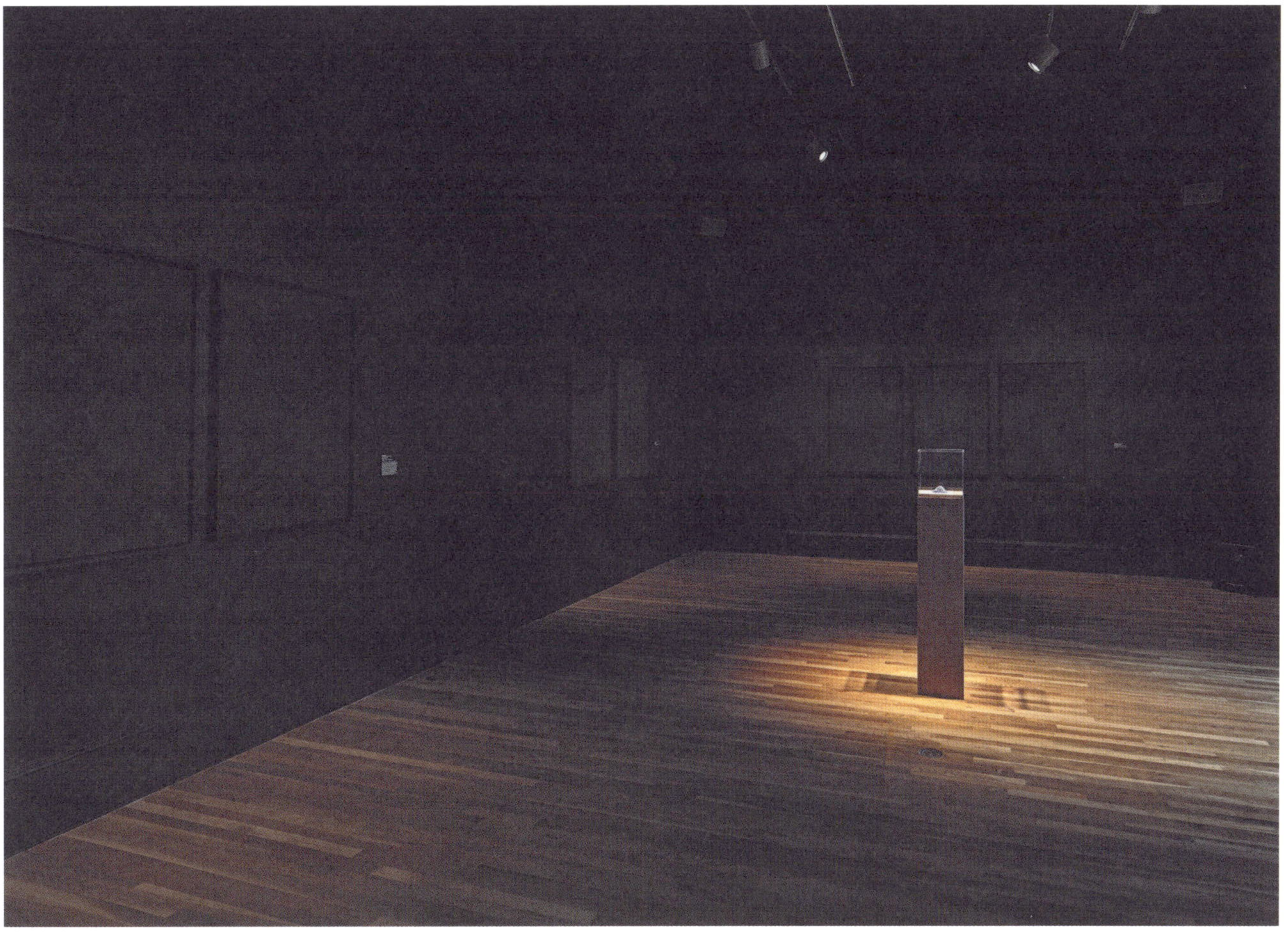

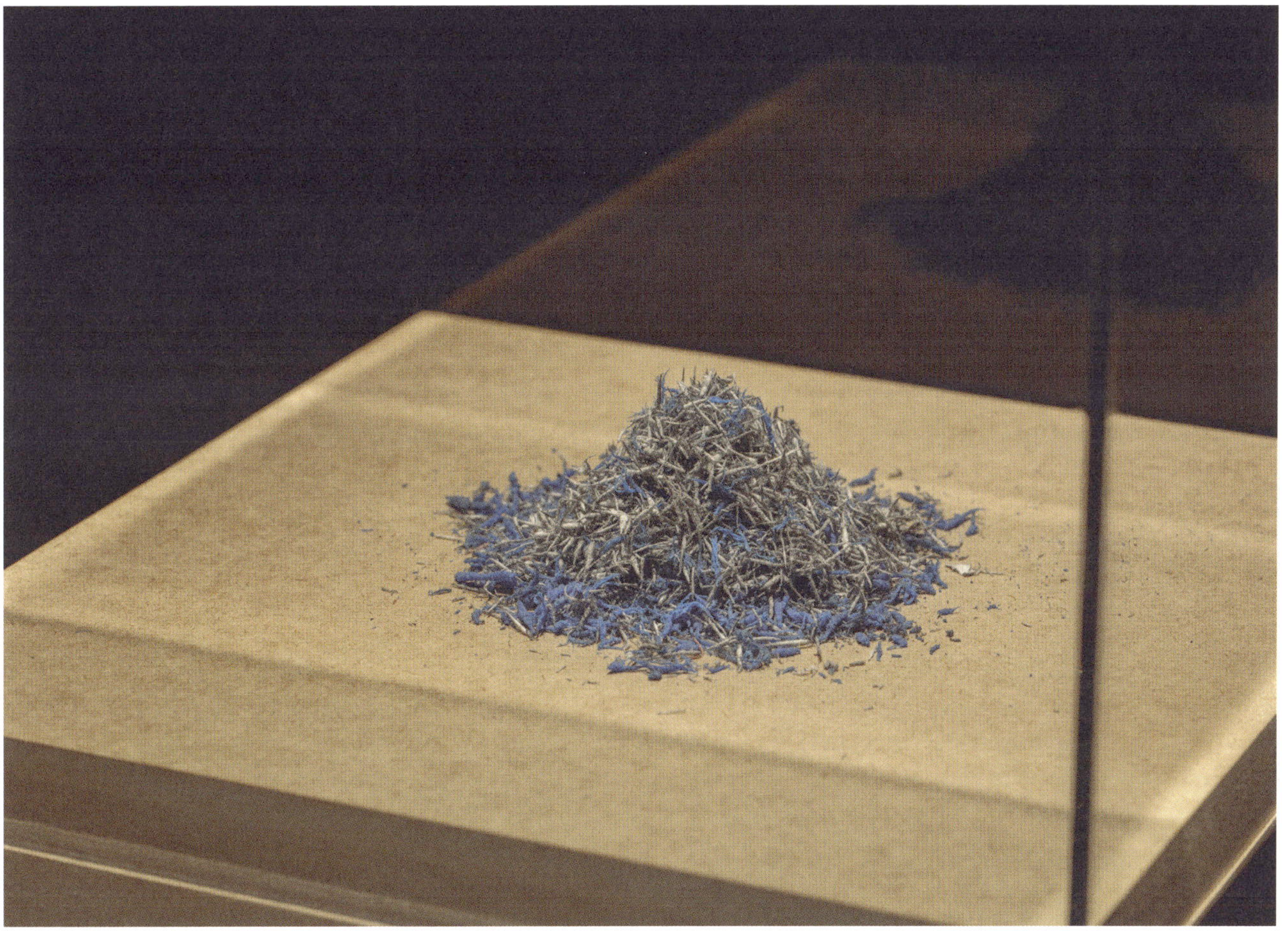

Top: Installation view at Newcomb Art Museum of
Tulane University

Above: *Moby Dick, Vol. 3*, 2024 (detail)

Myrlande Constant

b. 1968, Port-au-Prince, Haiti; lives in Port-au-Prince, Haiti

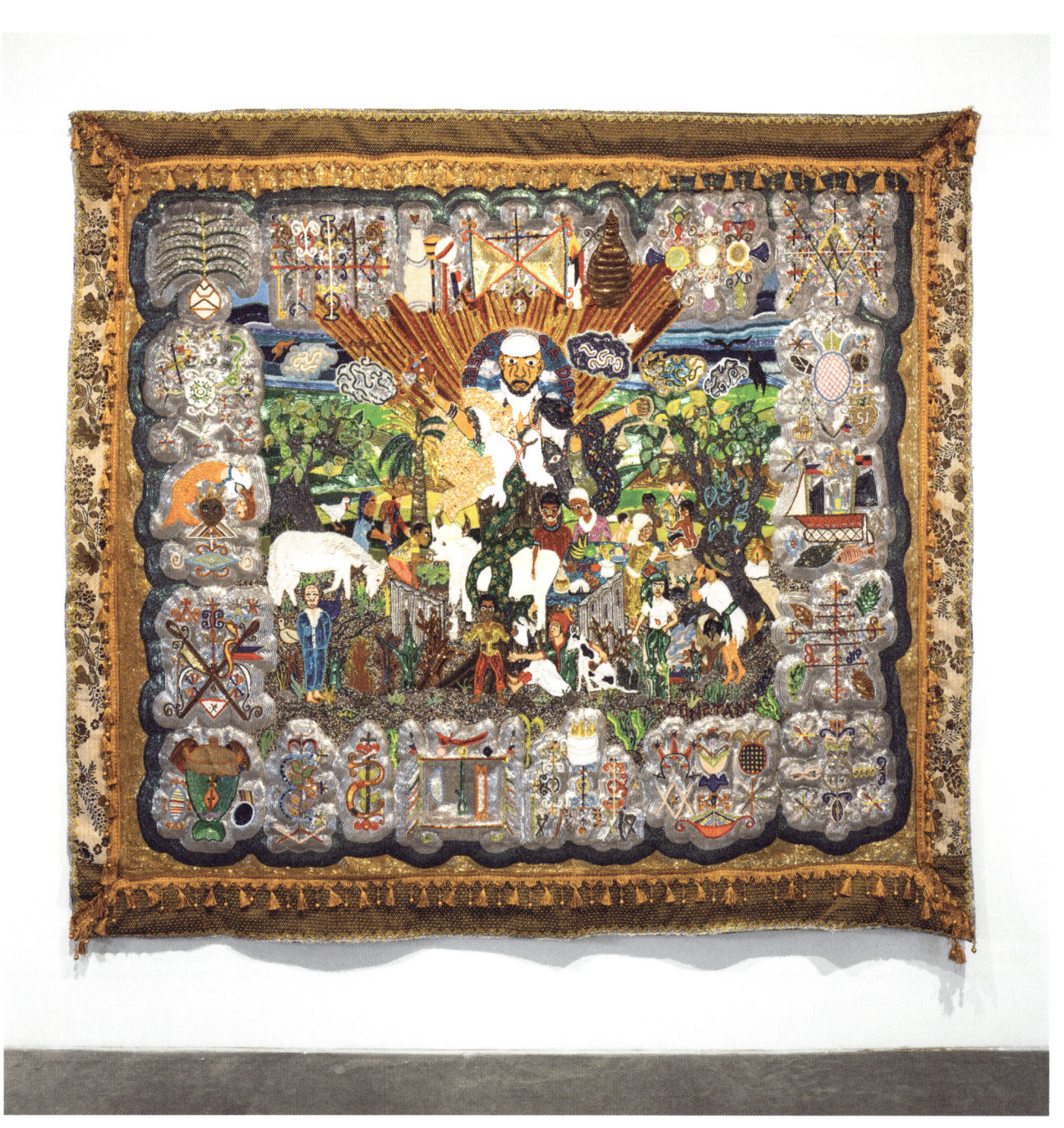

Sosyete Radha, 2024

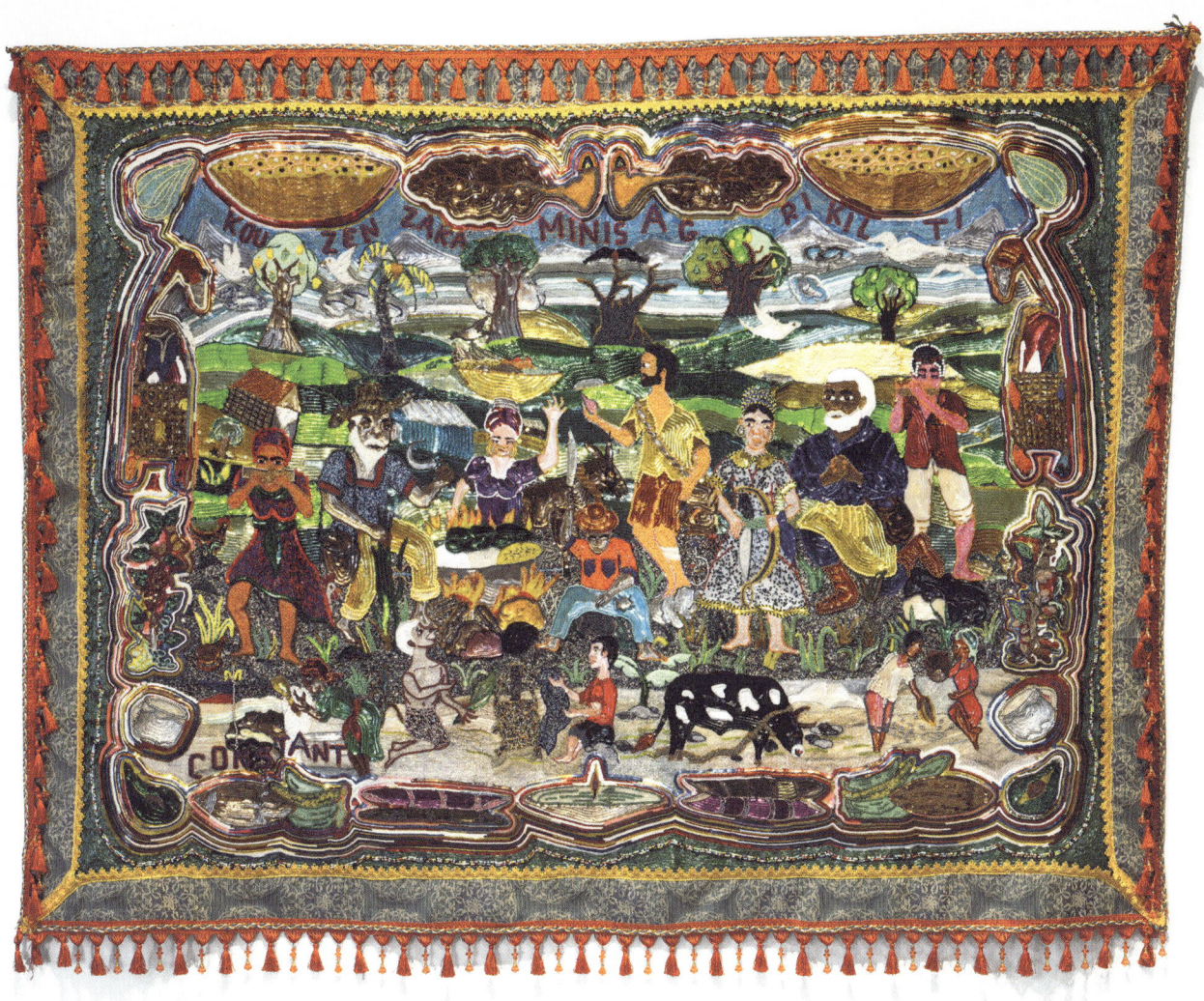

Myrlande Constant's thirty-year career as an artist was shaped as a young girl alongside her mother while working in a wedding dress factory beading lace. Later, she began experimenting with various beading and stitching styles and patterns. As her drawing and craft skills sharpened, the size of her panels increased and her compositions grew more complex. The size of her atelier also expanded, becoming a familial, communal space where young men and women work side by side. Her artworks at Prospect.6, *Sosyete Radha* (2024) and *Kouzen Zaka Minis Agrikilti* (2022), capture the vibrancy of *drapo Vodou*, the embroidered flags used in Haitian Vodou ceremonies. They offer vignettes of daily and spiritual life in Haiti.

Constant comes out of a tradition of Vodou flag-makers, whose drapo were placed in an *ounfò* (temple) as ritual flags and ceremonial banners to entice the *lwa*—deities—to enter the space of worship. Her large-scale drapo include tiny, hand-stitched beads and sequins that portray humans, saints, and spirits engaged in moments that are sacred, and at other times, intimate and humorous. Constant's labor is both a creative and creating process imbued with Haitian aesthetics. By "Haitian aesthetics," I mean the practice of using expressive and religious traditions to create and maintain Black life worlds—a livability. The practice is a proclamation of existence and a refusal to be obscured, a radical aesthetic that is filled with fugitivity—a desire to break free, to escape from an imposed, racist ontological logic, and to visualize a Black humanity that creates emancipatory possibilities through the visual arts.

Kouzen Zaka Minis Agrikilti, 2022

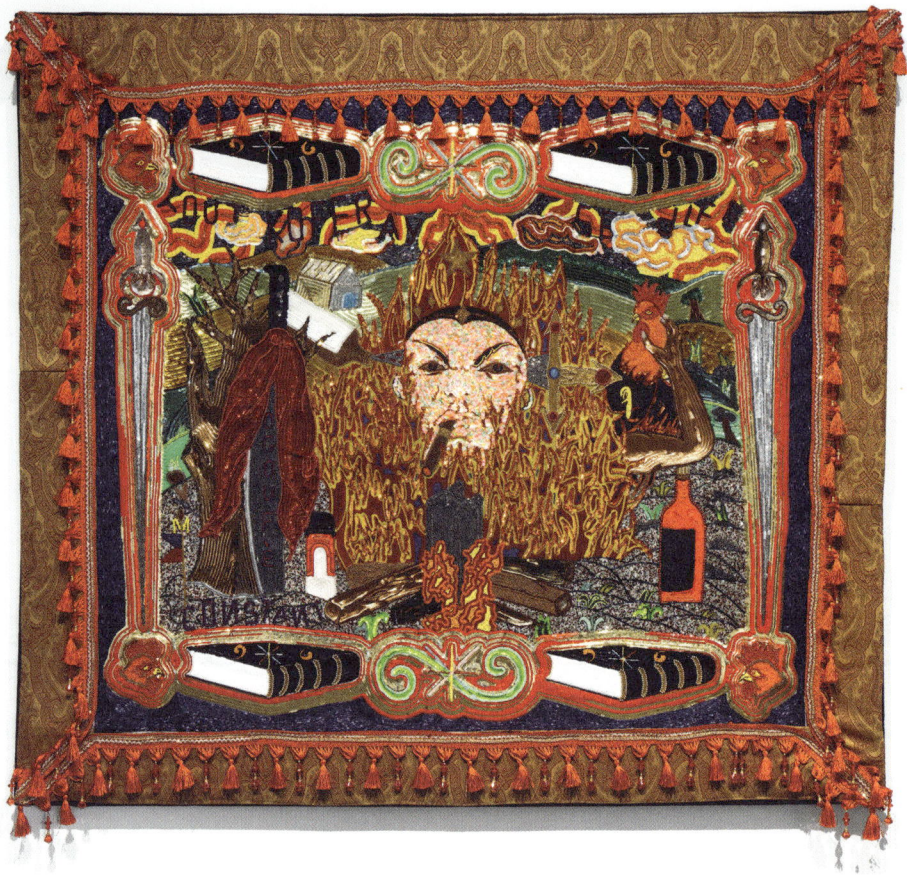

Constant's meticulous attention to detail in each stitch, bead, and sequin—to form a figure, object, or a *vèvè* (sacred symbol)—enables the viewer to comprehend the vitality and beauty that the material culture of lived religion and spirituality reveal. Both *Sosyete Radha* and *Kouzen Zaka* explode with bold color and texture, and there is no clear demarcation between foreground, middle ground, or background. It is as if you can almost *feel* the presence of the lwa. In *Sosyete Radha*, three bead-encrusted *Danbalas*—one of the most significant lwas in Haitian Vodou—take center stage as they protectively intertwine themselves around the figure in the center. In *Kouzen Zaka*, the lwa of agriculture, Kouzen Zaka, watches over the harvest as others enjoy and thank him for his *benediksyon*. Curiously, Constant has represented two Kouzen Zaka figures in this composition.

Visually and narratively, the figures in these drapo live on the border between real and imagined. Constant situates these subjects and their stories within a Vodou epistemology, and as part of an ideological and aesthetic project that moves beyond art-historical boundaries and hierarchies. These beaded drapo resonate on multiple levels, imagining not only "Haitianness," but also a Black postmodern world that defies Western conventions of representation that associate Vodou, Haiti, and Blackness with abjection and inhumanity. Constant's maximalist aesthetic in the tight pictorial space seeks not to define the world, but rather to explode its reductive classifications and representations, and emphasize humankind's inherent complexity and interconnectedness, which resides on the border of otherworldliness. Her works are bound together not only by their display of Vodou iconography, but by the inclination to dwell imaginatively within literal and figurative thresholds. Combining the compositional skills of a painter with the technical skill of a textile artist, Constant creates layered compositions with dramatic effect that transcend a regional and national understanding—one that places Haiti as central in the Black Atlantic visual aesthetic.

by Jerry Philogene

Christopher Cozier

b. 1959, Port of Spain, Trinidad and Tobago; lives in Port of Spain, Trinidad and Tobago

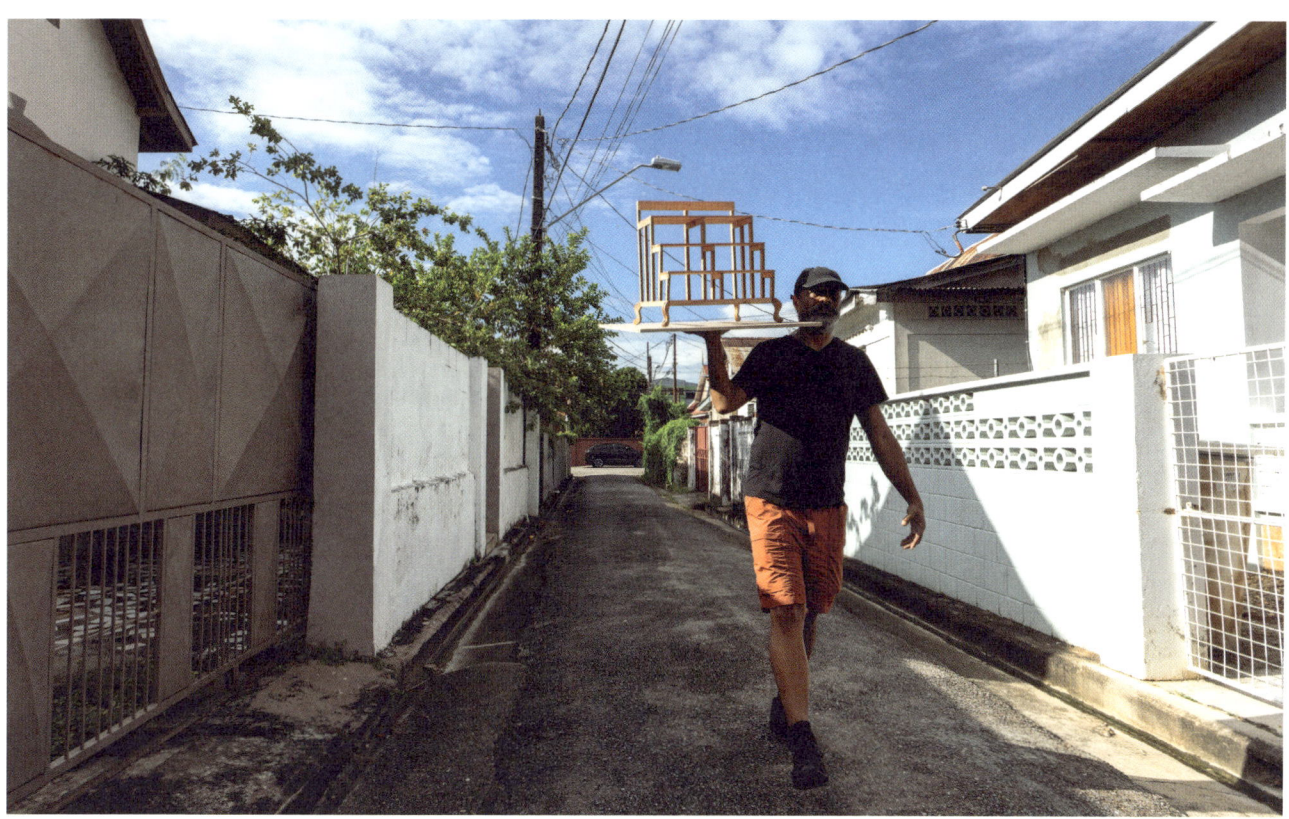

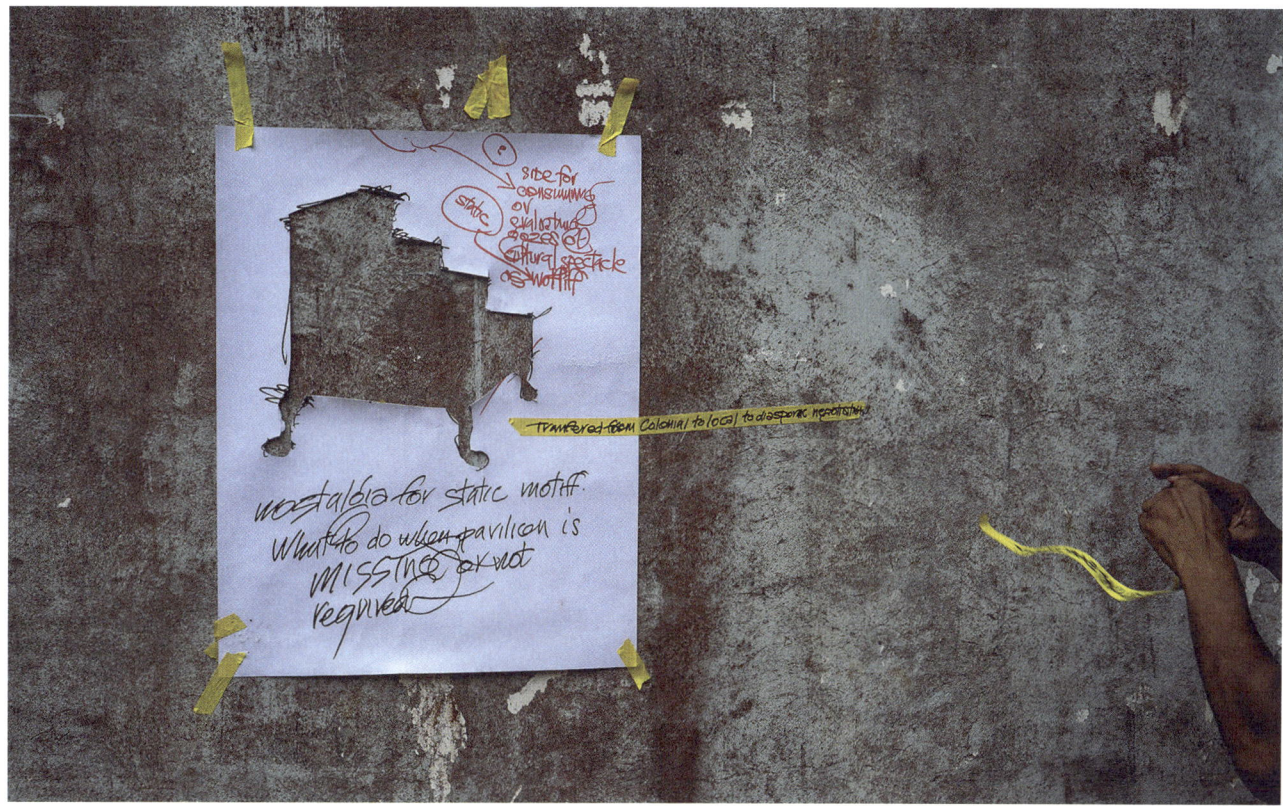

it has already been decided...Notes, 2024 (video stills)

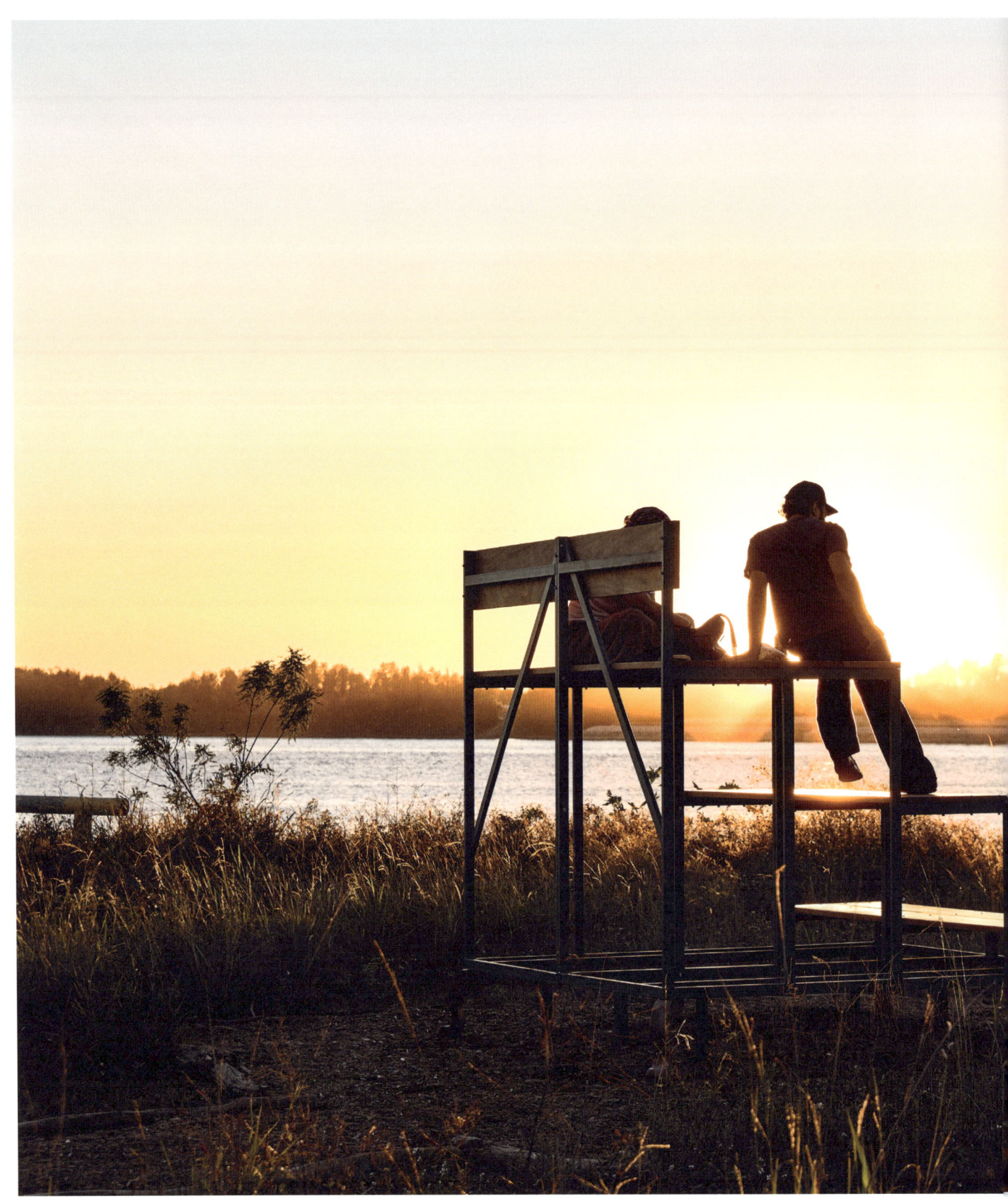

it has already been decided..., 2024

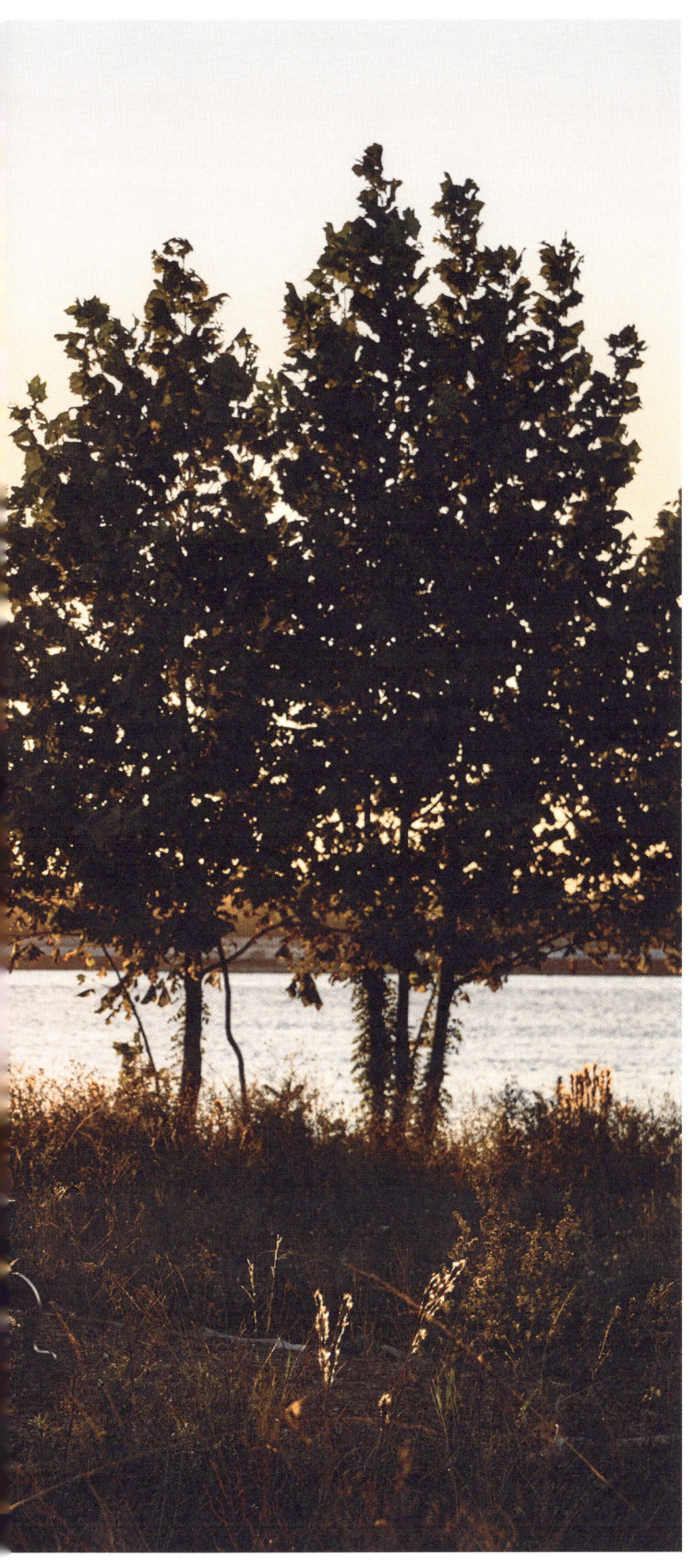

Christopher Cozier's new public commission and related drawings, sculpture, and video, *it has already been decided...* (2024), stands at a crossroads of colonial history, cultural performance, and the shifting narratives of place. A readymade sports bleacher, placed atop legs that evoke nineteenth century Victorian furniture, the pavilion-style seating suggests the continuity of the colonial encounter, and a place to witness the big and small makings of a nation be performed. Installed at The Batture, on the banks of the Mississippi River, Cozier's installation invites viewers to contemplate the idea of empire.

An artist, curator, professor, and writer, Cozier works from a distinctly Caribbean cosmology to render the entanglements between the Caribbean and the world. Ranging from drawings, installations, video, and sound pieces, Cozier's work engages with the evolving narratives of postcolonial Caribbean realities in the global context, through the objects and imagery of daily life in his home country of Trinidad and Tobago.

it has already been decided... is born from the pavilion seating of Cozier's youth. For anyone from Trinidad or New Orleans, this work will evoke memories of Carnival and Mardi Gras. But in this work, it is not the cultural performance that comes into focus. Instead, Cozier puts the

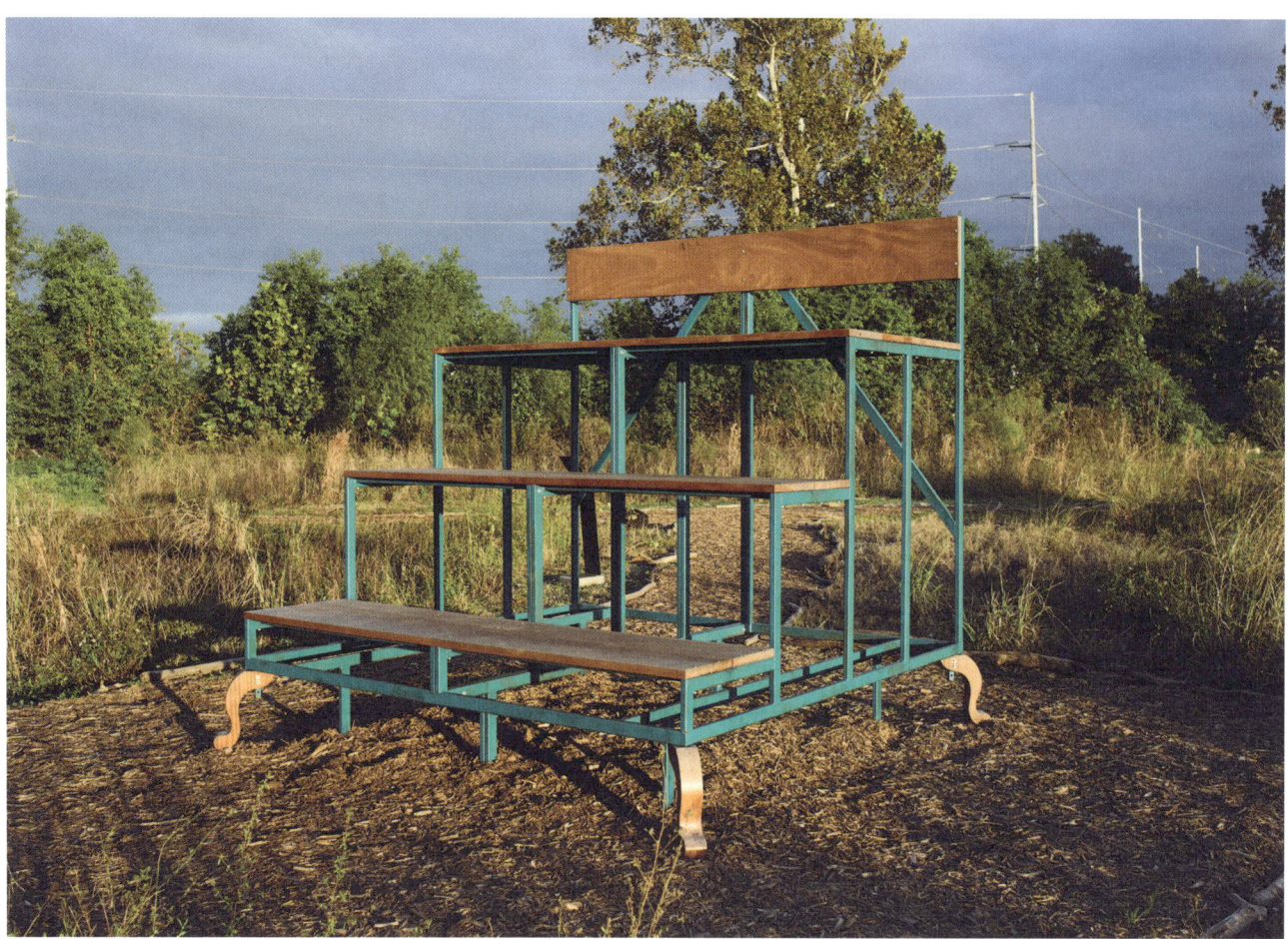

function of the spectator on display. Evoked in the work's title, we are asked to consider: What is predetermined? Is the transfer from colonial rule to neocolonial resource-grabbing simply the grim reality of how history repeats itself under new guises?

Like Trinidad, New Orleans moved from a plantation economy to one dependent on the oil, gas, and tourism industries. Installed on the Mississippi River, a site marked by its own layers of historical and contemporary industrial land management—from the devastating impact of Hurricane Katrina to the region's role within the Gulf South's petrochemical industry—*it has already been decided...* sits in an industrial yard slated for redevelopment. The public sculpture is placed in a reclaimed site formerly associated with a river transport and tugboat business known as E.N. Bisso & Son, which is now destined to become a riverfront park with restaurants. Here, at the edge of the city along the Mississippi River, visitors, maybe unknowingly, watch the tensions between visible gentrification and the invisible traces of colonial extraction—this area is one toxic node in what's known as "Cancer Alley."

Here, Cozier's installation invites viewers to see the site itself as an everyday theater of relations. This is what Cozier and his colleagues at Alice Yard, an art space in Port of Spain he co-runs, call "off veranda." While the veranda symbolizes enclosure and colonial control, life "off veranda" is emergent, participatory, ever-evolving. *it has already been decided...* is a prompt to consider the (im)possibilities that emerge when gathering, especially as sites for Black sociability. This seemingly simple work raises critical questions about spectatorship. What are we watching? What narratives are predetermined? Here, at The Batture, is the witness asked to contemplate the sins of empire, or to make a way out?

by Diya Vij

it has already been decided..., 2024

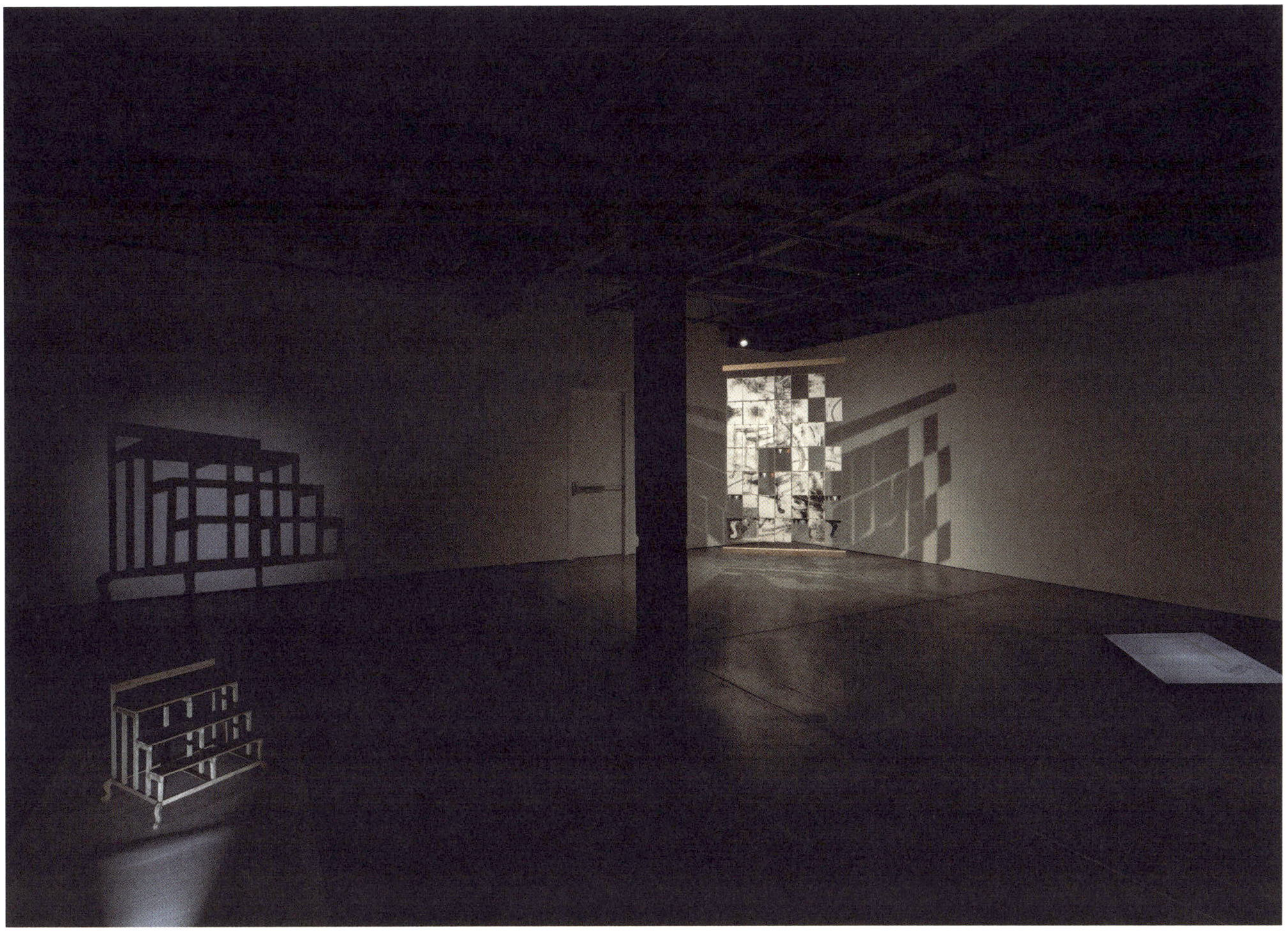

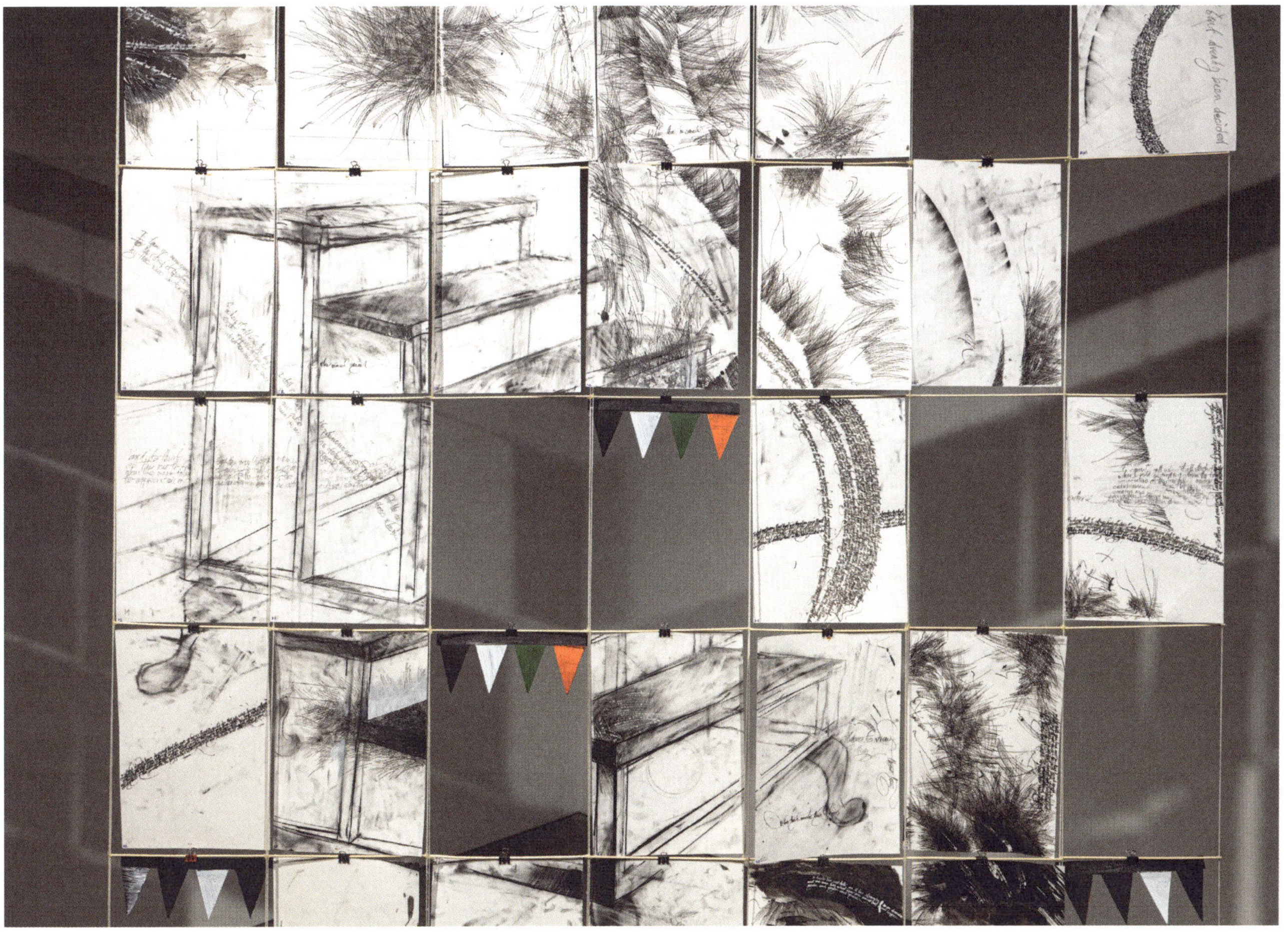

Top: Installation view at Contemporary Arts Center,
New Orleans

Above: *it has already been decided...*, 2024 (detail)

Ronald Cyrille aka B.Bird

b. 1984, Guadeloupe; lives in Guadeloupe

Born in Guadeloupe in 1984 to a Dominican mother and a Guadeloupean father, Ronald Cyrille moved to Dominica at eight months of age to live with his grandparents. His grandfather was a fisherman, and his childhood was spent closely tied to nature in Dominica, a place of lush forested mountains and fertile lands surrounded by the bounty and beauty of the sea. At nine years old, Cyrille returned north to Guadeloupe and became immersed in the urban density of the French Caribbean archipelago. It was here that Cyrille first began his art practice, drawing popular cartoon characters like Goku from *Dragon Ball Z* and Scrooge McDuck. After completing his secondary education, Cyrille moved to Martinique, where he earned a Master of Fine Arts degree from Campus Caribbean Des Arts in Fort-de-France in 2012. Returning to Guadeloupe, he emerged under the alias B.Bird as a major figure in the street art scene, executing murals that commented on Caribbean cultural history and socio-political realities in an expressionist style, saturated with bright color and populated with fantastical mythic figures.

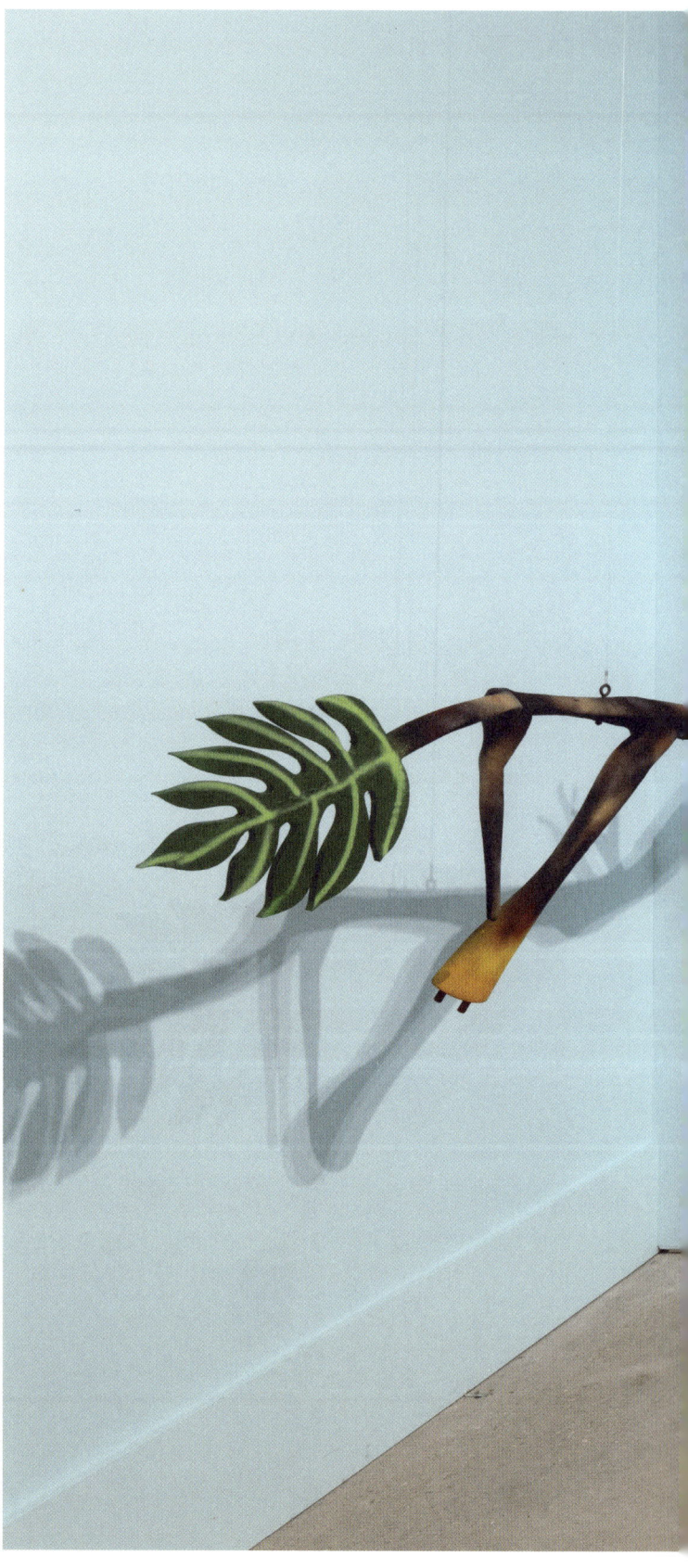

L to R: *Nature-elle la connexion*, 2024 and
Odyssées d'une exile, 2024

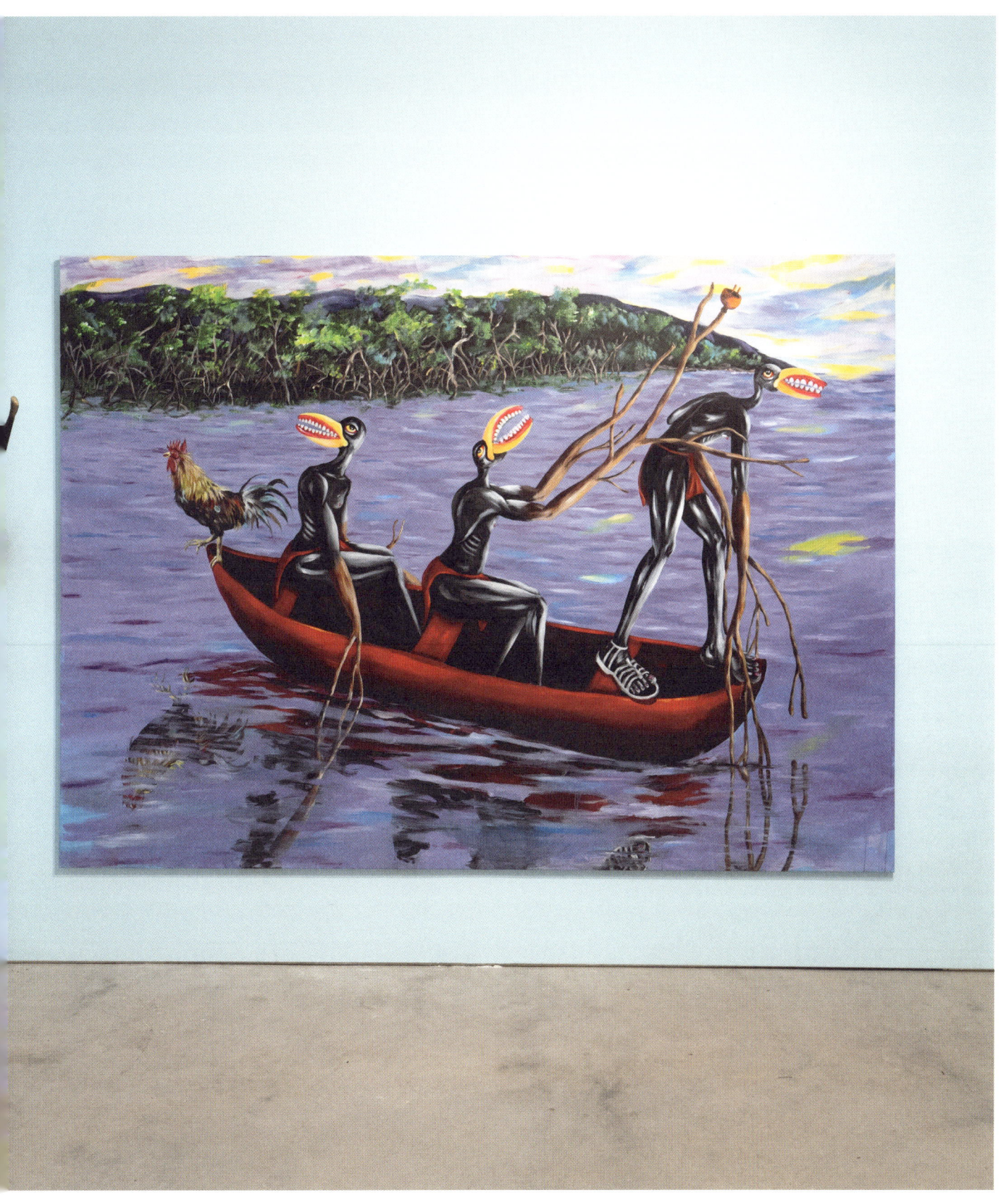

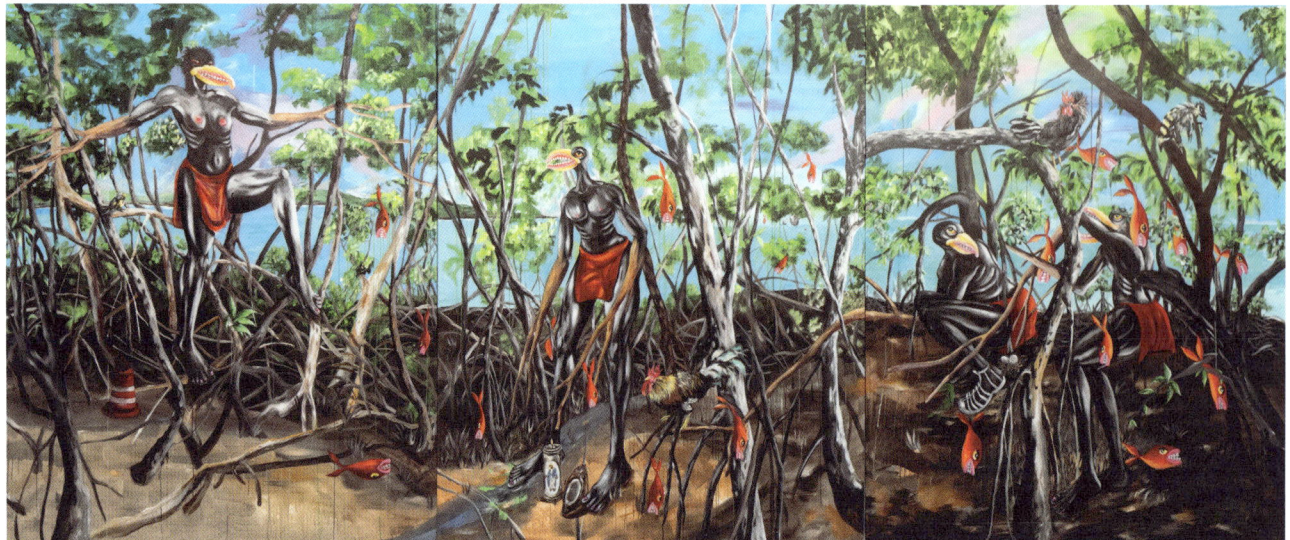

Ronald Cyrille's painterly practice exists both in the streets and in the studio he maintains in Guadeloupe. While spray paint is his primary medium on the street, his studio practice is expansive, and includes collage, oil, acrylic, and watercolor. His work expertly balances formal considerations with narrative intention, and moves fluidly between abstraction and representation. He draws inspiration from his own imagination and personal history, the landscape, mythologies, culture, and history of the French Antilles, as well as contemporary challenges facing the Caribbean, including climate change and the persistent legacies of colonization and slavery. His canvases are populated with a private symbolic bestiary that includes creatures both real (Creole dogs, roosters, bees, fish) and imagined (plant-humans, dog-humans, bird-humans). The symbolic meaning of each creature can change within the context it is presented.

Cyrille's work challenges stereotypical notions of the Caribbean as a pastoral para-dise, drawing attention to the real challenges of contemporary life while celebrating the diversity of cultures in the region. Though his work is deeply personal and autobiographical, it also opens dialogue with a broad audience about issues related to immigration, globalization, the history and persistence of colonization, the recovery of ancestral knowledge, and, perhaps most significantly, the relationship between humankind and the natural world. By telling his own story in paint, allowing his unrestricted imagination to guide the way, his work becomes universal in its message and appeal.

New Orleans is often called "the northernmost city in the Caribbean." The food, architecture, music, religions, mythologies, and people of New Orleans all resonate to varying degrees with the thirty three political entities of the Caribbean. South Louisiana also faces similar existential challenges: How do you maintain cultural authenticity while embracing a tourism economy? How do you overcome the persistence of colonialism and the legacy of enslavement? How can a place so vulnerable to climate change and environmental destruction survive this moment? Cyrille's paintings do not posit answers to any of these questions. They do, however, engage in these crucial conversations. By showing these paintings during Prospect.6 in New Orleans, Cyrille's visual narrative expands the dialogue around our shared histories, cultural practices, and contemporary challenges. They invite the viewer to consider concepts of home, displacement, family, and our crucial yet fragile connection to the environment.

by Bradley Sumrall

The unknown land, 2024

Raúl de Nieves

b. 1983, Morelia, Michoacán, Mexico; lives in Brooklyn, NY

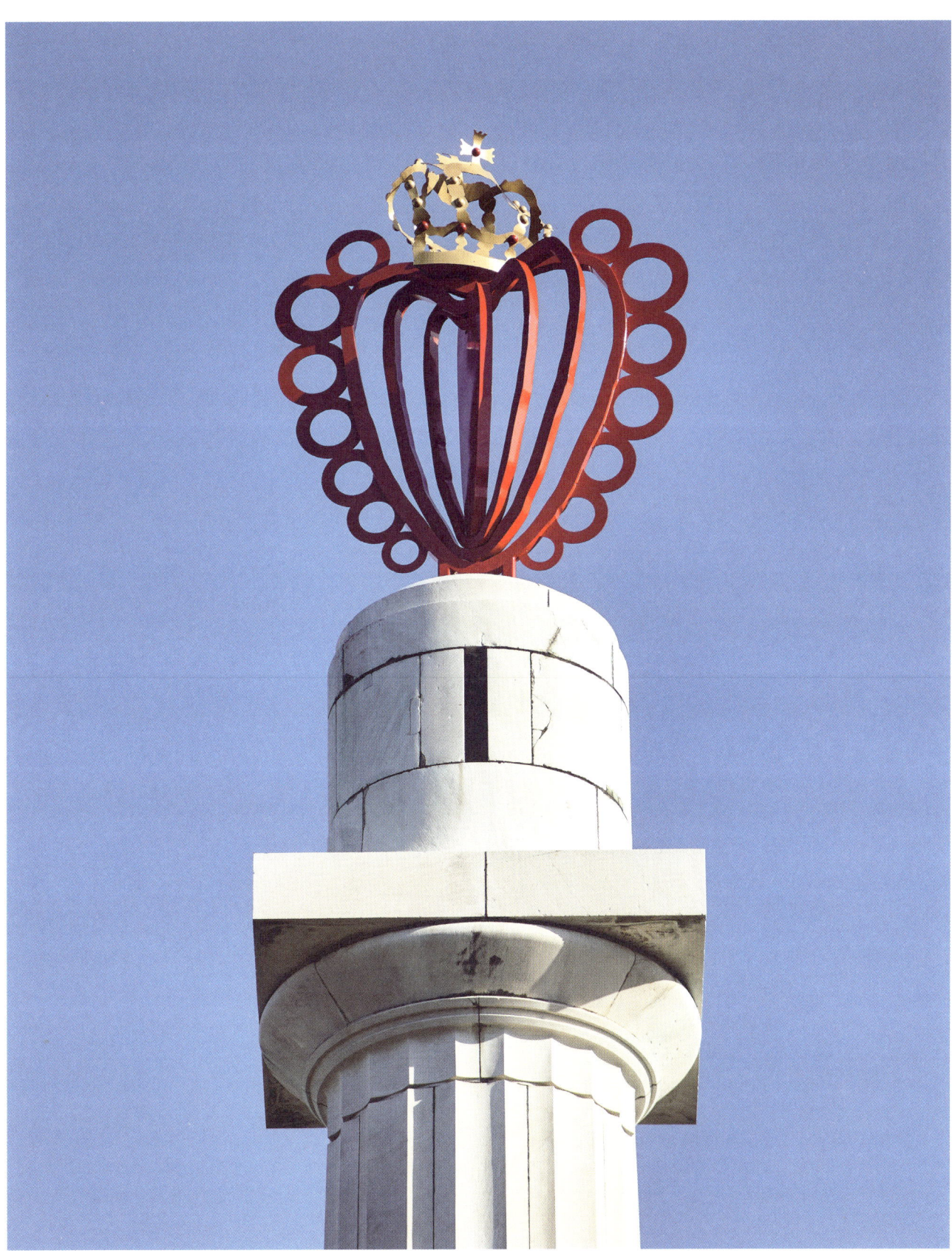

The Sacred Heart of Hours and the Trees of Yesterdays,
Today, and Tomorrow, 2024 (detail)

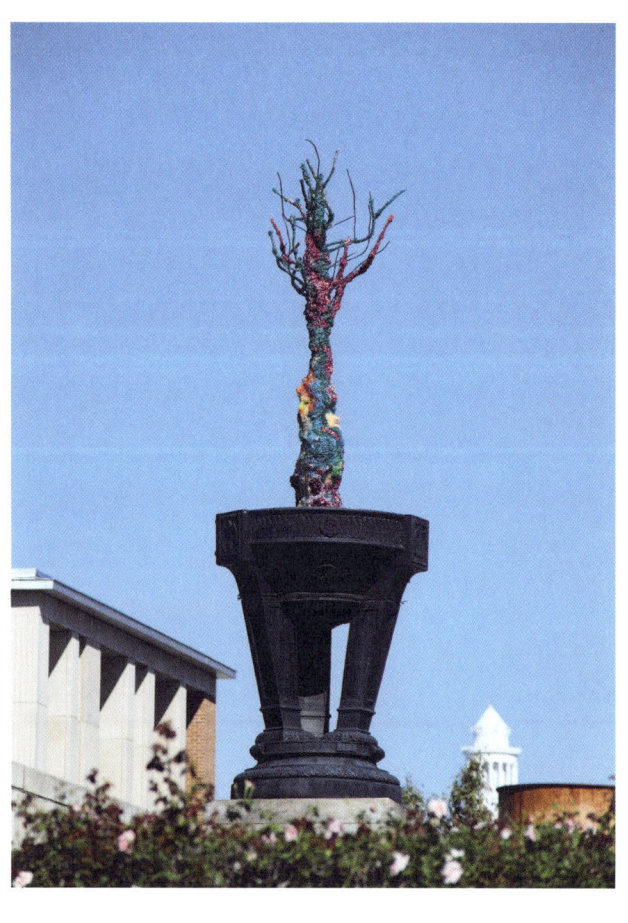

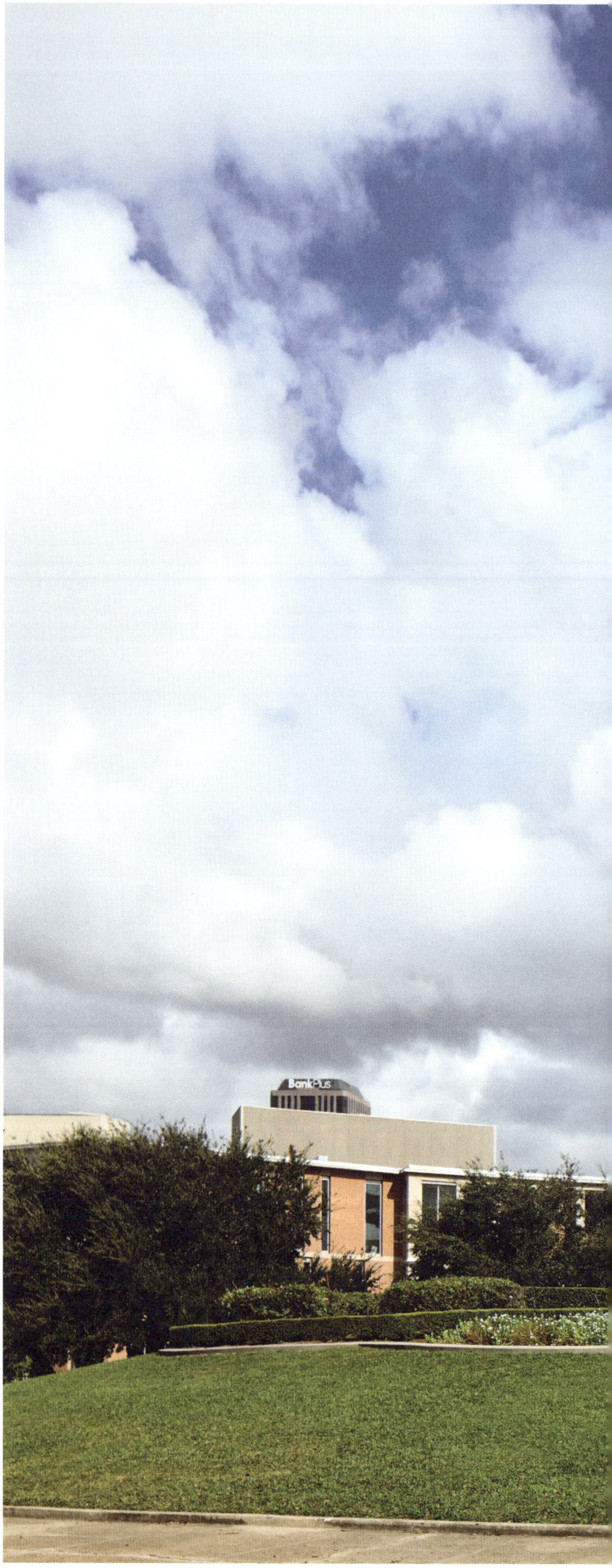

The Trees of Now (Justice), 2024

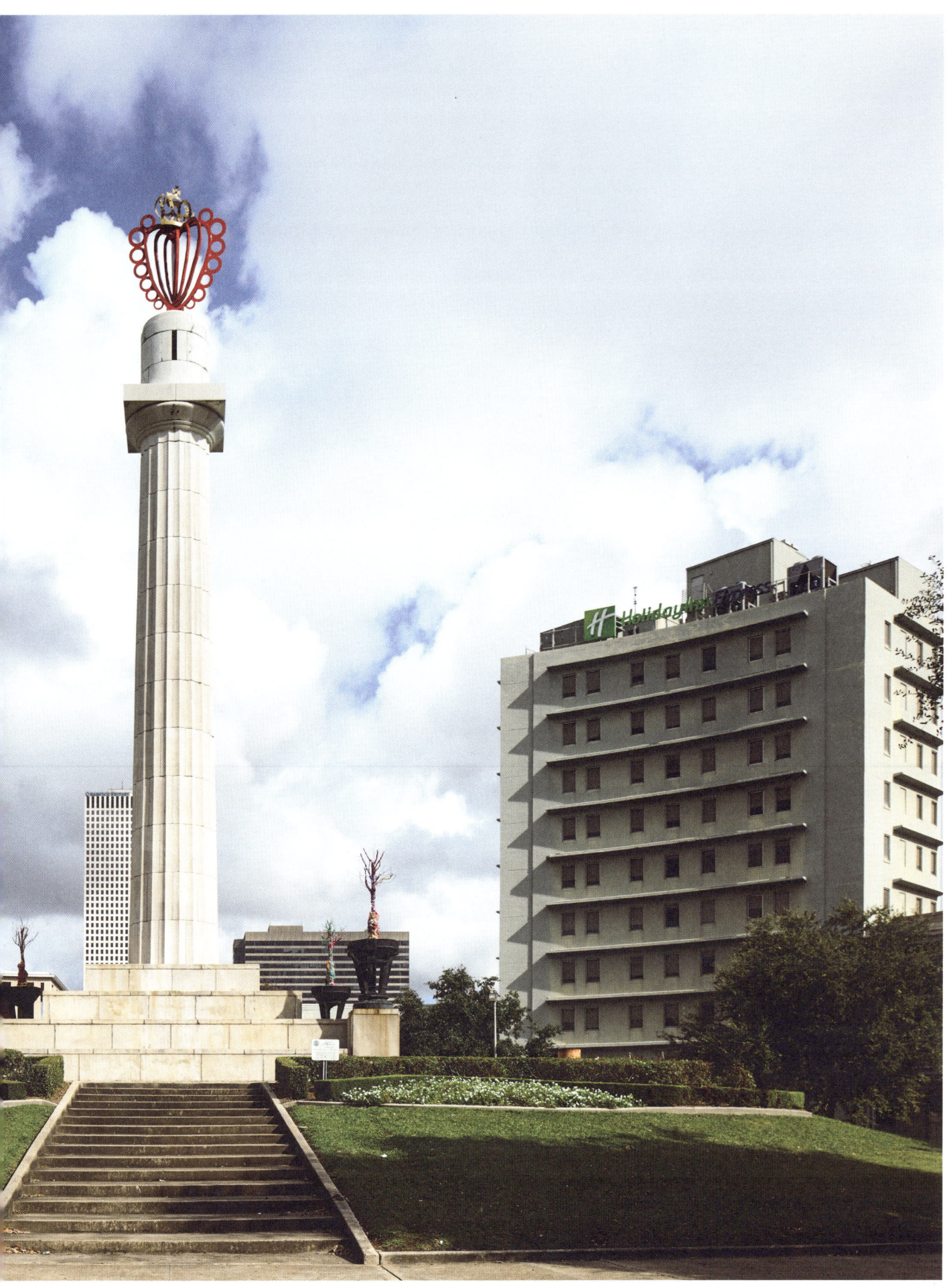

The Sacred Heart of Hours and the Trees of Yesterdays,
Today, and Tomorrow, 2024

Raúl de Nieves's multidisciplinary practice, spanning sculpture, performance, and music, vividly demonstrates the power of transformation and becoming. He is most widely known for his use of homespun materials—sequins, beads, trim, and rhinestones—to create dazzling sculptures and installations. Starting with a single bead and employing a meticulous adornment technique, his sculptures evolve into vibrant, fantastical figures. Similarly, his room-sized "stained-glass" installations are crafted through the laborious layering of hundreds of hand-cut acetate sheets and tape. Through these material metamorphoses, de Nieves reveals the latent potential within even the most humble materials, embodying a profound sense of hope and optimism while encouraging viewers to reconsider what has been discarded, overlooked, or undervalued.

For Prospect.6, de Nieves extends this exploration of hope and transformation to the site of the former Robert E. Lee Confederate monument in New Orleans'ss Harmony Circle. Erected in 1884, Lee's monument was one of the earliest of its kind in the South, and stood until 2017. Presented with the opportunity to engage this historically significant and emotionally charged public site, de Nieves kept returning to the same question: "What comes next?" He considered not only the aftermath of dismantling the commemorative and racist statue, but also what must emerge and be unearthed in the evolving cultural reckoning of our time. Indeed, as Indigenous scholar Lou Cornum (Diné/Bilagáana) poignantly reminds us, "History is never behind but below: the land we build on."[1] To that end, both the land and remaining pillar that Lee's statue once stood upon contain haunted histories and contradictions.

In response, de Nieves envisions this civic circle as a portal for collective imagination and healing, shaped in the form of a fifteen-foot-tall crowned heart, aptly titled *Sacred Heart of Hours* (2024). Resting atop the sixty-foot-tall marble column that once supported Lee's statue, de Nieves's monument offers multiple layers of meaning in this prominent public space, informed by the site's history and daily interactions with its users. While the red heart is commonly recognized as a symbol of love and romance, the crowned Sacred Heart of Jesus carries significant meaning in Catholicism, with

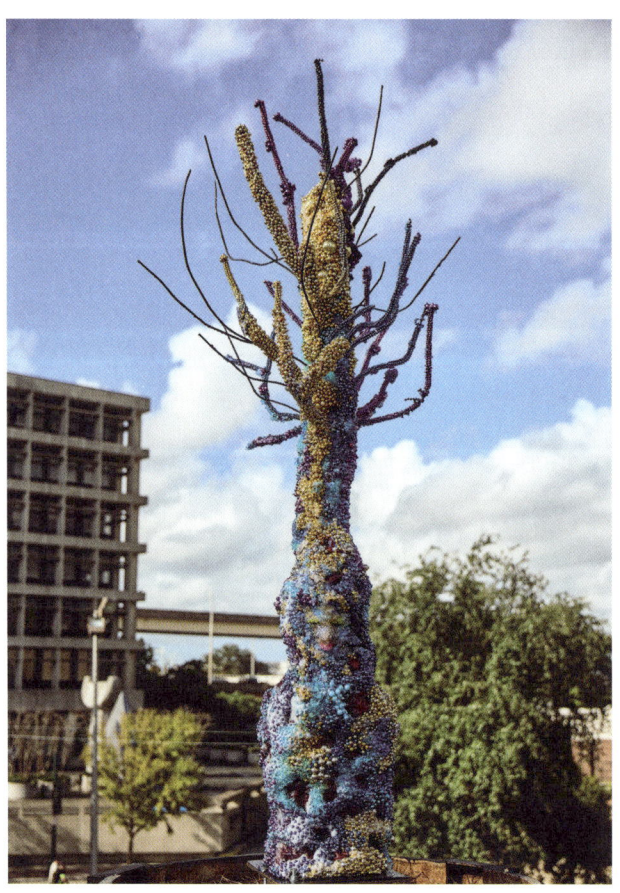

The Trees of Today (Diligence), 2024

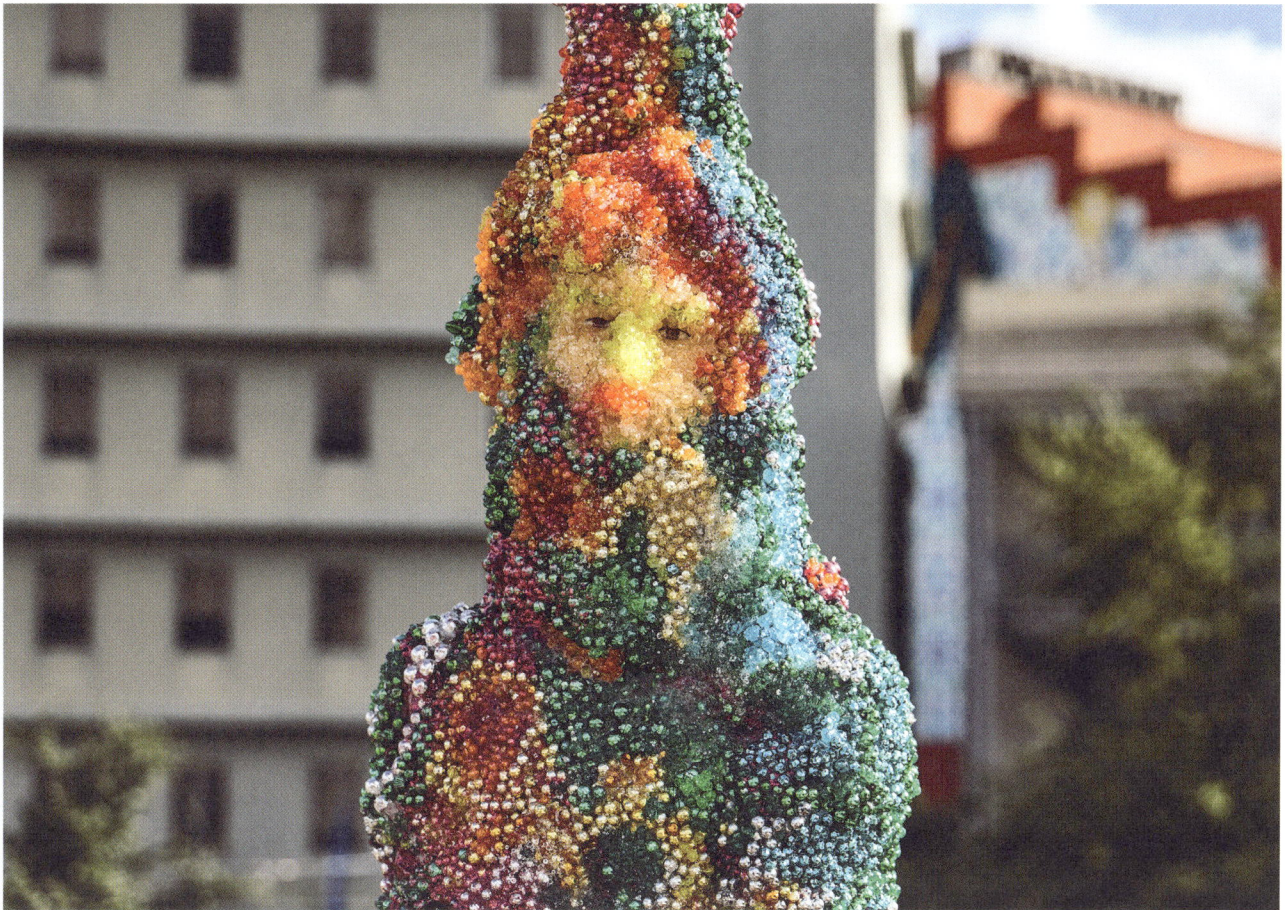

deep roots in Mexican culture, recalling New Orleans'ss own history of Mexican influence. During the city's Spanish colonial period, Mexican traditions were intricately woven into the cultural fabric of New Orleans, a bond strengthened by the Mexican-American War and subsequent waves of migration, which left indelible marks on the city's music, cuisine, and festival traditions.

For de Nieves, whose work often explores Catholicism and Mexican folklore, and who migrated from Michoacán, Mexico to the United States at age nine, the element of devotion is present, though not prescriptive. Instead, he hopes this sacred portal, soaring to a height where it meets the sky, with the clouds as its natural backdrop, will inspire a collective embodiment of love and a devotional practice of unity during this era of societal fractures.

At the base of the column, de Nieves reimagines the four historic bronze urns as vessels for anthropomorphic trees sculpted with thousands of recycled Mardi Gras beads. Titled *The Trees of Now (Diligence)*, *The Trees of Today (Justice)*, *The Trees of Tomorrow*

(Strength), and *The Trees of Yesterdays (Faith)* *(2024)*, the sculptures' beads were acquired in collaboration with the Krewe of Muses—the first all-female Mardi Gras krewe—and carry the impressions and memories of the Carnival parades and participants.

The result is a celebration of the city's cultural roots, with the trees symbolizing the interconnectedness of all life. Their metaphorical roots extend deep into the earth, intertwining with the city's history, while the heart's energy pulses up in the sky and travels into the ground itself, forging a portal between past and future, material and spiritual.

by Kaitlin Garcia-Maestas

1   Jess Wilcox et al, *Monuments Now*, exhibition catalogue, Socrates Sculpture Park, 2020-2021.

The Trees of Tomorrow (Justice), 2024 (detail)

Lafayette, Louisiana native Thomas Deaton paints semi-fictive New Orleans cityscapes populated by clowns and supernatural denizens who have been the subject of various moral panics: witches, ghosts, vampires, and cannibals. These figures mill about their lives, blithely slipping between the clutches of more everyday people. In 2016, people around the US and Western Europe began reporting sightings of "evil" clowns in unexpected settings. A cultural oddity of the transitional era after the global financial meltdown, some experts believe the clowns signaled a kind of mass hysteria, not dissimilar to the Salem witch trials. This was a time characterized by zero-interest money, which developers and corporations profited greatly from. The era of cheap capital caused further cracks in the US's social, political, and economic systems, creating divides that today read like unbreachable chasms.

Depicted in the background if depicted at all, in Deaton's work skyscrapers are stand-ins for financial hubs. Though they don't always appear in the picture plane, they nevertheless sit at the center of his psychic geographies. For Prospect.6, Deaton created *Last Megalopolis* (2024), a tryptic of three views that maps the built environment of different communities and reveals how classes relate to unseen powers. The left panel depicts a wealthy suburban development of single-family homes. Physically distanced from the urban core, placing it out of frame, these houses paradoxically highlight their inhabitants' close relational proximity to

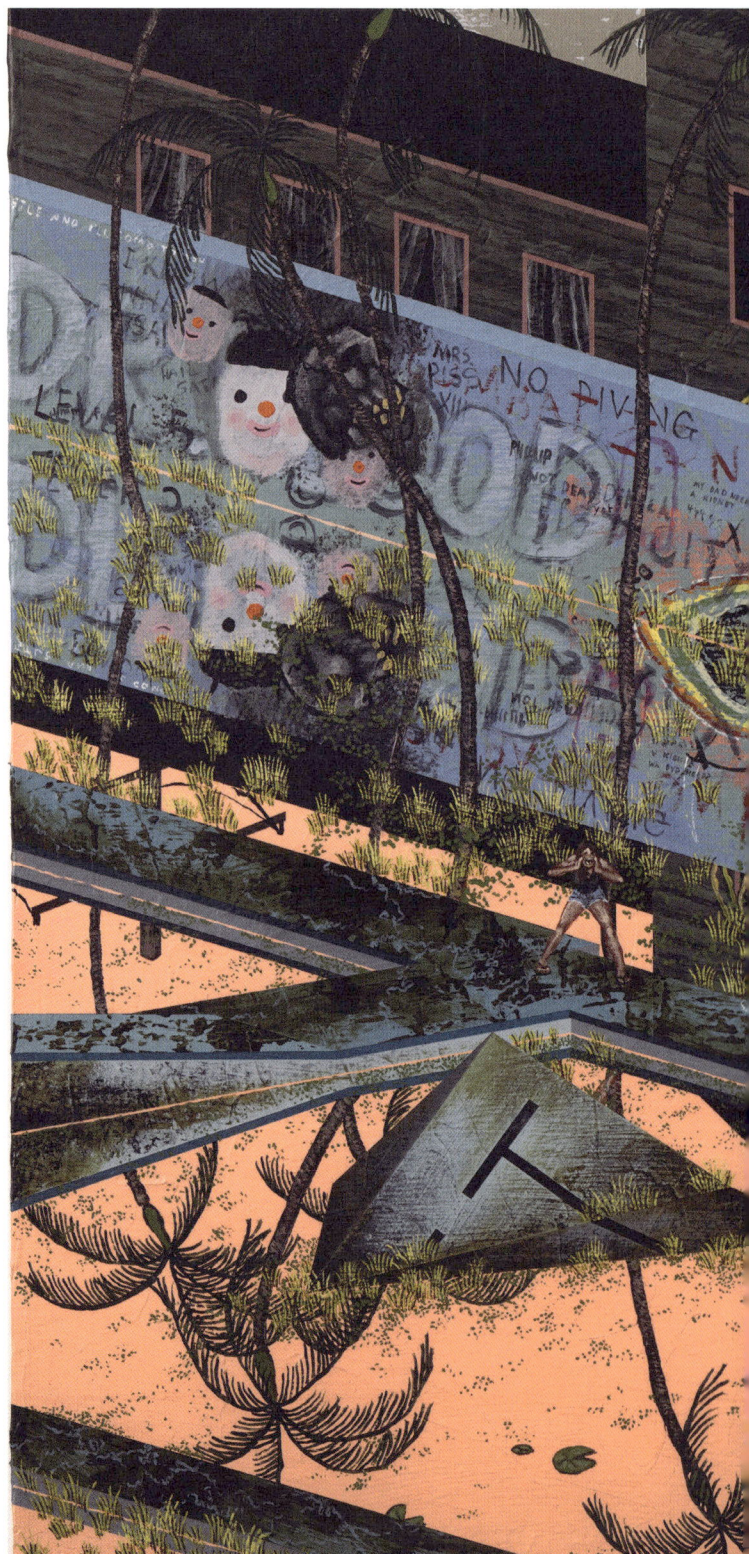

Last Megalopolis, 2024 (detail)

Thomas Deaton

b. 1988, Lafayette, LA; lives in New Orleans, LA

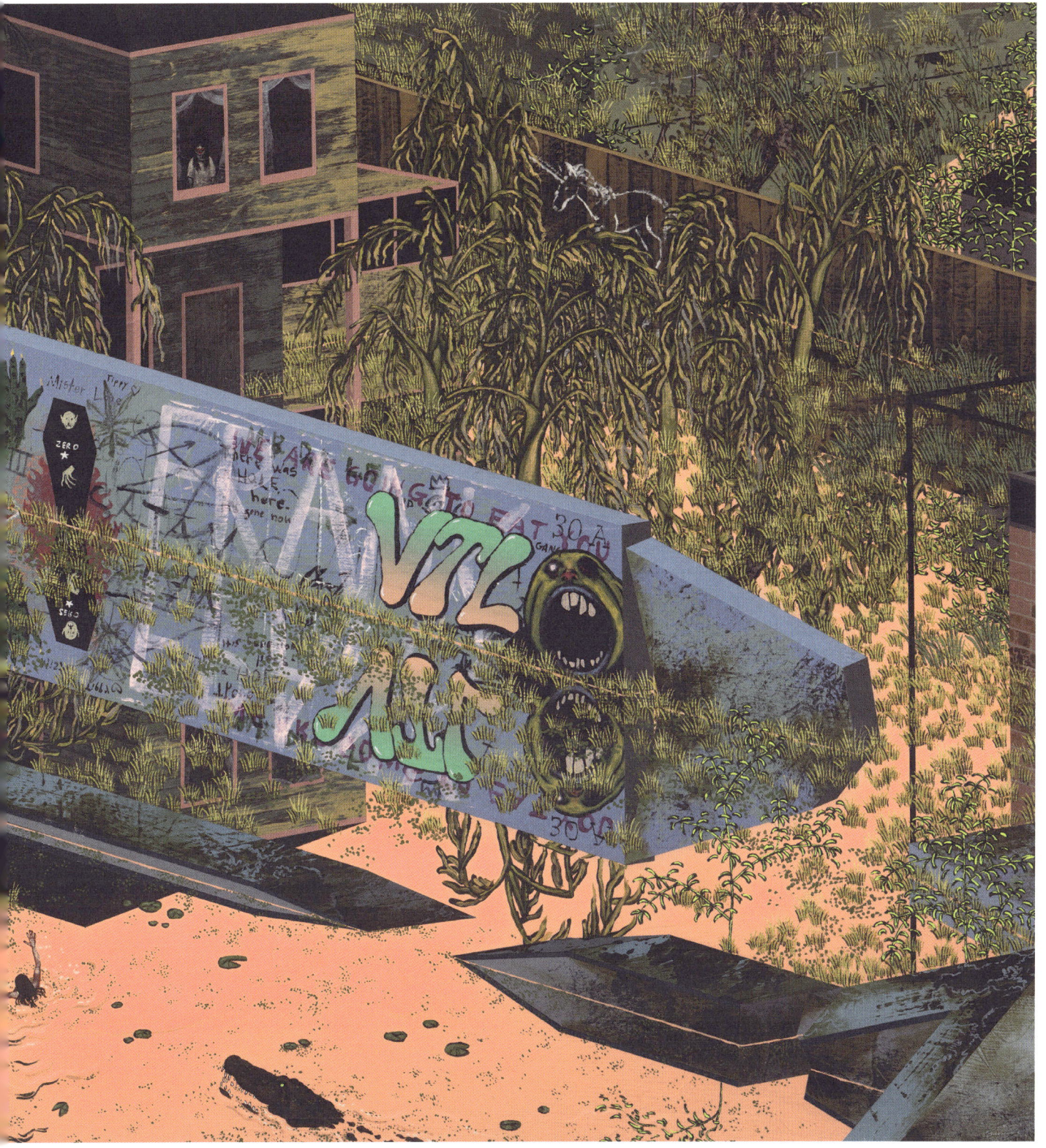

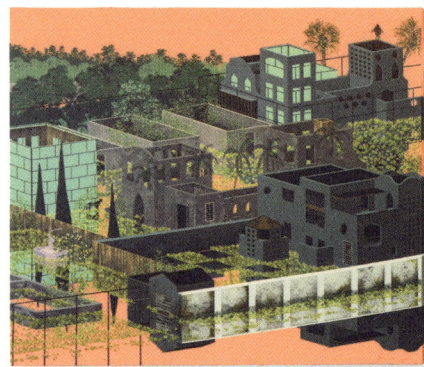 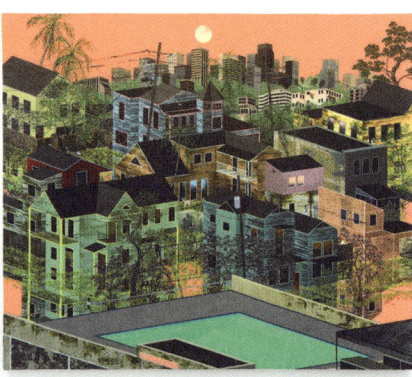 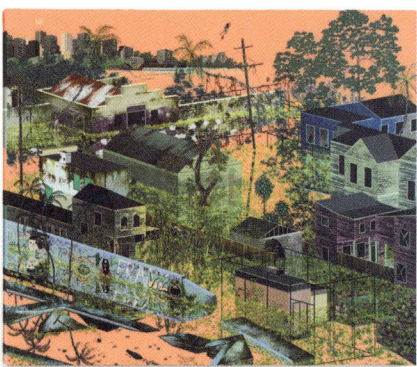

high-rises. They imply that the owners' ability to afford these homes means they are unseen scions moving money and making decisions. The center panel renders a mixed-use, multi-family community in front of the high-rises. This view positions the low-density community in the foreground in a relationship with the city that has not (yet?) tipped into either cynicism or nihilism. On the right, a blighted zone where ghouls run amok is set behind the high-rises, in what Deaton refers to as "the other side of the river." This view highlights the disaffected communities on whose backs the comforts of privilege and power tend to rest.

In *The Garden of Earthly Delights* (1490–1500), Hieronymus Bosch famously presents what Deaton describes as "heaven on the left, Earth in the middle, and hell on the right." He uses this format to unravel how developers and politicians in New Orleans traffic in ideas of heaven and hell by crossbreeding the jazz-inflected veneer of a city that has perfected romanticizing perpetual decay and morally rebuking the quotidian hardships of urban blight. While the right panel features a concentration of witches, clowns, and

cannibals, the extraction that built the homes in the left panel provokes the question: Who are the real vampires?

In the context of political, economic, and ecological crises, Deaton's romp through derelict urban and suburban uncanniness is unmistakably affectionate. His reference to the Bosch triptych is used to question: What paradise? Where? And for whom? As decades of under-investment in public infrastructure fails to meet the demands of a world threatened by the volatility of climate change, the surrealism of the everyday takes on a new pall. Suddenly, flood-affected communities turn to corporate assets as a public good, like using fast food apps to identify electricity outages. P.6 opens during the charge of an election year shot-through with a moral panic reminiscent of 2016. It's a year that may prove to be definitive for the country, local communities, and democracy itself. Finely attuned to this moment of fears both real and imagined, Deaton's paintings ring loud. "The clowns," he says, "are just a smoke screen."

by Kim Córdova

Abigail DeVille

b. 1981, New York, NY; works in Bronx, NY

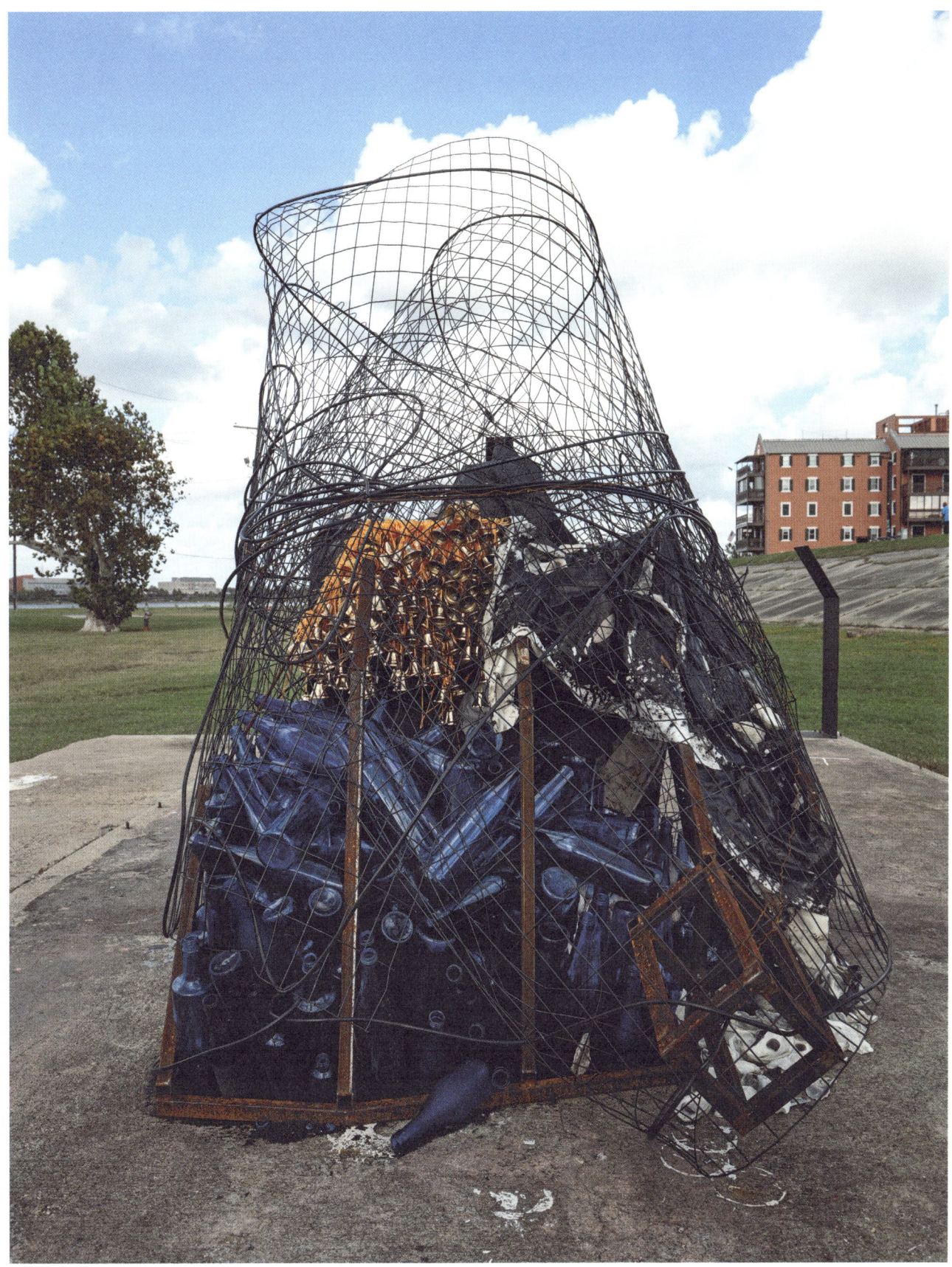

Carbon, 2024. Algiers Point

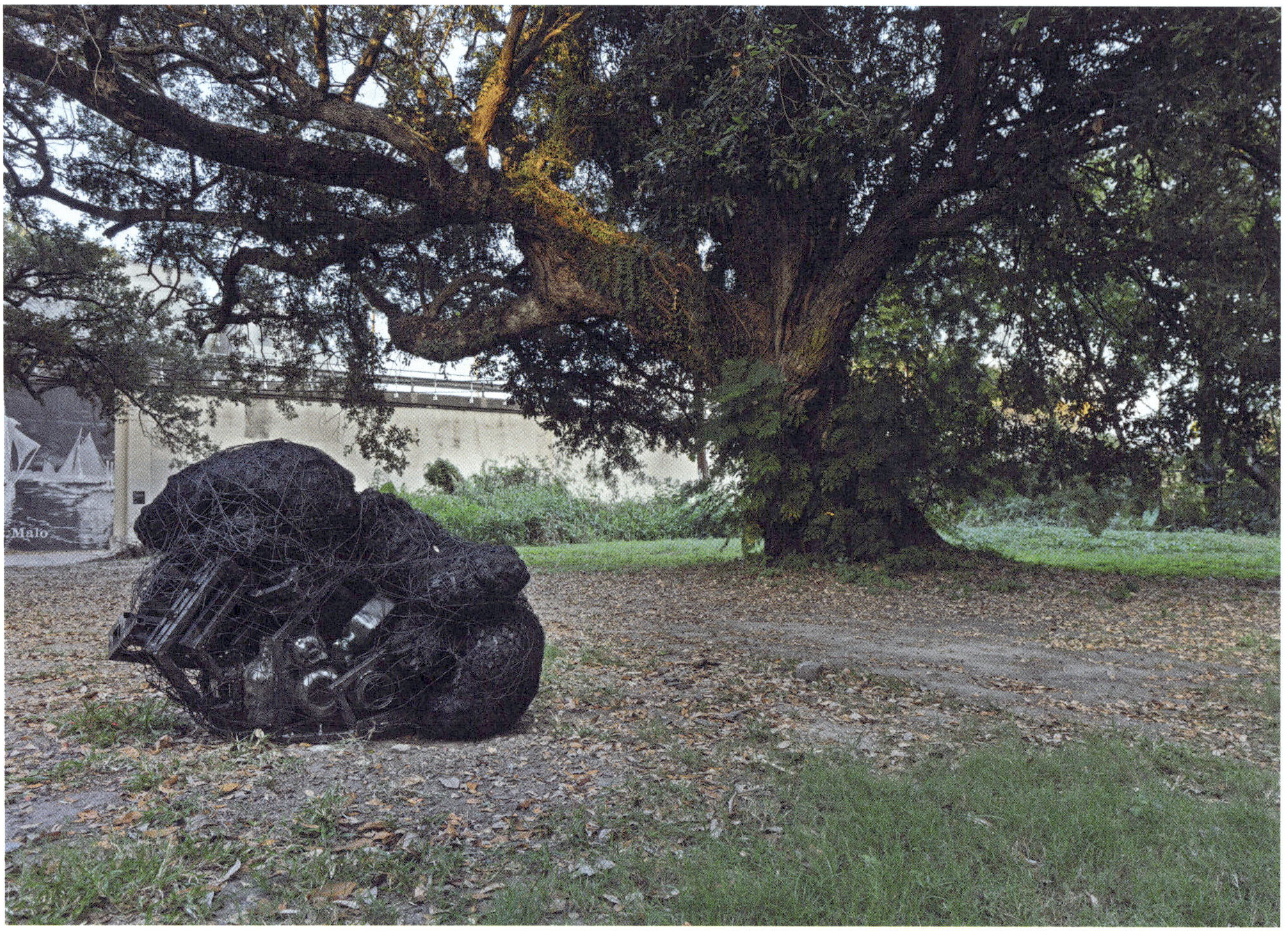

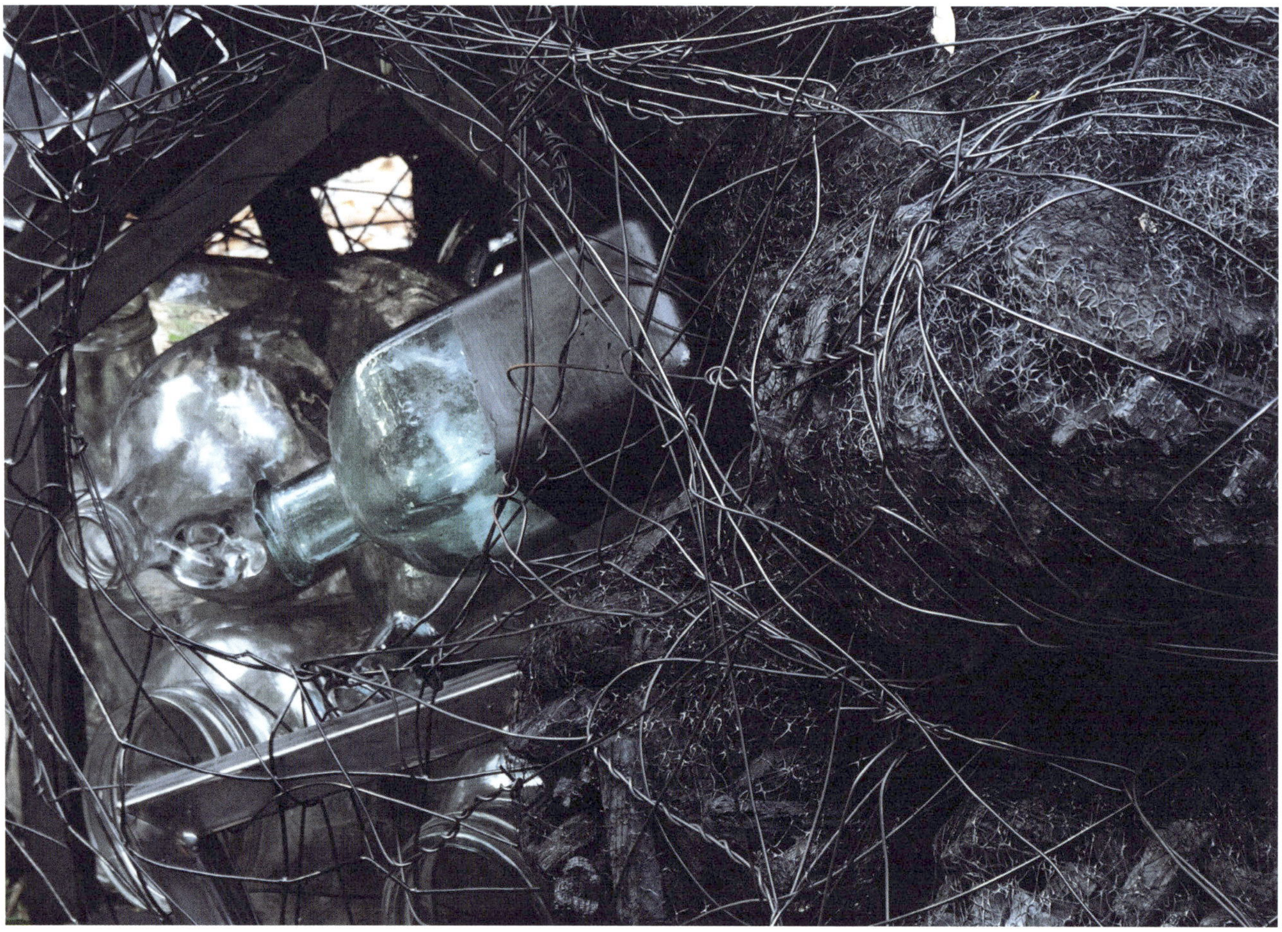

Top: *Carbon*, 2024. Music Box Village

Above: *Carbon*, 2024. Music Box Village (detail)

Working between sculpture, video, assemblage, and installation, New York-based artist Abigail DeVille's practice is one of site-specificity. The site itself can take many forms, from which the artist resituates forgotten or erased narratives within broader historical timescales. For her multisite installation at Prospect.6, she maps a cross-temporal narrative of Black movement and migration across the landscape of New Orleans.

Carbon consists of four anatomical heart-shaped sculptures installed throughout the city. One is located on the shore of the Mississippi River at Algiers Point, an area established by the French in 1719 as a plantation. Another sits near the station where, in 1892, Homer Plessy, a mixed-race man, intentionally boarded a segregated train in an act of civil disobedience, which led to the landmark Plessy v. Ferguson Supreme Court case. The other two sculptures are housed outside the performance and art space Music Box Village and on the campus of the New Orleans African American Museum.

The installation takes as its point of departure a series of shipping manifests filed in New Orleans from 1807 through 1860. These documents track the arrival of approximately 135,000 people of African descent sold in the largest slave market in the Deep South. The manifests, accessible via the US Customs Service archive, list the names, ages, and physical traits of the people forced aboard the ships from other states throughout the US (the transatlantic slave trade was banned in 1808, though slaves were shipped domestically). These personal details are incorporated into an evolving sound piece that accompanies each sculpture, forming unique sonic environments.[1] In probing this archive, DeVille unveils the violence of such indexical representation, but she also troubles the misapprehension that the lives of enslaved people are lost to history. Rather, their stories are hidden in plain sight, though often relegated to a space of subliminal darkness.

DeVille's materials often speak to the intangibility of historical narratives. For *Carbon*, the artist was particularly drawn to coal, which primarily consists of carbon, one of the most ubiquitous elements on the planet, from which all living matter emanates and returns. Each heart-shaped sculpture varies in dimension, approximately corresponding to the size of a human body at different life stages. The structures house various materials—coal, rope, steel, and glass bottles stuffed with copies of the manifests, all encased in a porous chicken wire exterior. In drawing on the material ecology of carbon—a time-keeper, a relic, a capsule that transcends temporality—*Carbon* memorializes erased histories of Black subjects, poetically operating at a similar threshold of liminal visibility.

Voids and porous boundaries often figure into DeVille's work. They embody the continuous processes of making and unmaking from which all things form, and from which history is written. "America has numerous black holes in which it tries unsuccessfully to bury the bodies of its many democratic operatives," the artist has reflected. "I use black holes as a loose metaphor for historical erasure. Black holes eviscerate matter, but the gravity of the matter remains to be discovered, interrogated, and recognized."[2] For DeVille, a black hole—an abstraction of an opening, an aperture, or an ellipse—represents a space of persistent misrecognition from which a veiled subject might emerge.

DeVille's work suggests that if the written record doesn't capture our histories, then a new visual language must be written. Symbols of nationhood and identity can similarly be rewritten, or bear alternating meanings across time and space. The felt experience of diaspora may conceal certain narratives from official histories, but, as DeVille reveals, these narratives can be uncovered, if one only knows where to look.

by Re'al Christian

1   The sound piece, entitled *The heart knows its own bitterness (Manifest)* (2024), combines singing, instruments, environmental and bodily noises. DeVille collaborated with composers, musicians, and artists Courtney Bryan, RA Washington, Jadele McPherson, and Justin Hicks.
2   Jane Ursula Harris, "Fault Lines: Abigail DeVille Interviewed," *BOMB Magazine* (June 14, 2021).

Christian Việt Đinh

b. 1992, St. Petersburg, FL; lives in New Orleans, LA

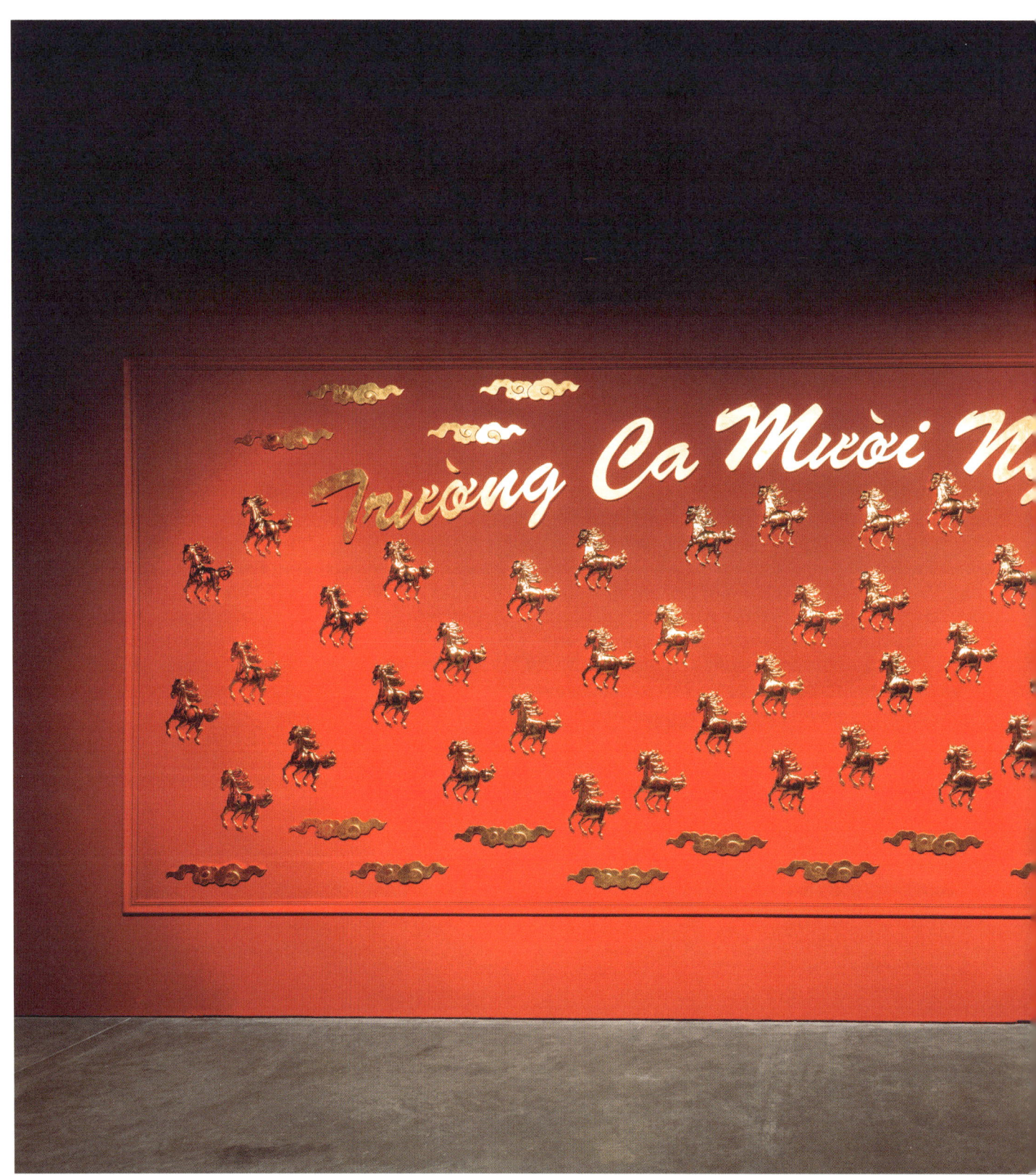

Trường Ca Mười Ngàn Năm (A Song of 10,000 Years), 2024

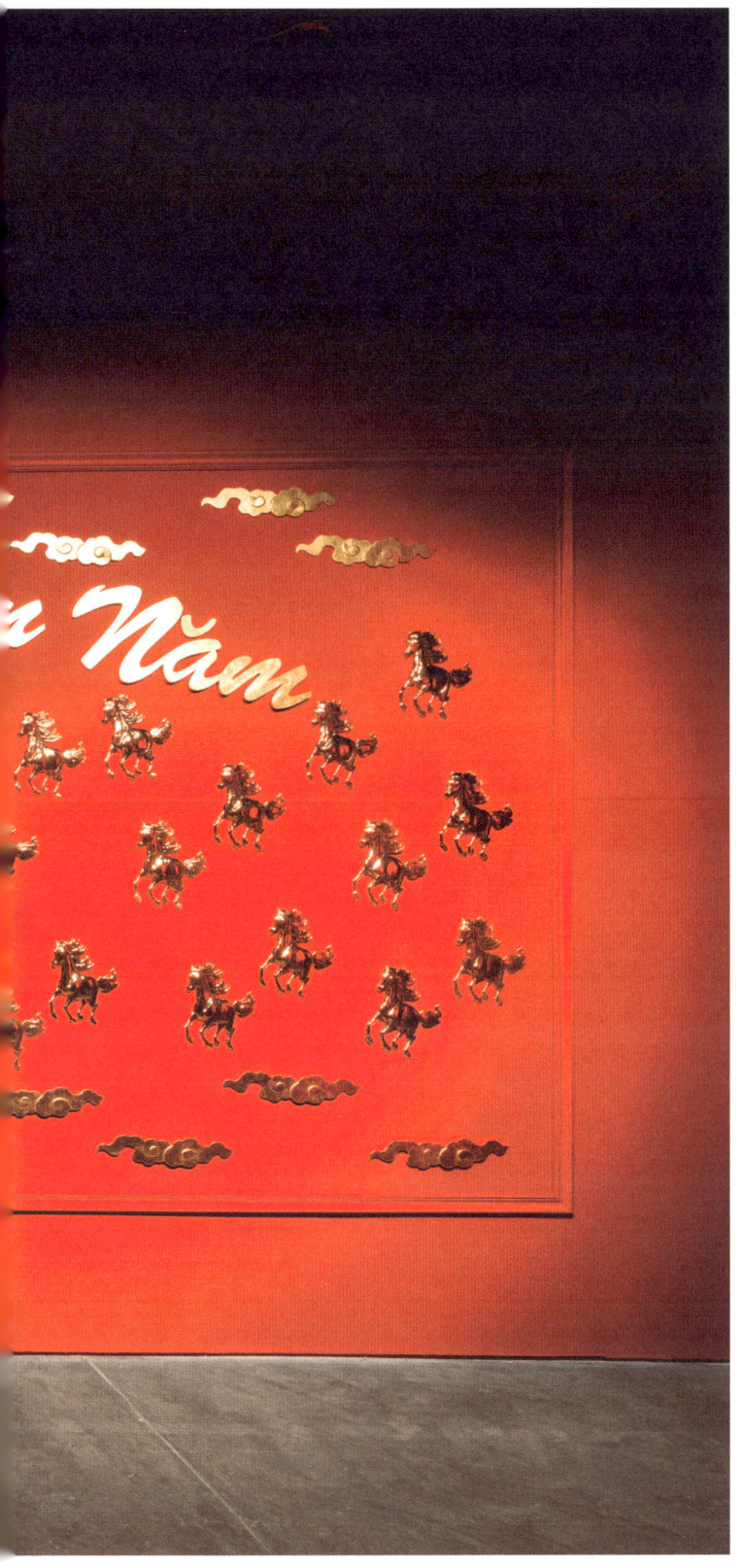

In May 1975, waves of Vietnamese refugees began to arrive in the United States after the end of the Vietnam War. Many found their way to New Orleans through sponsorship from charitable organizations, laying the foundation for the largest Vietnamese American community not only in Louisiana, but in the entire Gulf Coast region. Fifty years later, artists like Christian Việt Đinh are reflecting on the war's aftermath, which triggered the vibrant evolution of these communities across the United States.

Đinh's practice aims to reclaim the rich heritage and unique identity of Vietnamese Americans. Raised in Southern cities with significant Vietnamese American populations—and now based in New Orleans—Đinh's upbringing has deeply influenced the exploration of his community's diasporic identity. Commissioned for Prospect.6, Đinh's *Trường Ca Mười Ngàn Năm (A Song of 10,000 Years)* (2024) commemorates the fiftieth anniversary of the establishment of the Vietnamese community in the United States. Encompassing an entire room, the work melds influences from imperial Vietnamese aesthetics and cultural symbols tied to the Vietnamese American community in a space that articulates and honors the legacy of the diaspora.

This reverential space is sumptuously toned in red and gold, evoking the altar rooms at the imperial city of Hue in Vietnam, where royalty traditionally made offerings to their ancestors. Arranged in horizontal registers constructed from ceramic elements, the installation contains ceramic relief sculptures of horses, painted cloud motifs, and prayer-like poetic

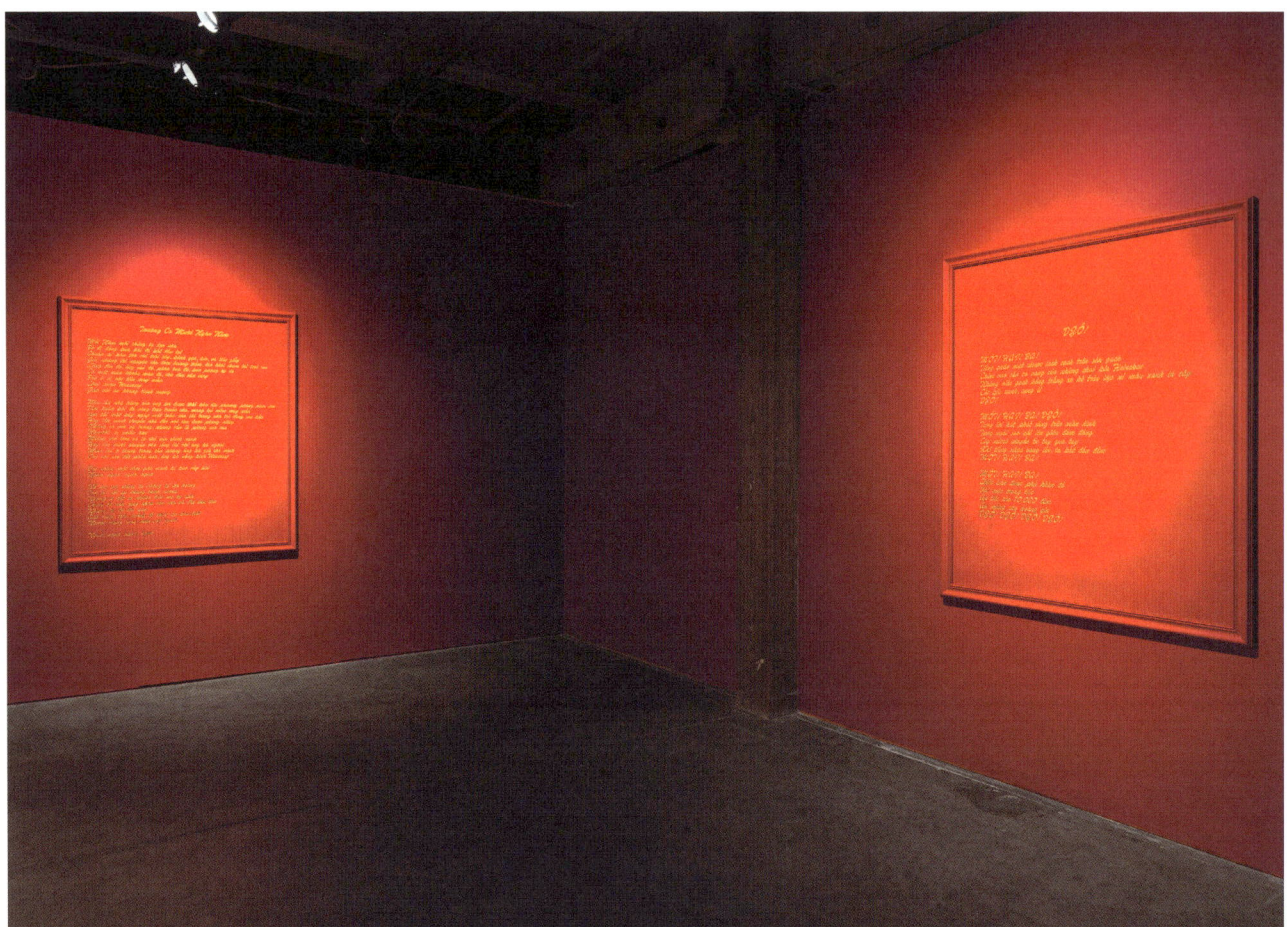

texts written by Đinh. Together, the elements in *Trường Ca Mười Ngàn Năm* visually mark the journey, progression, and development of the Vietnamese American community, crafted from amalgamated cultural influences.

Fifty ceramic horses finished in a golden luster glaze embody a form of diasporic patriotism. The horse is a potent symbol in both Vietnamese and American culture, denoting resilience, perseverance, and freedom for both, while emblematizing American rugged individualism and, in Vietnamese iconography, community strength. Đinh's horses are surrounded by cloud motifs signifying ascension across the liminal space between earthly and celestial realms. Together, the clouds and horses underscore the community's arrival at a once-aspirational, now tangible place, encapsulating a narrative that transcends the passage of a mere fifty years.

The last section is inscribed with poetic texts by Đinh himself, rendered in gold foil, expressing gratitude to his family and community, and reflecting the spiritual dimensions rooted in both Vietnamese and Catholic traditions. These texts not only evoke the opulence of imperial Vietnamese traditions but also resonate deeply within Vietnamese American communities, where *khánh vàng* (commemorative and celebratory plaques) are common in businesses and homes, symbolizing wishes for prosperity. This blending of aesthetic traditions from imperial Vietnam with the everyday realities of working-class Vietnamese Americans bridges historical narratives and reframes the community as a contemporary dynasty, forging a new legacy in a new country.

The placement of *Trường Ca Mười Ngàn Năm* at the Contemporary Arts Center—rather than in areas with larger Vietnamese American populations, like New Orleans East and the Westbank—underscores Đinh's intention to elevate and center the experiences of this underrecognized community within broader civic and artistic discourses. By doing so, Đinh not only celebrates the resilience and contributions of early refugees, but also sets a hopeful trajectory for the future, inviting reflection and dialogue on the evolving identity of Vietnamese Americans.

by Leilani Lynch

Trường Ca Mười Ngàn Năm (A Song of 10,000 Years), 2024

Jeannette Ehlers

b. 1973, Holstebro, Denmark; lives in Copenhagen, Denmark

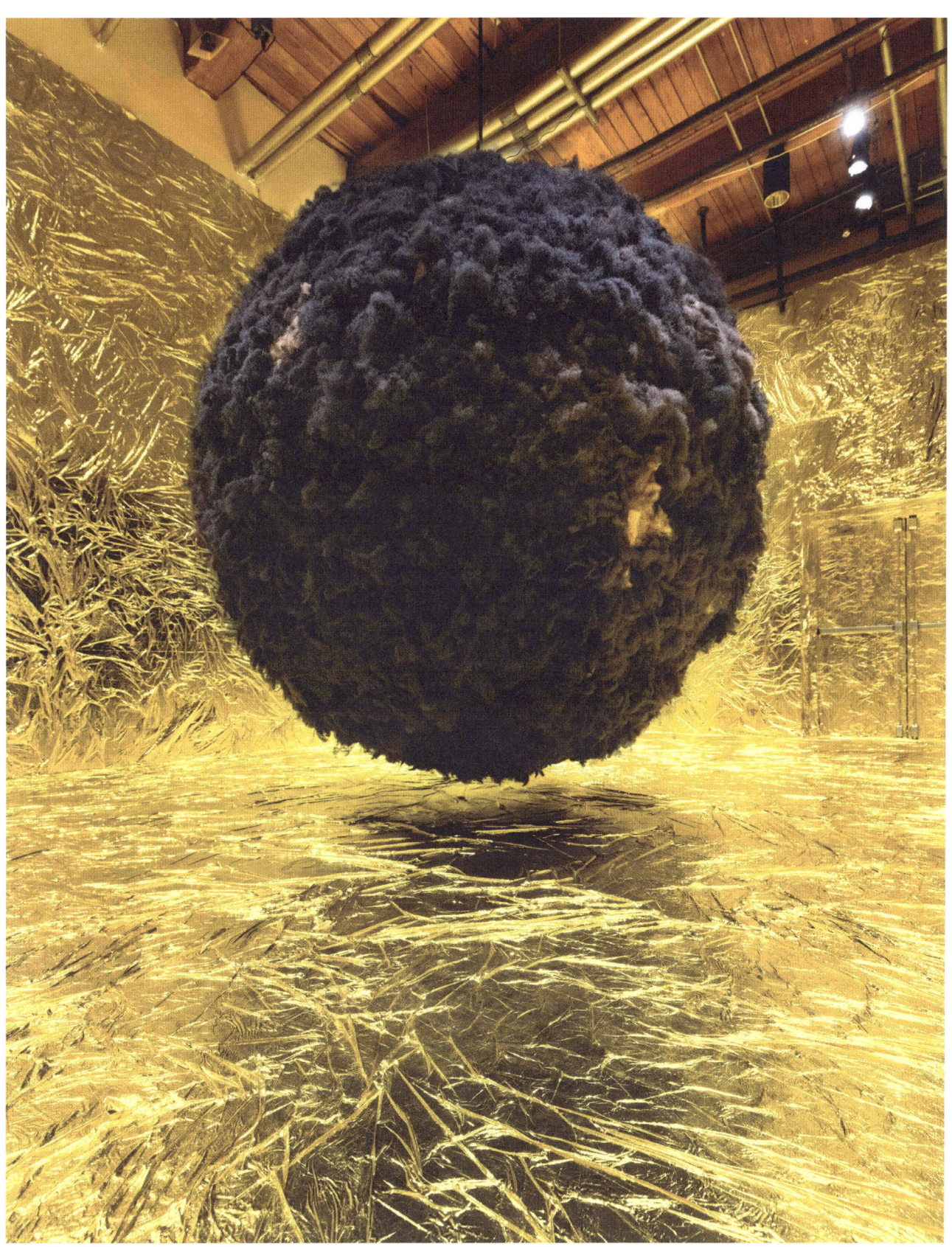

We're Magic. We're Real #2, 2020/2024

In the cavernous expanse of bygone industrial fluorescence—the Ford Motor Company Assembly Plant in Arabi, Louisiana—Danish-Trinidadian artist Jeannette Ehlers's *Hoist and the Unseen: Journeys Through Tempests in Times of Hunger* (2024) poetically reckons with Denmark's history of slavery and colonialism. One-half of a giant, antique pulley wheel is installed on the ground, adorned with braids of afro hair that tentacularly extend into the former auto assembly plant. Ehlers replicated the pulley wheel from the West India Warehouse, a building on the Copenhagen Harbor that received the majority of incoming goods from Denmark's Caribbean colonies. Her engagement with the enormous pulley wheel, which occupies the upper two floors of the warehouse, represents an expansion of her attention to colonialism and exploitation in the Danish imperial context: The wheel was driven by unpaid prison laborers to move the valuable colonial goods from the harbor into storage.

Ehlers's model of the wheel connects the enslaved labor of African peoples and descendants on the Caribbean plantation with the exploitation of the proletariat in the US. The braids that bedeck the wheel are a recurring feature of Ehlers's practice and speak to the diffuse centrality of Blackness in liberation struggles throughout the diaspora. For instance, in the 2023 performance *Diasporic Frequencies*, Ehlers hosted a braiding workshop (a common collaborative facet of her practice) to produce a set of seemingly endless braids that were braided into her own hair, then attached to the rafters of a barn at Rønnebæksholm, a former royal manor in Denmark. With *Hoist*, the wheel serves as a symbolic focal point to crisscross the Atlantic and over two centuries of Black history: from the Danish Caribbean plantation to the metropole, to the Fordist boom in American industry manifest in the architecture of the assembly plant. Importantly, Ehlers bifurcates the wheel, presenting only the top half. When replicated and installed on the floor of the former assembly plant, *Hoist* invites the spectator to imagine what lies beneath.

Installed in the Contemporary Arts Center, Ehlers's second contribution to Prospect.6, *We're Magic. We're Real #2* (2020/2024), is a sphere made of synthetic afro hair that slowly rotates in the reflective space of the gallery, accompanied by a soundtrack with a droning pulse and percussion that lulls the spectators into the looped sequence. Hung low to the ground, it seems to offer a rapport with the viewer's own body. Yet, the sphere's two-meter diameter exceeds individual corporeality, and synecdochically signals the capaciousness of Africa and its diaspora through hair. The sphere's slow rotation evokes the Earth's own rotation and further extends Blackness into the global. In *We're Magic. We're Real #2*, afro hair is a formal element that revels in textural variation and complexity, and speaks to the significance of hair for those in the African diaspora who were long discouraged from wearing natural styles.

The shiny reflectivity of the walls and floor in this installation form a stark contrast to the matte depth of the afro-hair sphere: They are covered in emergency blankets. As with the associative transtemporal connections in *Hoist*, this juxtaposition gestures toward the ongoingness of colonialism's effects from the perspective of Blackness. The textured rippling of these emergency blankets evokes the oceanic trauma of both the Middle Passage and the contemporary migrant crisis in the Mediterranean. As recurs throughout her practice, the material elements of *Hoist* and *We're Magic. We're Real #2* foreground the wounds of colonial history and extractivist capitalism alongside the promise of a radical futurity from the perspective of African diasporic Blackness.

by C.C. McKee

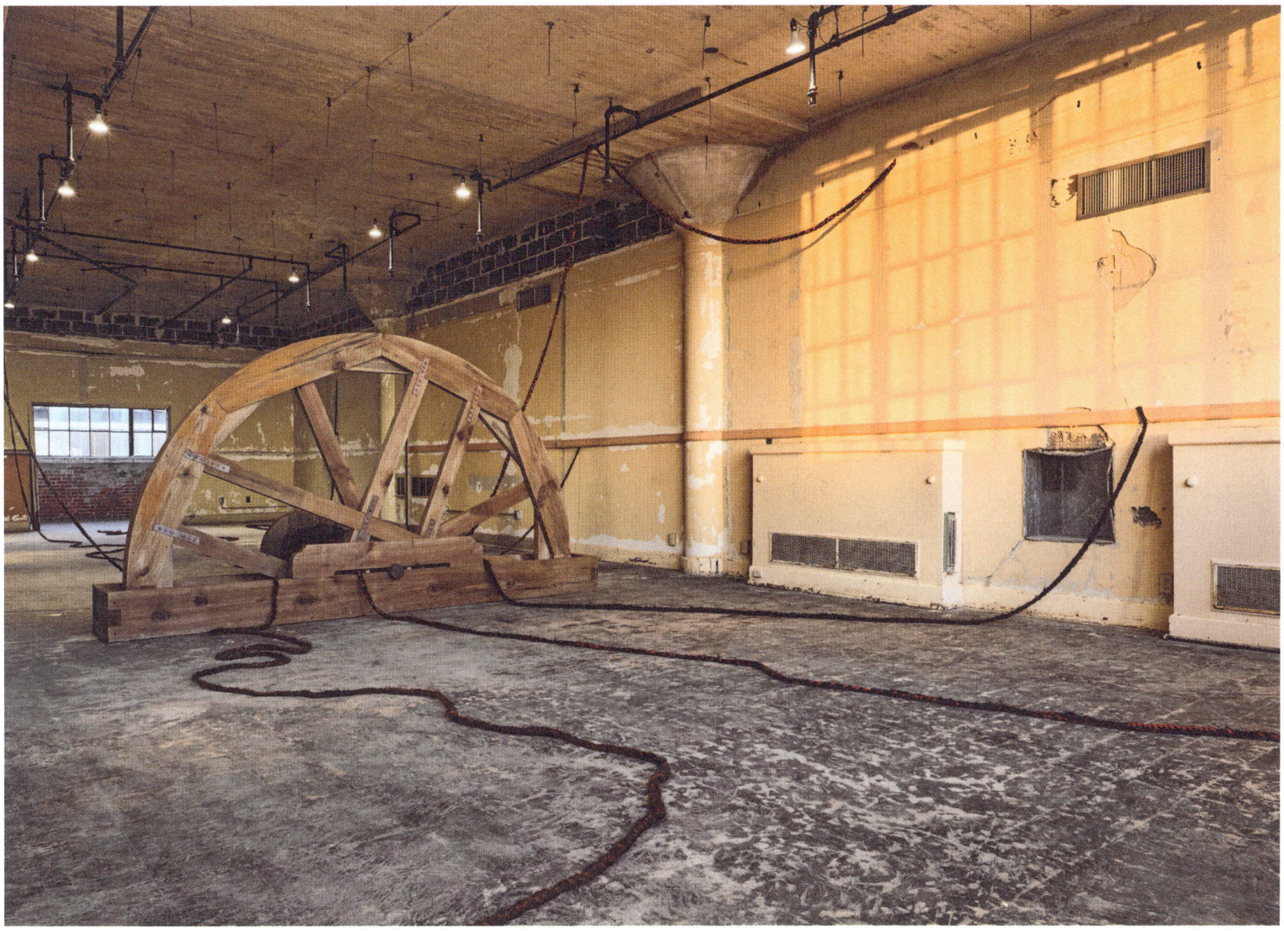

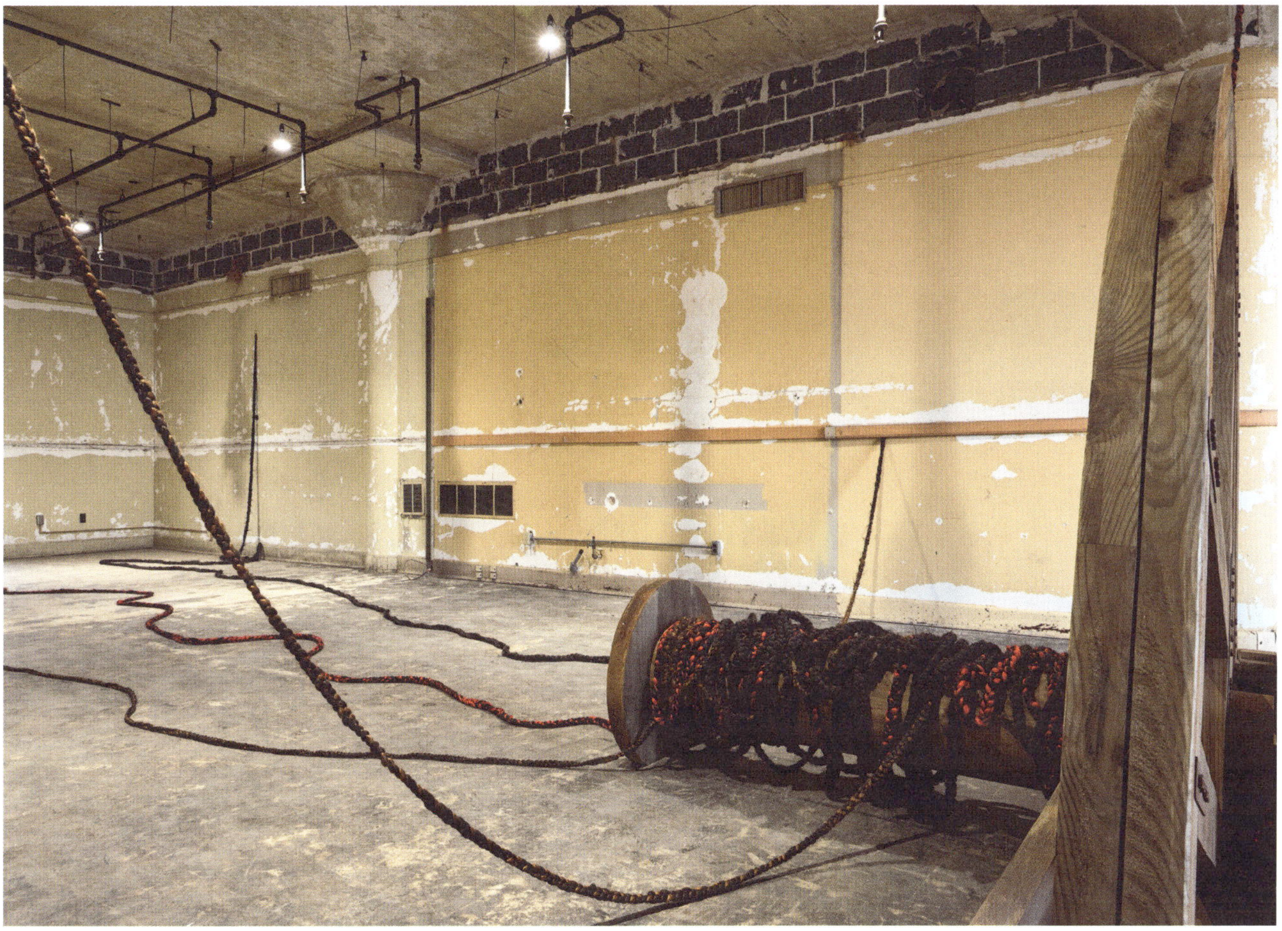

Hoist and the Unseen: Journeys Through Tempests in Times of Hunger, 2024

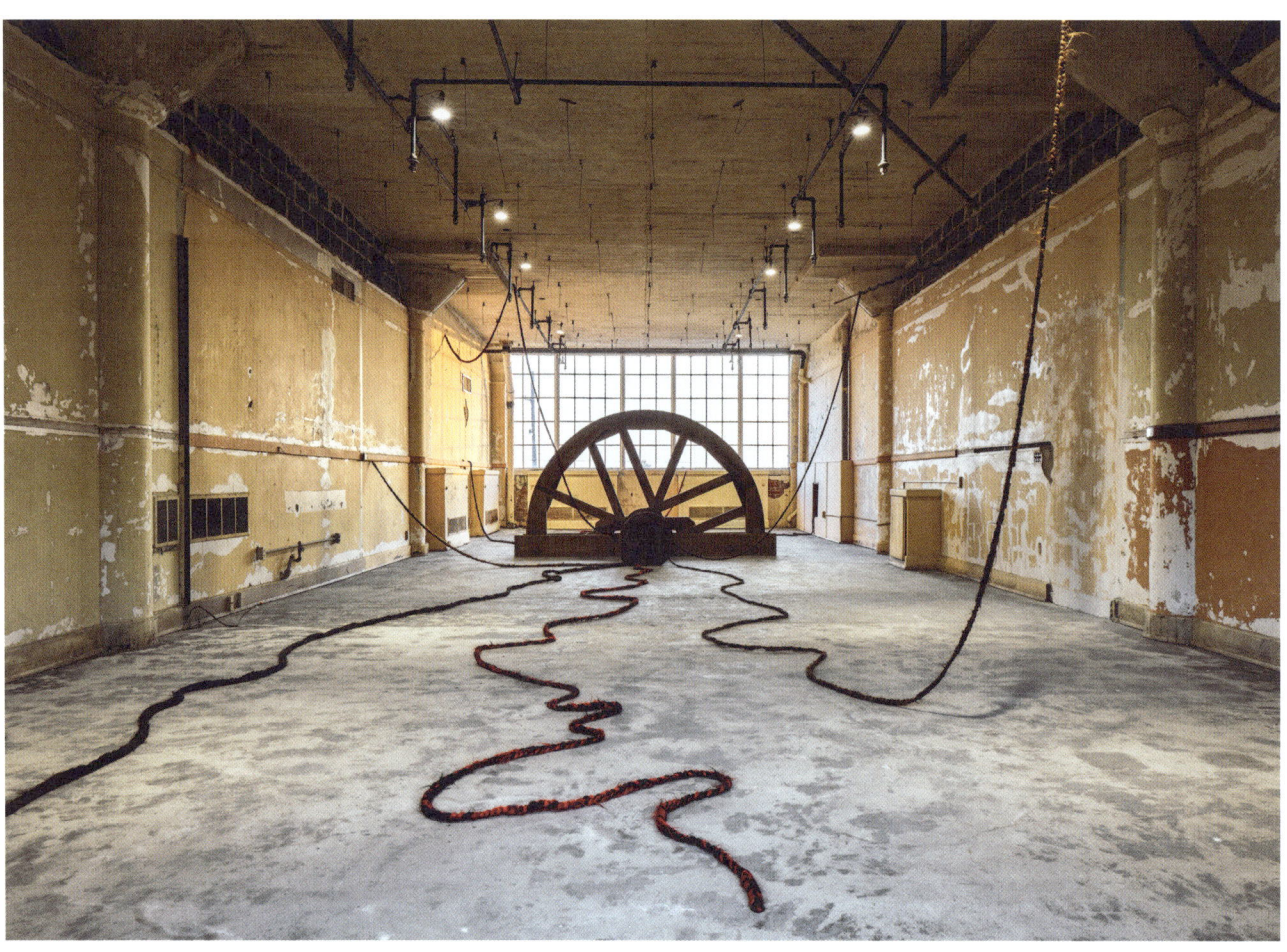

Hoist and the Unseen: Journeys Through Tempests
in Times of Hunger, 2024

Bonded by Magic Goo
Quintron

Speculating on "New Orleans in one hundred years" is making me crazy and a bit depressed. Keeping your head in the sand is a survival skill in this town, but I suppose we all must come up for a look around every once in a while. An obvious tone choice for this piece would be to go full-throttle dystopian due to the very clear writing by all of the elephants in all of the rooms on all of the walls regarding climate change, rising ocean temperatures, and the reliance upon antiquated man-made pumping systems to keep our architecture from slipping back into the mud. The weather-gods have been whipping handfuls of bright orange ping pong balls into the Gulf of Mexico at an ever increasing rate, making it logical to assume that the next big one is not a matter of if, but when. We can only be heroic and resilient for so long before it looks like collective insanity.

So what do we do and what will it mean to be a New Orleanian a hundred years from now and what even *is* that special thing that makes us who we are? What if we moved this entire city five hundred miles upriver? Can you transplant a soul from one body to another? Can you dress up a town in gumbo, liquor, and jazz and tell everyone, "*That's* NAWLINS baby!" Obviously no, but if the procedure were handled with the utmost care for those ethereal currencies which make up the *real* DNA of our interlocking neighborhoods and communities, New Orleans in one hundred years could potentially exist anywhere, right? Ack! This is too hard! Please, may I go back to the sand now? Anyways, that line of thought is a cavernous sci-fi rabbit hole, so why don't we leave such imaginings to the Asimovs and go a different, slightly sunnier direction.

Let's say that the whole hurricane thing gets fixed. The science people, realizing that global reductions in carbon emissions ain't happening because humans gonna human, figure out how to temp-blast sea waters and diffuse escalating storms. Let's also say that they figure out how to re-freeze the polar ice caps in order to keep rising sea waters at bay, and just *maybe* they also engineer some clever method for manipulating nimbostratus rain clouds in order to keep them from pissing all over one geographic location for days on end.

Great, but what about the invisible goo, made up of the unique bylaws and generational rituals that distinguish New Orleans as a safe haven for the corporeal wizards who thrive here? A town which embraces and respects the practice of art and music as human *behavior* rather than as mere entertainment. What toll does a hundred years take on this precious goo? Is it not also in jeopardy and in need of preservation? The way I see it, New Orleans has always been a sort of futuristic utopia, insomuch as it has always valued matters of body and soul over wealth and progress, embouchure and tone over muscle mass and speed. Bliss-functionality is our protective moat and I fear that it is slowly getting filled with sand one thimble at a time.

The science people, with their bubbling beakers and pointy pencils, can't help us with that one. Nope, we are on our own as citizens and elected leaders to defend our castle from the storms of logic, greed, and hard-hatted sharks-with-golden-shovels—all threats that have plagued us in the past and are sure to continue as long as there are dollars and men.

So, if you are a person who has been made whole by this city, a person who is validated and held together by the magic goo, then you understand what is at stake here. Dust off your suit of armor, gaze into the reverse-crystal-ball of our collective past, and prepare thyself for a bloody rumble. There will be beer.

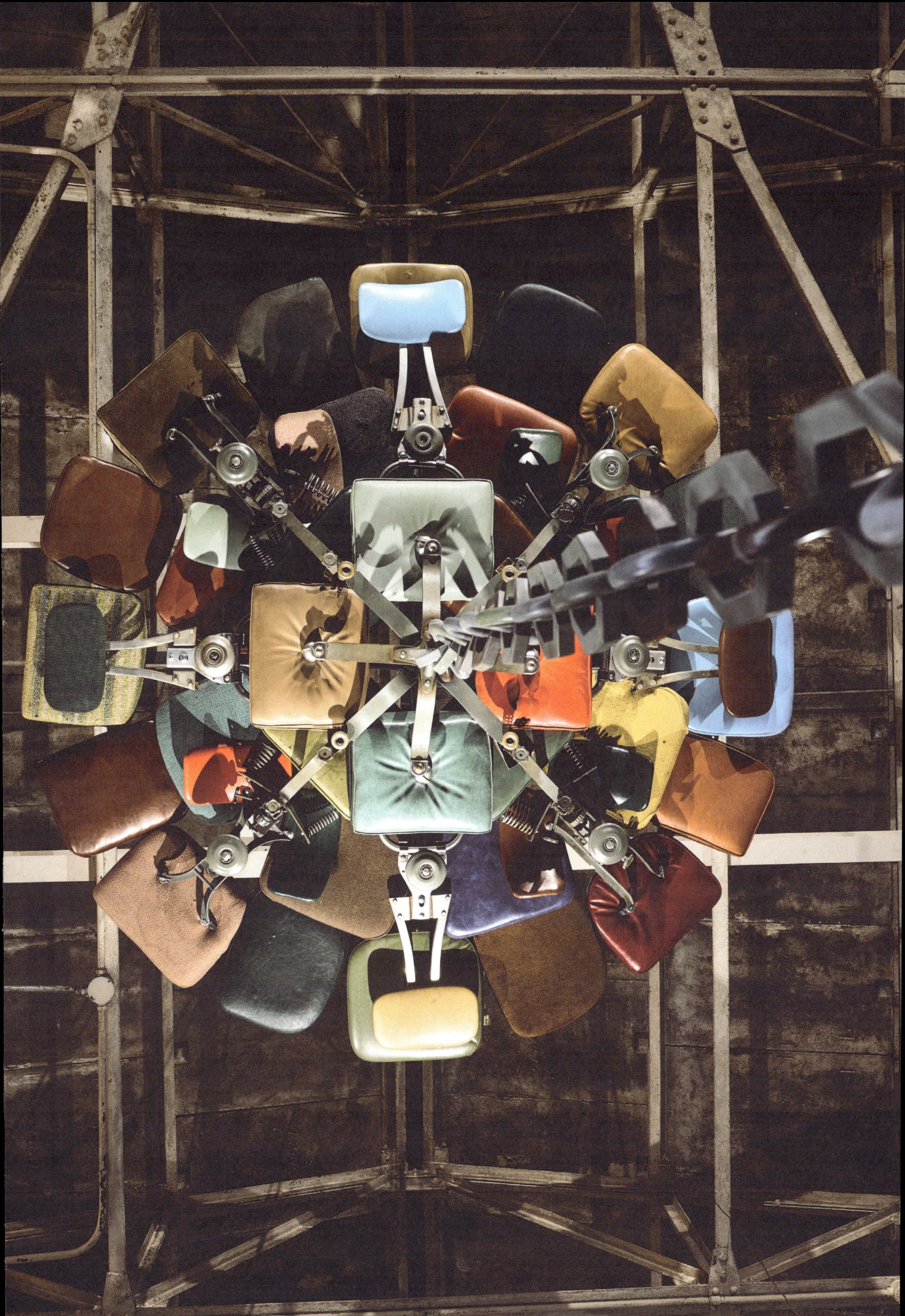

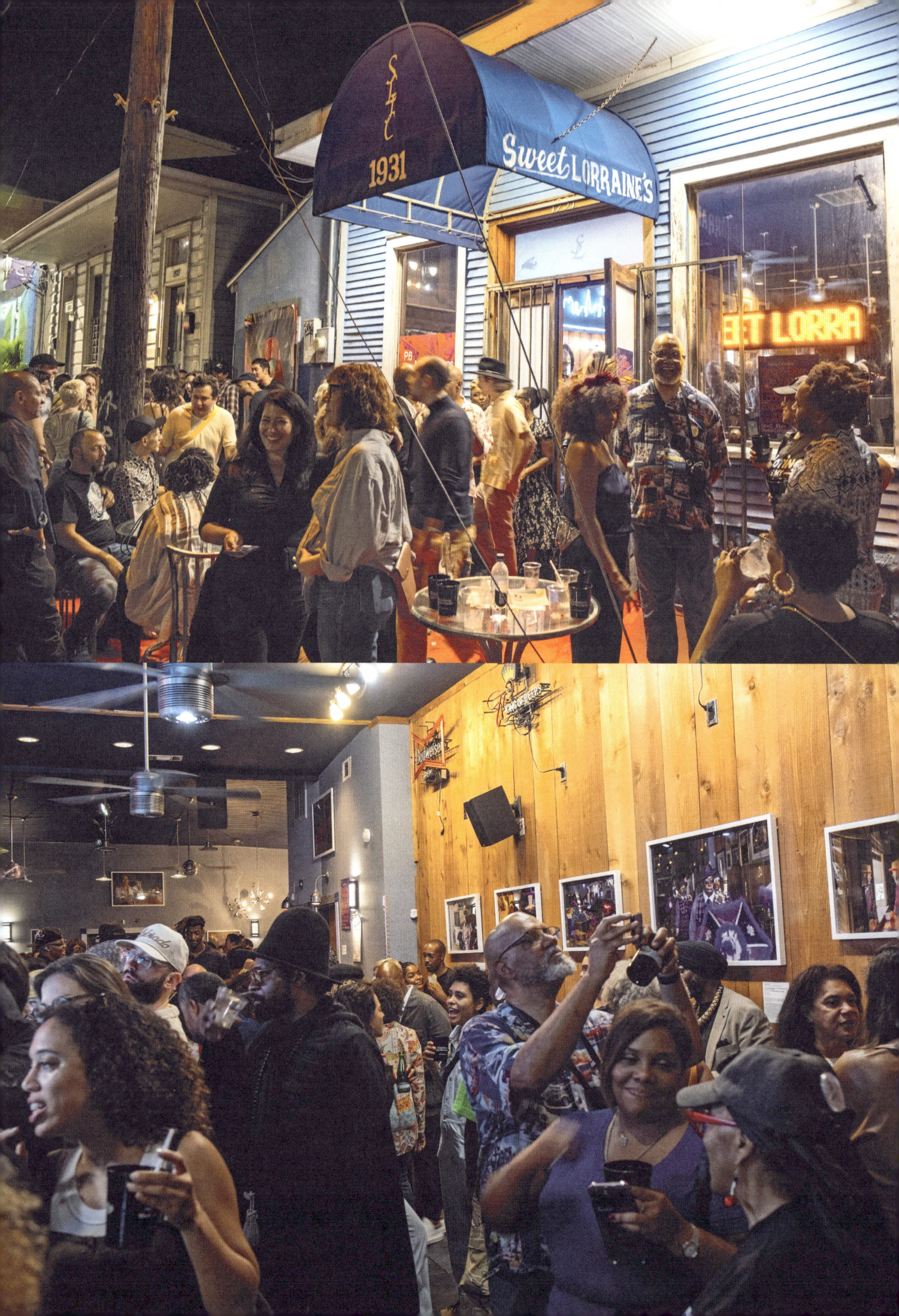

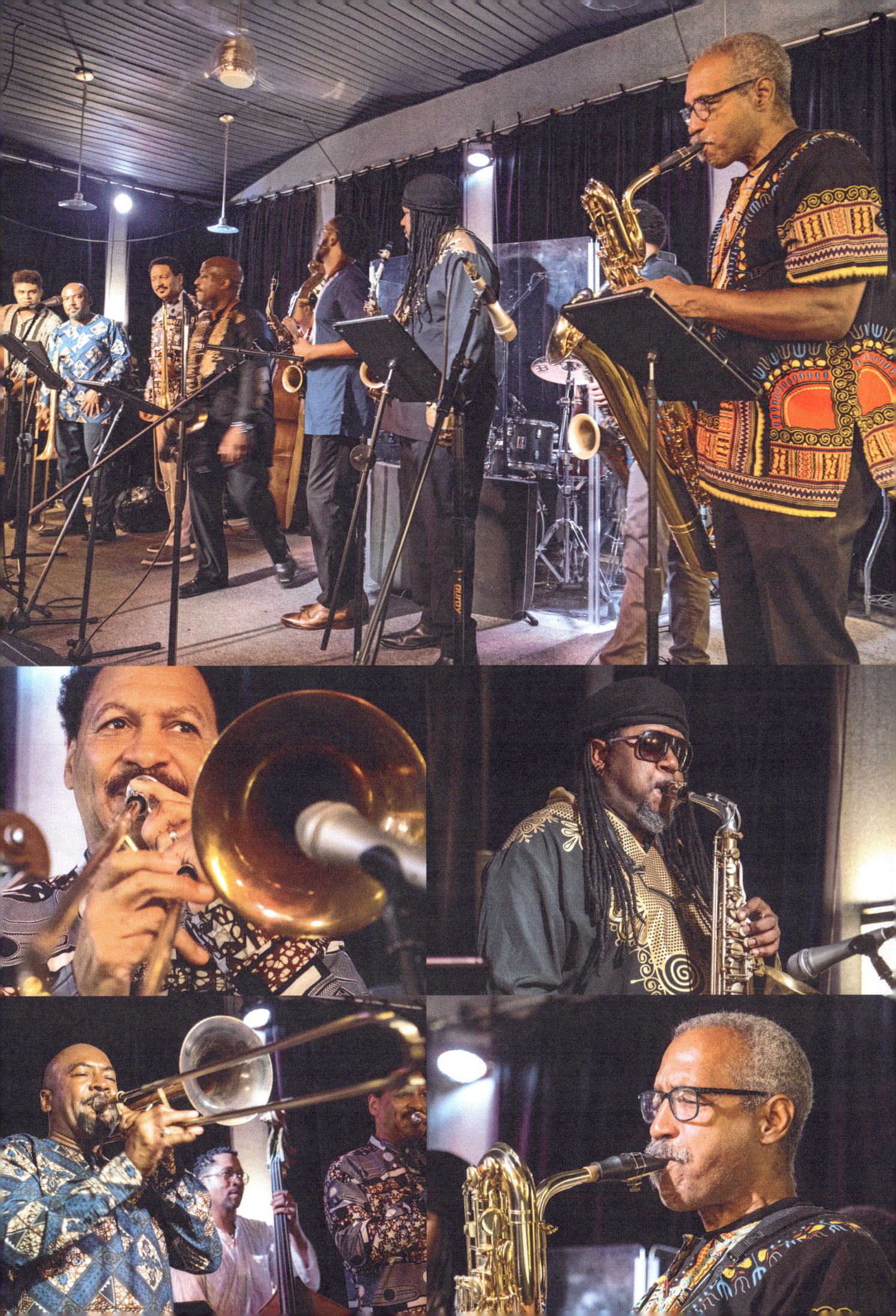

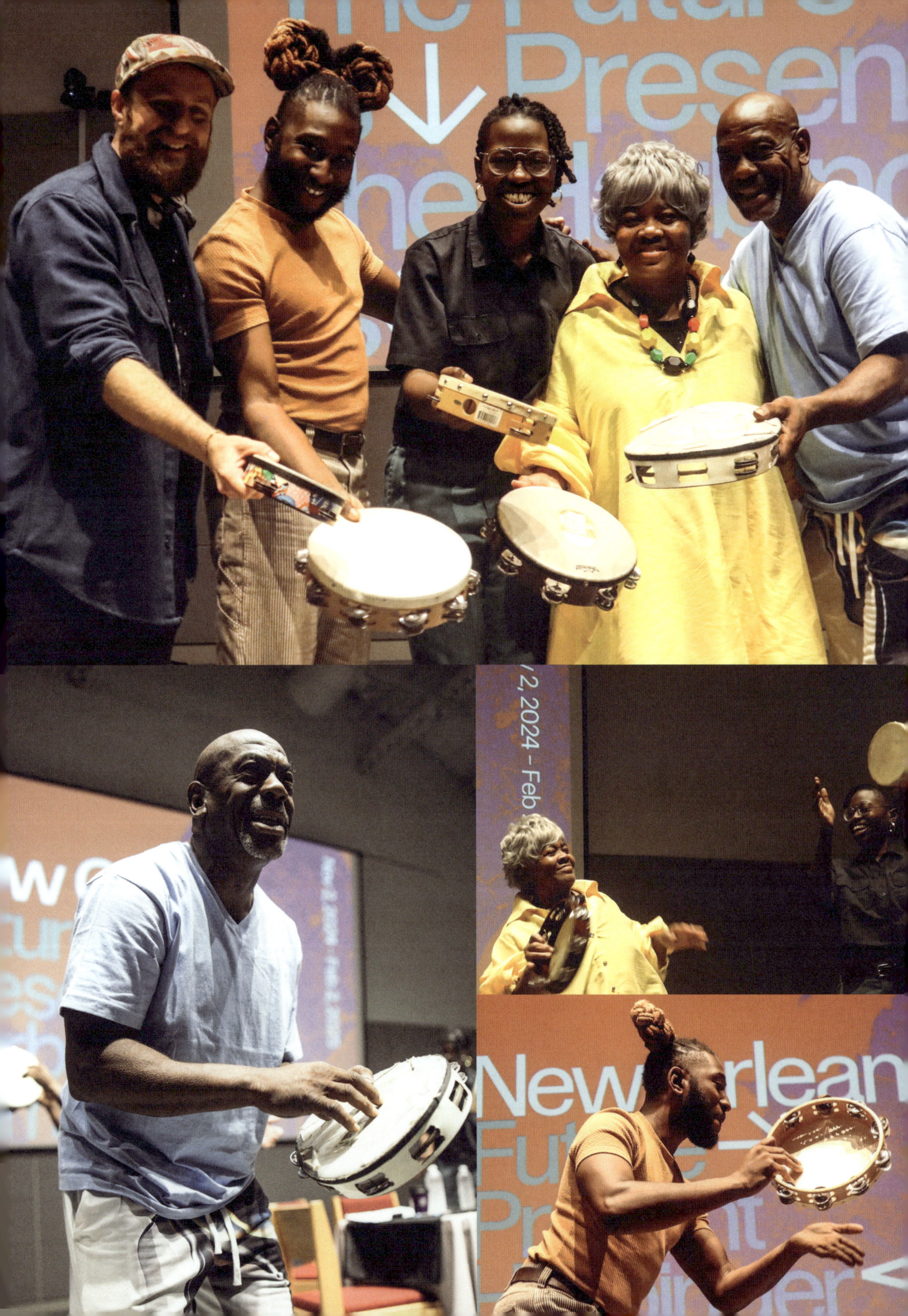

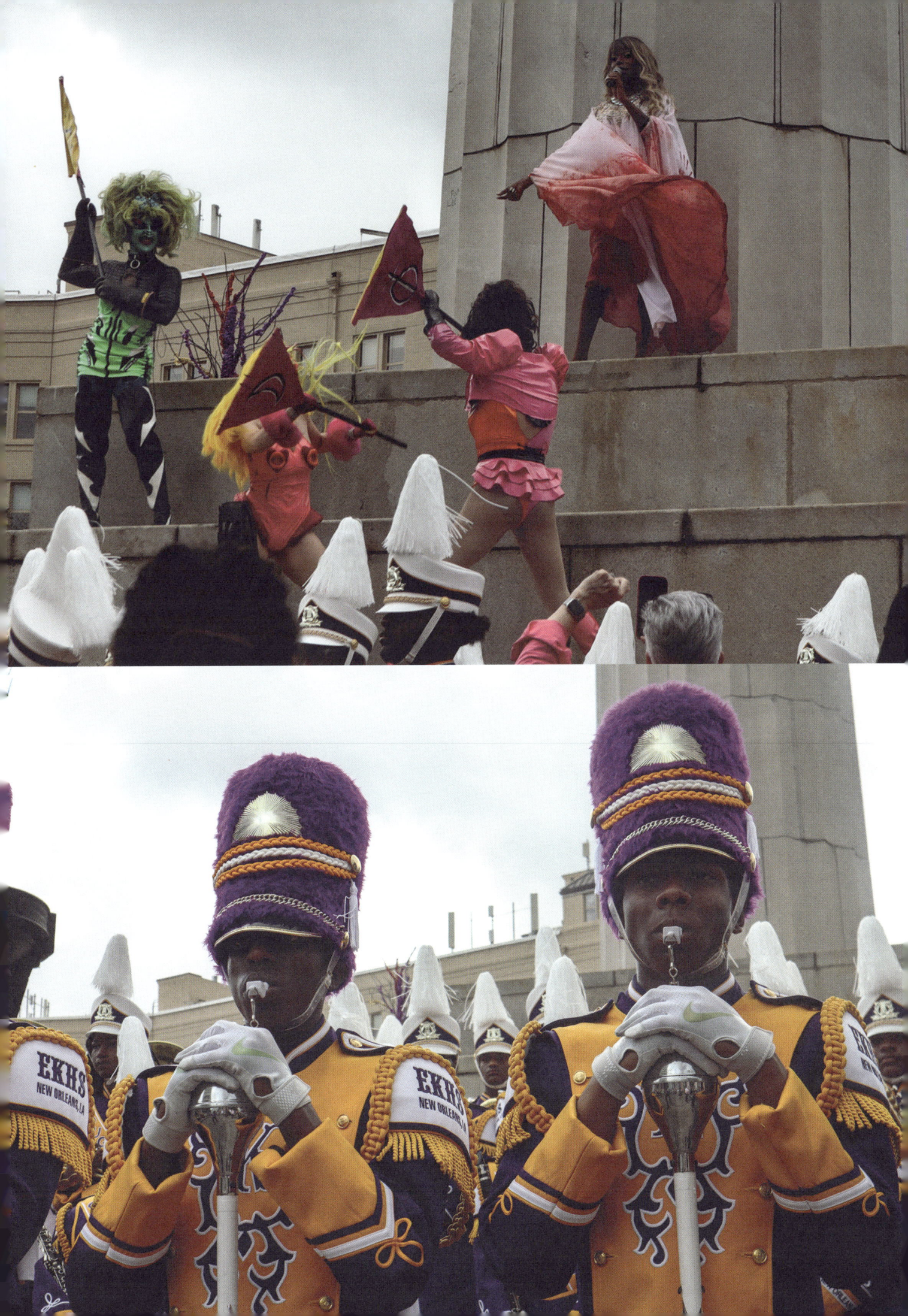

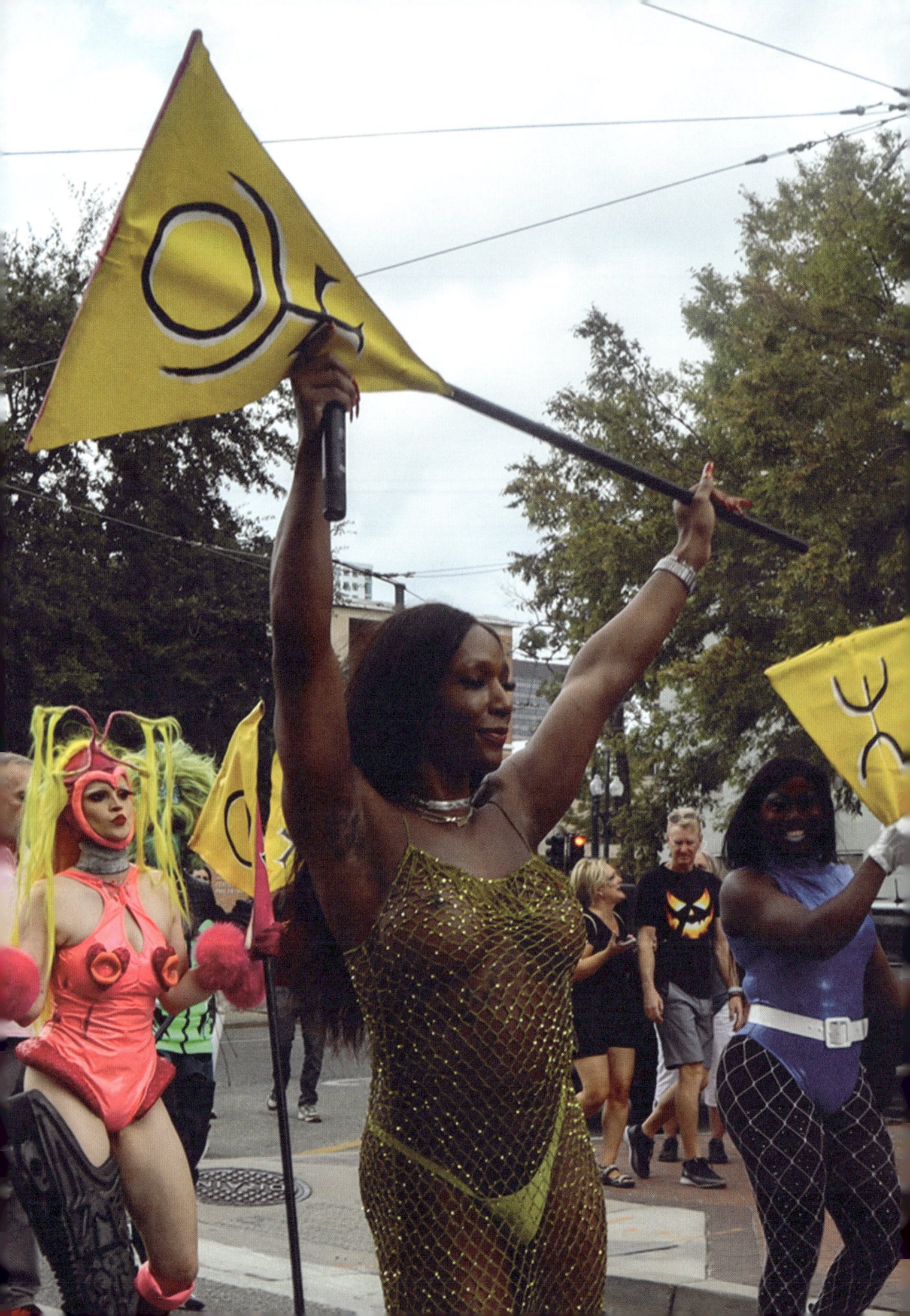

When I Say Creole

Kei Miller

What I mean is, a mixing—

which is, of course, the new way

to say it. Which was once to say,

a contamination, a soiled white sheet.

Which is to say, a darkening, the setting sun.

Evenings could be considered creole.

When Isobel exclaims 'bloodclawt'

in *The Book of Night Women*, the salt

syllables of her patois thrown against

that same setting sun—she reveals

her own créolité. Which is to say

home, which is to feel the slow shift

between there and here, which is to consider

the tragic dispersals, the magic diasporas

of our world. Which is to say, Jerusalem.

On the Mount of Olives is the place where

the Messiah launched himself towards Heaven,

like a rocket. Now, in the Islamic quarter, this site

is improbably called the Mosque of the Ascension.

And I would call this 'creole,' which is to say

an accommodation, the way we might pat

the empty space beside us, invite a stranger to sit.

Four Time Zones / Three Artists

Ebony G. Patterson, Christopher Cozier,
and Tuấn Andrew Nguyễn

EBONY G. PATTERSON
I had sent you all a couple questions or rum-
inations ahead of time. There's always a part
of the interviewer in the interview. These
questions, for me, are also pertinent, because
they're questions that I'm also thinking about.
I'm going through growing pains, so to speak.
Hopefully they didn't seem too fluffy and poetic
and waxy, in their indirectness. But I thought
that they were open enough that we could kind
of meander, and that maybe other questions or
considerations might come up for us as we have
this conversation. *Was your home your choice?*
***And how would you describe your home?* Who**
wants to start first?

TUẤN ANDREW NGUYỄN
But Ebony, it's going to be a conversation,
right? It's *not* an interview. Christopher, would
you like to start?

CHRISTOPHER COZIER
When I read the questions, I wasn't sure
if I could parse it, break it up. Because I
think about the concept of home . . . I think,
especially coming out of my particular
experience growing up in the Caribbean—not
just personally, but in terms of my family

* This is an excerpt from a series of conversations that took place with artists who live in multiple time zones and geographies: Christopher Cozier in Port of Spain, Trinidad; Tuấn Andrew Nguyễn in Ho Chi Minh City, Vietnam; and Ebony G. Patterson, Co-Artistic Director, Prospect.6, in Kingston, Jamaica and Chicago, Illinois. It's a candid conversation, the type that often happens with artists when they are with each other. Sharing considerations not so much about practice, but about the things that embed practice: home, community, family, the pursuit of personhood, health, and safety. This conversation includes political, historical, and social unpackings, the implications of being an artist in these geographical zones, and tears of deep frustration. This is a 'round' flowing in and out of internet disruptions.

story—I think home is always something that's relational. It's conjured. And in my own practice, I've brought up concepts of home and sanctuary very often. When I was younger, I thought about home in economic terms, places where I felt some kind of prospect, some place where it was possible. When I left Trinidad to go to art school, it was very clear to me that there were economic possibilities out there. But I never felt at home, I never felt safe as a Black person, a migrant, living in the United States. It always felt like a zone of contention. But at the same time, coming from this hemisphere with our particular history, the prospect of safety, or sovereignty, or sanctuary, is always contentious. Because these places, the way they were created, they were not designed to be homes. They were labor camps trying to evolve into societies, *'civil places.'*

I've been through many conceptualizations of what could possibly constitute home. Maybe the internet has caused this, but I feel that home has a lot to do with the places where people assemble, and how they assemble. So it's linked to some concept of assembly, and a kind of conjuring or sanctuary, or the spaces between spaces, so to speak. And it could be any place where that is possible.

TUẤN

I think that was a really beautiful response, Christopher. You mentioned this idea of safety. We have this very poignant kind of relationship to this idea of home. It's not just a place. I think for many of us, certainly in my case, this idea of safety comes up, and the idea of choice, or not having a choice of where we called home. This was especially true when I was younger. I was a child when we left Vietnam with my family. Their decision, I wouldn't say it was quite a choice, but it was a decision for them to leave because of this idea of safety. I appreciate you bringing this up, because it didn't even occur to me before, when I would think of their journey and my journey with them, that they were trying to find safety. So, for a very long time in my own life, I never considered home as a choice that we made. A series of decisions, possibly, but never a choice. It wasn't until I was in my late twenties, when I had finished graduate school, and I had some sort of independence financially—I mean, I was in debt, after all my school loans—but it was then that I made a decision to return to Vietnam. I've been here for twenty years. I was in the US for about twenty four years. So, the time that I've been in Vietnam versus the time I was in the US, has been approximately the same. This idea of, do we have a choice, do we choose home, is really complex. Beyond those choices, I think there's a whole series of currents that kind of ebb and flow, and kind of push and pull us into different places, psychologically, politically, and also physically. Yeah, I was very tired of the politics of the US at that time. It was 2003, 2004. I also very much wanted to be with my grandmother, who I never grew up with, but I heard so many amazing stories about her as I was growing up. My grandmother was a poet, and she managed to get most of her children out of the country after the end of the Vietnam/American War, a time that was a very dangerous time for many people, especially the people in the south. She was this wonderful, amazing woman that I never got a chance to know, and I wanted to know her. And maybe through knowing her, I would know a little bit more about my own journey, about my own kind of conception of home, possibly. I don't know. There's so many other kinds of under-lying things that are so deeply seated, that, after twenty-something years, I'm still kind of slowly unpacking.

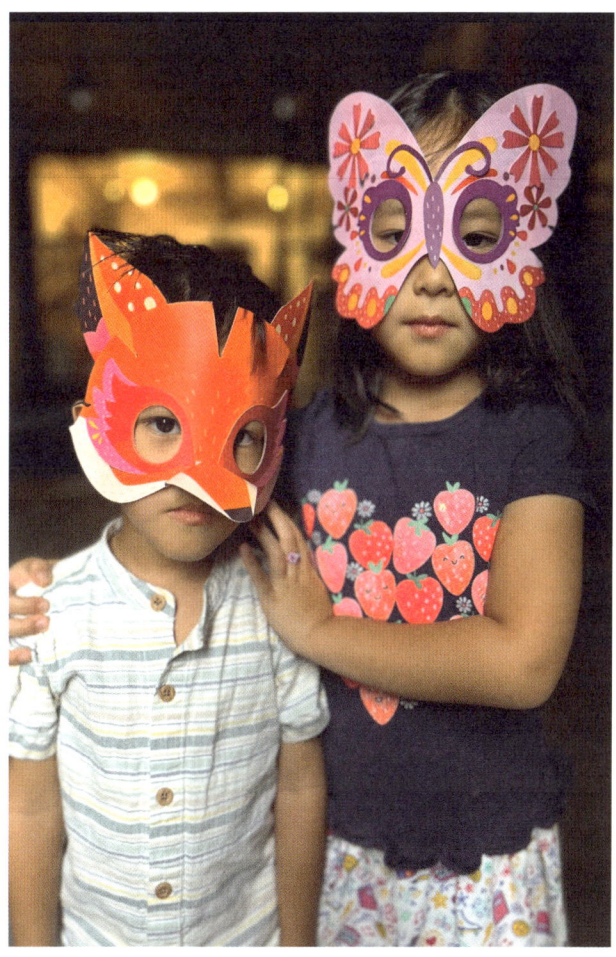

L to R: Talan Anh and Aiyana Thư Linh, children of Tuấn and his wife, Vân Anh. Ho Chi Minh City, Vietnam, 2023

CHRISTOPHER

I like the conceptualization of putting *choice and decision* both on a weighing scale. What I've been struggling with is that, even when one perceives a sense that it may be a choice, it's almost like an illusion. Because I think the engine is kind of in slow motion, it's gradual. And I think, as artists and thinkers who make certain choices or decisions to stay at the center of this engine, or to go to what was once called the peripheries of that engine, the zones of extraction and crisis, it's actually out of a kind of optimism. We are still searching for something. But what are we doing? Are we trying to slow it down? Because it speeds up sometimes, and we don't seem to be so sure of what's going on around us all the time, because it could just be ecological. I mean, ecological isn't random, it's linked to the things we've done to the environment. *I'm going to give it a try*. The calling, I suppose, is linked to the notion of hope and optimism that I think you underscored. But I'm not really resolved in my mind about the notion of choice, because choice could also be an illusion. Because we may be responding to forces around us that we are not always fully cognizant of. And then we make decisions. There's no resolution to this, but I really liked the way you expressed that.

For a moment Christopher and Ebony go back and forth about when Ebony was a student at the Edna Manley College in 2001, in Kingston, Jamaica.

TUẤN

And so, Ebony, to bring the question back to you—did you choose, was home your choice?

EBONY

I had all kinds of negotiations after high school about where I wanted to do my undergraduate studies. I had this fantasy of traveling from home very early on because I always wanted to know what the rest of the world looked like. [Begins to cry] I always wanted to know what the rest of the world looked like, and was also very aware of how hard that was going to be, because of the passport that I had. I remember first looking for schools in the UK and realizing how incredibly expensive it was to go to the UK. And even though I had a middle-class upbringing in Jamaica, that does not translate to middle-class in the places that I had an interest in going to. I really wanted to go to

school in Cuba, but could never really figure out information about art schooling in Cuba. Even though the internet was around, accessibility to the internet during the mid-to-late '90s in Jamaica was still novel. So I ended up applying for school at Edna Manley College of Visual and Performing Arts in Kingston. But I thought that, within my first year, I was going to figure out how to get to school in Cuba. I was really excited when I realized I had two Cuban professors. Anytime I would ask them about going to school in Cuba, they were like, "Why the hell would you want to do that?"

Because they escaped the regime in order to live, the idea of going back or encouraging anybody to go to Cuba seemed insane to them. But I did have an incredible time in my undergraduate life, and I credit my undergraduate life in Jamaica for the way I practice as an artist. I knew I was going to have to leave if I wanted to gain further understanding about what it meant to be the artist I needed to be. But then I ended up in really strange places. I went to grad school in St. Louis, then I ended up living in a tiny town in Virginia. Then I was in Kentucky for twelve years. Being in these places, I was deeply disconnected from anything that was familiar. It was really hard. It took me a long time to realize the impact it also had on my health

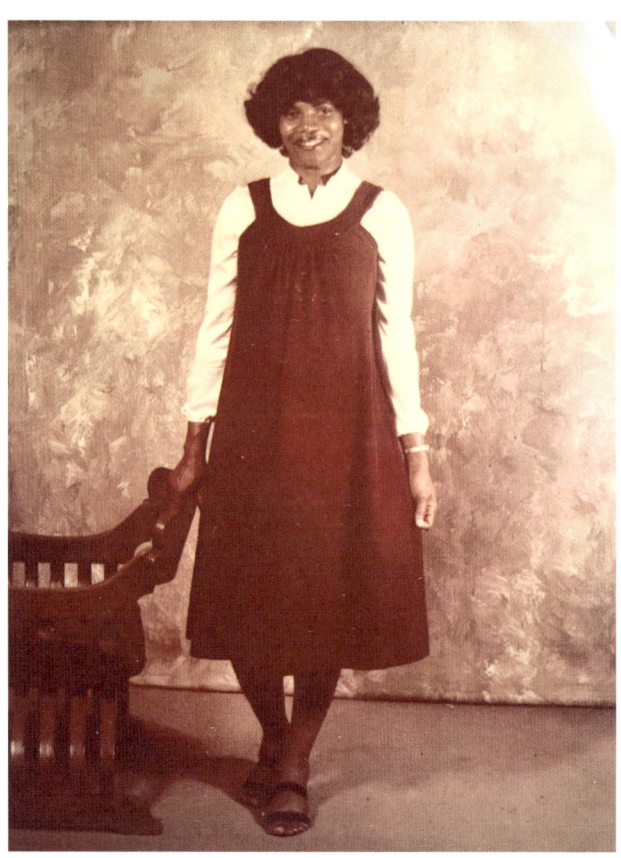

Ebony's mother, Thelma, pregnant with the artist. Kingston, Jamaica, December 1980

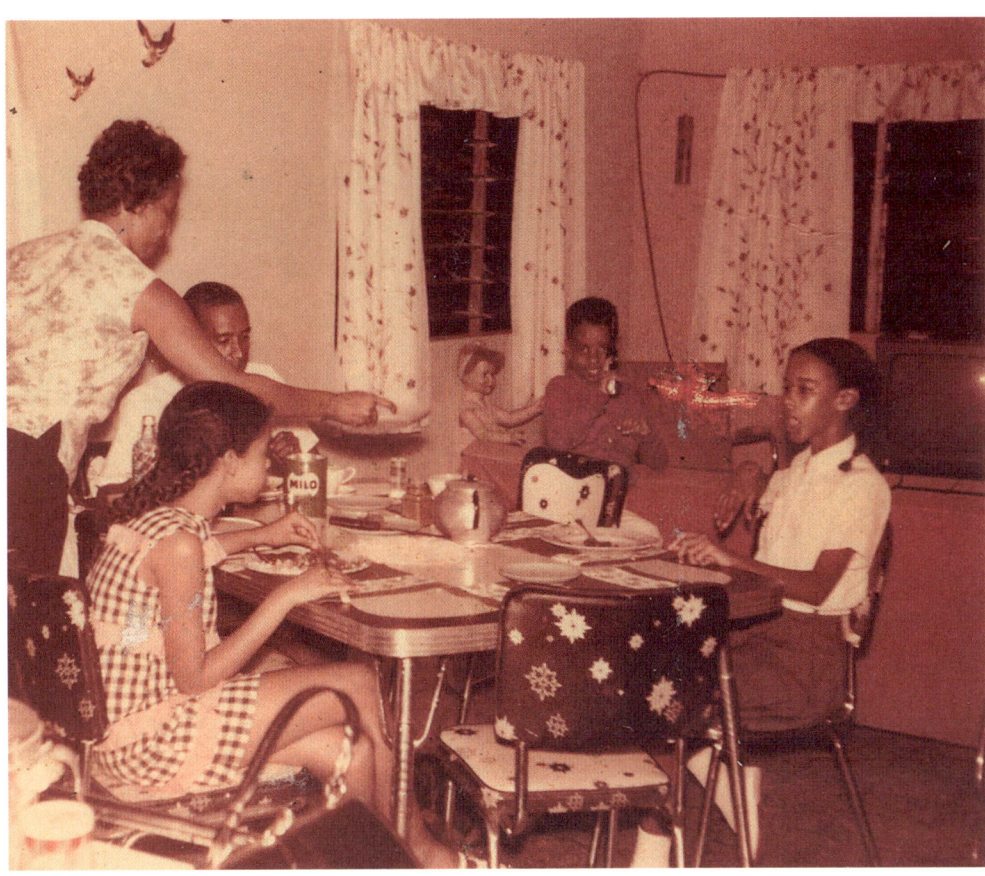

mentally. I also recognized, along this journey, when you're in a place like Jamaica, where your Blackness is never in question because you are the majority, one doesn't have to validate oneself in that regard. And then, coming to the US, where it's an immediate point of engagement. This was not my lens of understanding myself, or people who looked like me. There is a flatness, in terms of how Blackness was held or understood here—the idea that there's only one under-standing of Blackness, one that is through an American lens. As I've gone on in my time here, I also understand that people generally are insular, regardless of the bigness of a place. People are incredibly used to and comfortable in their footprints, and anything beyond that is impossible for them to imagine or conjure differently.

I would often argue with people when I would say I lived in two places. For a long time, I would never say that I lived in Kentucky, even though I lived there for twelve years. I would write that I worked in Kentucky, and worked and lived in Kingston. My only social experiences happened when I landed with people who came from the same zone that I came from, or when I went home physically to Jamaica. My experiences of being in the US

is totally grounded in work. Which for me has been a real challenge on multiple levels, and came with the recognition of certain deficits that I didn't think I would have. And going home was always the thing that I said was going to happen. The US was never going to be home for me. I've always thought of home as wherever my mother is. My mother is my home. There's too much discomfort in this place for me on too many levels for me to ultimately see it as home. But I also find that I also wrestle with home too, because there's also a lot of discomfort there for me too. And as often as I may go back to Jamaica, and for as long as I may go back, there are times when it does feel further and further away. I've been trying to find all of these different ways to anchor myself. So yes, for the last couple of years I really felt rudderless. And that rudderlessness is very hard. Not feeling grounded anywhere makes everything feel impossible. And now it's gotten to this place where even making feels impossible. Making does not feel good anymore because grounding has always been really important to me and my work. I've been doing this duality for so long, but then now it almost feels like nowhere feels good, and that's really hard. [Cries]

Chris around age eight at dinner with family at his parents' home. Diego Martin, Trinidad, 1967

TUẤN
That's actually quite a beautiful line though. And it's beautiful because it could be read in so many different ways: *Nowhere feels good*.

EBONY
Another thought I had was: *Does leaving home ever feel like you're entering or exiting a portal of some sort? And is there anything that you think you have to resist at home?*

TUẤN
I think my practice comes from intrigue. I'm intrigued with people who have dealt with this idea of home, um, or who have been challenged by the idea of home. Most of the communities I've worked with outside of Vietnam are communities that have been displaced. So, you know, even the communities that I worked with in Australia, they were displaced from their country, their native land, their native territory, and were displaced onto other, different parts of Australia, basically for slave labor.

I'm intrigued by what it means for people to have to leave a place, what it means for people to have to adapt to a different political environment, but also to a different physical landscape. And I'm intrigued by how people deal with it through art making, and the stories they tell. But somehow it all comes back to this idea, this curiosity of what it means to have a home and what it means to have lost a home. Last week I was talking about how important it is for us to feel at home everywhere, it's a very Buddhist, philosophical approach to being present, and being compassionate. But I thought about it more, and when I mention this Buddhist approach to the idea of home, I don't wanna disregard the kind of political ramifications that so many people are dealing with now. Millions and millions of people have been displaced in the twentieth and twenty first centuries. So this idea of home is actually very heavily weighted in the political situation that we have been dealt, right? And a lot of that comes from colonialism and comes from war, and now a lot of it comes from environmental catastrophe. I think my practice revolves around that.

CHRIS
I was thinking about my *Home/Portal* project, a project I first did in Boston at an organization called Design Studio for Social Intervention. I used a sculpture of red steps, based on chattel housing architecture. It represents the place

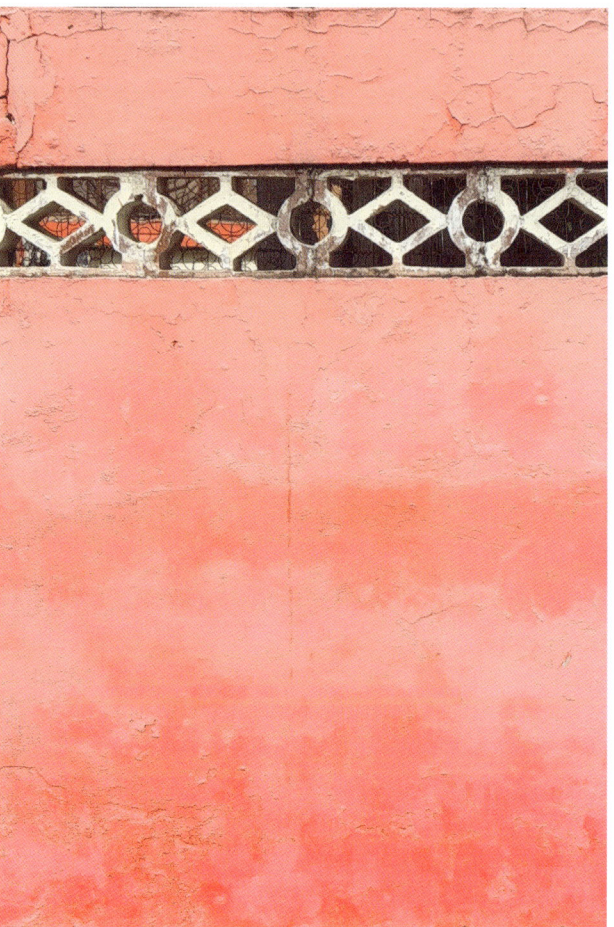

that you are always leaving and never quite returning to. I think there's a kind of way that we live in a state of perpetual departures [laughs] and possible arrivals—but arrival doesn't seem right, it feels almost utopian. People started showing up, you know, and asking, *What's this step doing here?*

Because the step reminded them of the kind of back step you see in a lot of colonial chattel architecture in the Caribbean, and the whole project evolved out of that. I was thinking about that as a vocabulary, how all of us are traveling with this concept of displacement. But *are we?!* Or is it just simply a strategy of being? I'd like to backtrack to something that has been haunting me from earlier in our conversation, which was this notion of choice and decision. I feel like maybe we need to tease that out some more. I think all of us, from different perspectives and histories, are juggling this concept. I really struggle when I think about it. I remember I was with [visual artist] Marcel Pinas in a canoe one time [laughs], going up a river in the Amazon, going up the Cottica River in the interior of Suriname.

And we were going past an Indigenous person, who was standing in an encampment.

A wall with breeze bricks. Belmont, Port-of-Spain, Trinidad and Tobago, 2012

He was standing there with a group of women and small children, along with some animals, and there was a field, a thatched hut along the riverbank, and a canoe. He had his gun, he had his bow and arrow, he had everything! [Laughs] But the way in which the man stood on the land, and the way in which he looked at us, I don't think I've ever been looked at by another person like that. Even though he was far away, us in the river, him on the bank, his look was like, "What's your business? Are you passing or are you slowing down? This is my family, this is my land, this is mine." It almost felt like I had to explain to him why I was even in his presence. It has stayed in my mind like a—like a picture, you know, I took a mental picture. Because I've never had a feeling like that, that's never been available to me.

It's not even a desire, you know—I'm coming from my particular history, I'm spread out across all these continents and I don't really know what it's like to stand on ground like that. I notice there's a big romanticism about all this, but it was just a weird encounter between us in the boat. But Marcel was indifferent, because he passes there all the time.

EBONY
That's interesting that you brought that up. I've been thinking about what you said about the history of the Caribbean, or places like the region, being a labor camp. And then you said, the truth is, "We don't really come from here either." It made me think about how elephants never forget their path. You put a house in the path, they go through it. And we now understand that trauma is also something registered and passed on down to generations, so why can't memory also be related in that way? And so if you are cut off from that kind of grounding . . . then that sense of place splits, right? So is rudderlessness, or never feeling quite anchored in any one place, does that then just become a part of your fabric?

CHRIS
It's a methodology. I think that's what I am trying to grasp. Because one of the things that I picked up on that canoe trip, and what some modern anthropological and archaeological work has shown, is that most Indigenous people are mobile, they move—because it's a way of not burdening the land. The enterprise of "civilization," whatever it's worth—that's when you start kinda mashing up the land, right?

TUẤN
Yeah.

CHRIS
It's a mashing up of space, an ordering of people, establishment of law. So there's a kind

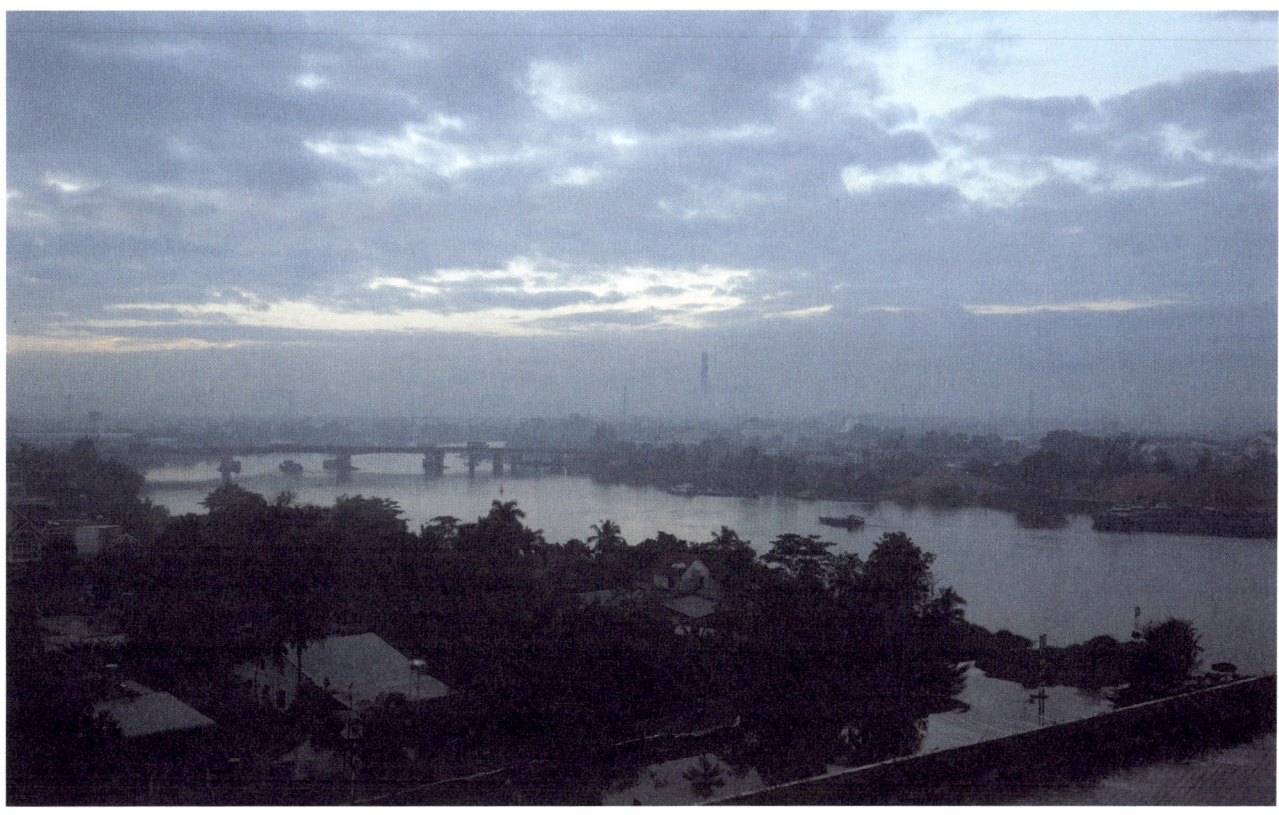

View from the hospital where Tuấn's son, Talan Anh, was born. Ho Chi Minh City, Vietnam, 2020

of thing where I feel that we have been made insecure, right? I was in a debate a couple of years ago, and a young woman from the US sort of looked at me disparagingly and said, "Oh, that sounds like Heideggerian debris." [Laughs]

TUẤN
[Laughs]

CHRIS
Something that crossed my mind when you talked about travel: *How* do we travel? We read about explorers, we read tourist magazines, and all that kind of tourism and going to resorts sort of thing, it doesn't really factor us in. We're just serving, right? How do we travel? Even traveling for leisure, where are the stories about that?

EBONY
It's funny, people keep telling me I need to travel more, and I'm like, "When?" [Laughs] I remember once, a friend said to me, "Yeah, I don't see you as the kind of person to do that— you would not just get up and go somewhere without having some kind of a purpose there." During the COVID lockdown I saw articles about Americans or other so-called 'first worlders' traveling. I wasn't seeing any articles about Jamaicans traveling elsewhere from Jamaica. [Laughs] Also the idea of traveling out of the region, generally to places that *we* would see or understand as being exotic—it takes so much to get there. One, you have to get a visa [laughs]. That's the first thing. For some people, a visa costs a month's or more salary. And then you might get turned down, and you need ties to the place you're going to, and ties in the home you are traveling from. Passports are transactions, and it takes more to be able to do leisure.

TUẤN
Right. There's a kind of historical specificity in regards to how people have imagined traveling away from Vietnam. When the refugee crisis started in '75, people left without knowing where they were gonna end up. So a lot of people ended up being picked up by Australia, countries in Europe, particularly France, because Vietnam was a French colony. And the United States too, of course.

A lot of people had served, in some form or another, under the US military. My dad, he was drafted during the very last six months of the war. He had spent many years in law school, trying to avoid the drafts, and

suddenly he was drafted. But lucky for him, it was only the last six months and nothing happened. Then we ended up in the US. So that imaginary, I think, stayed with people here. The youth in Vietnam throughout the '80s and '90s were always thinking about Europe, Australia, and the US. No one thought about South America, no one thought about Africa. They were just thinking about these places that previous generations had traveled to. But, over the last twenty years that I've worked in Vietnam, working with younger generations of local artists, they never even thought about traveling internationally because that wasn't a possibility, there weren't any resources available to them. It wasn't until a few young artists had come through our program at Sàn Art [an artist-run space in Ho Chi Minh City] that they kind of broke through and thought this was possible. Now younger artists are more ambitious. They believe that they can actually make it, and travel like these other artists do, which is a good thing. But before that, I don't think many artists even thought that they could, or thought they had a chance to travel. Um, yeah.

And this idea of insecurity, Christopher, is so striking. It brings me back to the question Ebony posed, "Do you feel like home is a portal?" And when I think of a portal, I think of a port. And when I think of a port, I somehow think of immigration automatically. There's nowhere more exaggerated than the sites of immigration. When I travel to different places, I feel a certain level of insecurity, right? And I can kind of rank it. Like, when I travel to the US, my insecurity level as I'm passing through immigration heightens. It's the most insecure I'll feel. I'll travel to other countries and I'll feel a little bit more welcome, right? I think this level of insecurity is reflected in the infrastructure of

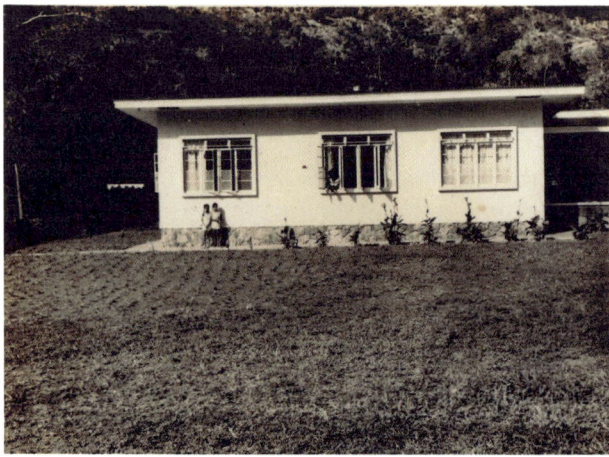

Chris's sisters, Lyn and Eleanor, and grandmother, Evelyn, at the artist's parents' home. Diego Martin, Trinidad and Tobago, 1963

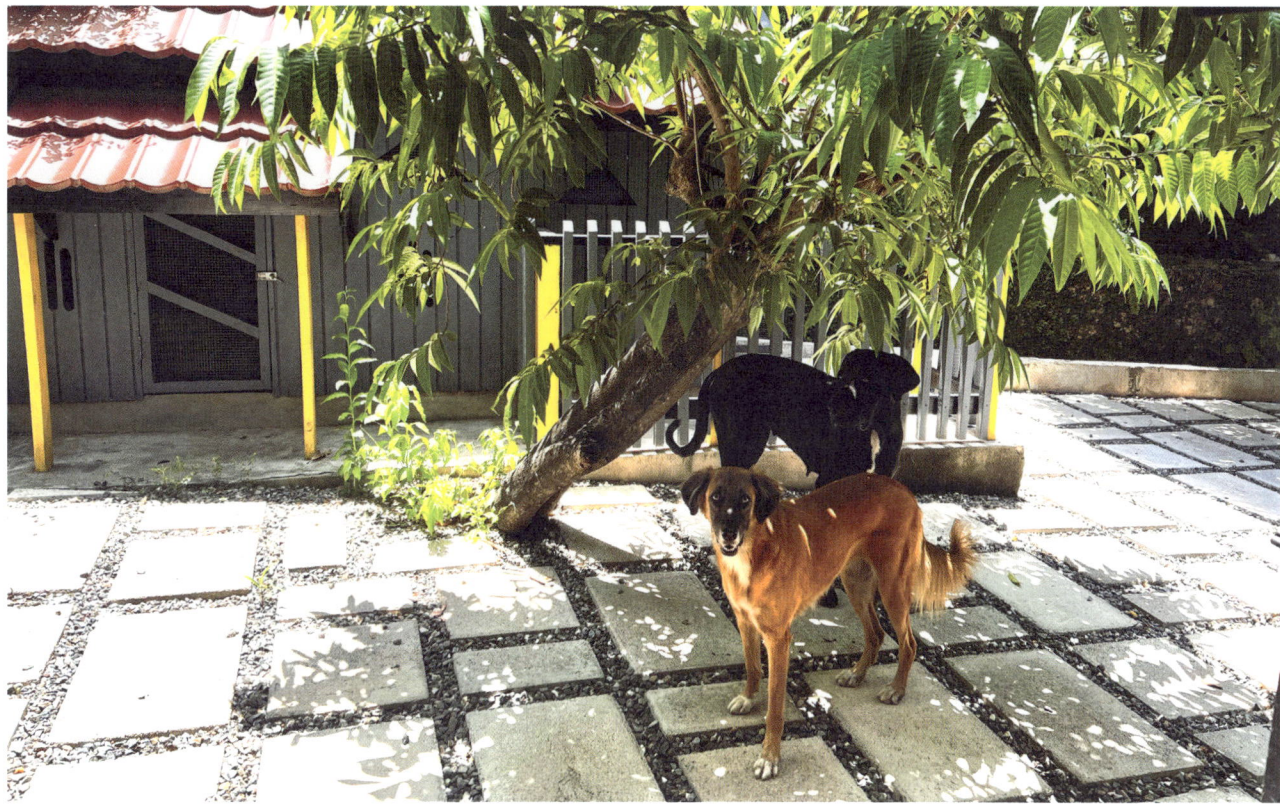

that country. The US is not a welcoming place, and you feel that. I'm also reminded of this book, called *Imagined Communities*, by Benedict Anderson, where he kind of deconstructs this idea. "Imagined communities" is the term he uses to talk about the nation-state. What it means to be a nation, he kind of deconstructs it and breaks it down and explains how this is all kind of mythological, as Christopher has mentioned. This idea of nation, this idea of country, this notion of home inside this context of a nation is all fabricated. It's all imagined. I always return to this notion of an imagined community, as I think about where it is that we try to locate home, or a sense of home.

CHRIS
I kind of grew up in the nationalist period—Trinidad had become independent in 1962. Coming out of that colonial history, there was this sense for the first time, at least for my parents' generation, that we have the right . . . that we could take on this responsibility of nation. But in my lifetime, the struggles were not administrative or structural. It was with those who had taken on that responsibility, it was a discipline-and-punish kind of environment, because now you couldn't argue with the state, because you had to be grateful for all they had done for us. They had delivered us from colonialism and now—what more

could you want? But I think for all of us, there's this problem of culture, there's this problem of the state, and then there's the zone of the imagination, right? Which is what brings us into conversation now. How does it all fit into this project?

I feel strongly that itinerancy is a part of it, because it's a kind of a refusal. And I don't mean in a romantic way, because I know when I interviewed some of the early artists from this period, the protagonists around nationalism, I was a much younger artist. I said things to them like, "Oh, this is about self-expression." And I remember one of the protagonists, Carlisle Chang, who was a descendant of Chinese immigrants, who became very enamored by the nationalist movement in Trinidad, and was very active between the 1940s and '60s. I remember talking to him and he just stopped me in my tracks. He said, "No, it's not just about the self. It's about a lot more than that." He had this sense of art being a responsibility.

But the funny thing is that he got jilted by that same mechanism that he sacrificed and sublimated so much of his creative desire for. As an Asian man, as a queer man, in a certain period of history, he was literally destroyed by the state machinery that he himself helped and dedicated his life to. And, actually, it had really impacted his practice, and I found that really strange. I don't know how I should

Ebony's girls outside of their house at the artist's home.
St. Andrew, Jamaica, 2023

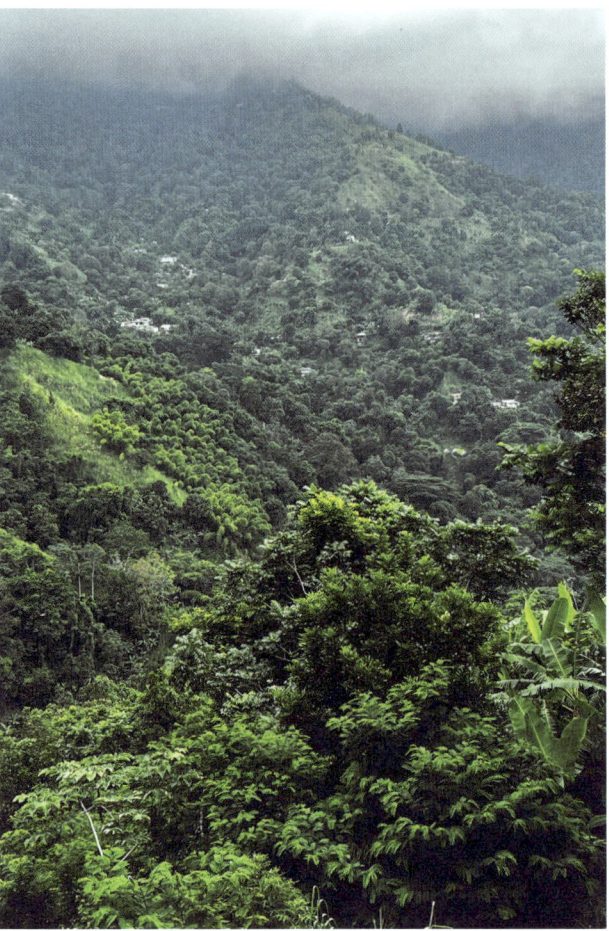

feel about this. Is it just . . . Is it elitism? Is it indolence? Is it idiosyncrasy? I just don't feel that pressure, I don't have a problem with not really being able to settle. Even though I made the choice to be here, it feels very personal-sense based . . . Ontological is too strong a word, but, you know, it's a place where I feel some, um, sense of purpose in a way. But I can't quite find all the right words for it because it'll get soppy. [Laughs]

EBONY
But that's fine, Chris, if you get soppy.

CHRIS
No, no, no, no—I agree with that. I just don't wanna speak for you all as well. I'm just telling you, I am very conflicted about this. Like, this is a choice that I've made, but there are times when I feel really confused because we live in societies where the question I asked was about ambition, right? Because sometimes, when I meet people, and I say I'm living in Trinidad—it means you have no ambition. You're supposed to move to New York or London or Berlin, right?

TUẤN
Mm.

CHRIS
You know, that's why I asked the question, are there sites of ambition within the world on your side of the planet Tuấn, are there other zones, other big cities? How do people imagine that? Or is everybody just running away?

TUẤN
It's hard to put a finger on a general ambition. I have friends that have moved back to the countryside or moved back to smaller cities after having practiced in Ho Chi Minh City, which is the biggest city in Vietnam, or Hanoi. I feel like people are kind of withdrawing to smaller communities, maybe because they also feel the same thing that you and I feel. Like they have more impact there. I'm not sure. I don't wanna put words in people's mouths, but I think the idea of ambition—where do we project ourselves mentally? Where do we want to go physically, but also in our careers as artists? Is the museum the space that we want to occupy? What art world do we wanna speak to, right? And so, when you bring up this idea of ambition, as artists, that's what I think about. It's an interesting question, and, and it's gonna be the forever question for artists who work in places like the ones we work in, right? Because we're always struggling with the question of which art world we want to engage in.

Are we engaging in the Western art world, or do we wanna kind of totally disregard the Western art world? Or do we have some sort of negotiating process where we're always one foot in and one foot out? Curators in the past have asked me, "Why did you move to Vietnam?" But my friend, who had actually moved to Vietnam several years before I did, he was like, "Tuấn, you know, if you're making good work and it's interesting work, you could be making work under a rock, and a curator who's a good curator will find out." And I think that's the state of the art world now, right?

CHRIS
Yeah. That's a really important part of it. But sometimes I think also about the concept of being found [laughs]. It's such a weird—

TUẤN
Right! Like, discovery, you know, discovery of the—

CHRIS
Found and discovered aren't quite the same.

TUẤN
Yeah.

CHRIS
There's that American sort of concept: Because we are looking, something is happening, but if you're not looking, it's not happening.

One of the questions that Alice Yard [the art collective Cozier is a member of] had for *documenta* was: What can we talk about when no one else is in the room? Like, how do we get beyond the performative and the self-explanatory postures? In terms of exposure, you guys have probably had a lot more exposure than I've had, with certain kinds of platforms. I feel like I'm being removed from a petri dish or something. There's a uniformity to these platforms and a uniform condition and reception as well, in which the world just moves. I'm supposed to feel that this is meaningful, but I have a lot of doubts. There are times when you feel like a fraud. You don't know where you are. Why am I here? And it has links to the concept of ambition as well. Like, maybe be careful what you ask for. [Laughs]

EBONY
I remember when I was in undergrad in Jamaica and I had to do an interview for a small bursary and the panelists asked, "Where do you see yourself in five years?" I remember Hope Brooks, who is a seminal artist back home, saying, "Well, don't you wanna be an art star?" I said, "No, I just wanna be able to make my work. I just wanna figure out what that means." I remember, really early on, I had all these goals about being able to just make my work, that

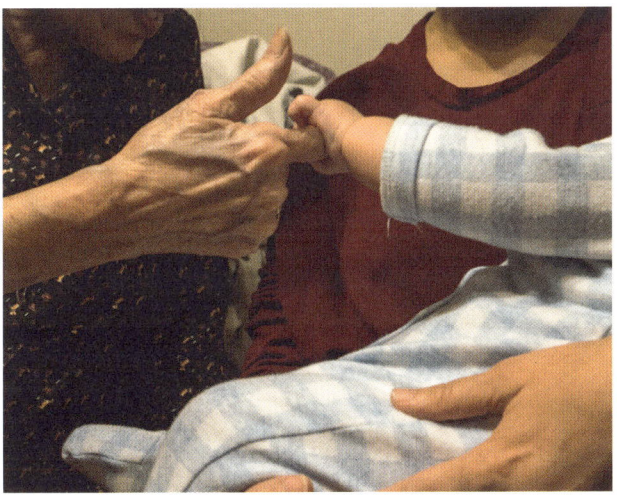

was all I wanted. I wanted to make my work and be able to, at some point, not just be in a classroom. It's why I left teaching. I wanted the dream that every artist has, but I didn't necessarily understand what that would entail. I thought when I quit teaching that I would have more time to make, and instead it was the opposite. I was on the road all the time and I'm like, "Where, when did this happen!?" I thought I cut one thing out so I could do more of the other thing, you know? [Cries]

CHRIS
It's dreadful, I know. Are you good? You're tired. Oh, lord. Too much, too much. Tell us when you're ready.

EBONY
I'm just really burnt out, you know? I am worried about my personhood, and my personhood being cared for. Not just my production.

TUẤN
It's a lot. It's a lot.

CHRIS
You just said it at the beginning of your comment: It's your person, it's your practice, and then there's the business of the art world. It's difficult to parse them, and I think each has its own requirements. But I think that, on the conveyor belt of your practice, your personhood is perhaps the least significant. Sorry to say, but it is.

EBONY
No, that's a fact. That's a fact.

CHRIS
What you're going through right now, you know, in terms of this uncentered feeling, I understand that part. I'm trying right now to travel less, but I was traveling because I was trying to maintain a family. You know, family, a home, that kind of thing. And I realized that the kind of work I was making and still make, there's no market for it, or there's not a large enough market to sustain it in this context. Trinidad has 1.3 million people living on it. This is a rock where there are maybe ten people who care whether I make work or not. So, obviously, it's important to step out of this environment because, in the Anglophone Caribbean, there's six million people. We should also talk about economies of scale, because a lot of young artists in countries like Brazil,

Tuẩn's grandmother, Thú Linh, wife, Vân Anh, and daughter, Aiyana Thư Linh. Ho Chi Minh City, Vietnam, 2018

Mexico, and other parts of the world can have careers, where there are economies around their practices without ever having to show in New York, London, Berlin. If you come from a small place like the Caribbean, Trinidad or Jamaica, inherently, you have to get on the road. The intinerancy is inherent.

EBONY
Yep.

CHRIS
And if we look into the lives of our ancestors, our parents, grandparents, you will see that people have always been on the move. Which brings us back to that point about choice and decisions, and this perpetual sense of departure, yearning to arrive somewhere. What you're feeling a lot of emotion about—maybe it's not a predicament. It may require something else from you, or us. Like, what is it requiring? What is this circumstance requiring of us? Tuấn, you talked about how, in the 1970s, people left Vietnam for very specific reasons that were harrowing . . . That's just an extreme moment within the system, one that heightens or exacerbates the need to move. But the desire to move is always there, you know? I don't know if I'm helping in any way . . .

EBONY
I mean, I've joked about going back to Kentucky, to be quite honest. But I can't go back to Kentucky. When I get to the root of what it is, it's about not being found. Things started to move for me before I came to Chicago, but I was out of reach. It's not that the work isn't accessible. It's just that I am less accessible. Me, my person. This feeling of not being anchored started when I moved from Kentucky to Chicago. It took me a minute to get settled in 2018, but I had to also move from my home and studio in Jamaica. So, all of a sudden I had, I had no pin . . . I didn't feel anchored in either place. Eventually when I finally bought my home in Jamaica, now almost three years ago, I thought, "Okay. Things will finally start to settle . . . " I feel great when I'm home, but I think I feel good when I'm home because I'm further away from whatever is here that creates a deep sense of anxiety for me. I'm able to just, like, hear myself, you know? And to be a person, not a thing, not a spectacle.

TUẤN
We often don't talk about the very pragmatic side of moving away from the art centers. What you were saying, Chris, and what you're talking about, Ebony, resonates with me deeply because I don't think I would be able to have survived for so long as an artist if I didn't move to Vietnam, for many reasons. I don't make work that circulates in the art world, and is friendly to galleries or collectors. Living in a place where the cost of living wasn't so demanding, that allowed me to continue to make the work that I felt most drawn to, work that was very challenging to make a living off of. But also, on the other side, I think psychologically separating myself from the "Western art world" helped me psychologically, because the Western art world has a way of consuming young artists and then chewing them up and spitting them out. And I have a lot of friends that have gone through so much pain and anguish and hardship because they've been dealt with in that way by the art world, and at such a young age. I'm sure we all have friends like that, and it's been so difficult to see them go through that process. I don't know if I would've survived in both those ways, economically and psychologically, if I didn't locate myself here in Vietnam. For very pragmatic reasons it's helped me to survive.

CHRIS
I was just thinking, something triggered in me, Ebony, when you said "I'm a person," the juxtaposition of this notion of personhood with the conveyor-belt environment of the art world. But I think linked to this construct of person is also the idea of home. Because I think the itinerancy is moving toward some kind of selfhood, right? But it's a selfhood that's dislodged from statehood, from cultural specificity, all those kinds of things. So, in a way, the anxiety that you expressed in a very emotional way around personhood is part of our journey, our mutual journeys, as well. I also feel like, in the practice of making work, it's like you're making something from nothing. So I always feel a little spurious when somebody gives me money for making art. So I take a portion of it and I try to buy work by younger artists. Last week I assembled three pieces that I just got. They came back from the framer and I put them up on the wall, and I sat down and looked at them and I felt such a sense of excitement. I could feel the desire

and the commitment of these three younger artists. And I felt a little less lonely. I felt like the world may have a future. Within all these gestures, there is a kind of architecture, a kind of imaginary world that's being built. They're like voices in the room. My interest in these works is not in their possible financial value for the future. My interest in these works is that, by looking at them, I feel motivated to keep going, you know? They challenge me in a way. I've had that experience through all the artists we interface with.

After the last Liverpool Biennial I was asked to participate in a program called "After Care." I agreed to participate in it, but I went in with a kind of weird position, because I said there's no before and after care. I think inherent to our way of being, coming from our historical experience, caring is perhaps the only way we can be. [Laughs] It is the cultural narrative. It is the radicality of our being. We look around the world and we can see many instances of people not caring. So, the notion of caring, it's an imagined sort of community where you have fellow conspirators, all trying to imagine something beyond, or put meaning on why we are doing what we are doing, or why we exist, or what we do. It isn't just a predicament. It has to become something more meaningful.

TUẤN
That's beautiful, Chris. I want to articulate something that I was having trouble with. This idea that everywhere is home is actually very connected to this idea of taking care of a person, of yourself, right? We travel. Our parents have had to travel to go out and find a living, to find sustenance, in very much the same way that we have to travel as artists to go out and find a living, to find sustenance. But, no matter where we go, we're with ourselves and we're of ourselves. And I think, when we can travel like that, everywhere is home and everyone around us is engaged in our home. Then, I think, is when we have maybe liberated ourselves and found home. I think that's—that's a really kind of beautiful way of connecting.

CHRIS
I don't know who the audience is for what we do. Is it us or them?

TUẤN AND EBONY
Both!

CHRIS
I mean, I don't want to get involved in a kind of petty binary, but like, what can we say to each other that is useful? And if we get into the depths of what we're saying to each other as people, as practitioners, how useful would that be to the superstructure? Because then we may go into these weird zones that we're going into now. We're just talking about ourselves and our struggles, you know? So it's got to be hard to . . . Like, what would the footnotes be? [Laughs]

EBONY
There are no footnotes. You are the footnote!

The conversation continues on WhatsApp.

An extended version of this conversation is accessible at prospect6.org.

rafa esparza   Zalika Azim   Dewey Tafoya

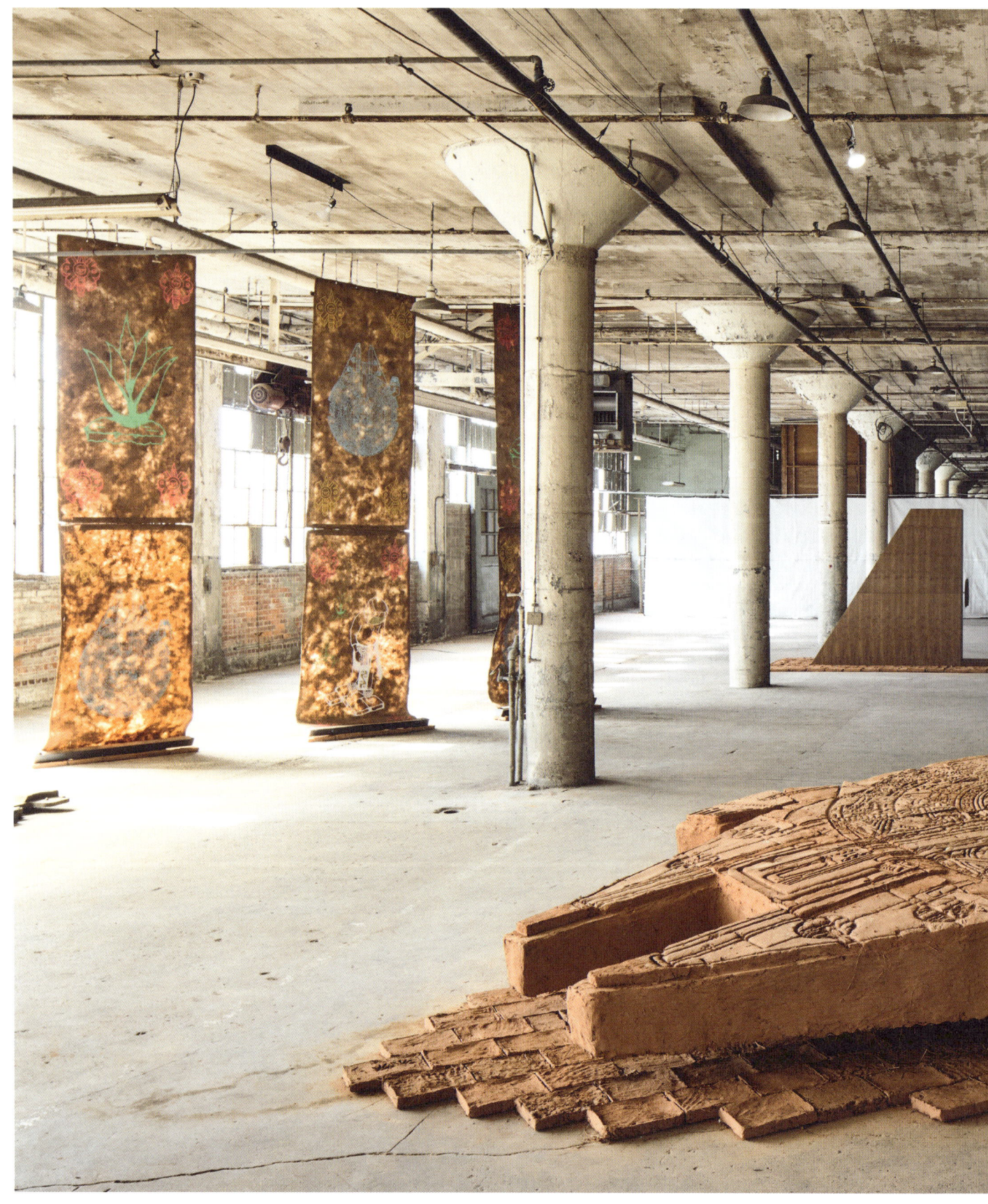

Proposals for Loops in Linear Time, 2024. A collaborative
exhibition by Zalika Azim, rafa esparza, and Dewey Tafoya

b. 1981, Pasadena, CA; lives in Los Angeles, CA (re)
b. 1990, Brooklyn, NY; lives in New York, NY (ZA)
b. 1970, Los Angeles, CA; lives in Los Angeles, CA (DT)

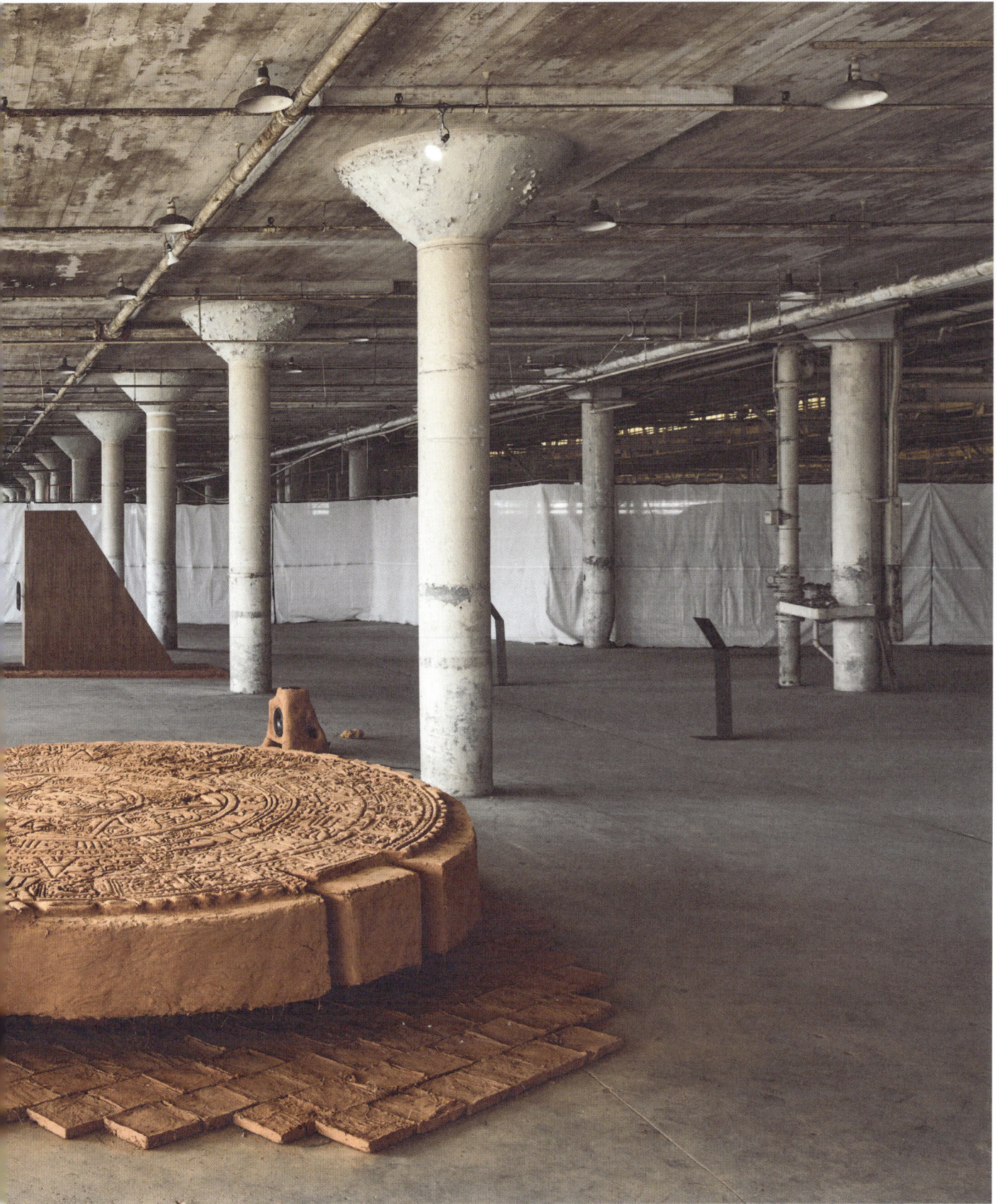

In 1923, Ford Motor Company constructed an assembly plant turned parts distribution center in Arabi, a place in St. Bernard Parish, Louisiana. Adjacent to the Mississippi River and railroad lines, it was an optimal node on the distribution route for the Southern Gulf region, but sat vacant after Katrina and now serves as storage for the film industry. For Prospect.6, the first floor was transformed into a site for a collaborative exhibition titled *Proposals for Loops in Linear Time* (2024) by rafa esparza, Zalika Azim, and Dewey Tafoya, one focused on migration, movement, and time travel, with ascension as the common thread amongst their artworks.

The trio has engaged with New Orleans'ss history, acknowledging the land's original inhabitants, the Mississippian culture who built earthen platform mounds, established elaborate trade networks and their own cosmology. The artists were interested in how this locale has for centuries been a place of convergence, either through consensual will or forced violence.

For this project, Tafoya and esparza hybridize Indigenous knowledge and cosmological beliefs with pop culture into a contemporary sculpture that transports them to a time where future humans are utilizing ancestral knowledge—land preservation, symbiosis, and nature connectedness. Meanwhile, Azim references early Egyptian and Phoenician civilizations and their connections to the present day street jump rope game of Double Dutch, considering the embodied knowledge that informs the movement and migration of Black people collectively and individually. Her work plays with gestures as metaphors for freedom, which allows reflections on the aftermath of fugitivity and gentrification.

Tafoya and esparza's work, *Mexica Falcon after Dewey Tafoya* (2024), is a sculptural re-creation of a 3D model of the *Millennium Falcon*, the fictional spaceship in the *Star Wars* franchise, integrated with designs of the Mexica people. esparza built the spacecraft, a seventeen-and-a-half-foot-long sculpture, which he affixed with mixed adobe then stamped with a print design by Tafoya, based on a hybridized remix of the Piedra del Sol (the Mexica sun stone), a late, post-classical Mexica monolith made of basalt. In this interpretation, the *Millennium Falcon* is transformed into the face of Xiuhtecuhtli, the lord of fire, with his protruding flint-knife tongue surrounded by an intricate design of lines and glyphs describing the Mexica's cosmogony.

Azim's kinetic sculptural work, *Ascension Device II* (*actions for earth...or some other oscillation...a haptic and sonic engagement...a breath...or an architecture for gathering between space and time*) (2024), explores the gestures of the jump and liminal space, a fitting companion to the *Mexica Falcon*'s capability to "hyperspace jump" and ascend through the cosmos. Set between two large trapezoids, the center of Azim's sculpture contains four spoked wheels, rhythmically turning ropes in opposite directions that hit the ground. For Azim, the jump also holds, in her words, "symbolic implications" of repetition, endurance, pursuit, and exhaustion. It is employed from a nuanced perspective, where there are simultaneous double meanings, histories, and images at work. It is an activity with the potential to unveil alternative understandings and new forms that center playfulness, leisure, and worldmaking via kinetic and bodily knowledge.

The trio's projects fluidly combine sculptural installations, audio work, and amate painting, offering connective queries about what they want to see and feel represented, presently and in a future world. Their mixing and blending of ancient and contemporary knowledge, hybrid forms of pop culture, and leisurely activities—with mechanical and laborious structures made of both natural and manmade materials—highlight the tensions, beauty, and openness of what could be, if only we took the time to be present and listen to those rhythms that help us ascend to a space beyond.

by Marissa Del Toro

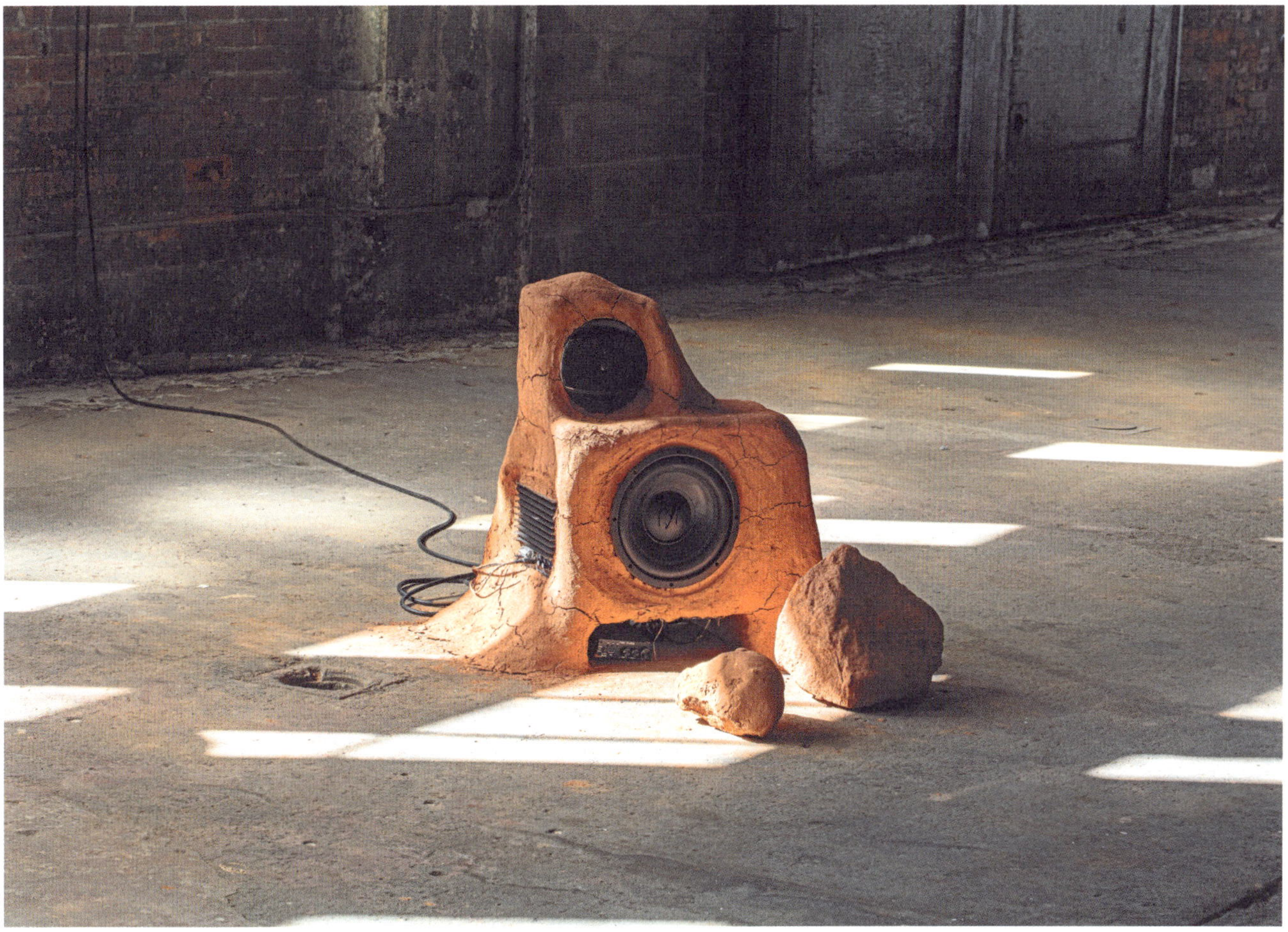

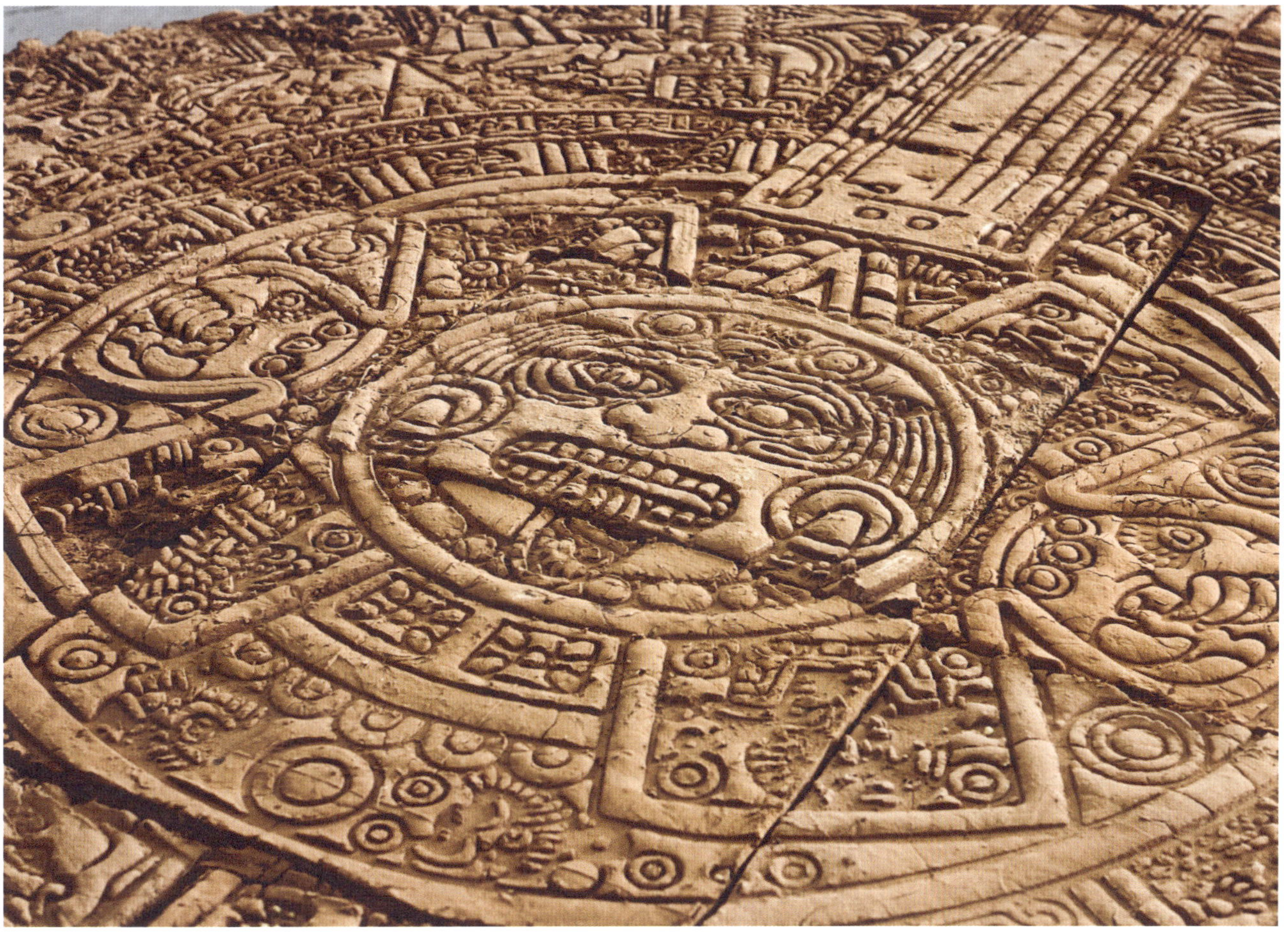

Top: Zalika Azim, rafa esparza, and Dewey Tafoya, *polysemous notes on geological time...or ways to steal from the workplace...a grounding...for an escape or an inhabiting*, 2024 (detail)

Above: rafa esparza, *Mexica Falcon after Dewey Tafoya*, 2024 (detail)

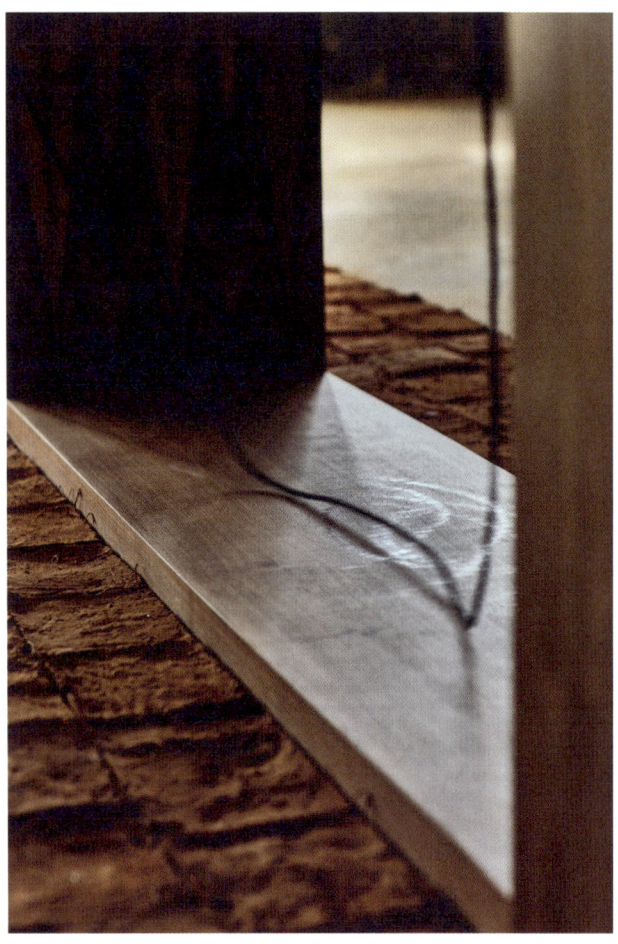

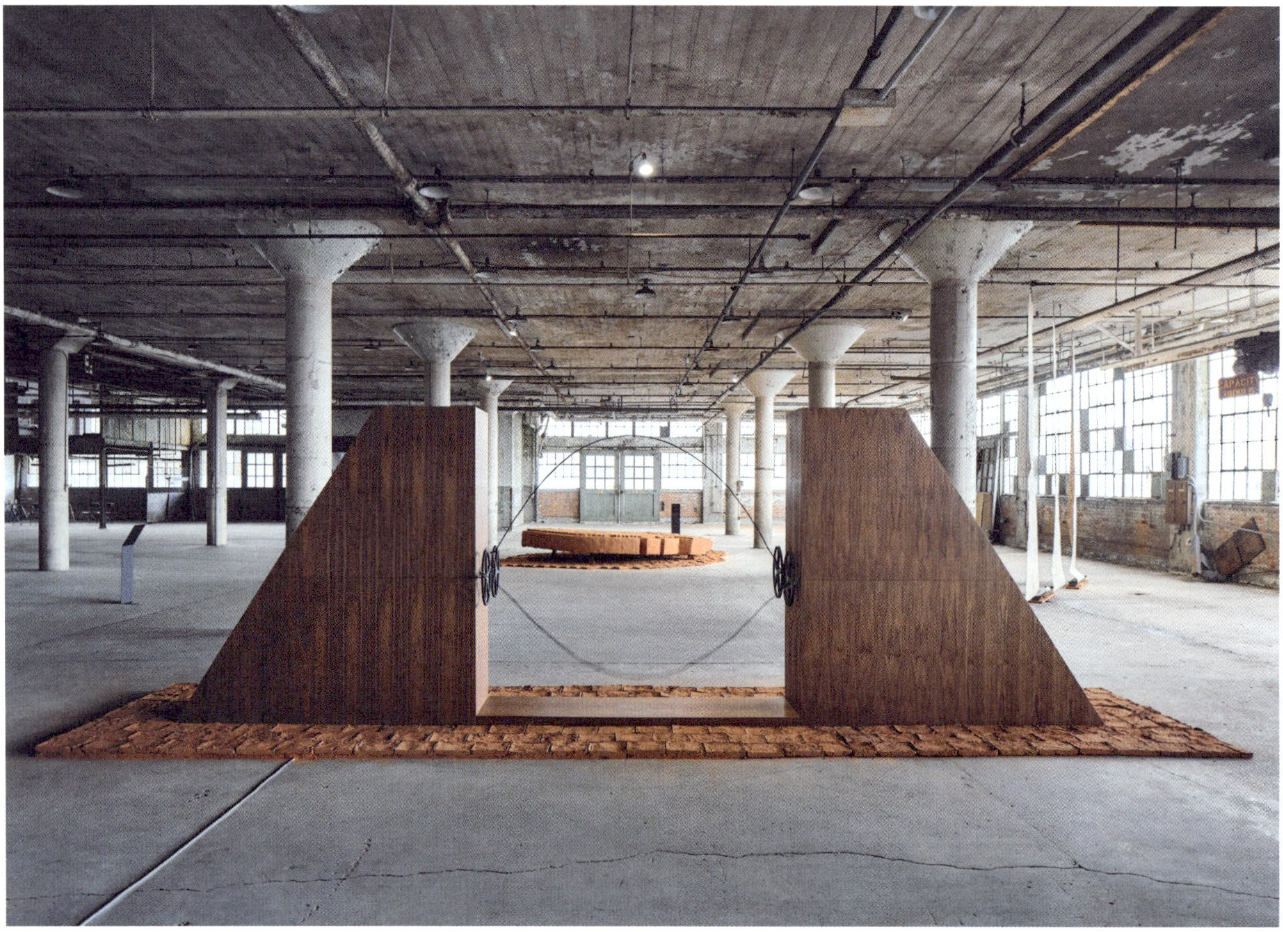

Top: Zalika Azim, *Ascension Device II (actions for earth... or some other oscillation...a haptic and sonic engagement... a breath...or an architecture for gathering between space and time)*, 2024 (detail)

Above: Zalika Azim, *Ascension Device II (actions for earth... or some other oscillation...a haptic and sonic engagement... a breath...or an architecture for gathering between space and time)*, 2024

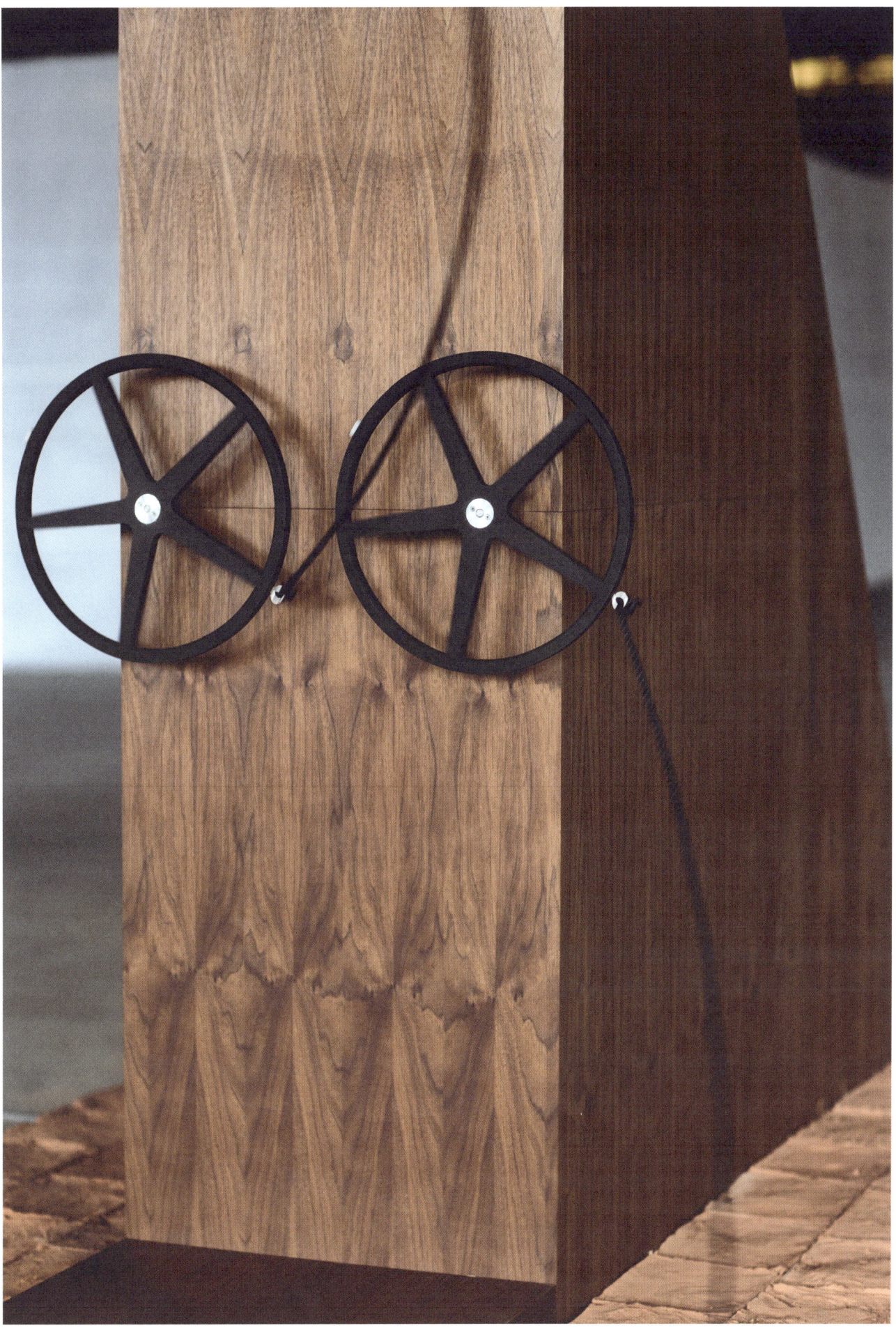

Zalika Azim, *Ascension Device II (actions for earth...or some other oscillation...a haptic and sonic engagement...a breath... or an architecture for gathering between space and time)*, 2024 (detail)

120

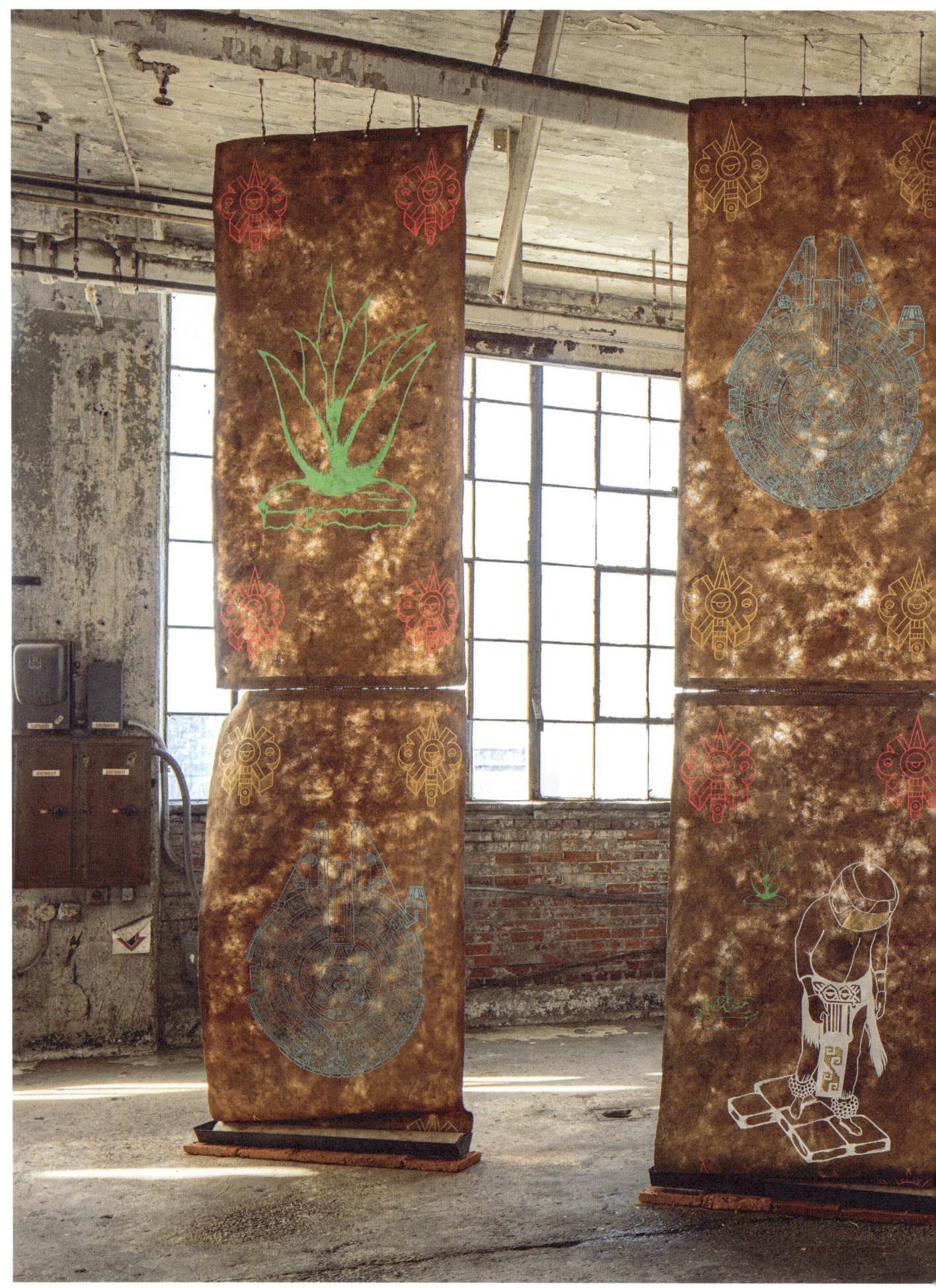

Dewey Tafoya, L to R: *Metl*, *Tlalli*, and *Milli*, 2024

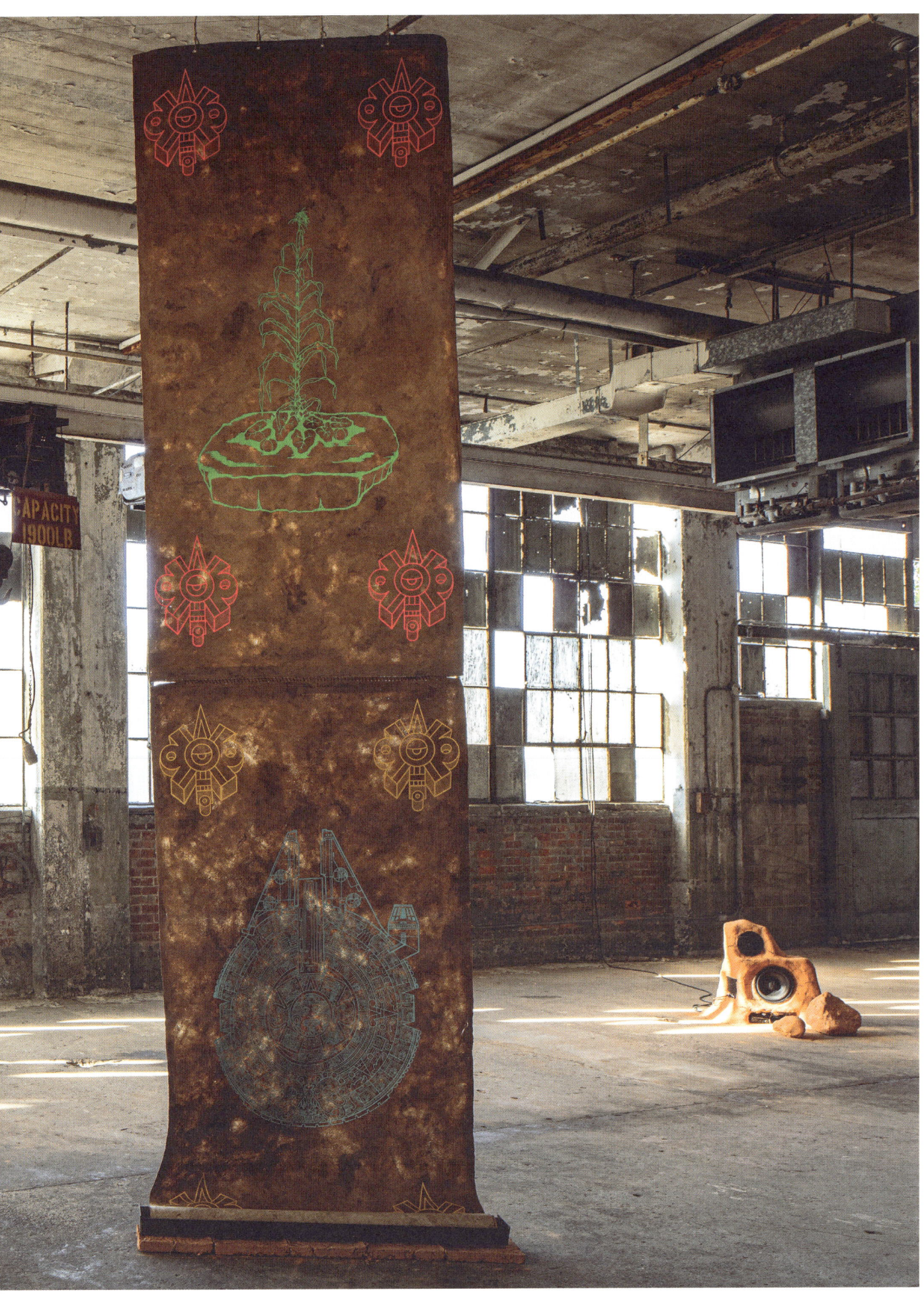

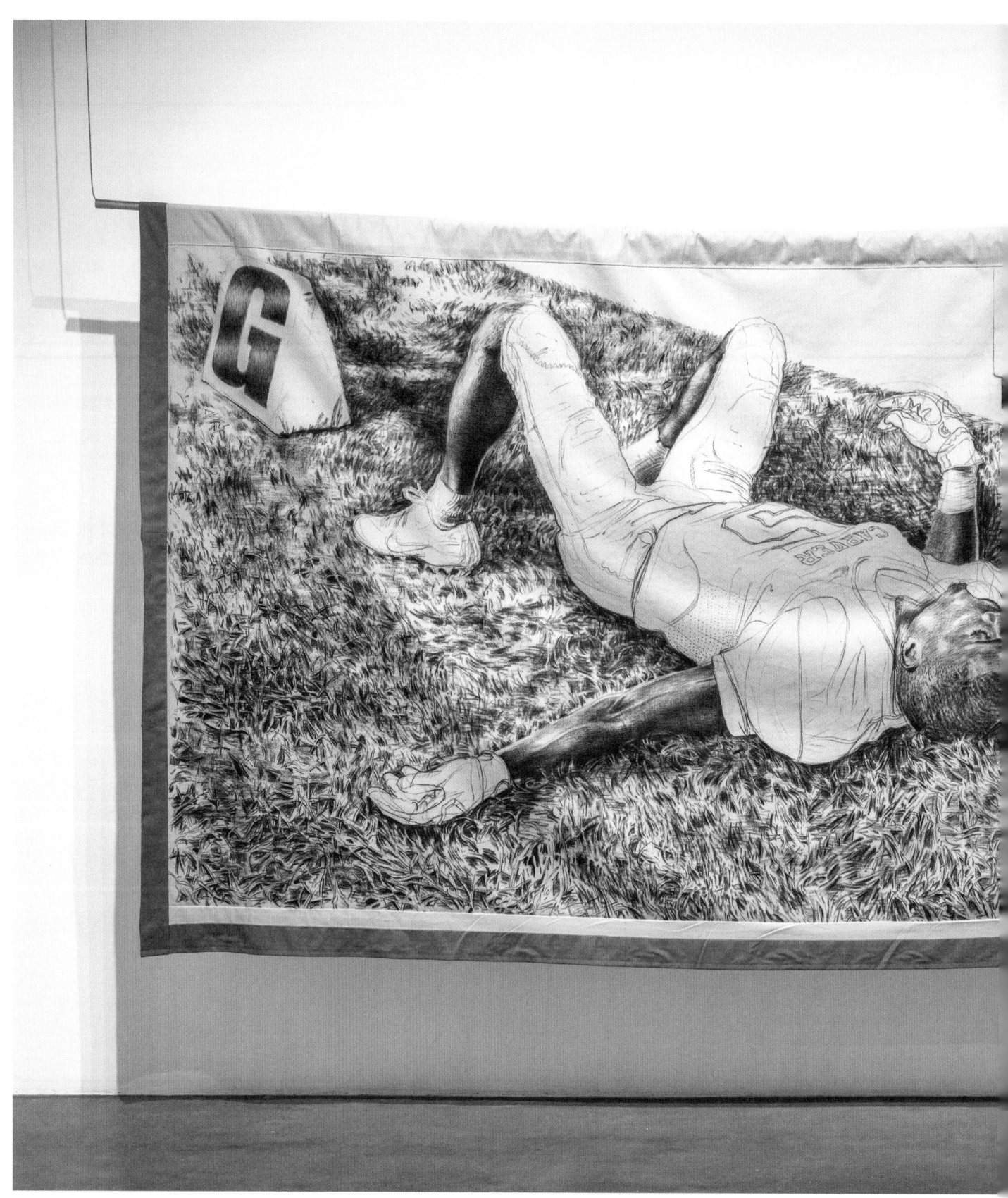

Three Down Back, 2019

Abdi Farah

b. 1987, Baltimore, MD; lives in New Orleans, LA

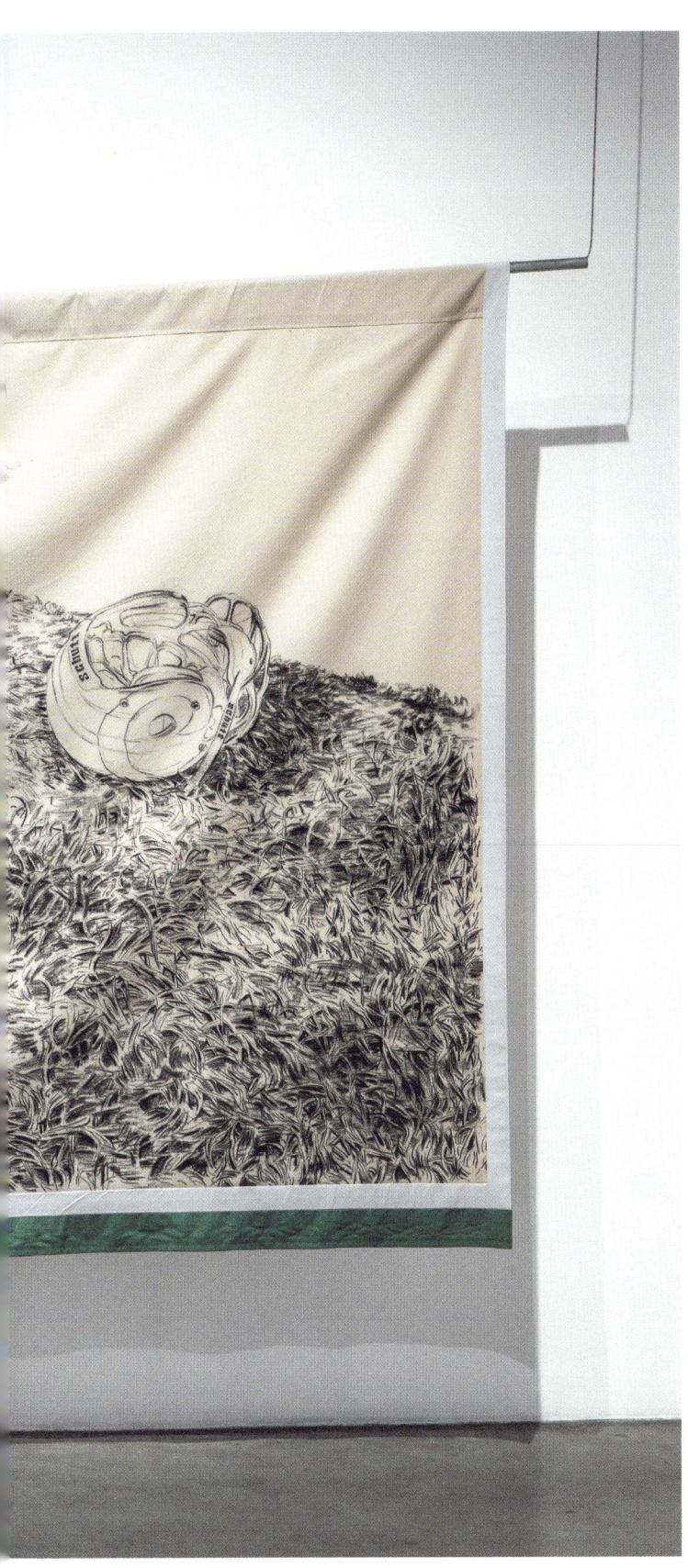

Abdi Farah works across textiles, painting, and sculpture, and believes that "the life of an artist feels parallel" to those of injured athletes.[1] Using sports as a metaphor for the struggles and successes in his artist life—pain, self-doubt, endurance, victory—Farah delves into Black American masculinity through figurative sculptures of young, Black male football players that incorporate fabrics, various paints, and other materials. He rejects hyper-masculinized, toxic stereotypes, and instead, his sports figures exude introspection and sensitivity. Born in Baltimore, he was raised by a Black American single mother and grew up obsessed with the NBA. He was shaped not only by basketball, but also by the Black Southern Baptist church he frequented in Baltimore County, and his local community. After obtaining a BA from the University of Pennsylvania, he received an MFA in painting from Tulane University, and has lived in New Orleans ever since.

Farah has worked with high school football teams in his adopted city for years, focusing his research on Black neighborhoods in the Seventh, Eighth, and Ninth Wards, and Algiers (the Fifteenth Ward) on the Westbank. Black male teen athletes—Farah's avatars—mirror his younger self, and serve as lenses inside New Orleans'ss robust high school football community. He eschews tired tropes, avoiding the hyper-performance of masculinity Black boys are expected to deliver on a football field, and instead, prioritizes vulnerable and pensive moments.

In *Three Down Back* (2019), a young football player lies on the football field in a moment of recovery. Farah portrays defeat, acknowledging that this stillness is only temporary in this charcoal on canvas piece. He works with used garments and also sews, a material and labor often gendered as "pink collar," as seen in the nylon-based textile pieces, *Indescribable Beast* and *Trojan Pride* (both 2017). He disrupts not only the masculinity of sports, but pays an ode to Black women as well—the single mothers, grandmothers, aunties, and others who support entire Black communities with their caretaking.

Pomp, pageantry, and peacocking permeate the theater of high school football, from its star players in-the-making, to its insatiable, cheering fans. In his artistry, Farah pays close attention to football's regalia, mascots, logos, and iconography. For Prospect.6, although the spectacle of high school football is present, he opts for more tender moments within the sport. His mixed media textile paintings of high school football players are rendered in scenes of quietude and rest. There's busyness and noise, but the adrenaline and brashness is replaced by sensitivity and emotion. Farah's constellation of

works included in P.6, self-described as a "three circle venn diagram,"[2] explores his church roots, team dynamics, and the emotional costs of navigating Black American male identity in America. In Farah's world, he offers young Black male athletes a meditative, soft place to land, draped in shiny and kitschy fabrics.

by Jasmin Hernandez

1   Conversation with the artist, May 29, 2024.
2   Ibid.

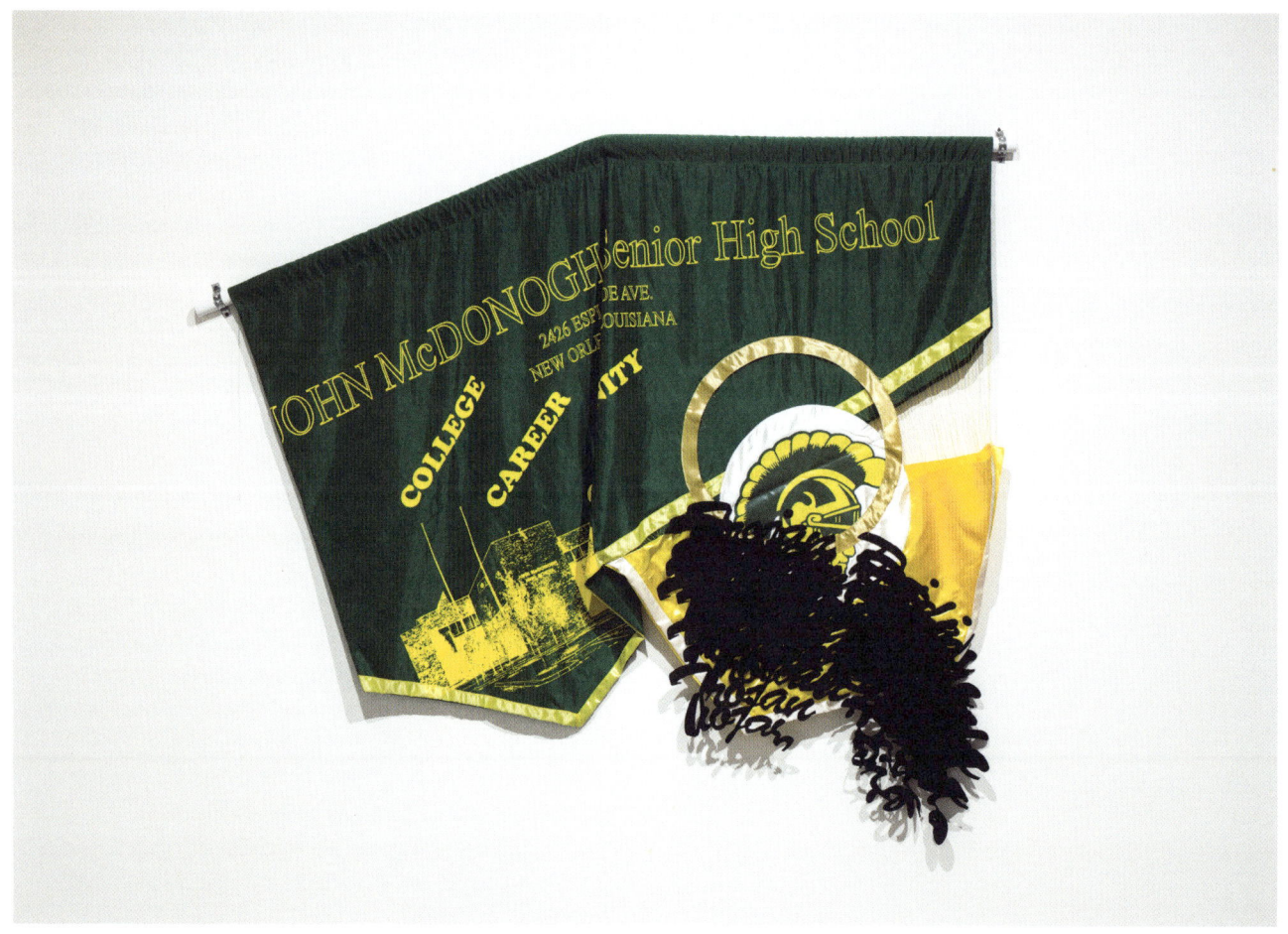

Trojan Pride, 2017

Abdi Farah

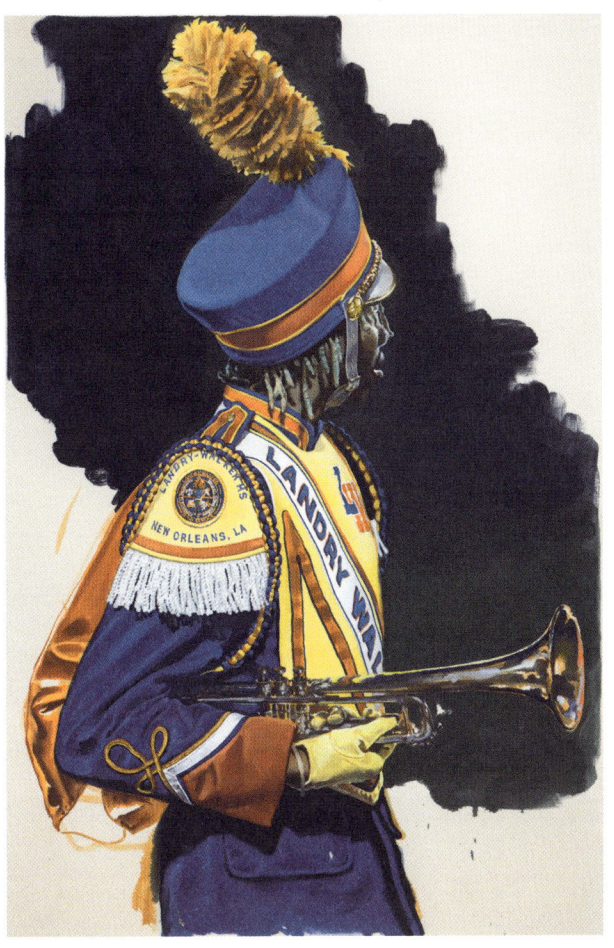

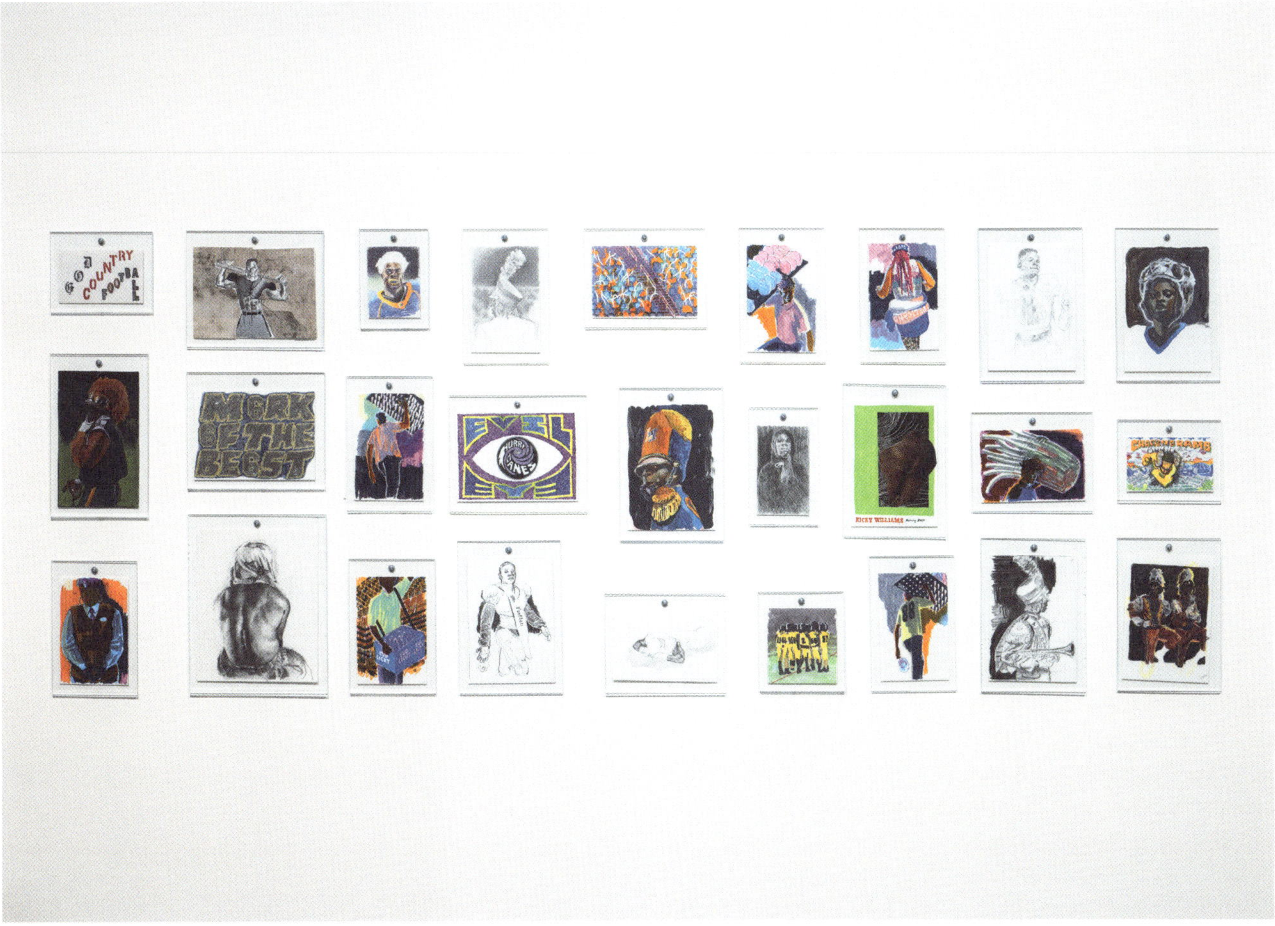

Top: *Plume*, 2021   Above: *Studies*, 2013–2024

Brendan Fernandes

b. 1979, Nairobi, Kenya; lives in Chicago, IL

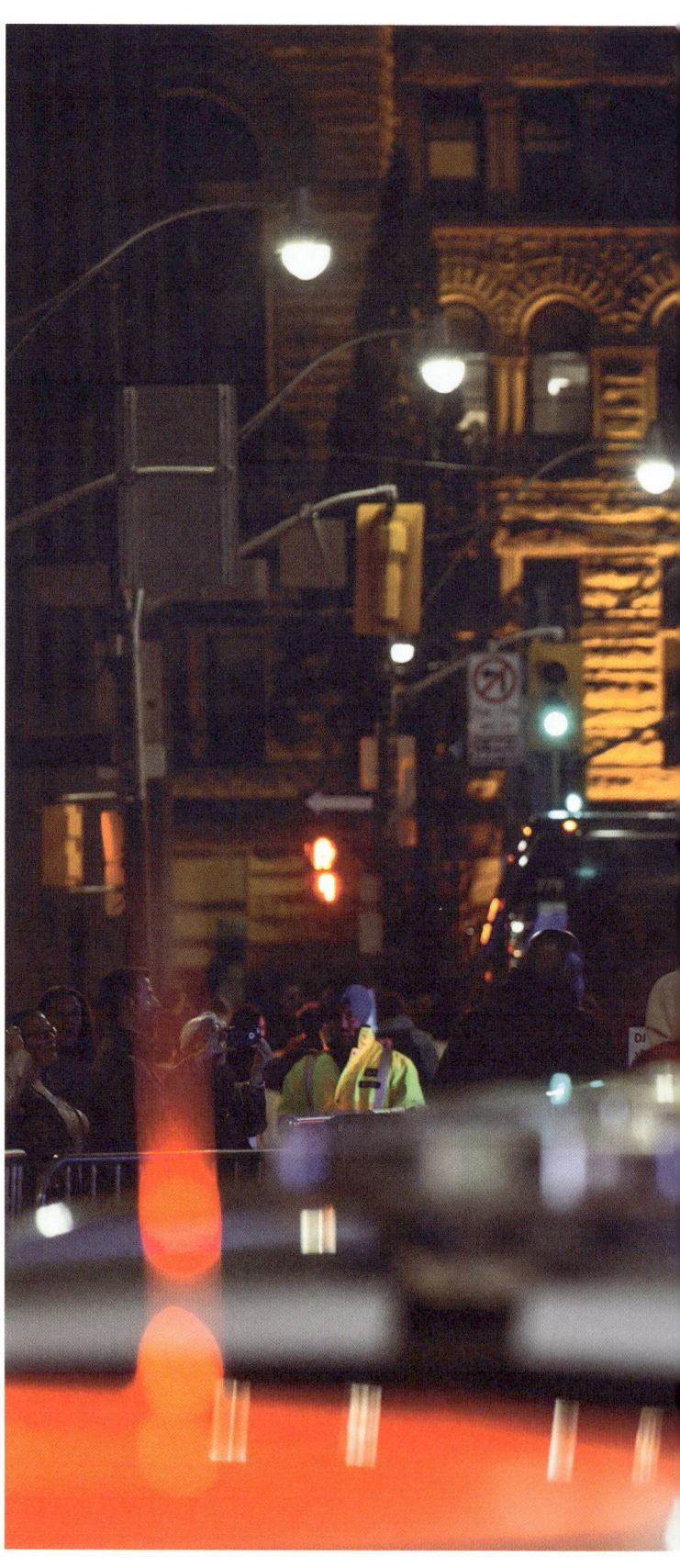

"My work is a form of protest and still looking at questions of freedom," states Brendan Fernandes. There is an urgency in Fernandes's work in how the artist examines broken structures. In his dismantling of oppressive systems. Fernandes's practice converges around dance and the visual arts. His work addresses issues of race, queerness, migration, protest, and forms of collective resistance. The choreographer Martha Graham and composer John Cage figure prominently in the artist's practice. In previous works like *Inaction* (2019-2021) and *Master and Form II* (2019), dancers perform a set of conditions, within and without architectural support to propel them. The works can be seen as a call to eradicate the violence instituted against queer selves. Bodies that resist conforming to certain measures. Where they *fall* or toil in the vestiges of freedom. Bodies call upon bodies to demonstrate or admonish connection.

On Flashing Lights is a light/sound/installation/ performance work originally commissioned by Nuit Blanche in Toronto. In the original piece, a barricade of police cars lined Bay Street, enclosing a scene of DJs spinning and revelers dancing. The lights of police cars flash, essentially to the beat, in discomfiting relationship to the communing happening around them. The work builds on Fernandes's

On Flashing Lights, 2018. Bay Street, Toronto, Canada. Commissioned by Nuit Blanche, Toronto

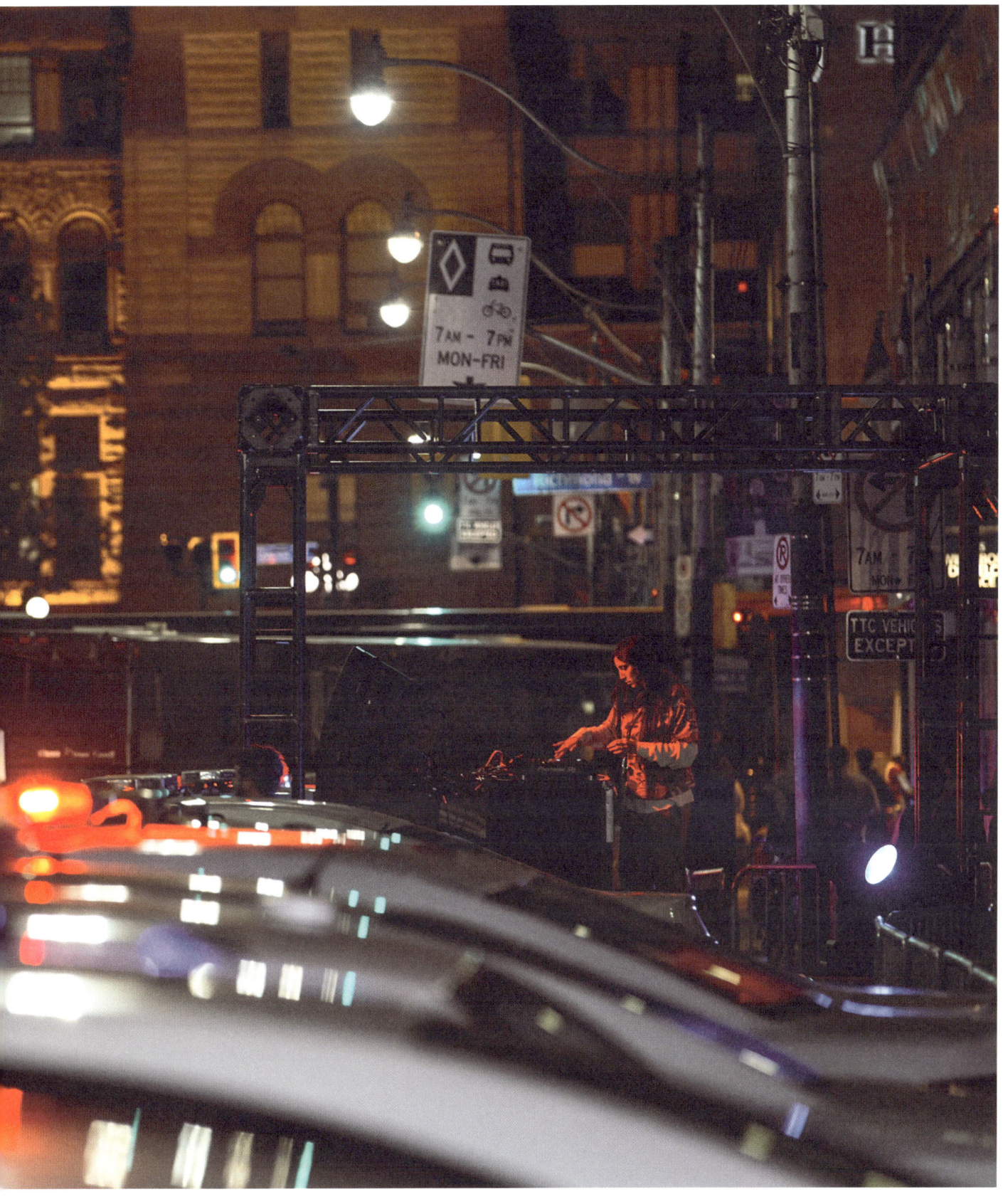

ongoing investigations of queer bodies and dance as acts of resistance. For Prospect.6, Fernandes is restaging *On Flashing Lights* in New Orleans in 2025. The artist is working with community members in New Orleans to negotiate what restaging this performance work in the city would mean. The artist asks himself, what's at stake here?

Fernandes wants to avoid extractive approaches to moving forward with a restaging of the piece within the context of a city with its own set of histories and connections. What does it mean to relocate the work to New Orleans? Fernandes is envisioning a collaborative relationship with community members to bring the performance to life. It's crucial that the work is explicitly, obviously staged: The police cars aren't actually police cars—they're painted prop cars used in movies. The sirens are both ornamentation and an emblem of alarm. Here, Fernandes plays with a symbolism and vernacular tied to regimes of power and suppression. Fernandes often speaks of "hegemonies" when talking about his work. Of shifting power dynamics—who's wielding power.

Fernandes reflects on the labor of dance—the body laboring to convey, to reconstruct: stasis, attenuation, mourning. The preponderance of claims against the self, where the body is forced to yield under the constraint of binaries and the regulations of late capitalism. What is a body to do? Resist. Recoiling under the weight of neglect or fervor, how bodies upend death.

Fernandes's practice is on a continuum, from the persuasive to the restorative. Delegations of form. There is an emotional calisthenics in the precision of attuning to bodies. How do we contend with death? How do we remain grieving? The body in alternate states of frenzy. This is the dance—how artists reframe the boundaries of tension—of how to effectively create the kind of work one is intending. "Bodies" are in peril. In real time. Fernandes asserts that *the club* is a "church," yes, but the body is a temple.

by Sherae Rimpsey

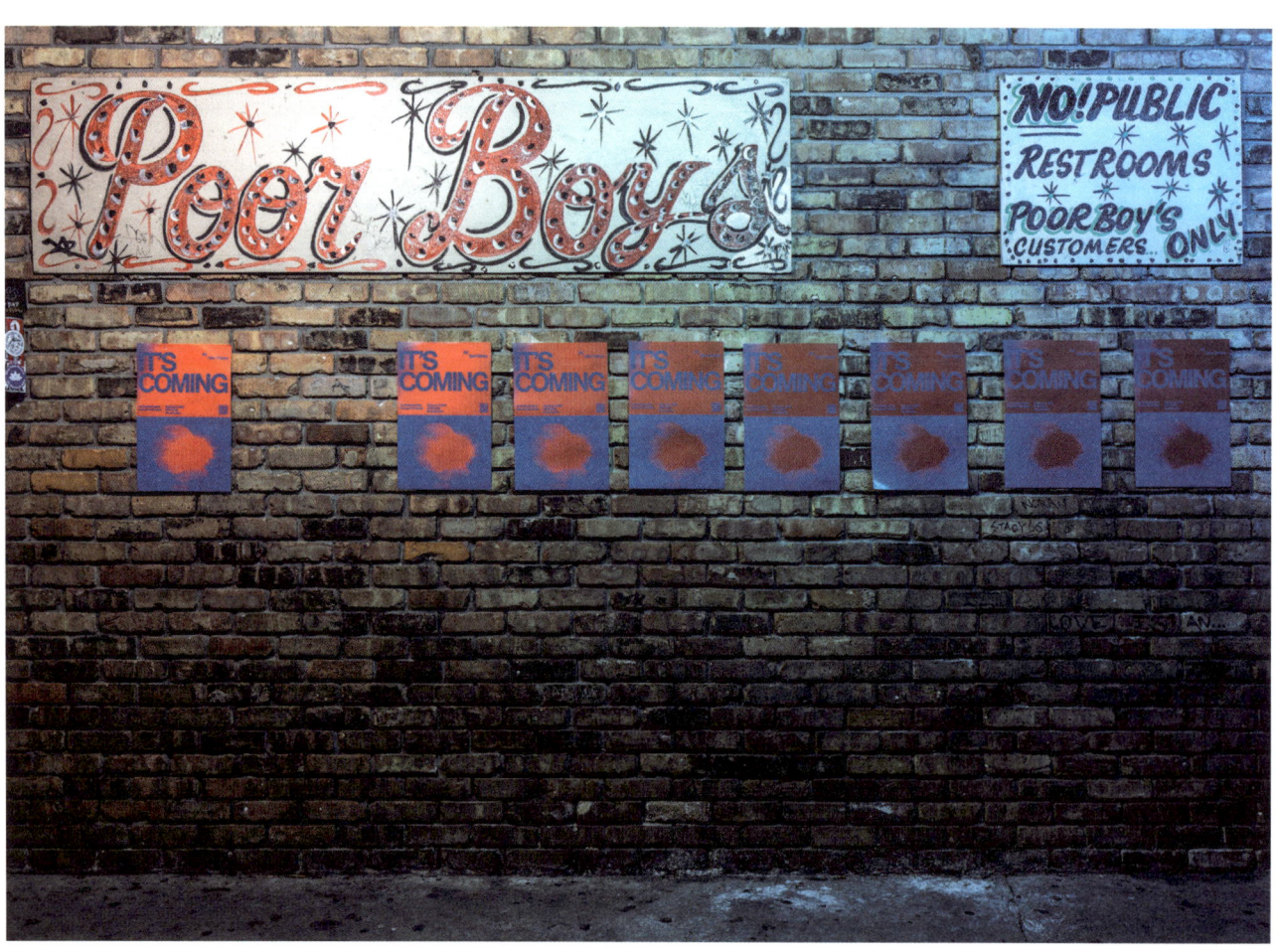

Posters for *On Flashing Lights* performance, 2024. Poor Boys, New Orleans, Louisiana. Poster design by Brett LaBauve

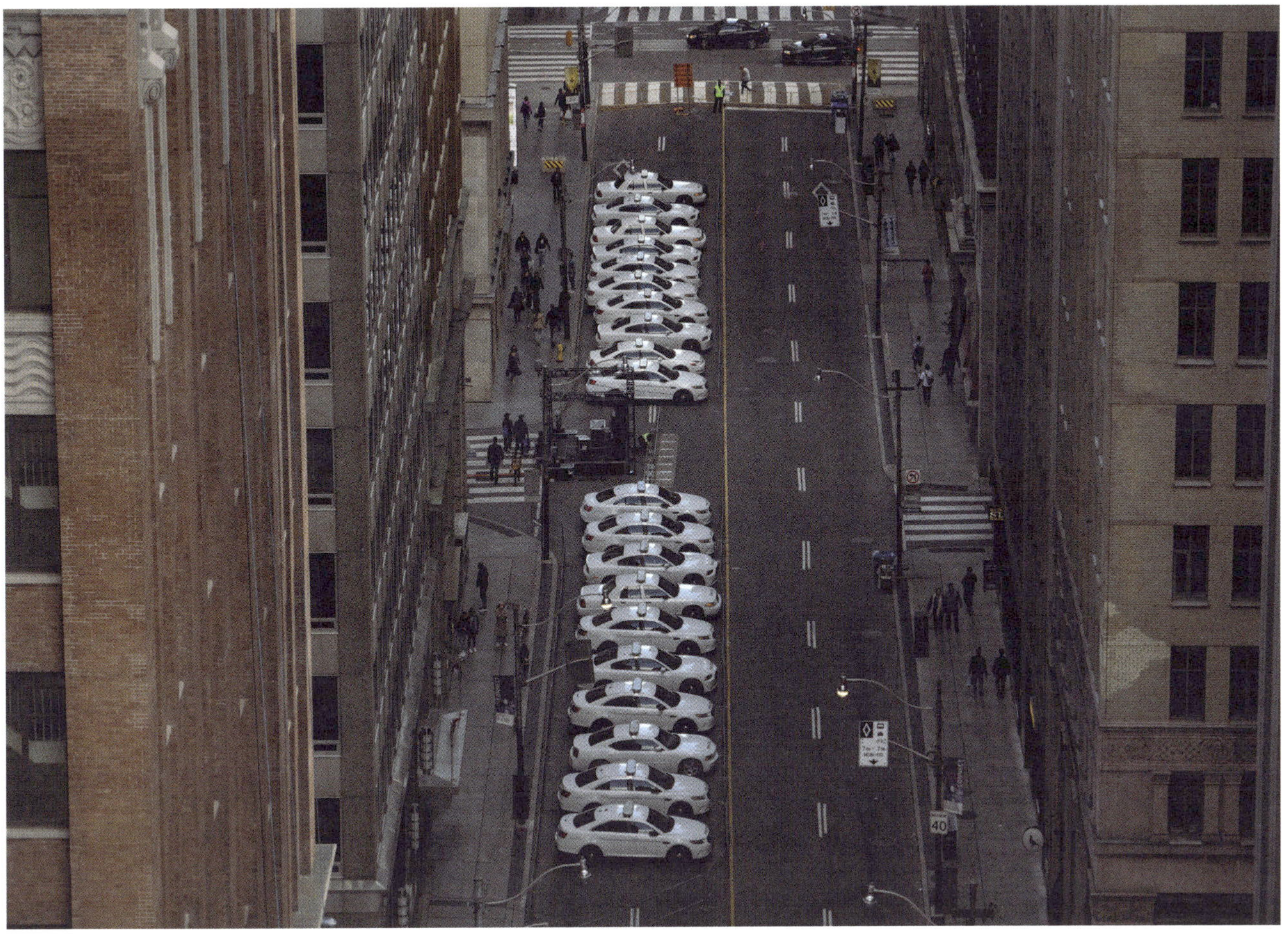

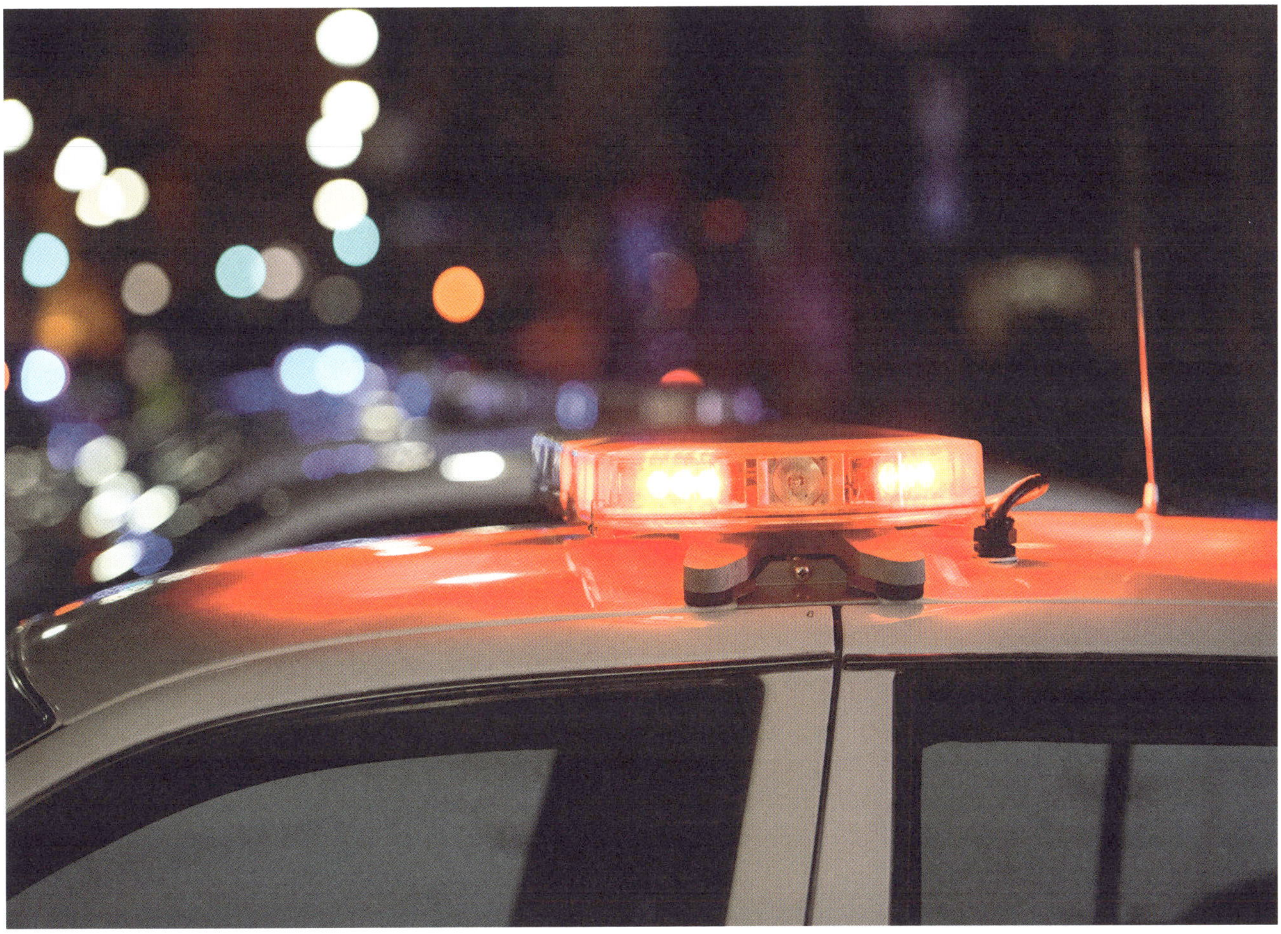

On Flashing Lights, 2018. Bay Street, Toronto, Canada.
Commissioned by Nuit Blanche, Toronto

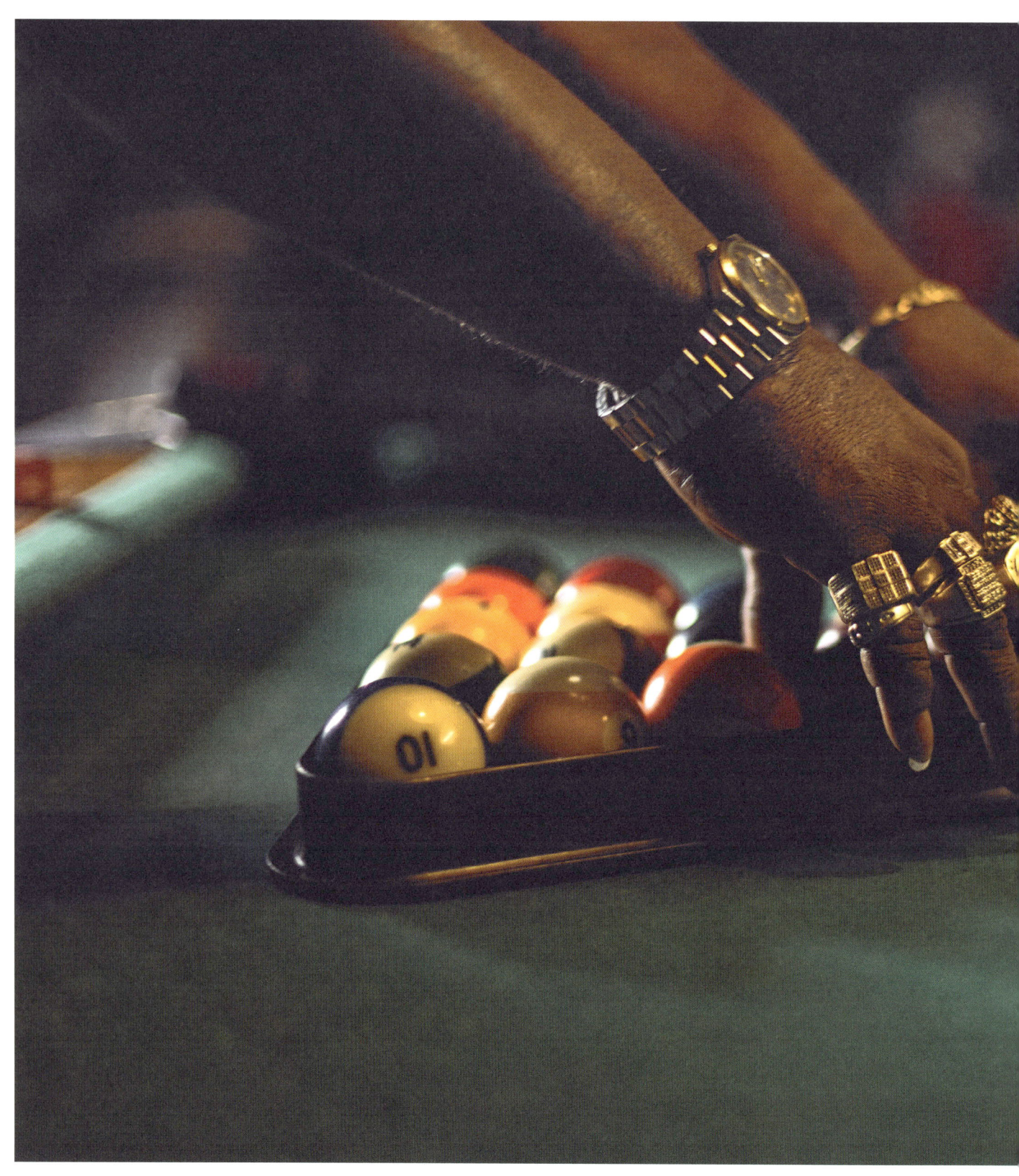

Rings, Rack, Win Dat Money Back (Mr. Ooooook Lounge),
Clarksdale, Mississippi, 2021, from the series *Vanishing*
Black Bars & Lounges, 2018–ongoing

L. Kasimu Harris

b. 1978, New Orleans, LA; lives in New Orleans, LA

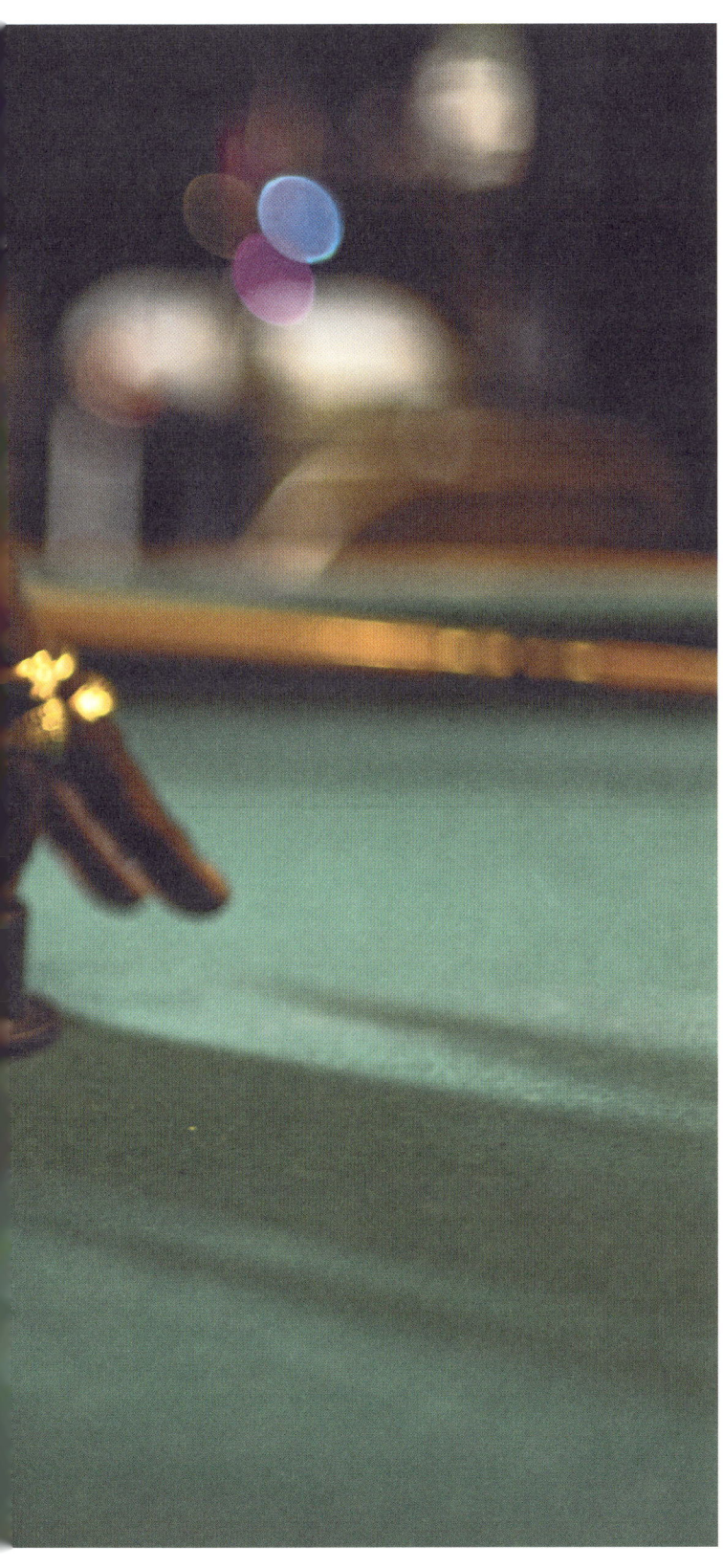

Photographer L. Kasimu Harris creates deeply descriptive, layered images that oscillate between portraiture, abstraction, still-life, and fictive constructions. Moving seamlessly between these generic modes and more—across sequences or even within a single image—Harris pursues visual rhythms, establishing patterns that challenge and draw viewers in for deeper exploration. As a storyteller and artist, Harris has never really been interested in easily digestible ideas, and instead has insisted on confronting complicated histories and urgent social issues, like the school-to-prison pipeline and racial inequity in healthcare. Even in work that examines systemic political problems, Harris's steadfast humanism has always made his photography emotionally resonant in ways that encourage thoughtful advocacy, without sacrificing any visual complexity or rigor.

Harris's series *Vanishing Black Bars and Lounges* (2018–ongoing) illustrates the vibrancy and generational importance of Black-owned bars in New Orleans, while also documenting how the post-Katrina displacement of Black New Orleanians and ongoing gentrification in the city threatens the existence of those establishments. Throughout the series, place-specific details, like snapshots of Black Masking Indians behind the register, anchor each photograph specifically in New Orleans. *The Set-Up, Unc's Hands, (Purple Rain Bar), New Orleans* (2019) presents a concise version of Harris's overall thesis and his sophisticated approach to crafting a picture. Embracing the ambient blue and red lights of the Purple Rain Bar, Harris uses the tones as compositional elements to split the frame. Formally and metaphorically, Harris routinely centers people that give life to the rooms he photographs. In this case, the bartender Precious's outstretched arm meets the hand of a patron in a pose evocative of *The Creation of Adam* in the Sistine Chapel. The Purple Rain Bar, Harris argues, also constitutes a sacred place. While this photograph evinces both the literal and emotional economy held between Black New Orleanians, the symbolism of the twenty-dollar bill at the center reminds us that capitalism also brings more sinister spirits. In *Purple Rain Bar into the Abyss of the Unremembered-Culture Persists. How Long?* (2023), Harris pictures a lonely figure standing in front of the dark and shuttered building, after new ownership took control of the bar.

For Prospect.6, Harris has installed the series in an actual Black-owned bar, Sweet Lorraine's Jazz Club, encouraging patrons and viewers in the real world (read: not the art world) to think about how they move in social spaces and the hospitality economy, as well as their own relationship to issues like gentrification. P.6 is debuting new works Harris made in Clarksdale, Mississippi, as well as Pittsburgh, Los Angeles, Chicago, and the Caribbean island of St. Lucia, connecting New Orleans to a diaspora of Black social spaces. Across that geography, Harris illustrates the importance of bars as third places for Black people to gather, build, and relax. Perhaps unexpectedly, the series demonstrates continuities in the economic stressors affecting historically Black neighborhoods, from Pittsburgh's Hill District to New Orleans'ss Tremé. Harris also

created a group of contemporary allegorical portraits based on real alcohol advertisements aimed at global Black consumers that might have been displayed in bars in the 1960s and '70s, featuring notable (real) figures from New Orleans'ss arts and hospitality industries.

The reimagined ads are cloaked in the visuals of conspicuous consumption, but overlaid with copy that slyly complicates the logic of capitalism, challenging us to support and maintain Black social and cultural spaces for the future. *Champers: 3 Beautiful Experiences* (2024), for example, stars bartenders Erika Flowers, J'Nai Williams, and Deniseea Head posed in the style of a vintage Champale poster. As the advertising copy tells us, Champers, like New Orleans and other shrinking cities, boasts the possibilities of "sparkling beyond recognition, bold changes, and vintage chocolate cities," but with a dire warning in the form of a slogan: "Better Savor It Now, It Won't Be There Later." For Harris and, one hopes, viewers of the work, the urgency of that challenge is as carefully considered as the photographs themselves.

by Brian Piper

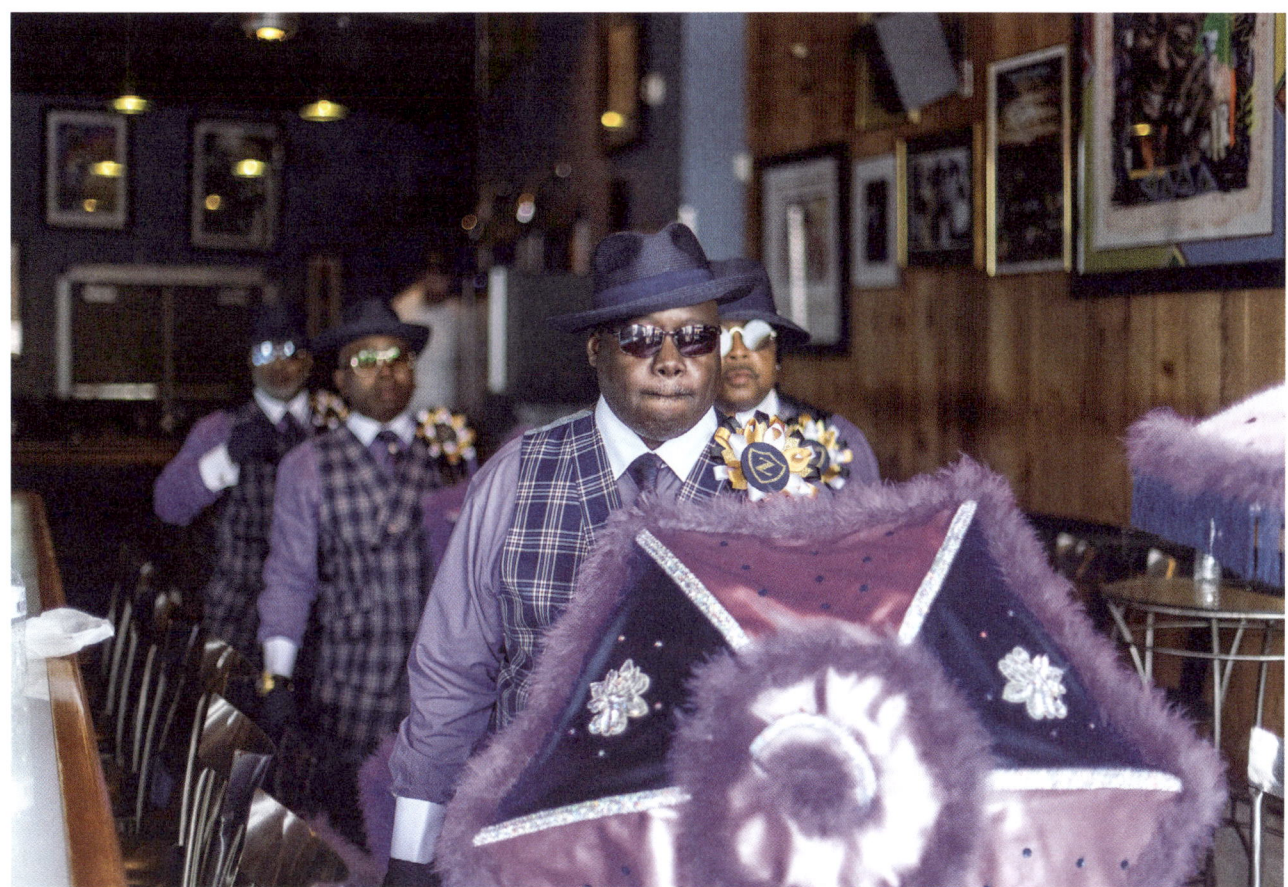

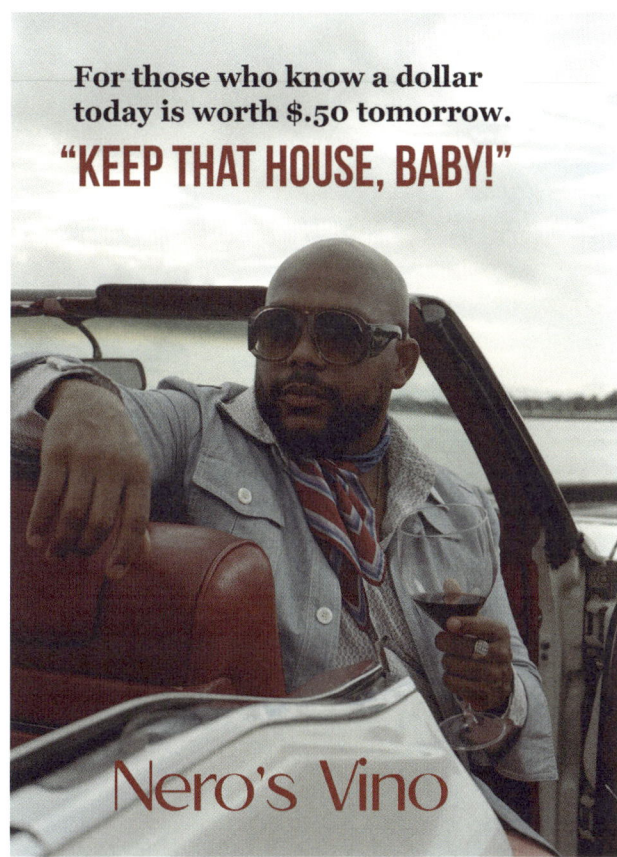

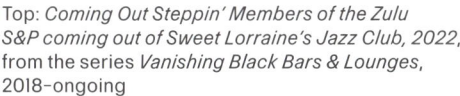

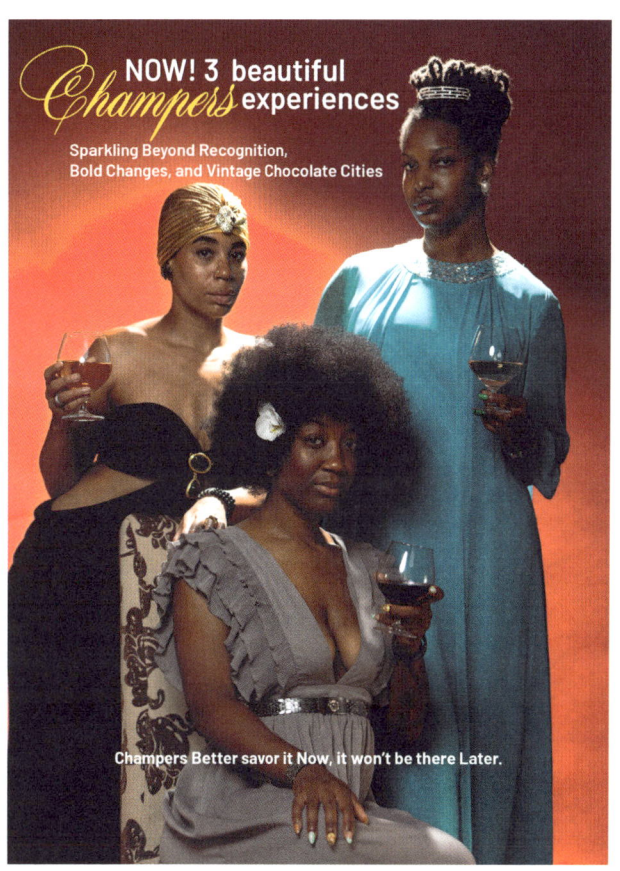

Top: *Coming Out Steppin' Members of the Zulu S&P coming out of Sweet Lorraine's Jazz Club, 2022*, from the series *Vanishing Black Bars & Lounges*, 2018-ongoing

Above L: *Nero's Vino*, 2024, from the series *Vanishing Black Bars & Lounges*, 2018-ongoing. Above R: *Champers, 3 Beautiful Experiences*, 2024, from the series *Vanishing Black Bars & Lounges*, 2018-ongoing

Nadia Huggins

b. 1984, Port of Spain, Trinidad and Tobago;
lives in St. Vincent and the Grenadines

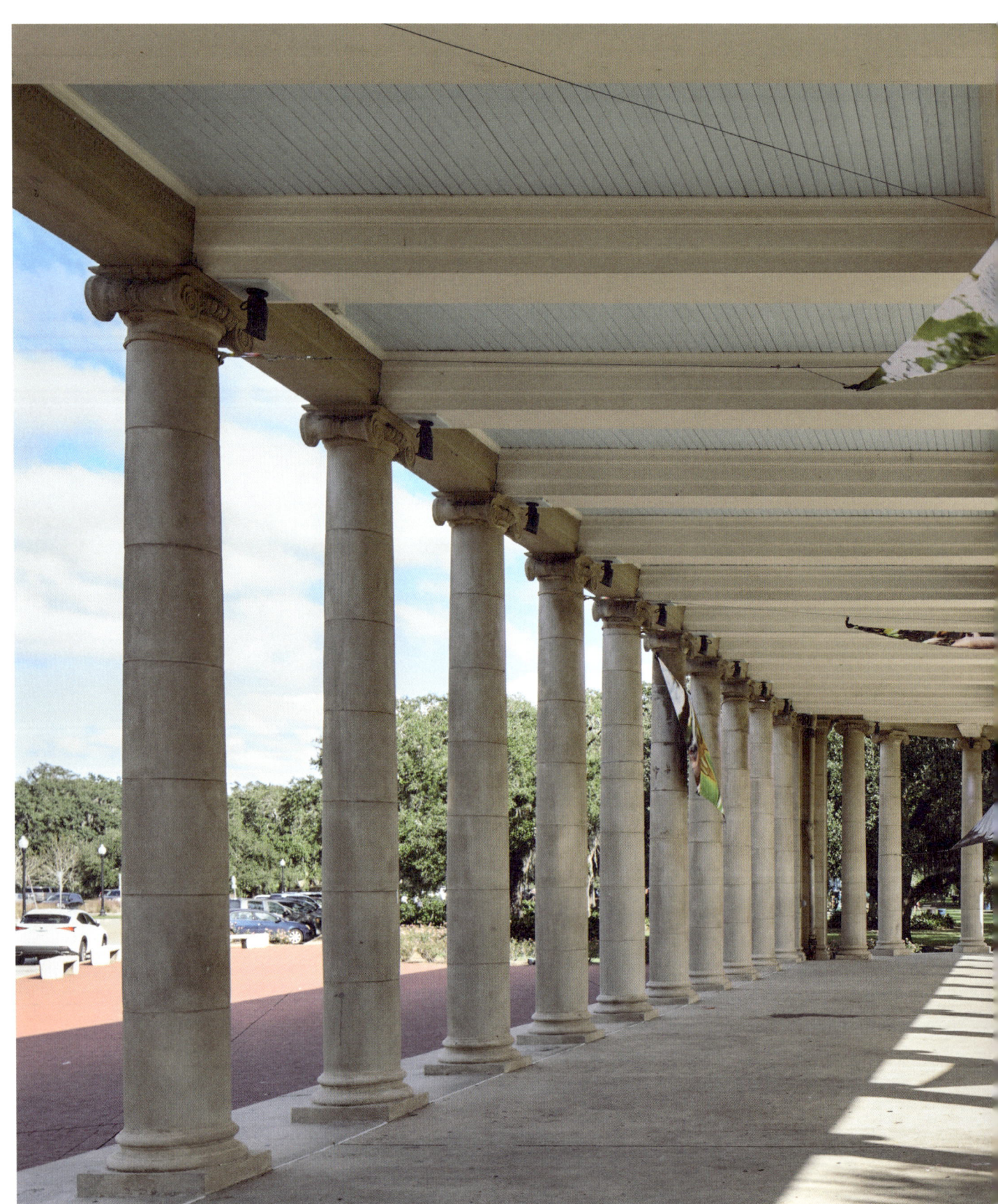

Birds of Paradise, 2024

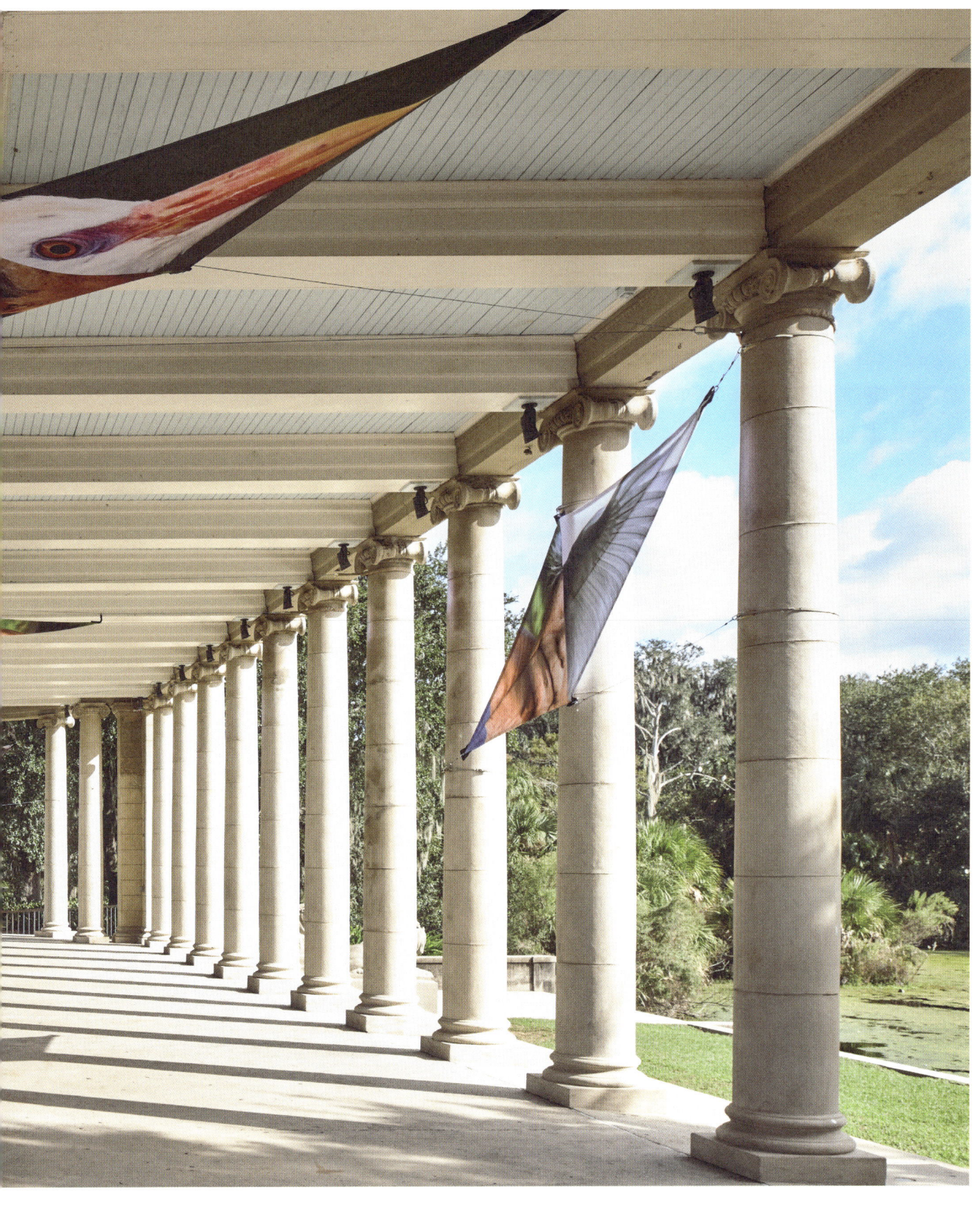

Flying creatures appear between granite colonnades. They descend from the ceiling of the New Orleans City Park Peristyle, caught in a dance with the winds. These floating beings are an amalgamation of pictured bodies amongst the classical architecture. Artist Nadia Huggins has made these kite-like artworks as a photographic offering, to honor family, home, and nature. Across Huggins's career, wonderment manifests in uncanny relationships within the natural world. She creates arrangements that reject the physical and biological seams between life-forms. She constructs these new realities through diptychs, transforming documentary photography into speculative promises of ungendered, interspecies communion. Descending from the peristyle ceiling is her latest conceptual study of bodies: the white egret, banana tree, and human form.

Born in Trinidad and Tobago, Huggins has long called Saint Vincent home. The island and the surrounding water have been her collaborators in photographic projects that document environments and climate change, and catalyze reparative human and nature symbiosis. In her series *Transformations* (2014-2015), Huggins photographed herself underwater and the oceanic fauna that surrounded her. She then stitched compositions together to create surreal images of her anonymized body compressed with sea animals. For Prospect.6, Huggins's photographs are an interweaving of different life-forms: An egret's wing is punctuated by a pale limb; nascent bananas extend into an elbow; a human profile transforms into a piercing eye and elongated orange beak. Time is a hovering character amongst these mythological creatures: Huggins documents growing bananas, the clockwork routine of the egret, and the silver hair and weathered skin of her own elderly mother. The temporality of these differing lives is then intertwined through Huggins's pairings, encouraging a contemplation of natural evolutions and the universally shared chronologies of birth and death.

In 2021, Huggins documented La Soufrière's sulfuric plumes and the ashen remnants that coated her beloved landscape. She describes the volcanic cataclysm as an experience of violence that simultaneously destroys but also births newness. This event dovetailed with

Huggins's family life and their relationship to abrupt change and loss, as the artist cared for her mother and grappled with the realities of parental fragility. Huggins was also inspired by Derek Walcott's *White Egrets*. In the poems, the Saint Lucian native offers elegiac stanzas, using the elegant bird as a metaphor for encounters with death. Titling her New Orleans installation *Birds of Paradise* (2024), Huggins similarly evokes notions of a collapsed human, plant, and animal experience—and the heavens beyond.

Just as Walcott's grief is shrouded in wordplay and the appearance of the egret, Huggins's photographic strategies do not offer clarity. The blended forms of plant, bird, and person create unknowns; they each appear as separates, only partially distinguishable when seen in conjunction with each other. This opacity echoes Huggins's interest in carnival celebrations, where festival accoutrements sometimes render people as animals and/or genderless, both of which are significant themes in her artistry. Like carnival, her fantastical compositions are a performance of coalitional possibility. While *Birds of Paradise* is heavy with the universal truth of loss—and the weight of collective care for the environment, not only by humans but by other species too—Huggins offers levity. The flock of photographs astonish with a carnivalesque joy, grand color, and the distinct vision and love of one's island home.

by Delphine Sims

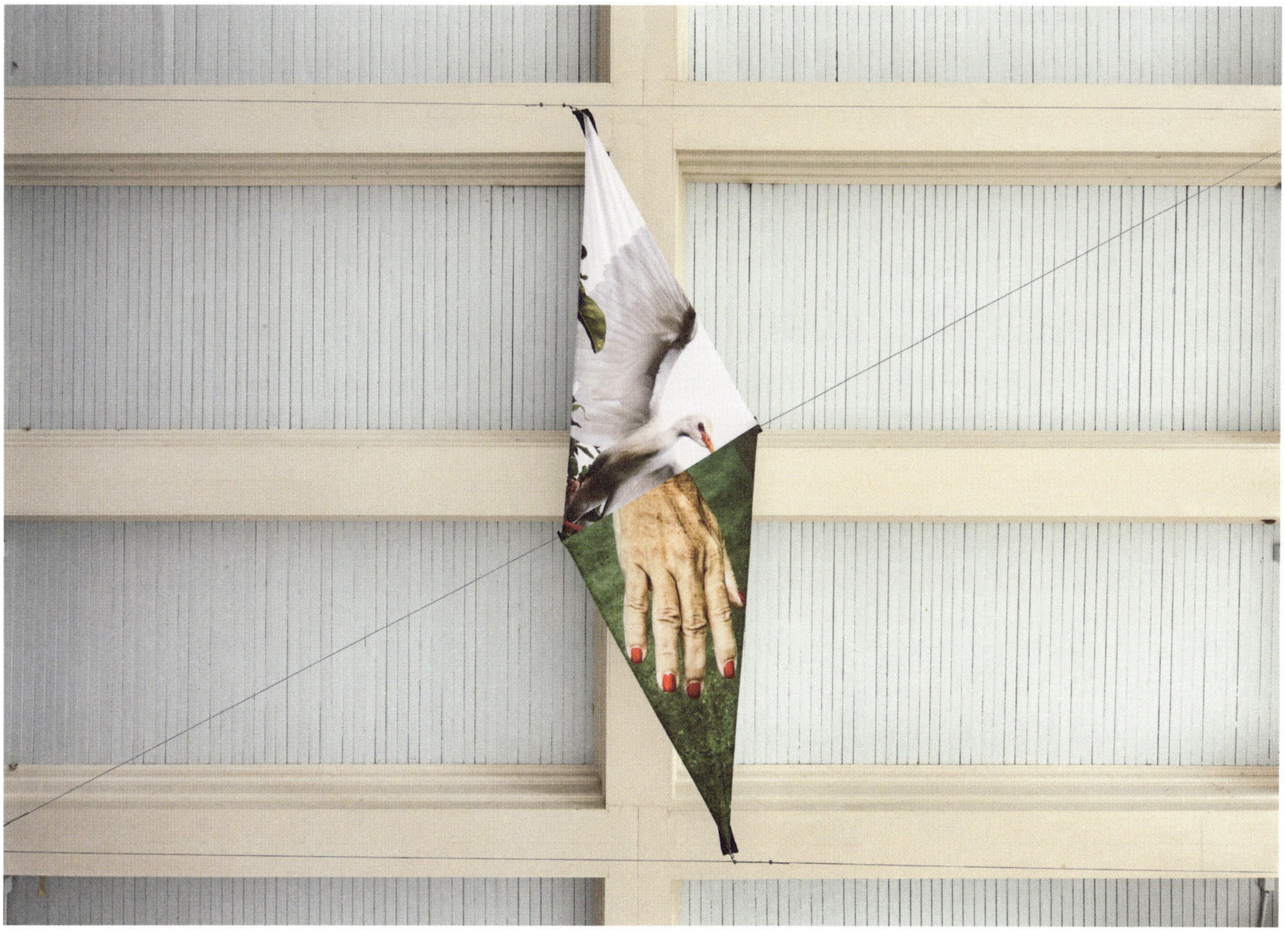

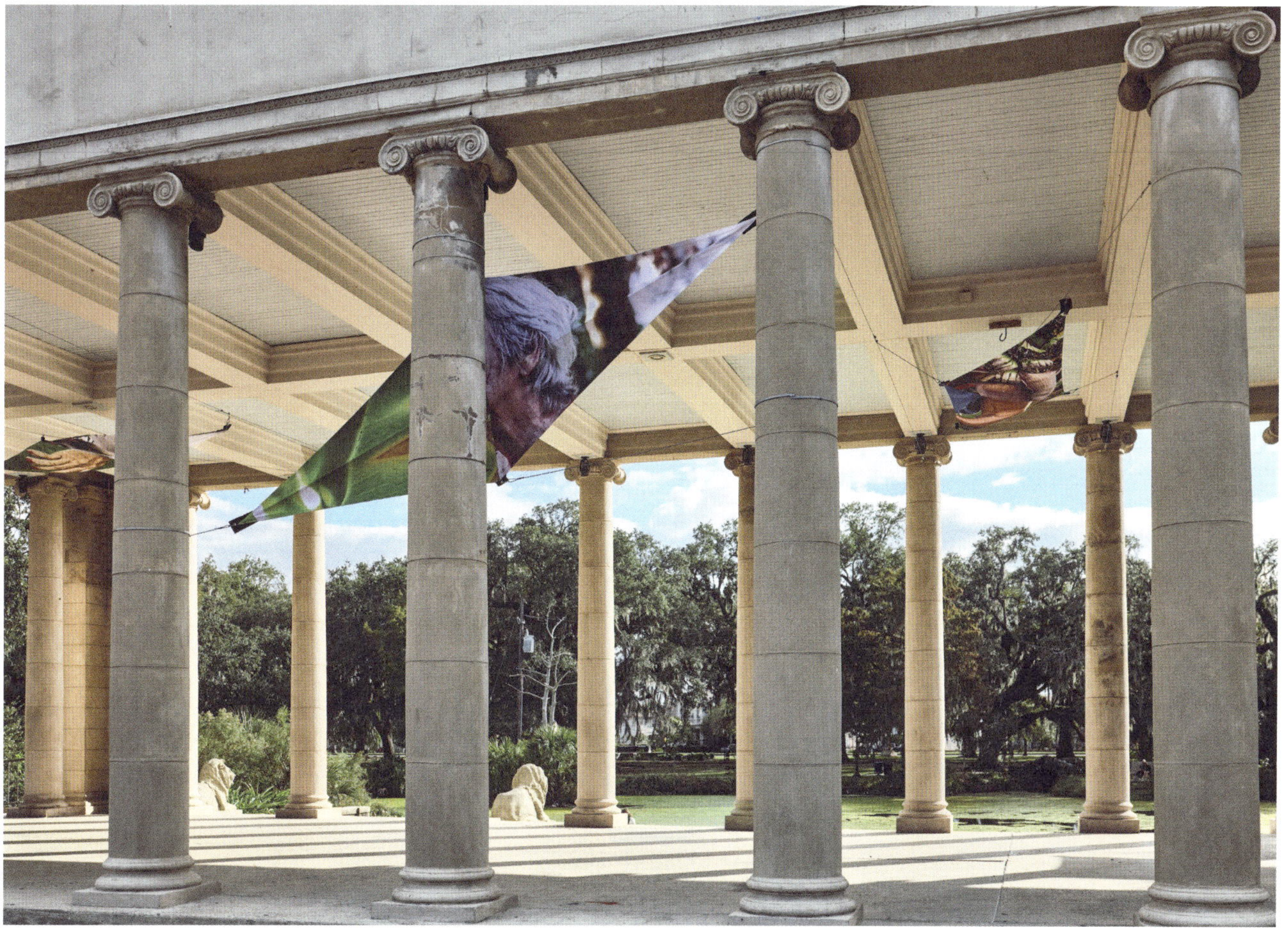

Top: *Birds of Paradise*, 2024 (detail)   Above: *Birds of Paradise*, 2024

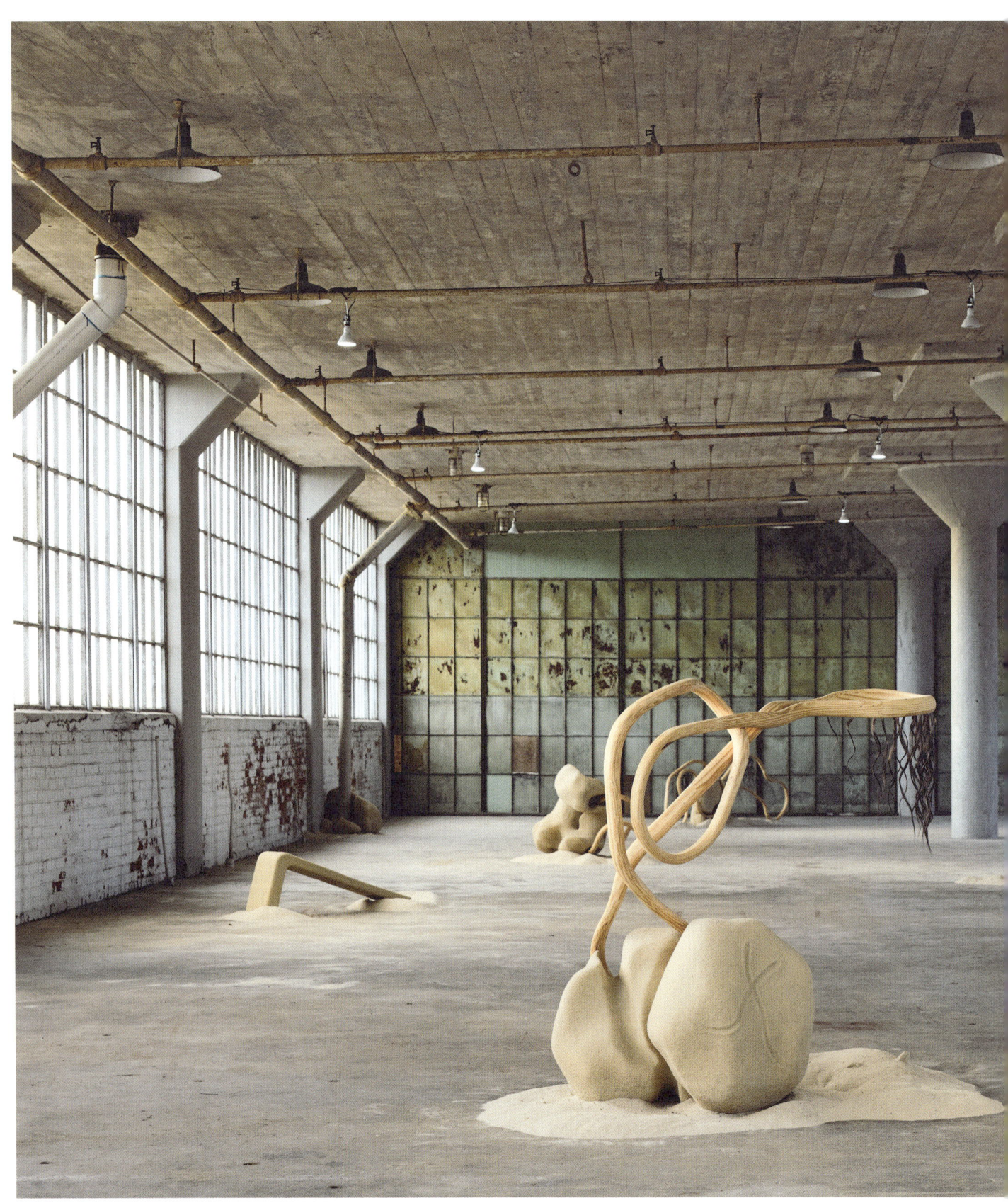

1,001,532 CE, 2023–2024

Blas Isasi

b. 1981, Lima, Peru; lives in New Orleans, LA

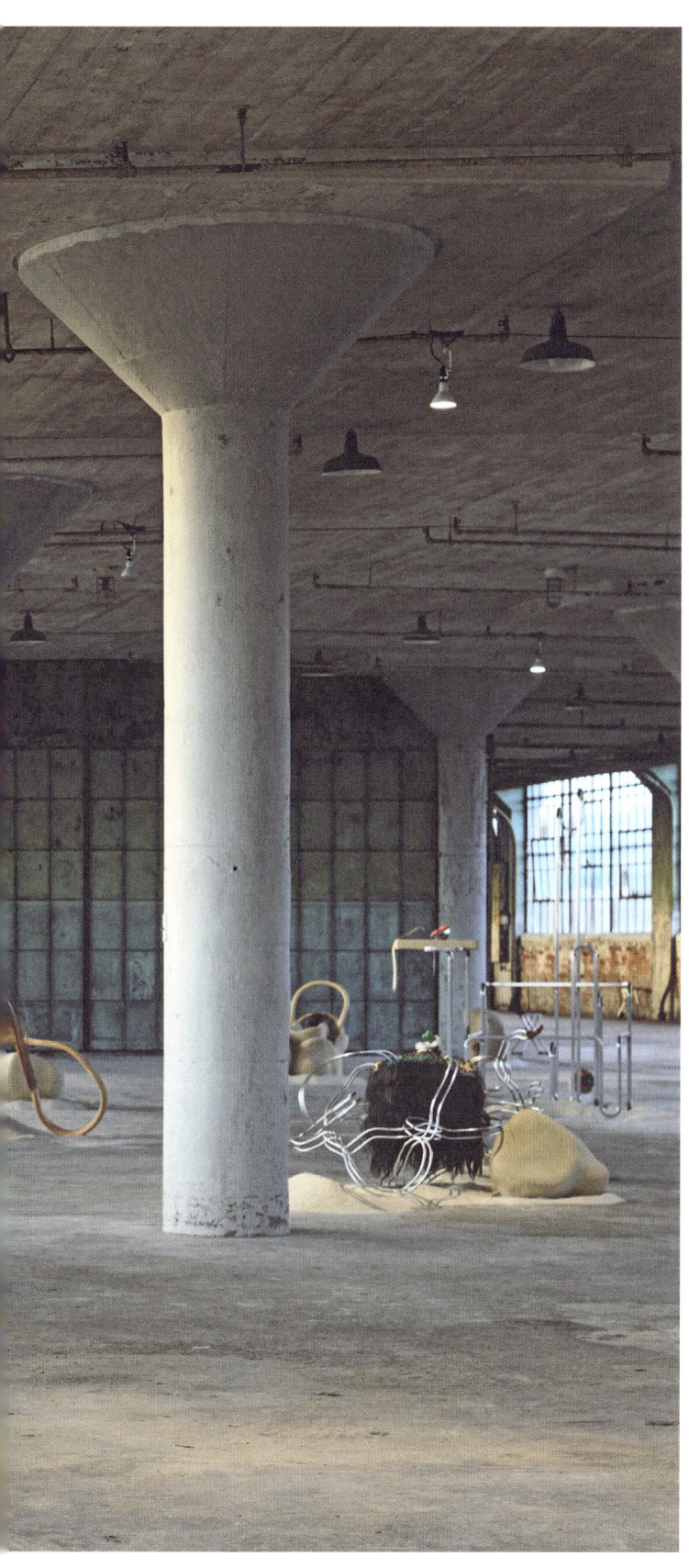

Blas Isasi's project for Prospect.6 stages a clash of conflicting cosmologies to model the intertwinement of land, bodies, and deep time in the ongoing processes of empire. Influenced by the cultural and geographical landscape and rich archaeological sites of his native Peru, Isasi's work is invested in the particular aesthetics of desert ecologies. After graduating from the Pontificia Universidad Católica del Perú and developing a practice as a photorealist painter, Isasi's postgraduate studies at Tulane University and the Jan van Eyck Academie introduced him to the posthumanist turn in Western philosophy. Isasi recognized that animistic epistemologies and traditions in places like Peru—where objects, materials, and nature have traditionally been understood to be invested with spiritual energy akin to human beings—predated Western civilization's "new materialisms" by thousands of years. This led to the development of a sculptural practice inspired by Peruvian traditions, including labor intensive and time consuming practices of weaving, carving, and wood joinery.

Isasi's installation for P.6 stems from his ongoing research into the so-called Battle of Cajamarca, the bloody massacre that followed first contact between the Spanish and Inca and prompted the collapse of the pre-Columbian civilization of Peru, which had dominated

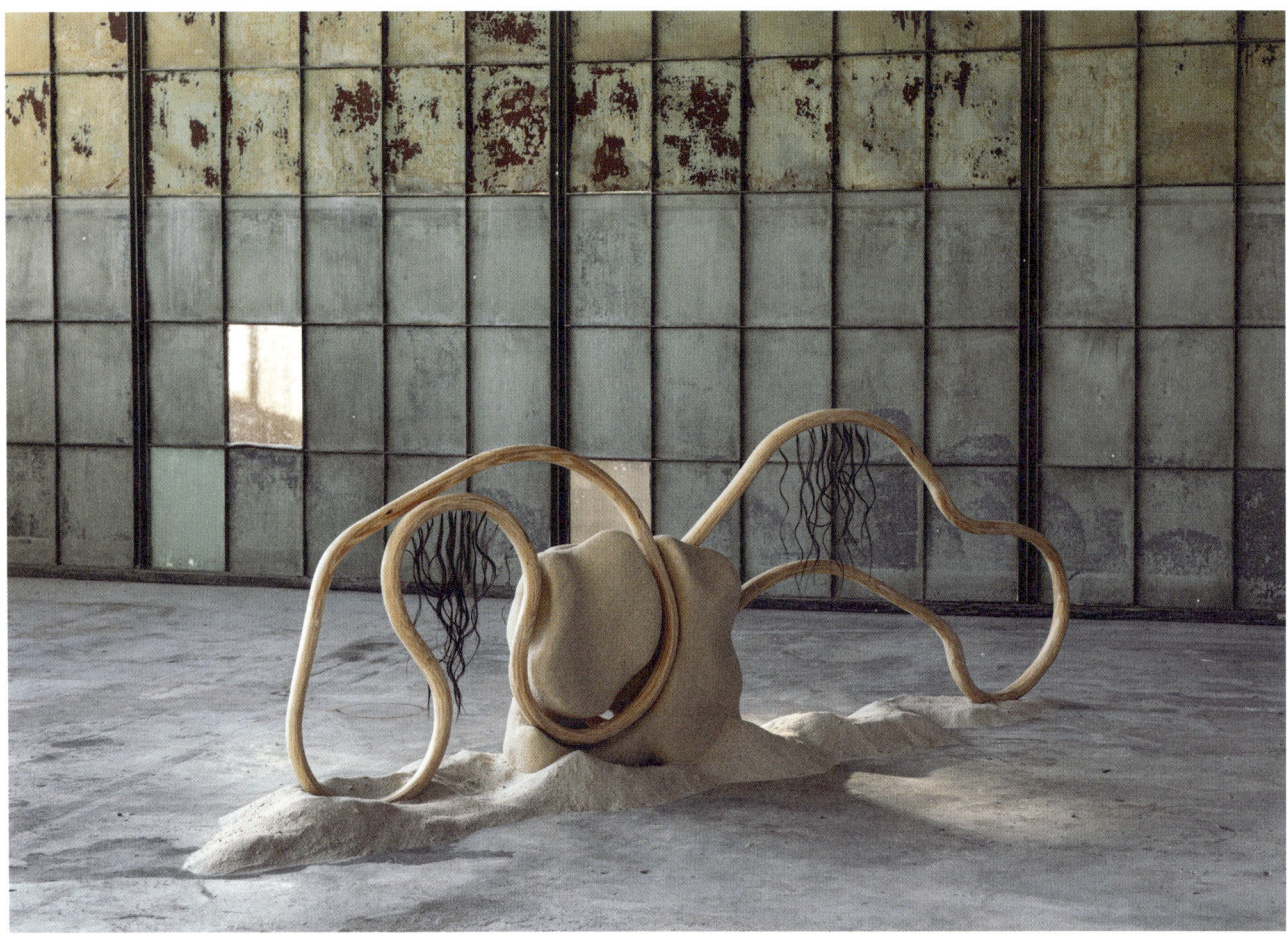

Andean South America for the preceding century. The Spanish victory granted the empire access to the silver and mercury mines that would become central to the Spanish colonial economy, fueling European colonization across the continent. Today, the Battle of Cajamarca is commemoratively reenacted by very remote communities in Peru's highlands, where it is cyclically re-performed and reframed to address the specific political concerns of the day. Its meaning, in other words, has been retooled and reinterpreted for centuries.

Inca cosmology traditionally conceived of time in half-millennium cycles; the conclusion of every 500-year cycle brings some kind of catastrophic, world-ending event. Counting forward from the Cajamarca Massacre, the current such cycle will come to a close in 2032. Isasi's project for Prospect.6, titled *1,001,532 CE* (2023–2024), sets the atmosphere for that moment to come, reimagining and re-staging the battle one million years after it occurred. Collapsing human histories and ontologies into a hallucinatory, posthuman landscape, *1,001,532 CE* crafts a poetic and symbolic account of the Battle of Cajamarca's ongoing ramifications.

Isasi's metabiotic forms meld organic, synthetic, and aggregate materials: powder-coated chrome tubes; branches made from bent, laminated pine, composed using joinery techniques to appear continuous; protrusions of hair and bodily appendages; and sculptures made from colorful Plastilina, a modeling clay that Isasi augments with added wax and paraffin. The Plastilina sculptures are a small but central element, merging Peru's three main landscapes—its coastal desert, the Andean mountain range, and the Amazon rainforest—into a swirling, composite topology. These sculptures, interspersed across an archipelago of sand islands, appear to grow like fungal blooms, at once suggesting chimerical bodies and a holistic, synthetic landscape. *1,001,532 CE* navigates the para-historical echoes of the Battle of Cajamarca, merging postcolonial critique with a speculative, posthuman geography to offer a visionary reflection on the cyclical nature of history and its future ramifications.

by Ian Wallace

1,001,532 CE, 2023–2024 (detail)

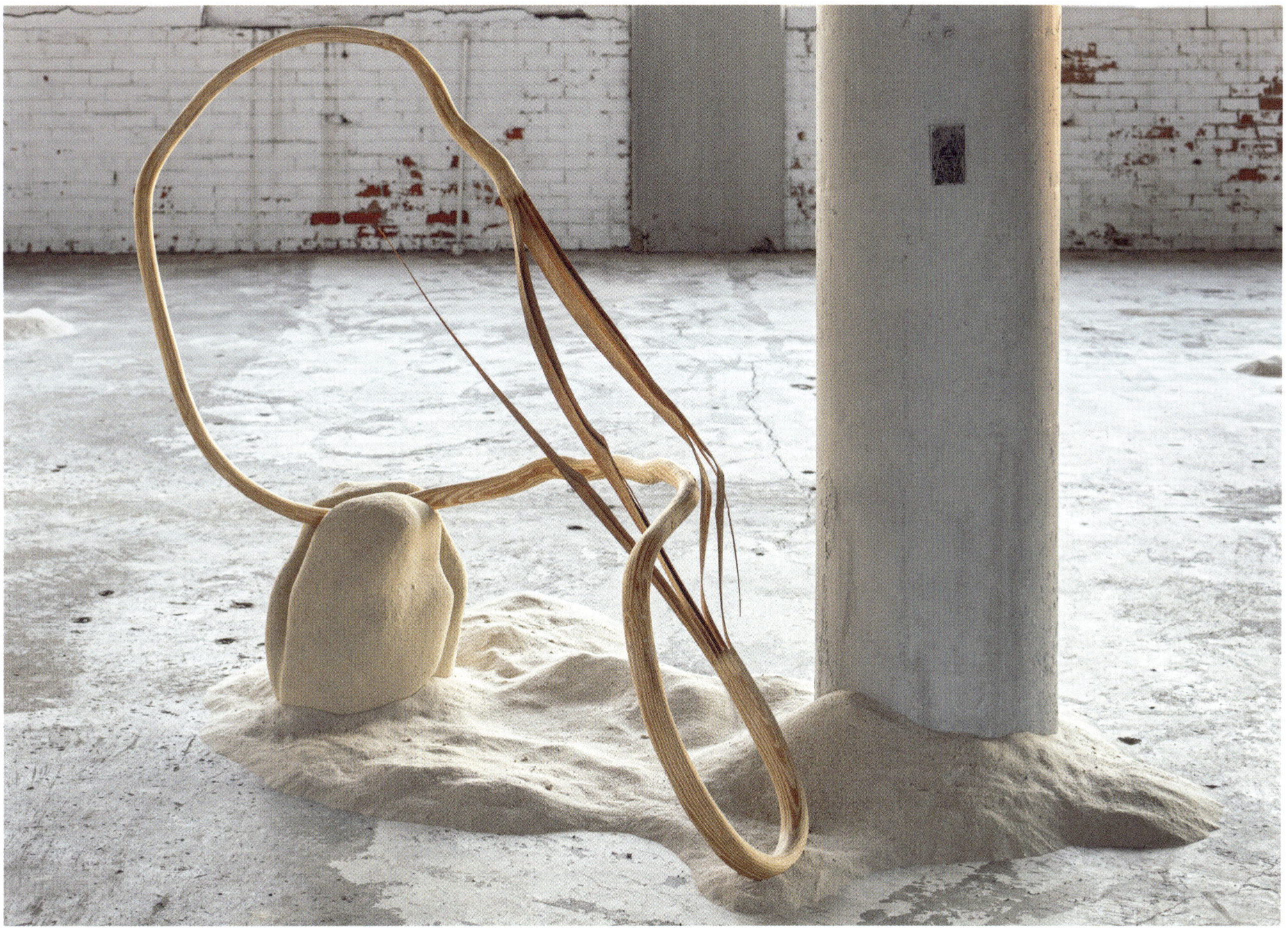

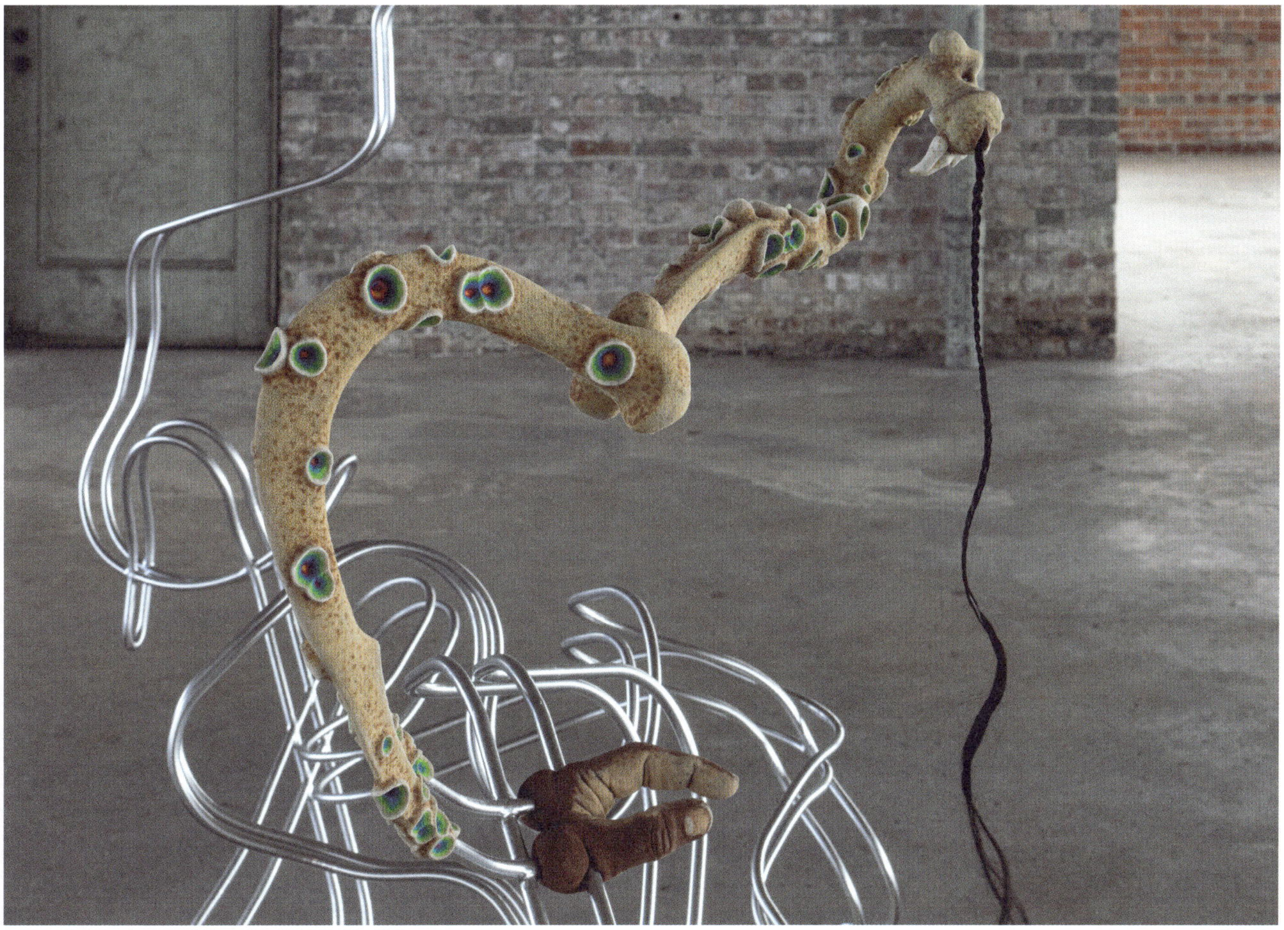

1,001,532 CE, 2023–2024 (details)

Deborah Jack

b. 1970, Rotterdam, Netherlands; lives in Cole Bay, St. Maarten
and Jersey City, NJ

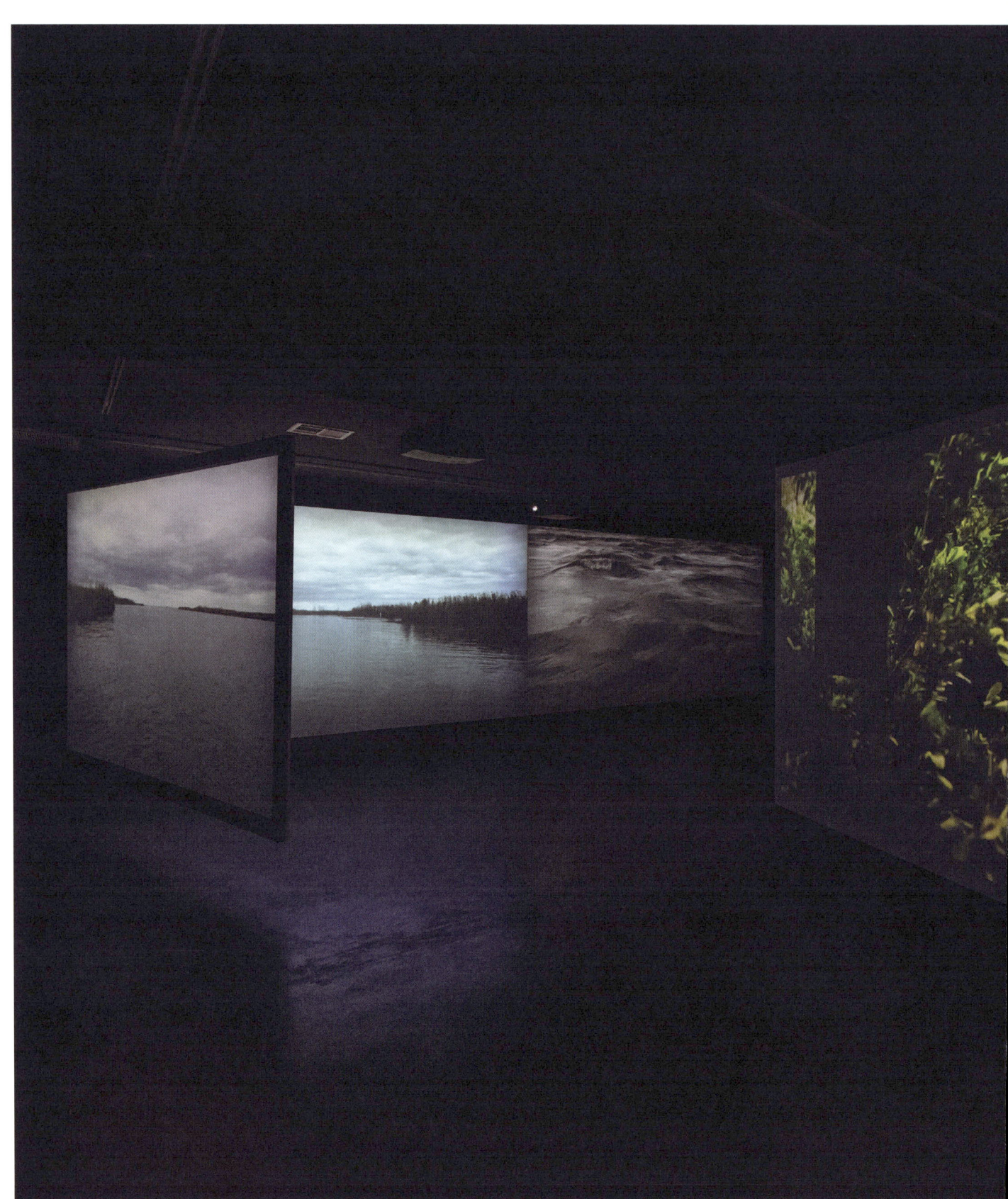

*a sea desalts, creeping in the collapse...in the expanse...a
rhizome looks for reason...whispers an elegy instead*, 2024

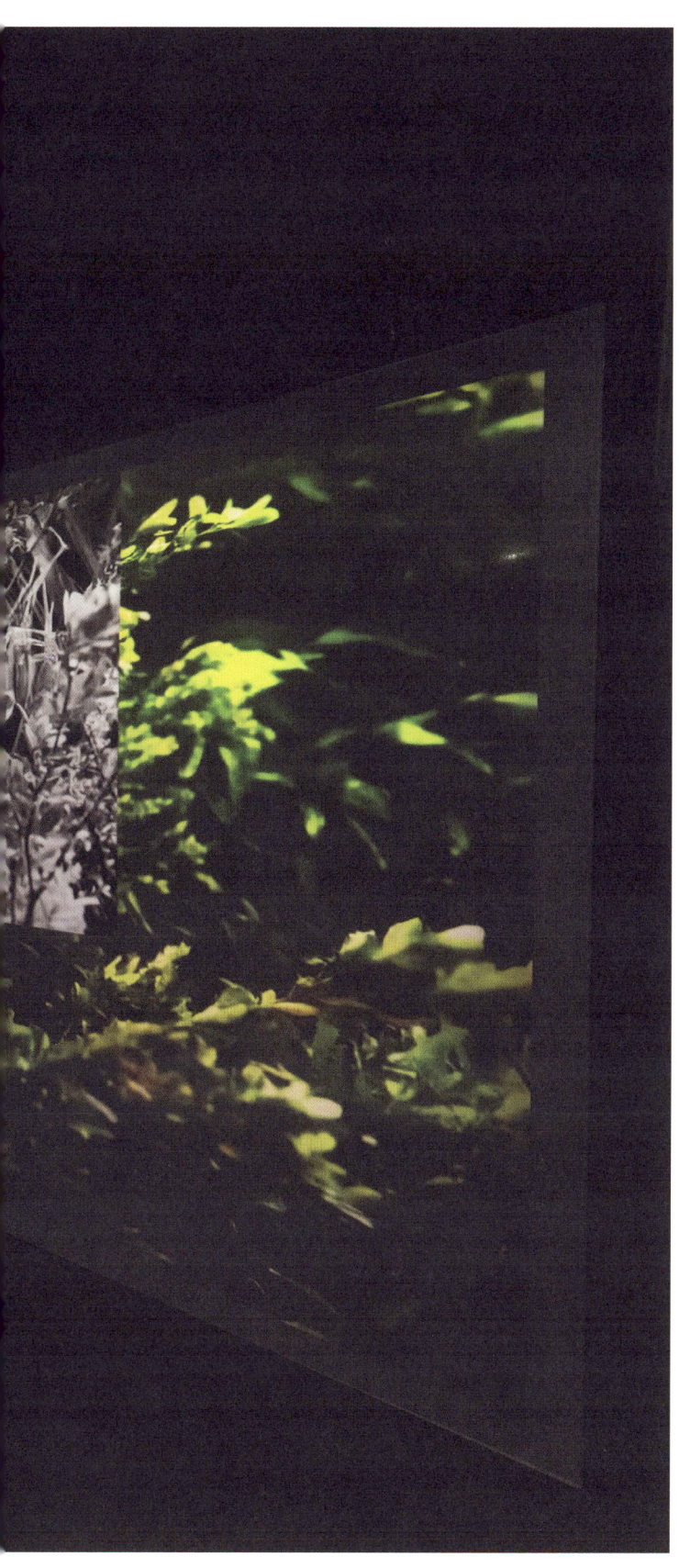

We speak first in the immediate aftermath of Hurricane Beryl, a Category 5 storm that narrowly spared her island of St. Maarten, and mine of Martinique too. She speculates about the number of times her home has surrendered its roof to the wind, having recurrently experienced the "destruction of everything I have." As if the valve that is her mouth has been temporarily replaced by a fountain through which her land can speak and spill, I realize this is an artist who means it with all her breath when she says "you can come out the other side of that"—the "you" here refracting beyond her own body and encapsulating a collectivity that is vulnerable to the sweeping whims of the twinned melodramas that are capitalism and its geological brainchild, the climate crisis.

Deborah Jack's contribution to Prospect.6, a sprawling video-based installation, sutures together footage of St. Maarten's mangroves, as well as topographies adjacent to New Orleans— including Lake Peigneur, Neptune Pass, and Quarantine Bay—and the coastline of York, Maine, all of which sing to one another across the tides of their shared inheritance. These are sites where the protective zones meant to keep unruly waters at bay have decayed, including

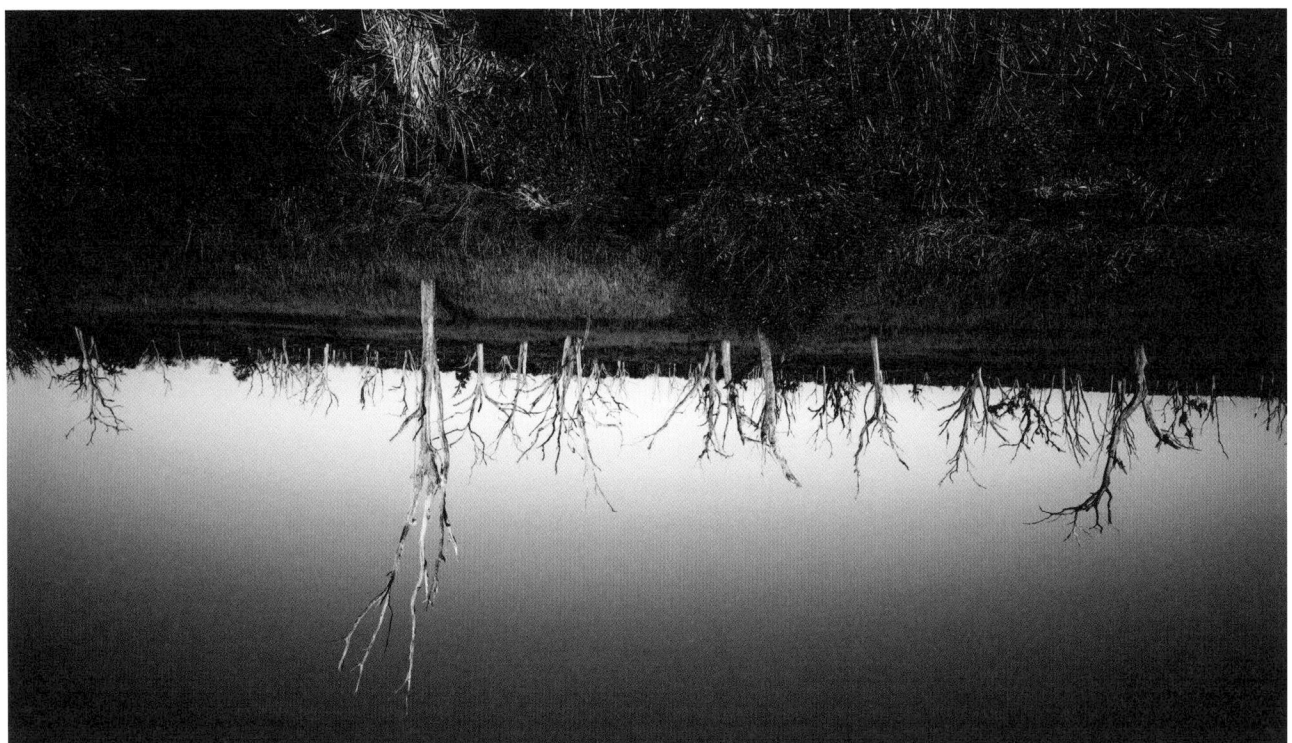

a mangrove in the case of St. Maarten, and the fickle, purposely neglected levee system that left New Orleans to flood in 2005. Also present are sites where the land has retaliated against human intervention, as in the case of Lake Peigneur, which formed as a result of a failed oil drilling operation, and the Gulf of Maine, which is warming at a rate triple the global average. Together, the images coalesced here prompt a consideration of how the land itself practices repair in the wake of erosion.

Jack and I speak from within the unrelenting crucible that is a Caribbean summer, during a time of year when the heat is implacable. We talk about how it deprives the air of humor and demands a recurrent surrender to an ever-pulsating sun. The sensory overwhelm of such weather is mirrored in Jack's installation strategy. Reaching across an architectural arrangement of six screens, the artist creates a condition of envelopment that harmonizes with the sweltering heat, raucous winds, and the imperial histrionics our islands have been subjected to. We might consider, then, the scale of this installation as a gesture of anti-erosion: accumulation as a means of repair.

This sensibility is felt acutely through the score, which was composed and performed by Diaphanous Ensemble. It bubbles and rumbles like roots growing triumphantly in the water, like protective barriers resuscitating themselves. This notion of revivification is visually reflected back most poignantly through the footage of Neptune Pass and Quarantine Bay, and, in concert with the score, elucidate how the landscape continues to insist upon itself. Since 2019, Neptune Pass has widened by over seven hundred feet, sending sediment into the water and forming a delta that is more resistant to erosion. In Quarantine Bay, teardrop-shaped islands have formed and begun to grow grass. Alas, the land is insisting upon itself.

In this work, Jack offers us a trembling portrait of willful resurgence in the face of forced decay. Indeed, a tear descends from the eye of the storm, plummets languidly down its cheek, and ordains the earth below in the shape of exalted endurance—all the while, our archipelago nods in ferocious agreement. *We will not be disappeared*.

by Camille Bacon

a sea desalts, creeping in the collapse...in the expanse... a rhizome looks for reason...whispers an elegy instead, 2024 (video still)

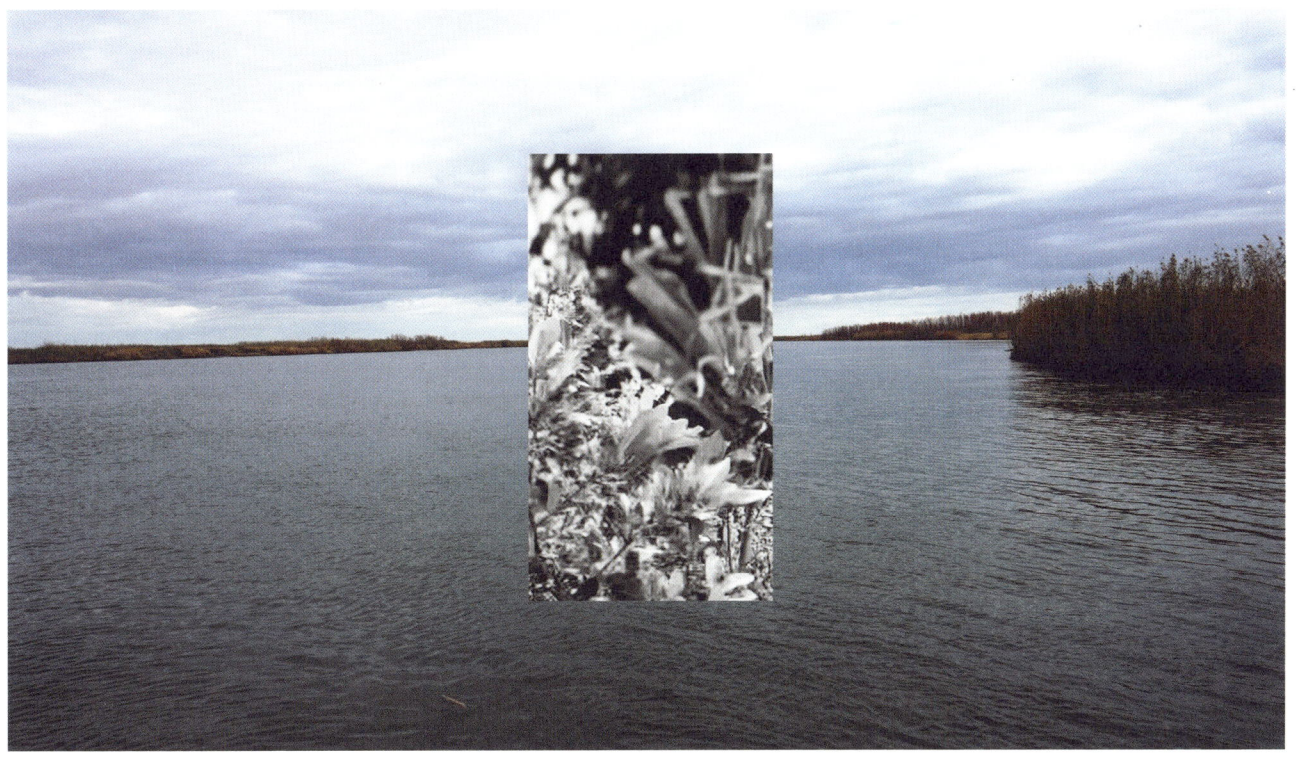

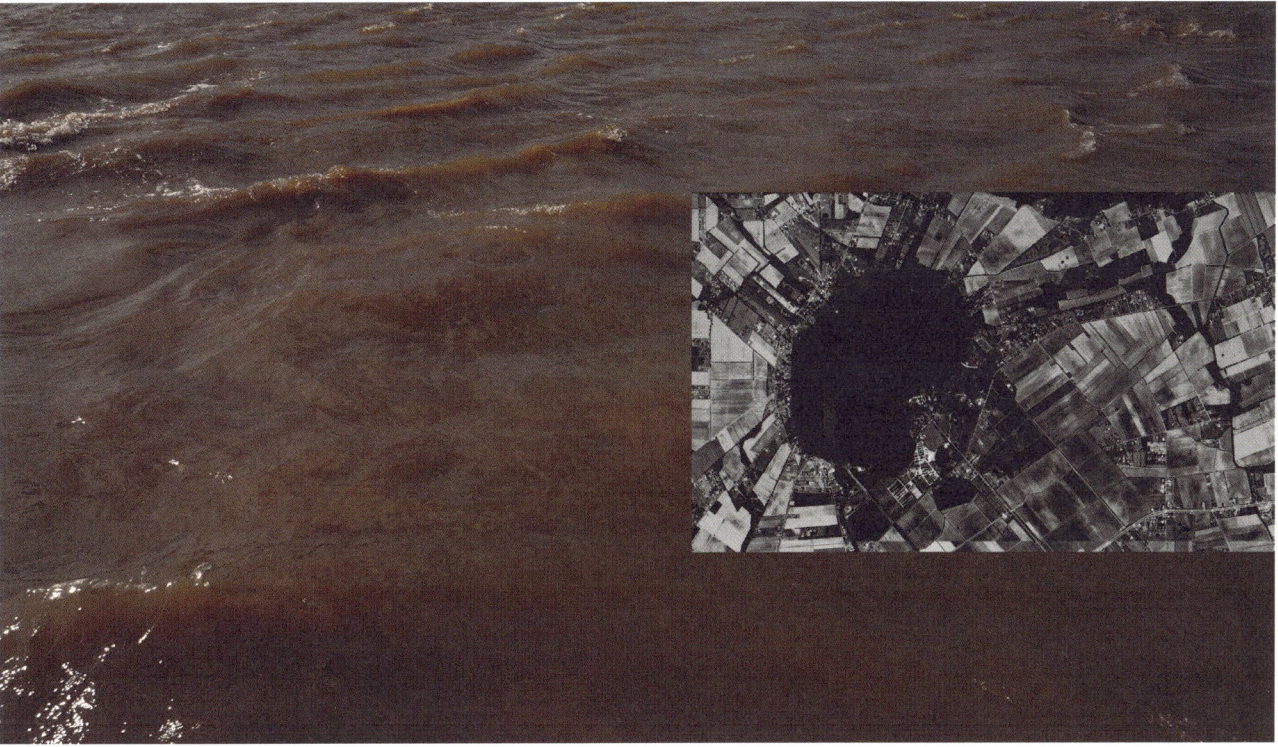

a sea desalts, creeping in the collapse...in the expanse...
a rhizome looks for reason...whispers anelegy instead,
2024 (video stills)

Eisa Jocson   Venuri Perera

Magic Maids, started in 2022, is a collaborative performance between artists Eisa Jocson and Venuri Perera that draws from research into the connections between the real histories of witchcraft and domestic servitude. Jocson, born in the Philippines, has been developing research in dance, performance, and audiovisual production related to notions of physicality and subalternity, including gender and the otherness created by immigration. Meanwhile, Perera, born in Sri Lanka, researches ways her body can be used to question gender roles using public space, create tension between class positions, and explore recent colonial histories in the region.

For the sixth edition of Prospect, the artists continued the project while doing a residency together in Basel, Switzerland. As the title suggests, it revolves around two major research interests: Firstly, the many narratives

Magic Maids, 2024

b. 1986, Manila, Philippines; lives in La Union, Philippines (EJ)
b. 1981, Colombo, Sri Lanka; lives in Amsterdam, Netherlands (VP)

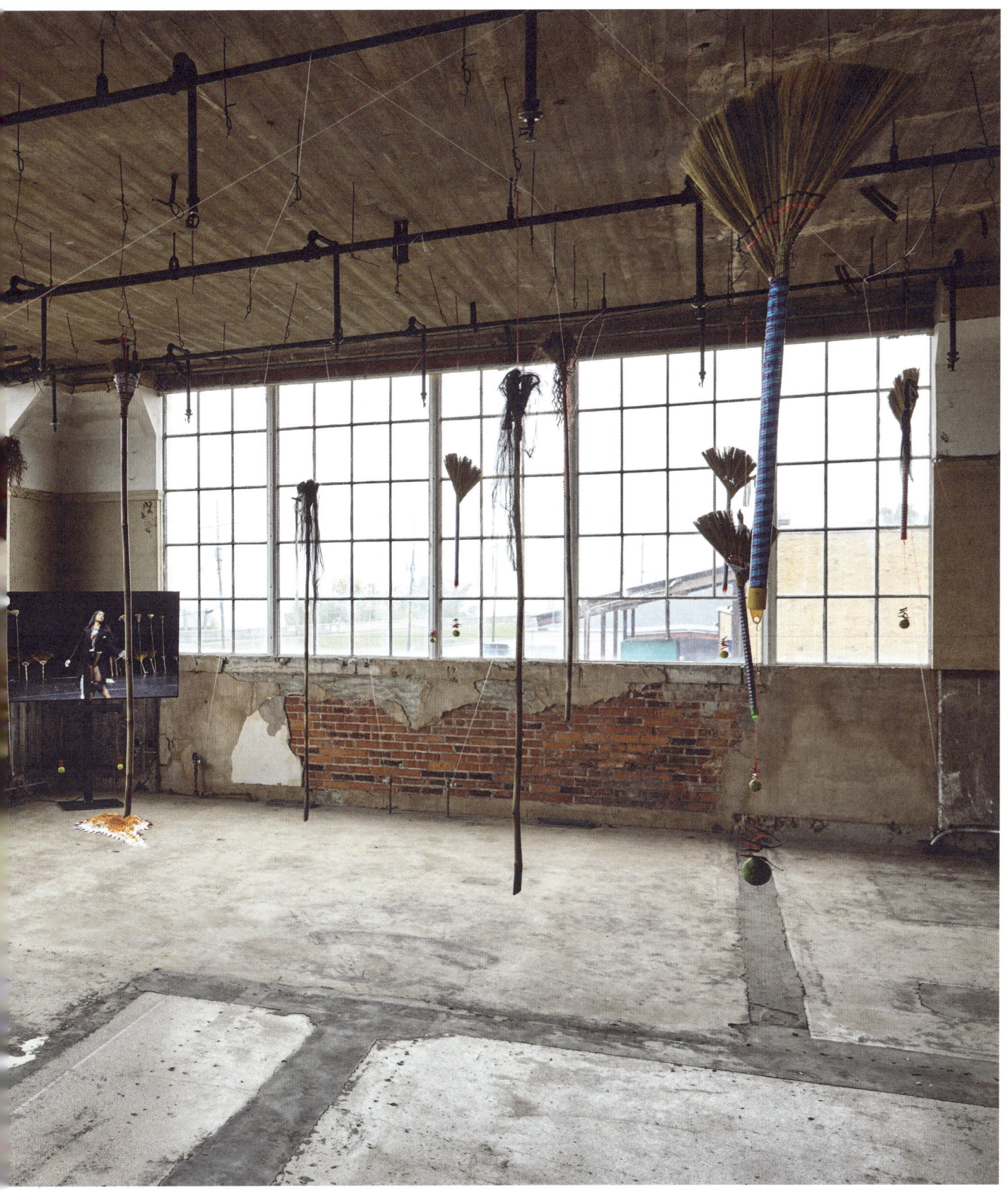

of women and witchcraft in Europe, where witch trials started in the fifteenth century. Secondly, the performance articulates the histories of non-White women from the Global South, and their migrations to work as domestic helpers in territories of the hegemonic North (and in the homes of the upper classes in their own countries).

There is an object that connects these two research interests: the broom. In *Magic Maids*, the object is used as an extension of the artists' bodies. Often held between their legs, its phallic aspect becomes a simultaneous exercise in eroticism and subversion. The broom that cleans the floor and makes circular movements is the same one that, in the audience's imagination, is used to take flight and warn of unknown territories—as in many popular culture images of witches. In this performance piece, the broom is also reduced to an element that at times borders on nonsense. Sometimes it is thrown into a corner from the artists' thighs and legs, other times it is an accessory used for quick gestures that refer to the notion of possession.

Existing between the sacred and the profane, between contemporary culture and the history of literal witch hunts worldwide, Jocson and Perera play with the spectator's imagination and, through their bodies, invite us to expand this interpretive background. Echoes of the performance can be observed in the United States, and New Orleans as well: the Salem witch trials of the seventeenth century, and the history of non-White bodies using brooms in servitude. As the provocative title of the works suggests, from their perspective, every maid needs a bit of magic to make life more dreamlike. Fabulation is an essential form of resistance.

by Raphael Fonseca

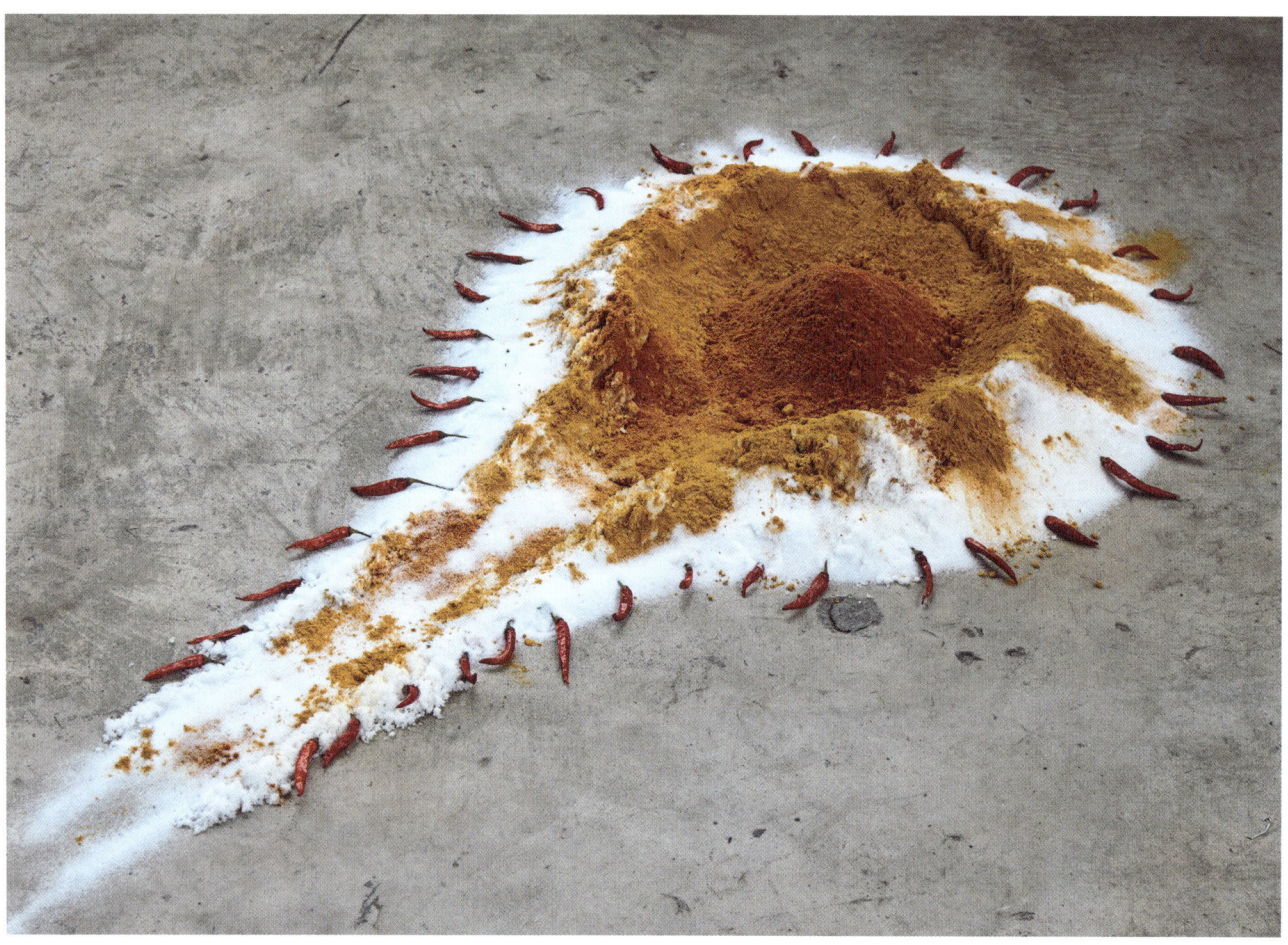

Magic Maids, 2024 (detail)

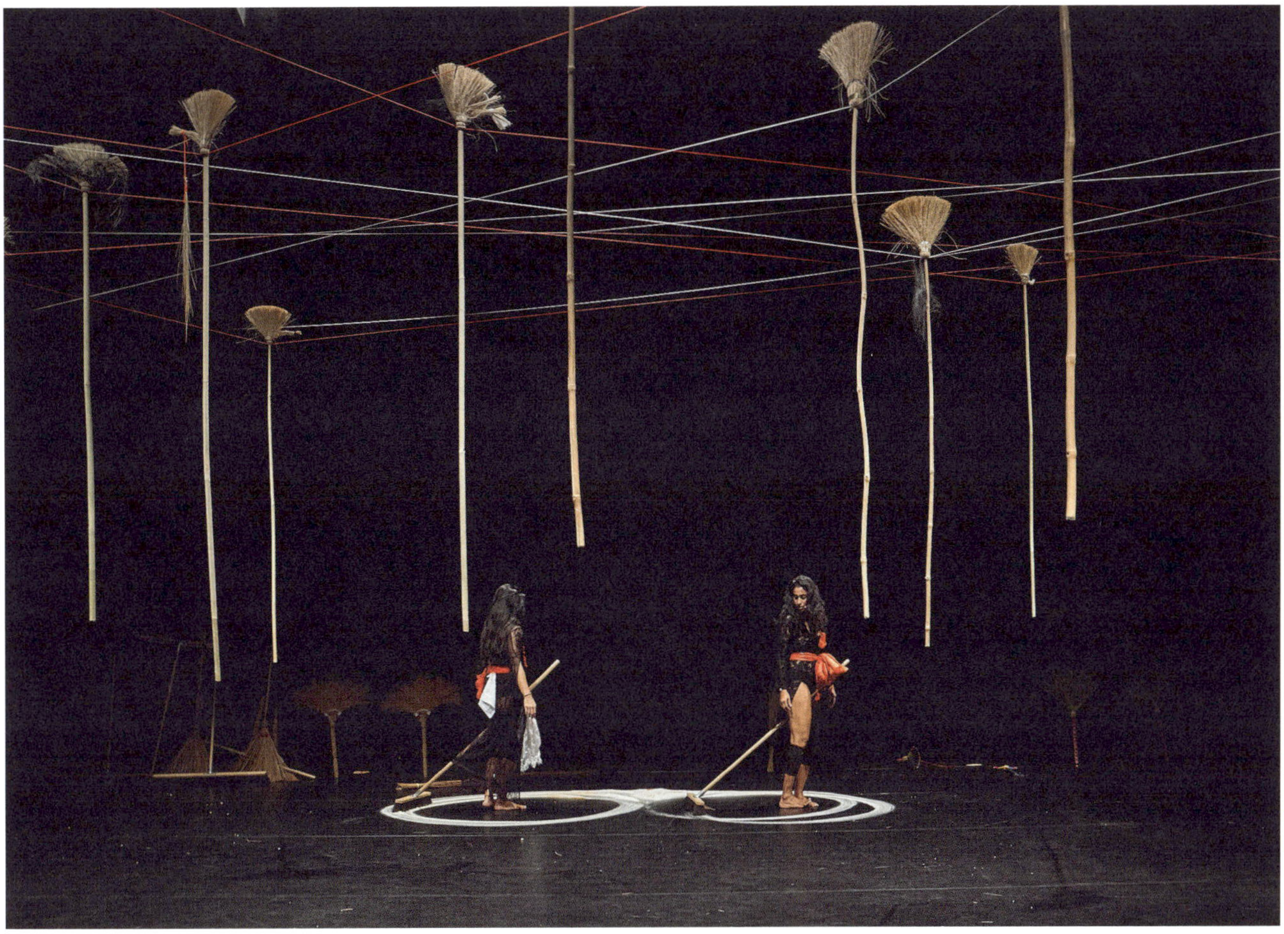

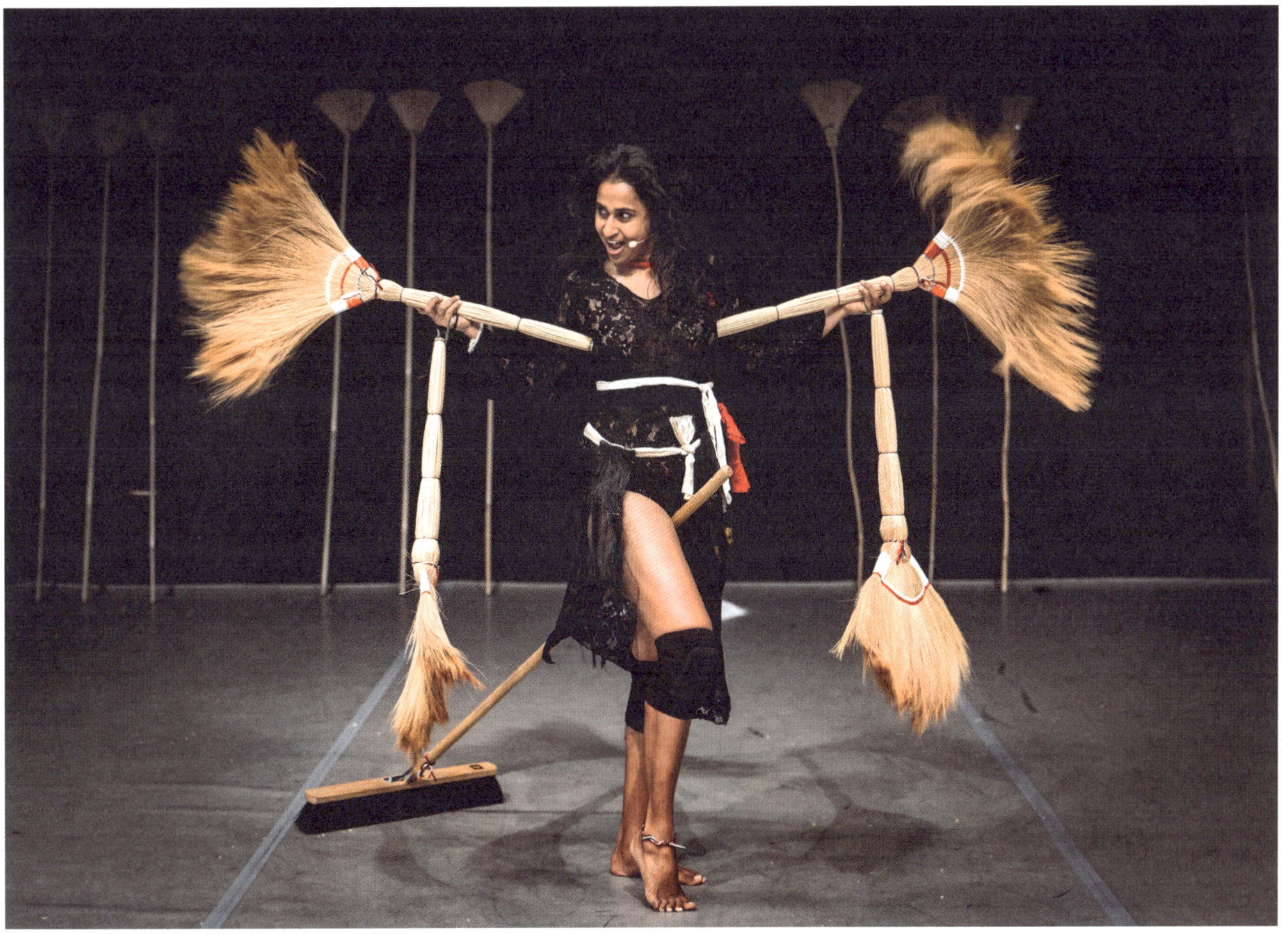

Top: *Magic Maids*, 2024. Performance documentation,
Künstler*innenhaus Mousonturm, Frankfurt

Above: *Magic Maids*, 2024. Performance documentation,
Esplanade—Theatres on the Bay, Singapore

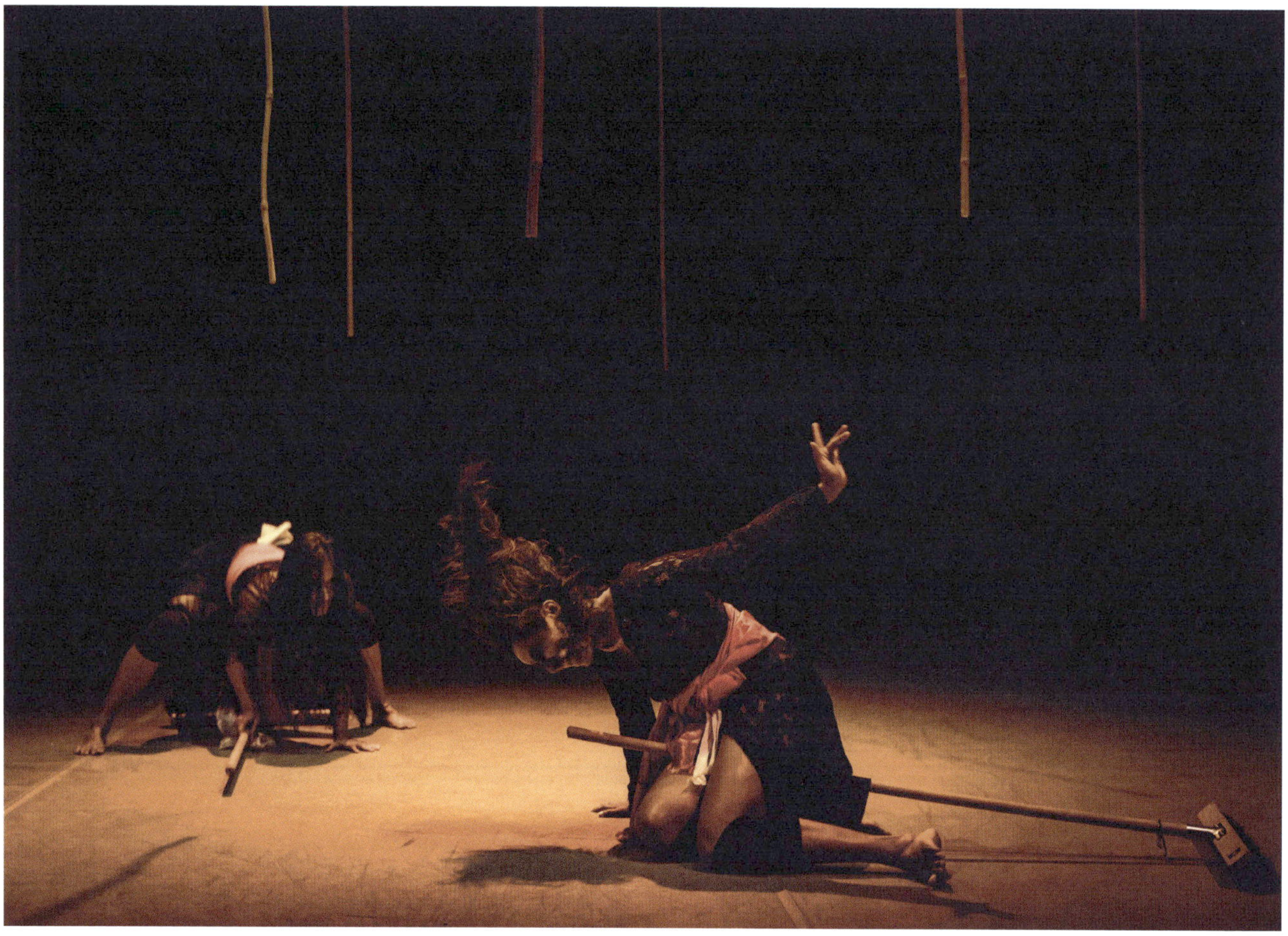

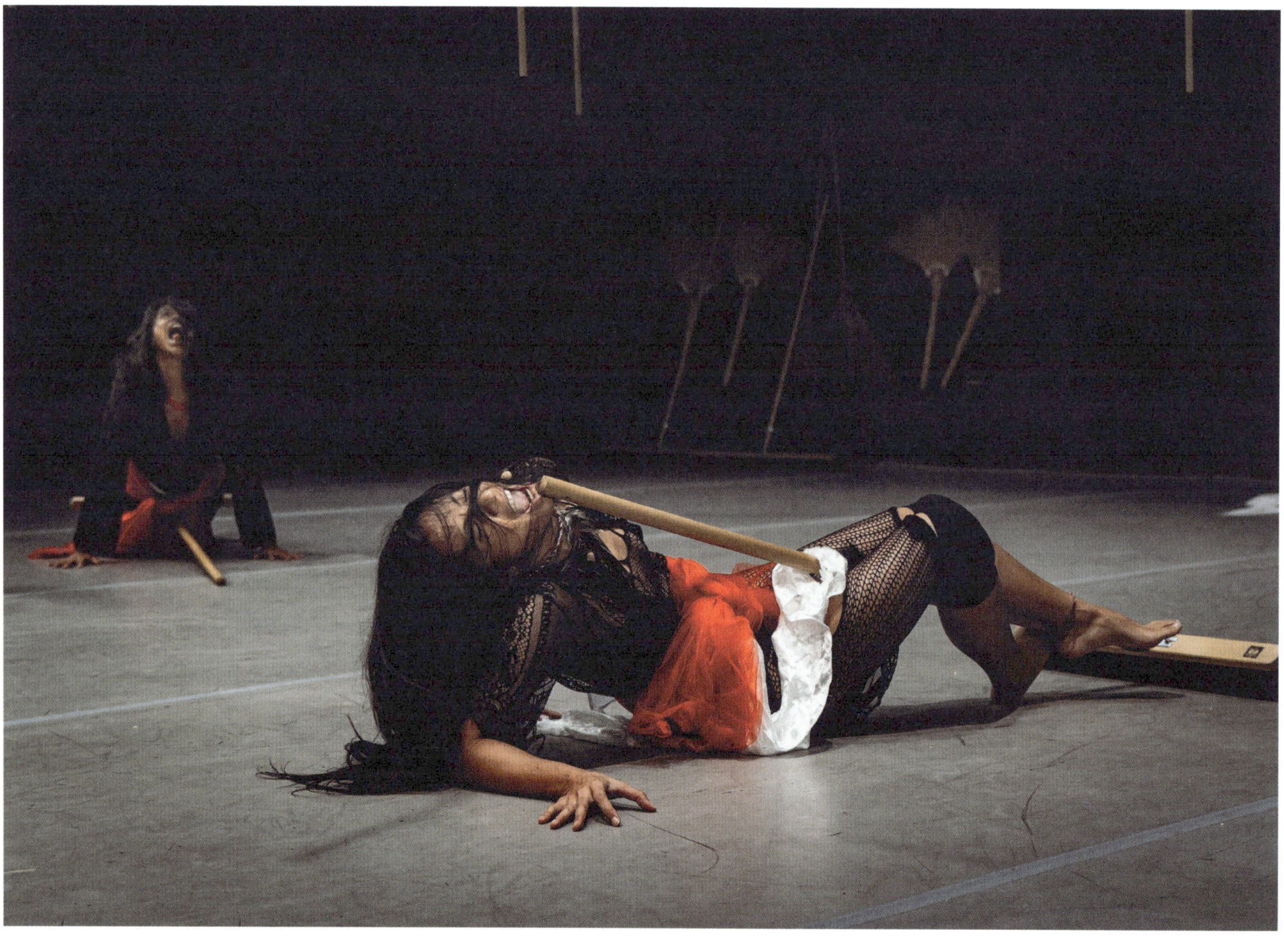

Magic Maids, 2024. Performance documentation,
Esplanade—Theatres on the Bay, Singapore

Joan Jonas

b. 1936, New York, NY; lives in New York, NY and Cape Breton, Nova Scotia

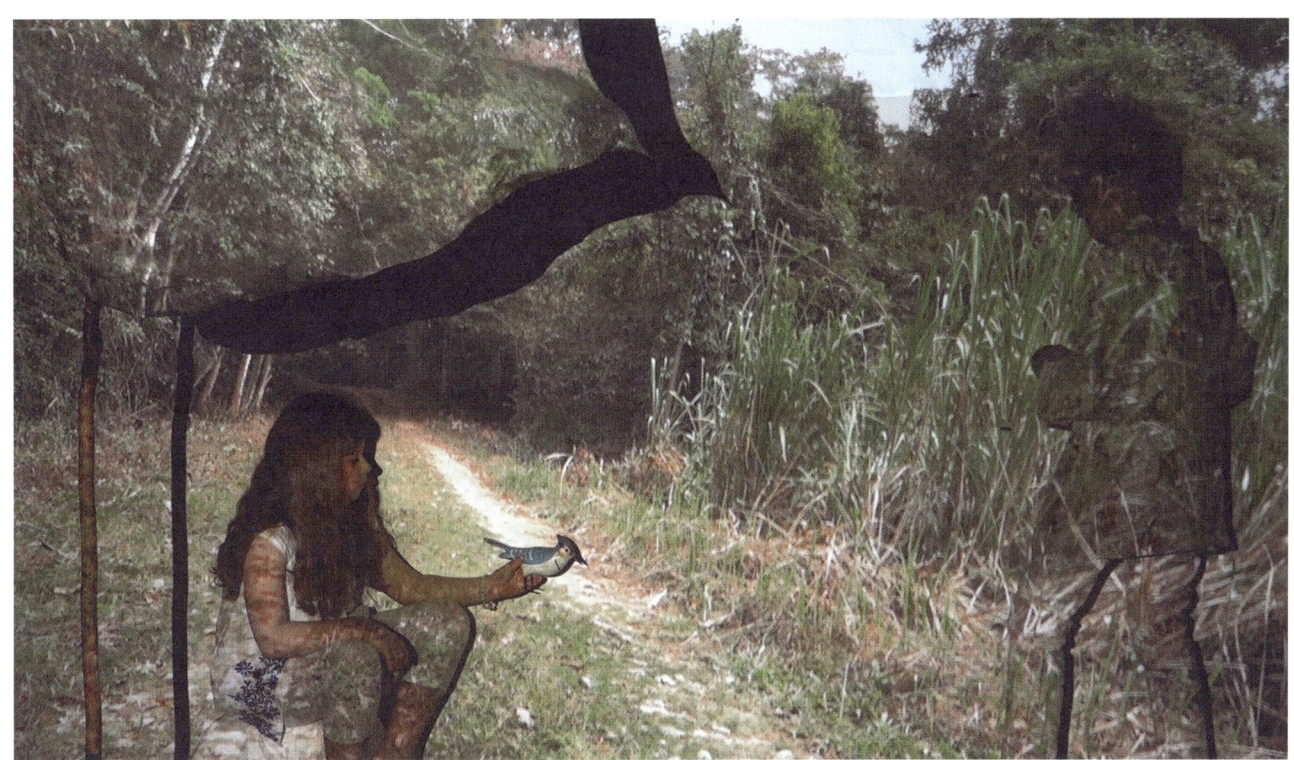

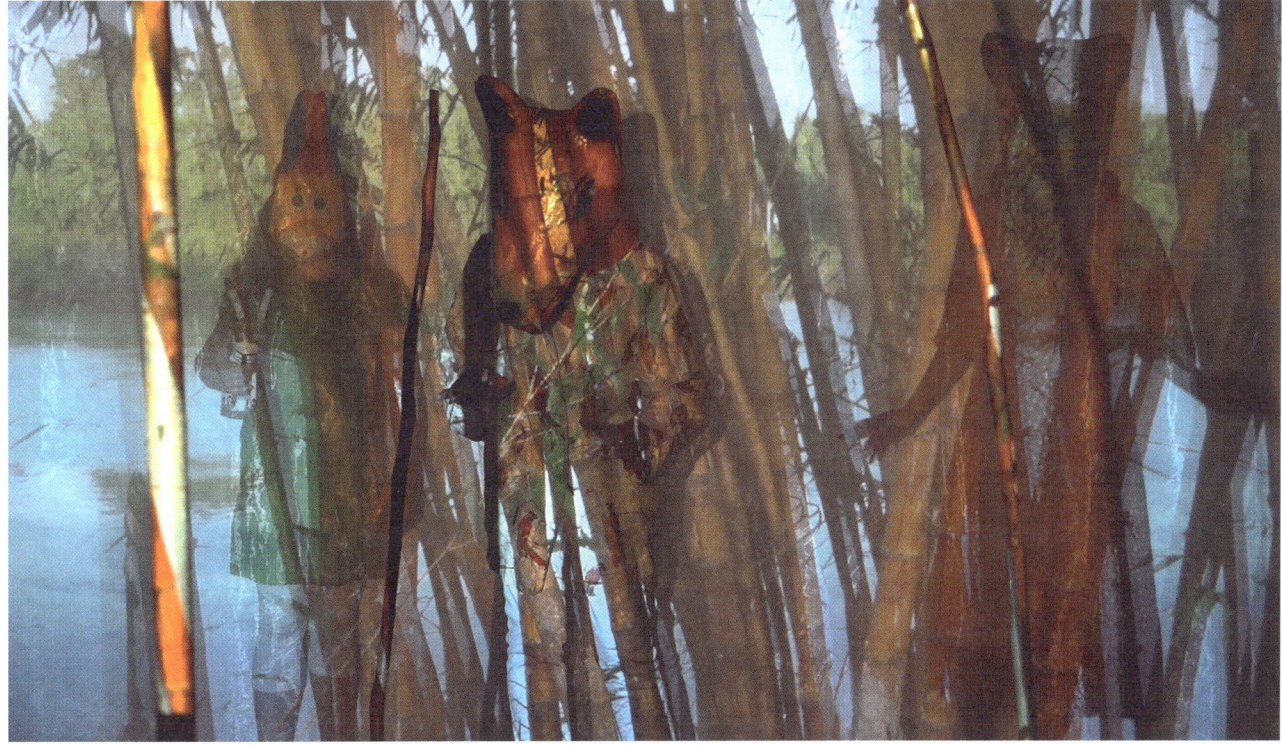

stream or river, flight or pattern III (Journey), 2016/2017
(video stills)

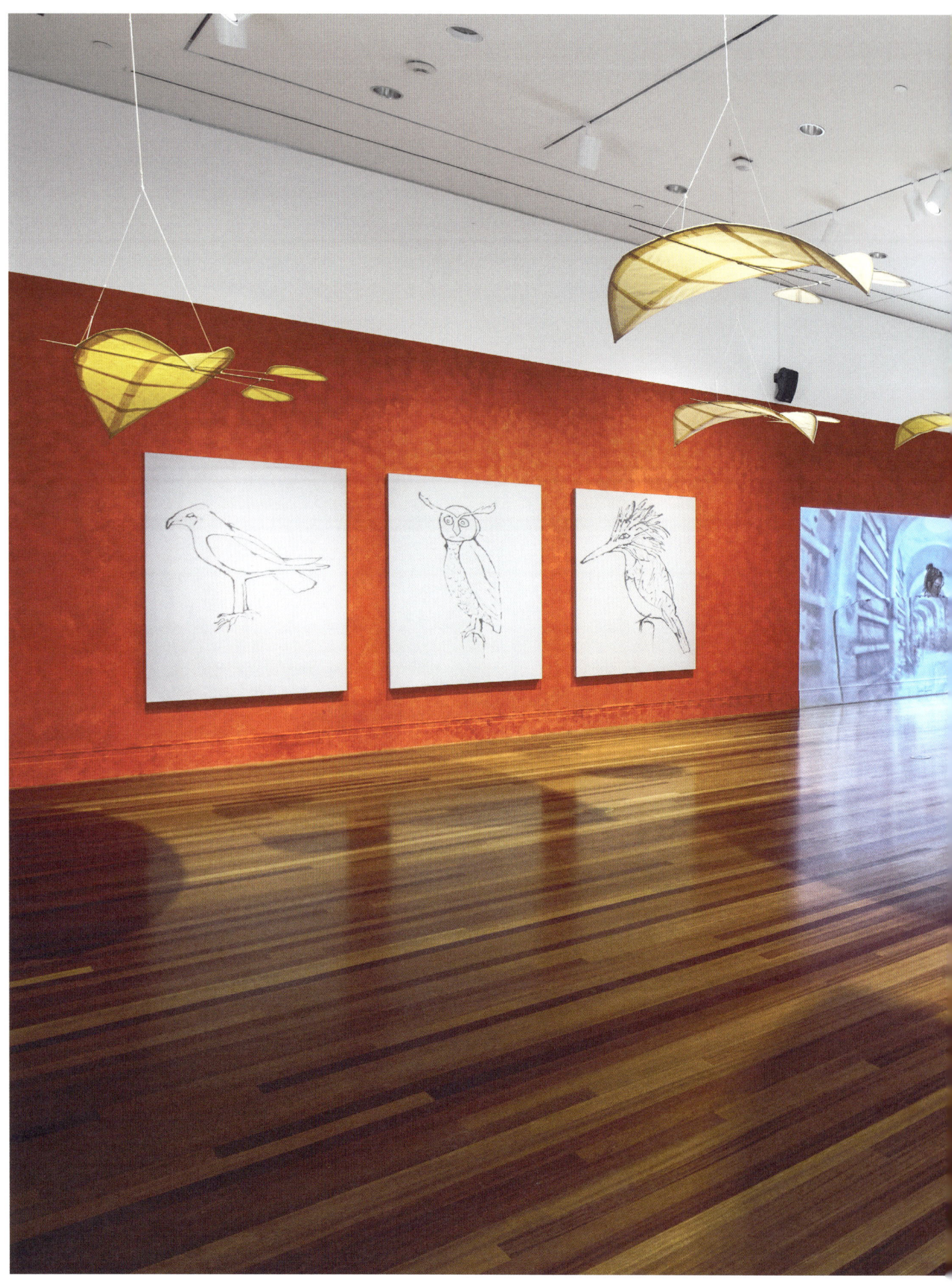

stream or river, flight or pattern III, 2016/2017

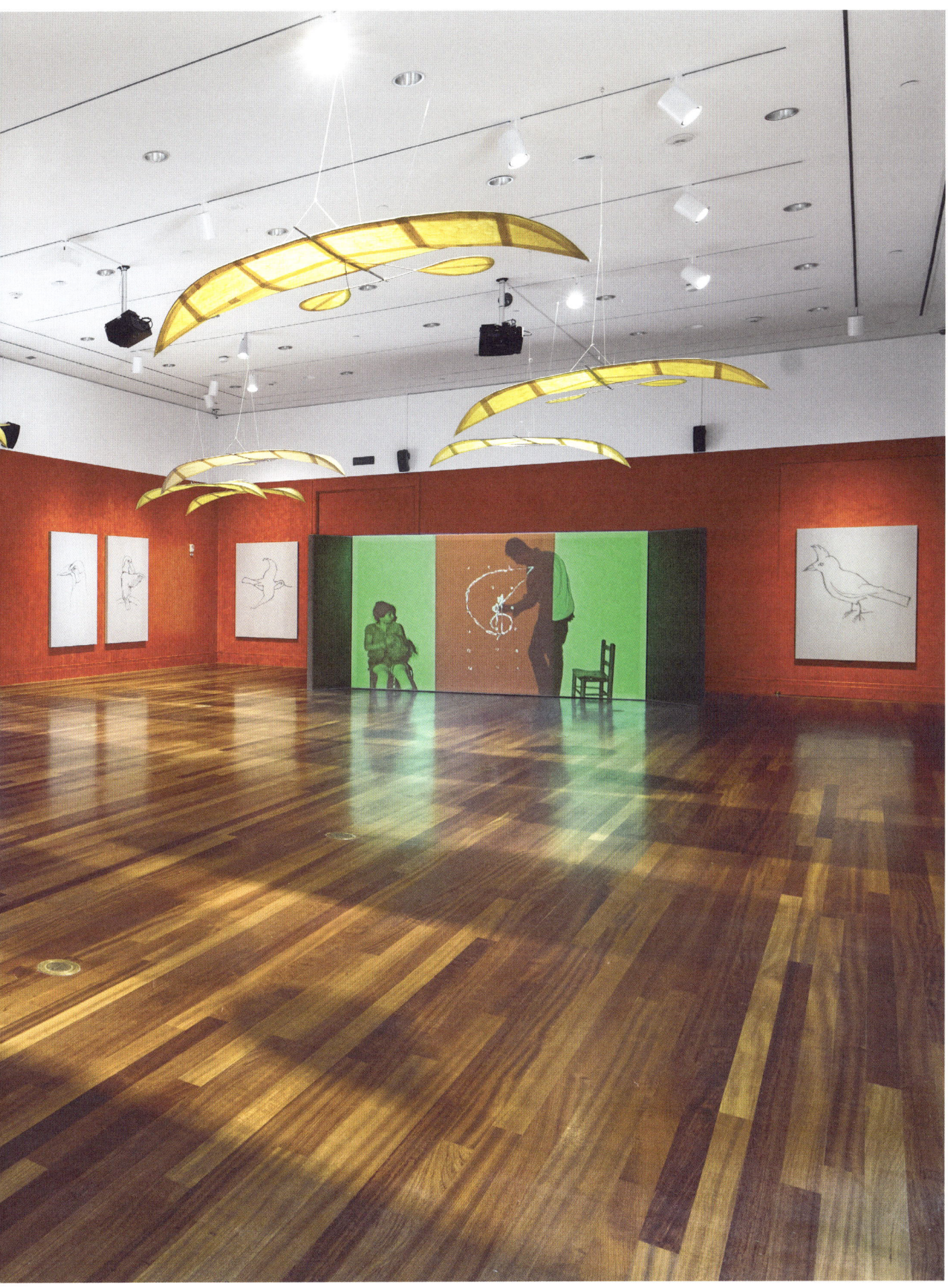

Widely regarded as a pioneer in performance and video art, Joan Jonas has profoundly transformed the ways artists engage with nonlinear narratives, nature, and the interplay of images and bodies in motion. Her work captures the ephemeral and the overlooked, drawing our attention to the delicate rhythms of the natural world while reimagining its fleeting qualities through her work. Interested in altered perceptions of spaces, Jonas's practice captures moments that feel timeless, yet remain tied to specific rhythms of nature and the human body. These influences emerge vividly in her use of layered projections, superimposed images, and recurring motifs that suggest cycles rather than conclusions. Her long-standing interest in Japanese Noh theater—a form characterized by its symbolic gestures, stylized movement, and expansive experience of time—subtly permeates her work. In Noh, temporalities coexist, allowing past, present, and future to intersect in a single gesture or performance.

At Prospect.6, *stream or river, flight or pattern III* (2016/2017) immerses audiences in Jonas's elemental world, where shadow and light, gesture and image, operate in a dance of interdependence. In the space, the viewer is invited to move through time and memory as though through a landscape, encountering Jonas's omnipresent touch—a continuous, shadowed thread of human and natural connection. The work weaves together large-scale drawings, suspended bird-shaped kites, and intricately layered video footage from diverse environments.

The installation integrates three video projections that traverse various landscapes. On one screen, projections of cityscapes and countryside views create a dynamic backdrop. Superimposed images introduce human shadows that interact with these shifting scenes, their movements forming a dialogue with the landscapes. These shadows transform, embodying humans, animals, and performers, often appearing to mimic or respond to the changing visual environment.

On another screen, video segments depict birds in their natural habitats alongside documentary footage of their behaviors in captivity. These are interwoven with the artist's hand-drawn sketches and scenes of flipping through sketchbooks and in-studio performances. These sequences are further layered with candid travel documentation from Jonas's journeys across California, Italy, Spain, Vietnam, Singapore, Cambodia, and her home in Nova Scotia. On the third screen, performers (including the artist) engage with props to animate the studio set in response to the projected images. In many of her projects, props play a pivotal role in guiding the performers' movements and enriching the narrative. Other frames in her work feature animals, cityscapes, and live drawings in nature by Jonas herself, punctuating the screen with travel logs, recorded performances, and observational footage.

The bird-like shapes suspended from the ceiling were created by sourcing delicate paper kites from a traditional kite-making village near Hanoi, Vietnam. Jonas painted and altered these kites by hand, transforming them into ethereal objects that challenge our perception of the relationship between sky and land, flying and grounded beings. At the core of her practice is the equal and active participation of living entities—animals, nature, and other actors. *stream or river, flight or pattern* challenges and expands our assumptions about the connections between these actors, inviting viewers to linger in a state of reflection and meaning-making.

by Daisy Desrosiers

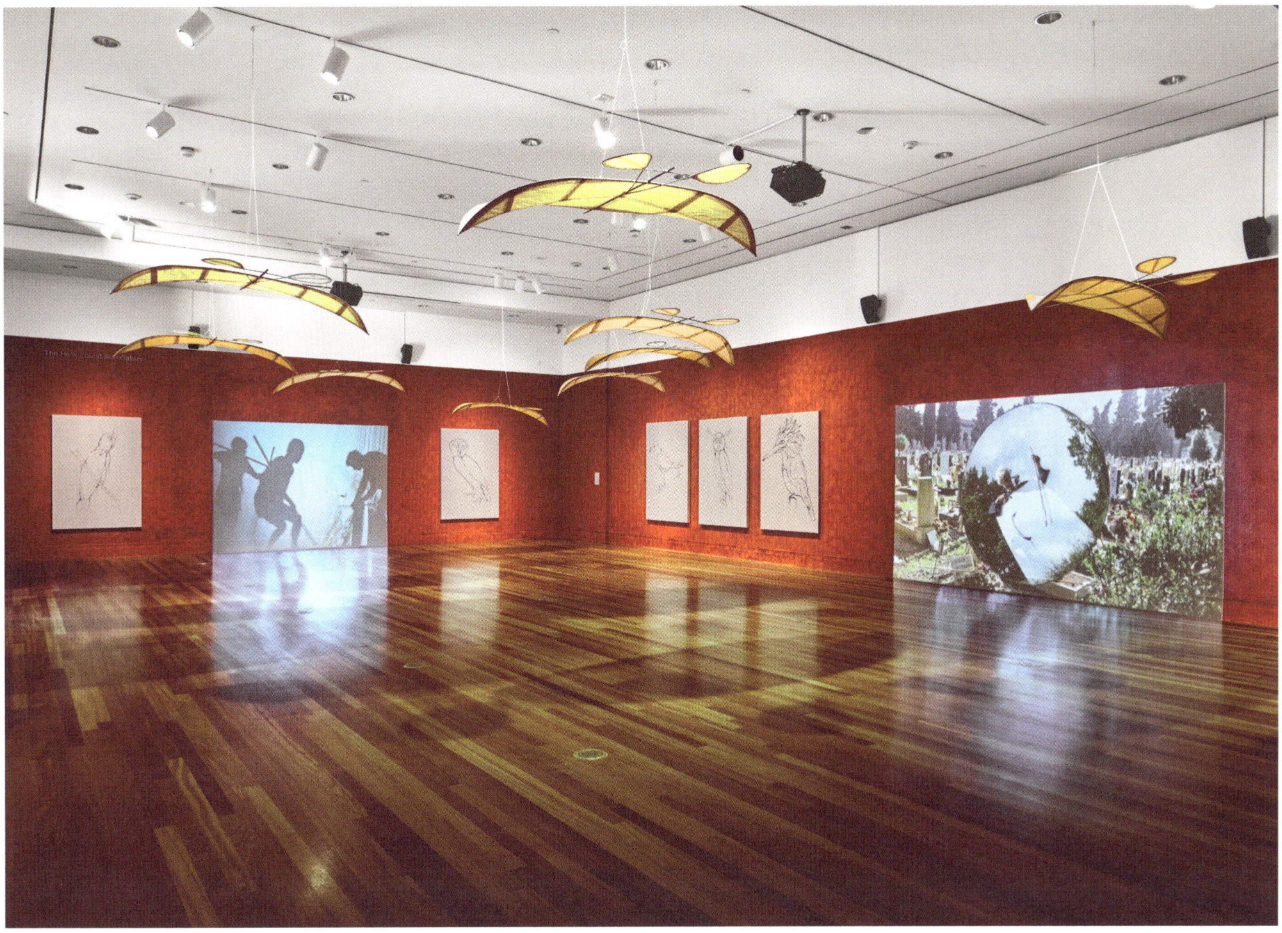

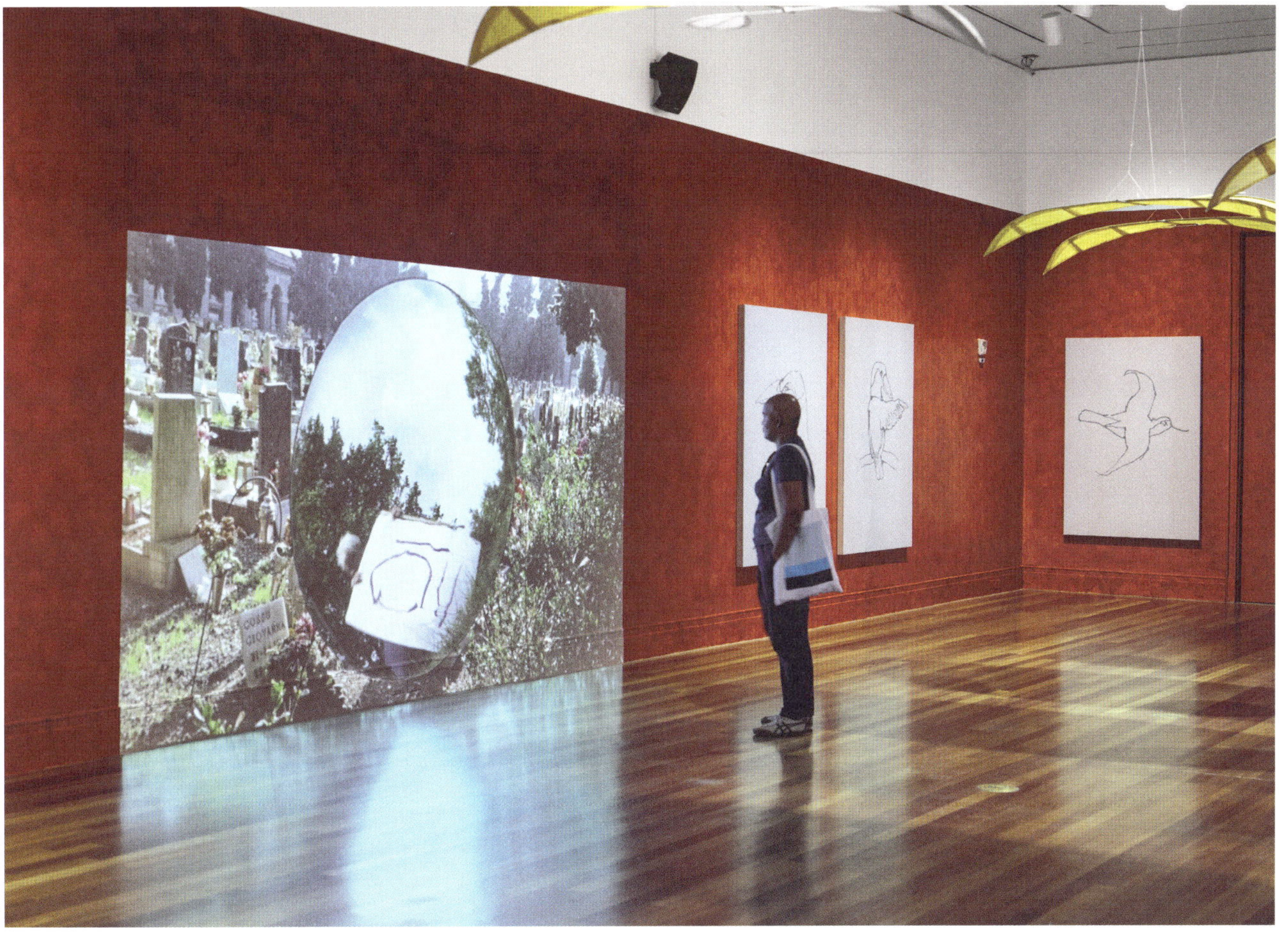

stream or river, flight or pattern III, 2016/2017

Brian Jungen

b. 1970, Fort St. John, British Columbia, Canada;
lives in Treaty 8 Territory, British Columbia, Canada

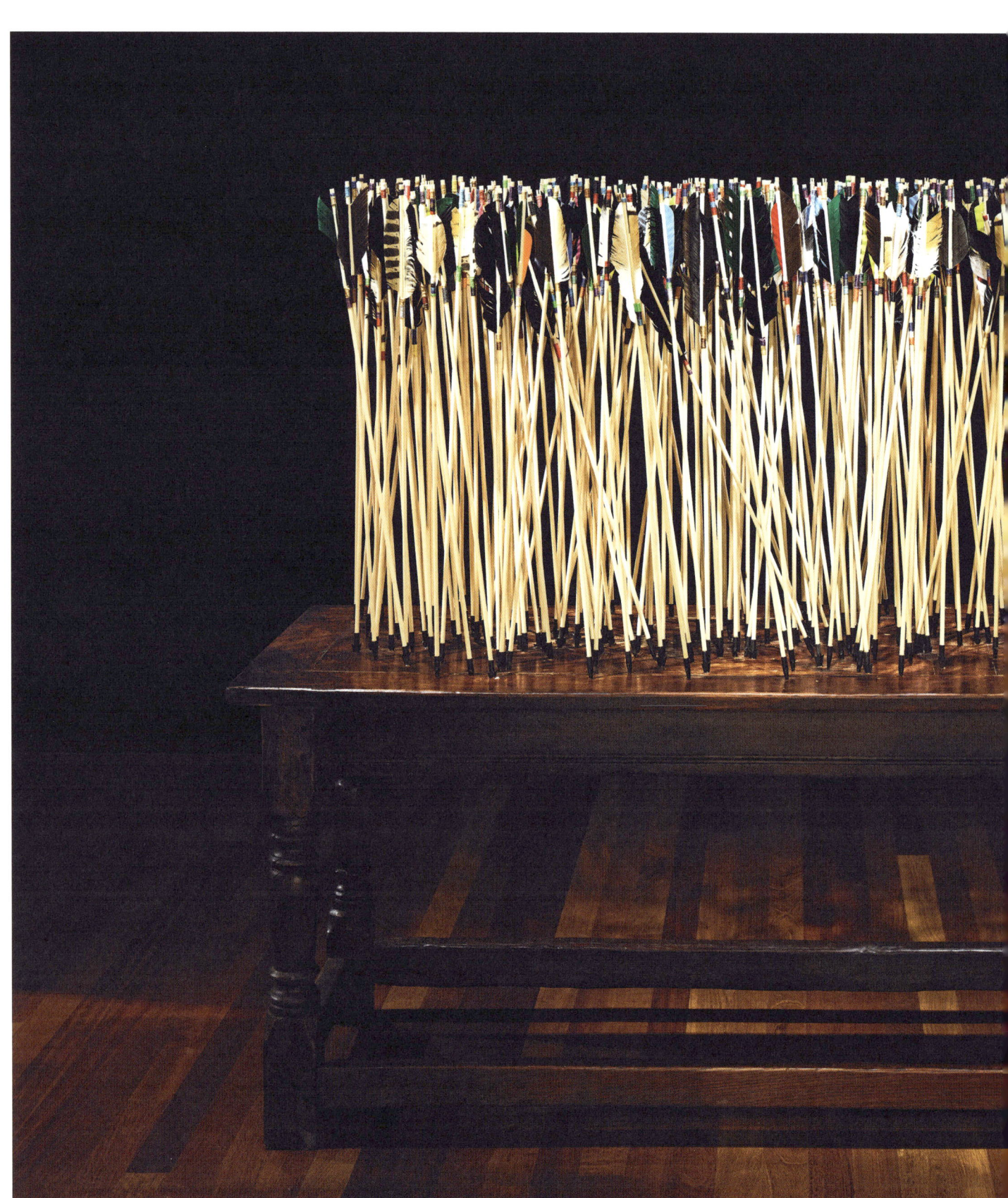

*The way of the world is to bloom and to flower and die
but in the affairs of men there is no waning and the noon
of his expression signals the onset of night*, 2024

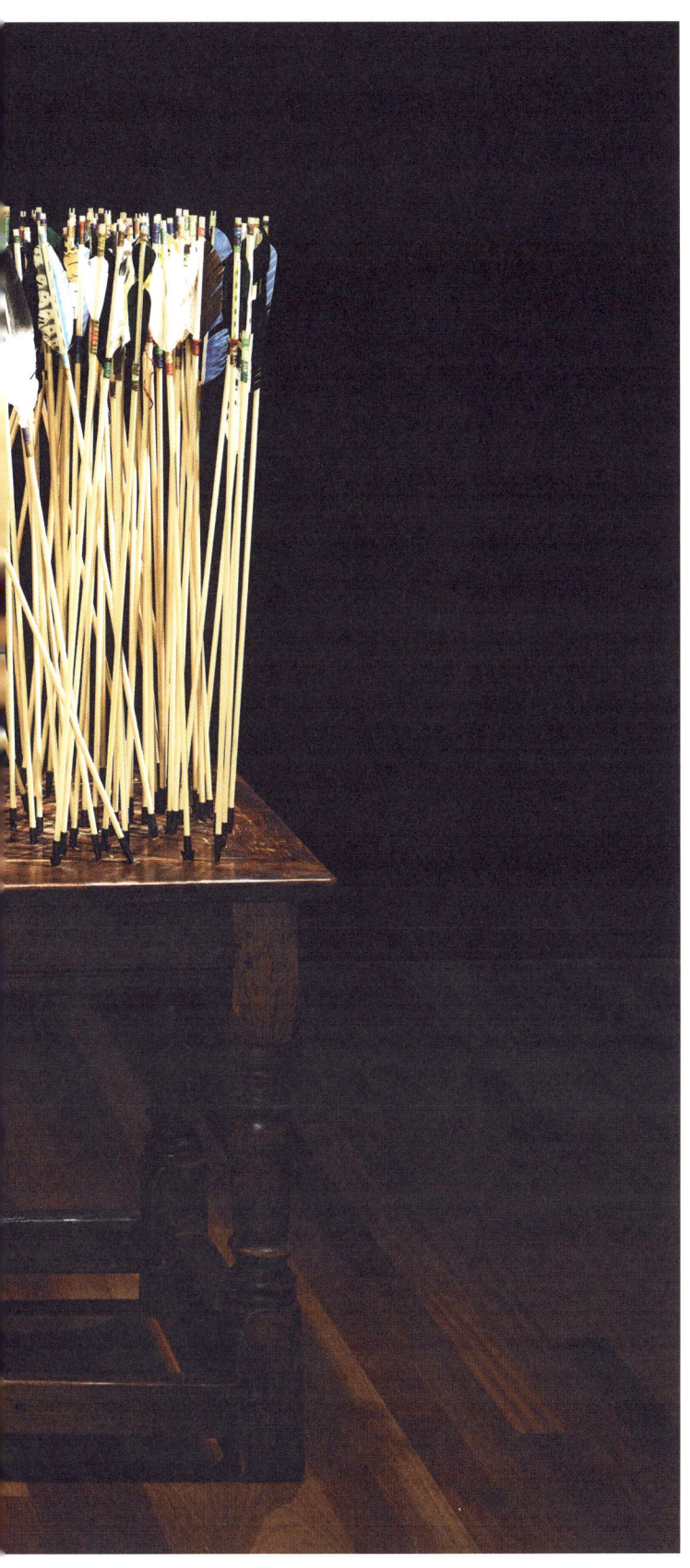

Brian Jungen's new sculptural project for Prospect.6 was inspired by his observations of ceremony, regalia, and colonial architecture in the French Quarter of New Orleans. Its title—*The way of the world is to bloom and to flower and die but in the affairs of men there is no waning and the noon of his expression signals the onset of night* (2024)—was taken from *Blood Meridian*, the 1985 novel by Cormac McCarthy. The sculpture explores the use and meaning of feathers for Indigenous people. By considering the legal complexities of the feather trade in the US, where the possession of certain feathers, such as the bald eagle, is largely restricted, Jungen considers how Native peoples attempt to access important elements of their cultures, and the limitations imposed on them by colonial governments, who force Native people to apply for permits, which are only made available for cultural purposes.

The way of the world involves shooting traditional arrows with hardwood shafts and bird feathers into colonial-era furniture, in this case, an eighteenth-century Louisiana table. This sculpture aims to make a bold statement about Indigenous authority and self-defense, combining aggression and beauty. It raises questions of power and the definitional limits of Native identity and culture. How are Native identities and cultures constructed? How do racial definitions and meanings change these constructions across time and place? And perhaps the most important question, what role do race and culture play in broader social and political systems?

Jungen's sculpture brings attention to the history of extensive hunting by White settlers and how this led to significant declines in

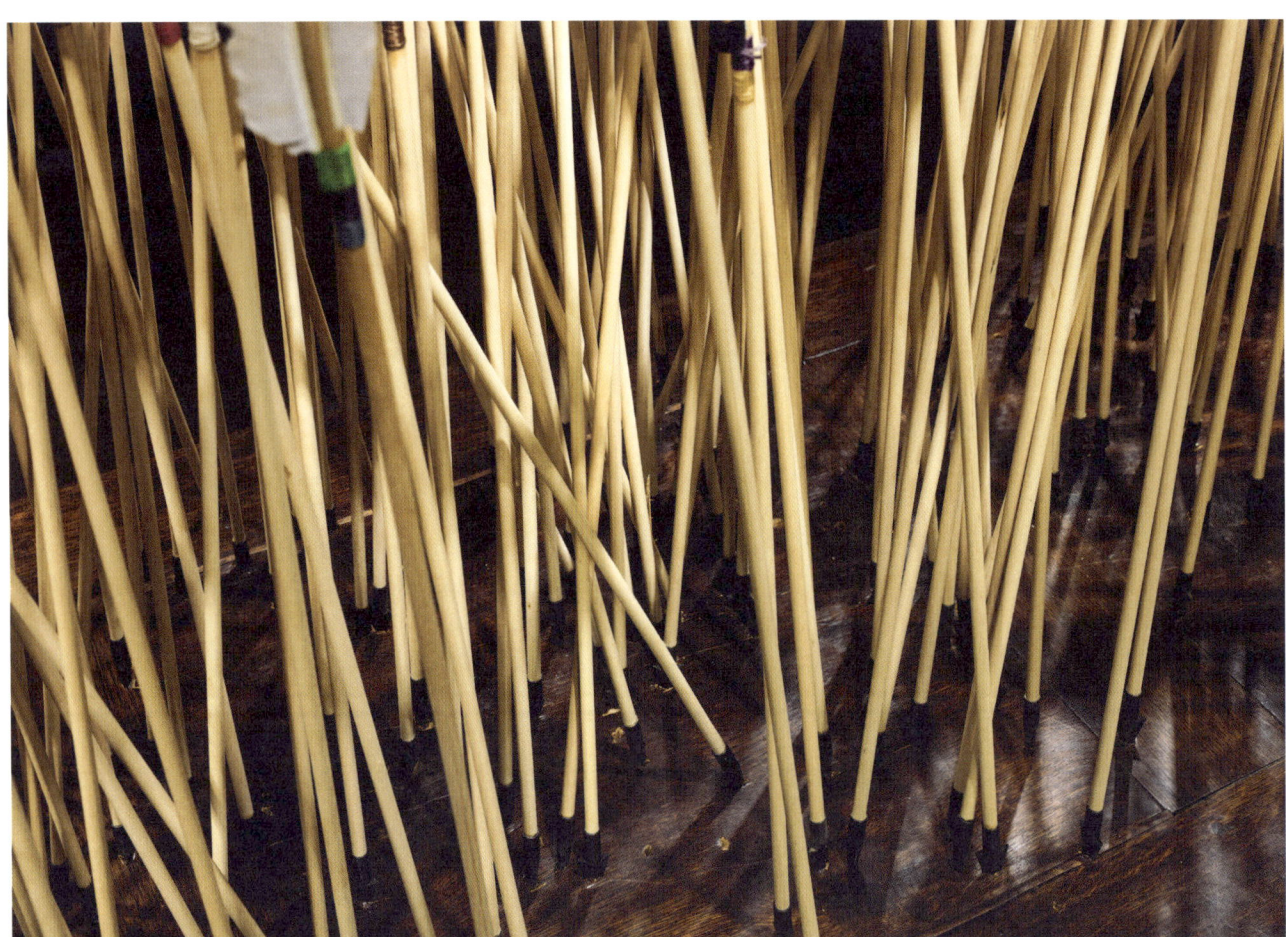

bird populations, severely disrupting the biodiversity of ecosystems. These events ushered in regulations that severely limit how Native peoples remain in relation with these nonhuman relatives through the use of feathers today. Jungen unites pasts, presents, and futures so that we might understand Nativeness otherwise. The variety of feathers and arrows, their sizes, colors, and designs, denote how Native agency and sovereignty are uniquely defined and enacted. The act of using feathers is not only representative of Native cultural and spiritual resilience, but also continued and ongoing resistance—the arrows break through Western definitions, ideas, limitations, and discourses, opening up a new channel of understanding and discourse.

Although we do not see a representation of the Native body in Jungen's work, how is it that our visual associations with the arrows in this piece symbolize Native presence? And, are we overlooking Native resistance to violence that ensures our futures, or are we instead leaning into a hypervisualization of stereotypical representations of "primitive" Natives in American Western films? Striking and powerful,

the cognitive shift occurs at the moment we consider who is viewing the work, and how the production of racial discourse becomes contingent on this relationship between race, representation, and looking.

Since the fifteenth century, the dehumanizing logics of colonization have marked Nativeness as a threat. For nearly six centuries, the logic of empire and White supremacy has been concerned with eradicating Native worldviews and lifeways. *The way of the world* critically challenges power and domination by reclaiming and reappropriating the aesthetics and semiotics of empire and expanding the possibility of Nativeness in moving us beyond ethnographic entrapment. Spiritually and physically, feathers hold power. In their fragility, feathers represent the sacredness of life, but in this sculpture, they become a form of protection against violence. We are encouraged to move beyond the fictitious representations of Nativeness and understand the demands of what it means to be and define our cultures, practices, connections, and truths.

by Larissa Nez

The way of the world is to bloom and to flower and die but in the affairs of men there is no waning and the noon of his expression signals the onset of night, 2024 (detail)

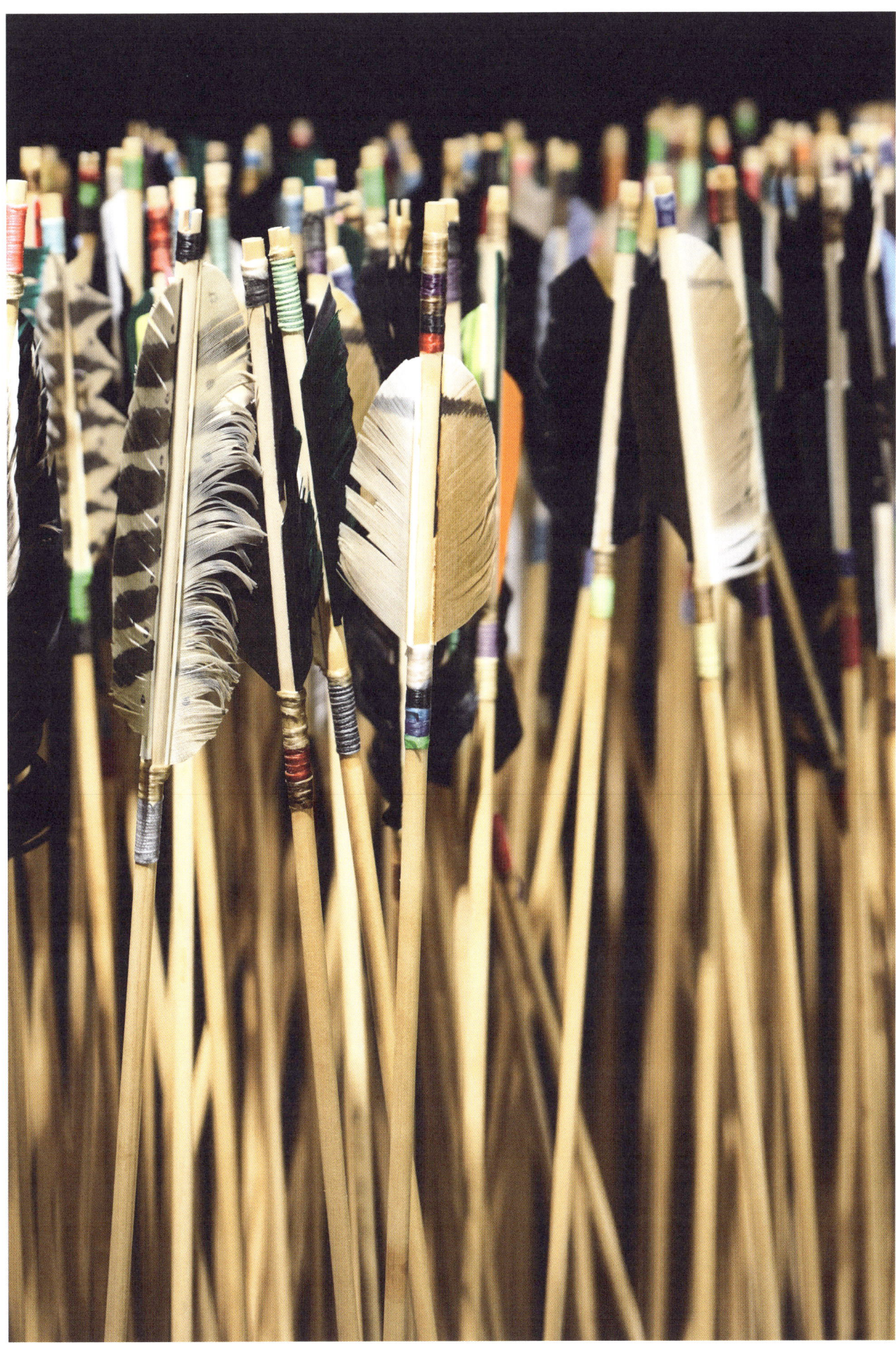

*The way of the world is to bloom and to flower and die
but in the affairs of men there is no waning and the noon
of his expression signals the onset of night*, 2024 (detail)

Artist Arturo Kameya grew up in Peru, and his paintings often refer to Lima's visual culture: pastiche mountain landscapes, a dental grill with the Batman logo, a banal plastic chair sitting in front of graffiti depicting a huge CD and cartoonish ocean foam. The paintings' soft edges and muted hues reflect the pixelation of low-resolution tabloid photos, or newscasts seen on low-fidelity television sets. There's a lack of polish, a candidness. But Kameya is actually interested in things that are *not* what they seem.

Kameya's work often deals with corruption in Peru, with an ironic twist. His source images include clandestine videos of politicians being bribed, Potemkin façades of fraudulent for-profit universities, papier-mâché political puppets burned during New Year's Eve, and comic book and horror movie costumes adopted by criminal gangs, drug dealers, and undercover police. Journalistic images purport to reveal the truth behind these masks, but Kameya's paintings use quirky cropping, awkward angling, and hazy focus to emphasize their unreality. Kameya further crafts an uneasy undercurrent by altering exhibition spaces around his paintings with lighting and materials such as sand.

While Kameya is best known for pop paintings in earthy color palettes, his medium is better understood as atmosphere building. His practice broadly centers site—places remembered, spaces transformed—in order to make palpable sedimented systems of belief that structure society.

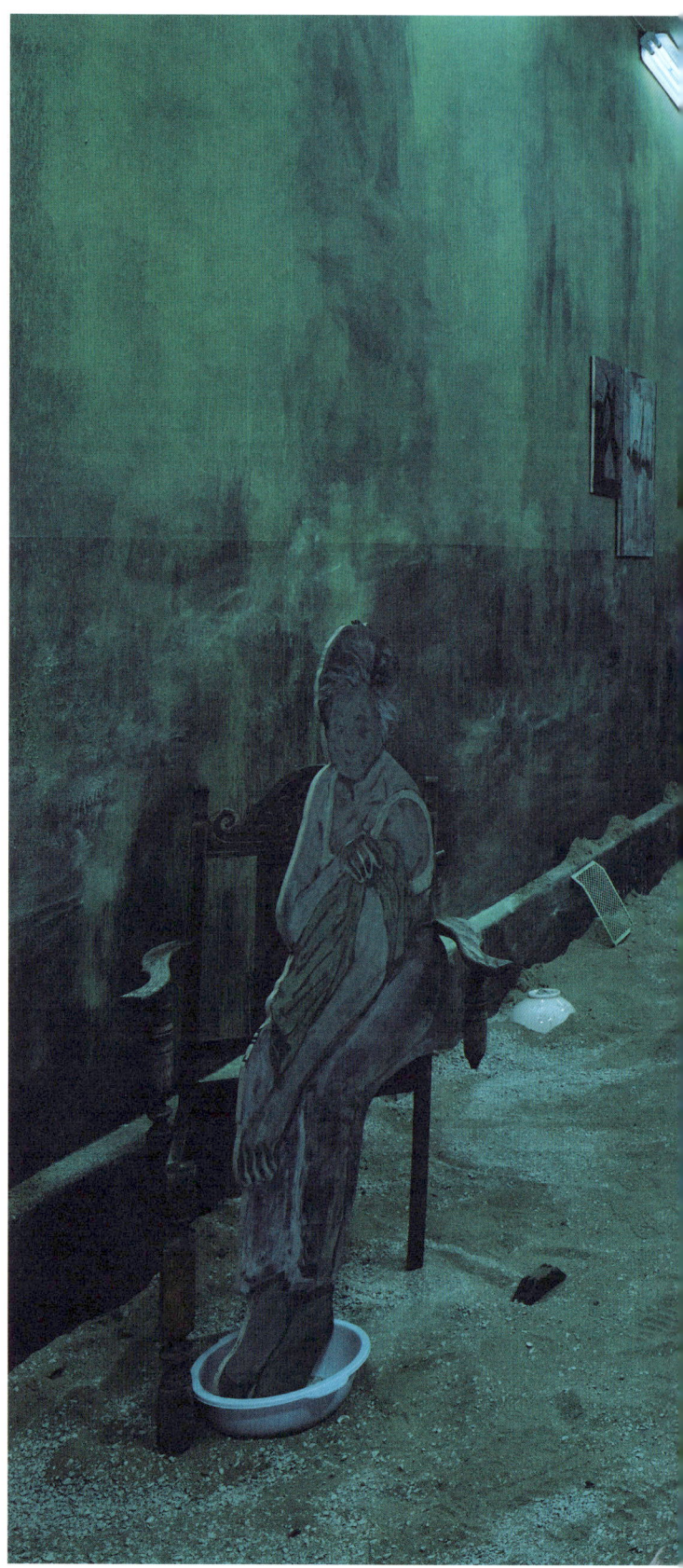

Whatever comes first, 2024

Arturo Kameya

b. 1984, Lima, Peru; lives in Amsterdam, Netherlands and Lima, Peru

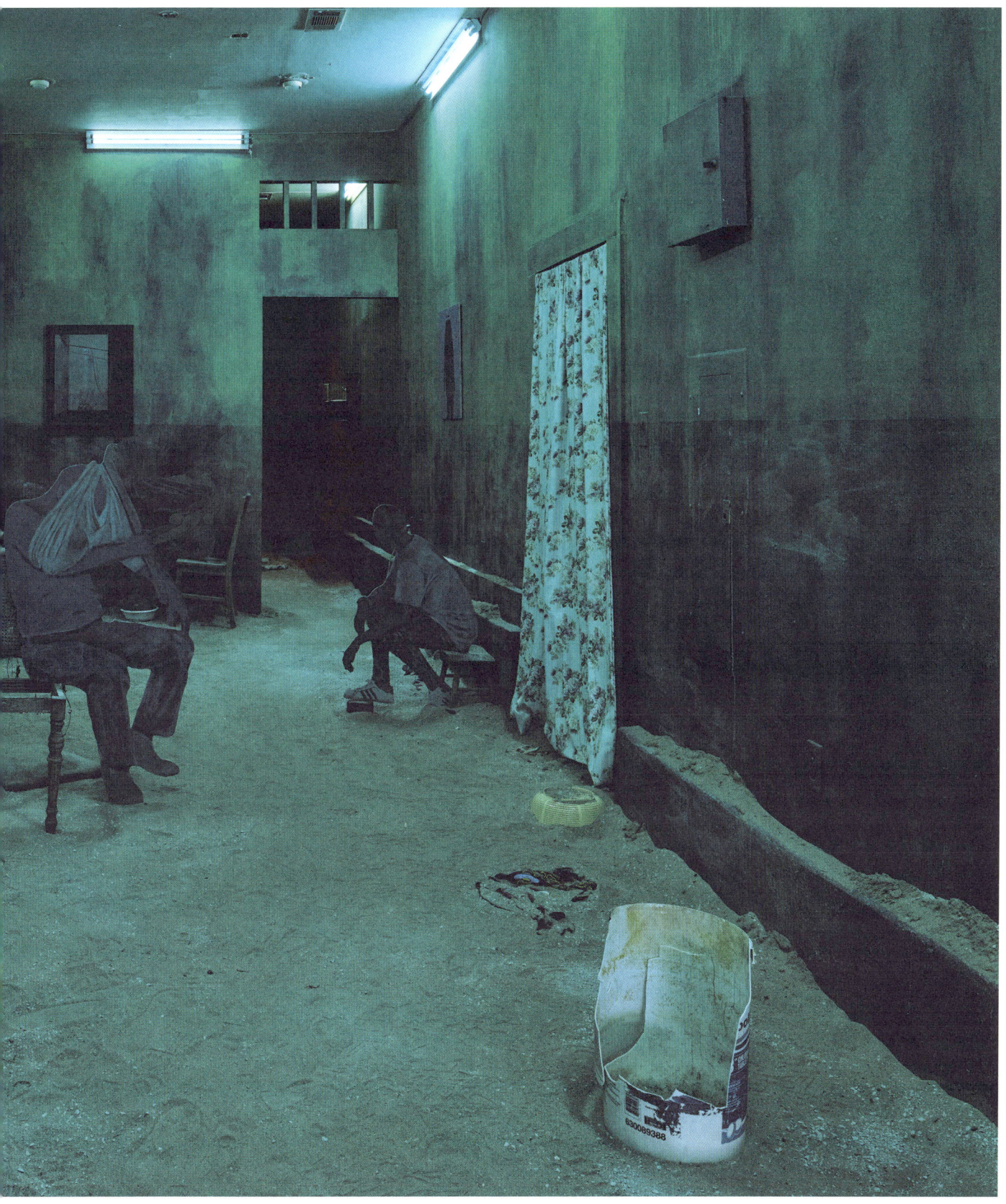

Kameya's works directly invoke Lima. His muted palettes refer to faded layers of paint, as well as the architectures—such as adobe or *quincha* (wattle and daub)—that historically characterized working class parts of Lima, such as La Victoria and other neighborhoods where Kameya grew up. These working-class communities of coastal Peru suffer from lack of investment in education and social services, and were some of the hardest-hit areas during the COVID pandemic. Additionally, the adobe dwellings of neighborhoods such as La Victoria are particularly vulnerable to earthquakes.

In his Prospect work, a sequence of dramatically lit, dirt-floor rooms containing painting and installation, Kameya draws parallels between urban transformation and precarity in Lima and New Orleans. The gallery's hallway-less layout alludes to intimate familial relationships, and to larger structures sliced into side-by-side housing for affordability (i.e., the New Orleans shotgun double). Inscribing urban space with additional sedimented meaning, Lima's working-class neighborhoods are often sites of Ichma *huacas*, historic sacred adobe structures, like

the Indigenous earth mounds of Bulbancha/ New Orleans. Layered religious currents emerge both in Kameya's use of earth and in his paintings: His source images include Google Street Views of Lima's Catholic funeral processions, which resemble New Orleans second-lines.

Drawing on Édouard Glissant's notion of the right to opacity among groups subjected to globalization, Kameya's installation analogizes religious and economic "belief" for precarious communities. Bringing together the ubiquitous plastic shelving of Chinese low-cost e-commerce site AliExpress, objects found in New Orleans, and Catholic devotional items, Kameya invokes interwoven obligations of the global system of debt as well as the "opaque spirits" of syncretic beliefs in postcolonial cities.

by Adrian Anagnost

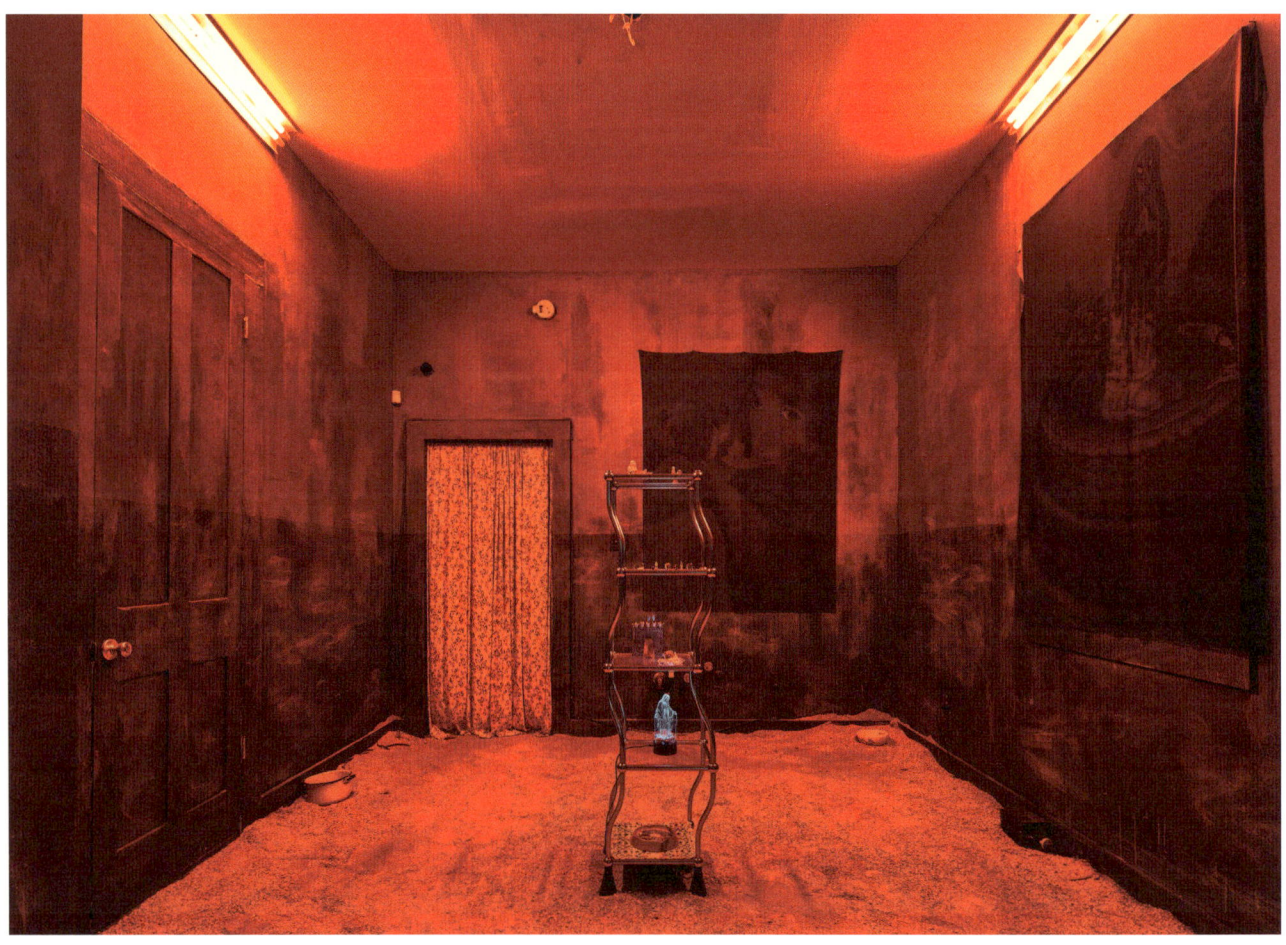

Whatever comes first, 2024

Maia Ruth Lee

b. 1983, Busan, South Korea; lives in Salida, CO

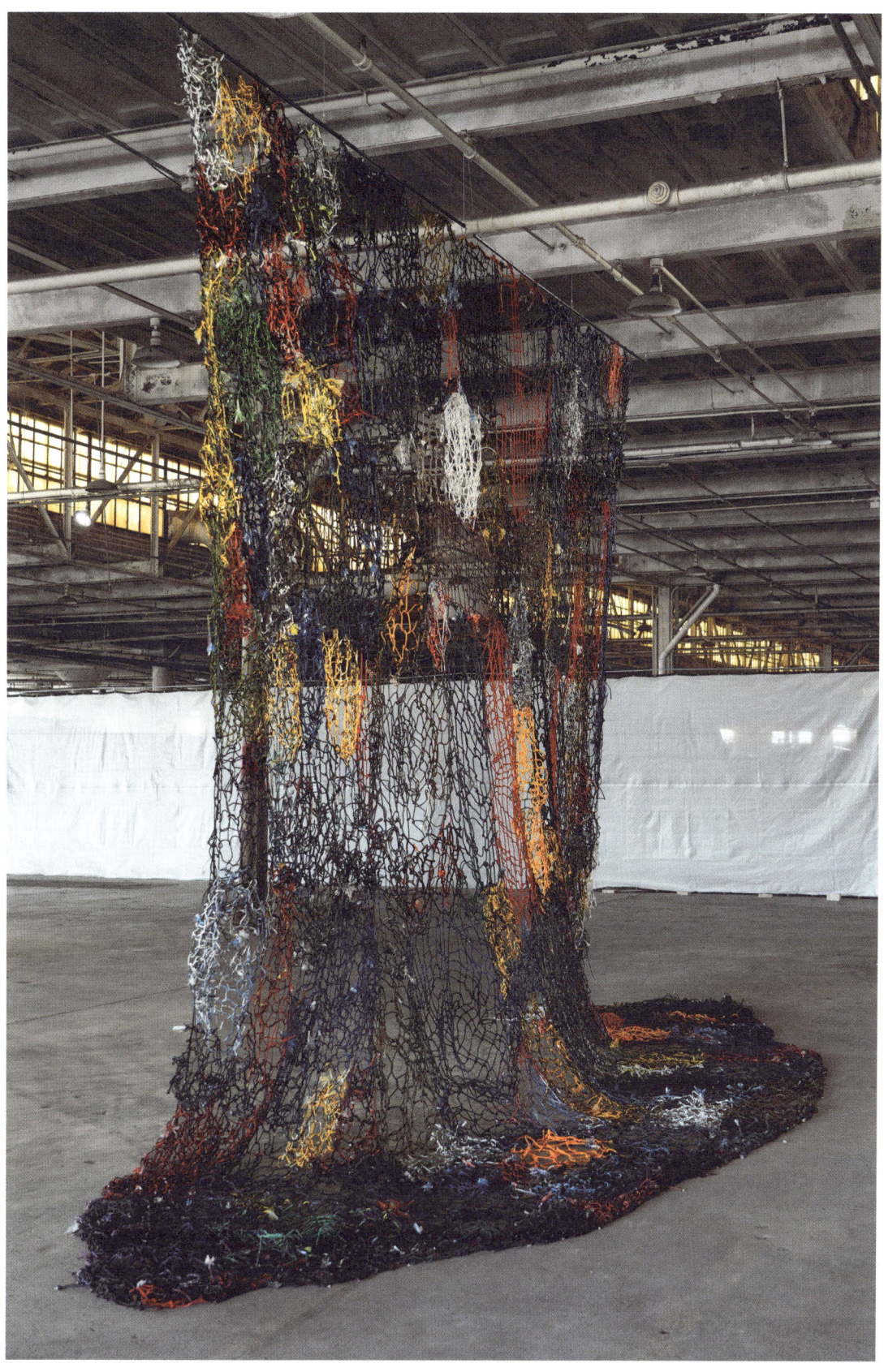

B.B.Rope_Time Loop, 2024

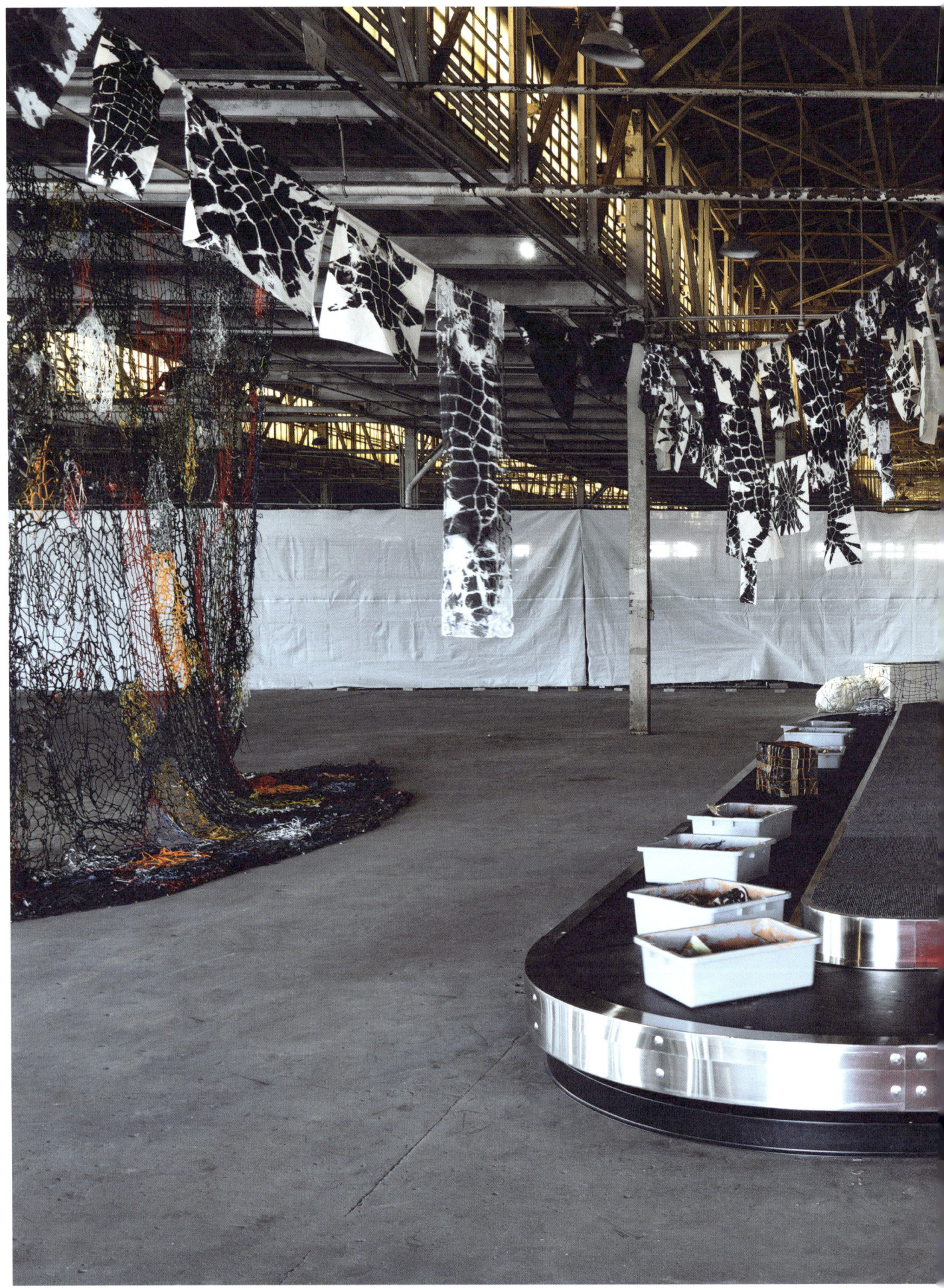

The Conveyor, 2024

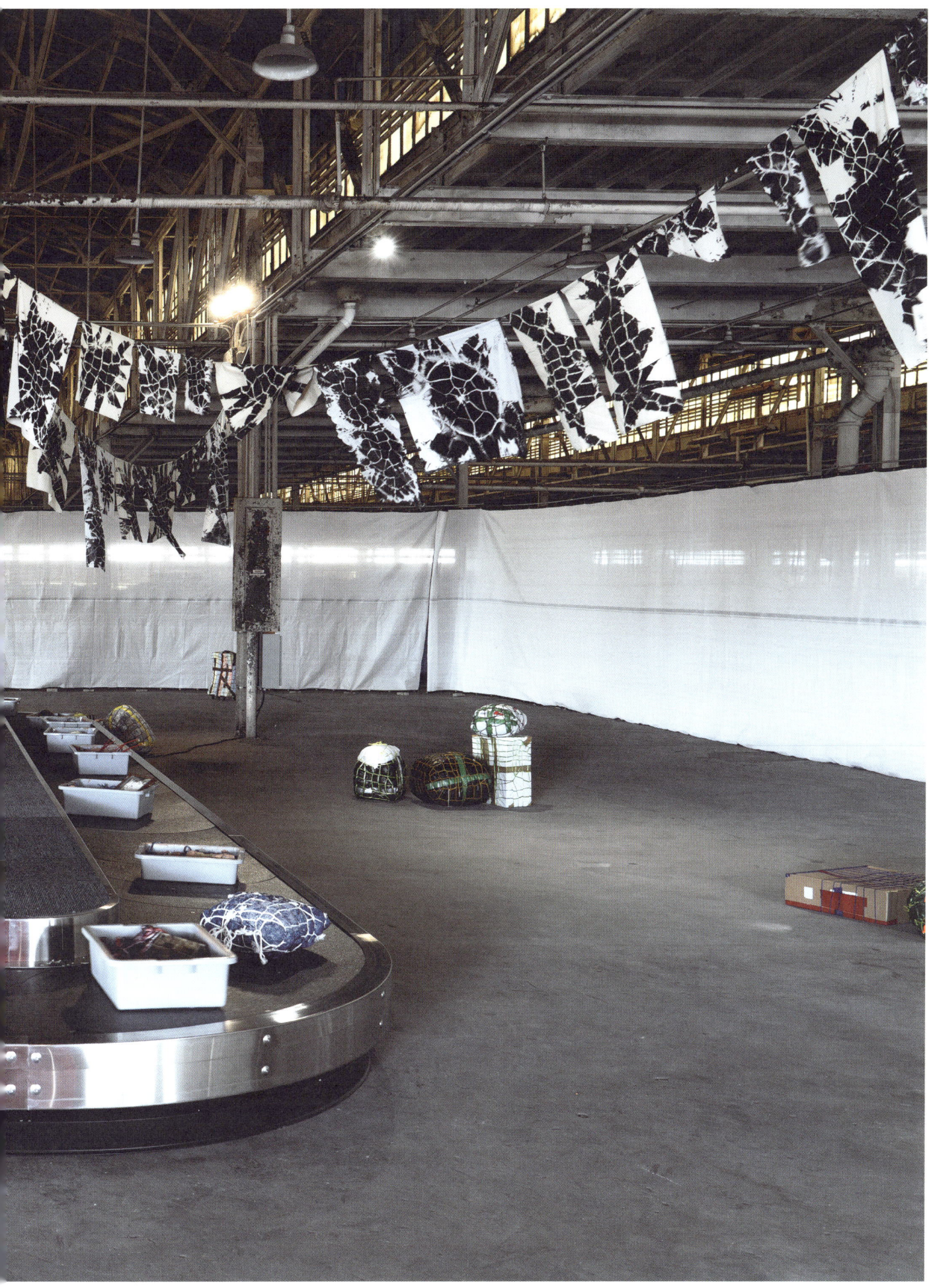

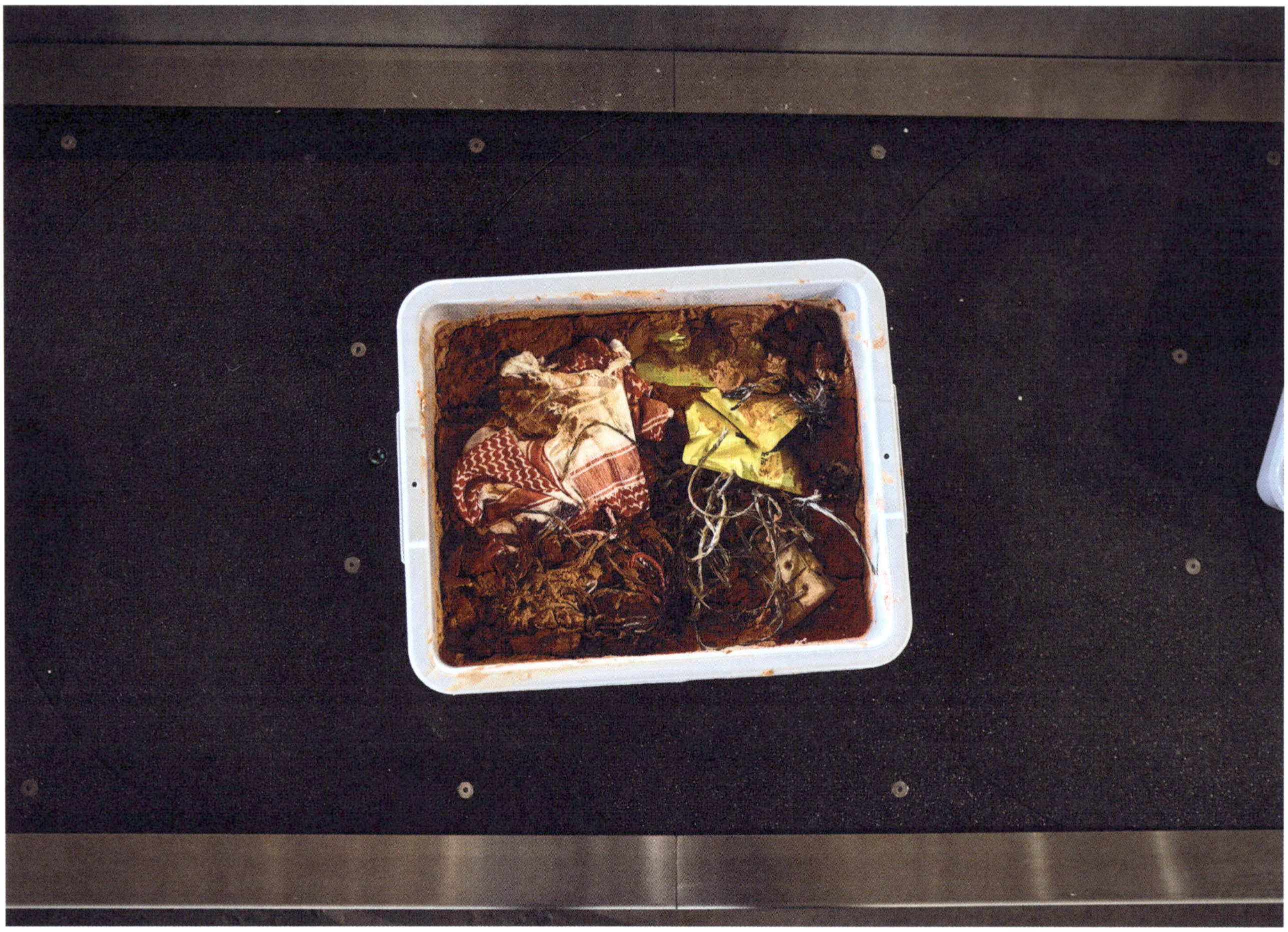

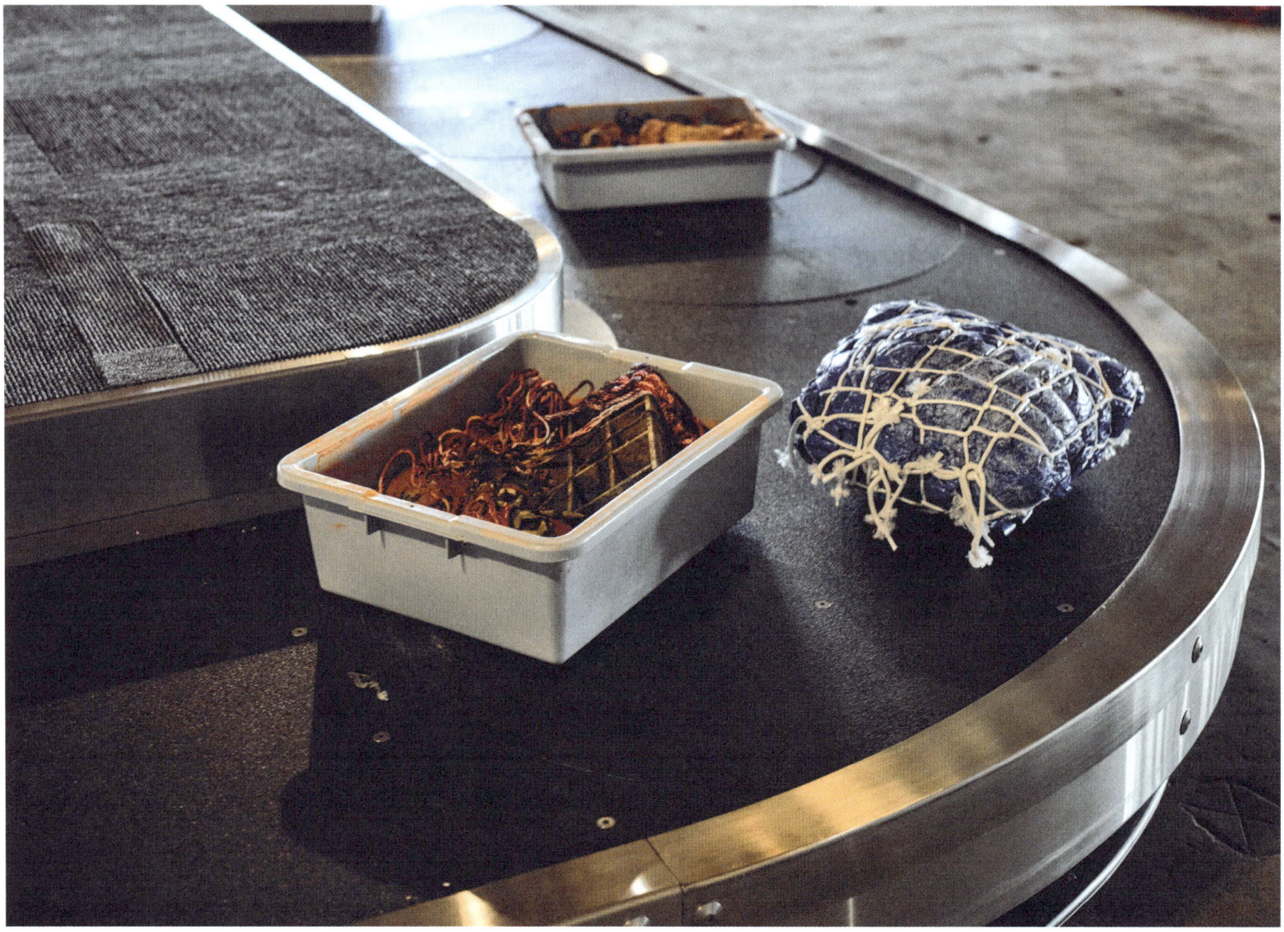

The Conveyor, 2024 (details)

"When I was little I thought people in airports lived there, like just lounging around reading books," a caption reads in Maia Ruth Lee's video *The Stranger* (2018). "Also that airplanes were like elevators. All the countries were just on top of each other, floor by floor." As these thoughts unfurl in yellow text, the camera pans across forested hillsides under lightly clouded skies, and a male narrator's voice competes with ambient noise. In the next scene, a woman, child, and two young men stand near a modest dwelling. Their baggage is tied up with string nearby.

Lee's father taped these scenes in the late 1980s-'90s in Nepal, where the family had moved from South Korea when Lee was a child. There, her parents spent years studying the local language in order to translate the Bible. *The Stranger* is the first of three short films collaged from her family's home videos; the captions, a viewer eventually realizes, are not direct translations of her father's Korean narration, but a collage of the artist's inner thoughts in the present and the older Lee's records of the past. That scene where Lee remembers her childhood understanding of air travel and geography juxtaposes her imagined ascension with an on-the-ground reality of migration. Already, then, we see Lee's central concerns as an artist—family, migration, language, translation, time, anticipation—which she explores through videos, sculptures, paintings, prints, and installations.

Lee's ongoing series of *Bondage Baggage* sculptures (2018–ongoing) was also shaped by her experiences in the airports of Nepal, where, for years, she took informal photographs of people's luggage, which tended to be covered with tarps and wrapped up in a grid of tied rope or tape—as seen briefly in *The Stranger*. This vernacular practice interests Lee as a convention of the "Global South" more broadly, often used by migrant workers bringing goods or gifts back home. In this sense, each netted bundle is representative of a person's life and labor—including, per the double meaning of "baggage," the inherited or psychological conditions they might carry. Her sculptures replicating this form are usually placed on the floor, huddled like bodies or lost bags.

In Lee's current installation at the Ford Motor Plant in Arabi, a suburb of New Orleans, titled

The Conveyor (2024), she revisits the scene of the airport itself. A baggage carousel slowly rotates within the immense warehouse, as if it were the forgotten baggage claim area of an abandoned airport. Atop the moving platform sit various plastic trays containing constellations of personal effects, which paint more visible (and perhaps more vulnerable) portraits than the baggage sculptures arranged nearby. These belongings circle in a perpetual loop, as if their owners may yet arrive. In the meantime, we inspect them to deduce the travelers' origins, destinations, needs, personalities.

Somehow the scene is not all mournful. The carousel is festooned with prayer-flag-like paintings hanging from the ceiling, evoking a site for ritual or celebration. In Tibetan Buddhism, Lee recalls, physical movement, whether by wind or water, ensures that prayers are in action, full of potential. In this light, *The Conveyor* reads as a meditation not only on the anxiety and complex geopolitical relations of actual migration, but also on the realms of desire, spirituality, and fulfillment.

by Mira Dayal

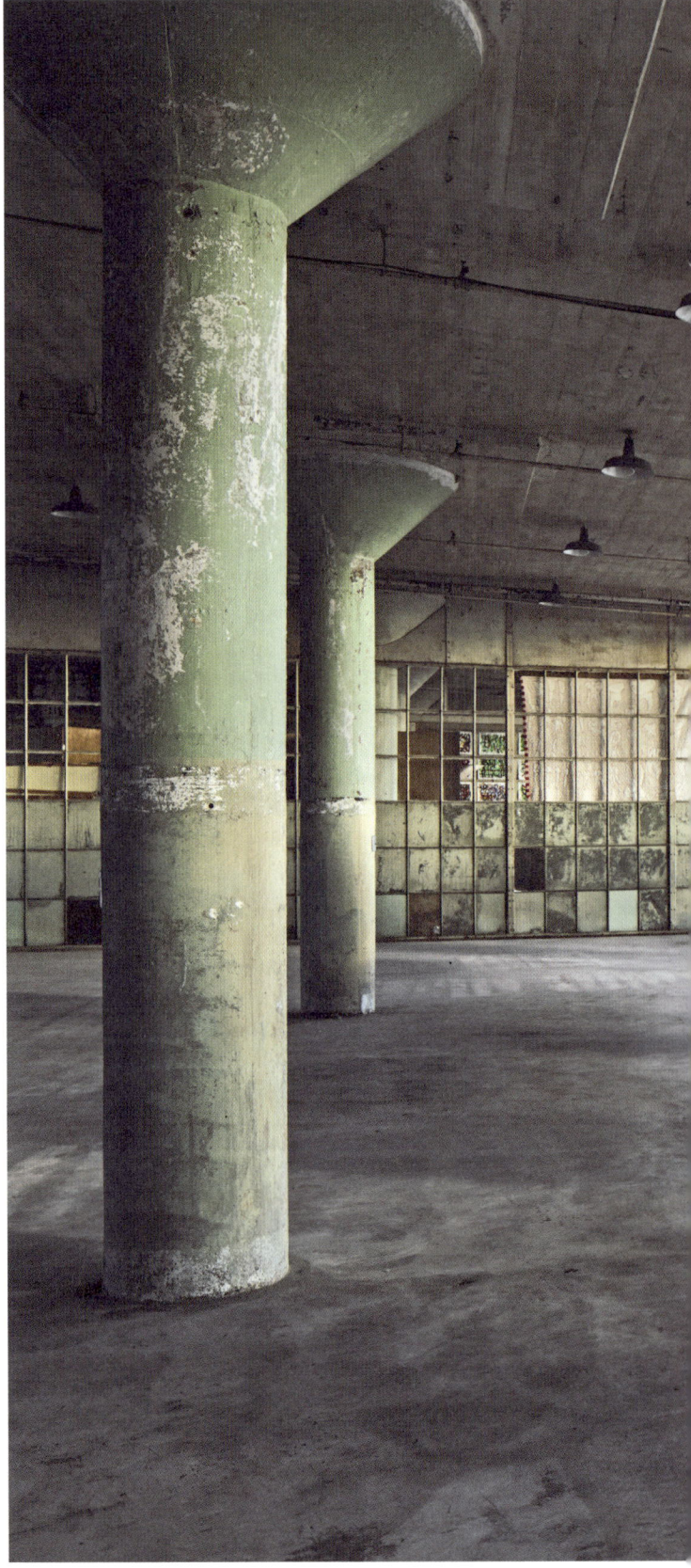

Kelley-Ann Lindo's Prospect.6 installation reconfigures an everyday object—a shipping barrel—as a sculpture that sparks discussions about distance and intimacy. In *Send Love Inna Barrel* (*V*) (2017-ongoing), the artist presents the shipping containers as a single suspended tunnel, measuring approximately thirty-two feet wide. Chairs are placed at both ends, encouraging audiences to engage not only with the object, but also with each other. What are usually mundane objects become mediators between visitors, funneling their vision and voices across the tunnel. Will audiences be able to maintain conversations through the barrels, communicating through whispers heard only by visitors on the opposite side? What will they notice about each other through the sculpture's span?

Send Love Inna Barrel considers how people sustain intimate connections across great distances, especially when relationships are tested by migration. Born in Kingston, Jamaica, and currently in the United States, Lindo strives to create a sense of community wherever she

Send Love Inna Barrel (V), 2017-ongoing

Kelley-Ann Lindo

b. 1991, Kingston, Jamaica; lives in Kingston, Jamaica and Providence, RI

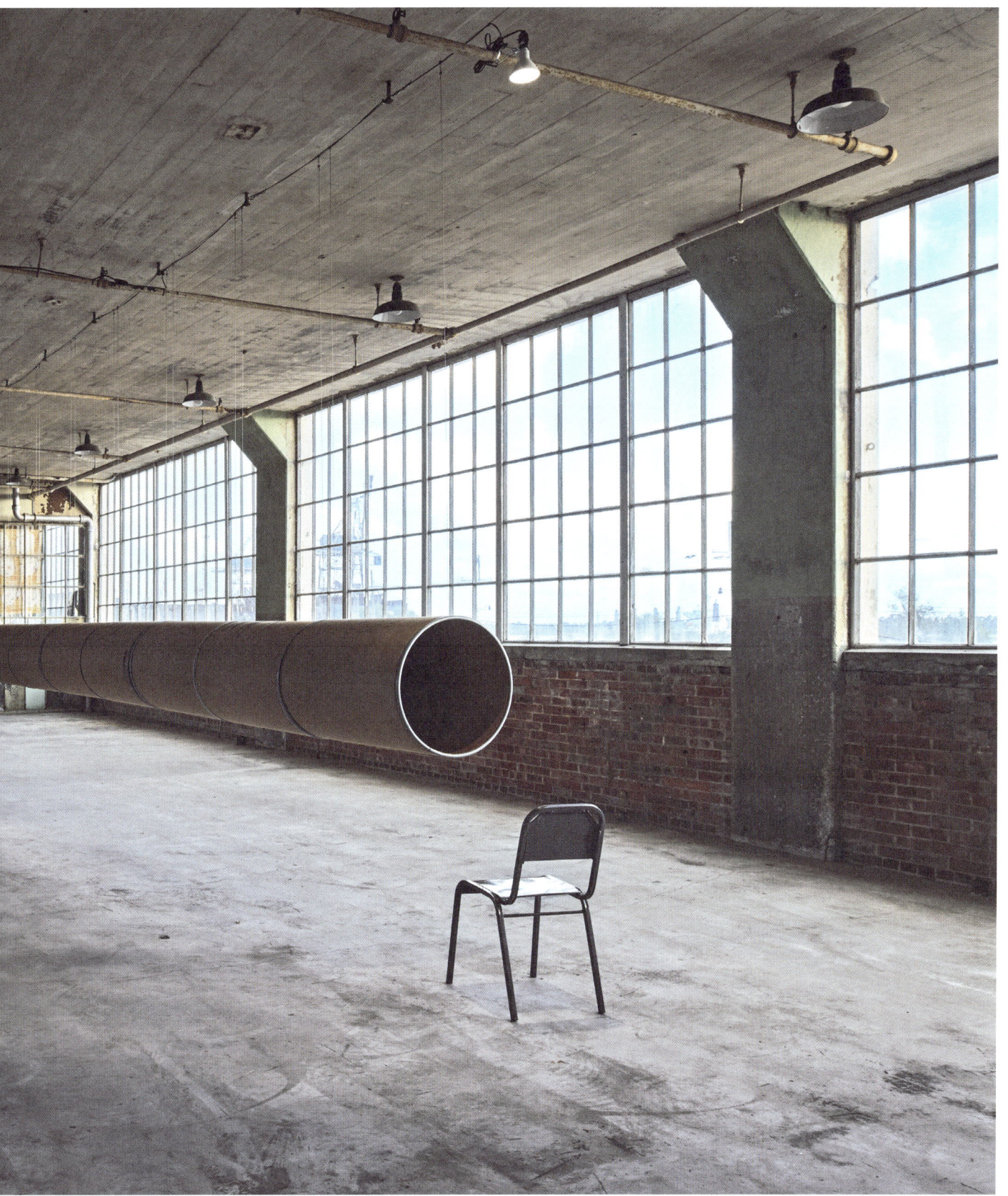

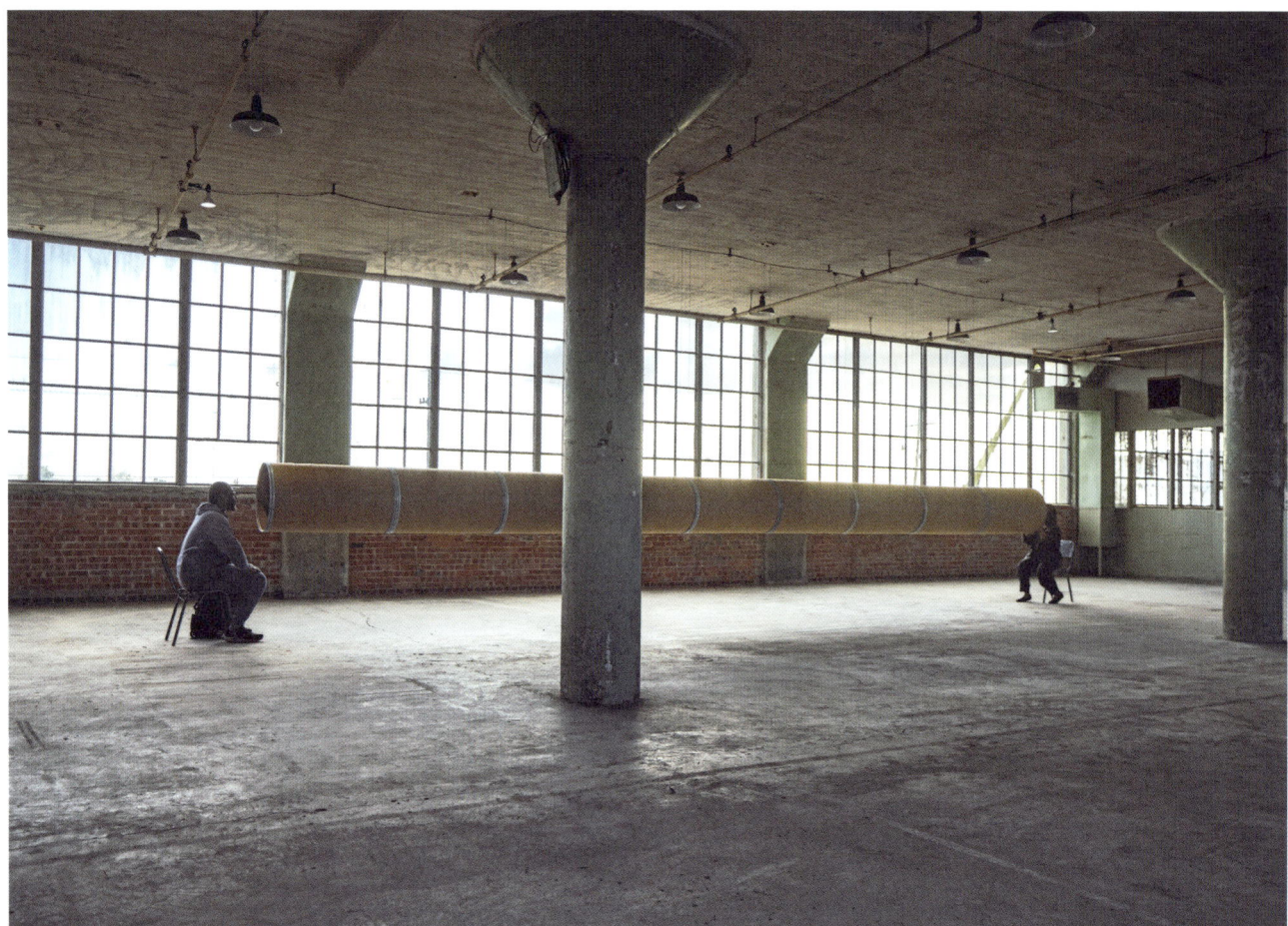

lands, which she credits as an integral part of her artistic practice and personal life. *Send Love Inna Barrel* reflects her upbringing in the Caribbean. It embodies the experiences of the region's "barrel children," which alludes to youth whose parents leave home in search of opportunities overseas. Parents often ship goods back home in barrels, like the ones used in the artwork. While migration may bring more access to resources, it also strains familial relationships. Caregivers and children are separated by borders and bodies of water that can be difficult to traverse, both physically and financially. Lindo's project explores how people communicate across these geographic gaps, with the barrels embodying the separation from loved ones and the care that one may not be able to express in person.

The artist's Prospect installation is her latest iteration of *Send Love Inna Barrel*. Lindo has described previous versions as studies for this moment where she is able to realize the project's full scale. The artwork was first shown in 2017 at the Jamaica Biennial in Kingston. Lindo attended this first showing and recalls speaking with a father who was visiting with

his son. The man became emotional when reflecting on his early life as a barrel child, his memories of receiving the shipping containers from caretakers abroad, and what it meant for him to view the installation as a parent. It was also an affirming moment that he was not alone in his experiences, a key intention of *Send Love Inna Barrel*.

Each successive version of the sculpture has grown in scale, expanding the gulf between sitters and making communication more laborious. In a time of increased globalization and movement across borders, *Send Love Inna Barrel* reminds audiences that care can take many forms, whether it's shared directly or through the parcel substitutes we send to those we cannot reach. Each iteration of the installation attests to the importance of fostering connection and community, even when the distance between us and our loved ones feels taxing: the work is worth it.

by Kendyll Gross

Send Love Inna Barrel (V), 2017–ongoing

Cathy Lu

b. 1984, Miami, FL; lives in Richmond, CA

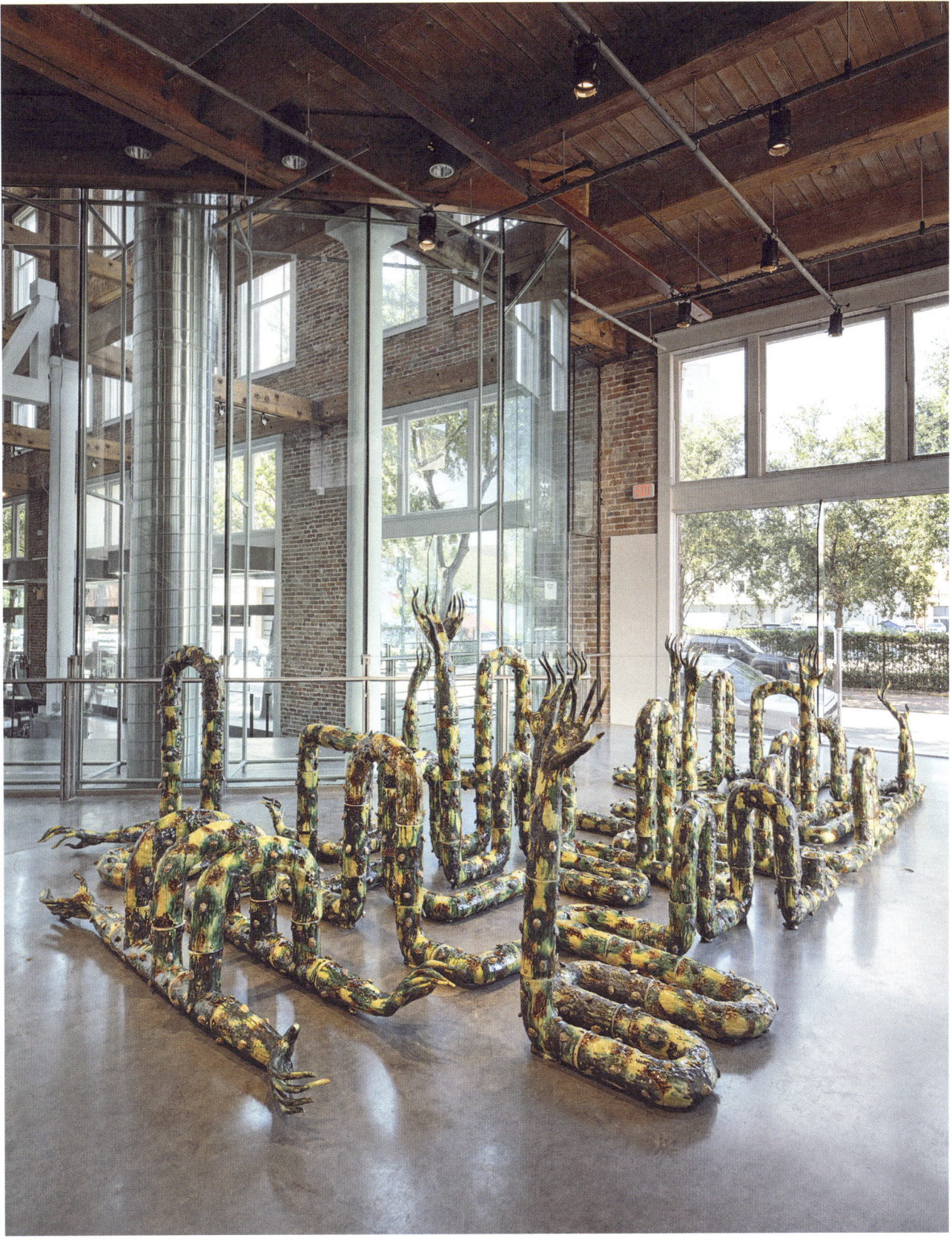

In her sculptures and installations, Cathy Lu examines notions of identity and cultural hybridity through a lens of Chinese diaspora. Informed by her and her family's experiences of immigration and assimilation, Lu's work investigates ideas of belonging—and conversely, otherness—while exploring the interconnections between culture, race, and gender. Growing up in Miami, Florida, to immigrant parents from Taiwan among a Cuban community, Lu recognized early on that her upbringing as an American was not considered mainstream. For over a decade, Lu has created sculptures of fruits—often bruised or rotted—and disjointed body parts in ceramic, drawing on Chinese symbols and imagery to consider her relation with them. Lu's work subverts preconceived definitions of what it means to be American and Asian, and considers the generalization of the term "Asian." Not always accepted by either group, Lu operates in a liminal space in a binary-dominated society, and in her art, she focuses on the journey and exploration, rather than a certain starting or end point.

For Prospect.6, Lu created a new, large-scale sculpture that expands upon a recent body of work developed during the pandemic and inspired by Nüwa, a mother goddess in Chinese mythology. With the head of a woman and a snake-like body, Nüwa created all humankind out of clay in the mud near a river. Lu also draws a connection between Nüwa and the role of the ceramist, as she notes both are "makers and creators—world builders and change seekers."

Measuring approximately five feet tall, nineteen feet long, and thirteen feet wide, this large-scale sculpture is an abstracted depiction of the spiritual deity, comprising numerous undulating, fragmented sections. The figure has sixteen hands—eight pairs—spread throughout, each with tapered fingers. Resembling colors of the earth, the yellow, green, and brown hued-glazes are Lu's chosen color palette, like the tri-colored glazed pottery from the Tang dynasty era.

The delicate looking forms, coupled with the pronounced fingers, vein-like markings, and pimpled body, project qualities of both beauty and grotesqueness, and thus serve to attract and repulse. The muted color is also characteristic of decay. In utilizing glazes of mixed colors, Lu's work comments on how people of color are portrayed and racialized. Simultaneously, Lu's work calls for possibility and hope. On the sculpture are hundreds of peach pits made of ceramic. Symbols of immortality and longevity, they also refer to the age-old Chinese tradition of carving scenes into the pits—the parts of the fruit that typically get discarded. Lu equates people who came from Nüwa with fruit that comes from seeds. With the peach as a recurring trope in her work, Lu also scrutinizes how singular objects become culturally specific, categorized, and commodified, such as in various markets— "Asian," "Chinese," or "American."

The fragmentation of parts alludes to the idea that history and narratives are in pieces, incomplete—just as her parents have built their lives in multiple places, all inevitably with physical vestiges and memories. Lu's complex installation further suggests a connection to water, as the sculpture resembles a piping system or fountain, bringing to mind a Chinese landscape garden, and a previous installation by the artist titled *Peripheral Visions* (2022), featuring large pairs of ceramic eyes of well-known Asian-American women with tears running through tubes, eliciting emotions of despair and hope. Throughout Lu's practice— including earlier watercolors, paintings, drawings, and sculptures that deconstruct assumptions of cultural authenticity and value in a hierarchical landscape—the artist creates tableaux that relate to everyday stories, people, and objects, prompting us to think about how we perceive ourselves and how we exist among each other.

by Eileen Jeng Lynch

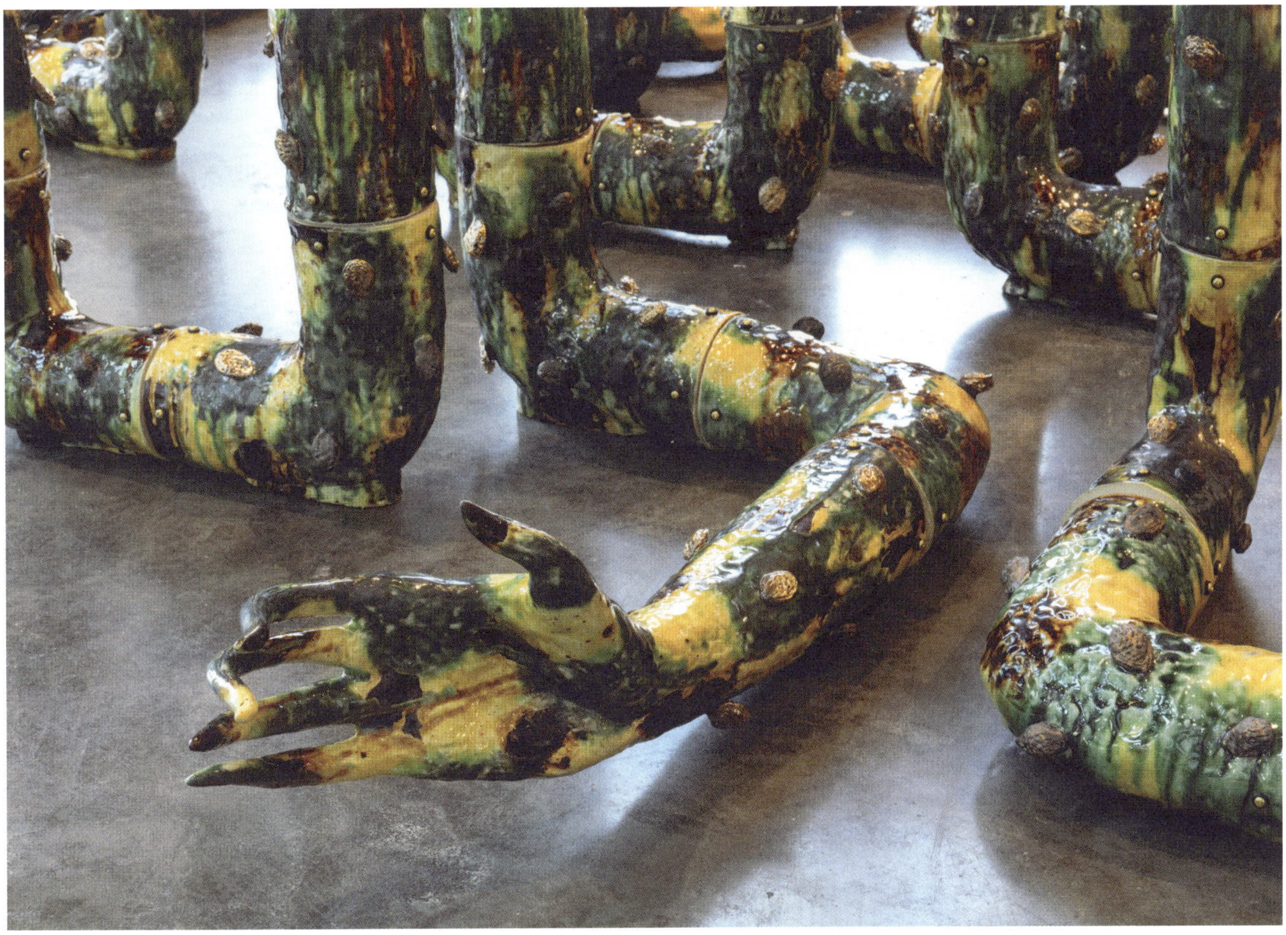

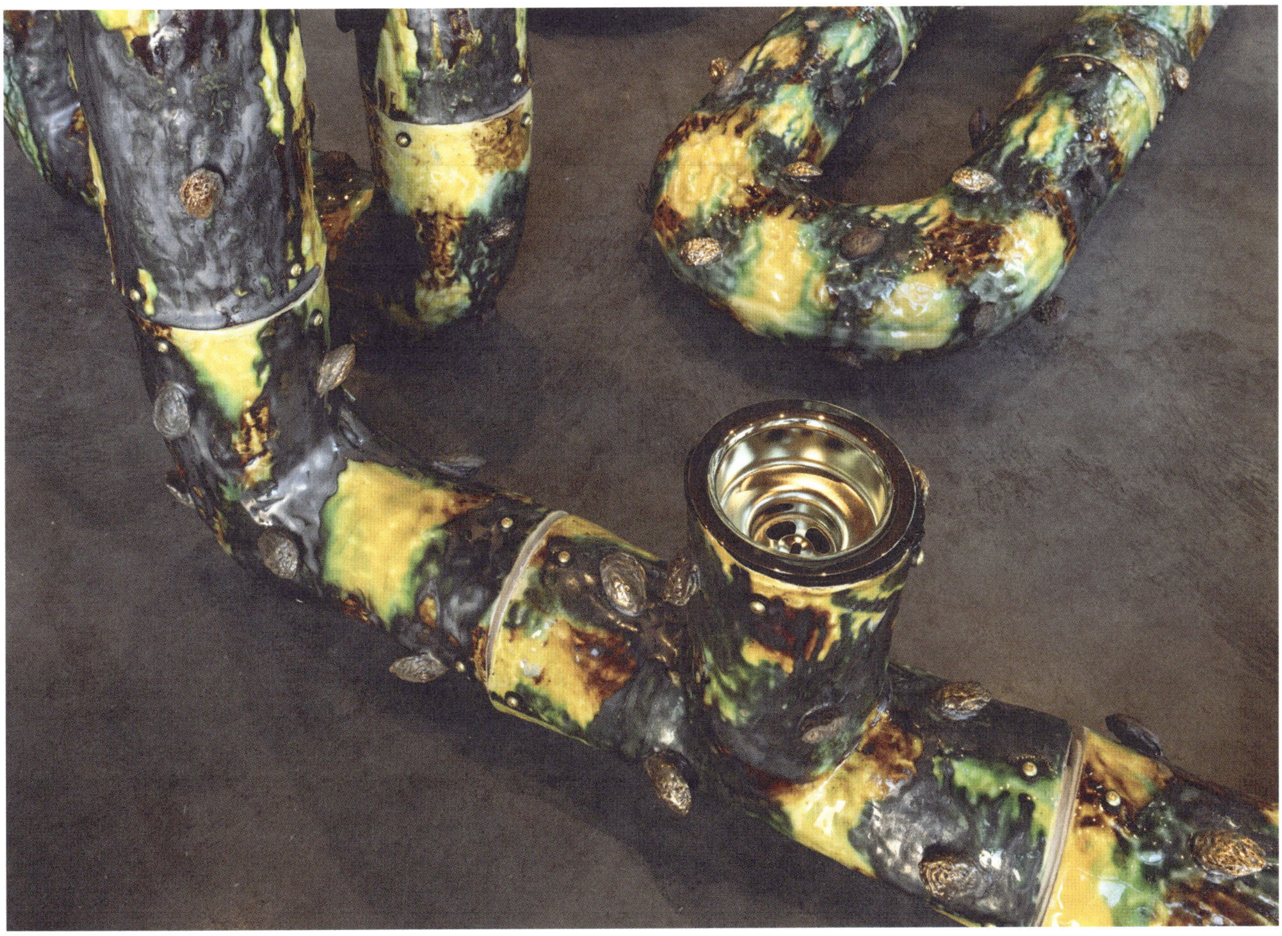

Passages, 2024 (details)

Tessa Mars

b. 1985, Port-au-Prince, Haiti;
lives in Port-au-Prince, Haiti and San Juan, Puerto Rico

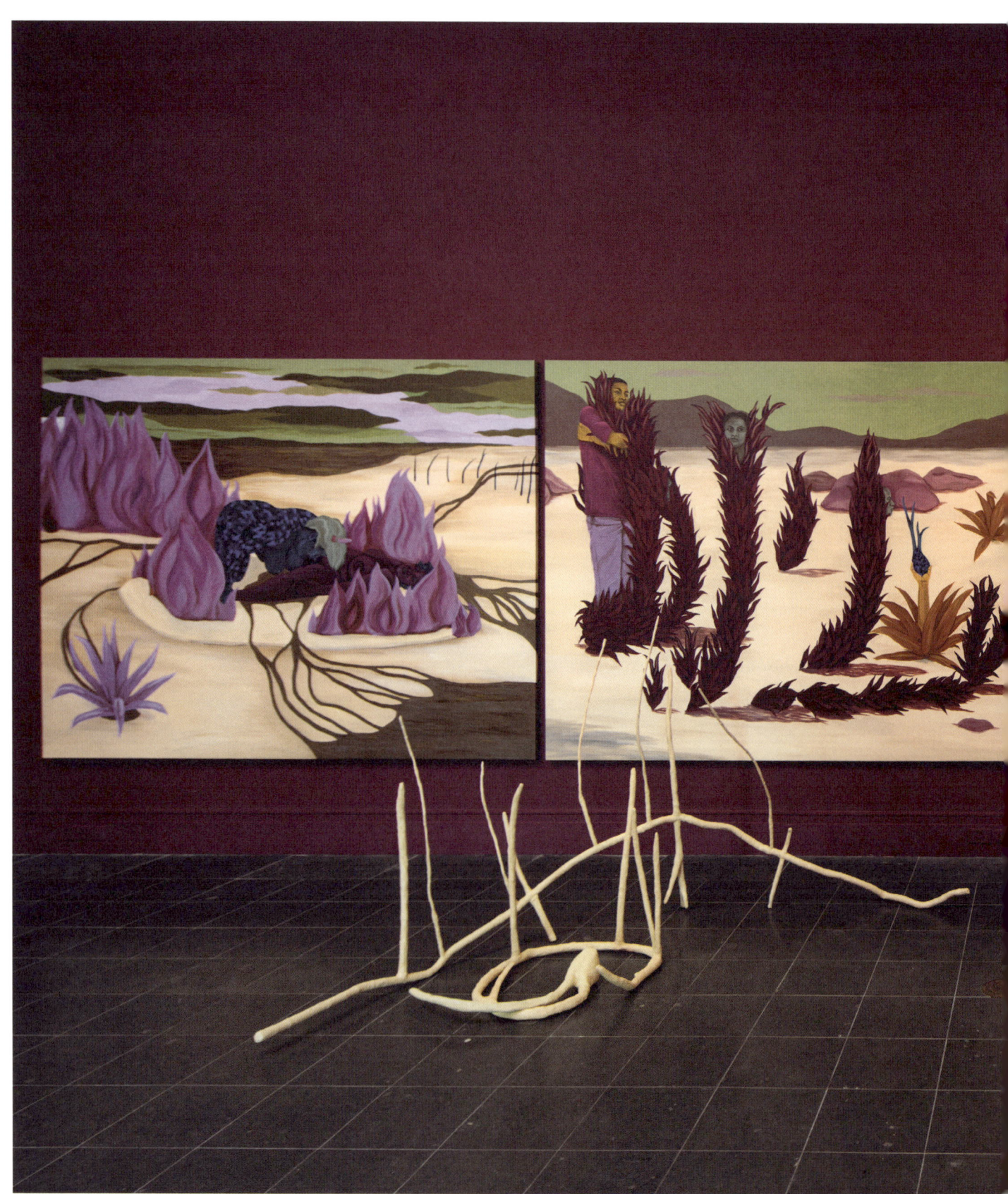

In a barren land we make dew, 2024

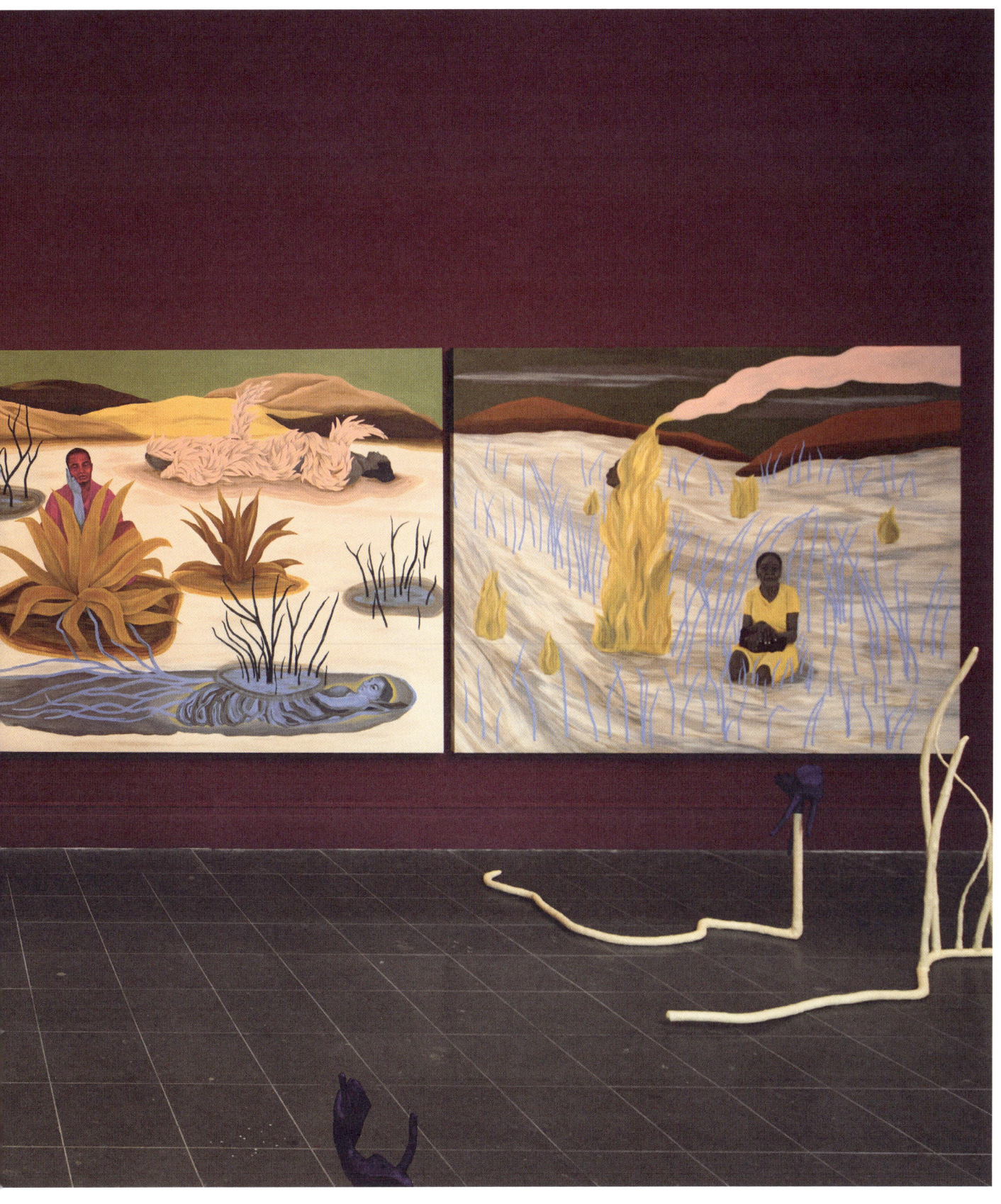

Tessa Mars's paintings, installations, environments, and sculptures are often barren landscapes, capable of surprise and sudden, forceful change. Their apparent silence infuses her oeuvre with a timeless aura, a critical dimension of the work. In her earlier paintings, subtle boundaries change color, suggesting a horizon or waterline. These transitional hues were initially intended to read as fractures or breaks, formal prompts that signified change. In her multimodal work for Prospect.6, *In a barren land we make dew* (2024), Mars conceptually mobilizes this healing power by embracing history, memory, and migration to imagine what may come.

This installation imagines migratory spaces as simultaneously tangible and intangible, holding death and creation, memorial and futurity in their grasp. Modern geopolitical boundaries interrupt this flow, but in this work, Mars's paintings and sculptures reimagine the swamps, seas, mangroves, deserts, and gardens as places of possibility. Consistent with her previous artworks, Mars inserts her alter ego Tessalines, an avatar that merges the artist with the persona of Haitian revolutionary Jean-Jacques Dessalines. *In a barren land* also includes depictions of the artist's family members. One sees people cultivating, gestating together, and caring for each other. Sculptures add dimension to painted landscapes and transform them into environments where, what may first appear barren and inhospitable to life, now sustains it.

These figures embody physical strength and freedom, pasts and presents. Both human and animal, expressing freedom and affirming life in myriad ways: body doubling, autoerotic sexual pleasure, and as provocateurs and guardians performing communal care. Here these bodies are free to move in the world without the constraints of time, gender, or citizenship.

For Mars, the emphasis on the Haitian revolution as a military victory has occluded the ways in which its success was only possible through community-building among slave and free, rural and urban, Black and mixed-race populations. This consensus building is embodied by the Haitian concept of the *lakou*, a kind of social cultivar, a community working together to live.

Earlier in her practice Mars's characters were often pictured alone or in communion with a single figure, but her work for P.6, exhibited in a city that was once a lakou for Haitians fleeing post-revolutionary uncertainty, embodies its values in the present. In drawing on Jacques Roumain's *Masters of the Dew* and the music of Cécile Mclorin Salvant for this work, Mars's multimodal installation redeploys lakou as a matter of life. The lakou that Mars puts forward is a space of togetherness that exists spiritually, acknowledging the Haitian communities that are not able to share physical space, as they are spread all over the world.

Avatars, mangroves, desolate lands, larvae, aloe and other medicinal plants speak life amidst uncertainty. *In a barren land we make dew*. We live. We make do.

by Erica Moiah James

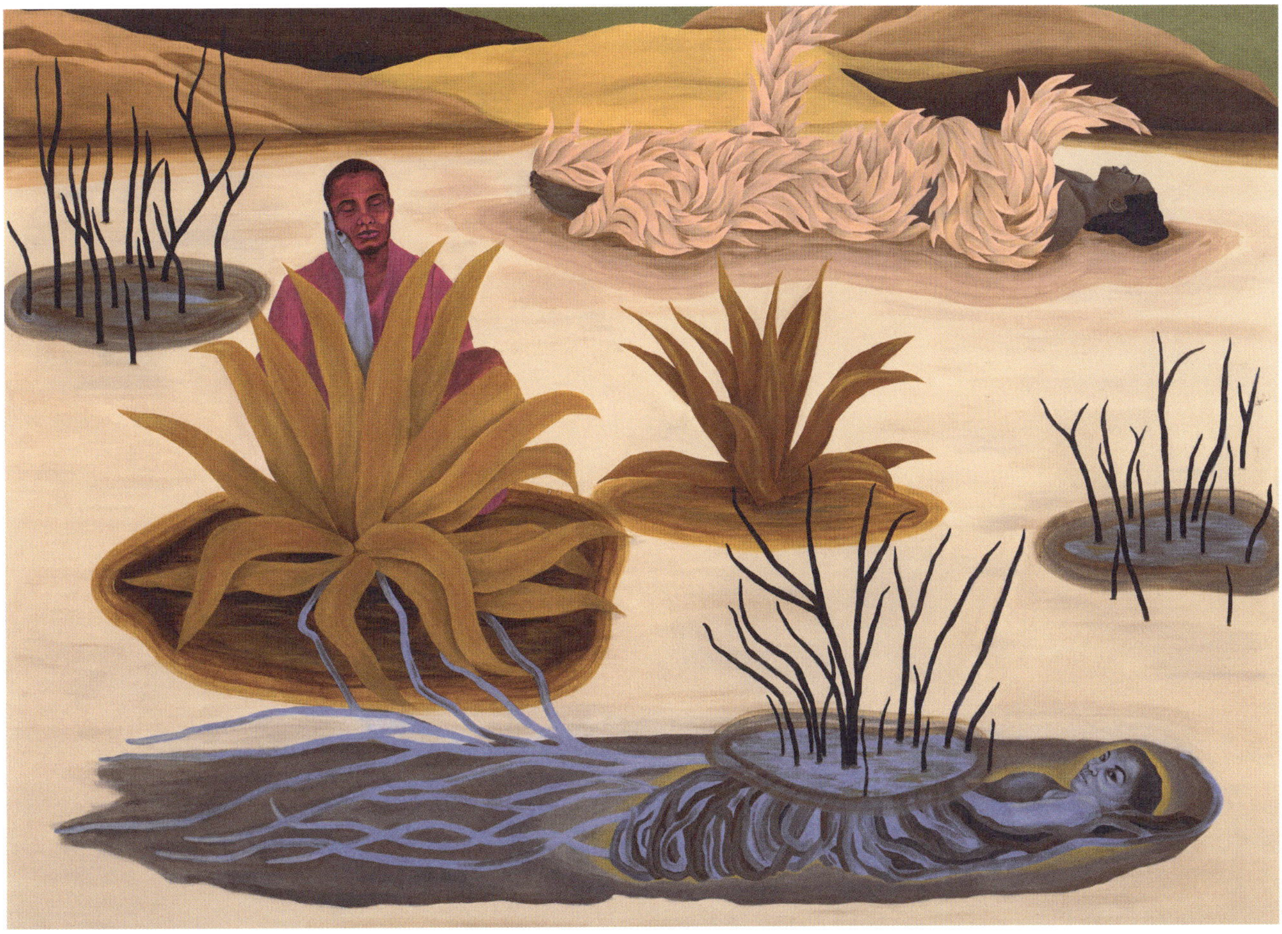

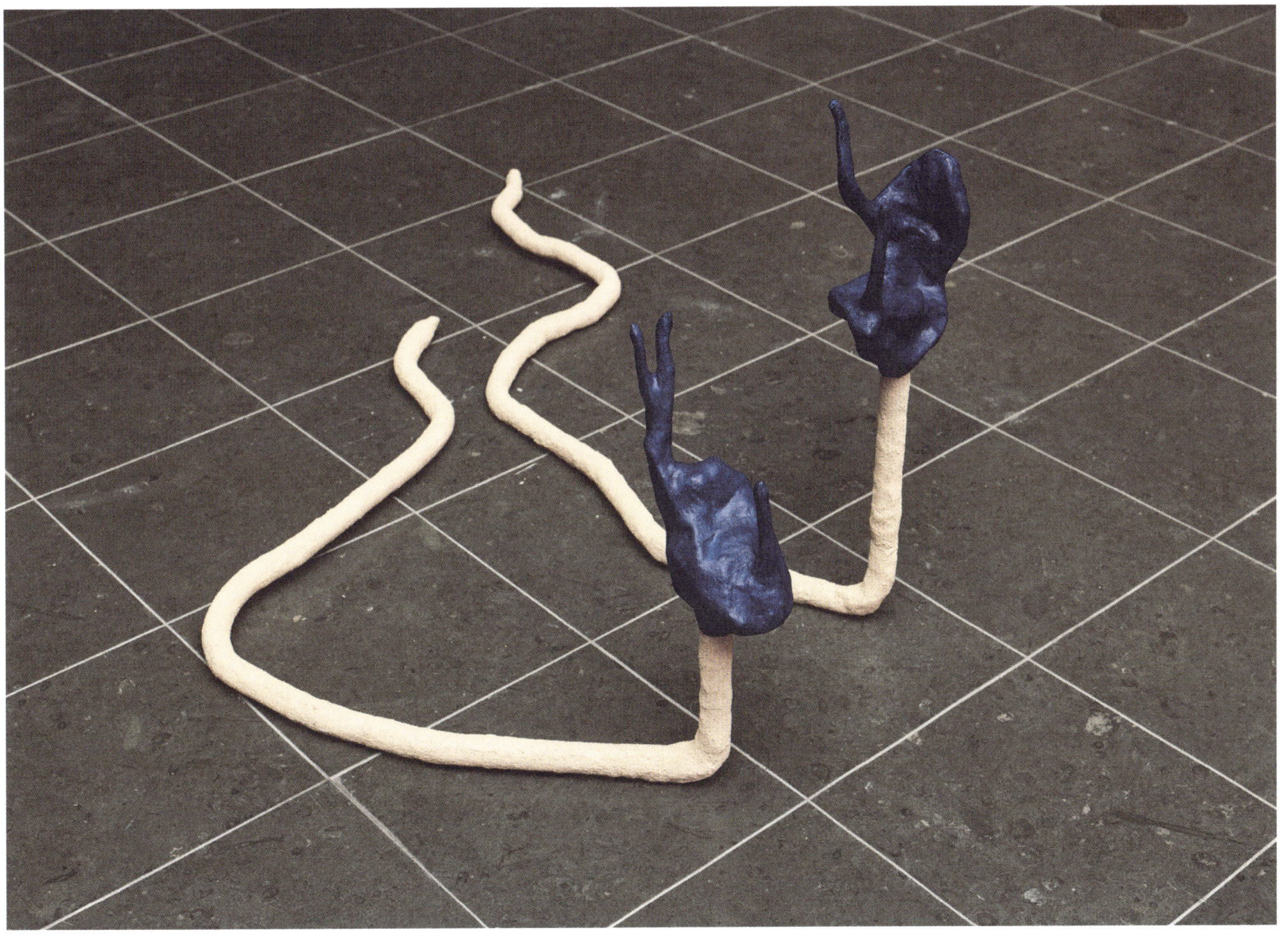

In a barren land we make dew, 2024 (details)

Jeffrey Meris

b. 1991, Saint-Louis du Nord, Haiti; lives in Nassau, Bahamas and New York, NY

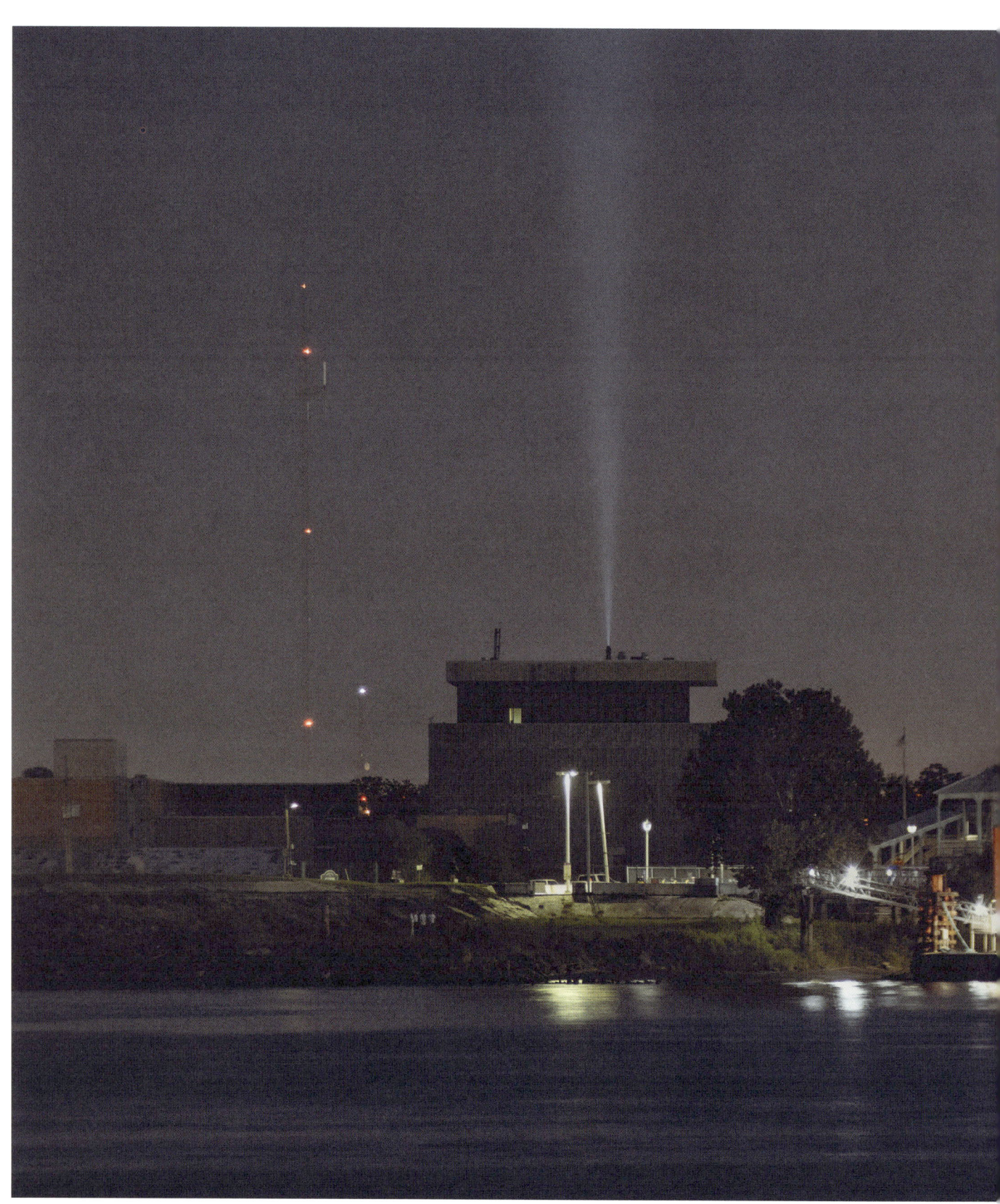

Our Moons Shine, For All the Worlds to See, 2024. Algiers Point, New Orleans

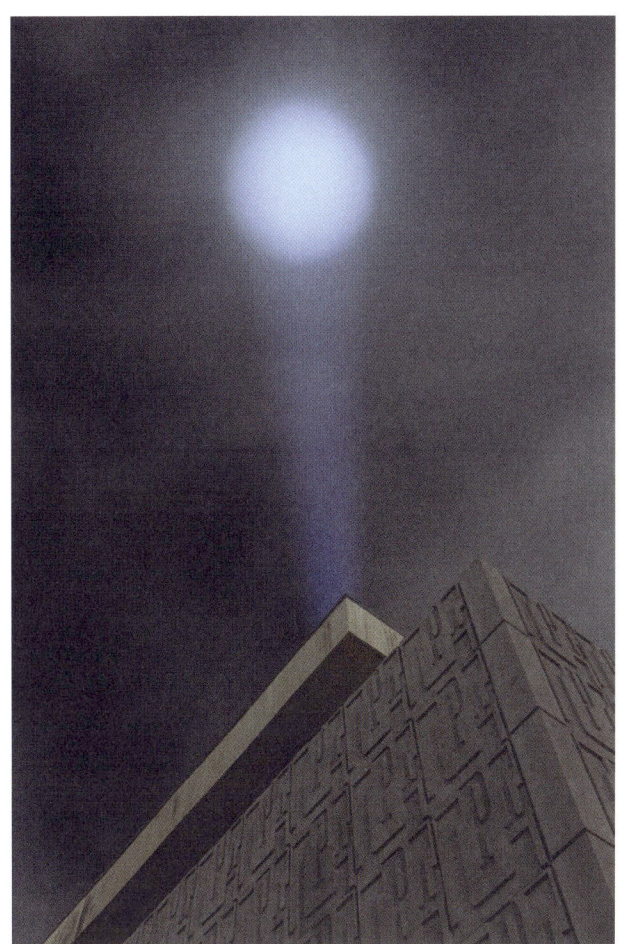

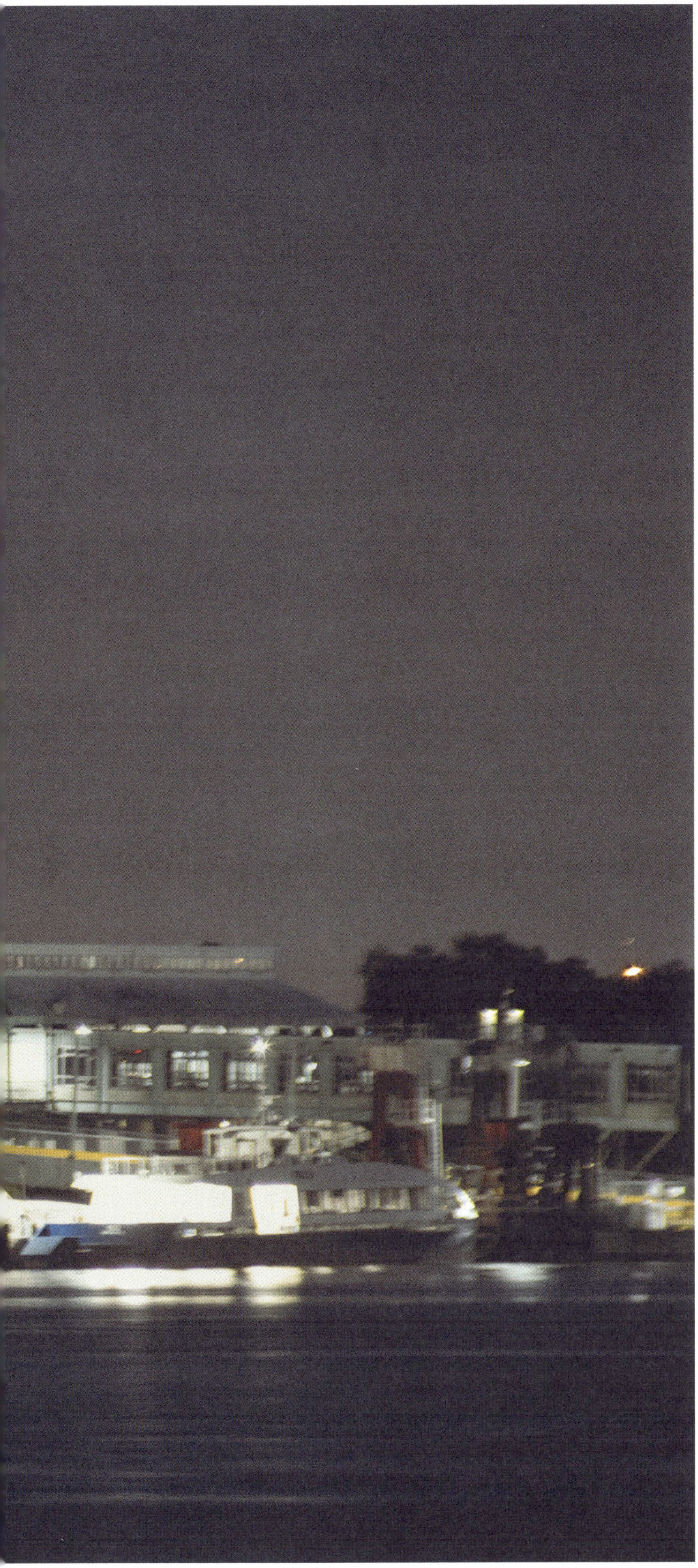

In Édouard Glissant's 1989 text *Caribbean Discourse*, the philosopher-poet synthesizes the animus of settler colonialism in one devastating footnote: "The West is not in the West . . . It is a project, not a place." For Jeffrey Meris—born in Haiti, raised in the Bahamas, and currently living in Harlem—this footnote provides fertile ground for thinking and creating in a critical, reparative mode. Attuned to the legacies of Anglo-American imperialism and its continual rupturing of Black life then and now, here and there, Meris's practice harnesses strategies of abstraction, material transformation, and acts of care to assemble expansive registrations of Black diasporic experience and futurity. Central to this work is the body—the artist's body, the bodies of loved ones, and the collective body of the Global Majority—and what it means to be in dialogue with Black re-presentation, without acquiescing to the violent desires or instrumental demands of the White gaze.

While Meris works across genres, his investments in sculpture and its traditions of seriality, casting, repurposing materials, site-specificity, and alchemy are emphasized in both two- and three-dimensional work. Meris's studio is thus a space of discovery and accumulation, a creative economy of production where nothing is wasted or lost, but involved in cycles of renewal and reclamation. A student of Caribbean history and activism, Meris's materials are selected for their political and poetic significance to the lived experiences of Haitian and Bahamian citizens. For example, the black roofing paper used as the ground for his metaphysical and cosmological series *I, Used to Be* (2021), is a nod to the destructive hurricanes and tropical storms that scatter the material across the landscape. The underarm crutches that form the rhizomatic corona shape of the sculpture *To the Rising Sun* (2023) reimagine the orthopedic aids as liberatory signifiers of Afro-Caribbean strength. Yet some materials can be traced directly to Meris himself, like the secondhand T-shirts and repurposed rags used to clean his copper sculptures in his series, *Shirt vs. Skin* (2021-ongoing), or the spider plants and orchids incorporated into the chandelier sculpture series *Catch a Stick of Fire II* (2021), which the artist tends and cares for in his studio and apartment.

Meris's two-venue installation for Prospect.6 takes up the call-and-response tradition of African diasporic cultures to connect New Orleans with his childhood home of Nassau in the Bahamas. Titled *Our Moons Shine, For All the Worlds to See* (2024), Meris projects a beaming light that emits "I am a possibility" in Morse code from the top of the old Louisiana Power & Light Building, nestled on the edge of the Mississippi River in Algiers Point, and "I am a promise" from atop the harbor-facing Fort Charlotte in Nassau. A nod to a popular Christian devotional sung each morning at Meris's childhood school, the title's hopeful message rubs against the historical use of the lighthouses and water towers scattered across the coasts of colonized lands. Built in the eighteenth century by British governor Lord Dunmore after the American Revolutionary War, Fort Charlotte was never used in battle, but stands as a reminder of empire nevertheless—and the ways colonial infrastructure continues to shape and interrupt Nassau's landscape and communal history.

Both of these structures were crucial to the development of global capitalism and the the global slave trade. In the aftermath of enslavement, migrants and tourists continue to make these journeys, fleeing from or running towards their destinies—each one of them a possibility, a promise, a vibration of light in a dark world.

by Jordan Amirkhani

Our Moons Shine, For All the Worlds to See,
2024. Fort Charlotte, Nassau, Bahamas

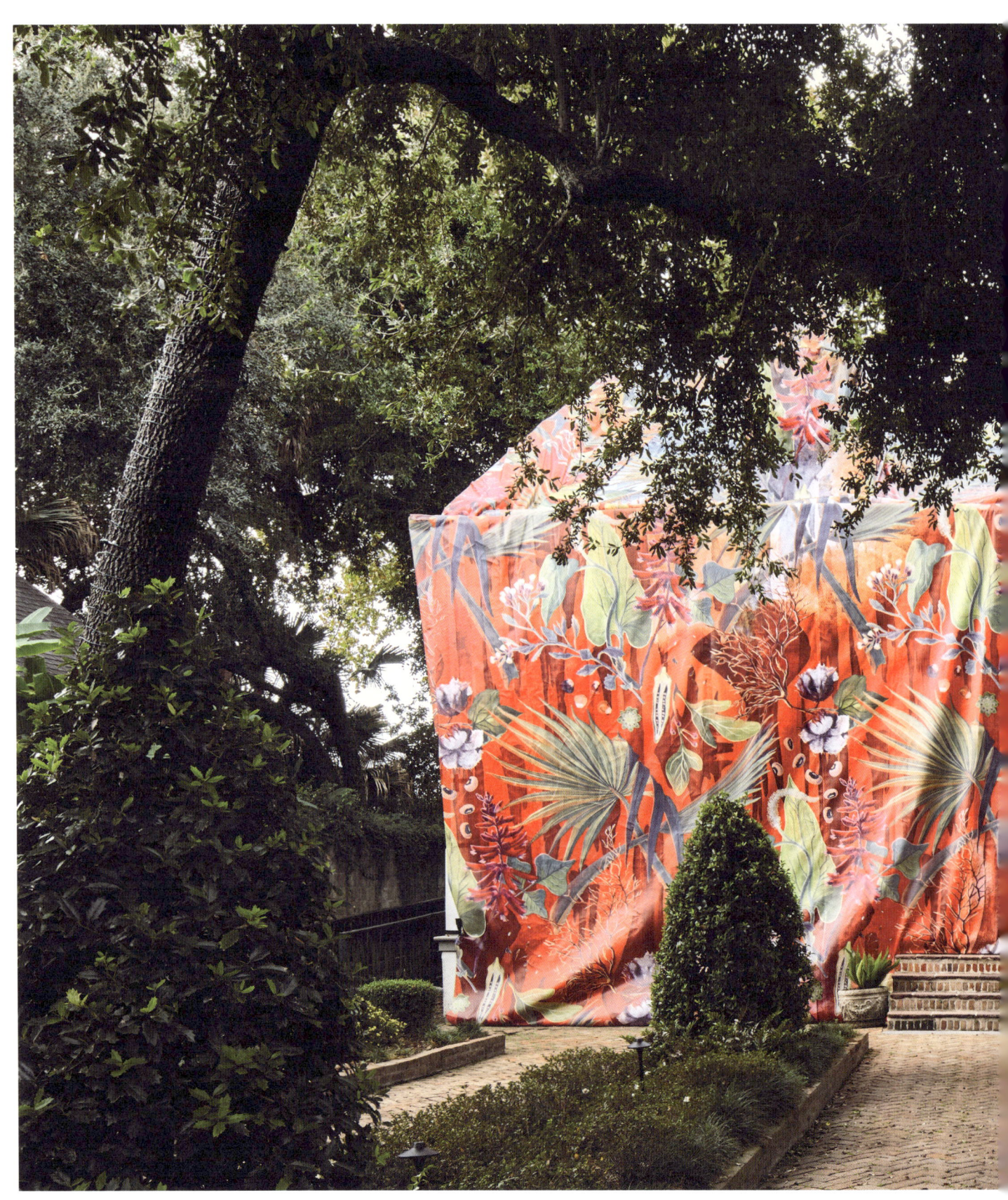

Fleurs de liberation: an ecology of resistance
(Cloaking of the Meilleur-Goldthwaite House), 2024

Joiri Minaya

b. 1990, New York, NY; lives in New York, NY

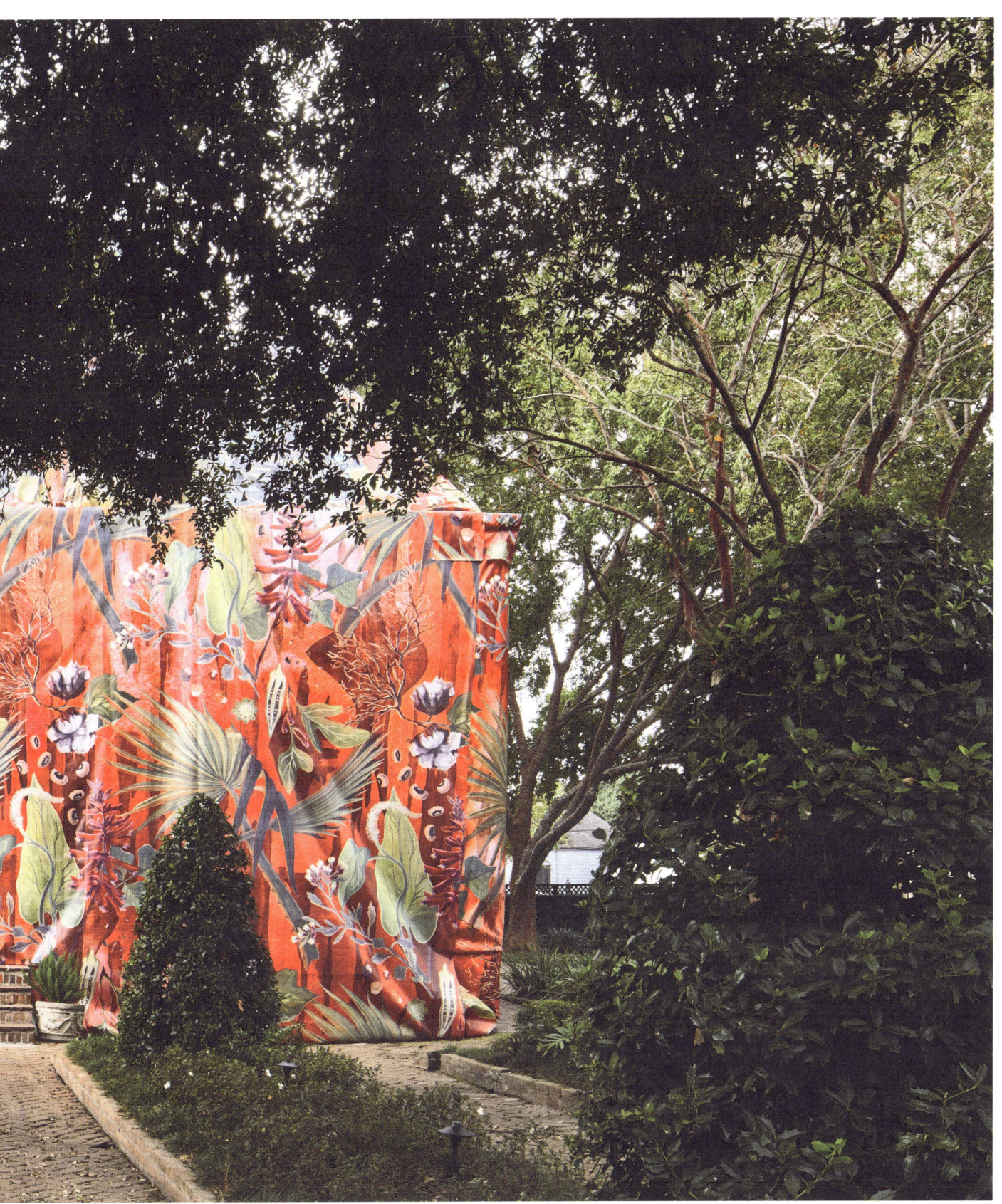

Joiri Minaya's new project for Prospect.6, *Fleurs de liberation: an ecology of resistance (Cloaking of the Meilleur-Goldthwaite House)* (2024), signals a new and evolving phase of public memory building in New Orleans. Minaya's outdoor intervention, concurrent with other P.6 outdoor commissions and Prospect's Artists of Public Memory program, complement the city's ongoing process of redefining which stories will be underscored in public spaces following a wave of Confederate monument removals in 2017. Minaya's cloaking envelops the Meilleur-Goldthwaite House in a vibrant red, blue, and gold fabric covered with a repeating pattern of plants indigenous to Louisiana and Africa. From afar the work acts as a visual exclamation point on the campus of the New Orleans African American Museum—an evocation of a plantation set ablaze. The work demands a reorientation towards the histories of the city's people of color.

Minaya's *Fleurs* builds upon her ongoing *Cloaking* series and is her most ambitious iteration. Her series began in 2017 with a proposal to cloak the statue of Christopher Columbus in front of the Government House in Nassau with fabric. When Minaya was denied permission, she created postcards featuring a rendering of her proposal. In 2019 Minaya cloaked Miami's statues of Columbus and Juan Ponce de León with fabric featuring patterns of tropical plants used by Indigenous people for healing and resistance. What was once reified in bronze, was sheathed, softened, and neutralized in a fabric that celebrates botanical knowledge that has survived centuries of colonization. Her aim of responding to and rewriting colonial narratives is underscored by the meticulous style of her plant renderings, which emulates the aesthetic of Western botanical catalogues from the eighteenth and nineteenth centuries.

In New Orleans, Minaya's pattern folds together Indigenous and African histories. For centuries before the French and Spanish arrived in New Orleans, the road in front of the Meilleur-Goldthwaite house—Governor Nicholls Street—was part of a portage route used by tribes who resided upon this land, including the Atakapa, Caddo, Choctaw, Houma, Natchez, and Tunica. Following the arrival of the French in the early eighteenth century, the house's site was part of the Morand Plantation.

In the nineteenth century, the land became part of Faubourg Tremé, a neighborhood comprised mostly of free people of color, including refugees from the Haitian revolution. The house's scale, and the still extant slave quarters behind it, indicates the relative wealth of its first inhabitant, Simon Meilleur, who was the city's jailer.

Minaya's pattern incorporates plants native to Louisiana, such as palmetto (used by many tribes for shelter and baskets) and cypress (whose forests provided building materials and refuge to maroons), as well as coral beans (used to treat viruses) and lizard's tail (used as an astringent and to treat wounds). Other plants include edible ones of Indigenous origins (corn and sassafras) or African origins (black-eyed peas and African wild rice). Her artwork's title, *Fleurs de liberation*, subtly plays upon the ubiquitous fleur-de-lis symbol that appears throughout New Orleans.

Like Christo and Jeanne-Claude's wrappings of buildings and monuments, Minaya's cloaking resignifies the site. In Minaya's work, however, histories of power and subjugation are more pointedly brought to the surface, as she unabashedly implicates the individuals and systems of power responsible for injustices. Her final product focuses not on the trauma, but on tools for survival. Embedded within her *Fleurs* pattern is cotton root. As nearly all abortions are currently banned in Louisiana, it bears remembering that this plant has been used since time immemorial as an abortifacient.

by Miranda Lash

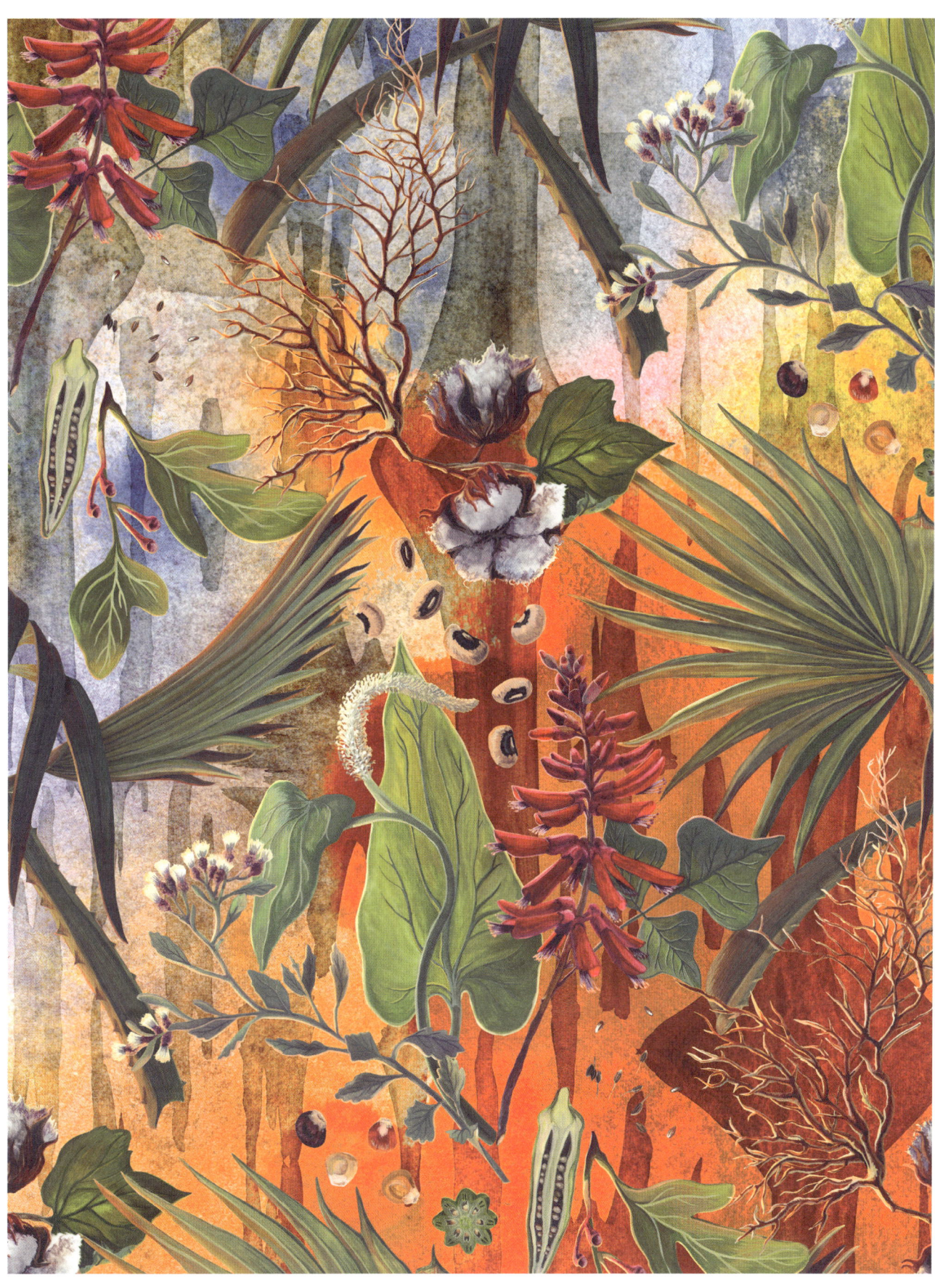

Fleurs de liberation: an ecology of resistance (Cloaking of the Meilleur-Goldthwaite House), 2024 (detail of digital pattern)

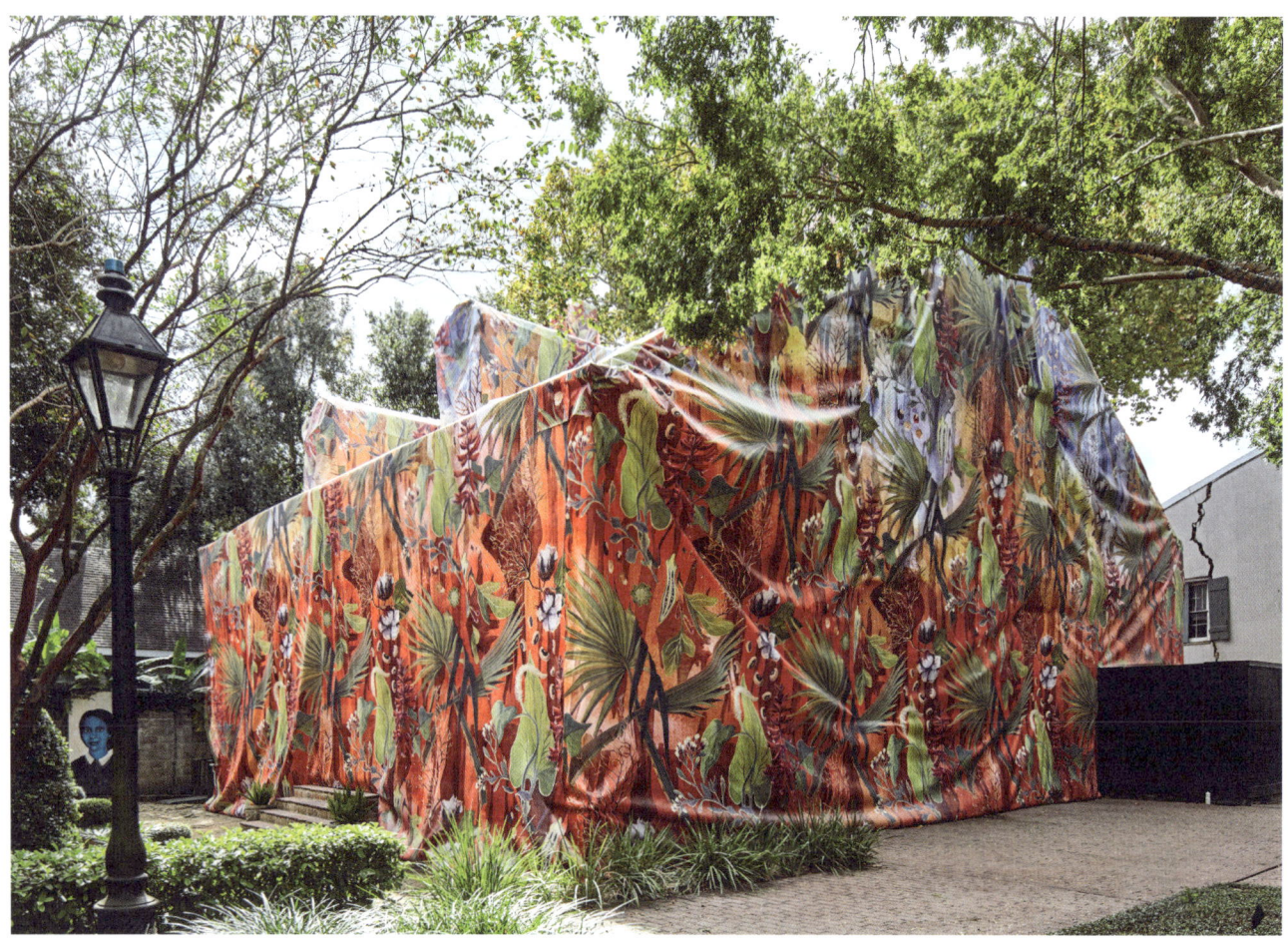

Fleurs de liberation: an ecology of resistance (Cloaking of the Meilleur-Goldthwaite House), 2024

Preparing for the Next Seven Generations

Lora Ann Chaisson

As told to Miranda Lash on May 29, 2024, in Pointe-aux-Chene, Louisiana

I don't know what the future holds, but I want our tribal people to be part of the solution.

It is my second year as Principal Chief of the United Houma Nation. We are building the tribe's future by focusing on a four-part policy called FACE: Federal Recognition, Accountability, Cultural Preservation & Education, and Economic Development.

We are recognized by the state of Louisiana, but are still seeking federal recognition as a tribe. In doing so, we honor our elders who worked on this endeavor while enduring discrimination. Both sides of my family fought for equal pay and equal rights. My mother worked on weekends, gathering paperwork for our application for federal recognition while all of us kids were fishing. As soon as I was elected chief, I put our team back together to focus on our federal recognition application. We're working with a blessed team consisting of Dr. Jack Campisi, Dr. William (Bill) Starna, and Ms. Arlinda Locklear, who's worked with our people for over forty years. Ms. Arlinda is the first Native American woman to ever argue before the Supreme Court and win. We also have our other tribal attorney, Jessica Duggan, from our own tribe, and Joshua Pitre, who works in policy. Many people don't understand what is involved in the application. Our last application to the Office of Federal Acknowledgement was many boxes. Right now, we are almost done with our application.

Accountability is critical to our future, so we ensure all our tribal funds are accounted for. When I arrived as Chief after Hurricane Ida, I made sure that the donations we had received for our tribal citizens to rebuild their homes were distributed. We created an independent ad-hoc committee to create criteria, then submitted those criteria to the Tribal Security Committee to be implemented for the applicants. We gave approximately $300,000 to citizens in $1,000 grants for rebuilding materials, furniture, and other needs. We started a pilot program for working with veterans who were houseless or close to being houseless, including legal fees for anything related to housing.

I was raised with a deep commitment to preserving our culture, dedicating my life to maintaining traditions such as basket weaving, beading, building traditional homes, keeping our herbal medicine, and passing down our oral history. My goal is to share the knowledge with the next generation. Our youth program features Jamie Billiot Dardar, a licensed teacher who conducts monthly Zoom sessions on history for groups of various ages. Although our service area spans six parishes, with most participants residing in Terrebonne Parish, we've recognized a gap between our older generations, who are rooted in oral traditions, and our younger, more digitally oriented youth. To bridge this division, we have invested in hiring elderly coordinators who specialize in fostering interactions between the youth and our elders, ensuring that both groups can engage and learn from each other effectively.

In December 2022, we hosted our first United Houma Nation Celebration. Because of COVID and Hurricanes Zeta and Ida, we hadn't hosted our elders' celebration or our Award Banquet for a few years. I thought it was time to bring our people back together—so we hosted a very successful United Houma Nation Celebration, with over four hundred people of all ages in attendance. We had a special memorial for the people we lost during COVID. Also, we had Spanish-moss makers, basket makers, net makers, stickball classes, and our first-ever White Bean Cookoff Cash Prize Competition.

Regarding economic development, we need to find ways to take care of our climate and reverse the changes that are happening so fast. We need clean energy jobs. We are exploring the possibilities of solar energy, and our agriculture department is currently developing green solutions, including a bee program and a pilot program with four other tribes for recording seeds and creating seed banks. Louisiana is known for its seafood, but we're flooded with imported shrimp right now, which is driving prices down. Our fishermen have steep regulations, but imported shrimp have none. This is putting our local shrimpers at a severe disadvantage. The alligator industry is facing its own challenges. We use every part of an alligator—

its hide for leather, fat for oils, head for tourist souvenirs, and the meat for delicious dishes. Personally, I make jewelry from the ridges on their backs. The decline in the alligator industry affects hunters, traditional practices, and the local economy that relies on these resources. It's time we stand up for our local industries and ensure they have the support they need to thrive.

Looking a hundred years into the future, climate change is very real. I've lived it, and I've seen it, and I'm still living it. Seeing the disappearance of my family and my land in my time, I would love to see a future down here, but the reality is that the government is not doing anything fast enough. The Army Corps of Engineers dammed the Mississippi River and stopped the natural flow of water. Lakes are no longer lakes, bays are no longer bays; you can't decipher the boundaries any longer—it all looks like the Gulf of Mexico. The oil and gas companies came and dug up our perfect hard land without permission, dug canals, and didn't dam the waters. Without damming the freshly dug canals, it allowed all the salt water to seep in, and since the Army Corps kept the fresh water out, there was no fresh water from the Mississippi River to replenish the salt water. Those two historical incidents have caused significant land loss in south Louisiana; man always thinks they know better than our Creator.

There is a significant disconnect between the broader society and Indigenous communities. While we need inclusion in discussions, we must take a leading role in these matters. This is our Mother Earth; we know what is best for her. Had our elders been at the table, we might not face the challenges we do today. With federal recognition, I envision land further north being put into a trust. I see a state-of-the-art hospital, museum, and store that sells our non-GMO produce, game, and seafood from our people. And we can't forget great restaurants; our people are excellent cooks! Ultimately, it's about unity and staying together.

To the future chief, my advice is this: Exercise patience and recognize that once you take on this role, your personal voice takes a backseat to the collective voice of the people. Your decisions should serve the needs and interests of the 19,000 individuals you represent. Remember, the choices you make today will impact not only the present but also the next seven generations. Always consider the long-term consequences of your decisions.

Sisyphus in the Swamp

Joshua Lewis

The largest coastal infrastructure project on the US Gulf Coast is hard to find. One must wind through crumbling, partially overgrown roads that serve a few industrial facilities in New Orleans East. Passing piles of discarded tires and egrets wading through clogged drainage ditches, the landscape gives little indication that you are approaching one of the most important and expensive federal infrastructure investments in the United States. The Inner Harbor Lake Borgne Storm Surge Barrier is a nearly two-mile-long expanse of concrete and steel, designed to prevent storm surges from overwhelming the region's eastern flank. Over six-hundred massive, black steel pilings are sunk diagonally some two-hundred feet into the marshy soil, each appearing to push against the hulking wall.

Each of these pilings stands like Sisyphus, the Greek mythological figure condemned to an eternity of pushing a heavy stone up a mountainside for his hubris. The storm surge barrier, known colloquially as "The Great Wall of Louisiana," embodies the hubris of human engineering in the face of a dynamic environment, and the tragedies such hubris can bring forth. The Great Wall was constructed in a reactive, urgent manner. The US Army Corps of Engineers desperately sought a solution to the flooding risk that their own past actions had created (primarily, the reworking of the city's eastern edge to serve navigation and industry). The immense scale of the barrier is less a testament to the promise of coastal engineering than it is an embodiment of the failure to protect vulnerable residents during the calamities of Hurricane Katrina—and our society's failure to balance the accumulation of wealth with the integrity of our ecosystems and health of our communities.

New Orleans is frequently—and tediously—referenced as a special and unique case of the confrontation between urbanization, nature, and

Photographs by Ben Depp

a changing climate, but this just isn't so. Perhaps we only arrived at the climate precipice a few steps ahead of our peers. New Orleans also (just as tediously) appears in the national conversation as a once-great city that has declined into an irrelevant backwater. Let us begin by considering the question: Is this region's place in the global economic order too modest, and its future too precarious, to draw any meaningful insights that can be applied to the other coastal metropolises of the twenty first century?

Let us first debunk the notion of New Orleans's supposed economic irrelevance. New Orleans is a critical node in the global economic system. Southeast Louisiana has long served as a control point for important global commodities—agricultural, mineral, industrial, and

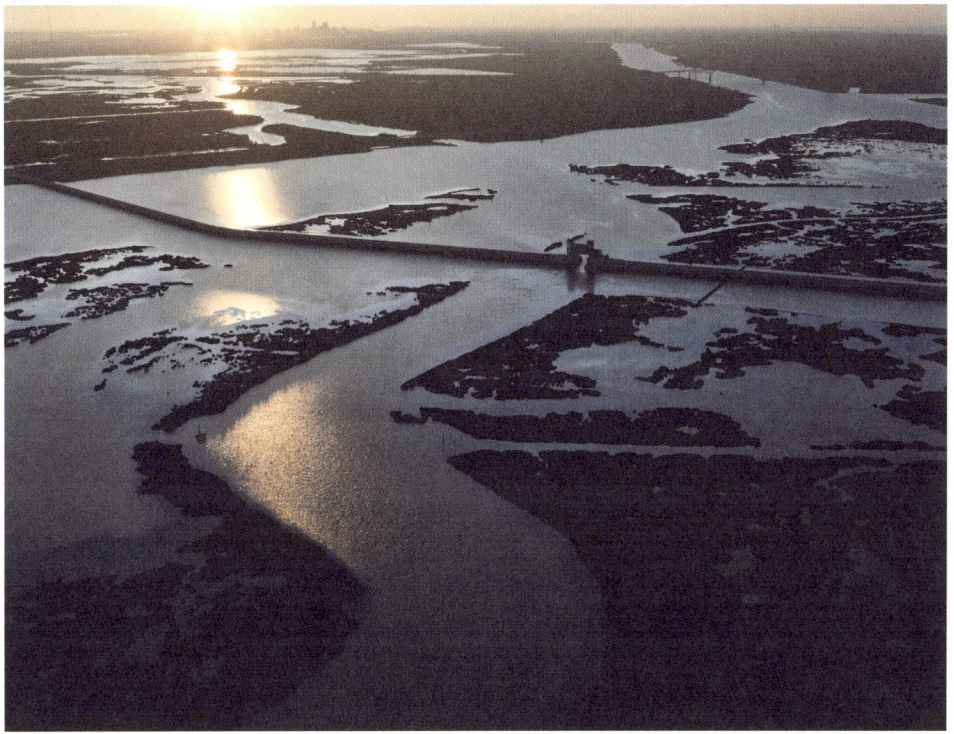

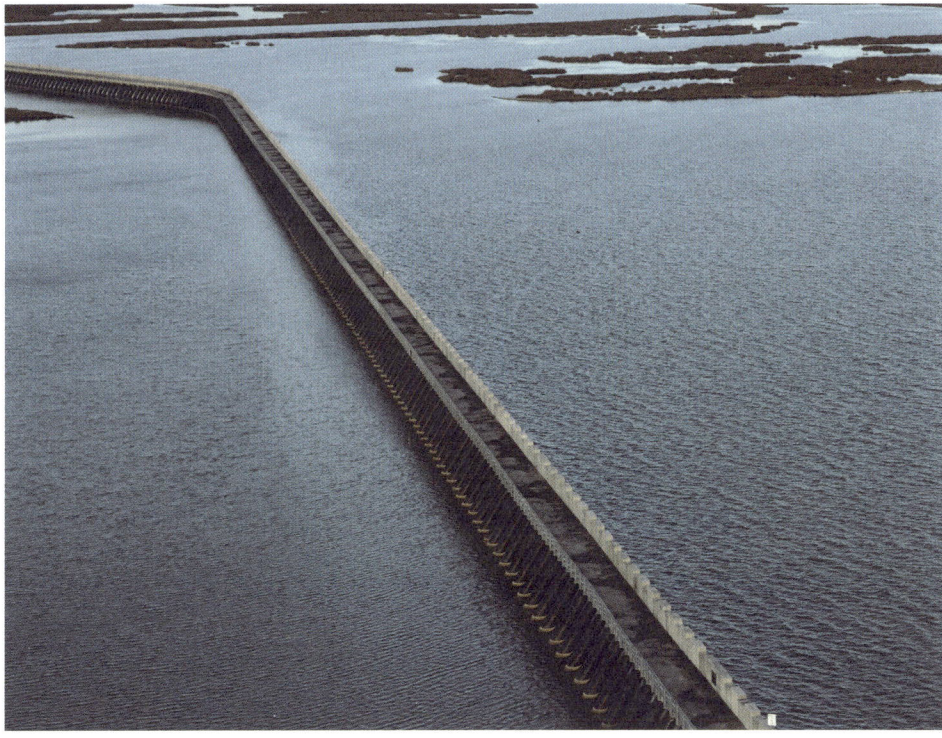

Top and above: Two views of the Inner Harbor Navigation Canal Storm Surge Barrier. The barrier is designed to protect the region from storm surges along its eastern flank. St. Bernard Parish, Louisiana, 2016

cultural. During the eighteenth and nineteenth centuries, the region was the nexus of the vast plantation agriculture system, circulating commodities forged through the removal of Indigenous groups, the transformation and disruption of ecosystems, and the brutal capture, transport, and enslavement of African peoples in pursuit of profit. These atrocities, combined with the city's position at the interface of oceanic trade routes and the Mississippi River's inland waterways, undergirded this growth. In 1860, New Orleans was not just the largest city in the Southern United States, its population was greater than the next five largest cities combined.

While the region's status as the dominant Southern population center gradually waned throughout the twentieth century, the region's position in the global economic system actually expanded and intensified. The region's wharves and refineries remain essential organs of global capitalism, directing flows of soybeans, grains, steel, and petrochemicals that are fundamental to the world economic system. If the port complex along the Lower Mississippi River were to cease operations, it could quite conceivably trigger a global food and energy crisis impacting billions of people. New Orleans has helped create, and continues to uphold, the patterns of economic exchange and land use across the entire Mississippi Basin and the rest of the planet.

The decoupling of economic growth from population growth in the region is not particularly unusual. Indeed, this points toward a broader phenomenon where increasingly automated and mechanized systems of economic production require less day-to-day input of human labor to function. Profits can continue to grow while the need for local labor shrinks. The benefits of economic growth are concentrated among a smaller group of elites, and fewer resources reach residents in the form of wages and public revenues, constraining upward mobility and creating few incentives for in-migration of new residents. Just as New Orleans found itself on the horns of the climate dilemma ahead of its peers, the million or so residents of the region arrived at this economic precipice only a few steps ahead of other cities, where the sophistication

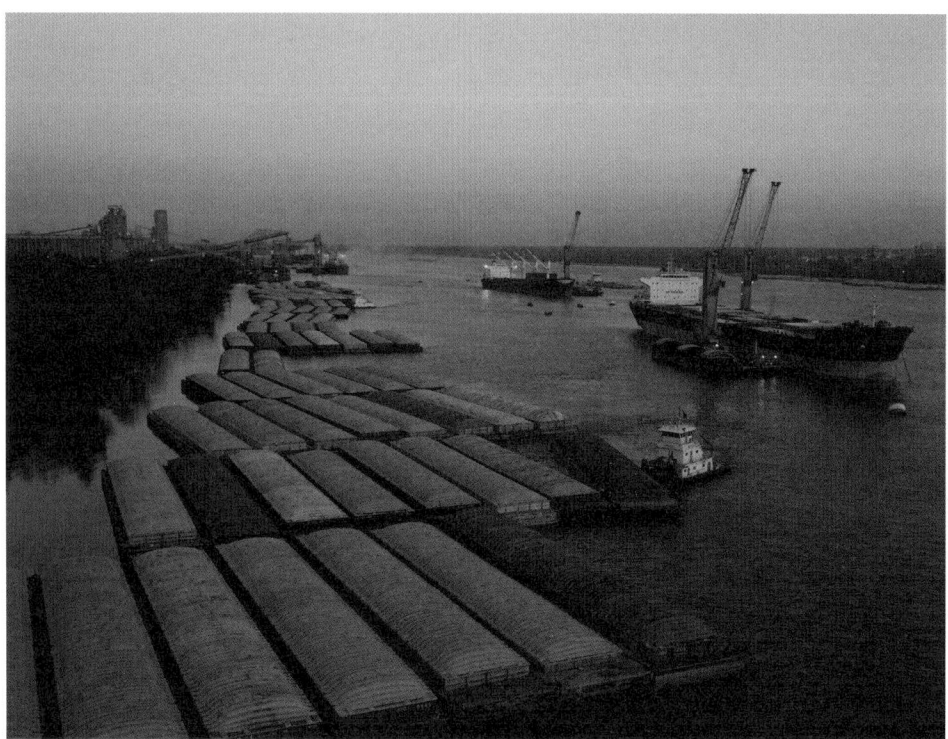

Barges lined up on the Mississippi River next to a grain elevator in Destrehan, St. Charles Parish, Louisiana, 2021

of automation and advent of algorithms and artificial intelligence threaten new economic sectors with a similar fate.

The gap between the region's economic importance and the daily lives of its residents is, and has always been, glaringly wide. A walk down the river levee can reveal someone fishing for catfish to put food on the table while their cork bobs in the wake of a ship carrying three million bushels of corn to the world market. In Plaquemines Parish, one of the largest liquefied natural gas (LNG) export terminals in the world is currently under construction, with thousands of mostly transient workers laboring around the clock to construct the massive facility. Meanwhile, Plaquemines Parish itself has undergone decades of population loss and declining public revenues, with daily life becoming increasingly challenging and untenable for many, and the new terminal seems unlikely to reverse this trend. The dredging of the Mississippi River's ship channel, which enables the ships full of corn and LNG to move freely, has likely exacerbated the risk of saltwater intrusion into drinking water supplies— as we witnessed during the summer of 2023—compounding threats to the region's quality of life. The national media's attention to the seemingly endless variety of catastrophes facing the region has, for decades, indeed centuries, engendered a sort of apocalyptic exceptionalism about New Orleans. Are we doomed in some mysterious and singular way?

One by one, communities across the world are arriving at the climate precipice alongside New Orleans. The complex effects of climate change and extreme weather events unfold every day along the world's coastlines. In many cases, these changes are outpacing the capacity of coastal communities to develop effective strategies for infrastructural adaptation. In 2023, the United Nations declared an adaptation emergency, urging world leaders to invest in new and innovative programs to prepare communities for an uncertain future. Mean sea level has increased 20 cm (about 8 inches) since 1900, and the rate of sea level rise is increasing. Projections put it at about a foot more before 2050, and up to 2 meters by 2100, according to a 2021 report from the UN Intergovernmental Panel on Climate Change. Many coastal areas are

A life ring floats behind a wrecked shrimp boat after Hurricane Ida in the fishing community of Cocodrie, Louisiana, 2021 also experiencing significant subsidence: Recent studies have shown that large swaths of the US Gulf and East coasts are sinking more rapidly than previously thought, compounding the risks presented by rising seas. Worldwide, coastal lowlands host large and rapidly growing populations, and are home to twenty one of the thirty three largest global megacities facing increasing flood risk. Urbanized river deltas like our own are particularly exposed, because subsidence rates in these settings can actually outpace sea level rise. This is a serious concern in many other nations too, including China, Vietnam, Bangladesh, and the Netherlands, to name only a few.

These challenges are emerging in low-lying coastal systems that are already highly engineered for hydrological control. Thousands of communities worldwide are protected by levees and other systems that are, in most cases, not ready for the climate of the twenty first century. Many of these systems were implemented decades ago, reflecting outdated science and engineering. As the gap between current infrastructural capacity and emerging extreme events widens, low-lying coastal regions are exploring and adopting strategies that deepen infrastructural complexity. Most commonly, these interventions produce greater hydrological (and potentially social, economic, and cultural) isolation by enclosing territory behind perimeter protection systems and complex drainage pumping systems. Transformative projects to enclose harbors and estuaries with levees and barriers are being pursued in and around major cities like Houston, Boston, San Francisco, and New York, as well as smaller cities with critical maritime and defense infrastructure, like Norfolk and Charleston.

Let's take a closer look at Houston, a city that eclipsed New Orleans in both population and economic expansion several decades ago, now joining New Orleans at the climate precipice. Following severe flooding during Hurricane Ike in 2008, Hurricane Harvey in 2017, and a series of major infrastructure failures in subsequent years, significant coastal adaptation initiatives are underway. The most touted solution for storm surge is a two-mile-long barrier across the harbor entrance, inspired by coastal defense strategies adopted in the Netherlands. Sound familiar? In addition to the gated barrier structure, known as the "Ike Dike" for the storm that spawned the idea, the plan also includes levees, pumps, and other protection structures extending dozens of miles, and is likely to carry a price tag of at least $34 billion—roughly thirty times more expensive than New Orleans's Great Wall, and more than twice the cost of repairing and upgrading the entire Southeast Louisiana flood protection system following Katrina. As I've mentioned, it's not just the Gulf Coast considering these approaches: Leaders in New York and Boston have proposed similar barrier systems following Hurricane Sandy in 2012. More coastal cities consider their Sisyphean future every year, as the economic and humanitarian stakes of flood protection in the twenty first century come into greater focus.

Discursively, the task of climate change adaptation is one that looks to the future, but its possibilities and constraints are firmly anchored in the past. In our highly unequal—and litigious—society, new investment in flood protection and coastal restoration animates grand visions as well as old disputes. Who receives protection and who is left exposed? Who profits from these major programs and who remains sidelined? What is to be done about the significant ecological changes that water infrastructure and coastal engineering will trigger?

We are familiar with much of this in Louisiana. Take, for example, the opposition to freshwater and sediment diversions that has emerged among some fishing communities downriver from New Orleans. Re-engineering dynamic coastal ecosystems and reconfiguring community life is riven with contradictions, trade-offs, and injustices. But to many, the scale of the threat calls for a commensurate response, even if new levees and constructed wetlands are built to protect fossil fuel infrastructure that helped give rise to our current predicament.

Climate adaptation projects in and around coastal cities offer important possibilities to address social inequality and climate risks simultaneously—and embed the promises and confront the perils of our Sisyphean future in our communities with greater fairness, awareness, and justice. The creative work of engineering ecosystems and coastal protection requires an educated workforce that understands the stakes of the work, and must draw from those communities most at risk and economically marginalized. It is important to recognize that the structures and landscapes we create through climate adaptation are never truly finished, and they require constant attention to remain effective.

Ribbons may be cut, press releases may scatter in the wind, but the real work involves monitoring, maintaining, and continually adapting these systems in the long run, while also embracing and nurturing more radical and unconventional remedies. Pushing the boulder up the mountain requires many hands, minds, and perspectives. Addressing flooding, for example, is a multi-scalar task that extends from a single new tree planted in a backyard to the vast ecological engineering projects that are in the making. But our best ideas for revolutionizing our relationship to

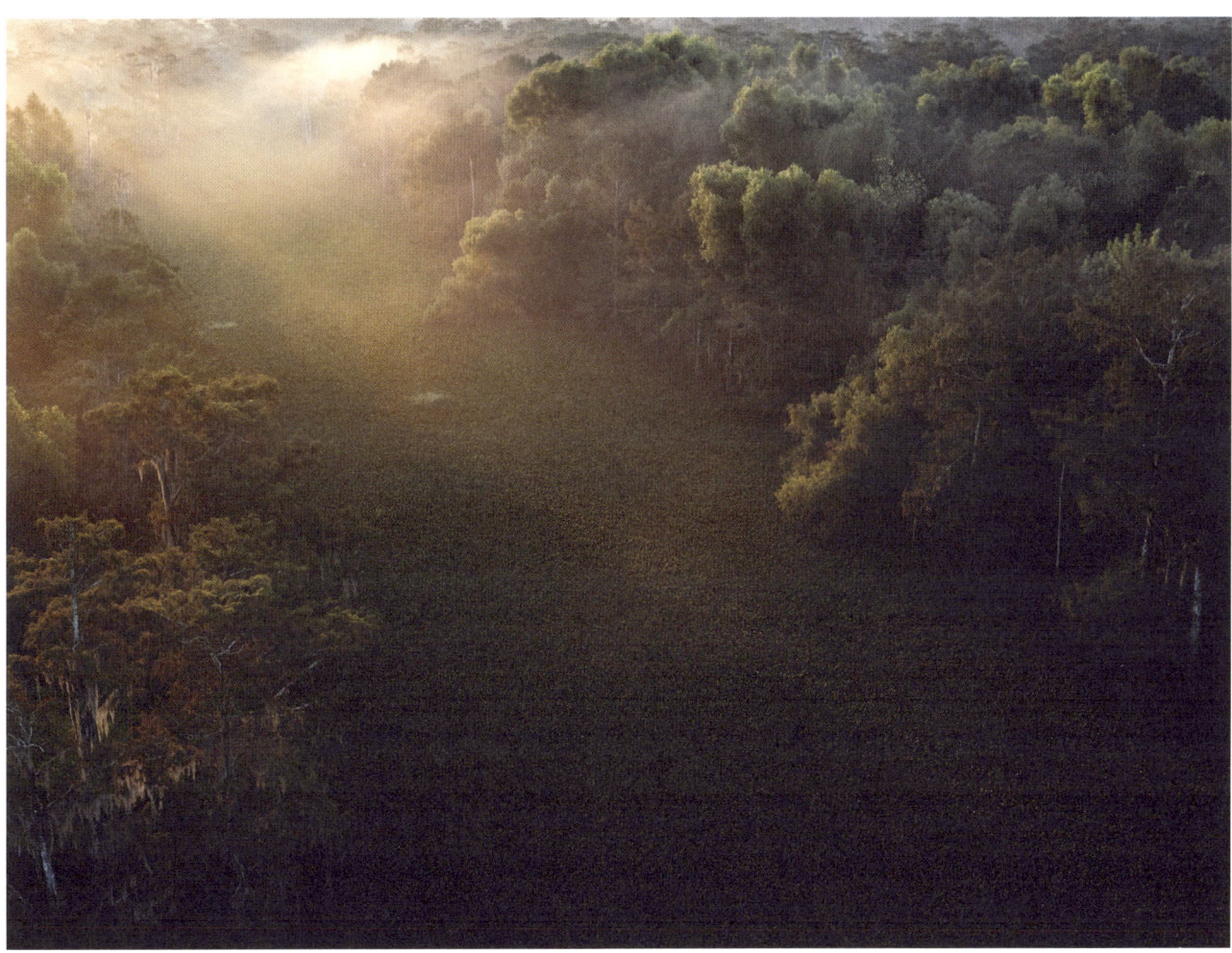

Cypress forest in the Atchafalaya Basin.
New Iberia, Louisiana, 2016

water haven't yet emerged. A fundamental duty in this regard is to ensure that the youth of New Orleans are supported as they explore and grasp our predicament, and are endowed with the resources, skills, and insights needed to lead and problem-solve.

One practical pathway to building our collective environmental and historical literacy is to make our infrastructural systems more accessible and legible to the public, despite—and indeed because of— the failure and tragedy they may symbolize. It should not require orienteering through overgrown post-industrial landscapes, as described at the start of this essay. Artifacts can reveal critical information about our past and what may lay ahead, and are indispensable and enfranchising public goods.

In this regard, artistic work is also critical for public sensemaking from the dizzying vantage point of the climate precipice, as Prospect.6 demonstrates. Hannah Chalew's installations, for instance, embody the chimeric and contradictory systems that define life in New Orleans, where history, industry, community, and the ecological world are intertwined in contested configurations. Ashley Teamer's collage work also coaxes us to encounter the social, ecological, and technological complexity that our future is tangled within. These artists invite us to reckon with our place and its precarity with a refreshing honesty, inciting experiences that might implicate us within—and maybe unbind us from—the seemingly inexorable circumstances we contend with. This sort of insight helps us to navigate our dilemmas with a sense of grounded curiosity, embedding the dismal task of Sisyphus in something more vital and panoramic.

New Orleans is not unique in the threats it faces. We are not a solitary figure heaving against a storm surge barrier in a forgotten marshland. As I've argued, we are perched alongside hundreds of millions of other coastal inhabitants worldwide, all of whom are gradually, if perhaps begrudgingly, accepting their place in our Sisyphean future. Realistically however, the apocalyptic exceptionalism foisted upon our city is not going away anytime soon. This outsized visibility, however ill-considered, carries with it a certain responsibility. Coastal people will look to New Orleans's plight to make sense of their own. As I've described, we did have a bit of a head start, and the stories we write in the coming decades will reverberate beyond our fraying coastline. If we are fated to be a harbinger for the world to learn from, I for one hope, and believe, that we can do so in a way that reveals a path of wisdom, prosperity, and justice for our coastal contemporaries.

The decisions that brought us to this precipice were forged through myopia and greed. But, unfairly or not, the task of Sisyphus is a collective one, and the story of New Orleans will always create a gravitational pull. The more ingenuity, muscle, and resolve we muster together, the greater our capacity to not only maneuver in an uncertain future, but to set forth an approach to climate adaptation that is as effective and egalitarian as it is imaginative and unorthodox. If our reputation must always precede us, let us deepen its resonance and sharpen its insights on our own terms.

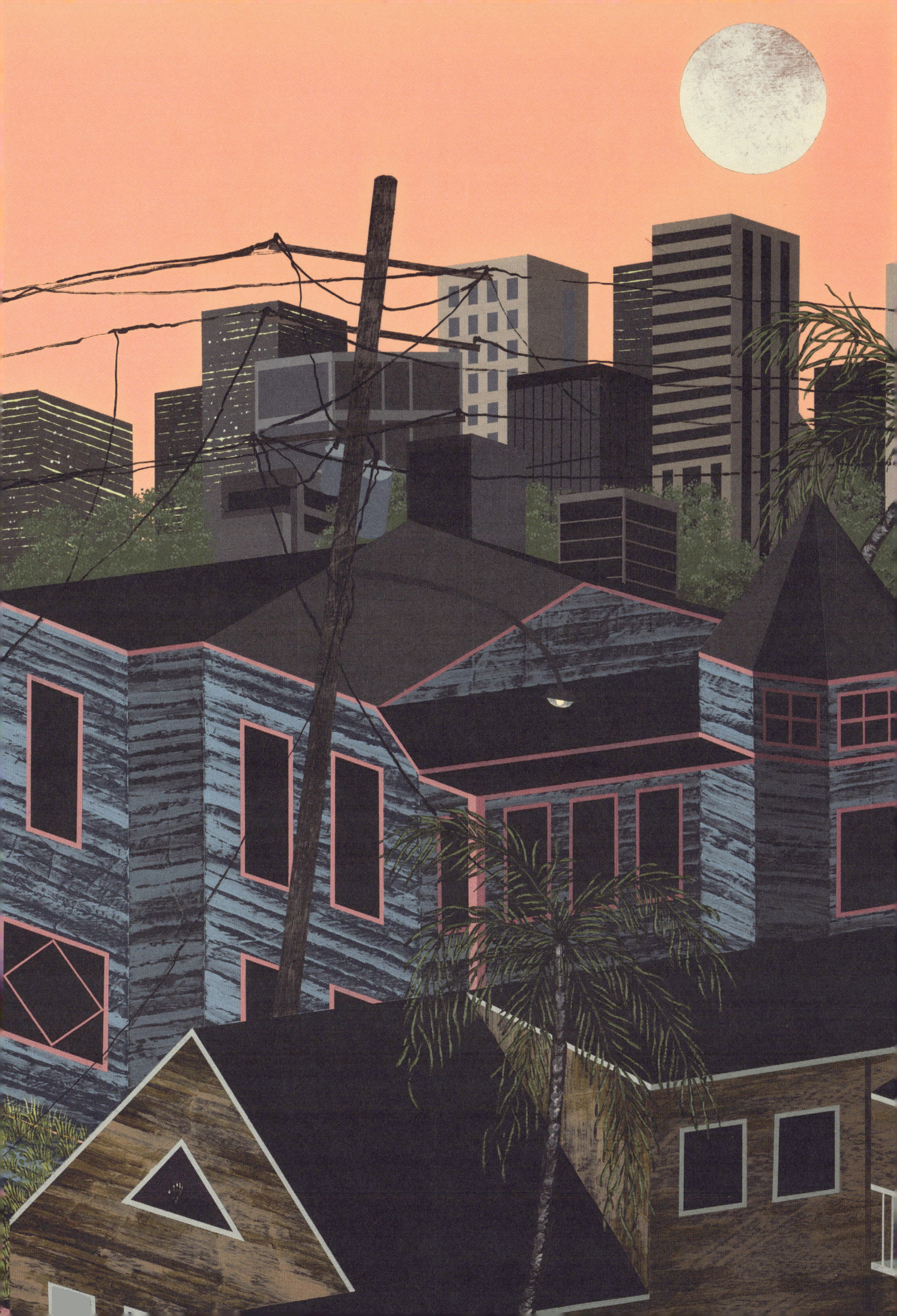

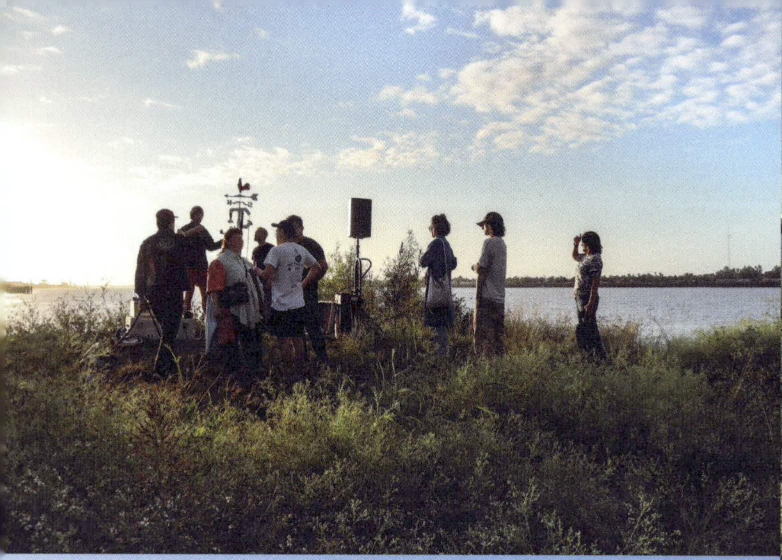

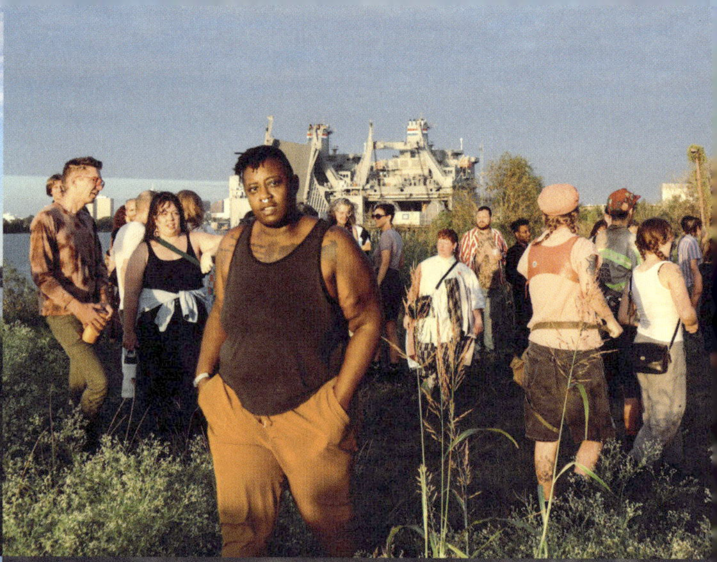

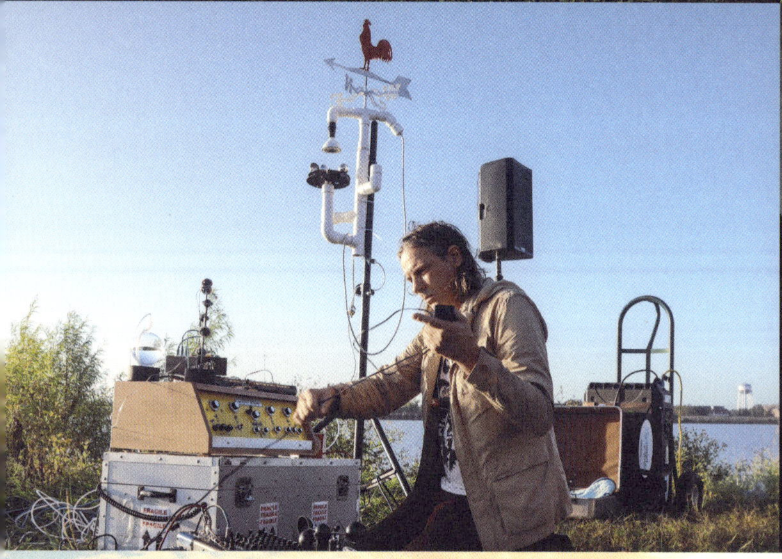

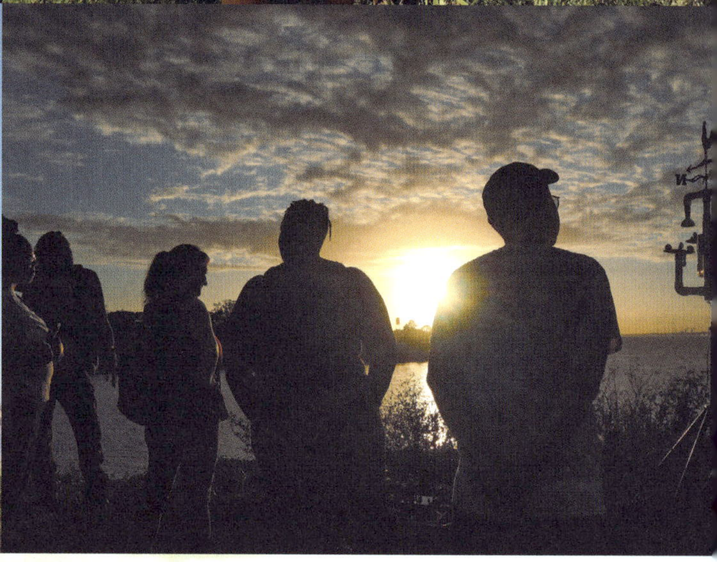

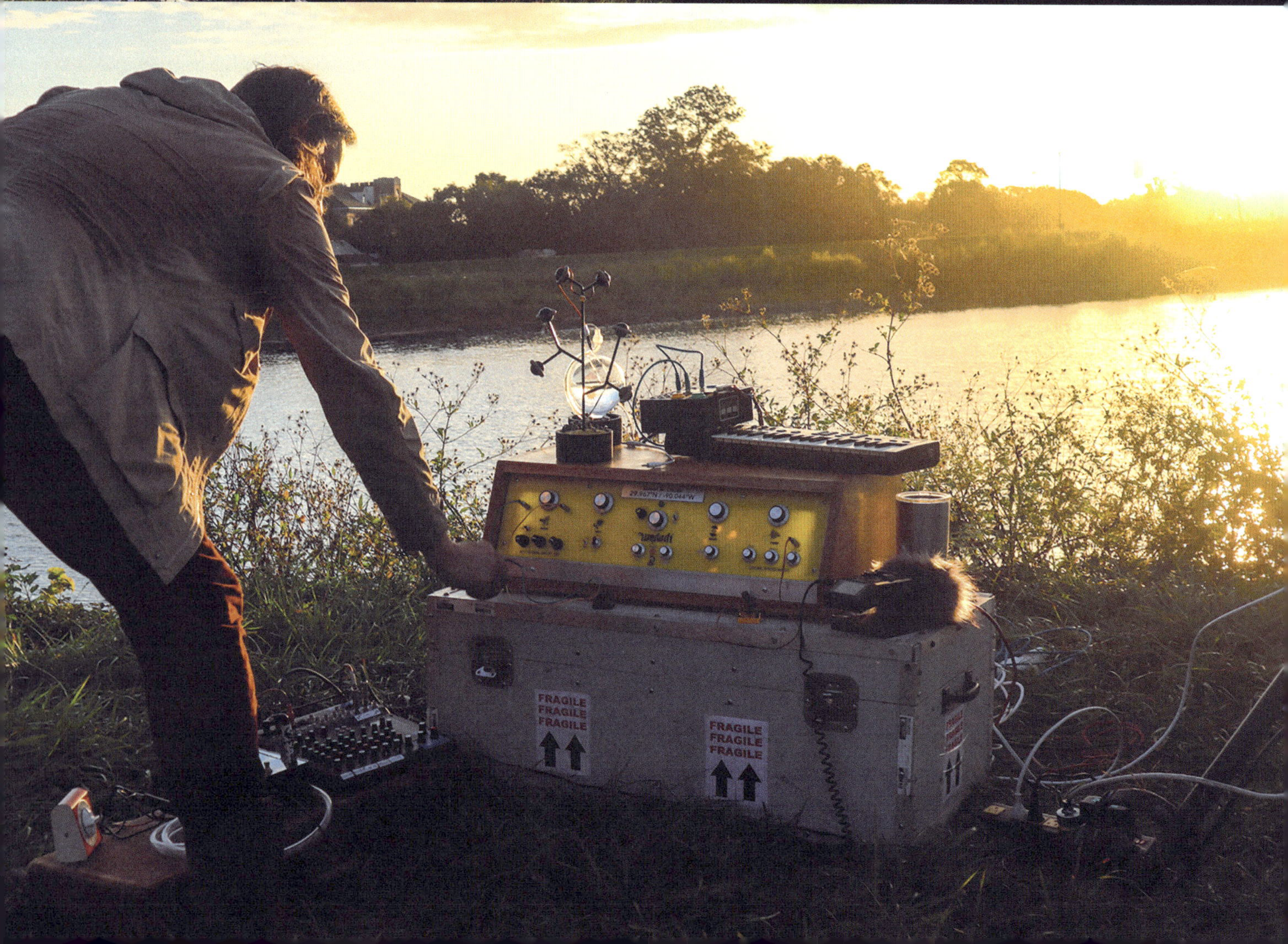
FRAGILE
FRAGILE
FRAGILE
FRAGILE
FRAGILE
FRAGILE

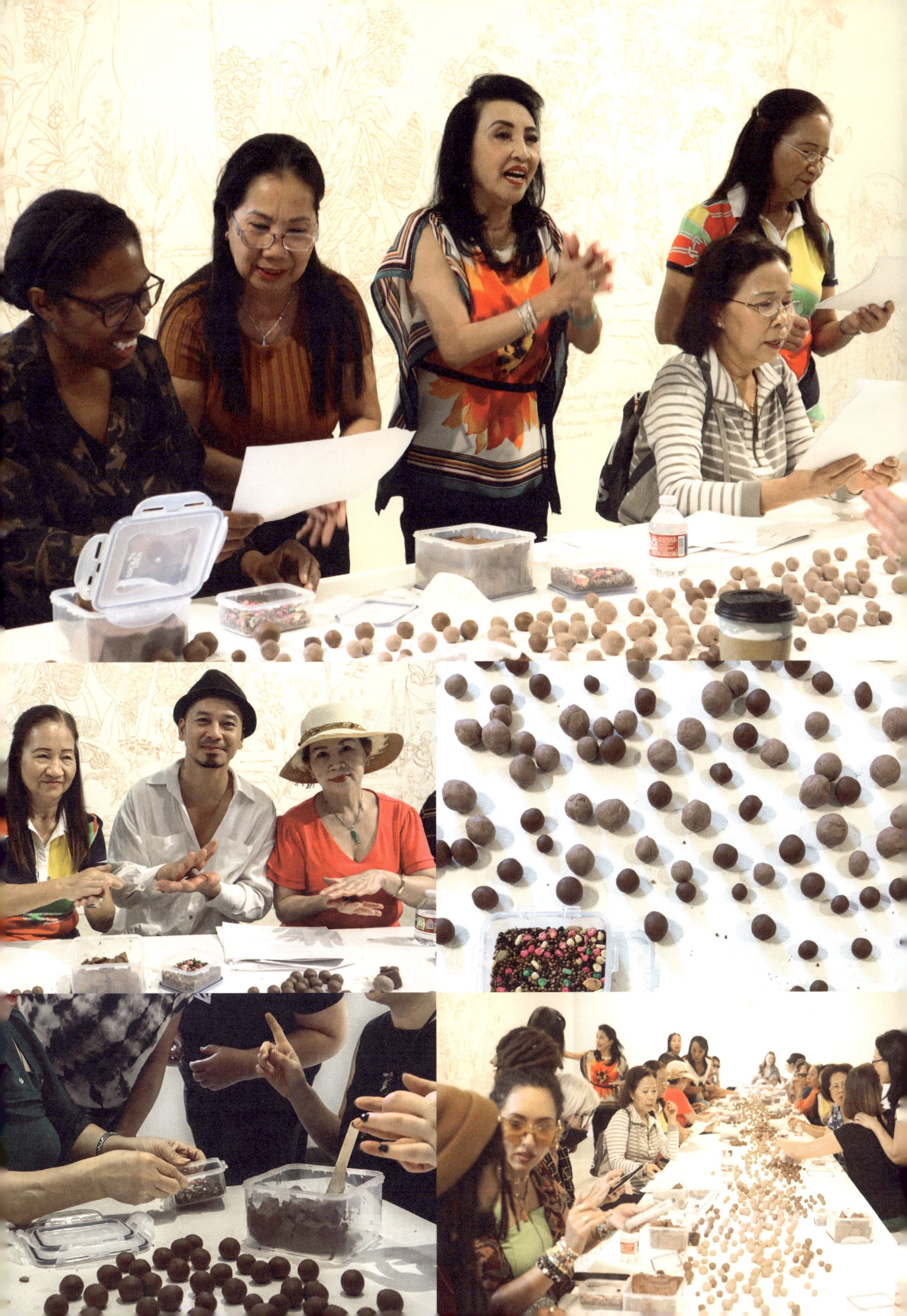

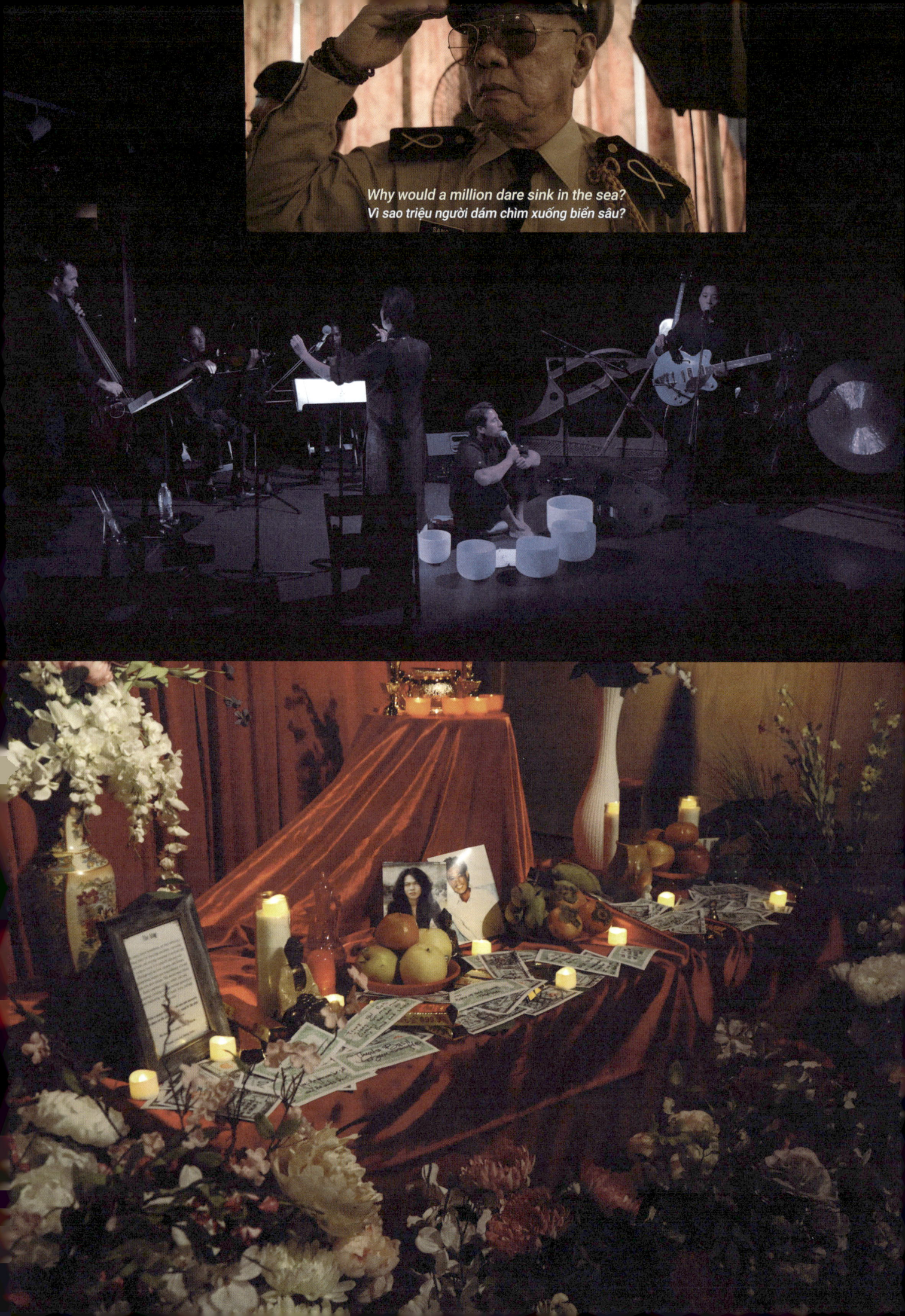

Why would a million dare sink in the sea?
Vì sao triệu người dám chìm xuống biển sâu?

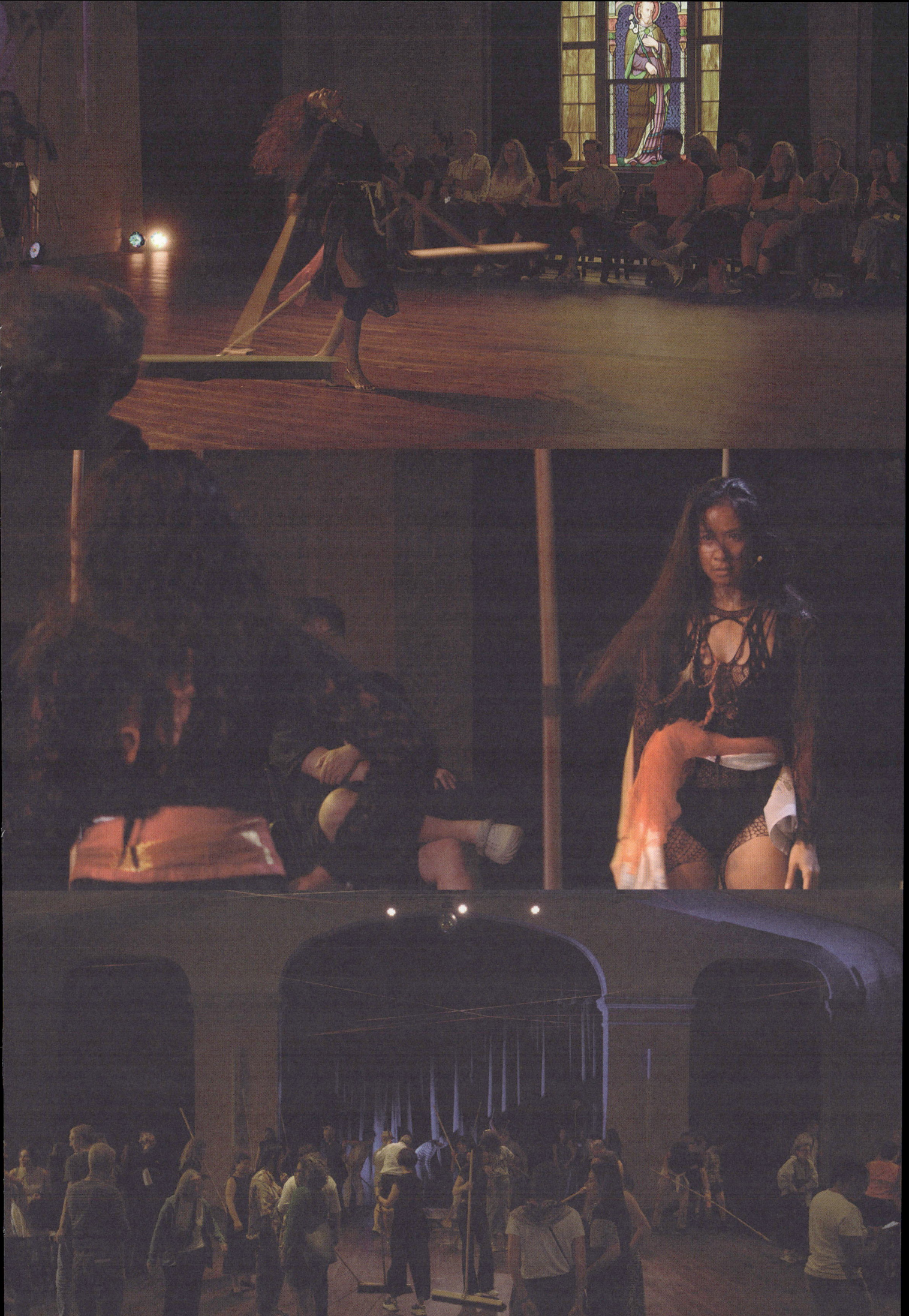

Meleko Mokgosi

b. 1981, Francistown, Botswana; lives in Wellesley, MA

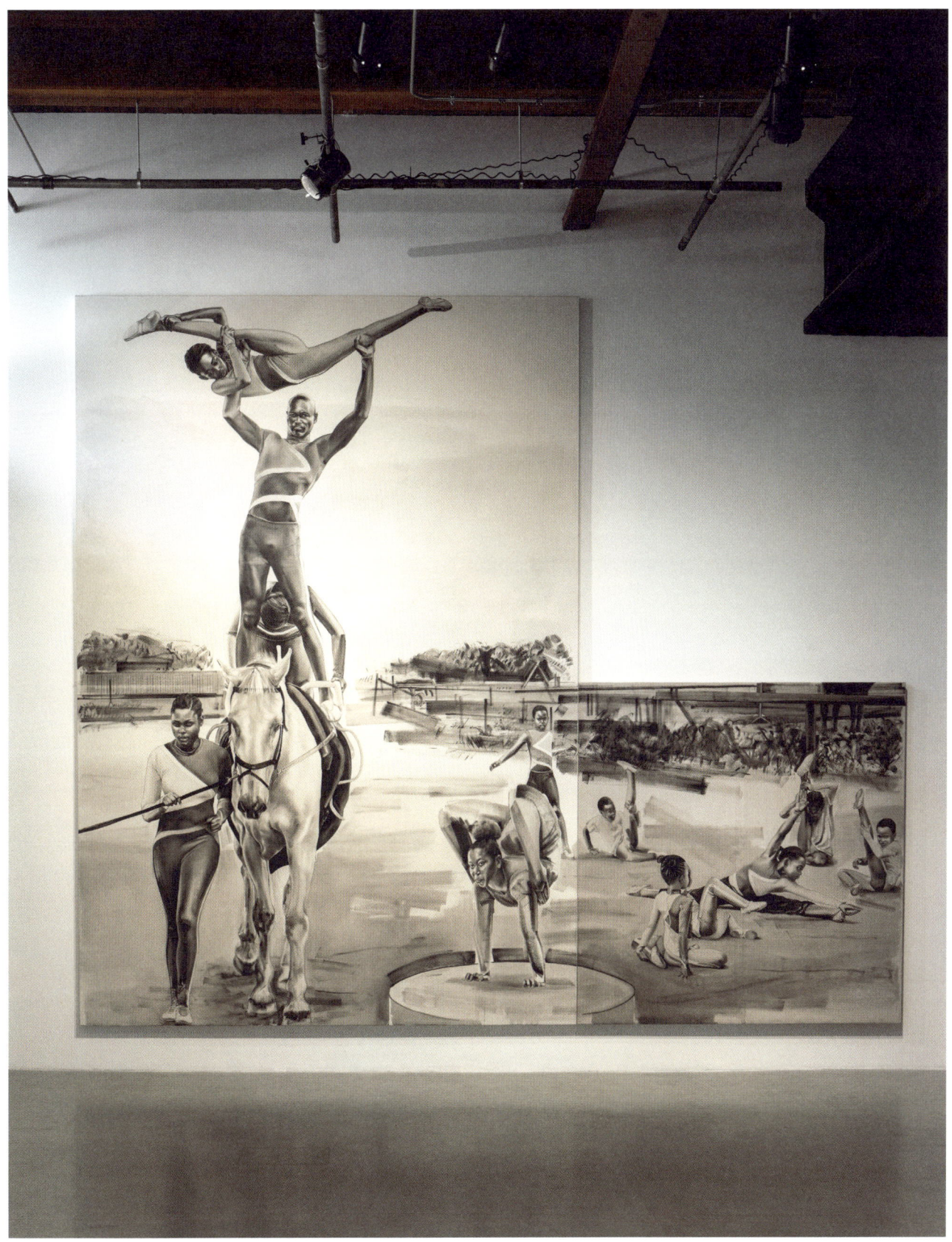

Spaces of Subjection: Appellations (Addendum III), 2024

Meleko Mokgosi is best known for painting large-scale scenes of Black life as a social inquiry into knowledge production about Black identity. These paintings exist in multiple panels and are continuous yet fragmented, containing multi-layered scenes about epistemic injustices and their links to coloniality. Mokgosi employs different painting techniques to investigate how discursive spaces such as art history, cinema studies, and psychoanalysis privilege Western thought at the expense of other cultures. He draws inspiration from vast Southern African historical archives—such as anti-Apartheid posters, family albums, magazines, and films—to highlight the lingering colonial legacies that insist on dominant Eurocentric narratives. His paintings illuminate the complexity of Black life, and highlight the inherent cultural biases and colonial power dynamics that continue to undermine Black culture.

For Prospect.6, Mokgosi turns his attention to the film *The Gods Must Be Crazy* (1980), written and directed by the White South African filmmaker Jamie Uys. The film was a commercial success, with mixed reviews from local and international audiences. Set in Southern Africa, the film explores encounters between members of the San (an Indigenous group of peoples in Southern Africa) and modern-day

Black and White cultures in South Africa. The film hilariously captures the misinterpretation and miscommunication that occurs between different cultural groups but fails to take into account the egregious problems of Apartheid. It portrays the San as simple and primitive; White culture as modern and civilized; and Blacks as violent and dangerous.

By turning his attention to this film, Mokgosi engages in the ongoing systemic denial, subjugation, and racism of today. He alters film stills of *The Gods Must Be Crazy* into a graphic storyboard configuration, with annotations on the margins to trouble the easy consumption of stereotypical tropes. Working on multiple panels, he draws our attention to how aesthetic practices objectify and commodify Indigeneity and Blackness. These cinematic vignettes become formal questions challenging the descriptive clarity of information that has consistently privileged White supremacy. Juxtaposed with several large paintings made by Mokgosi, these paintings focus on systematic othering as a method of social exclusion. Showcasing this work in New Orleans, a city known for its exceptional cultural integration, Mokgosi sheds light on the Black struggle for equity and power. He combines a range of images and symbols from European histories of painting and cinema to raise questions about who is othered, how this knowledge is consumed, and who benefits from such exchanges. The artist foregrounds Black figuration as a recurrent symbol that embodies knowledge about Black experiences. He examines elements of daily lived experience from Black life, which has been excluded and discriminated against. This work is part of an investigation into the politics of representation through the excavation of postcolonial memory and its imaginary futures.

Mokgosi's hyper-realistic paintings unfold like a storybook to expand the viewer's understanding of Black experiences. By depicting scenes from ordinary Black life, he transforms the ordinary into a spectacle, where Blackness is neither rendered as other, lesser-than, or threatening. Instead, Mokgosi plays up how Black representation can exist on its own terms.

by Tumelo Mosaka

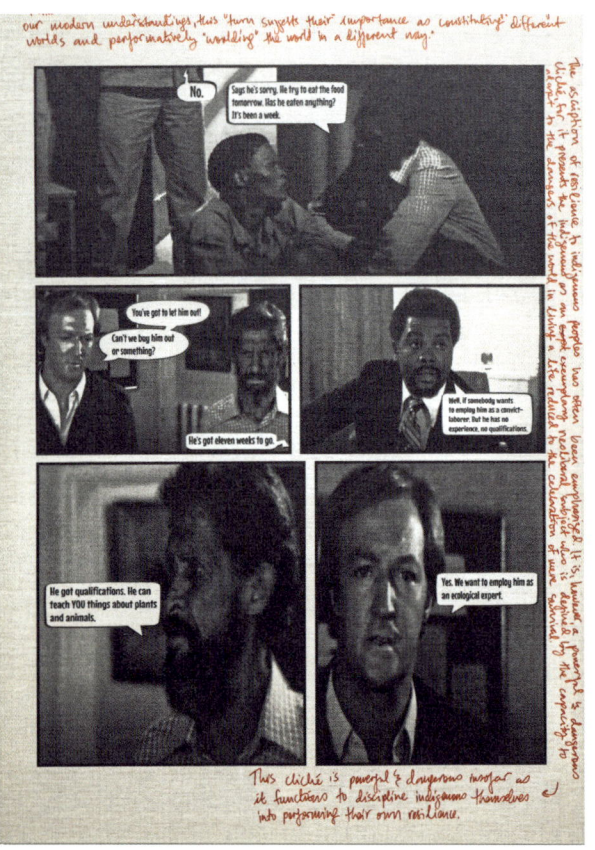

Spaces of Subjection: Appellations, 2024 (detail)

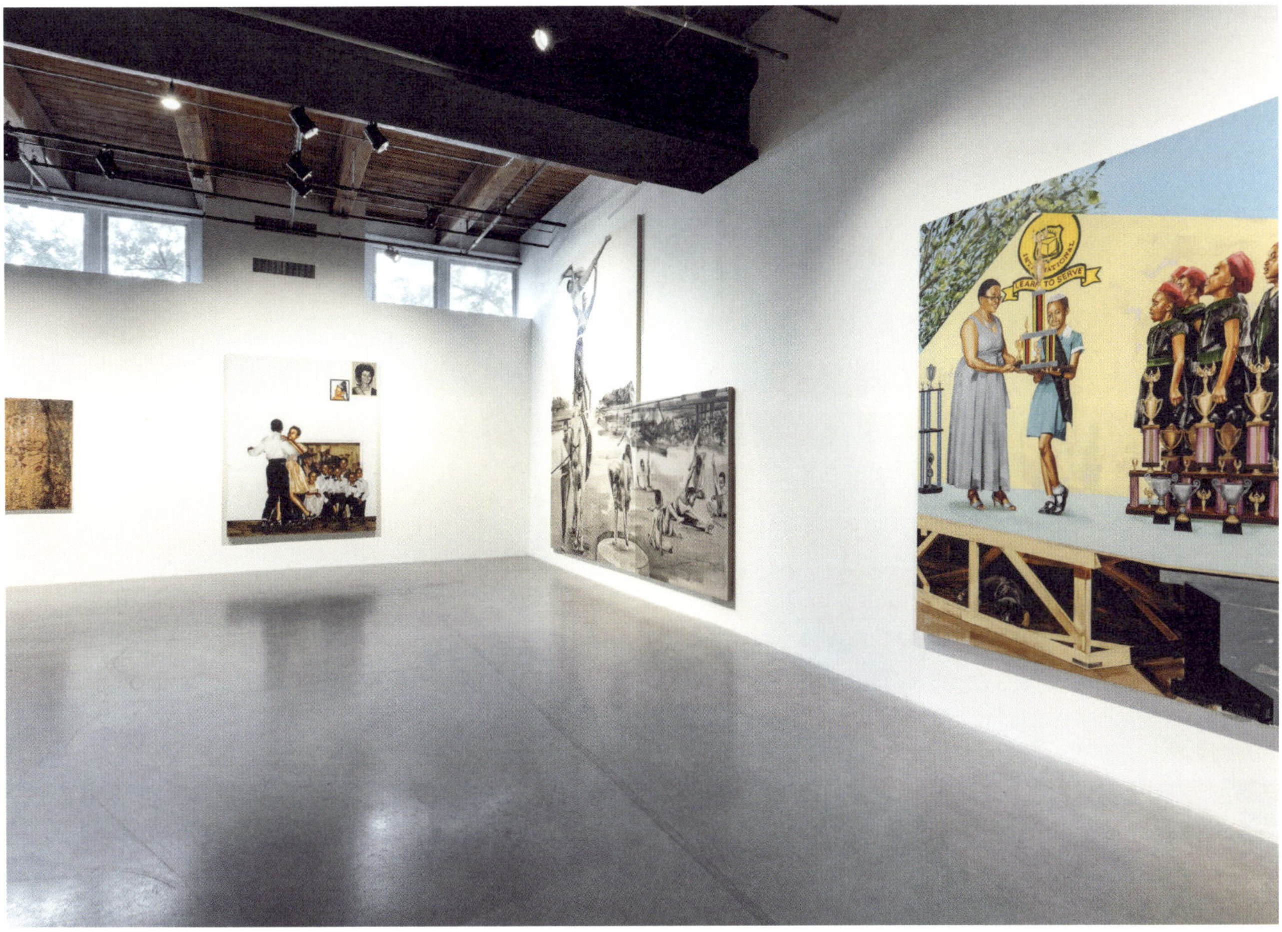

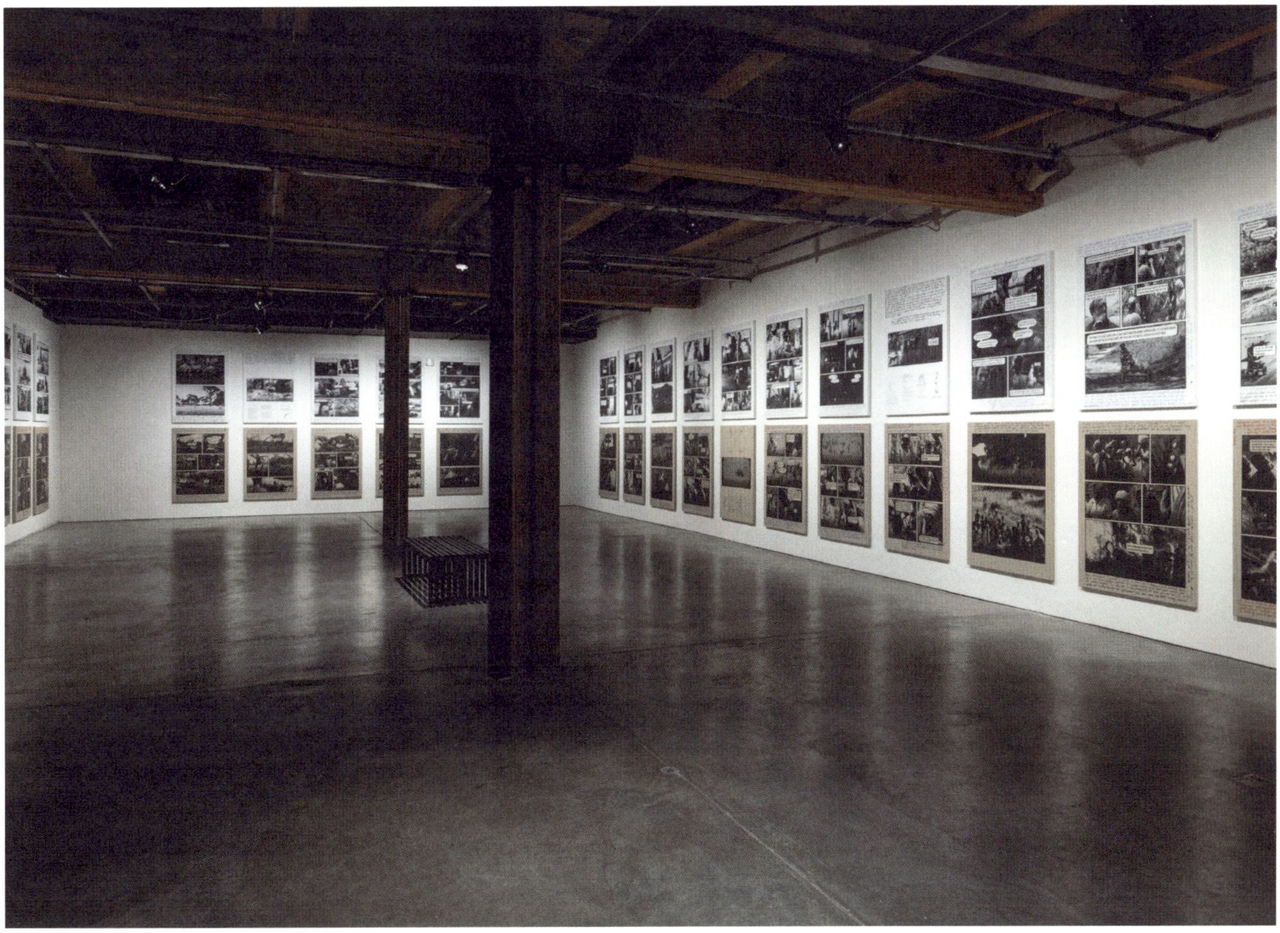

Top: *Spaces of Subjection: Appellations*
L to R: *Addendum IV, II, III, I*

Above: *Spaces of Subjection: Appellations*,
2024

Tuấn Andrew Nguyễn

b. 1976, Saigon, Vietnam; lives in Ho Chi Minh City, Vietnam

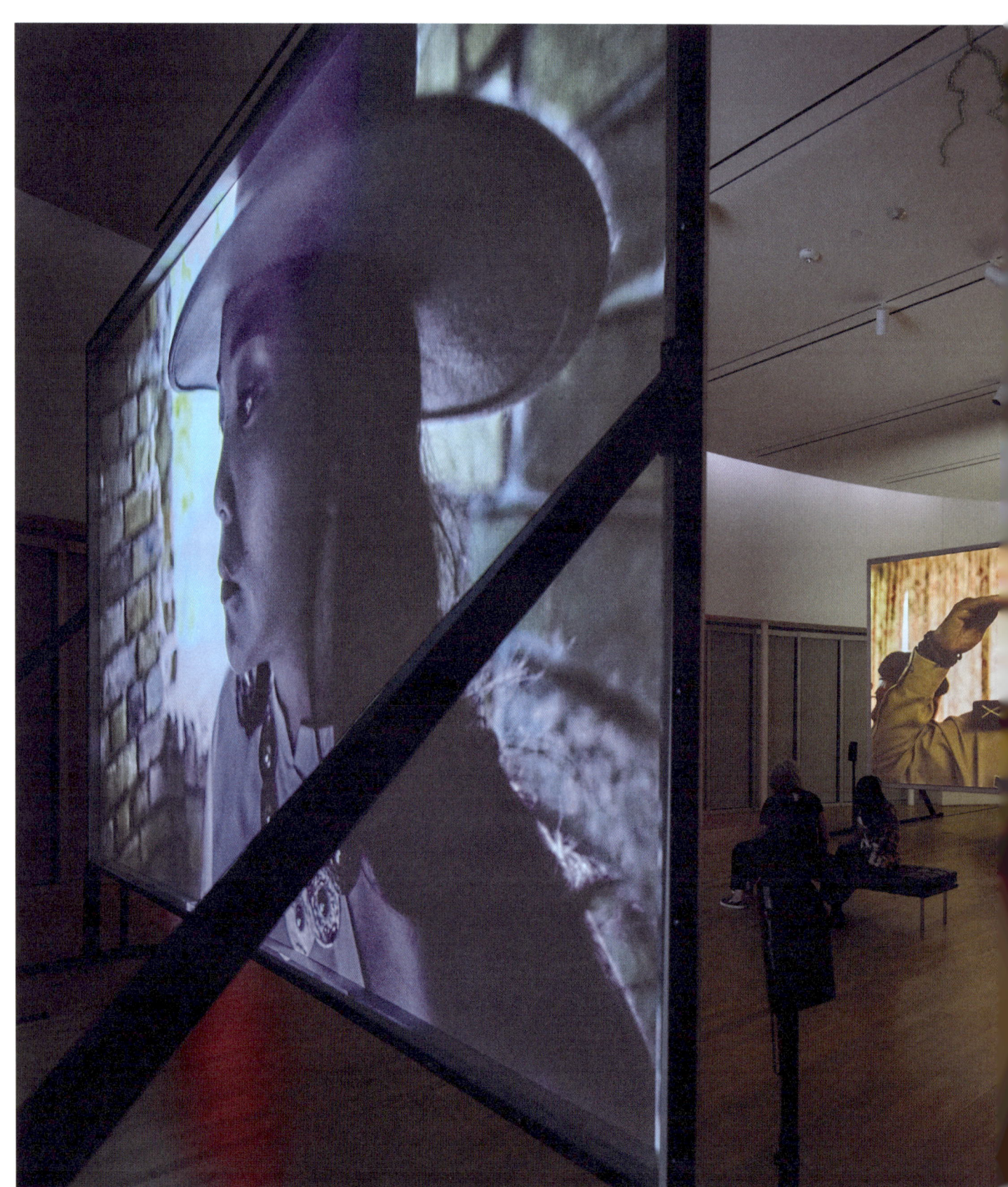

Amongst the Disquiet, 2024

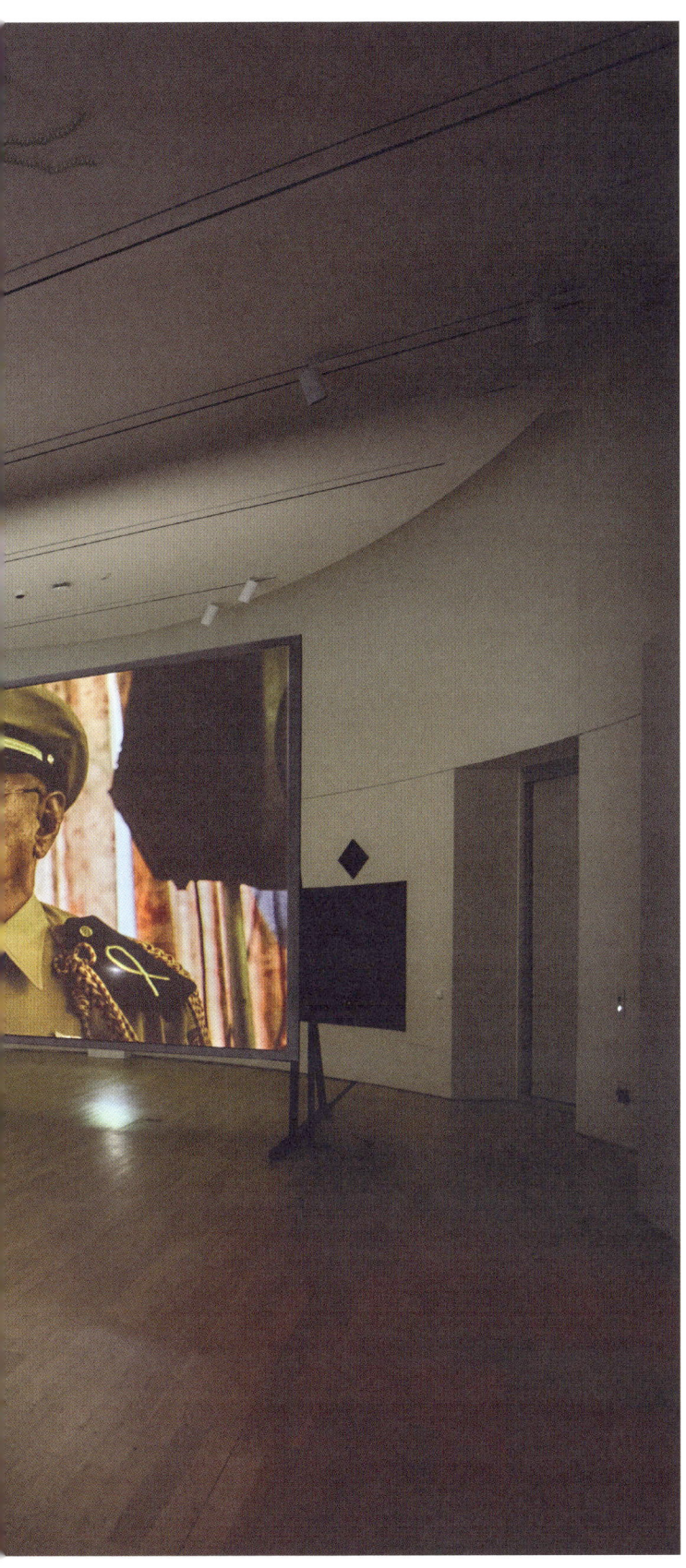

Over the course of the last two decades, Tuấn Andrew Nguyễn's work has been marked by what might be called an aesthetics of subterfuge, one where he reifies simply to invert, and stages only to redirect, the conventional mandates of a form. Through collaborative works, video, and installation, Nguyễn ostensibly gives the viewer what they have come to expect, then latently injects that recognition with different meaning. Such was the case with the early Benetton-esque piece, *Television Commercial for Communism* (2011–2012) promoting a commercialized, multi-cultural Vietnam, which is also at play in his piece for Prospect.6.

Made in collaboration with musician THAO (Thảo Nguyễn) and producer/director Marion Hoàng Ngọc Hill, *Amongst the Disquiet* is a mix of narrative, music, and documentary. Inasmuch as it shares some cinematic tropes with Adam Weingrod's documentary portrait of a hospice, *The Island* (2017), and Nguyễn's previous work *The Unburied Sounds of a Troubled Horizon* (2022), *Amongst the Disquiet*, from the outset, is queued to the hyperlocality of New Orleans as part of both the Global South and the US South. When THAO first appears in the film, her languid voice announces: "We are more than memory / come to haunt. / We are also haunted by the living / Endlessly returning / tumbling in the in-between." However, viewers can only arrive at this interstitial moment through a fleeting encounter with the sordid history of Jim Crow, as the camera moves through an opening in a brick wall, then through the thick brush, trees, and trash of what remains from the decaying ruins of the Lincoln Beach amusement park. In this way, Nguyễn collates the contemporary histories of Vietnamese immigration with histories of Black segregation that underpinned US racial formations.

Yet perhaps the most salient form of collation that Nguyễn employs is his use of dubbing to create the work's soundscape. Inasmuch as dubbing is the process by which new dialogue or other sounds are added to the audio track of a project that has already been filmed, Nguyễn whimsically plays with a figurative relay switch between aurality and visuality, as a reminder of the geopolitical role that cinema served in Vietnam throughout a long twentieth century that was layered over by French colonialism, Japanese occupation, and US militarism, among other forces. Like movie houses in other parts of the French empire, including Dakar in Senegal, Tangier in Morocco, and Les Abymes in Guadeloupe, those in Vietnam would often feature Western films that were dubbed.

While the production of the film itself constellates a certain generational network of global Vietnamese artists (with Nguyễn based in Ho Chi Minh City, THAO in San Francisco, and Hill in New Orleans), the performances themselves are not only the bringing together of two seemingly different communities, but an enactment of what the Barbadian poet Edward Kamau Brathwaite called "arrivant," insofar as "arrivant" is not simply the documenting of the past histories of migration and diaspora, but rather a harbinger of the kinds of kines-thetic energies and latent desires that will put bodies in motion in new relational futurities. The performances by Vietnamese practitioners, then, animate this latter iteration of "arrivant," of the arrivals or happenings that promise to remake New Orleans and perhaps remix received conventions about what constitutes contemporary "Vietnamese" art.

by Ivy Wilson

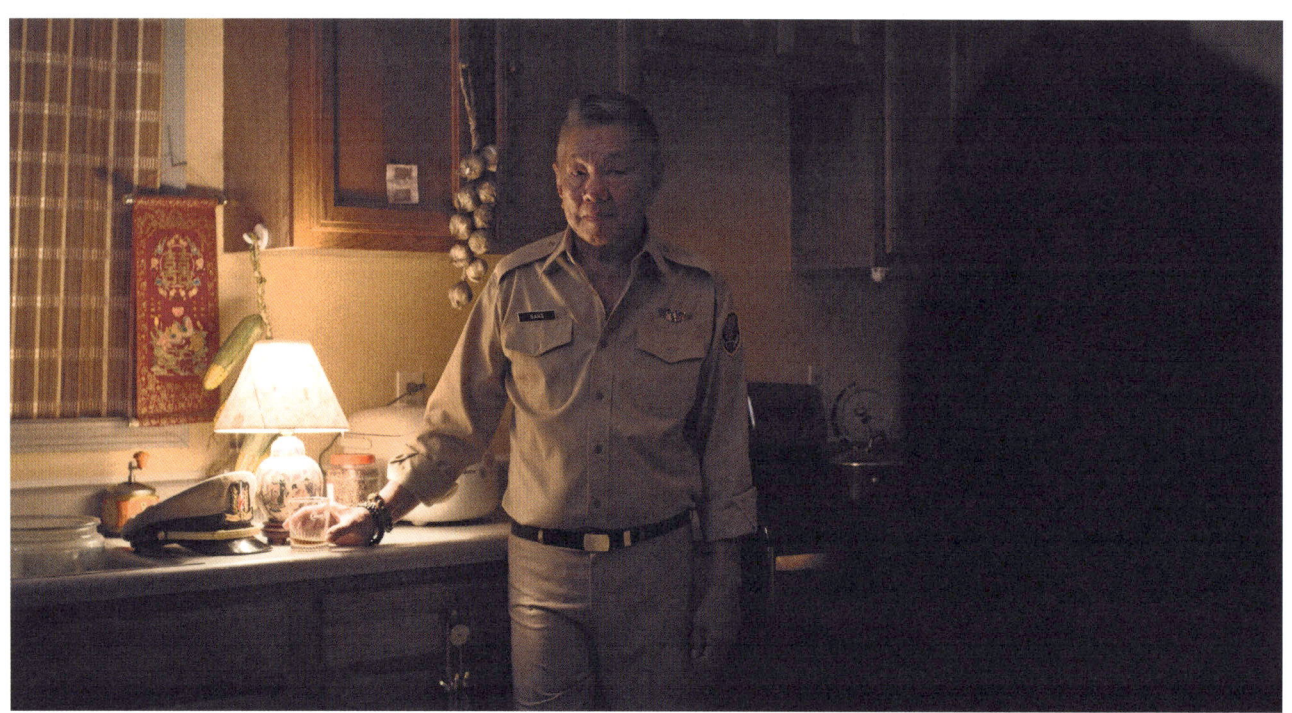

Amongst the Disquiet, 2024 (video still)

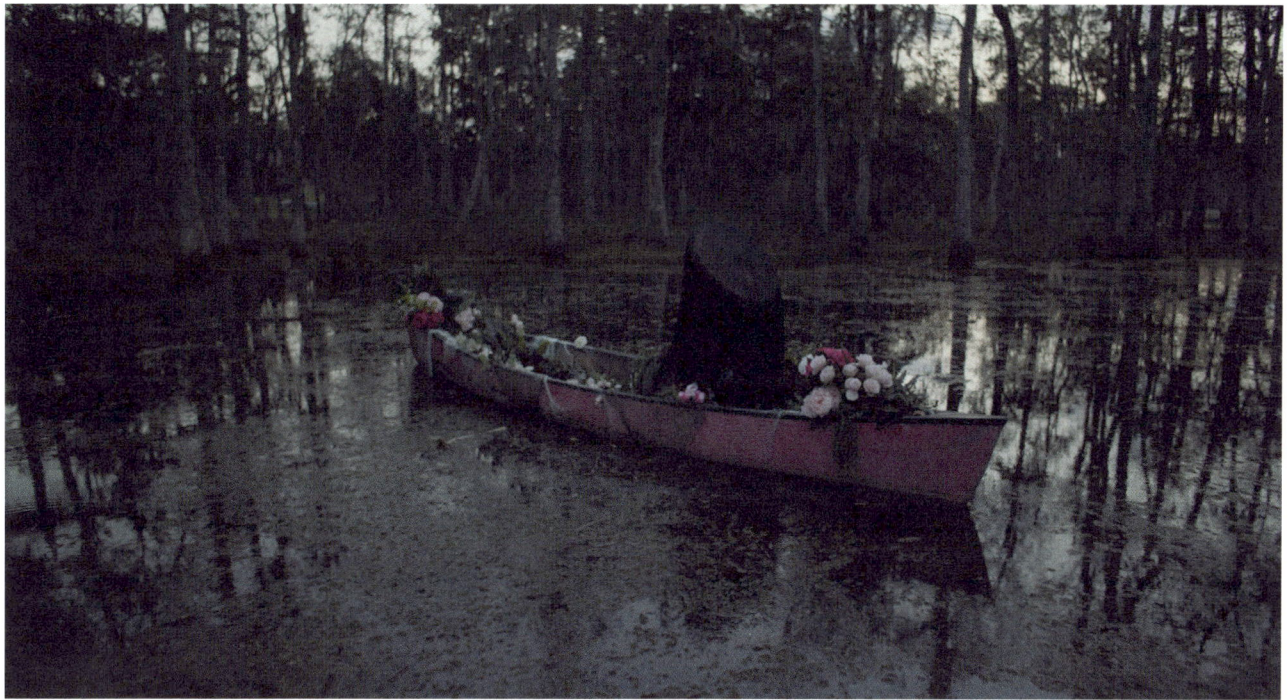

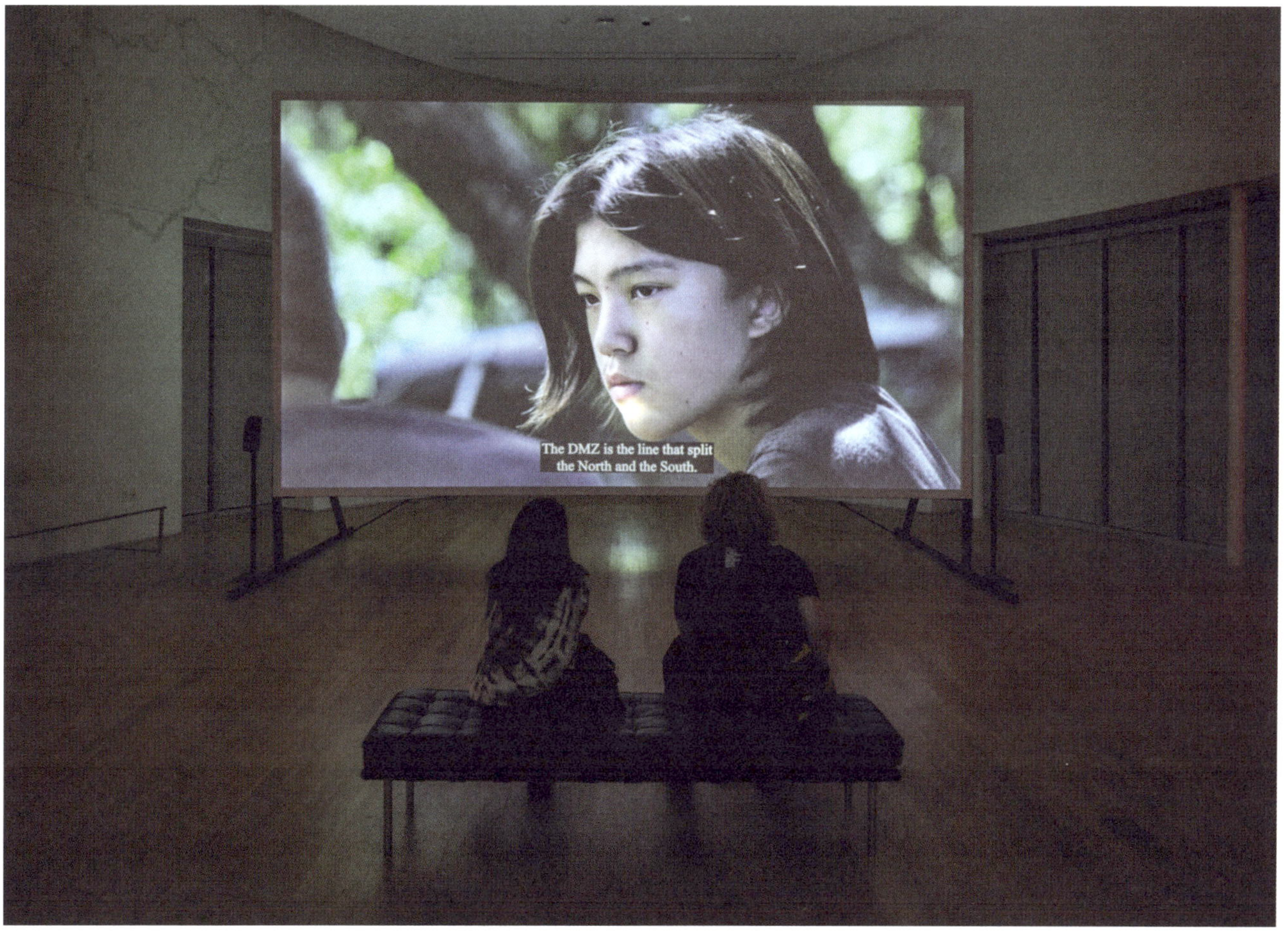

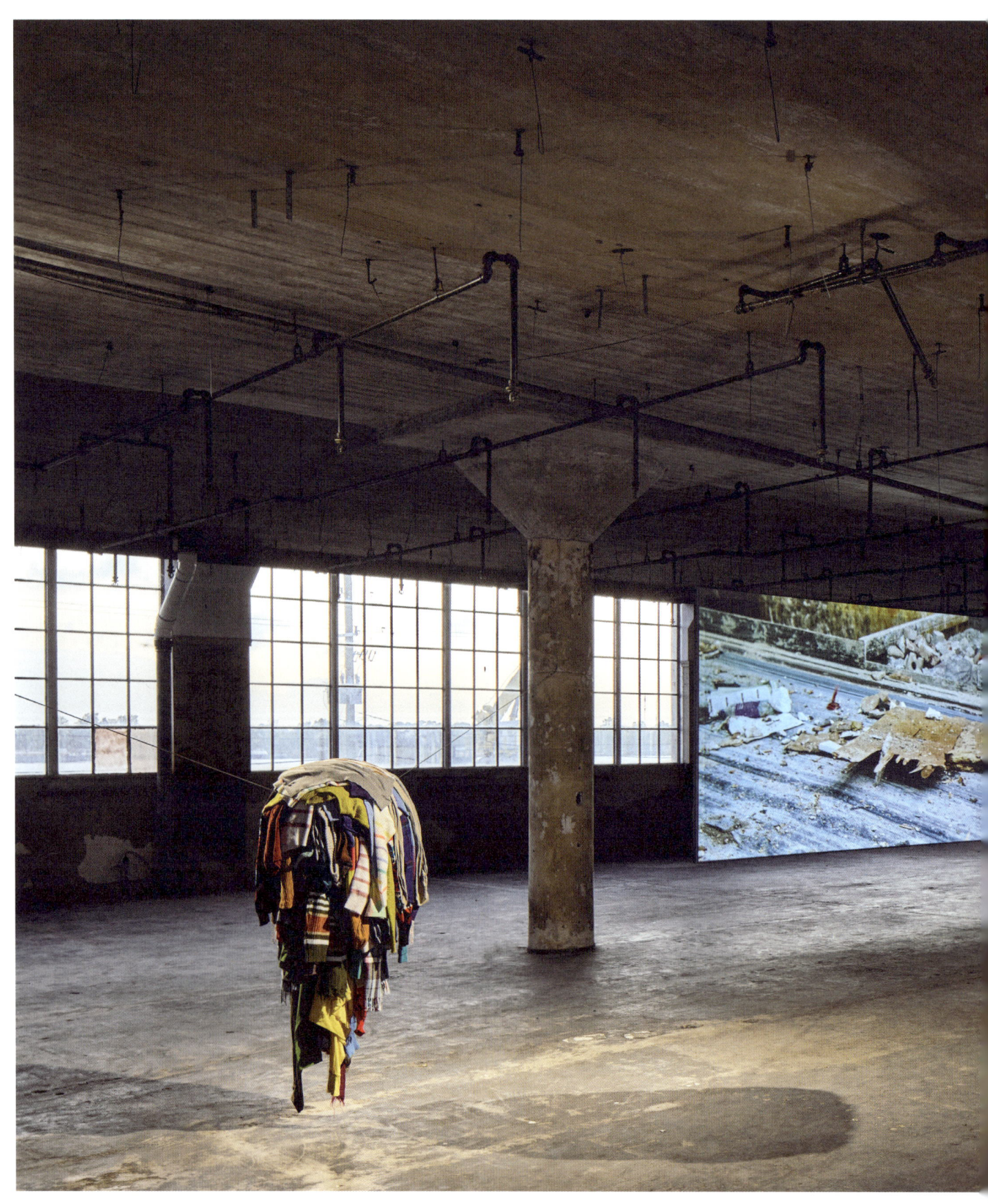

Installation view, L to R: *Winter hung to dry*, 2003;
Drift (Tributary), 2023; *Sampling (Need You)*, 2023

Karyn Olivier

b. 1968, Port of Spain, Trinidad and Tobago; lives in Philadelphia, PA

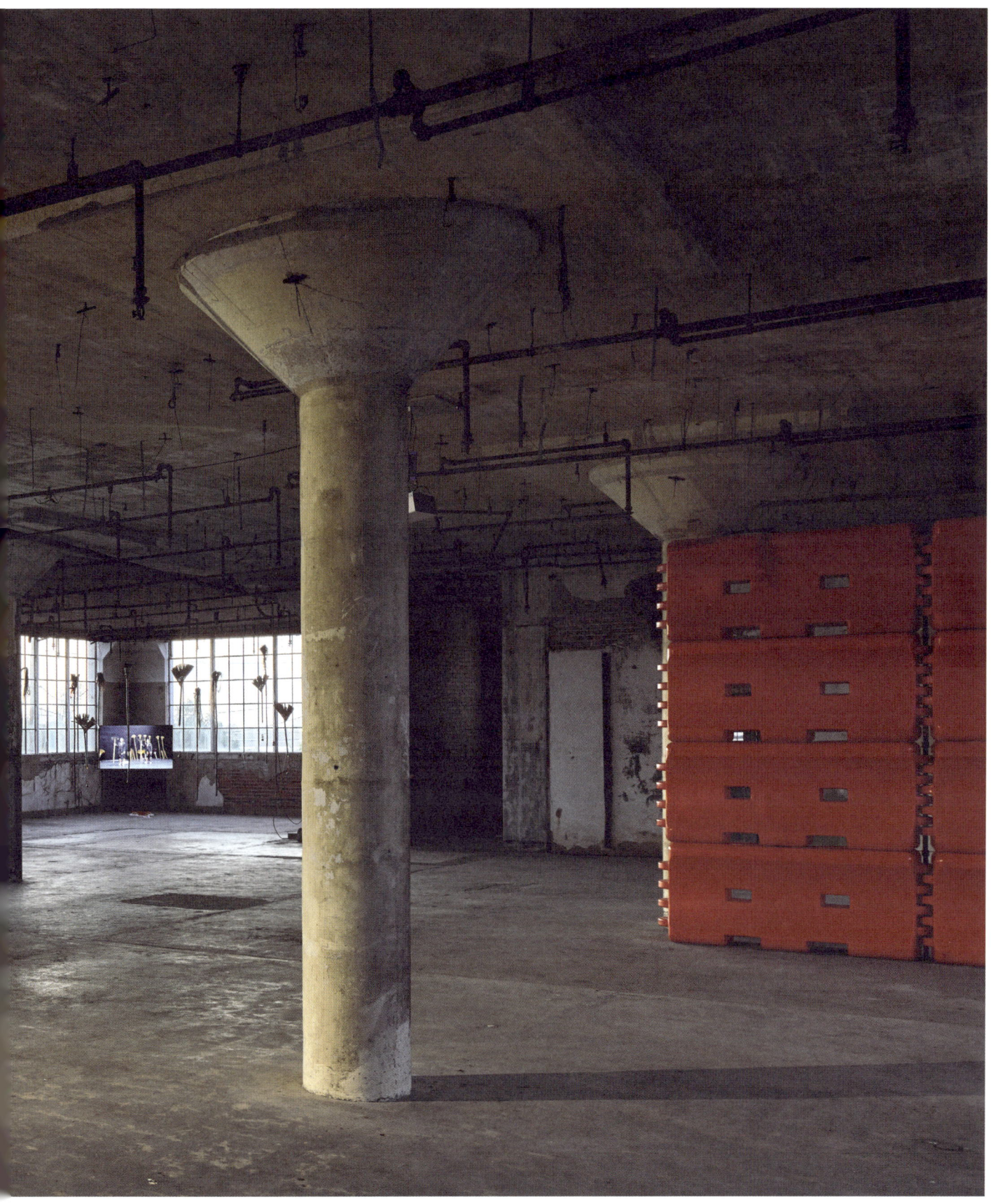

A quintessential aspect of living in an urban environment is encountering a site where a building is either being constructed, renovated, or razed to the ground. Other than the question of who will occupy the space or where the former residents might have gone, Karyn Olivier's work for Prospect.6 prods me to wonder who set the process in motion. Her installation *Sampling (Need You)* (2023) consists of orange traffic barricades—typically found around road repair and building construction zones—arranged into a wall, making explicit the implicit power they deploy. Noises from construction sites can be heard coming from these barricades, moving from one component to another. Recorded at construction sites in Philadelphia, Olivier's soundscape documents the continuous destruction, rebuilding, and expansion that occurs from building site to building site.

Barricades such as these mediate access; they wall some people in and others out, thus concretizing the binary opposition of either/or. Still, in the city landscape, the reasoning for erecting the barriers, or selecting the personnel permitted inside them, isn't necessarily clear to me, or other residents or passersby. The city's logic is both simultaneously visible and opaque. Olivier's film *Drift (Tributary)* (2023) prompts the same set of questions from a different vantage point. In the film, a river of construction materials flows by—processed by Revolution Recovery, a waste management and recycling center in Philadelphia—in a seemingly endless torrent. Who authorized all this destruction? For whom is this construction and destruction enacted? Whose homes were these and whose will they become?

The perpetual reconstruction of built environments is an enduring feature of modernity, and it suggests that someone, in an office somewhere, regularly makes decisions that change the texture of the places we live. They might make good decisions, or horribly destructive ones. Intuitively, I know I am subject to them either way. I can't countermand these choices, just as I don't have the power necessary to move and rearrange these orange barricades. Nor am I able to break down buildings. Historically there has always been tension between governing authorities, and the governed and citizenry have often developed paranoid fantasies about secret forces and hidden governmental agendas. Experiencing

Olivier's work, I'm reminded of the conviction that fuels belief in conspiracy theories—that clandestine forces will affect our lives in material ways because the state has control over the public order. Unless I have privileged status or access to those with municipal power, I will likely merely be a witness to its effects.

Alternatively, Olivier's *Winter hung to dry* (2003) makes a countervailing proposal— that contemporary life might be constituted by others we come to know. The work alludes to a sociality rooted in vulnerability: The positioning of donated clothes piled on a clothesline suggests that the contributors are willing to rub shoulders with strangers via the proxy of their clothing. This willingness stands in contrast to the aloofness and anonymity of the state's agents. Parts of these people's lives come under public scrutiny as items that are physically representative of their bodies are displayed. One line holds all their weight together, their personal experiences in a chaotic heap. And the cord thus constitutes a space where we can dwell with other humans, a place neither of fabrication, assembly, nor demolition, a space where we are just held together, for a moment, above the ground.

by Seph Rodney

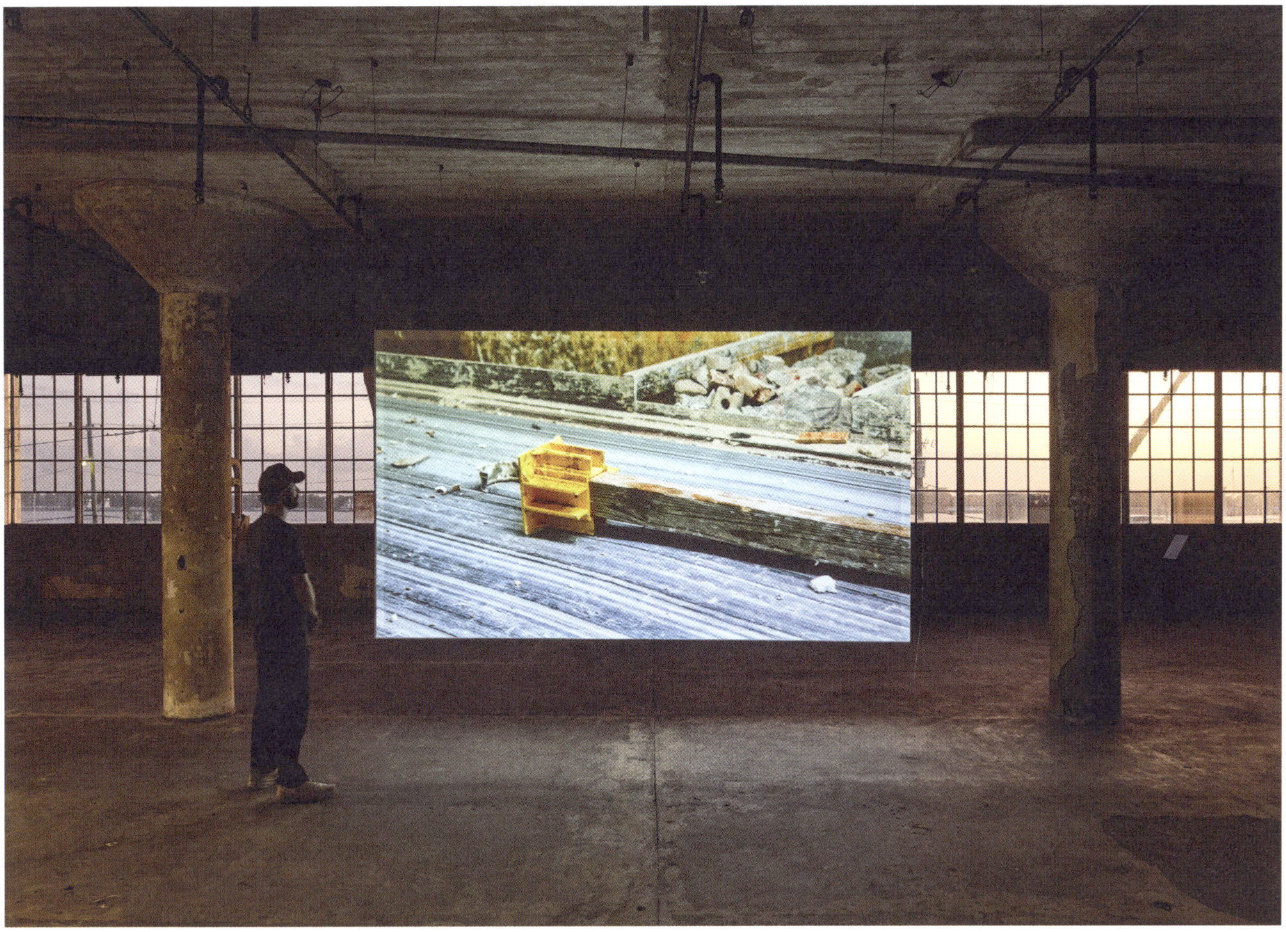

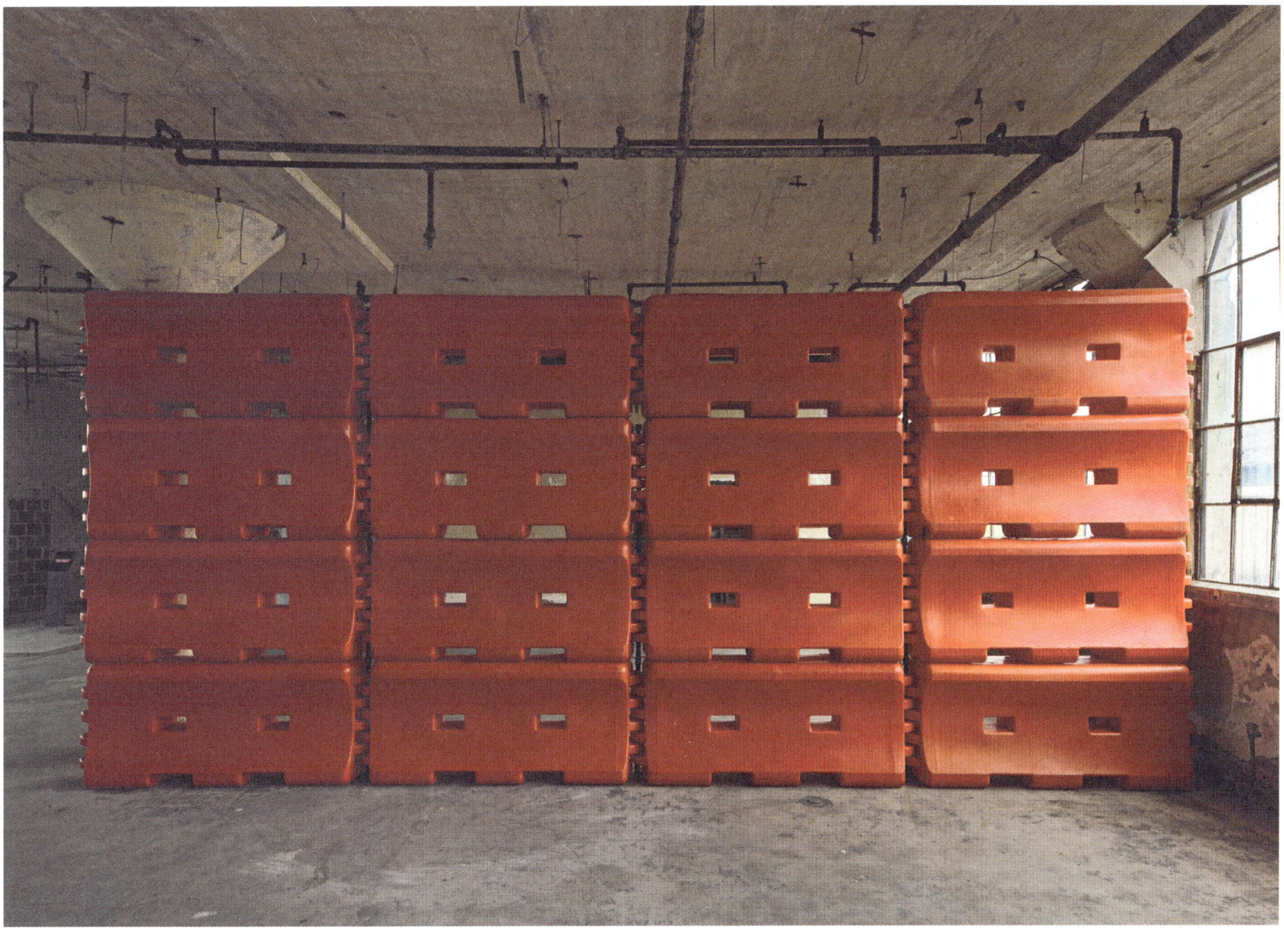

Top: *Drift (Tributary)*, 2023   Above: *Sampling (Need You)*, 2023

Ruth Owens

b. 1959, Augsburg, Germany; lives in Metairie, LA and works in New Orleans, LA

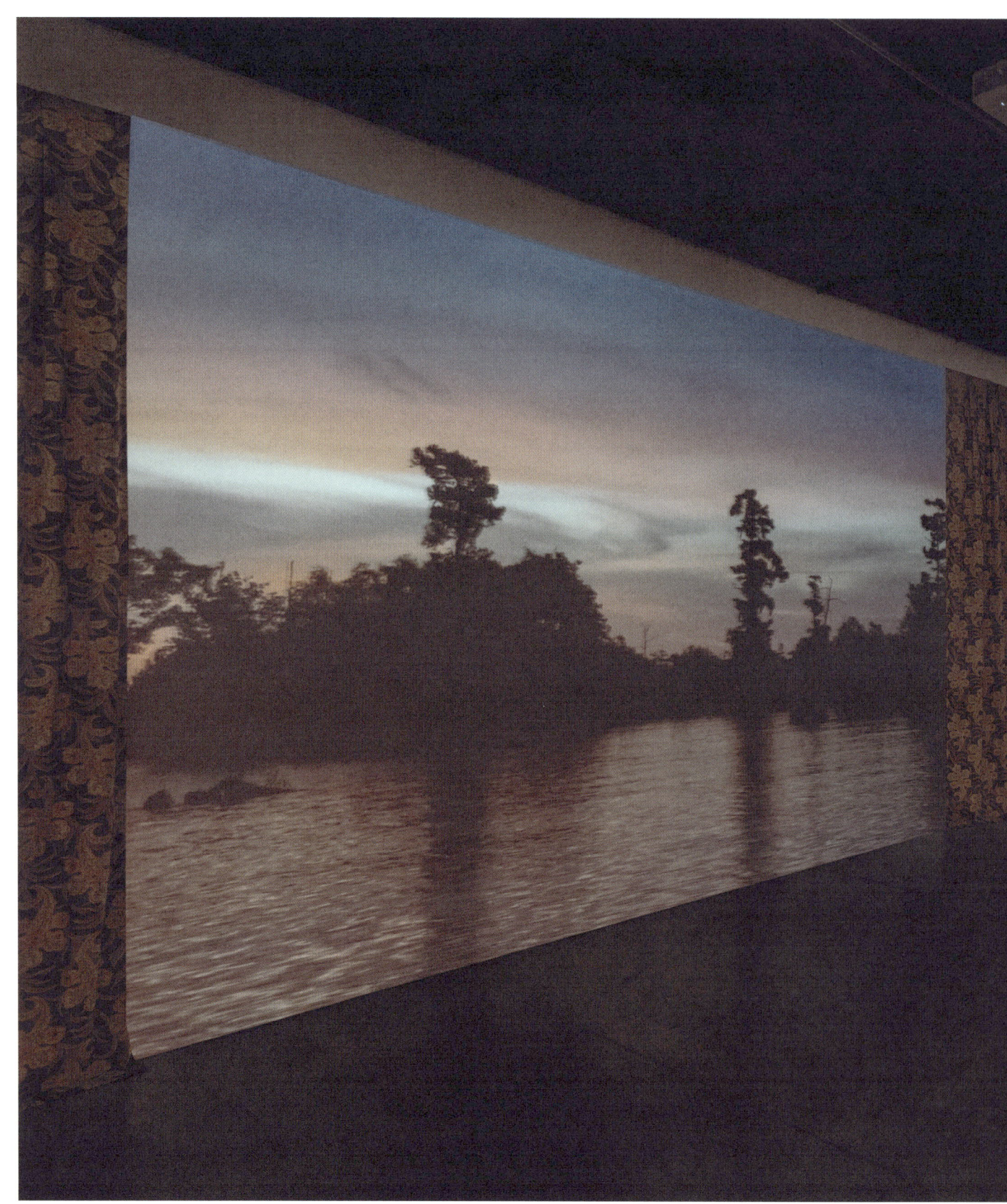

Black Delight, An Ecopoem, 2024

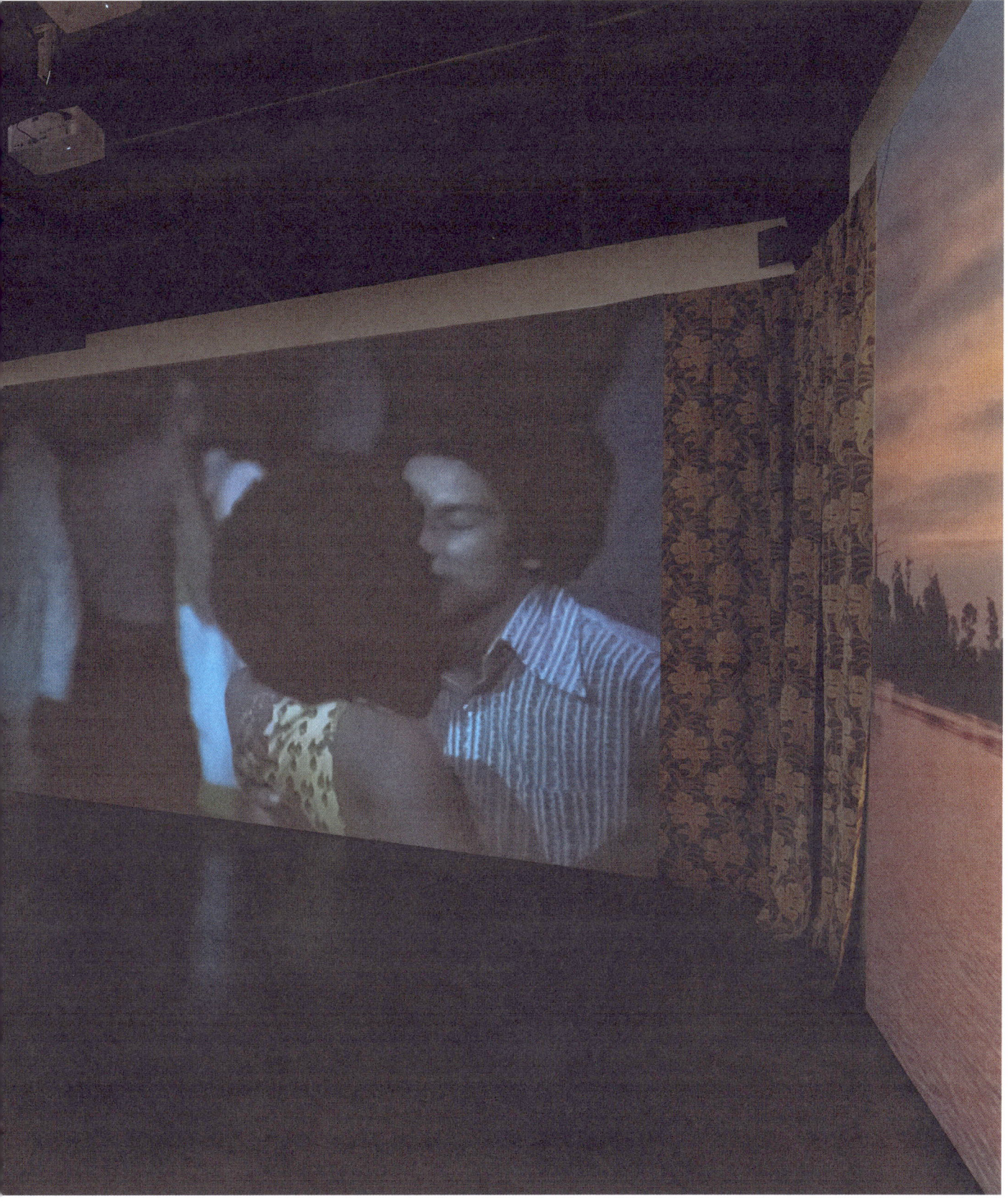

Black Delight, An Ecopoem, (2024) is an immersive, multisensory installation that inspires feelings of awe by emphasizing the tensions between the rising threat of mass extinction and the beauty of Black survivance—through the media of film and dance. Incorporating both made and found footage of social dance, a form of movement and social practice that prioritizes participation over performance, the installation allows audiences to witness the power of Black communal joy amongst the very landscapes that helped ensure their survival in the New World. Owens calls this work an ecopoem, a genre of poetry defined by a fundamental desire to reveal the interconnectedness of all living things. Ultimately, the installation makes an argument for the interdependent relationship between the bodies of Black people and the environments in which they live. By juxtaposing imagery of threatened coastal environments, such as Barataria Bay, with intimate scenes of a NOLA-style throwdown, the installation subtly emotes the complex facets of postcolonial Black existence in Louisiana and beyond. The peoples of Louisiana face coastal land loss at a rate averaging twenty five square miles per year due to rising sea levels and the loss of crucial barrier islands, marshes, and swamps. The air and waterways across the state are counted among the most polluted in the country. These abused ecosystems are victims of colonization and a century of extractive industrial practices and capitalist greed—much like the Black and Brown peoples who call Louisiana their home.

Black Delight is a continuation of Owens's exploration of the Kongo cosmogram, a two-dimensional tool used to illustrate the structure of the universe in the Bakongo religion of Central Africa. Its circular form presents the physical and spiritual realms as one world in constant motion, bisected by the sacred Kalûnga river. Life is created through the shifting relations between the elements of nature and the cyclicity of time. Owens places her audiences in the center of her shifting cosmogram, allowing them to feel the energy created when all is in synchronous motion—the daily movements of the sun in sync with Black social dances occurring across time and space. Viewers can traverse the defining line between the physical and spirit worlds, as scenes of found footage transition to crafted scenes shot on Super 8 mm film, intermingling the living with the dead. The sun's four motions, from dusk to dusk, are felt in the seat of the body as the slow drag of Erika Flowers' "Magickal" transitions to the up-tempo pace of Anjelika Jelly Joseph's track "Fya." What Owens proposes is the conflation of vulnerable ecological systems with the vulnerability of Black communities and the impending threat to continued Black survivance. This ecopoem not only demonstrates that connection, but goes so far as to offer audiences an invitation to surrender to the dance, not as separate human bystanders, but as humble members of diverse and delicate ecosystems.

Owens's perfectly balanced tension between unreconciled pasts and the present—between the archive and memory, what is known and what is felt, how it should be and simply how it is—offers an explanation as to why scenes of unquestionable Black joy can still compel us to break down and cry.

by TK Smith

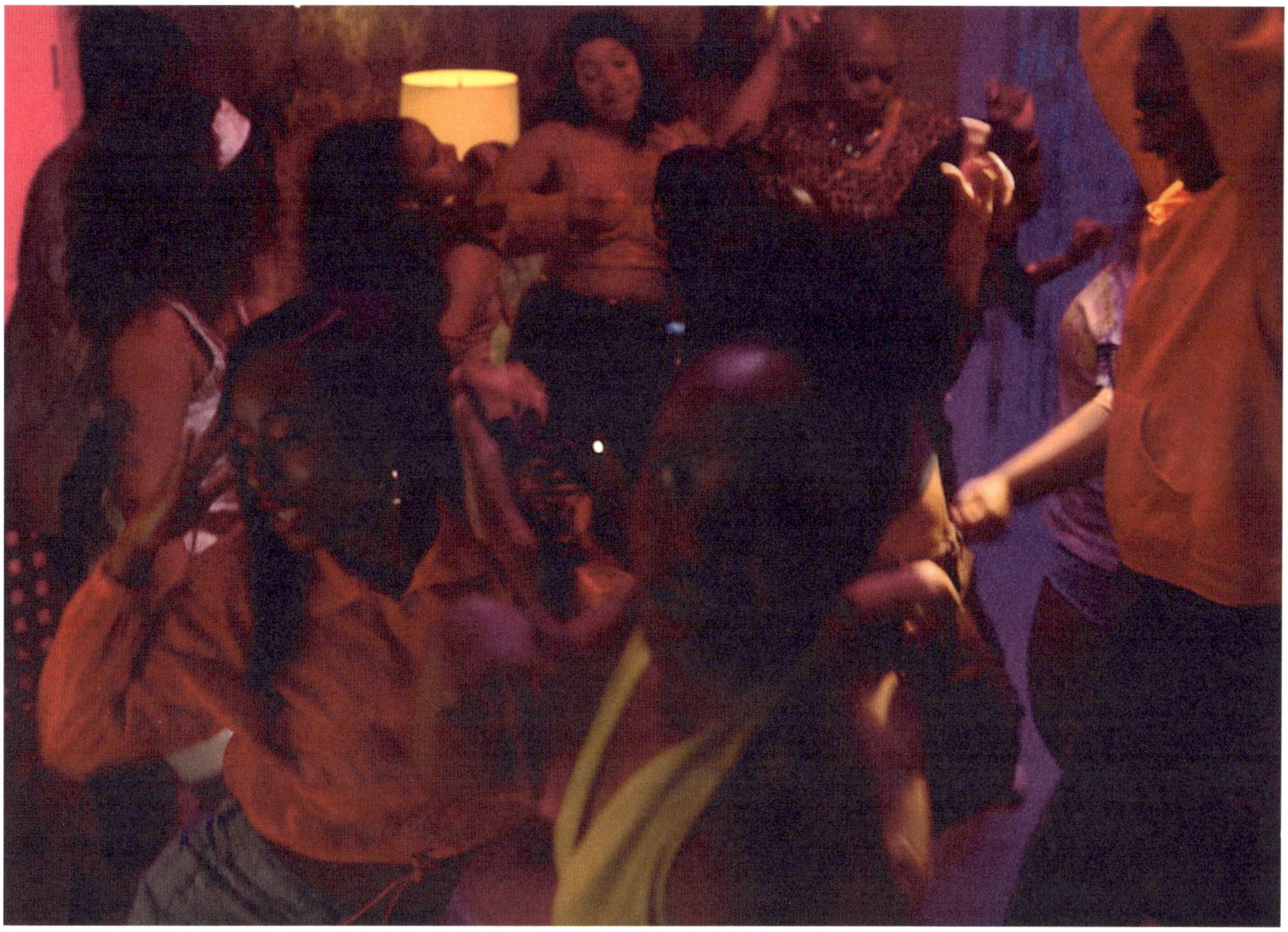

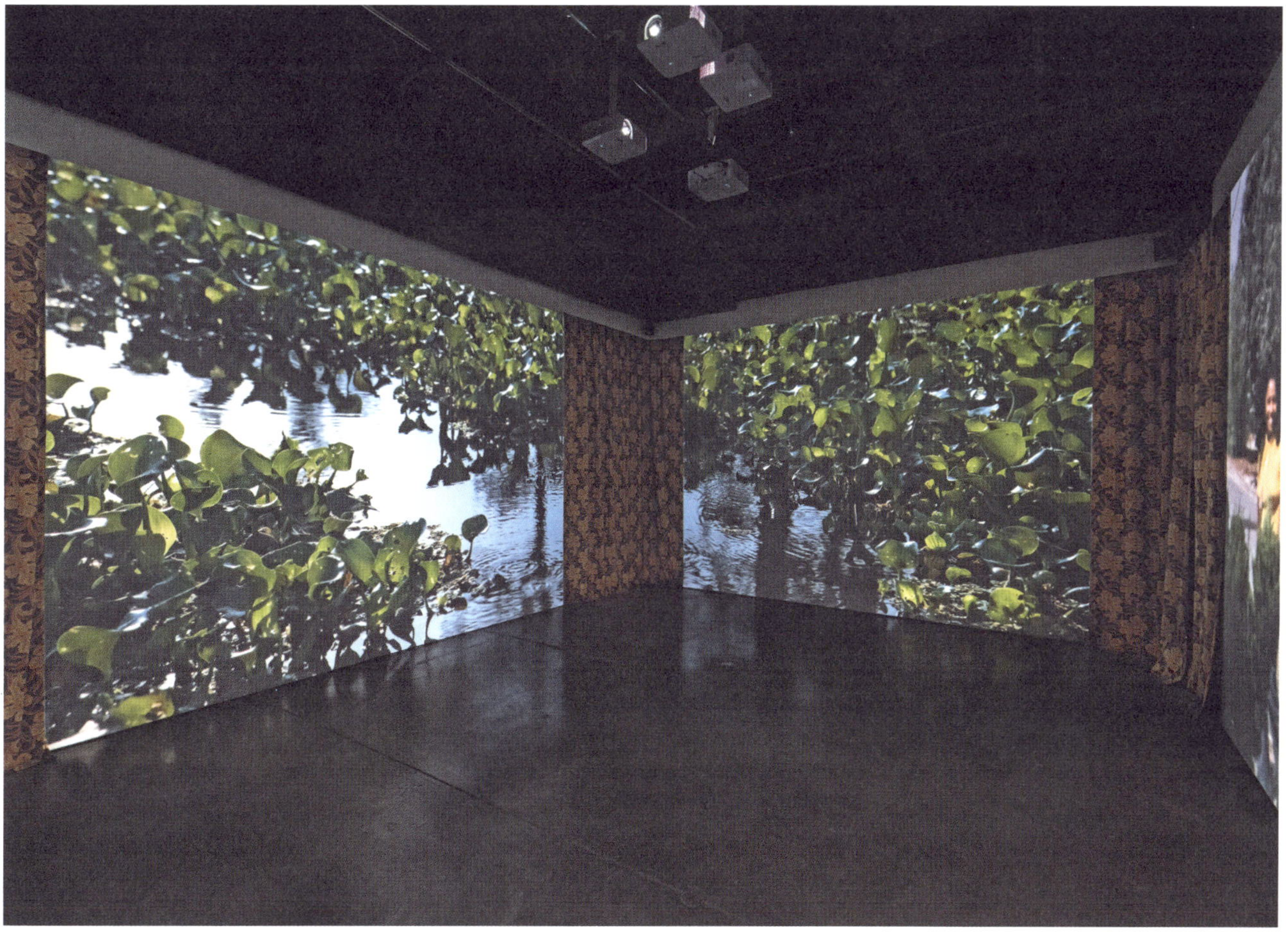

Top: *Black Delight, An Ecopoem*, 2024 (video still)   Above: *Black Delight, An Ecopoem*, 2024

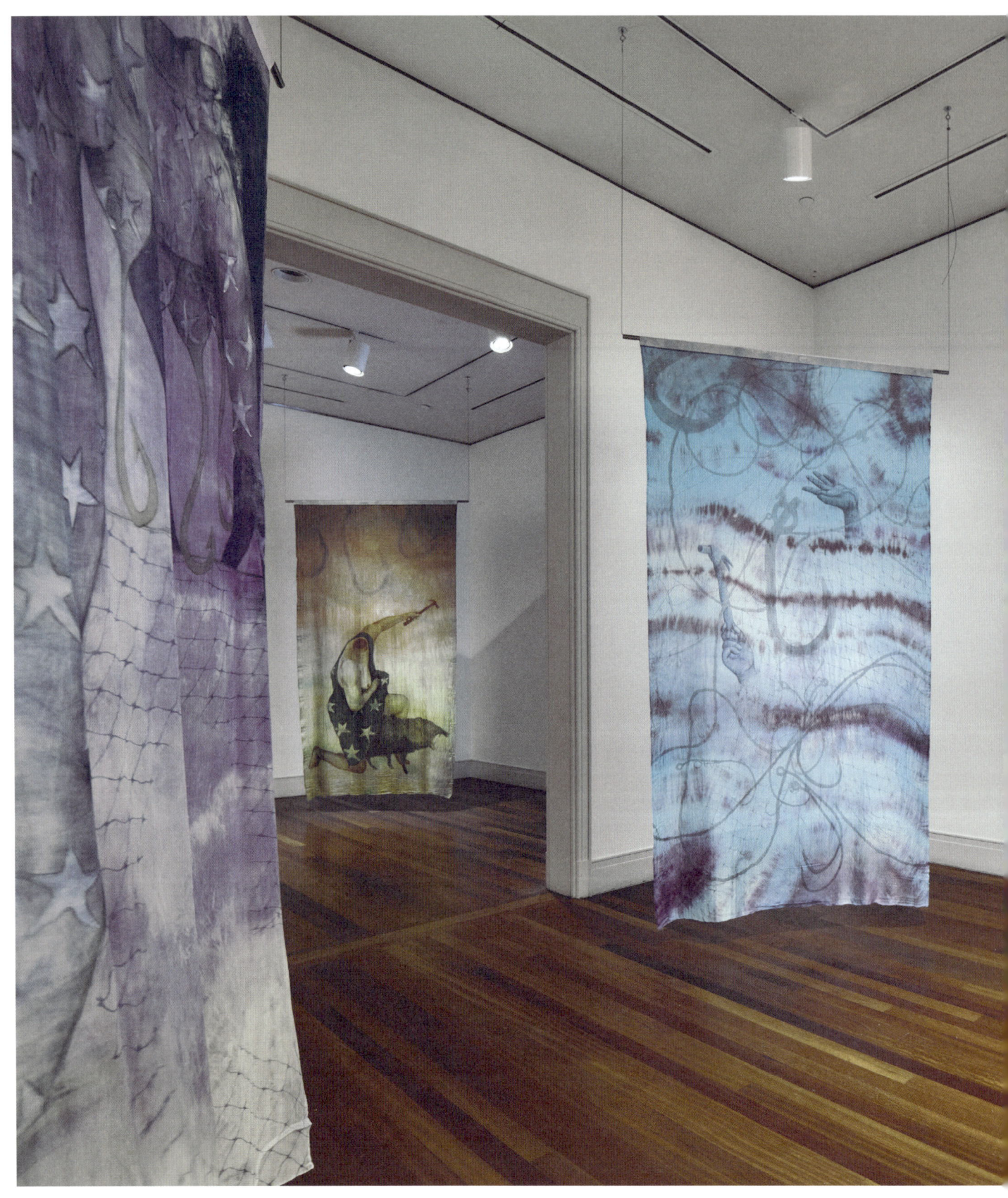

the hammeress in a state of disgrace, 2024

Ada M. Patterson

b. 1994, Bridgetown, Barbados; lives in London, UK and
Amsterdam, Netherlands

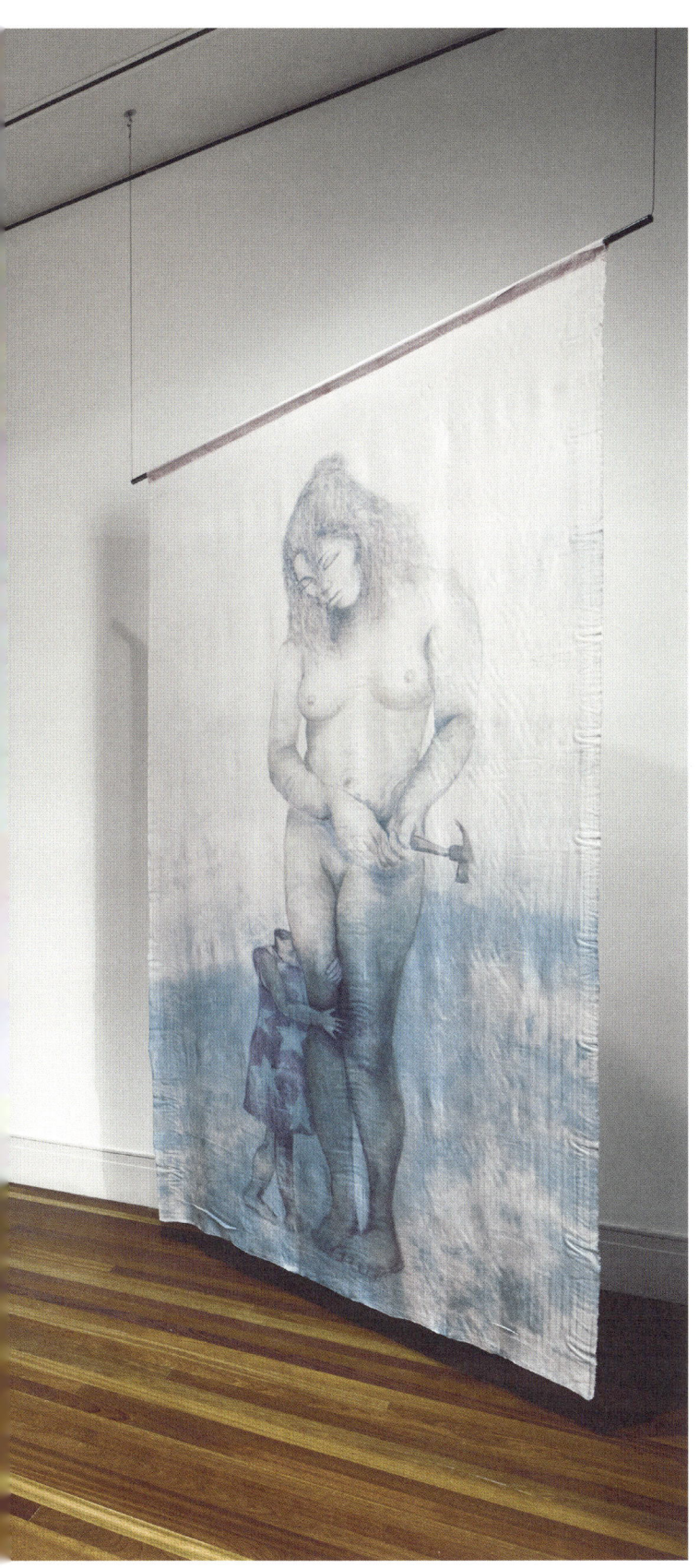

Over the last decade, Ada M. Patterson has
developed a multidisciplinary body of work that
includes masquerade, textiles, performance,
video, and poetry. Across these dynamic media,
she has been interested in confronting the
contradictions of living through crisis. In her
work, crisis is configured as a radical state of
indeterminacy that generates precarity. Under
such turbulence, Patterson often represents
social, cultural, and embodied transition as
a response to crisis. Transition, here, is less
about the eventual arrival at safety and stasis
and more about a mode of survival in which her
subjects demonstrate the fundamental capacity
to produce alternative forms of relations. And
yet, Patterson's work demonstrates that these
transitions do not always result in euphoria.
They are not always landscapes of utopia that
pale against a harrowing past. Sometimes,
transition spells disappointment, terror, grief,
failure, and even more uncertainty. Crisis
begets transition and transition begets crisis.

In this installation, which Patterson titled *the
hammeress in a state of disgrace* (2024), a
set of large-scale dye paintings on pongee
silk were created using her own body as the
initial point of reference. The paintings are

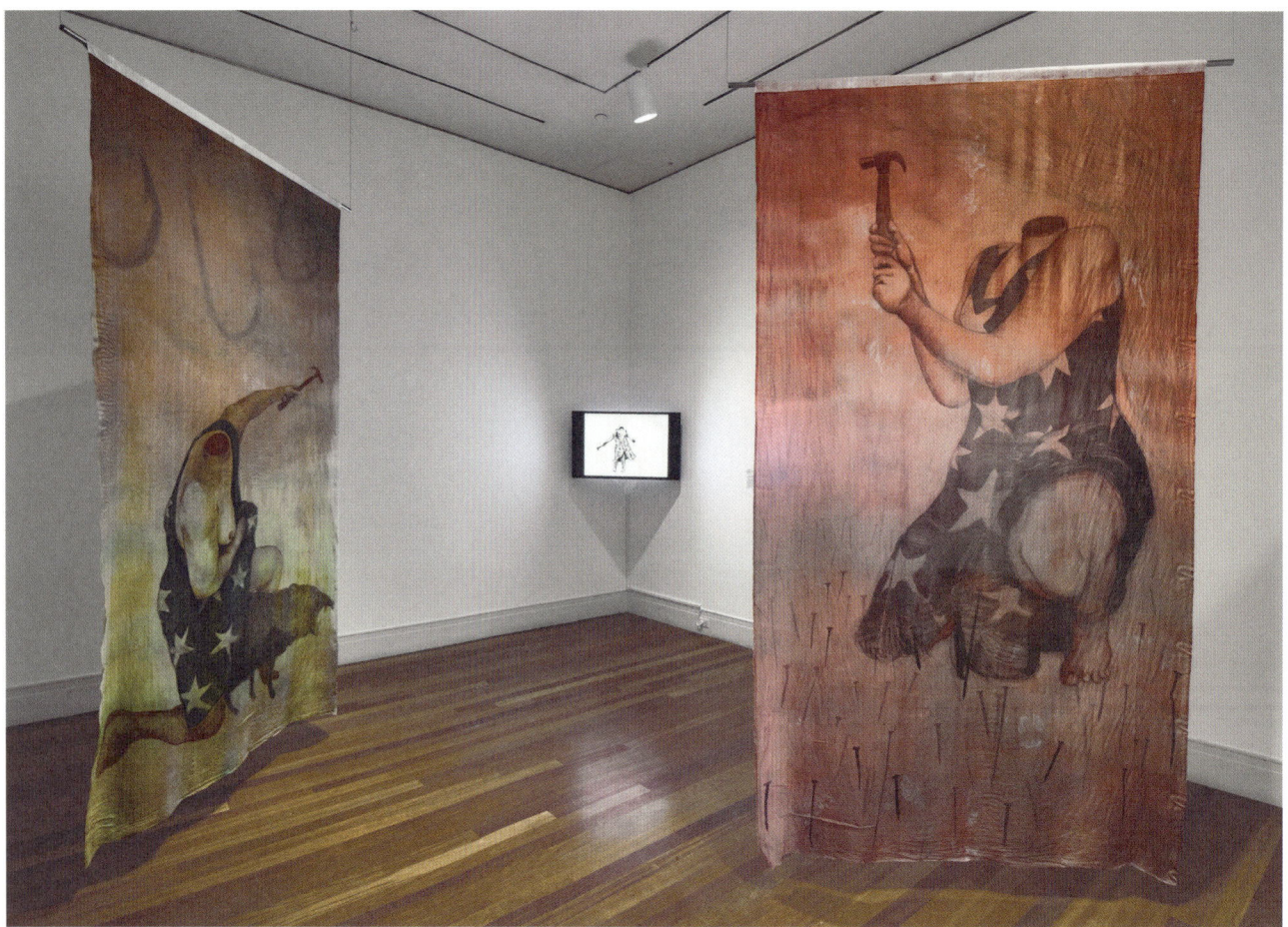

also accompanied by an enchanting video animation that features music played by her on steelpan. Throughout the images, the dismembered bodies of women scatter across a bare landscape as they take up postures of defense or defeat in a world characterized by a ubiquitous, yet ambiguous, sense of danger. Responding to these pervasive threats, these women wield the hammers as weapons and sever their own limbs to survive. They move through a state of becoming and unbecoming that speaks to their negotiation of a hostile world. In this gendered state of crisis, Patterson invokes the starfish, a signature motif that represents forms of life threatened by their environment. Like the women, the starfish also dismember themselves, sometimes fatally, in response to the catastrophic effects of the climate crisis.

Yet, there is a quiet utopian longing that the starfish signify in the paintings, particularly as they begin to resemble stars in the sky. In one scene, the hammeress poses like Nut, the ancient Egyptian goddess of the sky and the stars, who kept the primeval waters of chaos from crashing down on the Earth. And, as a master of transformation, Nut was known to swallow the sun and rebirth it every morning, a symbol of eternal renewal. But this hope is always haunted by ambivalence. In the video animation, the headless hammeress spirals to the looping rhythm of the steelpan, her dress coming undone. Without her head, it is difficult for us to decipher a sense of her interiority. Is she dancing in ecstasy, having escaped the surveillance of a world that demands her entire body? Is she in a state of delirium, turning again and again, stuck in repetitive anticipation of violence that might come from any direction? Headlessness, in the most Caribbean spirit of masquerade, affords these women a critical opacity that refuses easy interpretation. We are invited to witness, but never to determine. Ultimately, Patterson challenges us to ask: What futures can transition make, what futures does it foreclose?

by Jovante Anderson

the hammeress in a state of disgrace, 2024

Brooke Pickett

b. 1980, Shreveport, LA; lives in New Orleans, LA

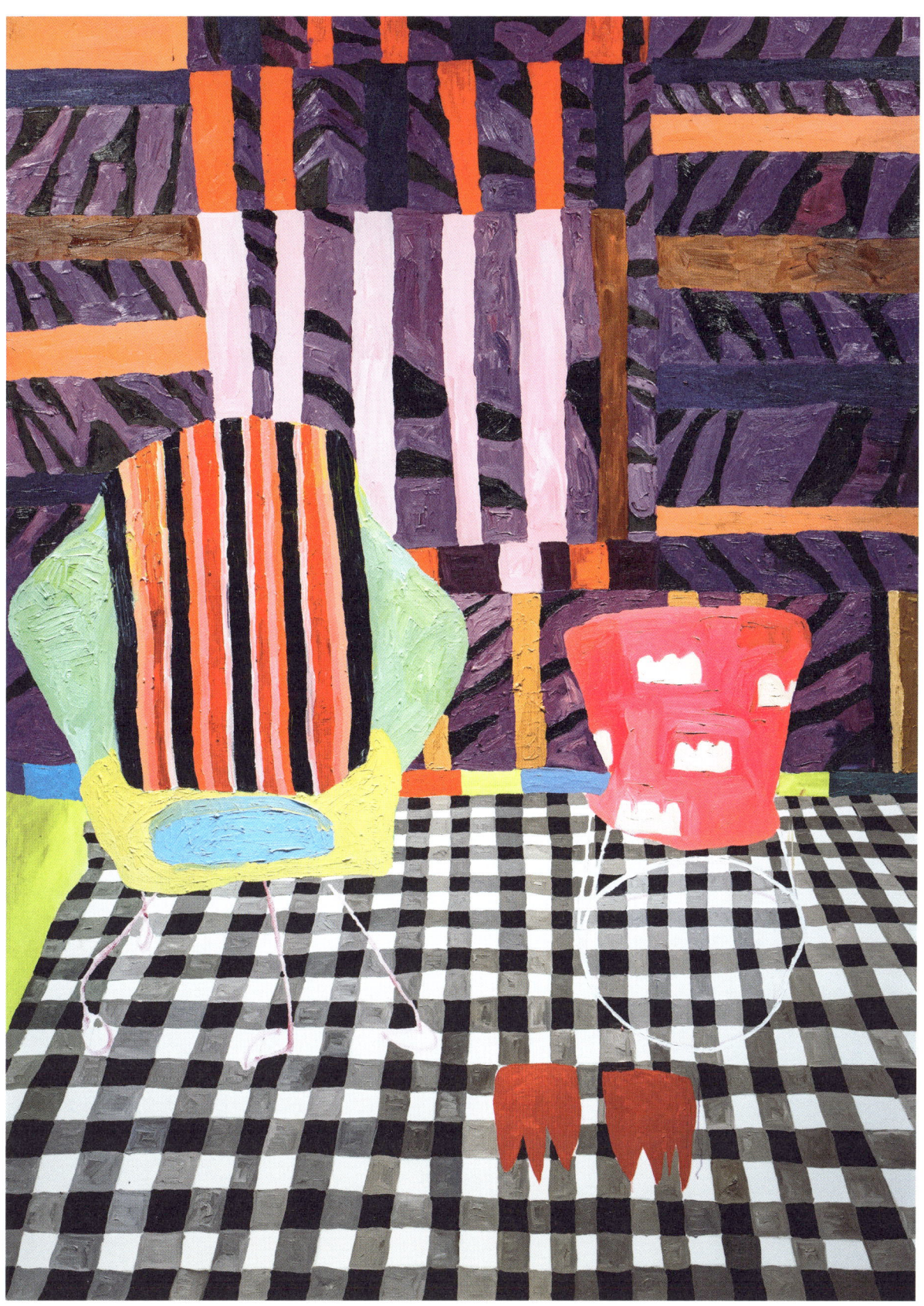

A Perpetual Search For The Perfect Place, 2024

Brooke Pickett's semi-abstract, monumental paintings explore the poetics and politics of domestic spaces, inspired by her native Louisiana as well as the years she spent away searching for the feeling of home outside of the South before returning. Through pattern play and thick layers of paint, Pickett creates narratives of shelter, memory, and life.

Pickett's painting process begins by arranging and rearranging items—draping a blanket over a chair and lampshade, or balancing precarious towers of textiles and children's toys. In creating these domestic scenes, Pickett points at our desire to create spaces that embrace, protect, and shelter us in the face of life. Drawn to imperfect items that have a purpose they can no longer accomplish, Pickett sources found domestic objects in need of fixing, mending, and saving, from thrift stores and her own home. Through heavy layers of oil paint, these fragile objects are rendered with a sense of permanence and given a second life. With each painting in Pickett's new body of work for Prospect.6, *What To Eat, What To Drink, What To Leave For Poison* (2024), Pickett aspired to work with a combination of colors she has never used before. Almost as if building a house, Pickett's layered paintings evoke solid structures, places where delicate narratives are memorialized on a monumental scale.

Pickett maps out all her titles before beginning a new series of paintings. With permission from the author, Pickett's new body of work takes its title from Camille T. Dungy's 2006 poetry collection of the same name. Pickett also drew inspiration from off-the-grid survivalist guides, and Catharine Beecher and Harriet Beecher Stowe's nineteenth-century treatise on homemaking for women, *American Woman's Home* (1869). Titles like *Retrofitted* (2024) and *A Powerful Transmitter* (2024) hint at the utilitarian, survivalist aspects of homebuilding, while the paintings themselves, with their punchy palettes, lush textures, and layered textile references, point to the ways home can sometimes be that special velvet pillow, or the lace curtains that are a little tattered after generations of wear.

A Perpetual Search For The Perfect Place (2024) captures the warm embrace of a comfy place to relax, wrapped in a quilted wall of vibrant purples and grounding tones of red.

In *A Powerful Transmitter*, moments of the real world, like the monster truck at center, meet unresolved abstraction, creating a tightness that just holds together a composition that creates its own unsteady sense of gravity while also feeling like it's on the verge of collapse.

Spotted neon panels in *How To Make Drinkable Water Out Of Air* (2024) pulsate on a purple door, beaming like warning lights behind a screen of dancing orange mesh reminiscent of materials found on construction sites. Intersecting these forms is a striped, reflective orange band that bisects the middle ground, creating pictorial planes evocative of the waterline left after flood waters recede.

With their own uncanny, internal sense of balance and bright colors that border on garish, Pickett's works hold all of the messiness and uneasiness that lives within the warmth and safety that home can offer. As climate catastrophe threatens traditional notions of place, Pickett captures moments and generations of life through objects, contemplating whether a painting can be a home.

by Caroline Cox

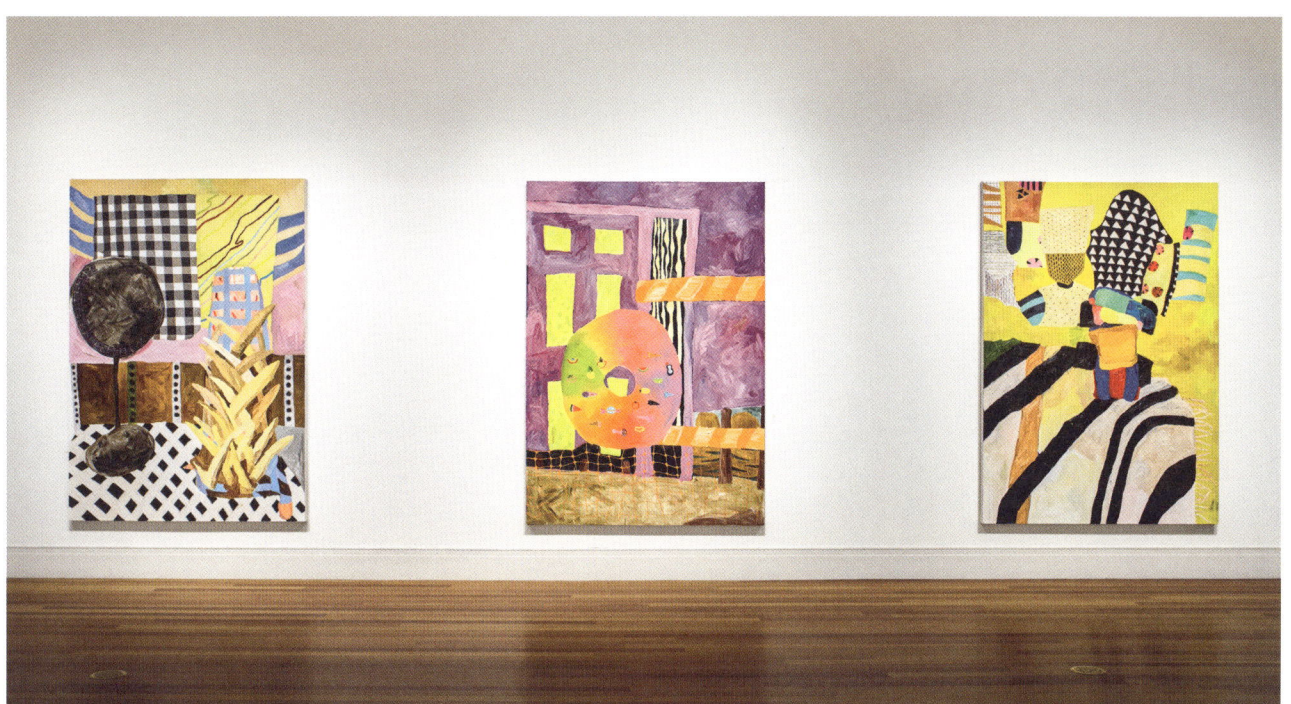

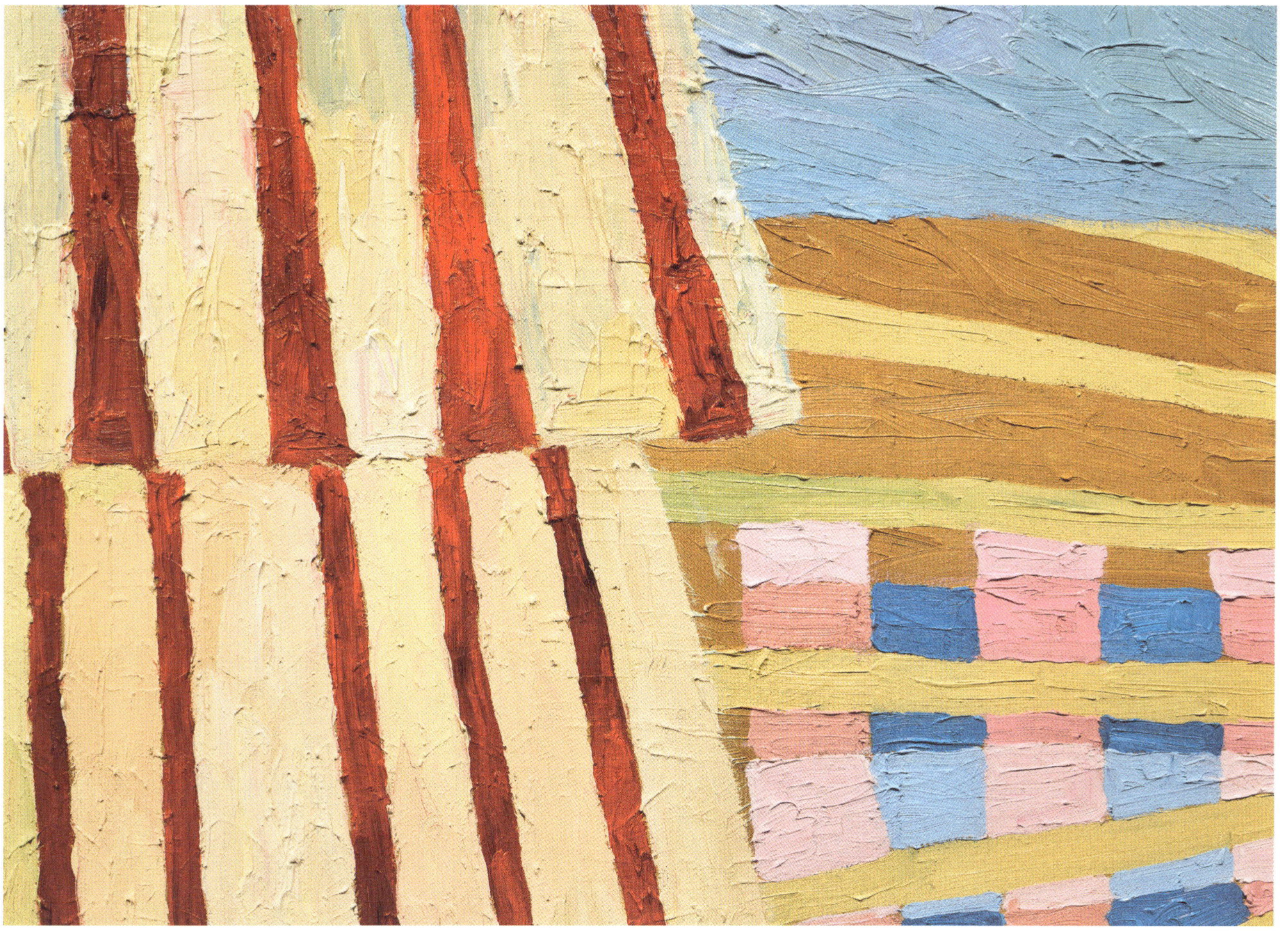

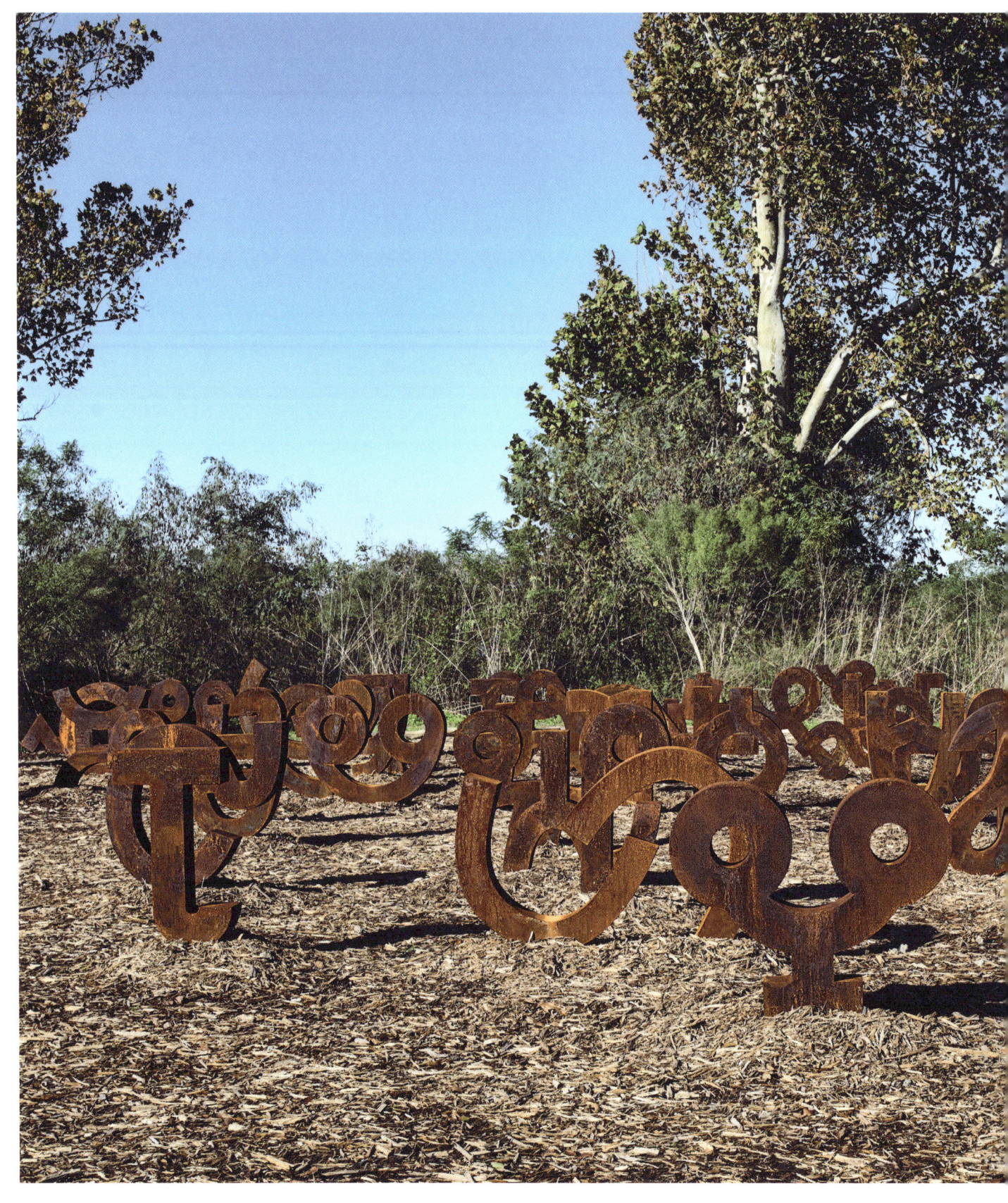

AFAKA BUKU, 2024

Marcel Pinas

b. 1971, Marowijne District, Suriname; lives in Paramaribo, Suriname

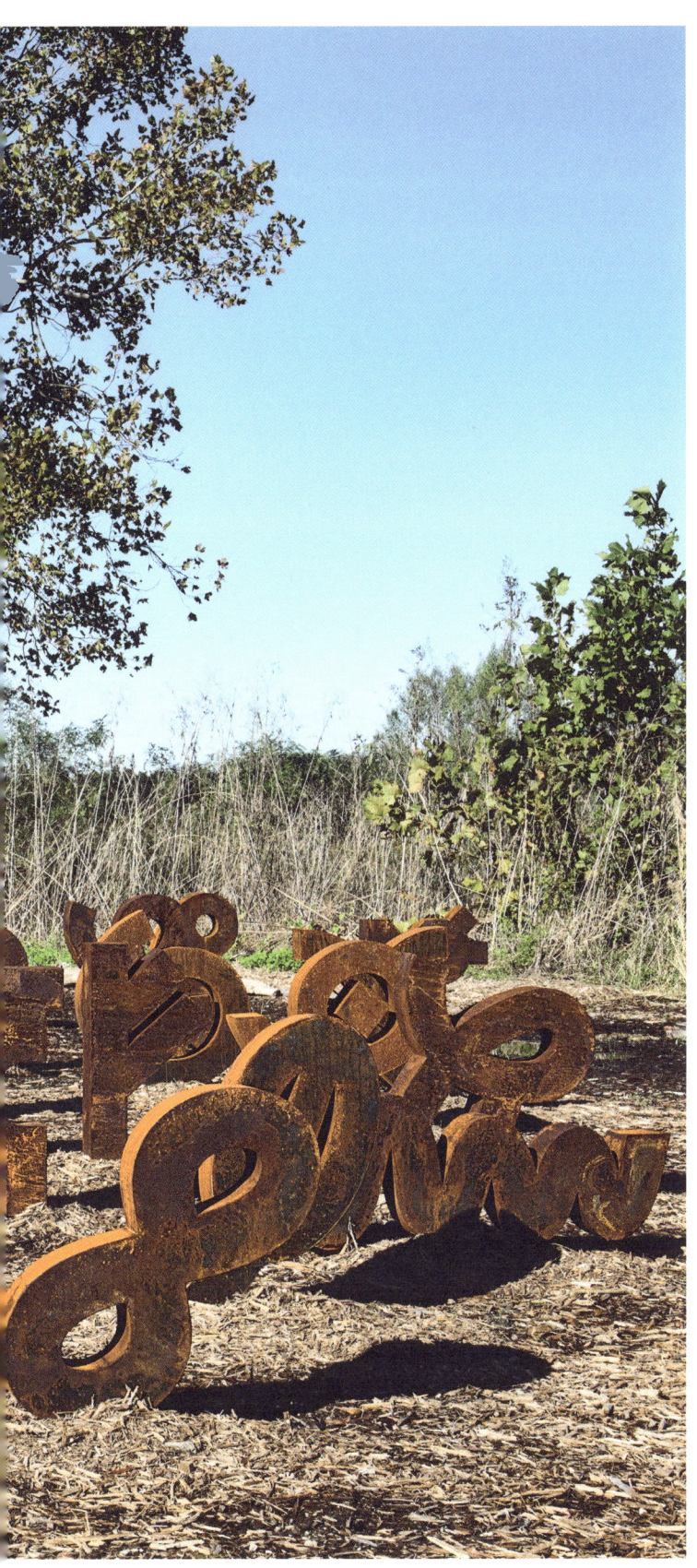

A 3,000-mile journey by water from Suriname's Marowijne District—where Marcel Pinas was born—to New Orleans would begin on the Cottica, a tributary of the Commewijne River flowing to the Atlantic. The route wends around numerous territories divided by language and politics, but all share a five-century history, from the coast of South America, through the Antillean chain and Caribbean Sea, then the Gulf of Mexico to the Mississippi Delta. Meandering upriver, you come to a stretch of shore near Audubon Park where, for the duration of Prospect.6, Pinas's *AFAKA BUKU* (2024) sculptures stood guard.

These Corten steel forms, in their deliberate jumble of angles and curves, are illegible to most viewers, but perhaps still recognizable as a pattern of symbols. They constitute, in fact, a text in Afaka script: a syllabary of fifty six characters used to write the Ndyuka language, named for its inventor, Afaka Atumisi.

It is impossible to discuss Pinas's work without implicating his Ndyuka identity, and dangerously easy to reduce the artist's prolific practice to mere representation of Ndyuka culture. It doesn't help that many visitors to P.6 (or other international art contexts where Pinas's work is encountered) will never have heard of the Ndyuka, of Suriname's other Maroon peoples, or indeed of Suriname itself— a small but dizzyingly cosmopolitan nation on South America's Atlantic shoulder.

Like other Maroon peoples across the Americas, including those of Louisiana, the Ndyuka are descended from enslaved Africans who escaped bondage and established and defended free communities outside the control of colonial powers. Their complicated, sometimes contradictory, and fully ongoing history cannot be adequately encompassed in the crisp summary of an art catalogue text.

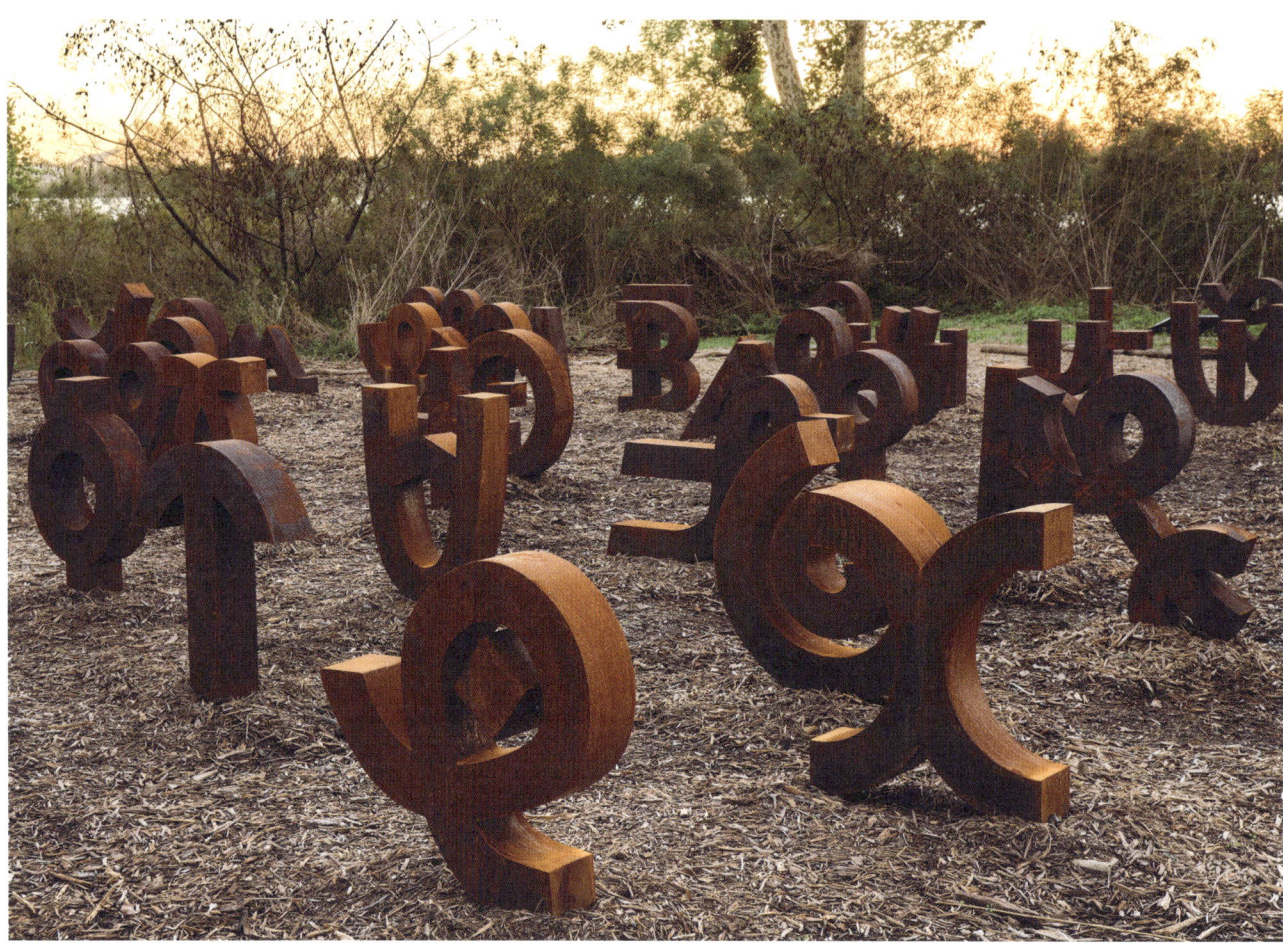

Over the past three decades, Pinas's work has ranged from boldly colored paintings and mixed-media collages to room-size installations and sculptural monuments. Afaka script, other Ndyuka symbols, and even physical artifacts are a persistent presence, deployed in an investigation of personal memory and collective survival. The Afaka syllabary is all but unknown outside Suriname, and few Ndyuka—one estimate says 10 percent—are fluent in the script. Even on home ground, most of Pinas's audience cannot literally "read" these works, but he has nonetheless insisted them into contemporary Suriname's visual environment, especially through public artworks like his *Kibii Wi Totem* (2006), totems made from black-painted oil drums, blazoned with giant aluminum Afaka characters.

Strategically located at key "gateways"—outside the seventeenth century fort in Paramaribo, once the center of Dutch colonial admin-istration, near the international airport, and along the highway that connects Marowijne to the capital—these totems spell out a plea for protection, addressed equally to ancestral presences and secular authorities.

For centuries, the Ndyuka and Suriname's other Maroon communities existed in a social reality outside (though immediately adjacent to) the Dutch colony and its successor independent state. Pinas's *Kibii Wi* works assert the Ndyuka—their knowledge and ethics, individual desires and collective demands—as integral, via literal inscription on the human landscape.

Located on the distant but not-so-different landscape of the Mississippi, once a highway for trafficking enslaved humans and plantation commodities, the characters of *AFAKA BUKU* are reminders of what Marowijne and New Orleans, Suriname and Louisiana, have in common. To inscribe a landscape by planting a flag, imposing a name on a map, or drawing a boundary line can be an act of simultaneous claiming and dispossession. The point of Pinas's inscription—against amnesia, against denial—is to claim without dispossessing. What we truly share, if we can recognize and name it, is what may protect us.

by Nicholas Laughlin

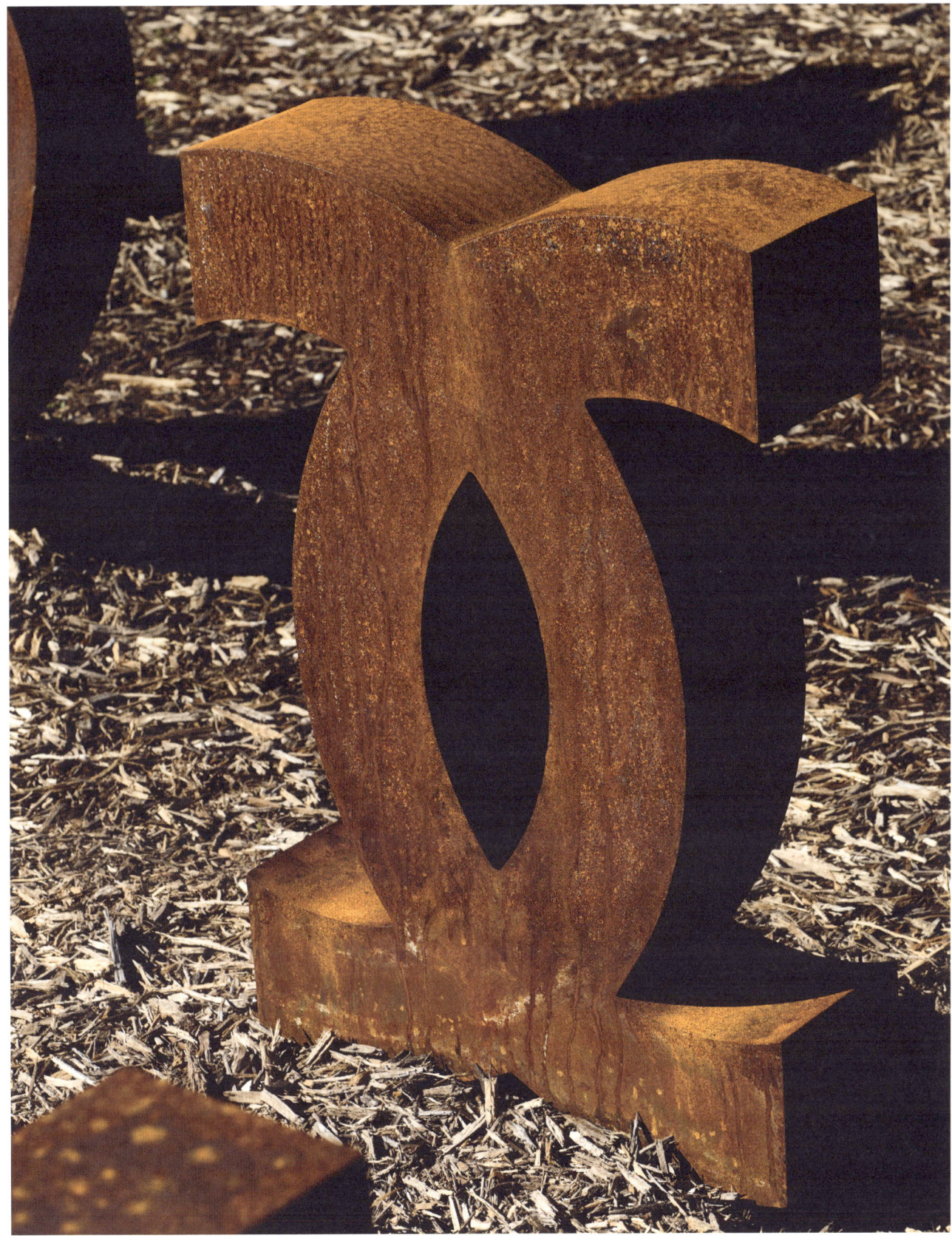

AFAKA BUKU, 2024 (detail)

Stephanie Syjuco

b. 1974, Manila, Philippines; lives in Oakland, CA

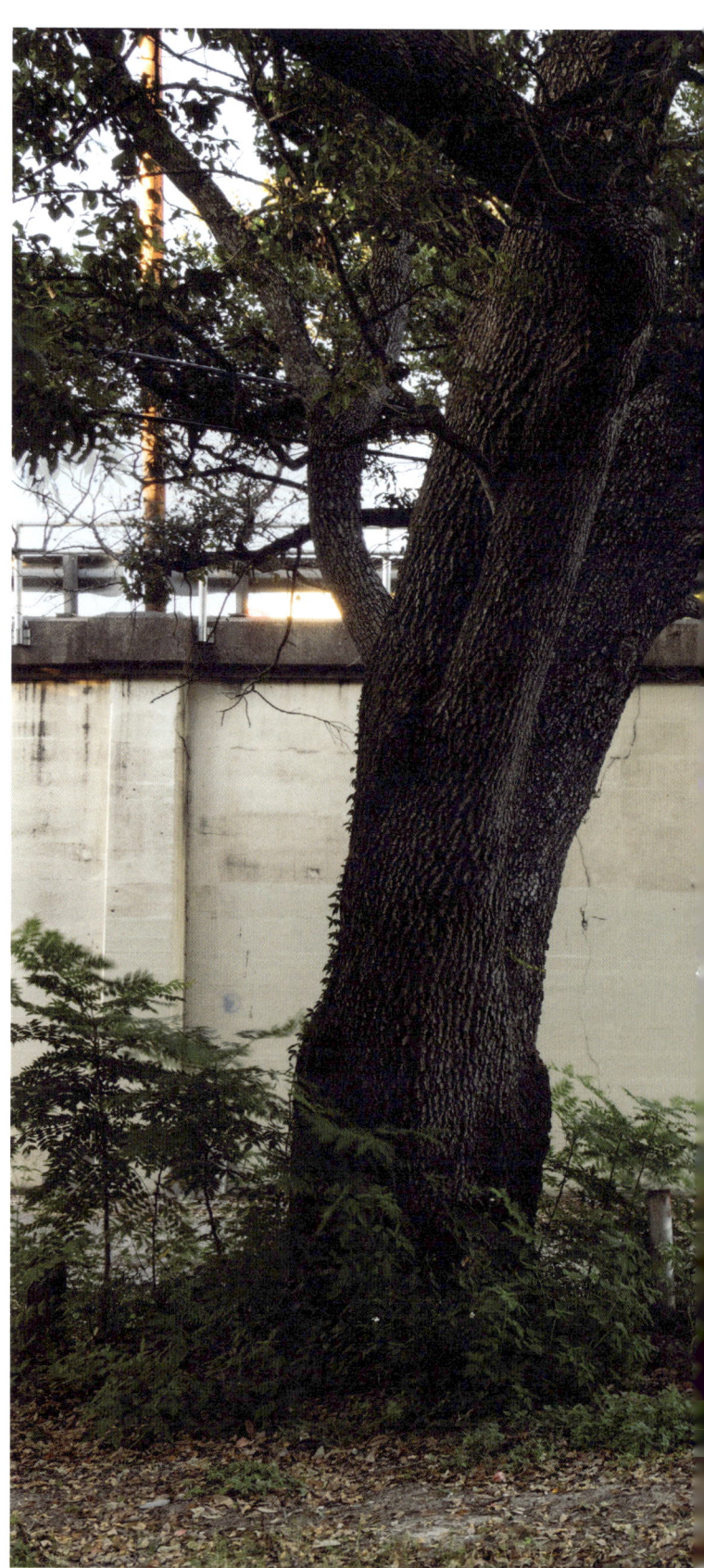

Born in Manila and raised and educated in the San Francisco Bay Area, Stephanie Syjuco is a conceptual artist who works in photography, sculpture, and installation, moving from handmade and craft-inspired mediums to digital editing and archive excavations. Recently, Syjuco has focused on how photography and image-based processes are implicated in the construction of racialized and exclusionary narratives of American history and citizenship. For Prospect.6, Syjuco engages with an important site/history in the Filipinx diaspora: St. Malo, Louisiana.

Located in St. Bernard Parish, St. Malo is where "Manilamen" from the archipelago—now known as the Philippines—jumped ship from Spanish galleons and built a fishing village in the first half of the 1800s. The exact date is unconfirmed. The actual village is long gone, which contributes to St. Malo's mythical or phantom qualities. The Manilamen built Native-style wooden huts on raised stilts, which provided shelter and communal space. Engaging with engravings of St. Malo created by Charles Graham (based on sketches made by J.O. Davidson), which accompanied Lafcadio Hearn's essay, "St. Malo: A Lacustrine Village," in *Harper's Weekly* (1883), Syjuco zooms in on important primary visual documents and the small details of Graham's images, which themselves are abstractions of the originals by Davidson.

Phantom Visions (The Lacustrine Village of St. Malo), 2024 (detail). Music Box Village

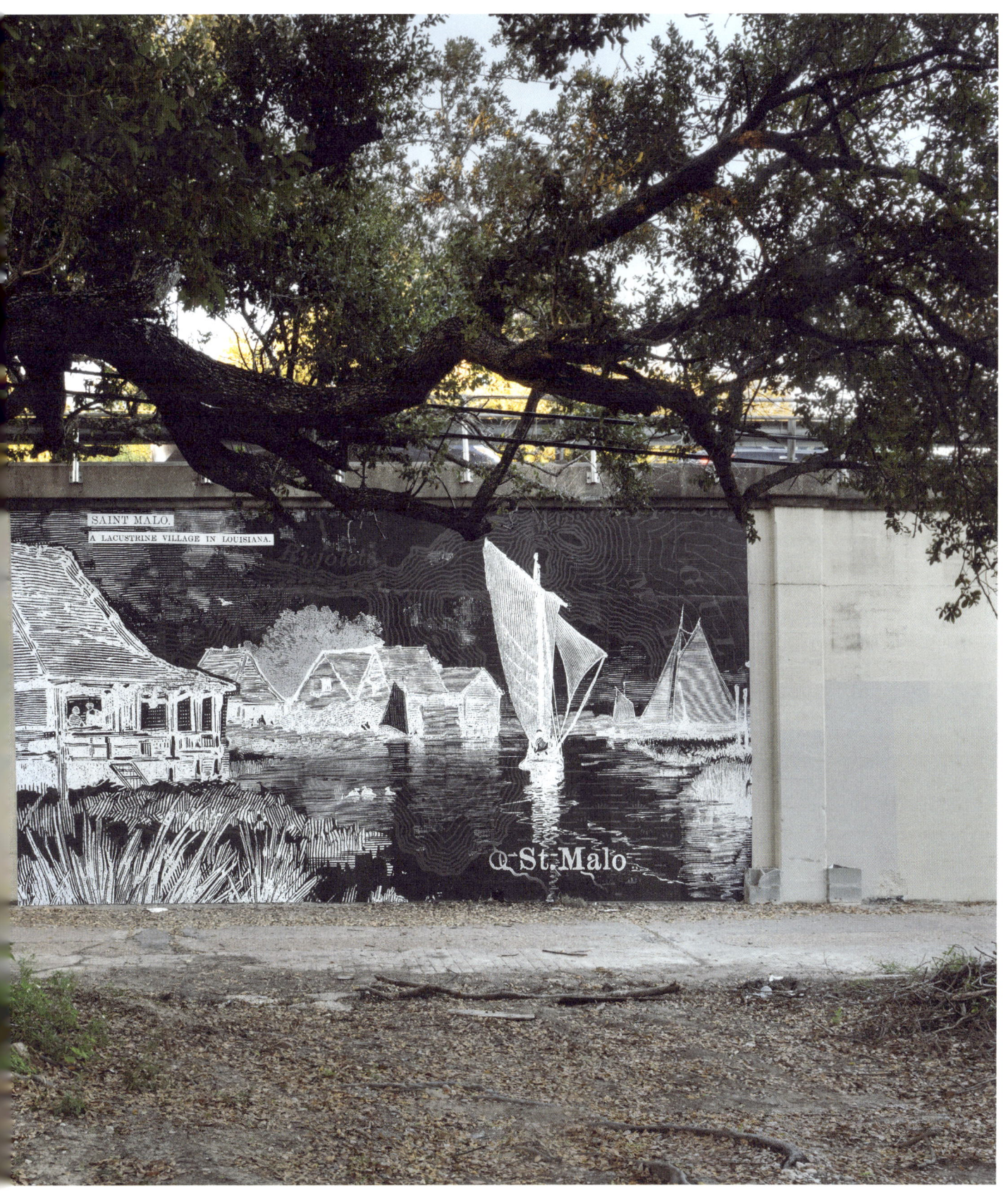

SAINT MALO,
A LACUSTRINE VILLAGE IN LOUISIANA.

St. Malo

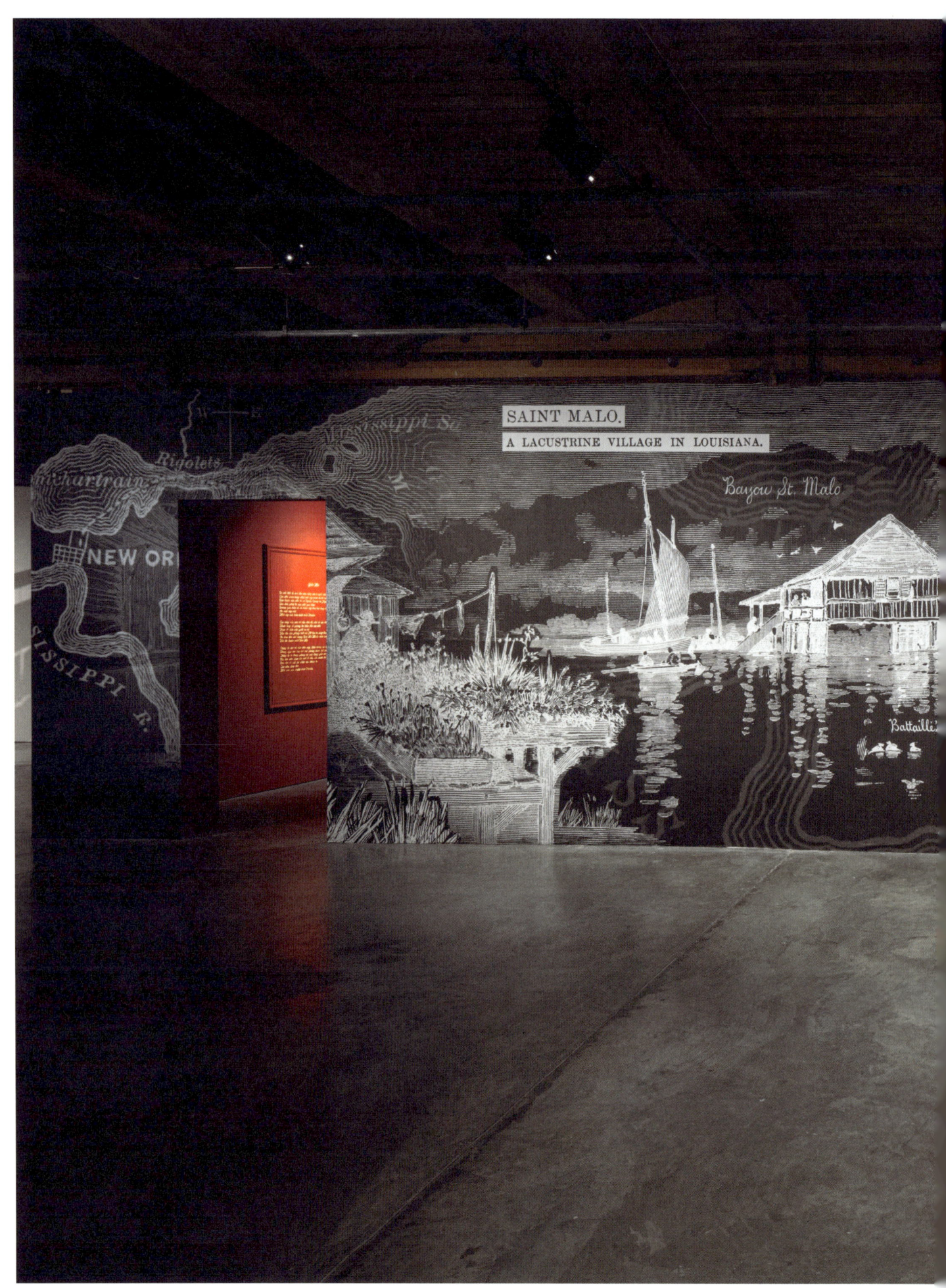

Phantom Visions (The Lacustrine Village of St. Malo), 2024.
Contemporary Arts Center, New Orleans

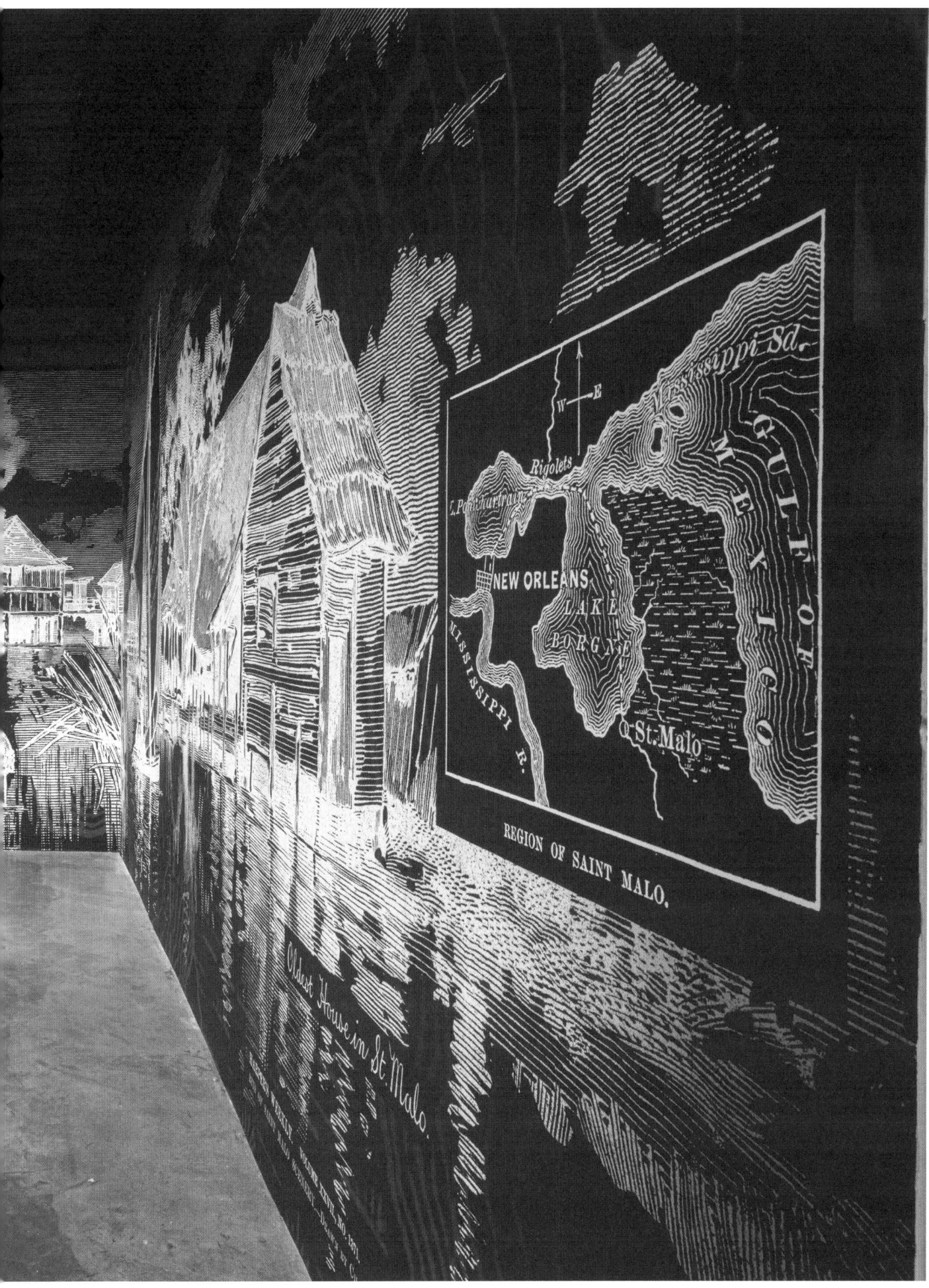

Syjuco also inverts the original images, which emphasizes their ghostliness and prompts viewers to wonder, "What am I looking at?" or, perhaps, *"Where* am I looking?" Moving from the micro to the macro, Syjuco also enlarges and places her images inside and outside of art institutions, having them wheat pasted at five sites throughout New Orleans. As the Manilamen's village at St. Malo is often understood as a historical, geographical, and racial "backwaters" in dominant US histories, Syjuco resists this temporal/spatial/social devaluation by transporting representations of historical/mythical St. Malo to the contemporary Crescent City. In doing so, Syjuco invites residents and visitors to become more curious about Louisiana's complex multiracial histories of placemaking, to question narratives that regularly racialize Asians as perpetual "foreigners" or "outsiders," and to reflect on the fluidities of St. Malo as a time-place.

Mirroring how *Harper's Weekly* was once distributed throughout New Orleans, Syjuco also created a smaller "giveaway" artwork that consists of a folded printed poster. On one side, details from Syjuco's projects are featured. On the other side, there is more information about St. Malo's capacious and fluid history, and Filipinx-American efforts to remember, memorialize, or re-imagine St. Malo. Also included is an excerpt of an interview with Syjuco about her St. Malo public art project. The poster was made free and available to the general public at different sites in New Orleans.

Scientists predict that in the next fifty years, St. Malo and other parts of the Gulf Coast will be largely submerged due to global warming. Just like St. Malo, in time, Syjuco's wheat pasted images will also deteriorate and be washed away by sunlight and rain, thunderstorms and hurricanes. Syjuco alerts art viewers to the past and present, while gesturing towards possible, but not inevitable, environmental futures.

by Kale Bantigue Fajardo

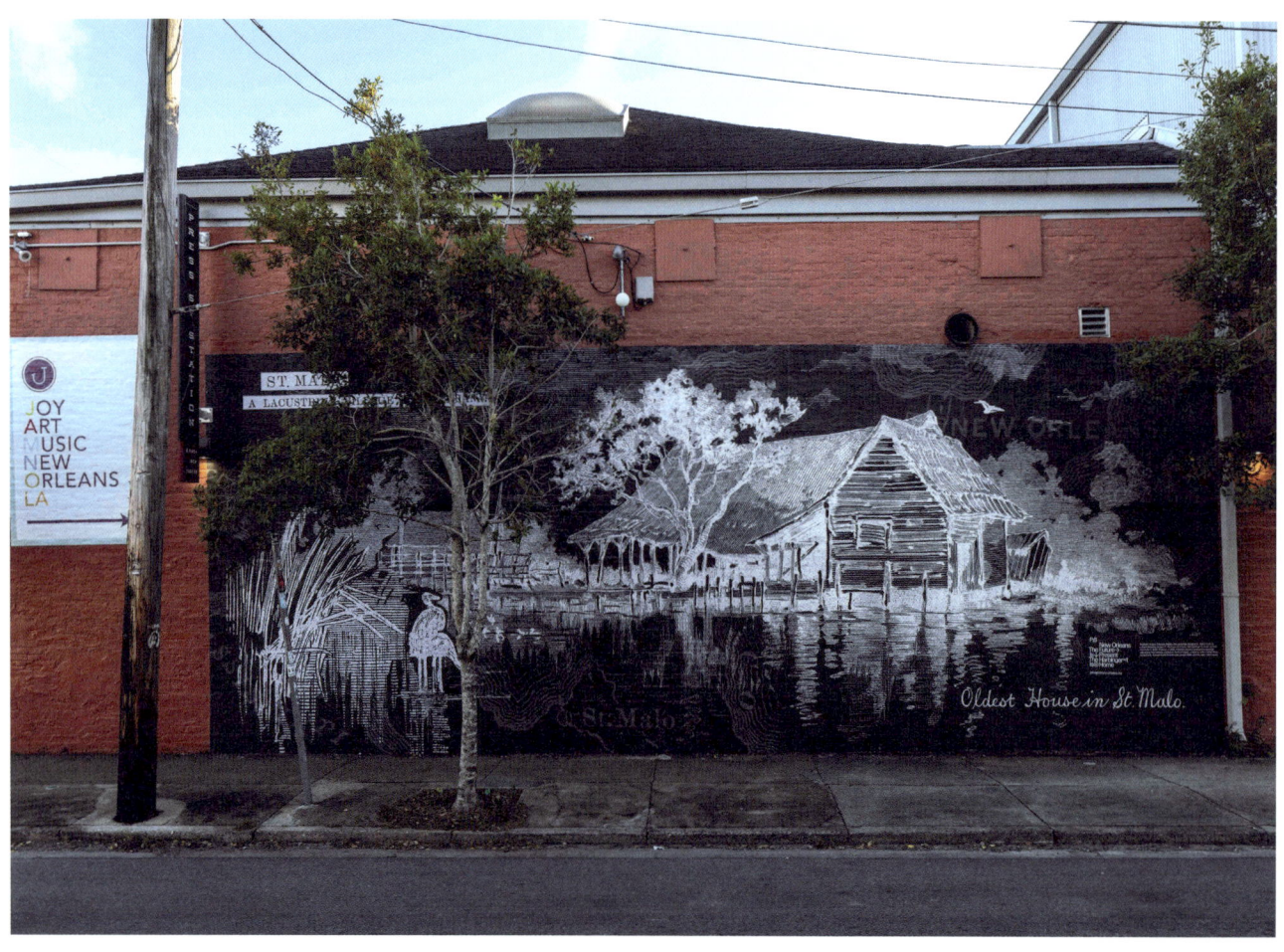

Phantom Visions (The Lacustrine Village of St. Malo), 2024.
New Orleans Center for Creative Arts (NOCCA)

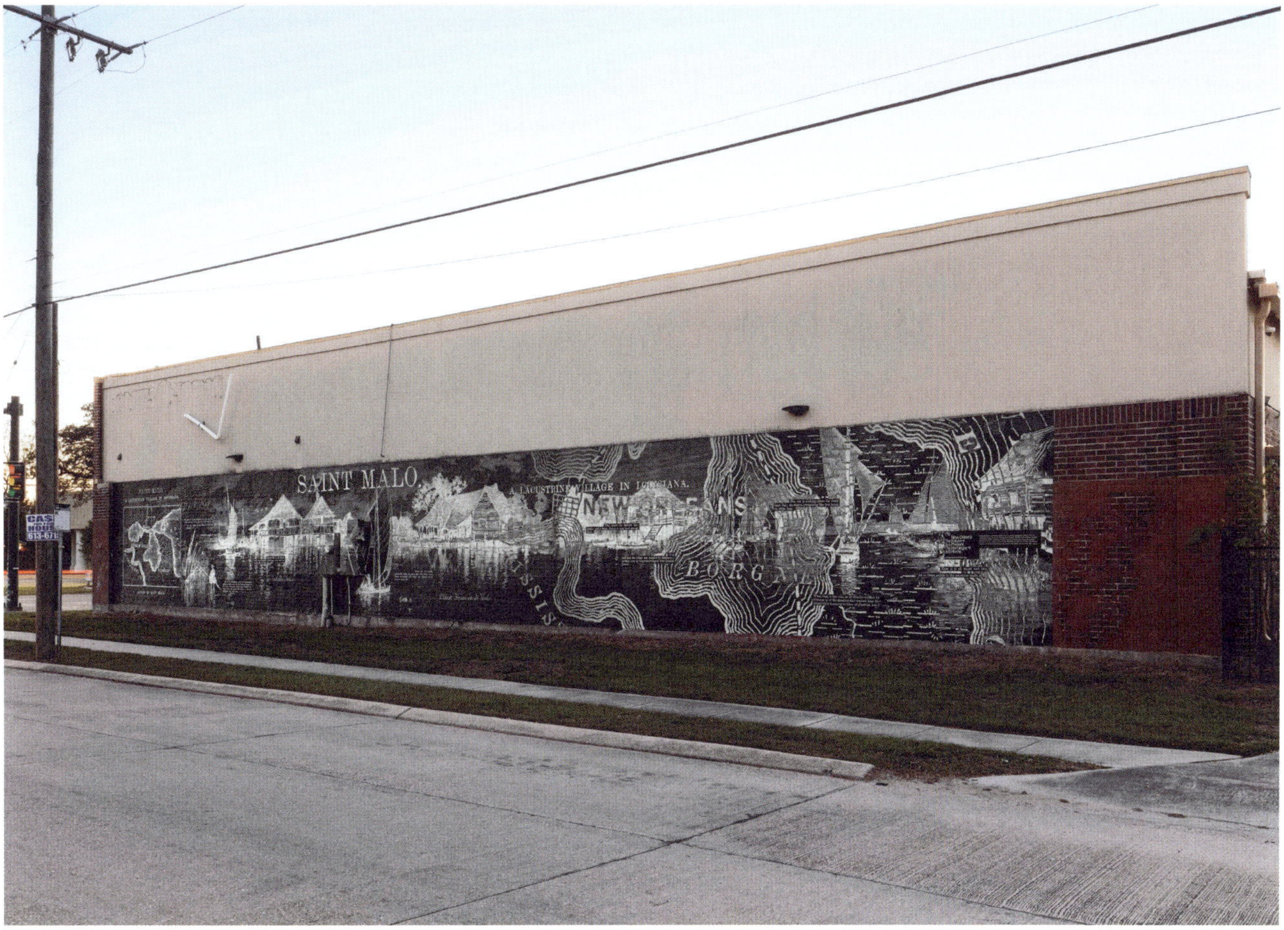

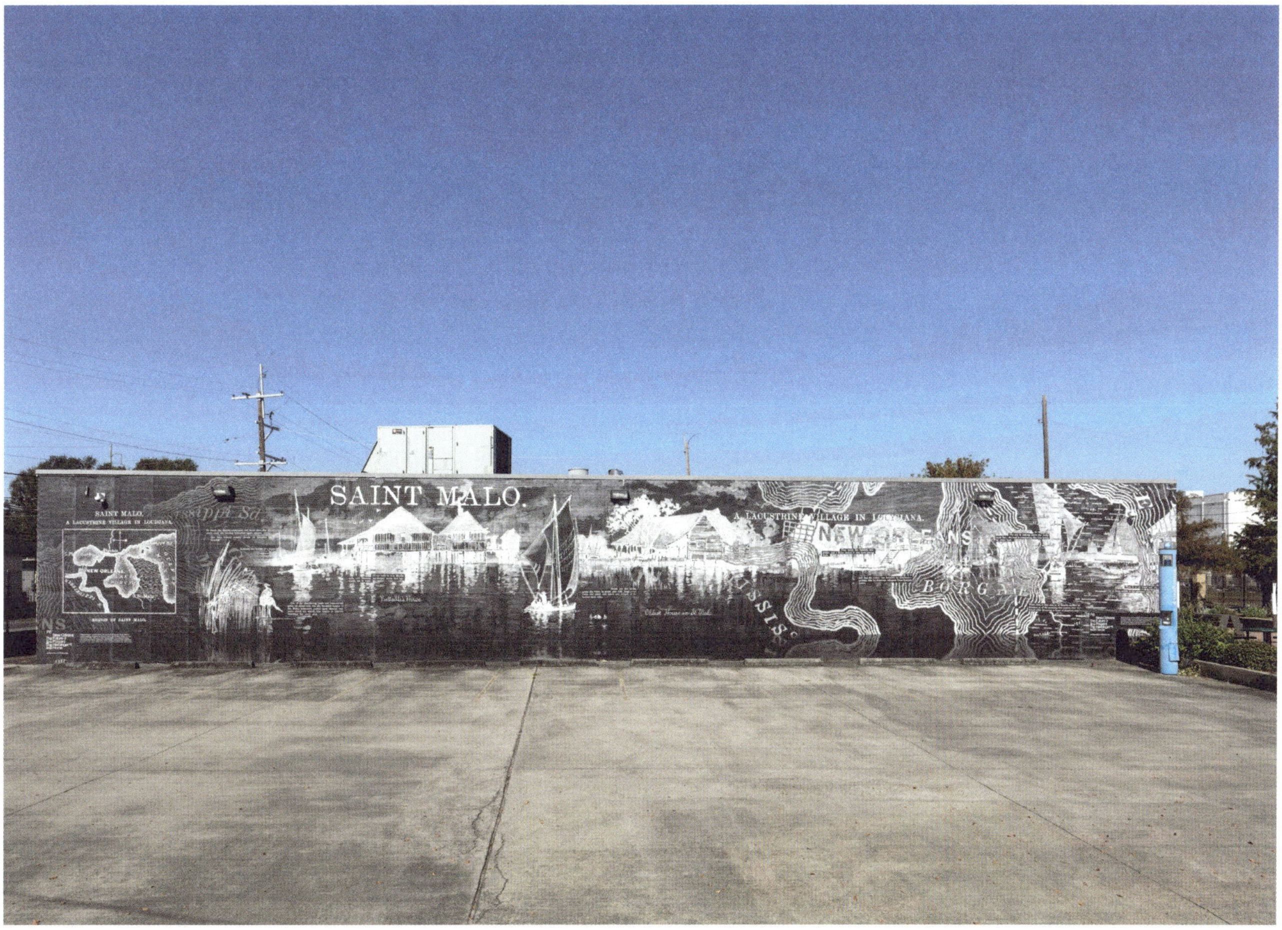

Top: *Phantom Visions (The Lacustrine Village of St. Malo)*, 2024.
5523 Saint Claude Avenue

Above: *Phantom Visions (The Lacustrine Village of St. Malo)*,
2024. Xavier University of Louisiana Art Village

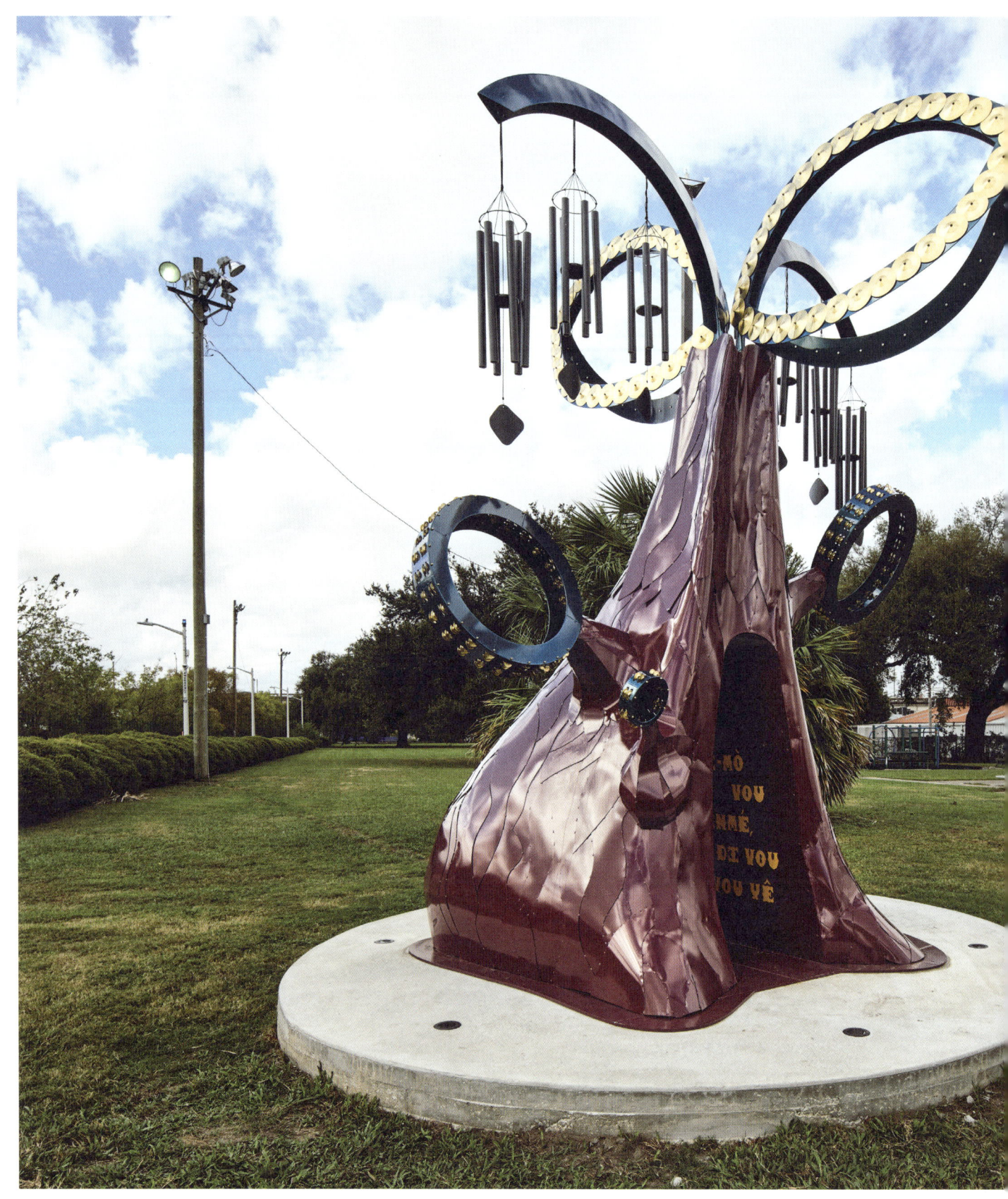

Tambourine Cypress, 2024

Ashley Teamer

b. 1991, New Orleans, LA; lives in New Orleans, LA and Brooklyn, NY

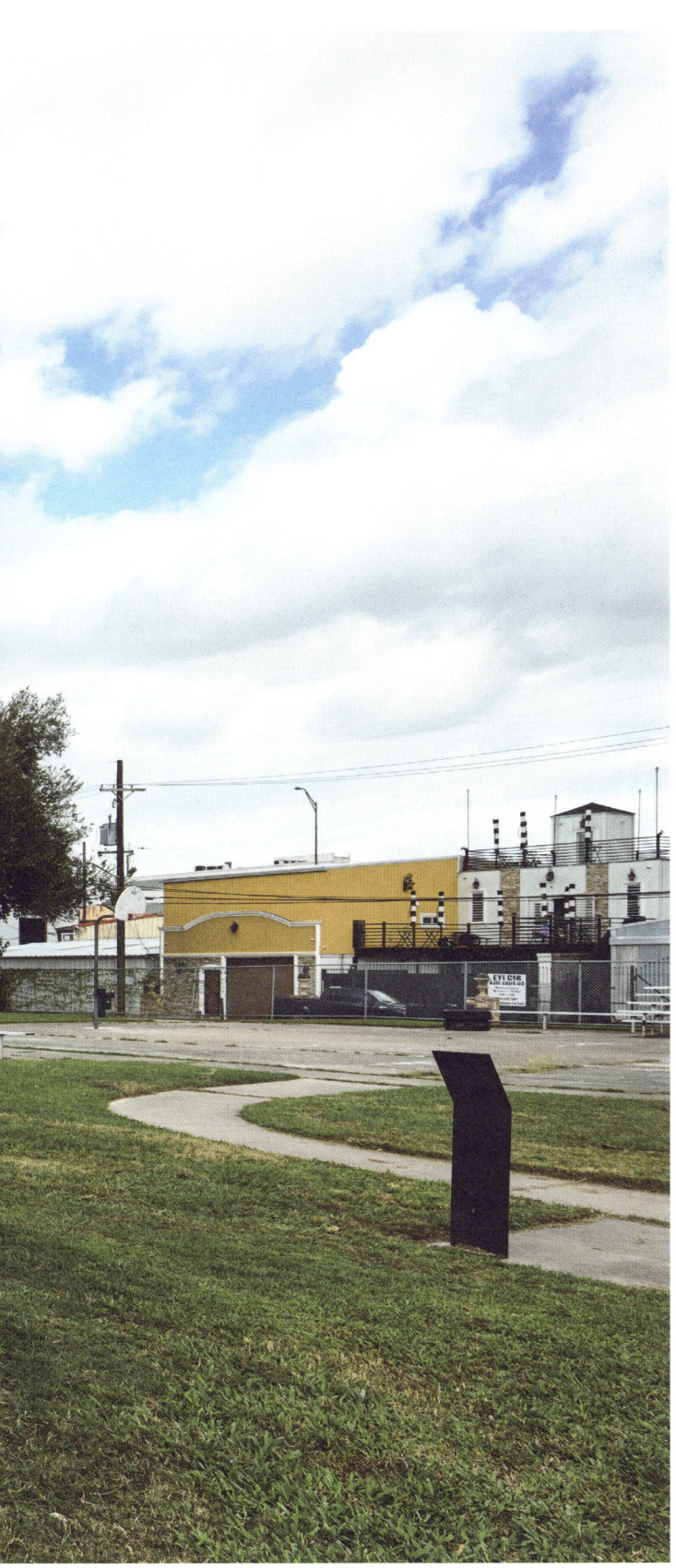

"I'm interested in putting art where people already are."[1] It's a sunny afternoon, and Ashley Teamer is walking me through her philosophy over burgers. Born and raised in New Orleans, Teamer works across disciplines, with a penchant for using sound, installation, and collage to explore the nuances of Black femininity in and beyond her hometown. She talks to me about her interest in public art, which has taken the shape of billboards, augmented reality monuments, and posters celebrating pillars of New Orleans's Black community.

In 2020, she and fellow artist/collaborator Annie Flanagan mounted a series of billboards around the city's Gentilly neighborhood, home of the HBCU Dillard University and where Teamer was raised. Each monumental display highlighted members of the Lady Bleu Devils—Dillard's women's basketball team—rendering them in vivid hues, and adorned with superhero-esque flourishes of abstraction. For Teamer, whose grandmother Mary Dixon Teamer founded the team in 1973 after the passage of Title IX, the project was both personal and an extension of her long-running interest in using the iconography of sports as a vessel for analyzing gender and power dynamics in pop culture.

Lately, Teamer's work has increasingly focused on the nuances and ecologies of the Gulf Coast, particularly its fraught history of water management. Collages like *London...My Double Vision* (2023) and *Tears Falling In My Pralines Under the Moonlight While Sitting by the London Avenue Canal* (2022) reference the Gentilly canal, which ruptured during Hurricane Katrina. It was one of the myriad levee breaches that led to catastrophic flooding in the wake of the storm, resulting in over 1,500 deaths and record displacement.[2] In *London...My Double Vision*, Teamer crafts a butterfly-shaped collage of images printed on fabric, its surface reinforced by stitching and grommets. An image of the

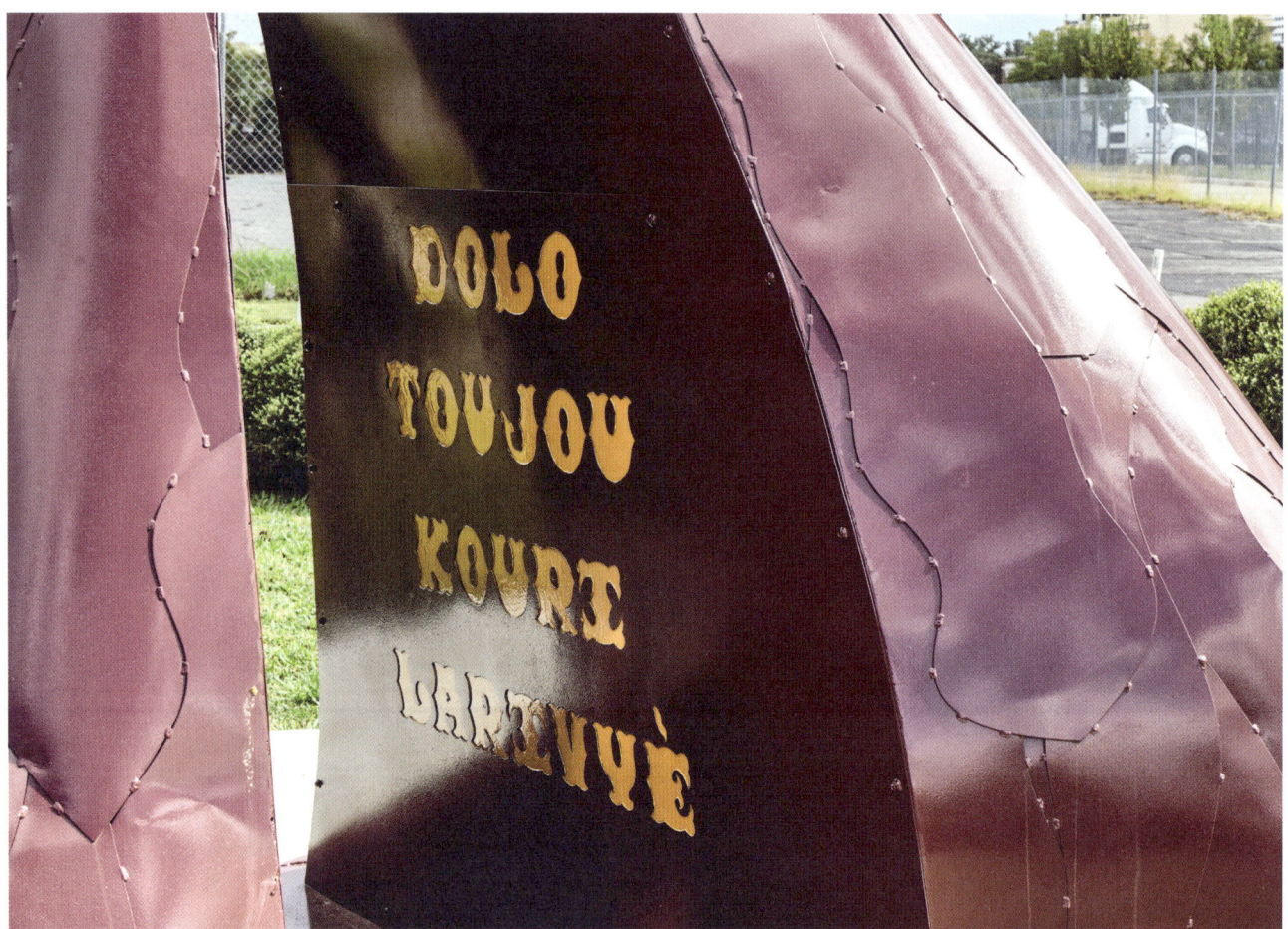

levee walls overlaps with lush florals and vegetation, gesturing towards hope for a future in which human beings practice a more harmonious relationship to water.

For Prospect.6, Teamer has created a major public art sculpture and two new collages that combine her ongoing interests. Her sculpture, *Tambourine Cypress* (2024), nods to the city's history of second-lines, a Black American tradition of brass band-led parades organized by local social aid and pleasure clubs. Teamer was inspired by the percussive instrument's ubiquity across Black, Indigenous, and Creole communities, as well as the performances of Rosalie Ashton-Washington, a local musician known as Lady Tambourine for her famously full-bodied performances with the instrument.

Teamer notes that she's always wanted to make an object that would also be an instrument, an outgrowth of her desire to create a "mechanism for engagement" that invites audience interaction beyond just passive looking. [3] Modeled after the cavernous cypress trees found across Louisiana and the southeast, *Tambourine Cypress* bears its

sound-making elements like fruit, with wind chimes and tambourines stretching from its branches. Installed along Tremé's North Claiborne Avenue, the work is also meant to lure passersby away from a toxic overpass, and towards the greenspace of Lemann Park and Playground. For Teamer, who thinks of art as a "site of possibility for different ways of being," the fact that the work will live on after the triennial closes (for seven years, due to a collaboration with Arts New Orleans) offers something particularly exciting. She's hopeful that the work will act as a threshold, through which visitors can experience "one foot in what has been, and one foot in what can be."

by Dessane Lopez Cassell

1   Conversation with the artist, May 12, 2024.
2   Sarah Pruitt, "How Levee Failures Made Hurricane Katrina a Bigger Disaster," History.com, updated August 25, 2023, https://www.history.com/news/hurricane-katrina-levee-failures
3   Conversation with the artist, May 12, 2024.

Tambourine Cypress, 2024 (detail)

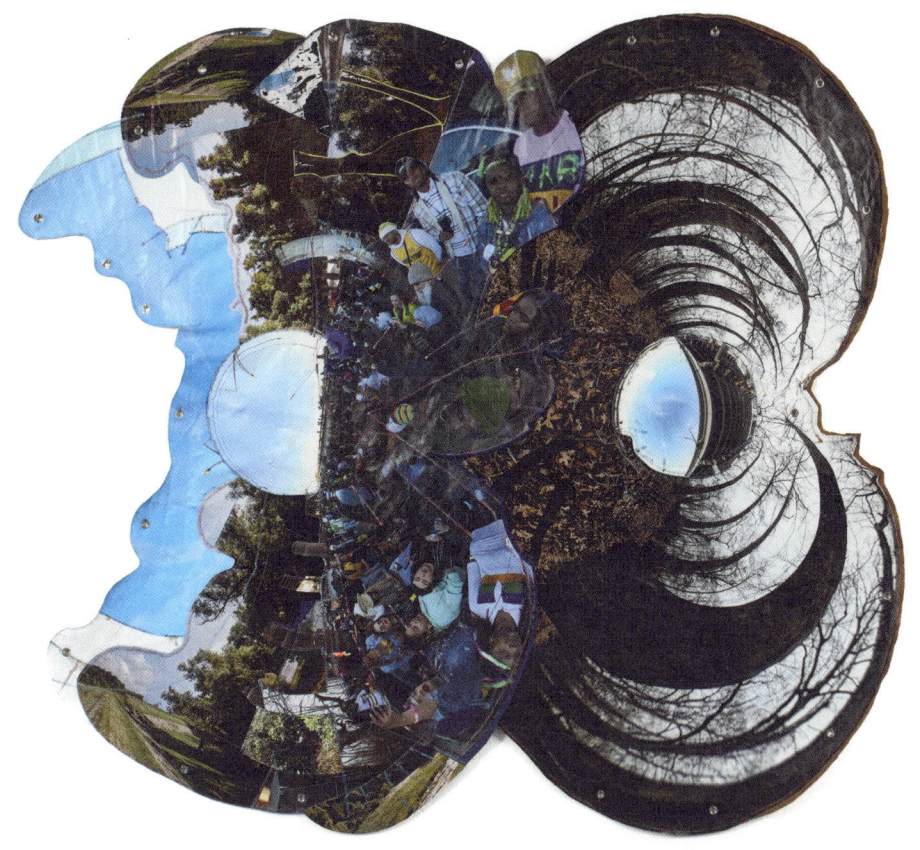

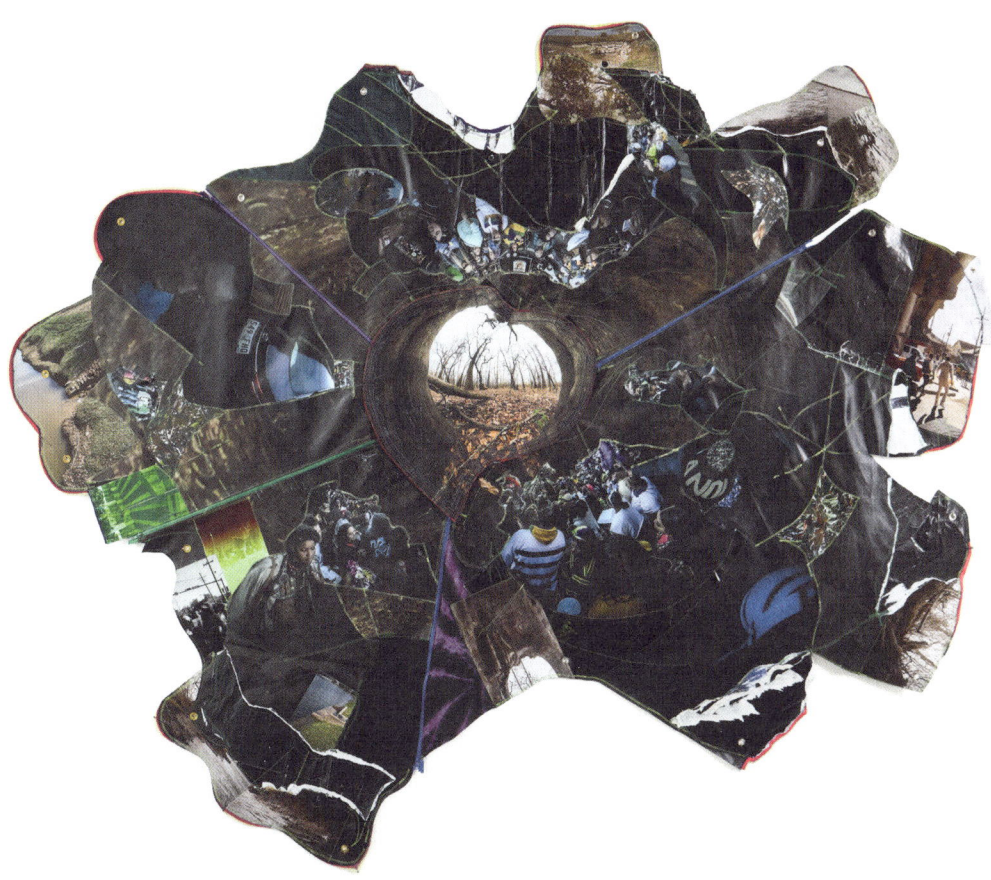

Top: *Claiborne: The Next Millennia*, 2024   Above: *Claiborne at the Epoch*, 2024

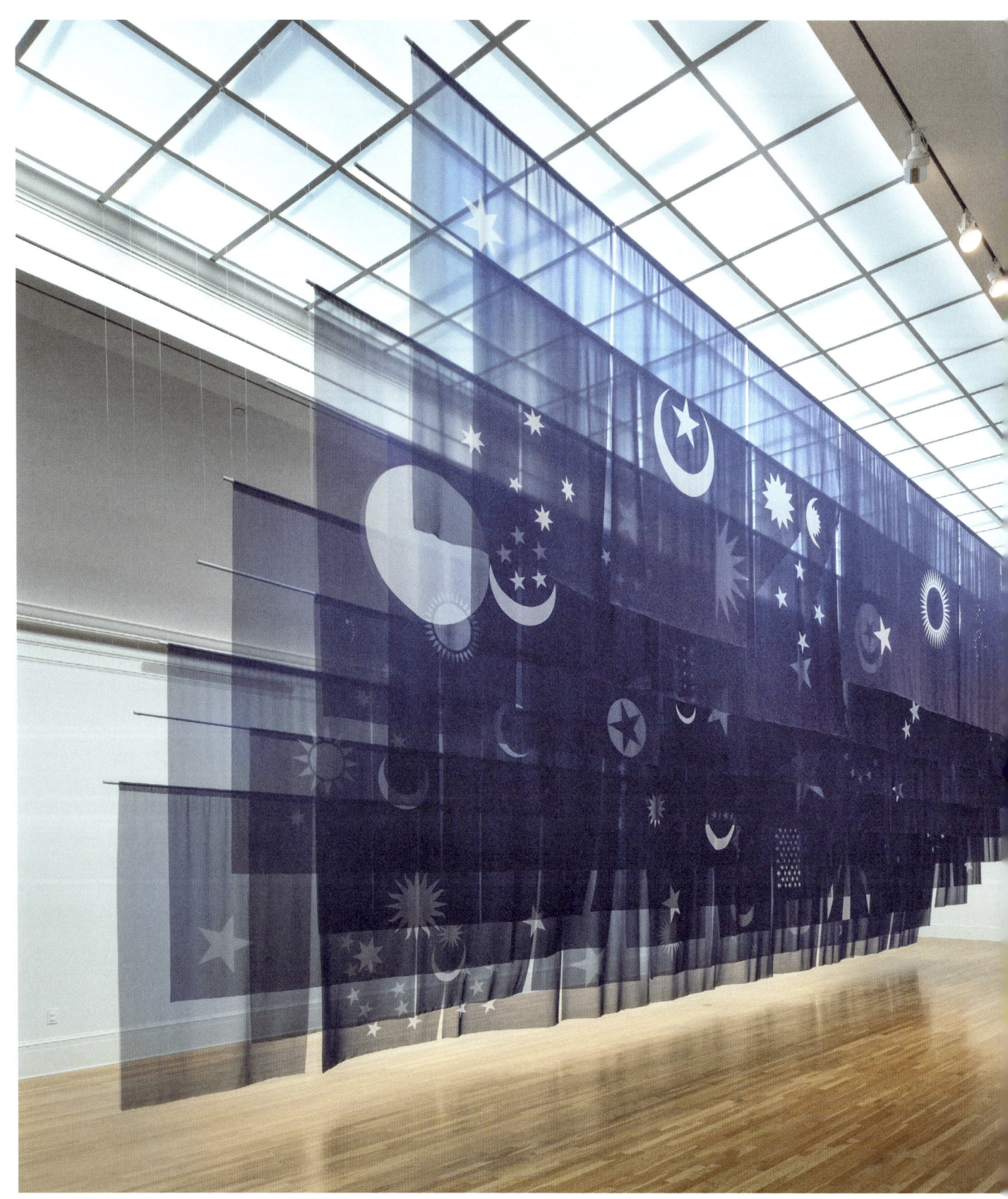

We are stardust, 2024 (left)

Clarissa Tossin

b. 1973, Porto Alegre, Brazil; lives in Los Angeles, CA

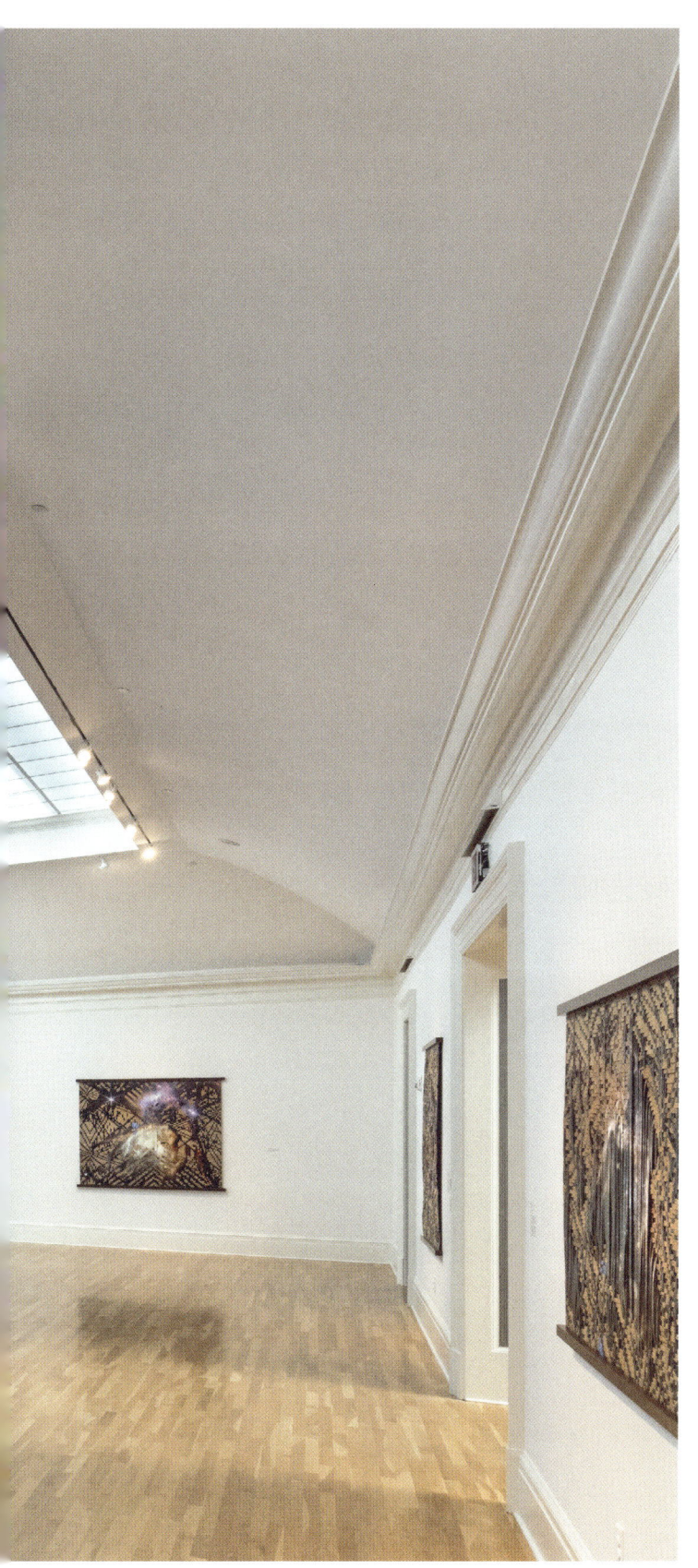

Twenty seven stars inside a blue orb adorn Brazil's national flag, making it a veritable star atlas. Including nine constellations, each star represents a state of the republic, and one star stands in for the capital of Brasília. Out of the constellations, the most recognizable is the Southern Cross, featured in the flag of Brazil with five stars. The *cruzeiro*, as the constellation is known in Portuguese, occupies a central place in the Brazilian imaginary—the cluster of stars is emblazoned on the passport; once the name of the country's old currency, the *cruzeiro* is now displayed on every coin of the Brazilian *real*. For various Indigenous groups, this particular group of stars has been an important signifier in their cosmovision. Its ease of visibility, especially in the Southern Hemisphere, makes the Southern Cross a herald of the greatness that lies above us.

Conceptual artist Clarissa Tossin includes the star atlas found on the flag of Brazil, her home country, in one of the eighty-six flags that make up *We are stardust* (2024), an installation commissioned by Prospect.6. Inspired by American astronomer Carl Sagan's quote, "The cosmos is within us. We are made of star-stuff. We are a way for the universe to know itself,"

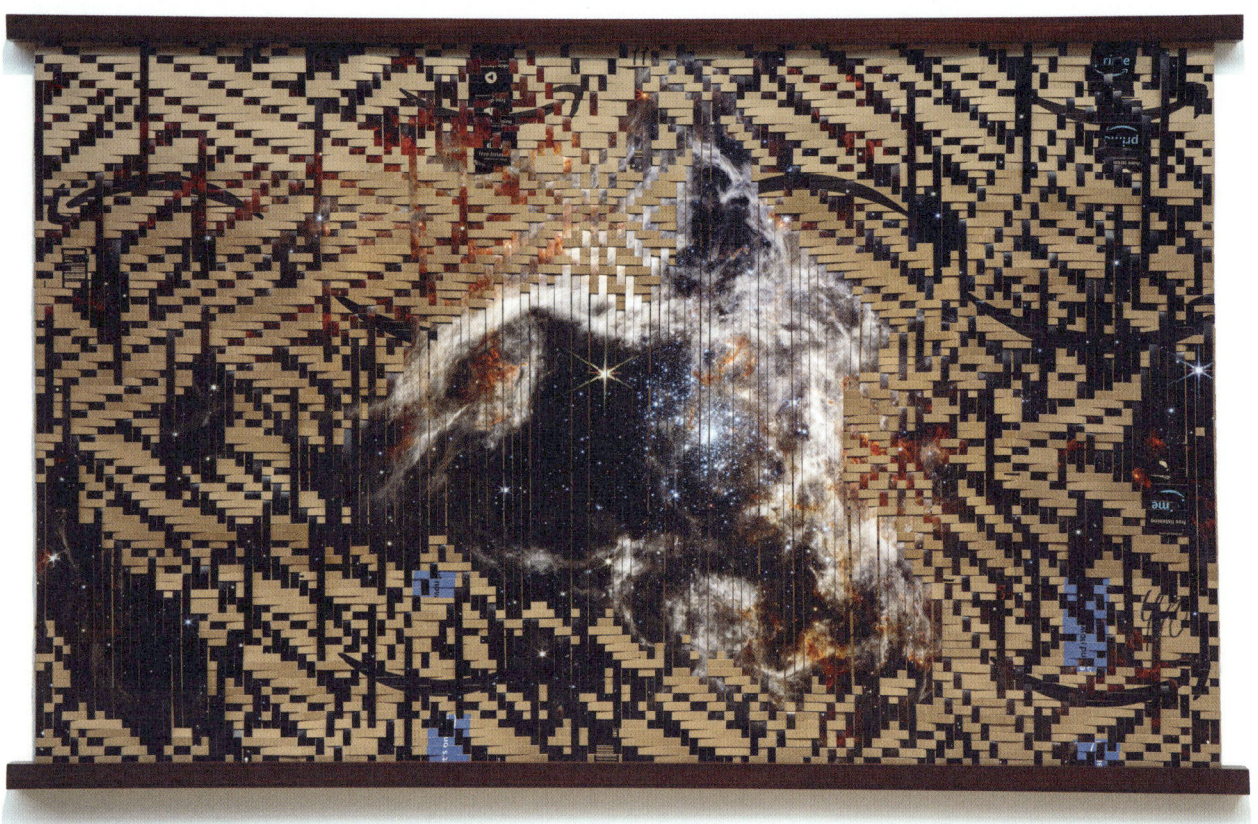

the title refers to scientists' belief that most of the elements in our bodies were formed in stars over billions of years. It stands to reason, then, that humans would seek in galactic space an existential meaning of life that is key to understanding who we are here on Earth. Imagery associated with space is found in the origin stories, myths, religions, and national symbols of many different peoples. It is as if to understand ourselves we must look outside of us.

In Tossin's *We are stardust*, the artist selected all the national flags bearing stars, the sun, and the moon in their original design, and erased all other graphic elements and colors, turning the background into a navy-blue night sky. Arranged into nine cascading rows of sheer, vertical flags, the installation reads as a unified constellation. The additive nature of her artwork emphasizes a shared cosmic origin—it resists jingoistic polarization and zealousness by reinforcing fundamental commonalities embedded in our makeup as humans. The work also proposes that, rather than speculating what resources will yield from space exploration, we should ask ourselves to think of our collective ancestry within the cosmos.

We are stardust continues Tossin's investigation of the space race and, as the artist wonders, "whether the abuses of land and people that have marked our time on Earth get perpetuated as we move out into the solar system." In other works such as *A Queda do Céu (The Falling Sky)* (2019), *The 8th Continent* (2021), and the series *Future Geographies* (2021–ongoing), also featured in Prospect.6, Tossin challenges the logic of greed and colonization inherent in the privatization of space exploration, the devastating effects of which are irreversibly evident on Earth.

by Marcela Guerrero

Future Geography: Tarantula Nebula, 2024

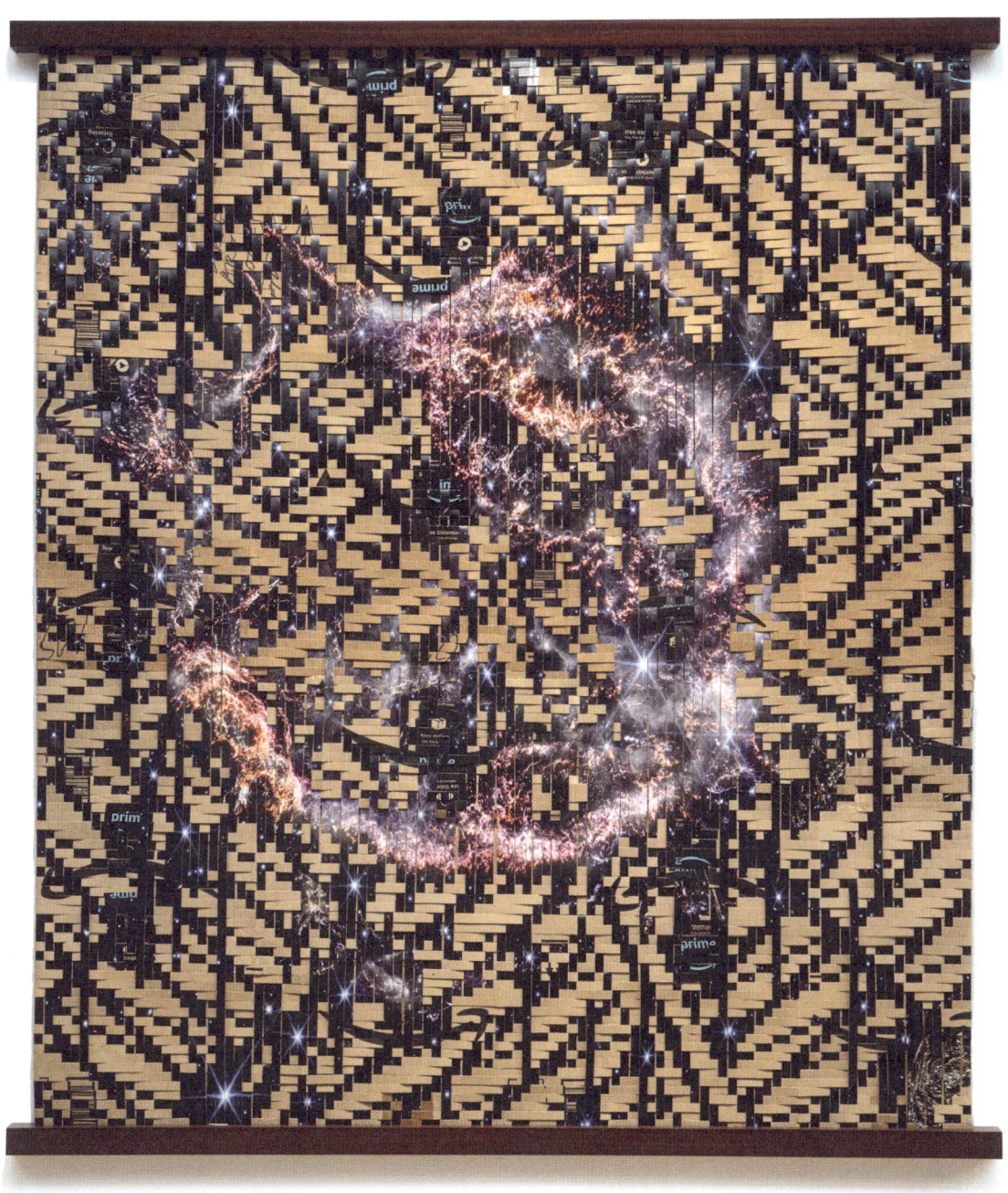

Future Geography: Cassiopeia A Supernova, 2024

Arlette Quỳnh-Anh Trần

b. 1987, Hennigsdorf, Germany; lives in Saigon, Vietnam

After the capture of Saigon by North Vietnam and the Viet Cong in 1975, two distinct Vietnamese migrant groups emerged in a divided Germany. The Federal Republic (West Germany) accepted refugees who fled for political reasons, while the GDR (East Germany) hired pro-communist workers on temporary contracts. The latter resulted from an economic agreement between socialist Vietnam and East Germany during the 1980s. Arlette Quỳnh-Anh Trần was born in the East German state of Brandenburg to parents from northern Vietnam in this context. When the Iron Curtain lifted, her family resettled in southern Vietnam, where the majority of Trần's childhood was spent.

Trần's art practice is grounded in modernist vocabularies of the Cold War. Her visual research acutely observes transnational currents, as she was trained in Vietnam as well as the Czech Republic, United States, and Germany. Recently, her investigations have increasingly utilized moving images and performance to navigate questions of heritage: What is Vietnamese identity? What external factors shape a belief system, and how does one arrive at truth?

For Prospect.6, Trần debuts a new time-based artwork, *The Curator Ghost* (2024). This monochrome fantasy film resembles a spy thriller and is set in Vietnam between the years 1960 and 2075. It tells the nonlinear story of an influential Saigon-based curator who contributed to the (real) exhibition *Art and Archaeology of Vietnam: Asian Crossroad of Cultures*, which traveled the US during the Vietnam War. Trần thoughtfully combines photomontage, animation, and reenactment to build a compelling portrait of Nghiêm Thẩm (1920–1979), an archaeologist who served as director of Vietnam's National Museum of History (a location in the film recognizable for its Indochinese architecture). Thẩm led

The Curator Ghost, 2024

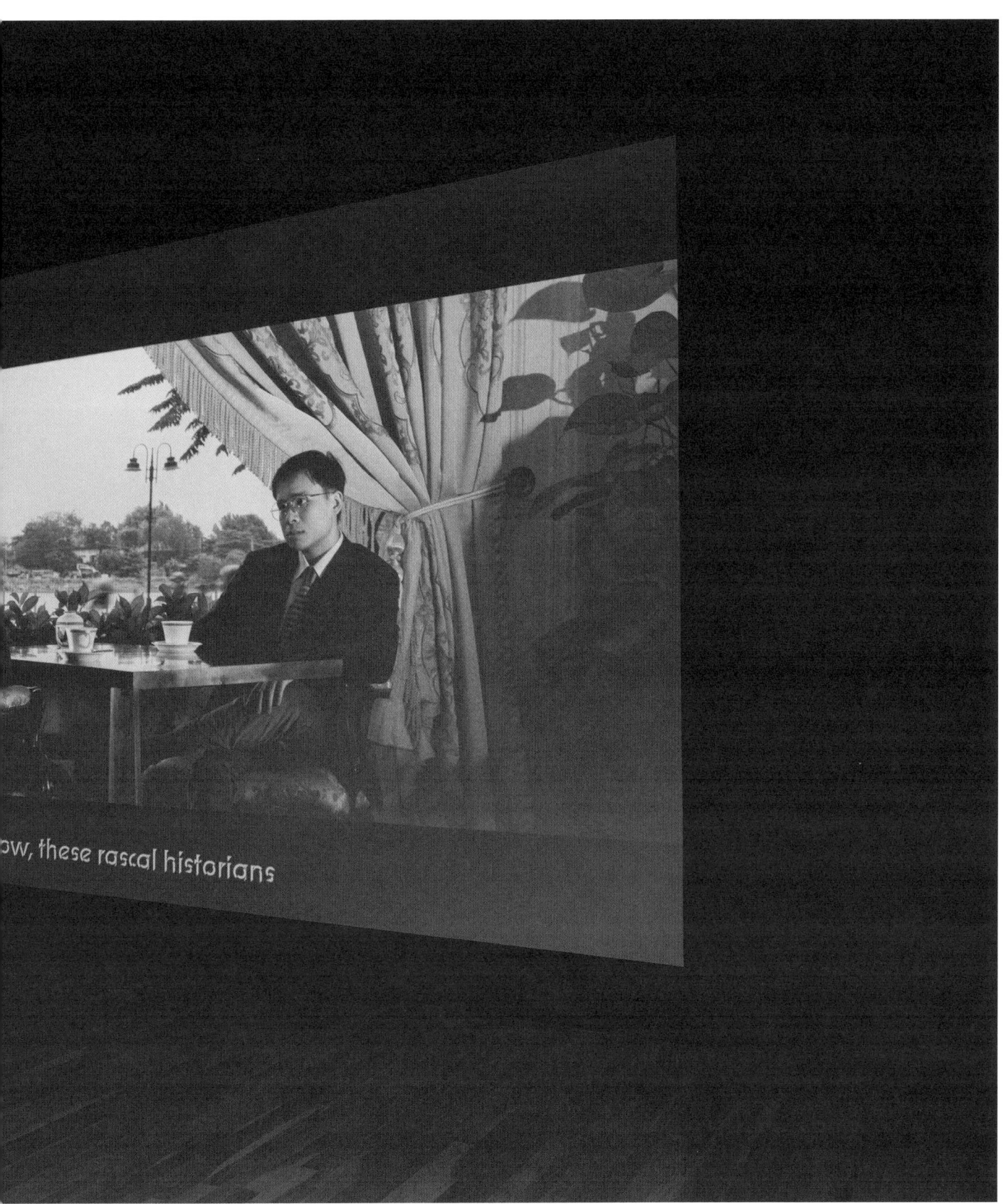

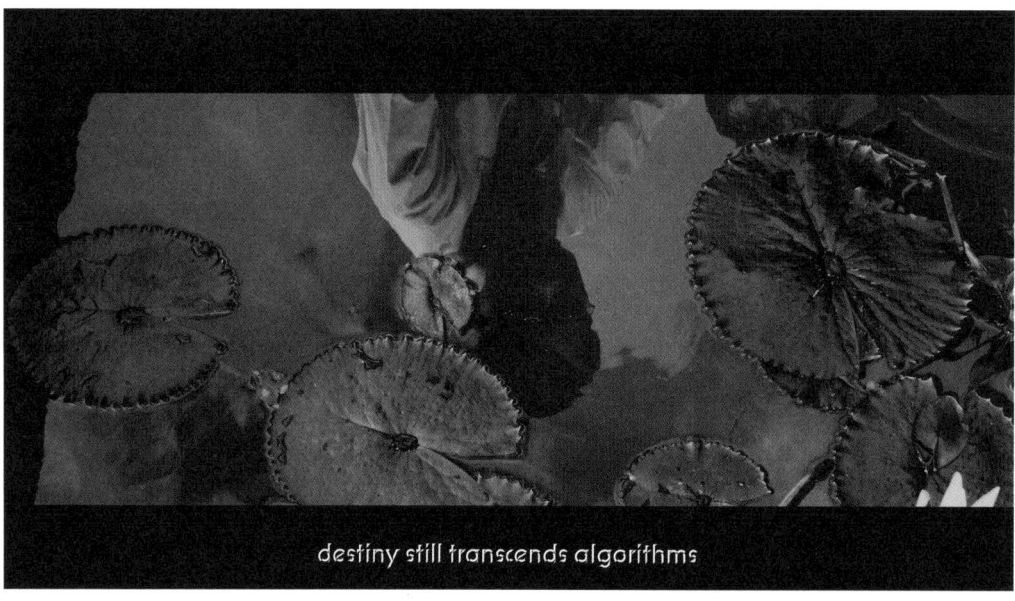

destiny still transcends algorithms

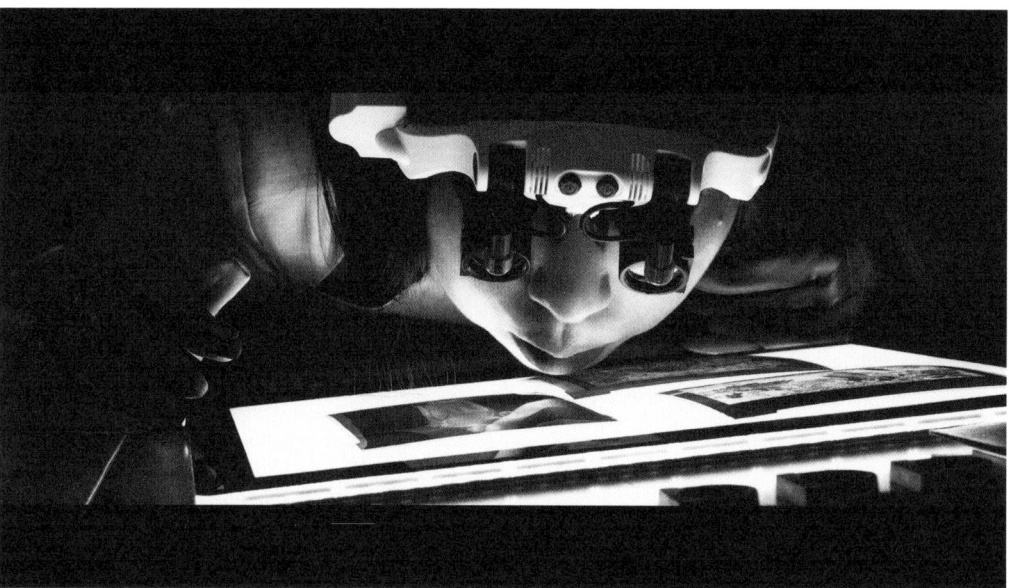

excavations in the Mekong Delta at the ancient port city Óc Eo, and he was an expert on the Funan civilization's role in connecting East and West on the Maritime Silk Road. New Orleans is a poetic site for tending Thẩm's legacy, particularly as it is home to over 15,000 people of Vietnamese heritage.

The Curator Ghost is steeped in the aesthetics of Thẩm's era, and integrates archival materials with content sourced from cyberpunk cinema. Based on the artist's research, the film brings Thẩm to life as an imagined memory from the future. The film's main characters are three time-traveling agents born in different generations. Modeled on Thẩm, Agent Sao is an archaeologist trained in France who remains in Vietnam after reunification under the Communist regime. Sao courageously

resists political coercion when a party officer suggests he author an unscientific essay to serve as propaganda. Trân's allegorical narrative portrays the machine behind Sao's politically motivated murder. His violent death is staged twice, as if the events were recounted by different sources—or perhaps to render a separation of his body and spirit.

The female protagonist of the film, Agent AQ, is played by the artist in her first on-screen role. As witness to Sao's destiny, she reflects on what it means to live with purpose and intention. Trân's work bravely stands as a memorial to the selfless act of safeguarding history, while it also reckons with a troubled past.

by Laura Blereau

The Curator Ghost, 2024 (video stills)

Tuan Mami

b. 1981, Hanoi, Vietnam; lives in Hanoi, Vietnam

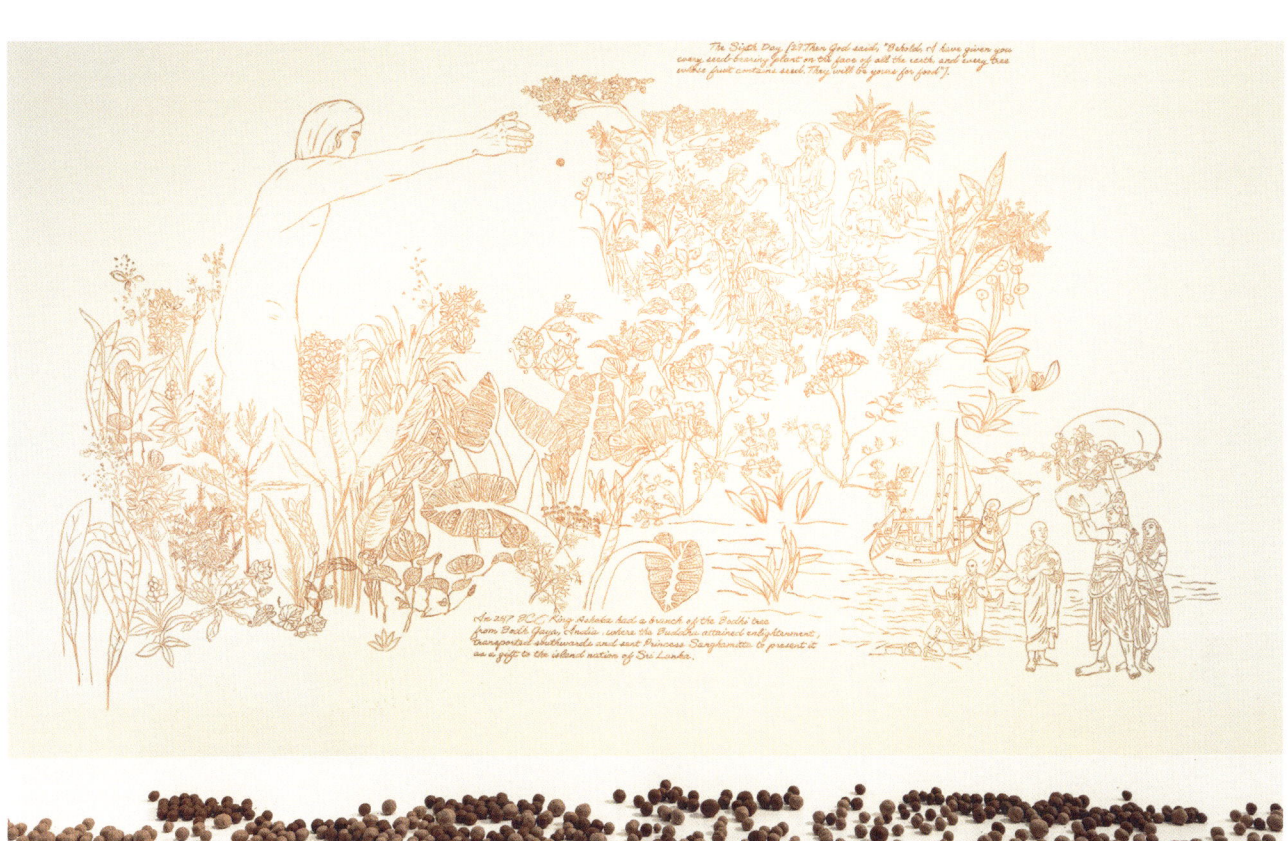

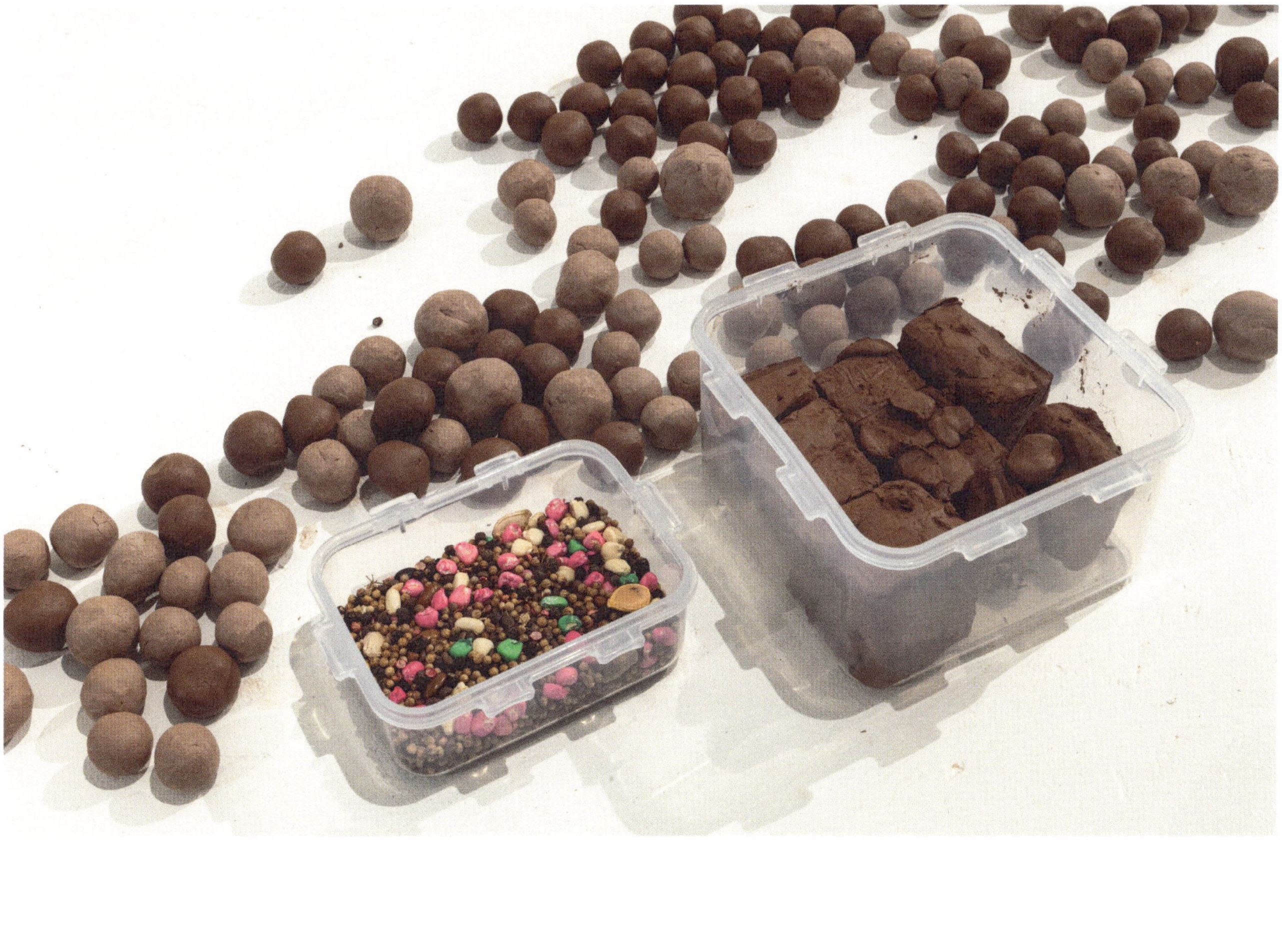

Seeding the Future, 2024 (details)

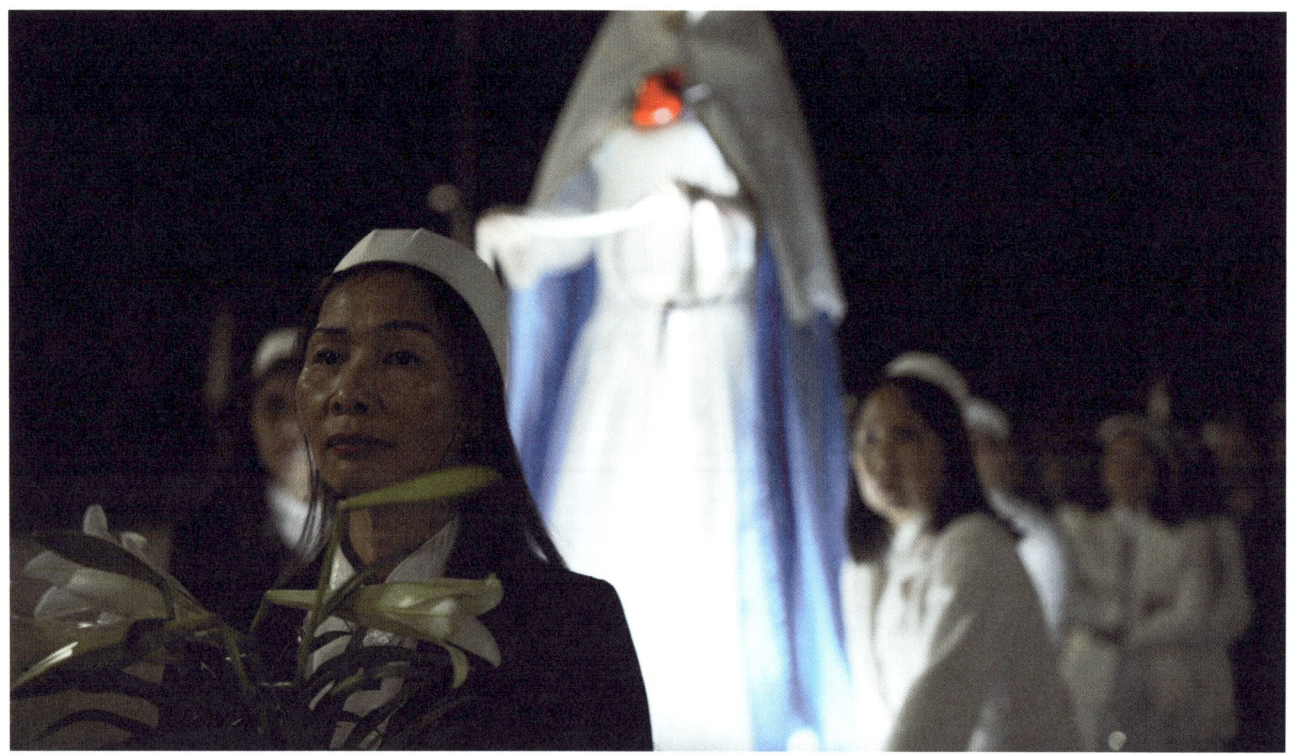

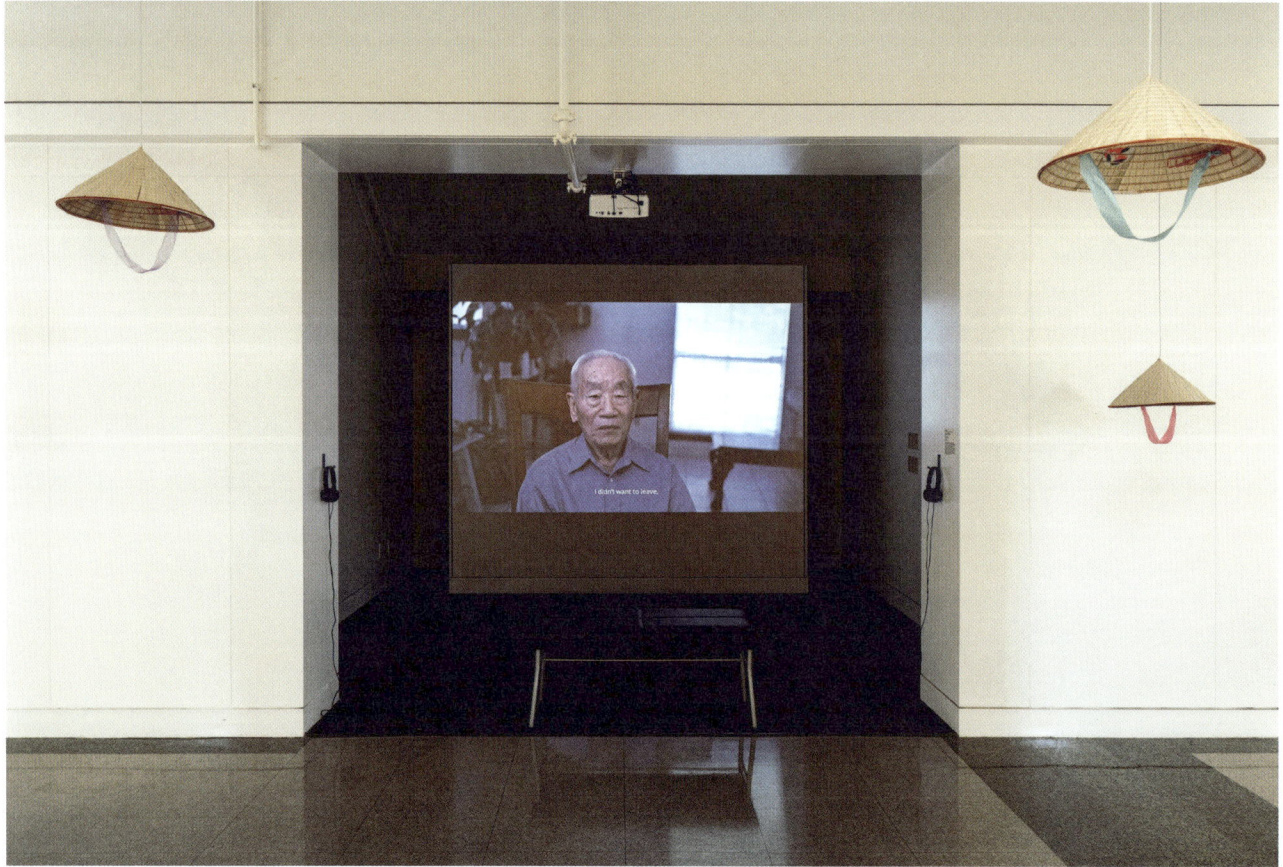

Top: *'Ngàn Dặm' THOUSAND MILES*, 2024 (video still)

Above, foreground: *Endless Home*, 2024;
center: *'Ngàn Dặm' THOUSAND MILES*, 2024

"I am a gardener, not an artist," says Tuan Mami. He has been fond of growing plants and observing their fascinating ecosystem for as long as I can remember. Much like a plant, the human body has the ability to adapt to new environments by forming intricate, entangled networks while negotiating their conditions with local organisms. For someone who lives and works across geographies, Mami is someone who can fathom the vast reverberations of physical dis/re-location.

Mami's interest in the politics and psychological nuances of human migration dates back to his 2011 residency at Hooyongri village in South Korea. The movement of the village's younger population to the city left Hooyongri nearly empty, bereft of commercial and social activities. This led Mami to ponder the impact of constant currents of migration on people's sense of place, memory, and intimacy. His rumination on this topic continued into another multidisciplinary project in Hà Nam province in Vietnam—the artist's hometown—where he observed how the economic apparatus of extraction caused environmental degradation, and consequently, people's displacement.

Vietnamese Immigrating Garden is an open-ended, collaborative project by Mami, articulated in the form of what he calls performative installations: an ensemble of recorded stories, conversational space, and culinary and medicinal plants collected and cultivated by Vietnamese immigrants in countries across the globe. By allocating equal weight to physical presentation and participatory events, the project seeks to create a social platform for encounters and exchange concerning human emotion, memory, and sense of belonging.

Mami's arrival at his performative installations are traced back to his earlier practice in performance art. In expanding the possibility of performance, the artist has explored ways to overcome its limitations, namely, its requirement of a present moment and restricted presentation modes. He has done so by creating circumstances through which the viewers' experience and interaction give form to the artwork itself. In the *Vietnamese Immigrating Garden* project, Mami transfers the site of interaction from his body (as often seen in his previous performance works) to a different form of living body—the garden. Instead of representing the garden in an artwork, Mami presents the garden itself. It has its own agency and the capacity to reshape itself in the exhibition space through the traces of intimacy, memory, and care left behind by its tenders.

Working closely with VIET (Vietnamese Initiatives in Economic Training), Mami's *Vietnamese Immigrating Garden* continues its journey at Prospect.6 with *Seeding the Future* (2024). The design of the space bears resemblance to a community hall, which comprises rooms housing collections of oral stories recounted by first generation Vietnamese communities in New Orleans and visual notes from numerous Vietnamese immigrant communities, joined by a connecting corridor designated for casual chitchats. Every Wednesday, an elder is on-site, making seed balls and placing them randomly. Visitors are welcome to pick them up to grow at home, and/or stay for conversation.

Unlike other iterations in Taiwan, Japan, and Berlin, there is no recognizable garden in sight. The garden, in this iteration, exists in the future, signified in the transmission of seedballs and the promise of their growth. The transfer of the seed balls into someone's home or garden facilitates the integration of life between plants, migrants, and other communities, formulating an organic and spiritual connection with its caretakers. Though silent and humble, they carry the expectation of life: a symbol of hope for a people whose migration journeys and assimilation into new lives have caused complex emotional residues.

by Lê Thuận Uyên

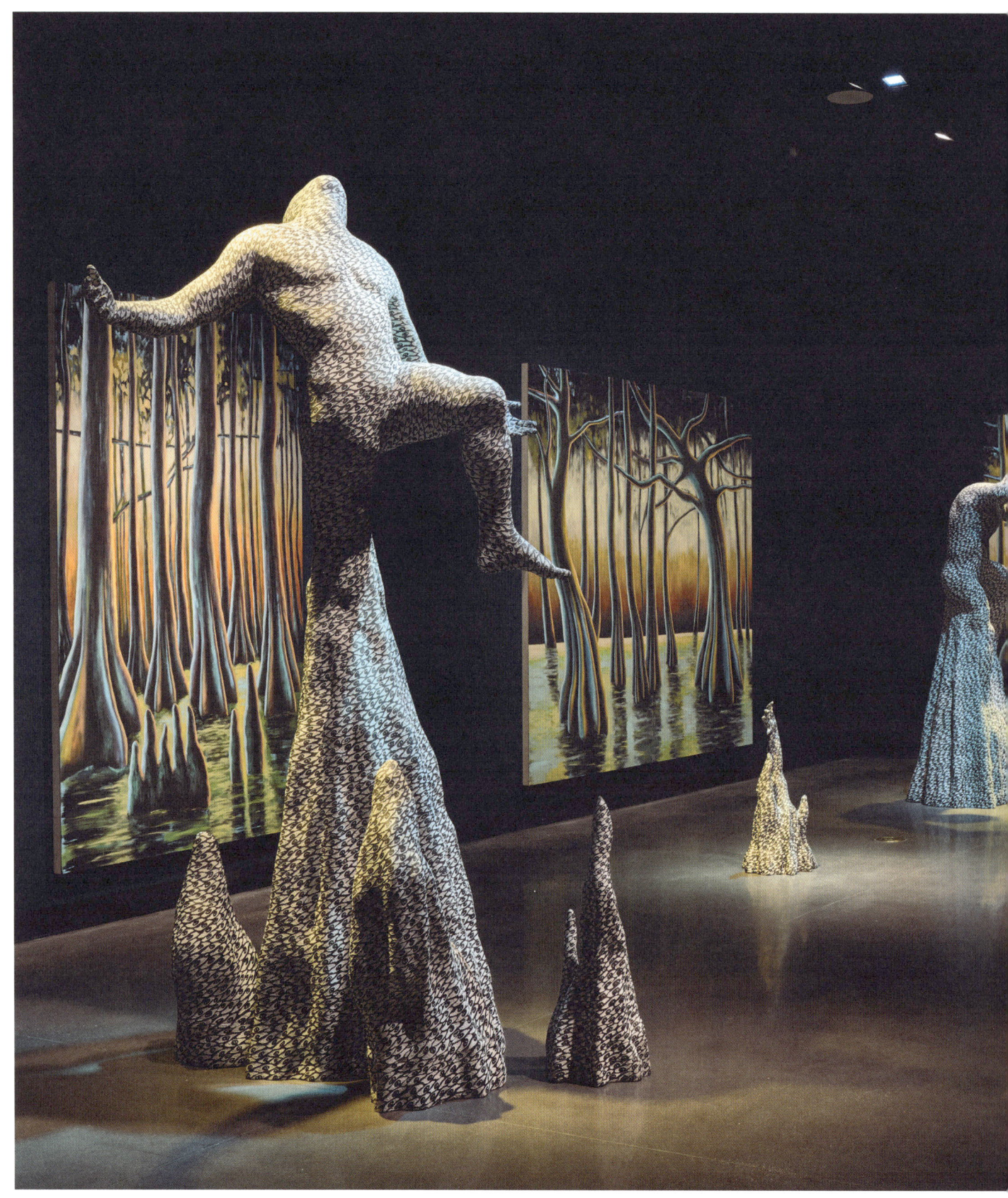

Gesture to Home, 2024

Didier William

b. 1983, Port-au-Prince, Haiti; lives in Philadelphia, PA

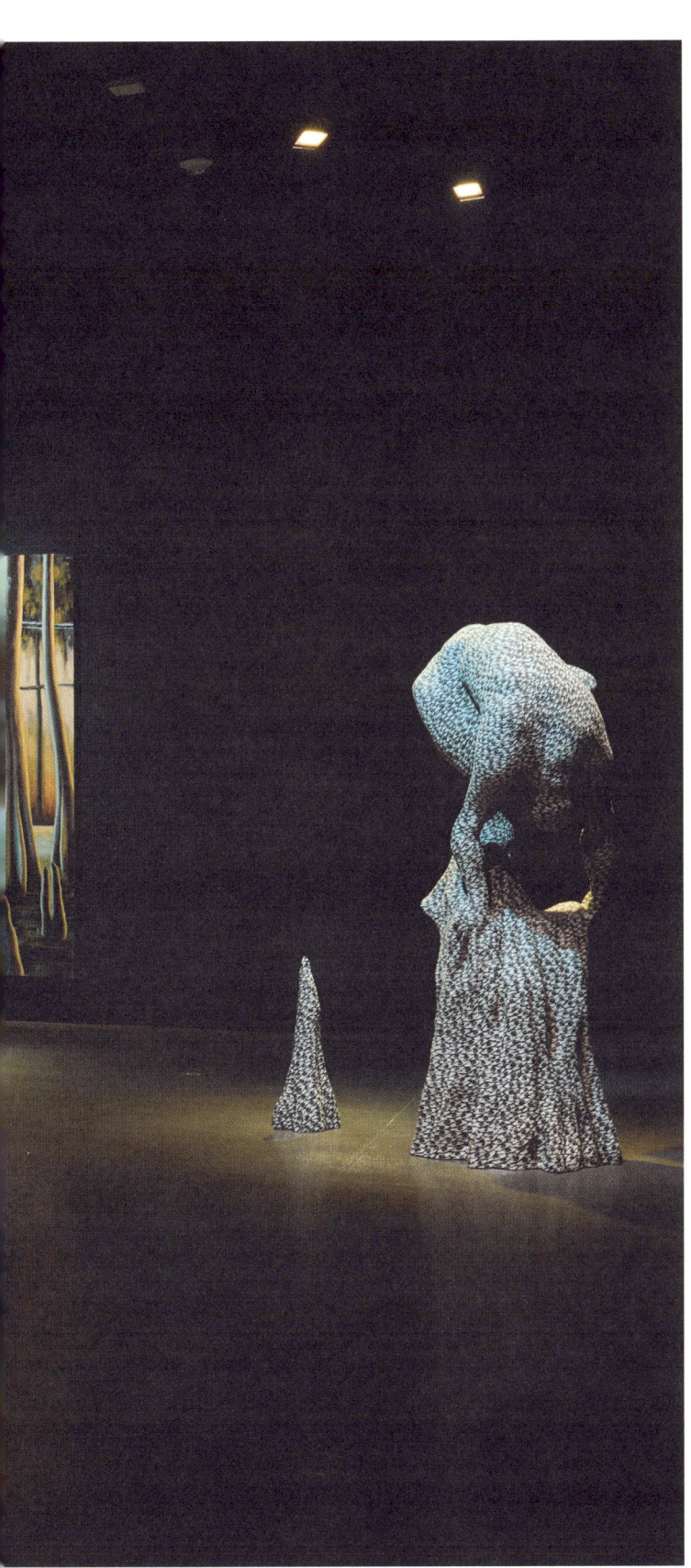

Haitian-American artist Didier William began carving eyes onto the surfaces of his figures as a means of enabling them to return the gaze of their onlooker, to challenge the viewer's curiosity. This signature eye motif has evolved into a kind of modular, secondary skin, an accumulated system that both builds and breaks down the body, an elastic means of rejecting categorizations of taxonomy. In a gallery in the Historic New Orleans Collection, on Royal Street in the French Quarter, four larger than life figures emerge from the skirts of cypress trees, their black and white skin carved with innumerable eyes. The muscular, humanoid forms stretch from rising tree trunks, their bodies towering over the viewer, pulling the gaze aloft. Five enormous acrylic paintings of trees surround the figures in a swampy golden hour, their branches extending far above the picture plane, their roots disappearing below the waterline. This is William's first foray into sculpture and installation—a piece whose figures might walk off into the bayou after closing hours, seeking out their natural habitat in the Atchafalaya Basin just beyond the city's edge.

The Gulf South's bald cypress trees, creatures that William calls "emotive, expressive harbingers of history," can live for over 1,000 years. "They are an artist's dream—strong, mysterious, enigmatic, and joyously flamboyant," says the artist. For many of these trees, still alive today, their trunks were standing before the onset of European colonialization, the transatlantic slave trade, the Haitian Revolution, and the Louisiana Purchase. This witnessing, beyond the human, is still occurring, rooted and oxygenating alongside us and the other critters of the wetlands. The knobby cypress knees that appear plentifully from the ground near the tree's base are not fully understood by contemporary botanists. Do the knees aerate submerged roots? Reduce soil erosion? Provide trunk stabilization? The secrets of the cypress are beyond scientific consensus or comprehension. In many ways, the trees know more than we do.

In William's installation, the ground is missing, or fractured, made up of fragile and symbiotic parts. Both the sculptures and the paintings visualize an unstable or absent ground, a flooding or loss of coastline, a disruption in gravitational homeland. "All my paintings are about looking for home, looking for ground," William shares. Perhaps this was a factor in the artist's conceptual pull toward the cypress tree, a deeply rooting plant that resists transplanting, that manifests and enables home for others. Historically, the tree is both a site of settler colonialism, plantation, and lynching, but it is also a place of leisure, a respite from heat, a being that enables breathing. William presents the tree not as a resource for capitalist, extractive profit, but as a living, knowing, and seeing titan. In this work and throughout the artist's practice, William visualizes new ways of knowing the human body as inextricable from plant and place. As ecofeminist scholar Donna Haraway writes, "We require each other in unexpected collaborations and combinations, in hot compost piles. We become-with each other or not at all." In the rooting, seeing realms of Didier William, we become-with.

by Emily Alesandrini

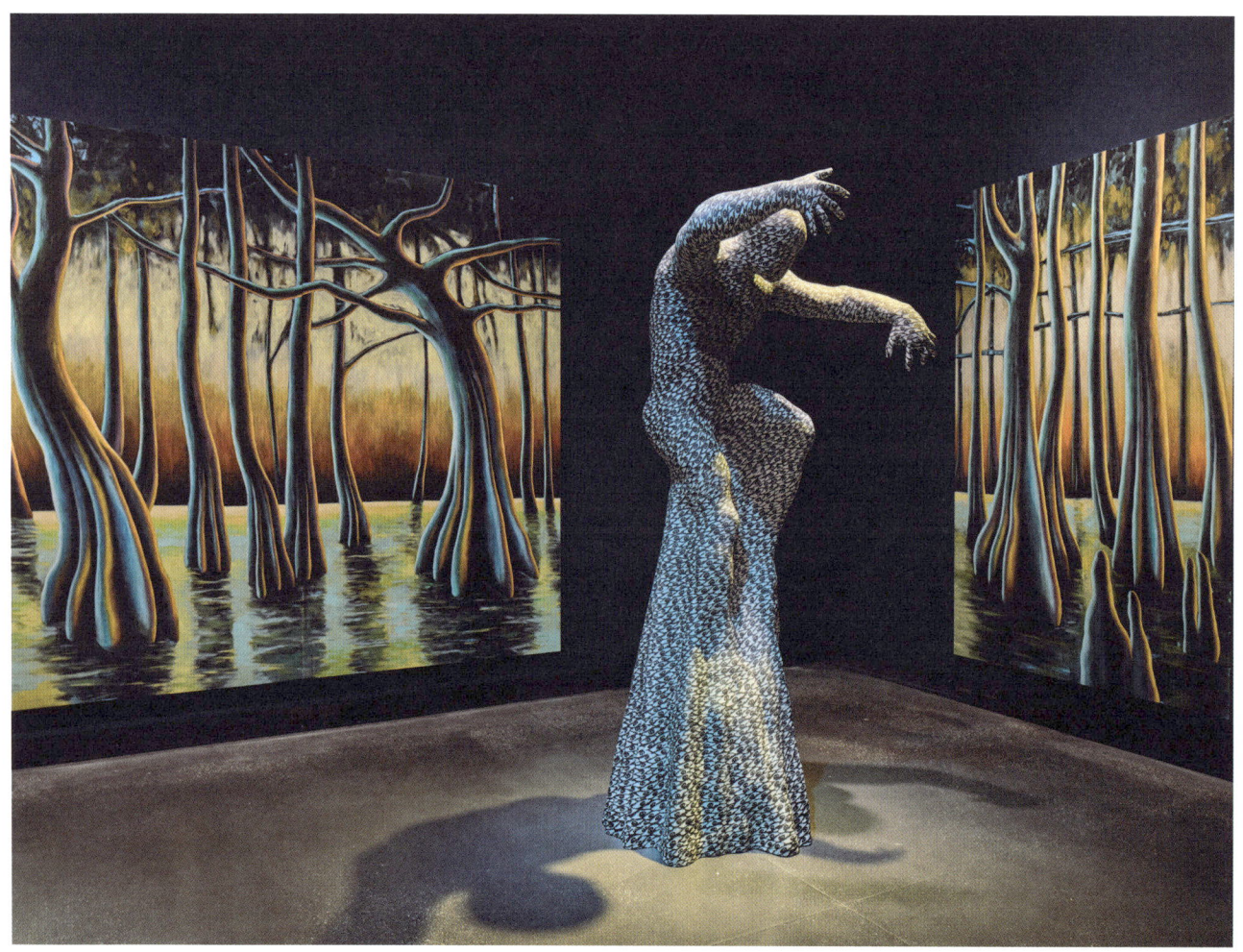

Gesture to Home, 2024 (detail)

Didier William

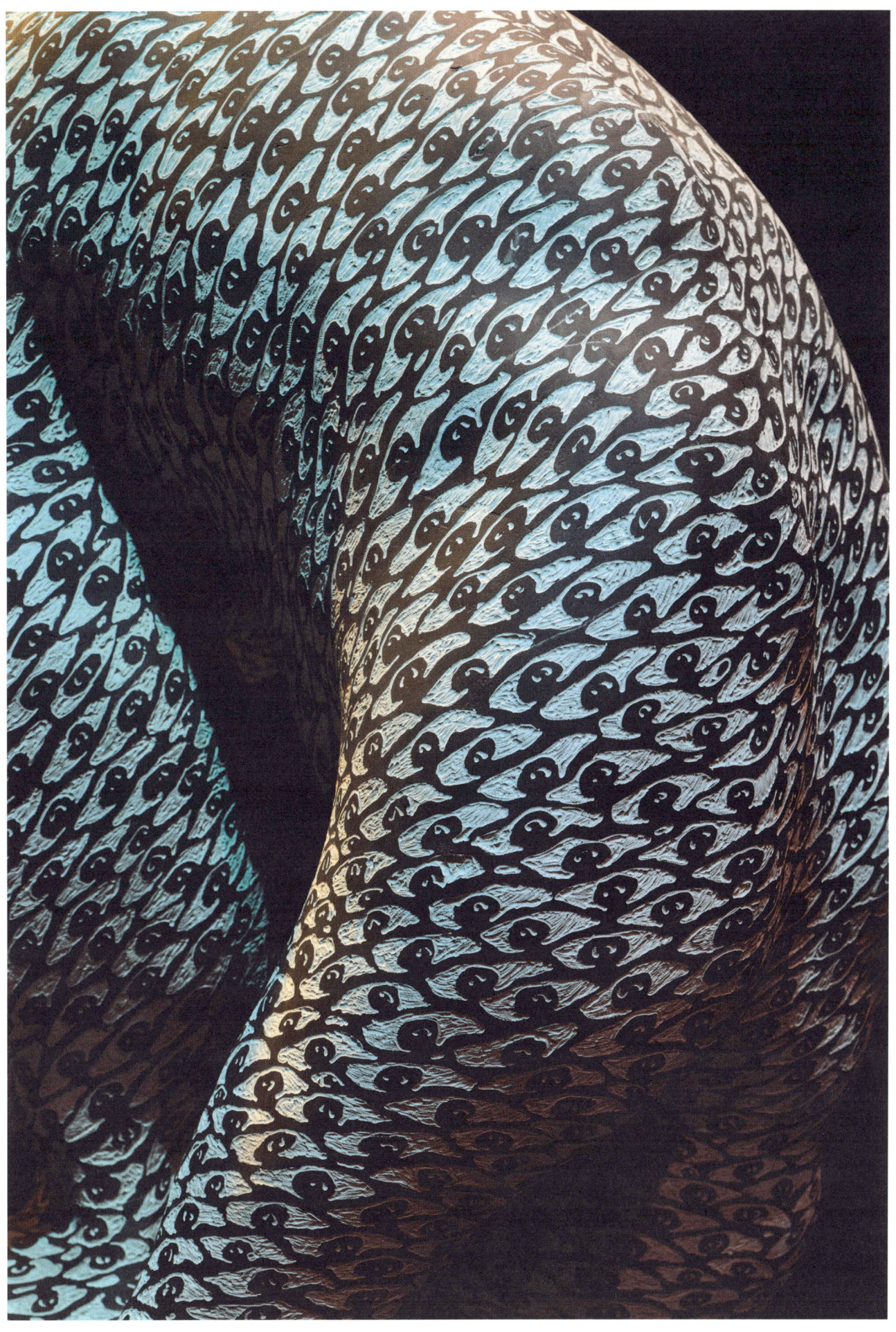

Gesture to Home, 2024 (detail)

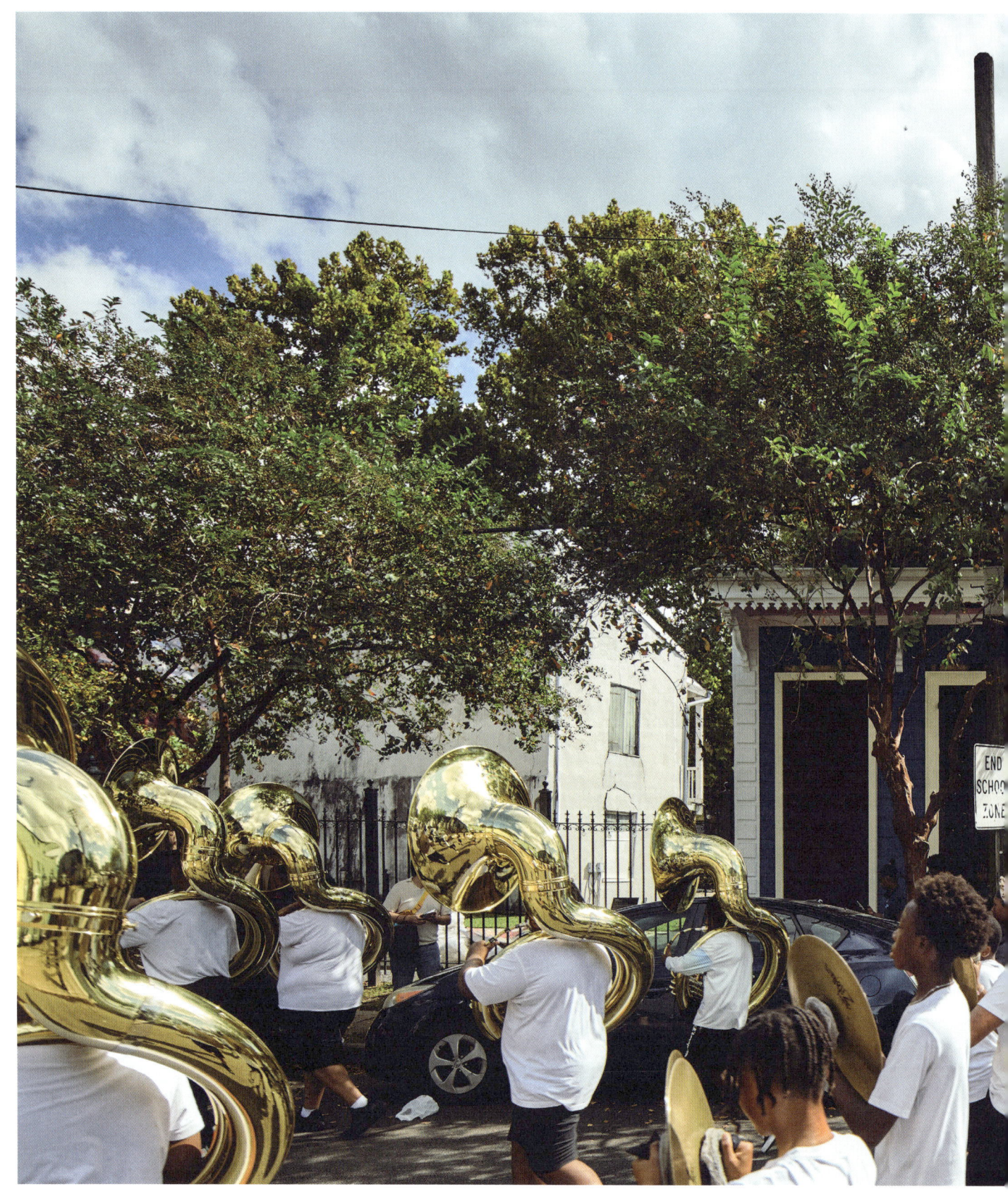

In Her Rich Deposits of (Blue), 2024. Local marching band practice, New Orleans African American Museum (NOAAM), November 2024

Amanda Williams

b. 1974, Evanston, IL; lives in Chicago, IL

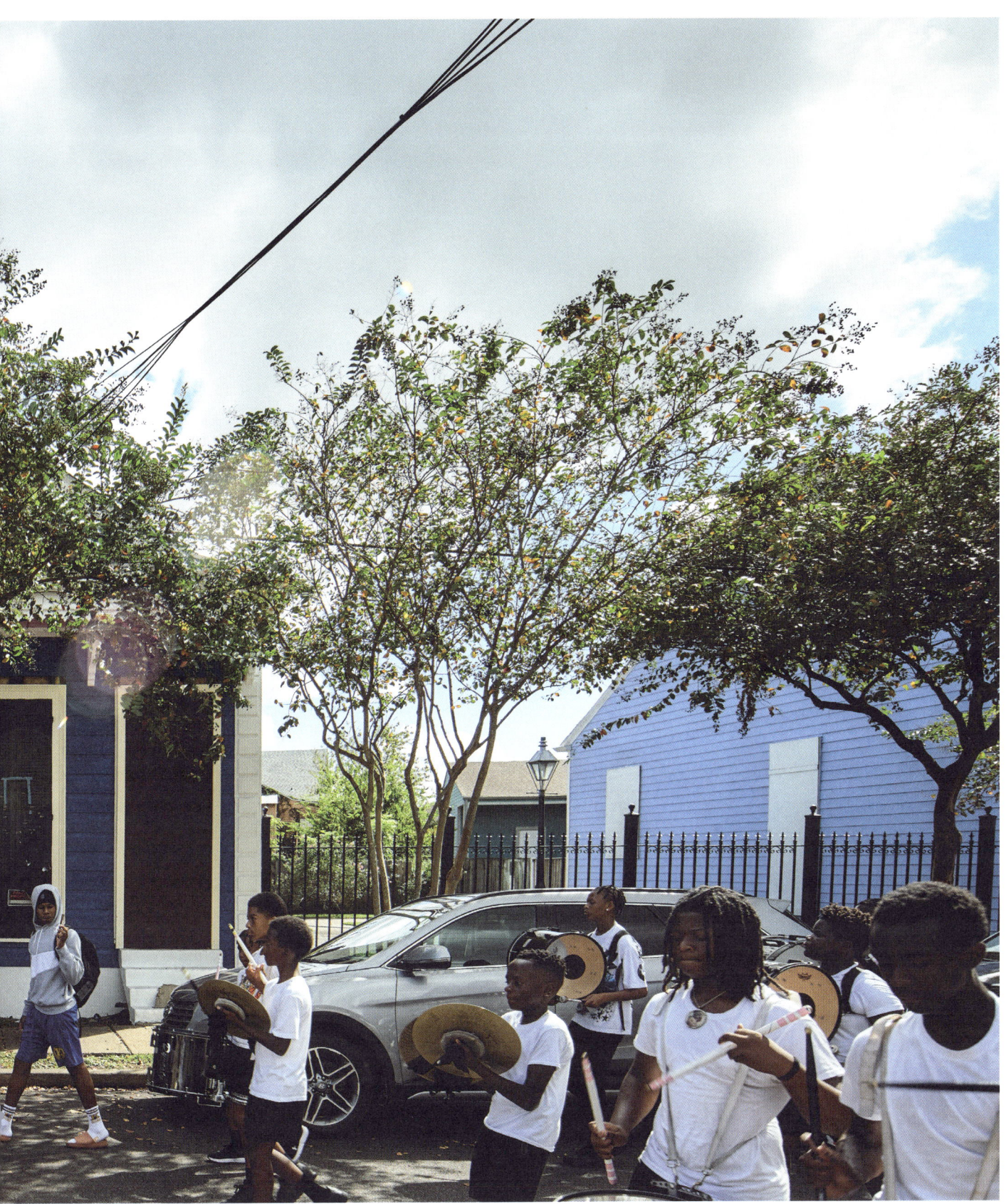

During a studio visit with Amanda Williams, the artist and Chicago native shared this definitive statement early on: "Black people, we are already great." It is a sentiment that encapsulates *In Her Rich Deposits of (Blue)* (2024), the title of her project for Prospect.6, along with her overall creative approach. As we continued our conversation, it was clear that Williams's passion involves reclaiming dynamic aspects of the Black imagination that are often unexplored, specifically our relationship to colors, in both history and gradient.

As Williams said of us Black people, "We pioneer things."

In her groundbreaking, multi-year series *Color(ed) Theory* (2014–2015), Williams, alongside a group of close friends, painted homes set to be condemned in rich, vibrant colors that signify elements from her childhood, such as Pink Oil Moisturizer Hair Lotion and Red Hots, all done in spite of the homes' ill fate. Examining the politicization of color within our everyday lives—especially legacies of disenfranchisement and displacement on the basis of race—is the central pursuit for Williams's artistic practice. George Washington Carver, the Black agricultural scientist whose passions included painting, became Williams's focal point for P.6. In the early 1900s, Carver spent over a year developing his version of blue by experimenting with natural elements like soil and clay, and monitoring chemicals for months on end. Eventually Carver extracted Prussian blue, a luminous combination of deep blue with a hint of the spring sky.

In collaboration with research scientists and chemistry students at the University of Chicago and Xavier University of Louisiana in New Orleans, led by the extraordinary expertise of Xavier chemistry student Nadia Caesar, Williams and her team began experimenting with Carver's recipe for Prussian blue. The team created a vial of color that Williams named Carver Innovation Blue, a lively and uplifting color with notes of indigo—a crop historically yielded by enslaved Africans. Like her *Color(ed) Theory* series, *In Her Rich Deposits of (Blue)* recalls this fraught legacy while signaling playfulness through its rich, boisterous undertone. "Understanding color is always chromatic and racial," Williams says. "I can't think of color and not think of both."

For P.6, Williams has brought a version of Carver's Prussian blue to New Orleans. She painted the Pink House, a historic Creole cottage at the New Orleans African American Museum, in Carver Innovation Blue. With student participation, Williams has also shrouded a building at Xavier University Art Village with the pigment.

Intent on amplifying the curiosity and complexity of Black people, Amanda Williams's *In Her Rich Deposits of (Blue)* instills a deeper look into the racial imaginary and the venerated yet under-discussed legacy of George Washington Carver. Williams's intentions with color theory honors the innovation and imagination of leaders in Black history, while paying homage to those whose hands tilled the soil, where many of these concepts were born.

by Erica N. Cardwell

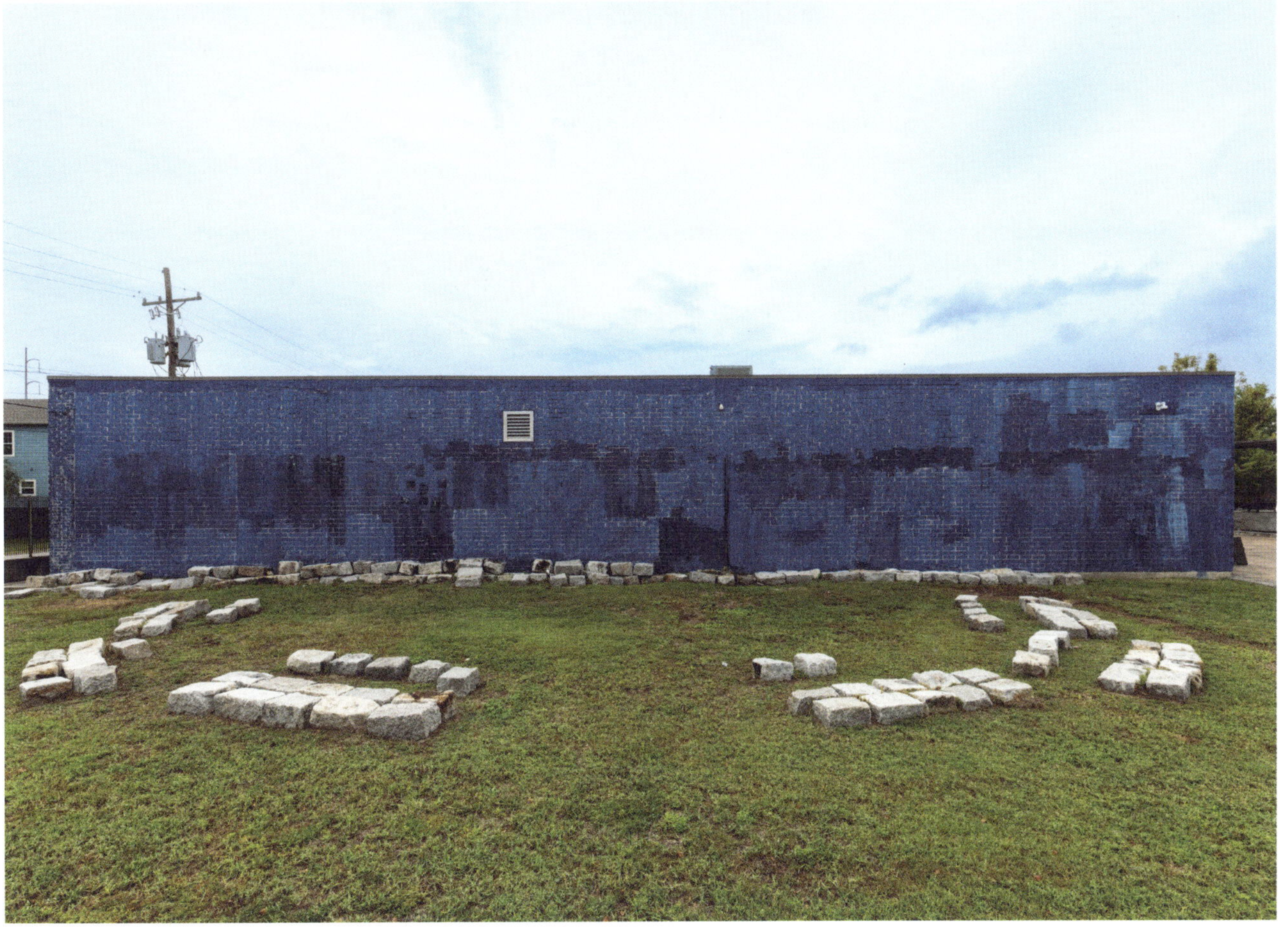

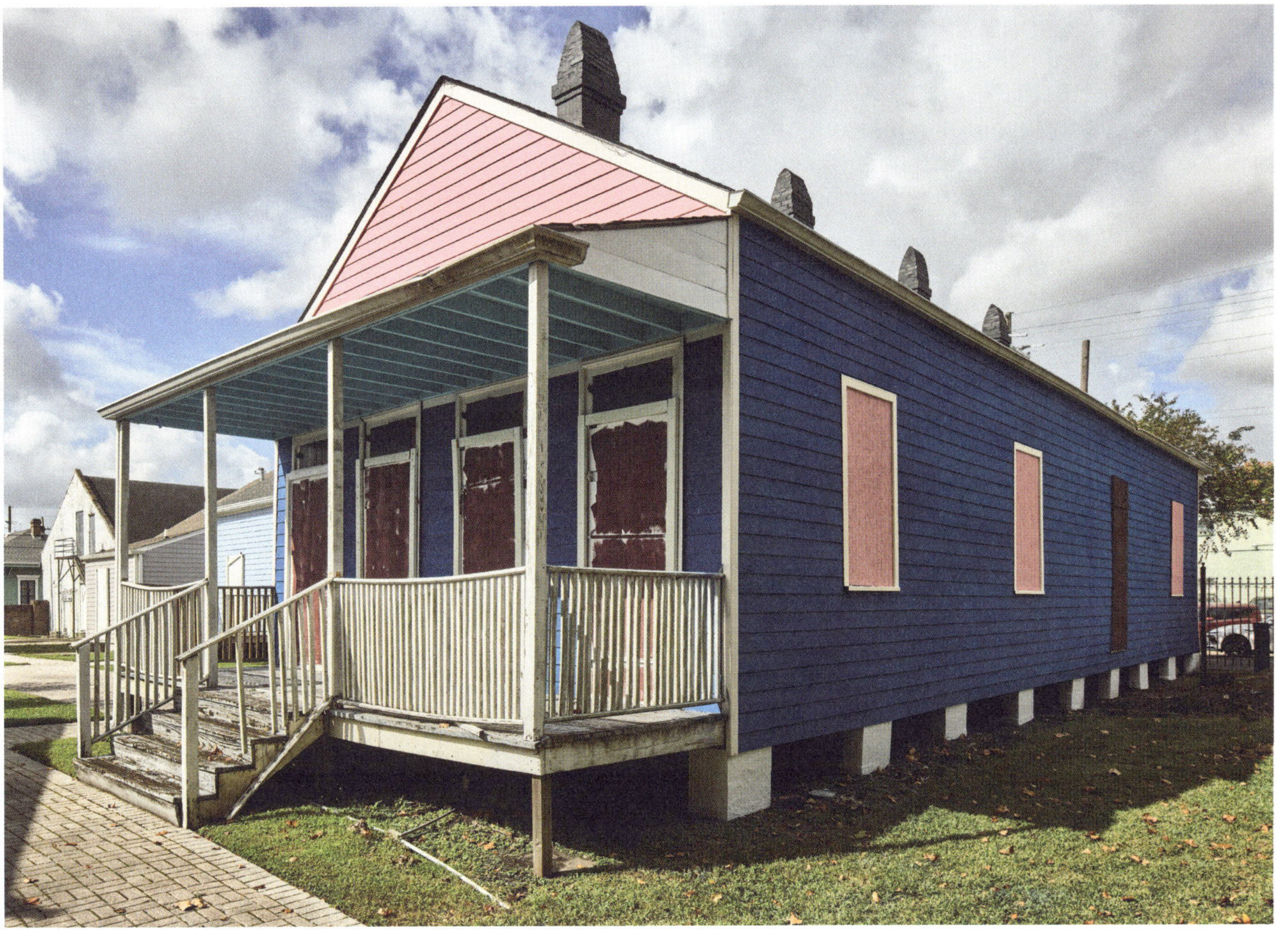

Top: *In Her Rich Deposits of (Blue)*, 2024.
Xavier University of Louisiana Art Village

Above: *In Her Rich Deposits of (Blue)*, 2024.
New Orleans African American Museum (NOAAM)

Yee I-Lann

b. 1971, Kota Kinabalu, Sabah, Malaysia; lives in Kota Kinabalu, Sabah, Malaysia

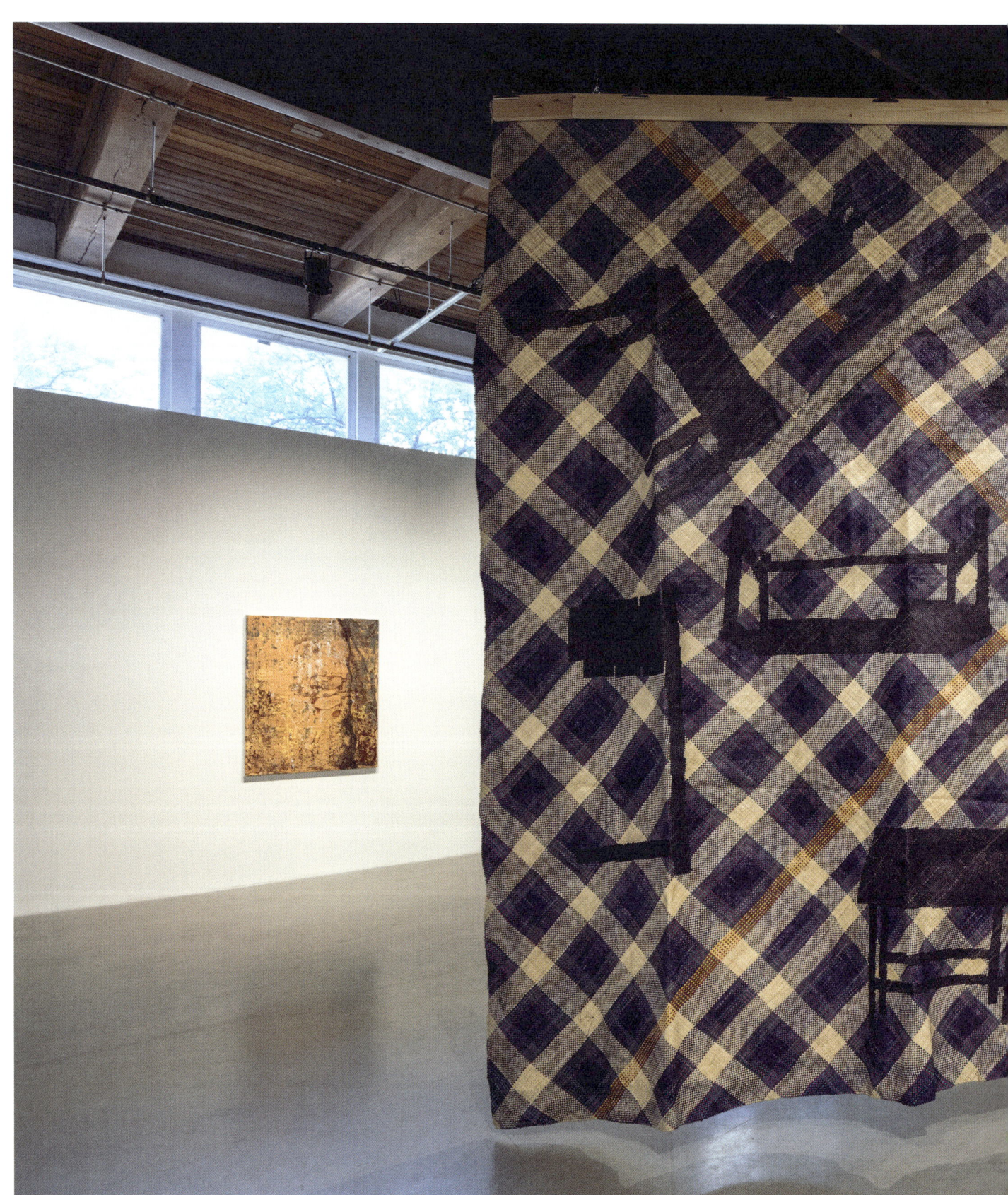

Tepo Aniya Nombor Na (Mat with a Number), 2020.
Installation view

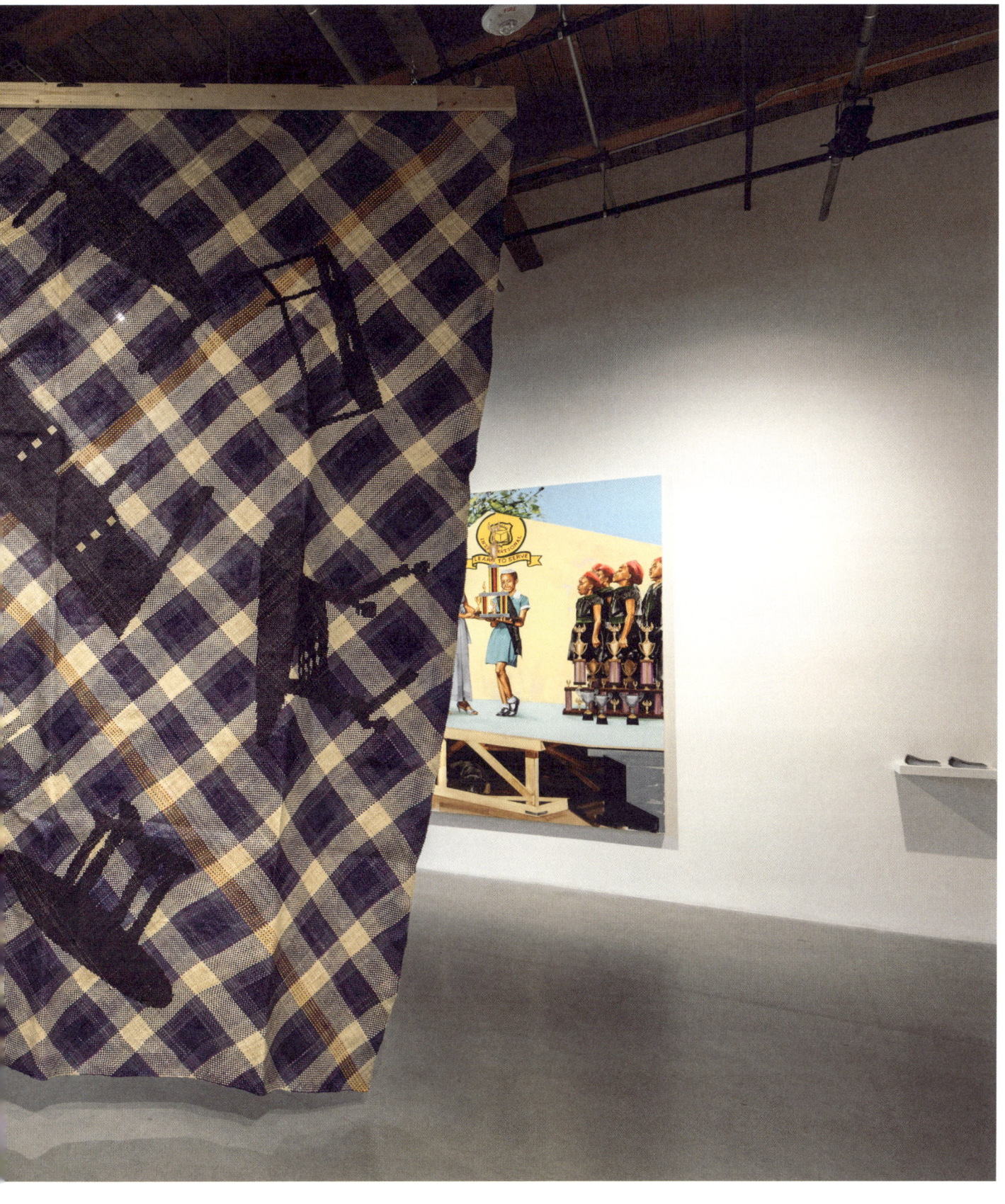

Yee I-Lann wants to flip the table.

She invites us, rather, to gather on and around the *tikar*—the woven mat resting on the floor—and imagine belonging beyond land and sea, beyond the powers of colonial administration. "Colonialism wasn't as much the violence of guns but the violence of a table," she shares over Zoom.[1] "[The table] is where colonialists made maps, surveyed the land, designed education systems, [determined] what was of value, what histories to learn, to preserve, to keep, to own. This insidious form of violence affects your very concept of self and is passed onto future generations."

While surveying thousands of colonial photographs from the Amsterdam Tropical Museum to create a previous body of work, *Picturing Power* (2013), Yee was struck by the recurrence and enduring violence of the table. This realization gave way to expanding her practice in 2018 beyond photomedia to include textile mats made in collaboration with Indigenous weavers from the mountains, plains, and seas of Borneo.

The weavers that Yee worked with to create *Tepo Aniya Nombor Na (Mat with a Number)* (2020) presented in Prospect.6 come from the Bajau Sama Dilaut, a seafaring community at Omadal Island, located between the Philippines' province of Sulu and Indonesian island of Celebes, in the seas northeast of Borneo. "When you are from the sea, you are not considered to be from a place—because they do not have a paper identity, they are stateless," shares Yee. "They are fluid."

The seafaring people are stateless because, when the nation-states of the Philippines, Indonesia, and Malaysia gained their independence after World War II, they were not registered as citizens in any of these countries. Thus, many do not have a registered nationality, do not hold identity cards or passports. Though they travel vast areas of water, they cannot legally enter any nation-state. Their crafts, especially weaving with pandanus leaves, became a way to express pride in their heritage and receive appreciation from people outside their immediate communities.

In this way, I-Lann's practice functions as a conjoiner, a bridge. "When you combine *tanah*' (land) and *air* (sea) into one word," she says, referring to the Malay language, "it becomes *tanahair*, which means homeland."

The checkered weaving pattern of the *tikar* is a motif shared by all maritime cultures of Southeast Asia. In the Bajau Laut language, this motif is called *kusta*. Bands of aquamarine blue, sandy yellow, and plum crisscross with smoky white. Embedded between the sheaths of color are the black shadows of tables, representing the omnipresent violence of administration that impacts this community.

Weaved on the reverse of the mat are the weavers' names: Sanah, Kinnuhong, Noraidah, Roziah, Darwisa, Enidah, Dela, Asima, Dayang, Tasya, Alisya, Erna, and I-Lann—the very present, prescient, and powerful women who contributed to the work. For some of them, it was their first time writing and seeing their name spelled. Weaver Kak Budi bestowed the mat with its title, *Tepo Aniya Nombor Na (Mat with a Number)*. In this act of self-determination, the collective establishes that even though they themselves are not acknowledged by any official state census, their lives and contributions count.

by Sadaf Padder

1   Conversation with the artist, July 15, 2024.

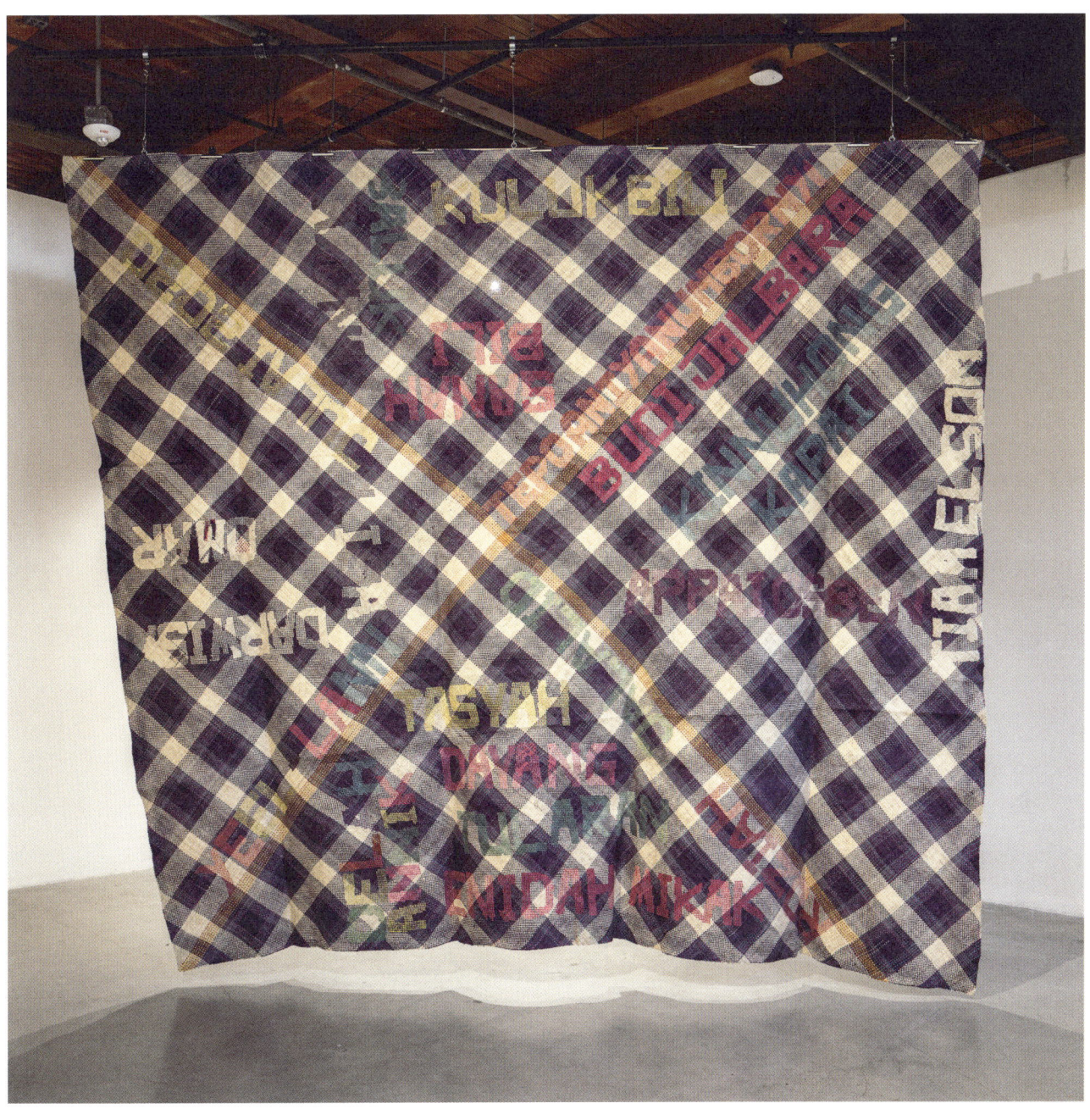

Tepo Aniya Nombor Na (Mat with a Number), 2020

New Orleans to Invite Billions of Participants for its Historic Congress of the Global Majority

Antawan I. Byrd, senior staff reporter for *The Prospect Dispatch*

New Orleans, Louisiana, June 15, 2038

The vibrant city of New Orleans is set to host the Congress of the Global Majority, a first-of-its-kind gathering planned for the summer of 2054. The garganTuấn event is expected to draw the attention and participation of billions worldwide and is poised to become the largest cultural-political event in the city's history. The Congress aspires to assemble as many people of Indigenous, African, Arab, Asian, and Latin American descent as possible, including those of mixed heritage. Organizers plan to extend invitations to this worldwide constituency of nearly 7 billion people, also known as the "Global Majority," who represent some 85% of the world's population.

New Orleans triumphed over six other cities that were shortlisted to host the gathering: Cairo, Delhi, Lagos, New York, Riyadh, and Santo Domingo. In a lively press conference held at the city's Ernest N. Morial Convention Center and streamed online for global audiences, local leaders and organizers celebrated the selection of New Orleans. "I do believe the people have spoken, and I am thrilled by what they had to say," exclaimed the city's mayor, Cheyenne Rivercane. "They say, ol' Bulbancha, our land of many tongues, is the best city for this historic Congress. They say we *are* the Global Majority! New Orleans will open its doors to the people of the world. Together, we will figure out a path forward for our collective salvation, and we're gonna have a helluva good time doing it too!"

The Congress of the Global Majority is organized and funded by a coalition of local and international organizations, grassroots movements, and cultural institutions dedicated to promoting global equity and cultural exchange. While it's too early to determine just how many visitors are expected to attend, organizers project about five million in-person attendees throughout the month-long Congress, with billions potentially joining the Congress virtually.

The sheer scale of the Congress echoes and amplifies the utopianism of other historic mass movements such as Pan-Africanism and Pan-Arabism. The Congress brings to mind as well histories of specific state-sponsored festivals, such as Nigeria's Second World Black and African Festival of Arts (FESTAC '77) as well as peripatetic cultural platforms such as the Caribbean Festival of Arts (CARIFESTA), ongoing since 1952. While these initiatives often sought coherence through ethnic affiliations and regional alliances, members of the Global Majority movement explicitly eschew labels that front-load race, ethnicity, or national identification. The twenty first century has thus far been saturated by culture wars and upheavals, which have catalyzed intense debates about language: Are terms such as "minority," "people of color," and acronyms like "BAME" (Black, Asian and Minority Ethnic) or "BIPOC" (Black, Indigenous, and people of color) appropriate for everyday use or national policy? black or Black? Hemispheric and regional terms like "Sub-Saharan Africa," "Black Atlantic," and "Global South" have also come under scrutiny or lost steam in popular culture and within academic industries increasingly motored by newly coined terms and critical theories seeking to meet the moment.

DEFINING THE GLOBAL MAJORITY

For some, the term "minority" is derogatory, or associated with willful efforts to diminish a subject's standing or a community's place in the world. "Language is really important, because that's the vehicle through which we conceptualize, we think, we speak, and we act," argues scholar Rosemary Campbell-Stephens who has been credited with coining the term "Global Majority" through her policy work on education in Britain during the early 2000s.[1]

The term has also generated impassioned detractors who view it as trendy, divisive wordplay. At the height of these debates in the 2020s, British journalist Nana Akua, derided the term as an attack on "white people, primarily white men" whereas the writer Sunder Katwala views it as "a step backwards for ethnic minorities, erasing their unique cultural heritage in the name of 'inclusiveness.'"[2] In response to critics, Campbell-Stephens stresses, however, that "it's really important that these conversations are had respectfully and not from a place of judgment or from a place of just wanting to slap-up White people a little bit for what's happened. I'm really commenting from a genuine place . . . When we deal with issues that pertain to the Global Majority, we're actually raising the level of the bar for *everyone* . . . "[3]

The Global Majority movement echoes historical efforts to mobilize the masses through blocs premised on shared experiences of imperial subjugation and systemic inequity. One thinks of the Dalit Movement in India, Civil Rights Movement in the United States, the Global Indigenous Peoples' Movements, LGBTQIA+ Rights Movement, Black Lives Matter, and the Anti-Apartheid Movement in South Africa. Even as these movements intersect with or take inspiration from social justice platforms other than their own, they are often circumscribed to national frameworks or appeals rooted in collective identities. One problem that unites them all is the persistent risk of internal division. While each takes unity and empowerment as their goal, they're often hampered by challenges related to class divisions and/or racial differences. Only a decade ago, the mainstream LGBTQIA+ movement was sharply criticized for not adequately addressing the intersectional nature of oppression faced by LGBTQIA+ individuals of color. Less so today, as a nationwide study, conducted in 2036 by *The Prospect Dispatch*, reported: Queer individuals of color experienced the largest decline in violence on record, and greater income parity when compared to their White peers. This is one measure of how the latest federal legislation—legal protections mandating equitable wages and accessible healthcare for the LGBTQIA+ community—is having an impact.

Writing in the early 1920s, American sociologist W. E. B. Du Bois lamented the lack of cooperation among the world's colored population, who, in his view, shared only experiences of oppression. Yet, he envisioned a future where these gaps could be bridged: "And yet quickened India, the South and West African Congresses, the Pan-African movement, the National Association for the Advancement of Colored People in America, together with rising China and risen Japan—all these at no distant day may come to common consciousness of aim and be able to give to the labor parties of the world a message that they will understand."[4] As Du Bois's vision remains unfulfilled more than a century later, one wonders whether the diverse voices gathered into the Global Majority will converge harmoniously at the Congress.

CONVENING THE PEOPLE

At the press conference announcing the Congress, organizers stressed that they would soon begin to implement an executive board, programming committee, safety and wellness council, logistics & environmental task force, and a cultural commission. Made up of local stakeholders throughout the city, these bodies will develop strategy and oversee planning, which will occur in phases over the next sixteen years. When asked about the goals of the Congress, spokesperson Frances Bechet stated: "This gathering is about the pursuit of cooperation. We want to bring together all the peoples of the world who have been historically dispossessed and disempowered in order to figure out a path forward. The stains of inequality have soiled our planet for far too long; it's high time we eradicate the practice and legacies of colonialism, genocide, fossil capitalism, and xenophobia."

Once word spread that New Orleans had won the bid to host the Congress, crowds of residents took to Congo Square to celebrate the news. "New Orleans has always been a city of convergence, where diverse cultures meet and create something truly unique, stated Mrs. Sookie Majesty, a resident of the city's Lower Ninth Ward. "We are honored to welcome the world and celebrate the shared heritage and future of the Global Majority. My great grandparents founded one of the oldest benevolent aid societies in this city, so hospitality and helping people is part of my DNA."

Elsewhere in the city, at Harry's Corner, a hip bar on Chartres Street in the French Quarter, a range of New Orleanians offered thoughts on the Congress. Alysha Randolph, an artist and curator, felt that the Congress as an idea was sufficient enough to pique her interest. "A lot of people are wondering whether it will happen, and I keep telling them it's not about that, it's about the strength of the idea and the conversations that it can catalyze." Yet even the idea of the Congress was enough for Ms. Randolph to envision how she might like to be involved. "Inclusive marketing is key. I would want to work with an artist to develop a series of

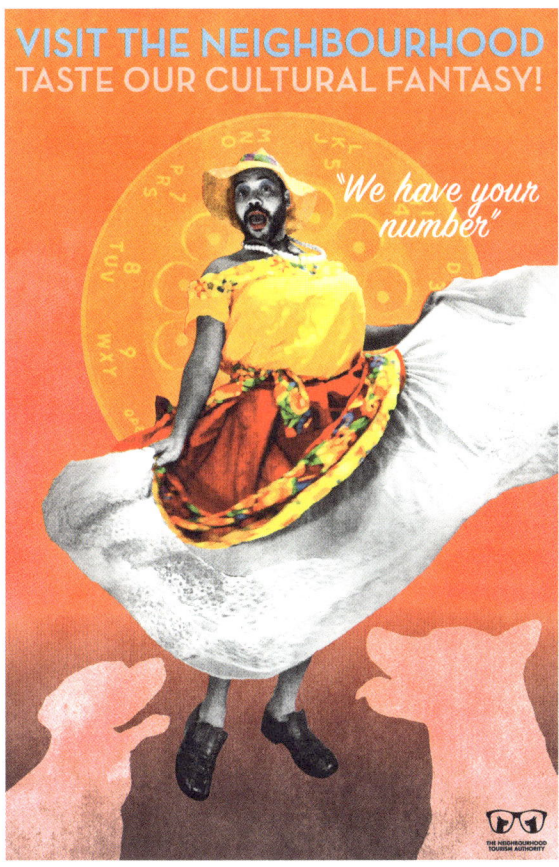
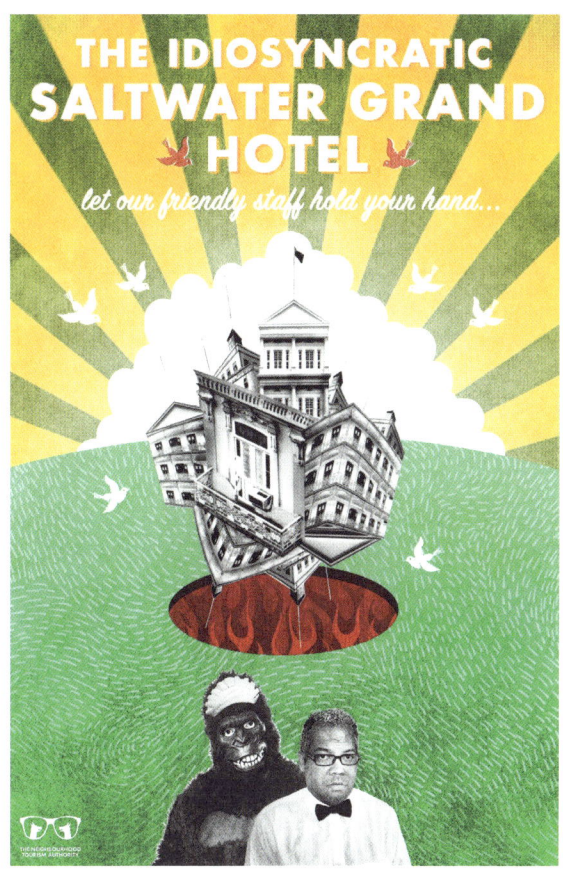

promotional campaigns. The Bajan artist Ewan Atkinson comes to mind. For the past thirty two years, he has steadily constructed a kind of parallel world through his *Neighbourhood Project*, which involves the development of characters and publications and maps, all of which address real-world issues. It's brilliant. I would invite him to make posters for the Congress, sort of like the ones made to promote his Neighbourhood."[5]

Hayden Brown, a jazz musician from Bayou St. John, believes the city's history and culture is its strongest selling point. "We have the Jazz and Heritage Festival, Prospect New Orleans, and of course Mardi Gras. We have been teaching the world how to—*and how not to*—host for centuries, long before Bienville crossed the Mississippi." When pressed about "how *not* to host," Brown recounted a story shared with him by his father who was a Garveyite and civil rights activist. "I'll put it to you this way. Growing up my dad told me that Marcus Garvey came to New Orleans in 1927 and thousands of Black people greeted him on the banks of the Mississippi. Later that day, all those people went to Algiers to hear Garvey speak. But the White police officers tried to shut down the whole rally, and before you knew it, Garvey was gone, deported; they shipped his ass back to Jamaica."

Implicit in Mr. Brown's illustration of how not to host seems a broader story about intolerance, about a time in the city's past—indeed, America's history—in which publicly platforming proponents of racial uplift and self-determination carried greater risks, especially when the stakes were as high as those set by figures like Garvey. His "mass movement," with all its connotations of "strength in numbers" and mobility—whether social, economic, or geographic—signaled a threat to the inequitable structures of power propped up by Jim Crow and the residual effects of the Middle Passage. Mr. Brown's anecdote seemed like a warning of sorts: Could solidarity and a unified vision among the majority

Ewan Atkinson, Posters from *Only in Our Imagination* (*The Neighbourhood Project*), 2015. These posters were commissioned by the Governing Body of The Neighbourhood Tourism Authority to advertise The Neighbourhood as a viable tourist destination.

of the world's population be perceived as a threat to the elite 2% that still holds a disproportionately large share of the world's total wealth? It also raises the question of the extent to which White people, in New Orleans and elsewhere, will participate in the event. Katherine Wearing, the owner of an online jewelry store and resident of Ascension Parish, when asked if she heard about plans for the Congress, spoke somewhat favorably of the project. "I think it's a great idea, but I am not sure it will ever happen," she said. "I'll believe it when I see it."

The incredulity expressed by some residents of the city could be found among those in local government as well, with some questioning whether sixteen years will actually be enough to host a convening of this magnitude. "This shit is huge, it's going to be crazy, there will be lots of challenges," stated an anonymous senior government official who was not authorized to speak on the record. Over the past decade, the city has been at the cutting edge of developing adaptive, modular architectural structures that can be easily assembled, and that automatically adjust their shading and ventilation systems to accommodate climate patterns. Since Mayor Rivercane's GREEN-ORLEANS bill passed, nearly every building in the city now has vegetative roofs and walls, which has significantly curtailed CO_2 levels, reduced heat island effects, and has improved air quality dramatically.

Still, how the Congress will impact these gains remains to be seen."We are going to have to transform this city in ways like you wouldn't believe," stated the anonymous senior government official. "We'll have to completely overhaul transportation, health and safety, the communication and technological infrastructure. I mean, even with the new 12G technology, we will still have to make sure that internet and communication networks can handle all those people—they'll be hacking hotspots and bootlegging WiFi."

However, a palpable optimism permeated the outlook of independent curator Mabel Ross, who has been working with a range of artists on public art projects. During a recent visit to her office, a series of miniature wood models had just arrived. "These are models

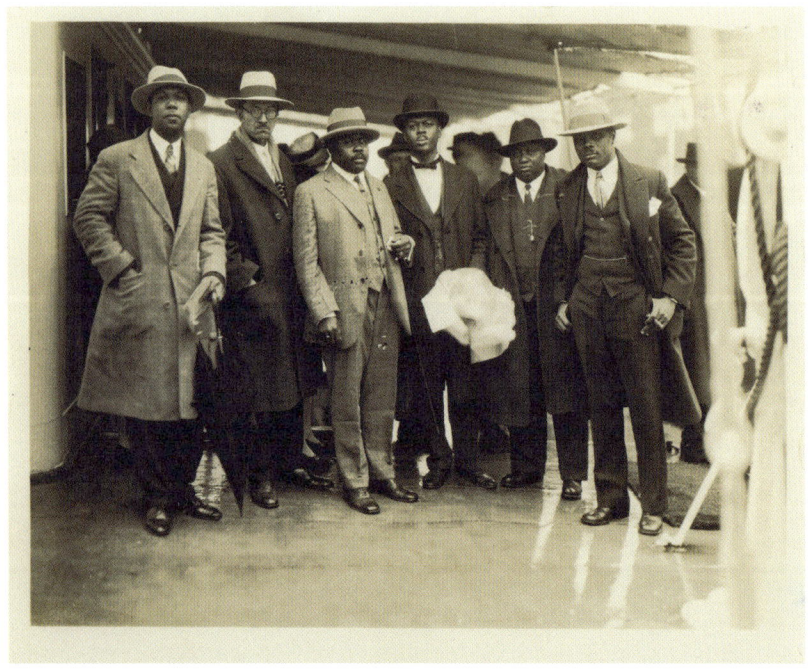

Arthur P. Bedou and Marcus Garvey with a group of UNIA-ACL (Universal Negro Improvement Association and African Communities League) officials minutes before deportation from the United States, 1927. Just before the SS *Saramacca* sailed out of the Port of New Orleans, Marcus Garvey posed on deck with a group of UNIA-ACL officials including, L to R: J.A. Craigen, executive secretary, Detroit Divisions; S.V. Robertson, president, Cleveland Division; Mr. Garvey; E.B. Knox, Garvey's personal representative; William Ware, president, Cincinnati Division; and Dr. J.J. Peters, president, New Orleans Division.

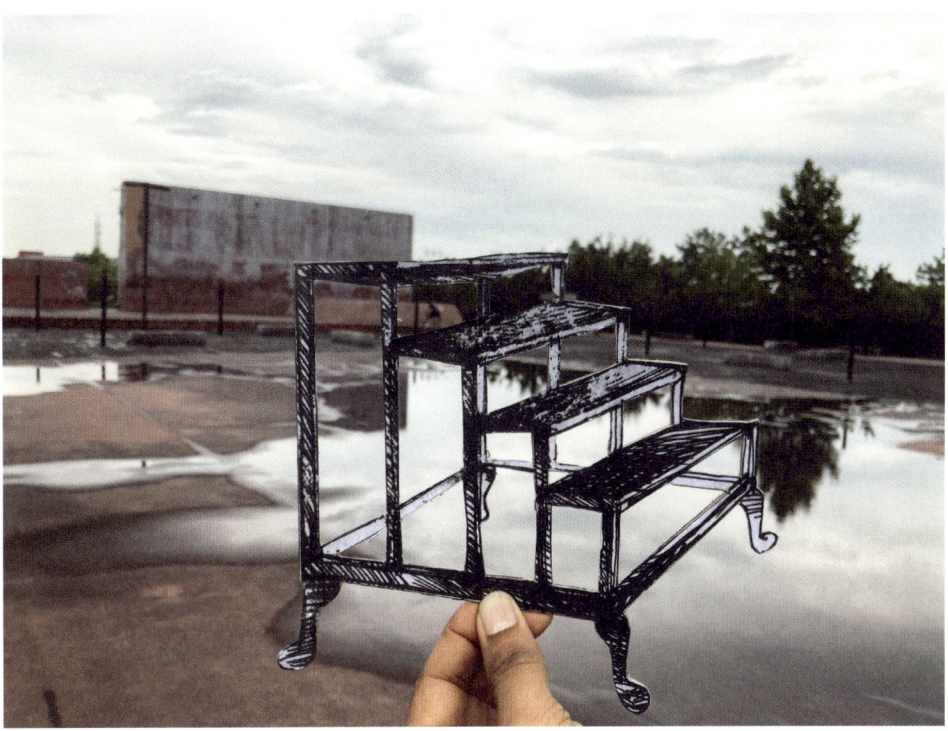

of bleachers created by the Trinidadian artist Christopher Cozier," she said. "Notice the ornate legs, they recall the scrollwork adornment found in Victorian-era furniture that was in vogue during the heyday of colonial expansion." According to Ross, Cozier plans to scale up the bleachers and produce them in the thousands for the Congress. When asked about the project's feasibility, she flatly stated, "People have to remember that this city has a long and storied history of pulling off the impossible. These bleachers are symbolic of this." Indeed, just as bleachers support spectators, enabling them to see and be seen, the Congress is set to illuminate the city of New Orleans, showcasing its capacity to welcome and unite those historically overlooked.

1   Rosemary Campbell-Stephens began using the term "Global Majority" in 2003 in conjunction with her policy work on the London Challenge Initiative, a multiyear project developed by the Institute of Education, University College London, to increase the number of the nation's Black and Asian educators. The term, according to Campbell-Stephens, was coined to reject the debilitating implications of being racialized as minorities. For a broader discussion of the term's emergence and mobilization, see Rosemary Campbell-Stephen's *Educational Leadership and the Global Majority: Decolonising Narratives* (London, UK: Palgrave Macmillan, 2021), 1–22.

2   Nana Akua, "The 'Global Majority' is a Sinister and Insulting Term for Anyone Who is Not White," *The Daily Mail*, 26 July 2023; Sunder Katwala, "Apparently I'm part of the 'Global Majority,' Now—What a Load of Nonsense," *The Independent,* May 17, 2024.

3   W. E. B. Du Bois, "Worlds of Color" (1925) in Adom Getachew and Jennifer Pitts, eds., *W. E. B. Du Bois: International Thought* (Cambridge, UK: Cambridge University Press, 2022), 89. My thanks to Adom Getachew for suggesting this reference.

4   Rosemary Campbell-Stephens, "Global Majority: Why Language Matters: A Conversation Between Rosemary Campbell-Stephens and Shereen Daniels," YouTube, November 26, 2020. <https://www.youtube.com/watch?v=F7MDqRH5Bxs>

5   Atkinson's *Neighbourhood Project* is distinct from but resonates with the work of the New Orleans-based nonprofit, the Neighborhood Story Project (NSP), which, since its founding in 2004 by Rachel Breunlin, has archived the multivalent stories of thousands of New Orleanians through a range of forms. For more on their work, see neighborhoodstoryproject.org/ as well as "The Neighborhood Story Project" in *Prospect.5 New Orleans: Yesterday We Said Tomorrow* (New York: Rizzoli Electa, 2021), eds. Naima Keith and Diana Nawi, 204–207.

Photograph taken during a site visit with Christopher Cozier for Prospect.6, New Orleans, July 2023

Sempiternal: To the Future of a Crescent City
Karisma Price

ending with a variation of a line by Frank O'Hara

Again, we are not simple. Say, it is a privilege to see our city this way: a bowl tuned to the sound of singing hands—the city that refuses to run from the mouth that will unmake it. Say, for right now, the towels are still, and above us, life grows from wine. Say, we will water it. Our mouth is the God that transcribes the drowning: *Who's been spoken for? Who keeps on the light? Who owns the door that holds a hole as small and significant as the prey of a meadowhawk?* We can see them. Trying to live is such a practice. Not far ahead, the swiftest of men will sprint on the painted field: A body knocks another. They cannot look back from the future, after their stiffness causes surgeons to hungrily split their skulls like swollen peaches. Tell us what to name our future. Have we taken from ourselves? What have we denied our teeth? Because we are speaking, the future turns its head like a misbehaved witness. Look back at us. *We no longer have to lie to each other to be immediate.*

"Sempiternal: To the Future of a Crescent City" by Karisma Price originally appeared in the *Indiana Review*.

Works in the Exhibition

Shannon Alonzo

Three Whistles and a Howl, 2024
Steel and wire framing, Poly-fil wadding,
cotton and synthetic fabrics, fiberglass
rods, thread, and paracord
Dimensions variable

Courtesy of the artist
Support for this project was provided by
the National Endowment for the Arts
Supported in part by Alice Yard Collective
Commissioned by Prospect.6

Eddie Rodolfo Aparicio

*Muñecas de transmisión (Bridge City/
Whitnall Hwy) (Blue)*, 2024
Families' clothes, Ceiba tree fibers,
thread, and paint on metal frame
138 × 60 × 60 in.

*Muñecas de transmisión (Bridge City/
Whitnall Hwy) (Green)*, 2024
Families' clothes, Ceiba tree fibers,
thread, and paint on metal frame
138 × 60 × 60 in.

*Muñecas de transmisión (Bridge City/
Whitnall Hwy) (Orange)*, 2024
Families' clothes, Ceiba tree fibers,
thread, and paint on metal frame
138 × 60 × 60 in.

All works courtesy of the artist
Support for this project was provided by
the National Endowment for the Arts
Commissioned by Prospect.6

Ewan Atkinson

*Stories from the Neighbourhood: The Great
Exposition*, 2015–2024
Mixed media
Dimensions variable

INDIVIDUAL WORKS

"Apple of Sodom" Plushie, 2024
Fabric and paper
Dimensions variable

Commissioned by Prospect.6

Exposition Pictography, 2024
Digital print on paper
22 × 30 in.

Commissioned by Prospect.6

Extra Extra, 2024
Digital prints on paper
Two prints: 25 × 18 in. each

Commissioned by Prospect.6

Fire on The Dock?, 2023
Found painting
12 × 13 ½ in.

Four Dogs, 2015
Gouache, watercolor,
and acrylic ink on paper
22 ½ × 30 in.

*The Magnificent Wigwam to
Wind up The Moon*, 2024
Digital print on paper
96 × 36 in.

Commissioned by Prospect.6

*A Man of Letters and His Scientific Genius,
Mr. R.H. Liard*, 2018–2024
Mixed media on paper
Twenty-four illustrations: 11 ¾ × 8 ¼ in. each

The Mysterious Magic Metal Mule(atto), 2024
Digital print on paper with collage
36 × 24 in.

Commissioned by Prospect.6

Neighbourhood Texture (Grass and Fur),
2015
Gouache, watercolor,
and acrylic ink on paper
Two drawings: 22 ½ × 30 in. each

*None of These Things Are Just like the Other;
A Comparative Study of Neighbourhood
Stray Dogs and Their Genitalia, Scratch 'n
Sniff Edition*, 2024
Digital print on paper
24 × 32 in.

Commissioned by Prospect.6

The Official Cereal of The Exposition, 2024
Digital print on paper
22 × 35 ½ in.

Commissioned by Prospect.6

Only in Our Imagination, 2015
Digital prints on paper
Twelve posters: 36 × 24 in. each

Peregrination, a Playable Reproduction, 2018
Digital print on paper, paper playing
pieces on wood stands, metal buttons,
candy wrapper, dice, plastic toys, and
found objects
Dimensions variable

*Places I've Been That Are Definitely Not
Here: A Photo Essay by Mr._____*, 2024
Digital prints on paper and photo albums
Two photo albums: 8 × 12 in. open, each

Commissioned by Prospect.6

*Sight Unseen No.13B (Inside a Cuckoo's
Nest)*, 2017
Digital print on paper
12 × 12 in.

Sight Unseen No.14 (The Key to His Heart),
2017
Ink on paper
12 × 12 in.

Sight Unseen No.22 (Peek-a-boo), 2017
Digital print and paint on paper and mylar
12 × 12 in.

Sight Unseen No.109 (Filler), 2024
Digital print on paper
12 × 12 in.

Commissioned by Prospect.6

Sight Unseen No.127 (Baby Dogoose Adrift),
2024
Digital print and paint on paper and mylar
12 × 12 in.

Commissioned by Prospect.6

Sight Unseen No.127 (Opinion Piece), 2017
Digital print on paper
12 × 12.

*Significant Pages From "How The Dogoose
Got Lost in Someone Else's Make Believe,"*
2024
Digital print on paper
31 ½ × 50 in.

Commissioned by Prospect.6

*The Spinster Sisters Made a Valentine (Of
Sorts)*, 2024
Digital print on paper, wood, glass, paper,
false eyelashes, false fingernails, plastic,
lace, human hair, and makeup
10 ½ × 8 ¾ in.

Commissioned by Prospect.6

*A Treatise Implicating Animalcule as
Catalysts for Tension During the Historic
Dog-Mongoose Hostilities*, 2019–2024
Mixed media on paper
Two drawings: 30 × 22 ½ in. each

*A True and Exact History of The
Neighbourhood, in Brevibus Anecdotis, Vol
I. (Obfuscated by Bleeding-Tooth Whelks)*,
2024
Digital print on paper
24 × 32 in.

Commissioned by Prospect.6

Woof, 2024
Digital print on paper
18 × 26 in.

Commissioned by Prospect.6

Yes, We Have No Bananas, 2024
Digital print on paper
60 × 40 in.

Commissioned by Prospect.6

All works courtesy of the artist

Zalika Azim
rafa esparza
Dewey Tafoya

Proposals for Loops in Linear Time, 2024
A collaborative exhibition by Zalika Azim,
rafa esparza, and Dewey Tafoya
Mixed media installation
Dimensions variable

*polysemous notes on geological time...
or ways to steal from the workplace...a
grounding...for an escape or an inhabiting*,
2024
Three-channel audio, mixer, subwoofers,
speakers, and adobe
24:56 min.
Composed by Uriel Valenzuela Ibarra

All works courtesy of the artists
Made possible through major funding from
the Mellon Foundation
Commissioned by Prospect.6

Zalika Azim

*Ascension Device II (actions for earth...or
some other oscillation...a haptic and sonic
engagement...a breath...or an architecture
for gathering between space and time)*, 2024
Wood, aluminum, polypropylene ropes,
spoked wheels, and electric gear motors
276 × 25 ¼ × 91 in.

Courtesy of the artist
Made possible through major funding
from the Mellon Foundation
Commissioned by Prospect.6

Teresa Baker

Beacon I, 2024
Willow, cardboard, and AstroTurf
53 × 8 ⅜ in.

Beacon 2, 2024
Willow, cardboard, and AstroTurf
33 × 10 ½ in.

Beacon 3, 2024
Willow, cardboard, and AstroTurf
43 × 12 ½ in.

Tracing the Dirt, 2024
Buckskin, willow, acrylic, and yarn on
AstroTurf
92 ¾ × 92 ½ × ¼ in.

All works courtesy of the artist and
de boer, Los Angeles & Antwerp
Support for this project was provided by
de boer, Los Angeles & Antwerp
Commissioned by Prospect.6

Andrea Carlson

Trade Canoe for Earthdivers to Come, 2024
Canoe, wood, paint, rope, and stone
Dimensions variable

Trade Canoe for Recollection, 2024
Gouache, ink, and acrylic on paper, wood
canoe, and paint
Canoe: 204 × 36 × 26 in.
Seven works on paper: 34 × 26 in. each

All works courtesy of the artist
Support for this project was provided by the
National Endowment for the Arts
Commissioned by Prospect.6

Hannah Chalew

Orphan Well Gamma Garden, 2024
Metal, sugarcane, disposable plastic
waste, lime, recycled paint, paper made
from sugarcane combined with shredded
disposable plastic waste ("plasticane"), ink
made from persimmon, goldenrod, indigo,
copper, and oak galls, pumps, irrigation
tubing, diffuser, *Fertile Rot* scent, living
plants, soil, and water
Dimensions variable

Courtesy of the artist
Support for this project was provided by
the Eugenie and Joseph Jones Family
Foundation, the Selley Foundation Fund,
the Ella West Freeman Foundation, the
Keller Family Foundation, and the National
Endowment for the Arts
Commissioned by Prospect.6

Mel Chin

Pool of Light, 2024–2025
Steel, industrial paint, aluminum, vinyl,
leather, and mid-century office chairs
Dimensions variable

Courtesy of the artist
Support for this project was provided by
Suzanne Deal Booth and Virginia Lebermann
Commissioned by Prospect.6

Bethany Collins

The Aeneid: 1971 / 1697, 2022
Ink on handmade paper with
Black Magic eraser in two parts
Diptych: 44 × 30 in. each

Courtesy of the artist;
Alexander Gray Associates, New York;
PATRON Gallery, Chicago

The Aeneid: 1981 / 2007, 2024
Ink on handmade paper with
Black Magic eraser in two parts
Diptych: 44 ¼ × 30 ¾ in. each

Courtesy of the artist;
Alexander Gray Associates, New York;
PATRON Gallery, Chicago
Commissioned by Prospect.6

The Aeneid: 2005 / 1990, 2024
Ink on handmade paper with Black Magic
eraser in two parts
Diptych: 44 × 30 in. each

Courtesy of the artist;
PATRON Gallery, Chicago;
Alexander Gray Associates, New York
Commissioned by Prospect.6

The Aeneid: 2017 / 2020 / 1885, 2024
Ink on handmade paper with Black Magic
eraser in three parts
Triptych: 44 × 30 in. each

Courtesy of the artist;
PATRON Gallery, Chicago; Alexander Gray
Associates, New York
Commissioned by Prospect.6

The Aeneid: 2021 / 1697, 2022
Ink on handmade paper with Black Magic
eraser in two parts
Diptych: 44 × 30 ½ in. each

Courtesy of the artist;
Alexander Gray Associates, New York;
PATRON Gallery, Chicago

Moby Dick, Vol. 3, 2024
Somerset paper and blue eraser
Dimensions variable

Courtesy of the artist;
Alexander Gray Associates, New York;
PATRON Gallery, Chicago
Commissioned by Prospect.6

The Patriot's Banner, 2024
Two-channel sound recording and ceiling
mounted speakers
105:30 min.
Sung by James Osby Gwathney
Arrangement and post-production by
Peter Christian

Courtesy of the artist;
Alexander Gray Associates, New York;
PATRON Gallery, Chicago
Commissioned by Prospect.6

Myrlande Constant

Kouzen Zaka Minis Agrikilti, 2022
Beads, sequins, and tassels on fabric
69 × 95 in.

Courtesy of The Clark Collection

Sosyete Radha, 2024
Beads, sequins, and tassels on fabric
96 × 109 ½ in.

Collection of the Akron Art Museum,
Museum Acquisition Fund 2024.7
Commissioned by Prospect.6

Tout Ko Feray Se Dife, 2022
Beads, sequins, and tassels on fabric
56 ½ × 65 in.

Courtesy of the artist and Fort Gansevoort,
New York

Christopher Cozier

it has already been decided..., 2024
Paper, ink, wood, and string
90 × 60 in.

Courtesy of the artist
Support for this project was provided by
the National Endowment for the Arts
Commissioned by Prospect.6

it has already been decided..., 2024
Wood
19 × 19 × 19 in.

Courtesy of the artist
Support for this project was provided by
the National Endowment for the Arts
Commissioned by Prospect.6

it has already been decided..., 2024
Steel, enamel, and sapele wood
96 × 96 × 96 in.

Courtesy of the artist
Commissioned by Prospect.6

it has already been decided...Notes, 2024
Video, color
1:54 min.
Produced with assistance from
Maica Gugolati, Shari Petti, and
Marlon Rouse

Courtesy of the artist
Support for this project was provided by
the National Endowment for the Arts
Commissioned by Prospect.6

Ronald Cyrille aka B.Bird

Lost in the vegetation, 2024
Acrylic on canvas
81 ½ × 122 in.

Nature-elle la connexion, 2024
3D printed acrylonitrile butadiene styrene
and spray paint
Dimensions variable

Nostalgie d'une rencontre, 2024
Ink on paper
84 × 78 ¾ in.

Odyssées d'une exile, 2024
Acrylic on canvas
80 × 112 ½ in.

The unknown land, 2024
Acrylic on canvas
Triptych: 97 ½ × 80 in. each

Where my belly button is buried, 2024
Ink on paper
78 ¾ × 84 in.

All works courtesy of the artist
Major support for this project was
provided by Hancock Whitney
Commissioned by Prospect.6

Raúl de Nieves

*The Sacred Heart of Hours and the Trees
of Yesterdays, Today, and Tomorrow*, 2024
Powder-coated steel
178 ½ × 132 × 43 in.

The Trees of Now (Diligence), 2024
Metal, fiberglass, leather, beads, and resin
Dimensions variable

The Trees of Today (Justice), 2024
Metal, fiberglass, leather, beads, and resin
Dimensions variable

The Trees of Tomorrow (Strength), 2024
Metal, fiberglass, leather, beads, and resin
Dimensions variable

The Trees of Yesterdays (Faith), 2024
Metal, fiberglass, leather, beads, and resin
Dimensions variable

All works courtesy of the artist and
Company, New York
This project was made possible through
major funding from the Mellon Foundation,
the Stephen Reily Family Fund,
Walda Besthoff, and the Teiger Foundation.
1800 Tequila is the exclusive corporate
supporter of this project
Commissioned by Prospect.6

Thomas Deaton

Last Megalopolis, 2024
Acrylic and mixed media on canvas
Triptych: 60 × 72 × ½ in. each

Courtesy of the artist
Major support for this project was provided
by The Helis Foundation.
Additional support was provided by
the Eugenie and Joseph Jones Family
Foundation, the Selley Foundation Fund,
the Ella West Freeman Foundation, and
the Keller Family Foundation
Commissioned by Prospect.6

Abigail DeVille

Carbon, 2024
Steel, chicken wire, coal, glass,
paper, galvanized wire, wire mesh,
rope, and charcoal
Four sculptures: dimensions variable

*The heart knows its own bitterness
(Manifest)*, 2024
Sound
Duration ranges from 10 to 60 mins.
Composed by RA Washington,
Jadele McPherson, Justin Hicks,
and Courtney Bryan

All works courtesy of the artist
Commissioned by Prospect.6

Christian Việt Đinh

*Trường Ca Mười Ngàn Năm
(A Song of 10,000 Years)*, 2024
Gilded porcelain and gilded wood
Dimensions variable

Courtesy of the artist
This project was made possible through
major funding from the Mellon Foundation
and The Helis Foundation. Additional
support was provided by the Eugenie and
Joseph Jones Family Foundation, the Selley
Foundation Fund, the Ella West Freeman
Foundation, the Keller Family Foundation,
and the National Endowment for the Arts
Commissioned by Prospect.6

Jeannette Ehlers

*Hoist and the Unseen: Journeys Through
Tempests in Times of Hunger*, 2024
Wood and synthetic hair
Dimensions variable

Courtesy of the artist
This project was made possible through
major funding from the Mellon Foundation.
Additional support was provided by the
Danish Arts Foundation and Pérez Art
Museum Miami's Caribbean Cultural
Institute
Commissioned by Prospect.6

We're Magic. We're Real #2, 2020/2024
Synthetic afro hair, aluminum, motor,
emergency blankets, and sound
Dimensions variable
Sound by Trevor Mathison from *Black Bullets*

Courtesy of the artist
This project was made possible through
major funding from the Mellon Foundation.
Additional support was provided by

the Danish Arts Foundation. Production
assistance provided by Saniya Alderson,
Carlos Alvarez Clemente, Ron Bechet,
Etelvina Benjamin, Kalea Cook, Dartanya
Croff, Denise Frazier, Deliam Frazier-
Nadalin, Nancy Hampton, MaPó Kinnord,
Ebony G. Patterson, Susanna Rantala,
Valesca Santos, Sharlene Sinegal-DeCuir,
and David Williams, with special thanks to
Morgan Mo'Beauty Dillon from Banga Headz

rafa esparza

Mexica Falcon after Dewey Tafoya, 2024
Steel, adobe, car jacks, and adobe tiles
210 × 149 × 25 in.

Courtesy of the artist
Made possible through major funding
from the Mellon Foundation
Commissioned by Prospect.6

Abdi Farah

Indescribable Beast, 2017
Assorted nylons and fabric paint
87 × 87 in.

Courtesy of the artist

Plume, 2021
Oil on canvas
72 × 48 in.

Private collection

Studies, 2013–2024
Mixed media
Dimensions variable

Courtesy of the artist

Three Down Back, 2019
Charcoal on canvas
72 × 132 in.

Courtesy of the artist

Trojan Pride, 2017
Plastisol ink, felt lettering, ribbon,
and thread on satin nylon
54 × 87 in.

Courtesy of the artist
Major support for this project was provided
by The Helis Foundation. Additional support
was provided by the Eugenie and Joseph
Jones Family Foundation, the Selley
Foundation Fund, the Ella West Freeman
Foundation, the Keller Family Foundation,
and the National Endowment for the Arts

Brendan Fernandes

On Flashing Lights, 2018/2025
Sound, light, and dance performance

Courtesy of the artist
Support for this project was
provided by Lambent Foundation
and Monique Meloche Gallery

L. Kasimu Harris

About to go get'em, Spy Boy Louis Thomas Jr. (Carnival Day, Purple Rain Bar), 2015, from the series *Vanishing Black Bars & Lounges*, 2018-ongoing
Archival inkjet print
16 × 24 in.
Edition 1 of 6, 2 APs

A Beloved Past, A Precarious Future Sandpiper Lounge, New Orleans, 2022, from the series *Vanishing Black Bars & Lounges*, 2018-ongoing
Archival inkjet print
16 × 24 in.
Edition 1 of 6, 2 APs

Champers, 3 Beautiful Experiences, 2024, from the series *Vanishing Black Bars & Lounges*, 2018-ongoing
Archival inkjet print and screen printed text
16 × 24 in.
Edition 1 of 4, 2 APs
Models: Deniseea Head, J'Nai Williams, and Erika Flowers, all bartenders; Screen Printing: L. Kasimu Harris, guided by Daniella Marx; Design and Layout: Vitus Shell; Wardrobe: Two Sisters

Commissioned by Prospect.6

The Circle of St. Joseph Night, for The Golden Blades at Silky's Bar, New Orleans, 2024, from the series *Vanishing Black Bars & Lounges*, 2018-ongoing
Archival inkjet print
16 × 24 in.
Edition 1 of 6, 2 APs

Commissioned by Prospect.6

Come Tuesday (Marwan Pleasant at Sportsman's Corner), 2018, from the series *Vanishing Black Bars & Lounges*, 2018-ongoing
Archival inkjet print
1 6x 24 in.
Edition 1 of 6, 2 APs

Coming Out Steppin' Members of the Zulu S&P coming out of Sweet Lorraine's Jazz Club, 2022, from the series *Vanishing Black Bars & Lounges*, 2018-ongoing
Archival inkjet print
24 × 36 in.
Edition 1 of 6, 2 APs

Exclave, 2024, from the series *Vanishing Black Bars & Lounges*, 2018-ongoing
Chromogenic print and screen printed text
18 × 24 in.
Edition 1 of 6, 2 APs
Model: Elliot Hutchinson; Screen Printing: L. Kasimu Harris, guided by Lauren Bailey; Producer: Ariel Wilson Harris; Design and Layout: Vitus Shell; Wardrobe: Two Sisters; Location: NightBloom Bar, New Orleans

Commissioned by Prospect.6

Farmer Hartford, 2024, *from the series Vanishing Black Bars & Lounges*, 2018-ongoing
Chromogenic print and screen printed text
18 × 24 in.
Edition 1 of 6, 2 APs
Model: Myron Hartford; Screen Printing: L. Kasimu Harris, guided by Lauren Bailey;

Design and Layout: Adrian Franks of FRNK Brands; Wardrobe: Two Sisters

Commissioned by Prospect.6

Feet Can't Hurt, When you got that Footwork (Derek Gardner) of the Zulu Go Getters (Bertha's Place Bar & Restaurant), New Orleans, 2022, from the series *Vanishing Black Bars & Lounges*, 2018-ongoing
Archival inkjet print
16 × 24 in.
Edition 1 of 6, 2 APs

From My Hometown, to Yours: Nina Compton Takes me to a "Fryday" in Gros Islet, St. Lucia at the Irie Bar, 2022, from the series *Vanishing Black Bars & Lounges*, 2018-ongoing
Archival inkjet print
16 × 24 in.
Edition 1 of 6, 2 APs

From Silky's to Sportsman's Corner, and the Streets in Between Harry G on St. Joseph's Night, New Orleans, 2024, from the series *Vanishing Black Bars & Lounges*, 2018-ongoing
Archival inkjet print
16 × 24 in.
Edition 1 of 6, 2 APs

Commissioned by Prospect.6

Get the Bag and "Meet the Browns." Is that you, Carl Winslow? (Mr. Ooooook Lounge), Clarksdale, Mississippi, 2021, from the series *Vanishing Black Bars & Lounges*, 2018-ongoing
Archival inkjet print
16 × 24 in.
Edition 1 of 6, 2 APs

How to Stand on Business: "Try Me Hoe," (Good Trouble Lounge), New Orleans, 2023, from the series *Vanishing Black Bars & Lounges*, 2018-ongoing
Archival inkjet print
24 × 36 in.
Edition 1 of 6, 2 APs

King Joe Lindsey and his Royal Setup (Roberton's Vieux Carre Lounge), New Orleans, 2022, from the series *Vanishing Black Bars & Lounges*, 2018-ongoing
Archival inkjet print
16 × 24 in.
Edition 2 of 6, 2 APs

King Joe Lindsey, in his Sunday's Best, every Friday and Saturday at Robertson's Vieux Carre Lounge, 2022, from the series *Vanishing Black Bars & Lounges*, 2018-ongoing
Archival inkjet print
16 × 24 in.
Edition 1 of 6, 2 APs

Last Call for COVID, Inside of the Zulu clubhouse, 2020, from the series *Vanishing Black Bars & Lounges*, 2018-ongoing
Archival inkjet print
16 × 24 in.
Edition 1 of 6, 2 APs

Louisiana Jones, Very Rare, 2024, from the series *Vanishing Black Bars & Lounges*, 2018-ongoing
Archival inkjet print and screen printed text

18 × 24 in.
Edition 1 of 4, 2 APs
Models: Troi and Ron Bechet; Screen Printing: L. Kasimu Harris, guided by Daniella Marx; Design and Layout: Adrian Franks of FRNK Brands; Wardrobe: Two Sisters

Commissioned by Prospect.6

NBA Playoffs on the Tube, Lee Morgan on the Juke (The Living Room Bar), Los Angeles, 2022, from the series *Vanishing Black Bars & Lounges*, 2018-ongoing
Archival inkjet print
16 × 24 in.
Edition 1 of 6, 2 APs

Nero's Vino, 2024, from the series *Vanishing Black Bars & Lounges*, 2018-ongoing
Chromogenic print and screen printed text
18 × 24 in.
Edition 1 of 4, 2 APs
Models: Courtney Nero and Nesby Phips; Screen Printing: L. Kasimu Harris, guided by Lauren Bailey; Design and Layout: Vitus Shell; Wardrobe: Two Sisters

Commissioned by Prospect.6

Never Too Young to Cut a Rug (St. Joseph's Night) Sportsman's Corner, New Orleans, 2024, from the series *Vanishing Black Bars & Lounges*, 2018-ongoing
Archival inkjet print
16 × 24 in.
Edition 1 of 6, 2 APs

The Pool Playing Proprietor, Jimmy Perryman, at his Spot: Mr. Ooooook Lounge, Clarksdale, Mississippi, 2021, from the series *Vanishing Black Bars & Lounges*, 2018-ongoing
Archival inkjet print
16 × 24 in.
Edition 1 of 6, 2 APs

Purple Rain Bar into the Abyss of the Unremembered-Culture Persists. How Long?, 2023, from the series *Vanishing Black Bars & Lounges*, 2018-ongoing
Archival inkjet print
16 × 24 in.
Edition 1 of 6, 2 APs

Rings, Rack, Win Dat Money Back (Mr. Ooooook Lounge), Clarksdale, Mississippi, 2021, from the series *Vanishing Black Bars & Lounges*, 2018-ongoing
Archival inkjet print
16 × 24 in.
Edition 1 of 6, 2 APs

The Set-Up, Unc's Hands, (Purple Rain Bar), New Orleans, 2019, from the series *Vanishing Black Bars & Lounges*, 2018-ongoing
Archival inkjet print
24 × 36 in.
Edition 1 of 4, 2 APs

The Silk Pressed Crown of Jay's Lounge, Pittsburgh, 2020, from the series *Vanishing Black Bars & Lounges*, 2018-ongoing
Archival inkjet print
16 × 24 in.
Edition 1 of 6, 2 APs

Sophisticated Jolly, 2024, from the series
Vanishing Black Bars & Lounges,
2018-ongoing
Chromogenic print and screen printed text
18 × 24 in.
Edition 1 of 4, 2 APs
Models: Drs. Rupa and TJ Jolly; Screen
Printing: L. Kasimu Harris, guided by Lauren
Bailey; Design and Layout: Vitus Shell;
Wardrobe: Two Sisters

Commissioned by Prospect.6

*Steve is Still Here, Honoring Louis, Theresa
and the Sacred Culture, New Orleans*, 2020,
from the series *Vanishing Black Bars &
Lounges*, 2018-ongoing
Archival inkjet print
24 × 36 in.
Edition 1 of 6, 2 APs

*Stories Can Live on Forever: Theresa
Elloie's Last Interview*, 2024, from the
series *Vanishing Black Bars & Lounges*,
2018-ongoing
Sound
14:36 min.
Edited and produced by Stephanie Serrano;
Engineered by Rahsaan "Adoni" Ison:
Edition 1 of 4

Commissioned by Prospect.6

*They Out There, Baby Myron Thibodeaux
Sr. & Jarvis Lewis of the Zulu Go Getters
Bertha's Place Bar & Restaurant, New
Orleans*, 2022, from the series *Vanishing
Black Bars & Lounges*, 2018-ongoing
Archival inkjet print
16 × 24 in.
Edition 1 of 6, 2 APs

*A Venerable Tradition, Footworkin' on a
Tepid Existence?*, 2022-2024, from the
series *Vanishing Black Bars & Lounges*,
2018-ongoing
Video, color, sound
27:24 min
Edition 1 of 4

*We Outchea, Thomas Pierce of the Zulus at
The Other Place Bar & Lounge* 2022,
from the series *Vanishing Black Bars &
Lounges*, 2018-ongoing
Archival inkjet print
16 × 24 in.
Edition 1 of 6, 2 APs

*When the Whole Bar is a Vibe, The Park,
Chicago*, 2024, from the series *Vanishing
Black Bars & Lounges*, 2018-ongoing
Archival inkjet print
16 × 27 in.
Edition 1 of 6, 2 APs

Commissioned by Prospect.6

*When Your Team is Losing, But You're
Still Winning (Tamila "Tammy" Pikes at
Licorice Lounge), Chicago*, 2024, from the
series *Vanishing Black Bars & Lounges*,
2018-ongoing
Archival inkjet print
18 × 24 in.
Edition 1 of 6, 2 APs

Commissioned by Prospect.6

*Who All Over There? (Licorice Lounge),
Chicago*, 2024, from the series *Vanishing
Black Bars & Lounges*, 2018-ongoing
Archival inkjet print
16 × 24 in.
Edition 1 of 6, 2 APs

Commissioned by Prospect.6

All works courtesy of the artist
Major support for this project was
provided by The Helis Foundation.
Additional support was provided by the
Norman and Emmy Lou Illges Foundation,
the Eugenie and Joseph Jones Family
Foundation, the Selley Foundation Fund,
the Ella West Freeman Foundation, and
the Keller Family Foundation

Nadia Huggins

Birds of Paradise, 2024
Digital photographs printed on fabric
Eight components: 164 × 55 in. each

Courtesy of the artist
Major support for this project was provided
by Pan-American Life Insurance Group
Commissioned by Prospect.6

Blas Isasi

1,001,532 CE, 2023-2024
Wood, steel, powder coat, modeling clay,
hair extensions, polystyrene foam,
unfired clay, spray paint, sand, and epoxy
Dimensions variable

Courtesy of the artist
Major support for this project was
provided by The Helis Foundation.
Additional support was provided by
the Eugenie and Joseph Jones Family
Foundation, the Selley Foundation Fund,
the Ella West Freeman Foundation, and
the Keller Family Foundation
Commissioned by Prospect.6

Deborah Jack

*a sea desalts, creeping in the collapse...in
the expanse...a rhizome looks for reason...
whispers an elegy instead*, 2024
Six-channel video, color, sound, 8:45 min.;
aluminum prints and vinyl
Display dimensions variable
Sound by Diaphanous Ensemble

Courtesy of the artist
Support for this project was provided by
the Dutch Culture USA program by the
Consulate General of the Netherlands in
New York and A Studio in the Woods
Commissioned by Prospect.6

**Eisa Jocson
Venuri Perera**

Magic Maids, 2024
Single-channel video, color, sound,
1:20:56 min.; salt, turmeric powder, chili
powder, chilies, lime, brooms, and red and
white strings
Display dimensions variable

Courtesy of the artists
Support for this project was provided by the
Dutch Culture USA program by the Consulate
General of the Netherlands in New York

Concept and performance by Eisa Jocson
and Venuri Perera; Technical Production
by Yap Seok Hui | ARTFACTORY; Music by
Soraya Bonaventure; Editing by Brandon
Relucio / *Magic Maids* is a production
of Künstler*innenhaus Mousonturm in
co-production with Frascati Producties
(supported by Ammodo), Tanzquartier Wien,
HAU Hebbel am Ufer, SPRING Performing
Arts Festival, Festival Theaterformen,
DDD - Festival Dias da Dança, Kampnagel,
Arsenic-Centre d'art scénique
contemporian, La briqueterie CDCN du
Val-de-Marne, Points Communs-nouvelle
scène nationale Cergy-Pontoise / Val d'Oise,
Maillon, Théâtre de Strasbourg—Scène
européenne and Esplanade—Theatres on
the Bay. Funded as part of the Alliance of
International Production Houses by the
Federal Government Commissioner for
Culture and Media and the Hessian Ministry
of Science and Research, Art and Culture.
This project was supported with residencies
by Kaserne Basel, Puón Institute Philippines,
Goethe-Institut Sri Lanka, Dance Nucleus
in collaboration with Studio Plesungan as
part of ARTEFACT Creative Residency, and
Colomboscope Contemporary Art Festival
2024. / With gratitude to the wonderful wise
working women who generously shared
their knowledge and stories with us.

Joan Jonas

stream or river, flight or pattern III, 2016/2017
Duration: 24:06 min.
Installation with three projected videos,
color, sound, fourteen China marker
drawings on boards, and ten handmade
paper kites
Dimensions variable

VIDEOS

stream or river, flight or pattern III (Shadows),
2016/2017
10:55 min.

*stream or river, flight or pattern III (Bird
Sequence)*, 2016/2017
14:59 min.

stream or river, flight or pattern III (Journey),
2016/2017
24:06 min.

All works courtesy of the artist and
Gladstone Gallery, New York
Support for this project was provided by
the Girlfriend Fund

Brian Jungen

*The way of the world is to bloom and to
flower and die but in the affairs of men there
is no waning and the noon of his expression
signals the onset of night*, 2024
250-year-old French colonial oak table from
Baton Rouge, wood arrows, carbon steel
points, feathers, and artificial sinew
64 × 75 ½ × 28 ½ in.

Courtesy of the artist
This project was made possible through
major funding from the Mellon Foundation
and the National Endowment for the Arts
Commissioned by Prospect.6

Arturo Kameya

Whatever comes first, 2024
Mixed media installation
Dimensions variable

INDIVIDUAL WORKS

El cuerpo es una culpa, 2024
Acrylic and clay powder on wood
Panel I: 25 ½ × 23 ⅝ × ½ in.;
panel 2: 17 ¾ × 15 ¾ × ½ in.

Gallinazos, 2024
Acrylic and clay powder on wood
19 ¾ × 17 ¾ × ½ in.

Juanetes, 2024
Acrylic and clay powder on wood
47 ¼ × 141 ¾ × ½ in.

Midnight Radio, 2024
Aluminum shelf with rotating
mechanism and found objects
Dimensions variable

Occupational Therapy, 2024
Acrylic and clay powder on wood
Dimensions variable

Plasticity, 2024
Acrylic and clay powder on wood
Panel I: 31 ½ × 25 ⅝ × ½ in.;
panel 2: 28 ¾ × 21 ⅝ × ½ in.;
panel 3: 19 ¾ × 13 × ½ in.

Pyramid I, 2024
Acrylic and clay powder on wood
19 ¾ × 17 ¾ × ½ in.

Pyramid II, 2024
Acrylic and clay powder on wood
25 ⅝ × 19 ¾ × ½ in.

Small fires, 2024
Prints on mesh
Two prints, 71 ⅝ × 55 ⅛ in. each

All works courtesy of the artist and and
GRIMM, Amsterdam, London, New York
Support for this project was provided by
the Dutch Culture USA program by the
Consulate General of the Netherlands in
New York
Commissioned by Prospect.6

Maia Ruth Lee

The Conveyor, 2024
Flat plate carousel, plastic tote trays,
mud, ceramic, found objects, rope, ink,
canvas, and mixed media sculptures
Dimensions variable

Courtesy of the artist
This project is presented in partnership
with Art Production Fund
Commissioned by Prospect.6

INDIVIDUAL WORKS

B.B. Check-in, 2023
Tarp, burlap, rope, tape, luggage,
used clothing, and bedding
Dimensions variable

Courtesy of the artist and
Tina Kim Gallery, New York
This project is presented in partnership
with Art Production Fund

B.B.Rope_Time Loop, 2024
Rope and india ink
192 × 210 in.

Courtesy of the artist and
François Ghebaly, Los Angeles & New York
This project is presented in partnership
with Art Production Fund

B.B.Time_Until Liberation I, 2024
Cardboard, canvas, foam, rope, and steel
26 × 107 × 28 ¼ in.

Courtesy of the artist and
François Ghebaly, Los Angeles & New York
This project is presented in partnership
with Art Production Fund

B.B.Time_Until Liberation 2, 2024
Cardboard, canvas, foam, rope, and steel
29 ¾ × 118 × 26 in.

Courtesy of the artist and
François Ghebaly, Los Angeles & New York
This project is presented in partnership
with Art Production Fund

Kelley-Ann Lindo

Send Love Inna Barrel (V), 2017–ongoing
Shipping barrels and metal chairs
Shippings barrels: 382 ½ × 24 in.
Chairs: 15 × 16 × 30 ¼ in.

Courtesy of the artist

Cathy Lu

Passages, 2024
Stoneware, glaze, and gold luster
232 × 158 × 62 in.

Courtesy of the artist
Support for this project was provided by the
National Endowment for the Arts
Commissioned by Prospect.6

Tessa Mars

In a barren land we make dew, 2024
Acrylic paint, canvas, papier-mâché, plaster
of paris, wire mesh, and PVC tubes
Four panels: 73 ¾ × 94 in. each
Sculptures: dimensions variable

Courtesy of the artist
Commissioned by Prospect.6

Jeffrey Meris

*Our Moons Shine, For All the Worlds to
See*, 2024
Proteus Maximus light and DMX electronics
Dimensions variable

Courtesy of the artist
This project was made possible through
major funding from the Mellon Foundation.
Additional major support provided by the
Charitable Arts Foundation and Lehmann
Maupin
Commissioned by Prospect.6

Joiri Minaya

*Fleurs de liberation: an ecology of resistance
(Cloaking of the Meilleur-Goldthwaite
House)*, 2024
Ink on vinyl fabric
Dimensions variable

Courtesy of the artist
This project was made possible through
major funding from VIA Art Fund and the
Mellon Foundation. Additional support was
provided by the Stephen Reily Family Fund
and the Graham Foundation for Advanced
Studies in the Fine Arts
Commissioned by Prospect.6

Meleko Mokgosi

Spaces of Subjection: Appellations, 2024
Inkjet and permanent marker on linen
Fifty panels
50 × 36 in. each

*Spaces of Subjection: Appellations
(Addendum I)*, 2024
Oil on canvas
96 × 72 in.

*Spaces of Subjection: Appellations
(Addendum II)*, 2024
Oil on canvas
96 × 72 in.

*Spaces of Subjection:
Appellations (Addendum III)*, 2024
Oil on canvas
Panel I: 152 × 108 in.; panel 2: 72 × 72 in.

*Spaces of Subjection: Appellations
(Addendum IV)*, 2024
Oil on canvas
50 × 36 in.

*Spaces of Subjection: Appellations
(Addendum V)*, 2024
Oil on canvas, framed
9 × 12 in.

All works courtesy of the artist and
Jack Shainman Gallery, New York
Support for this project was provided
by the National Endowment for the Arts
Commissioned by Prospect.6

Tuấn Andrew Nguyễn

In collaboration with Thảo Nguyễn
(performing music as THAO) and
Marion Hoàng Ngọc Hill

Amongst the Disquiet, 2024
Two-channel video installation,
color, stereo sound
50 min.

Courtesy of the artists and James Cohan,
New York. Support for this project was
provided by Duettist and the New Orleans
Tourism and Culture Fund
Commissioned by Prospect.6

Karyn Olivier

Drift (Tributary), 2023
Single-channel video, color, sound
12:31 min.

Sampling (Need You), 2023
Sixteen construction barriers, fifteen-
channel audio, amplifiers, and speakers
Approx. 294 ½ × 17 × 124 ½ in.
12:30 min.

Winter hung to dry, 2003
Winter clothes and line
Dimensions variable

All works courtesy of the artist and Tanya Bonakdar Gallery, New York & Los Angeles

Ruth Owens

Black Delight, An Ecopoem, 2024
Four-channel video installation with original soundtrack
14:02 min.

Courtesy of the artist
Major support for this project was provided by The Helis Foundation. Additional support was provided by the Eugenie and Joseph Jones Family Foundation, the Selley Foundation Fund, the Ella West Freeman Foundation, the Keller Family Foundation, and the National Endowment for the Arts
Commissioned by Prospect.6

Credits / Dancers: Elise Barnes, Sonata Yazmeen, Joshua Bell, Necai Byrd, De'Von Favorite, Daniel Gray, Anjanaé Hassell, Lauren Hughes, Amari James, Myrtle Croson, Emma Lean, Matthew Lee, Nondi, Melani Martinez, Adrian Peters, Amaya Smith, Jelani Smith, Johari Smith, Isadora Yassir, Florence H. Young / Music: Water Seed, "Dance Until The Dawn" (2021); Erika Flowers, "Magikal" (2018); Anjelika "Jelly" Joseph feat. HaSizzle, "Fya" (2022); Sava Wolf, "My Name Is Sava Wolf" (2021) / Narration: "Danse Africaine" (1922) by Langston Hughes, read by Zandashé L'Orelia Brown; Additional narration by Johari Smith, Jelani Smith, and Necai Byrd / Crew: Director and Editor: Ruth Owens; Producer, Assistant Editor and Assistant Camera, Environment: Varvara Degtiarenko; Producer: Kelsey Scult; Director of Photography, Dance: Bron Moyi; Director of Photography, Environment: Ben Depp; Dance Coordinator: Chanice Holmes; Music Supervisor: Brandon Lattimore; Sound Designer: Lee Garcia; Supplemental Sound Designer: Sasha Masakowski; Production Sound Mixer: Derek Roque; Colorist: Bradley Greer, Kyotocolor; VFX: Alexander Wiltz; First Assistant Director: Charles Jones; First Camera Assistant: Noell Dominick; Second Camera Assistant: Justin Thomas; Chief Lighting Technician: Mason McGuire; Key Grip: Thaddeus Mitchell; Wallpaper Design: Dina Cintura, Women Who Wallpaper; Costume Design: Christine M. Hamilton; Hair and Makeup: Niala Howard; Catering: Chef G. Adriane; Production Assistant: Fred Olaleye; BTS Photographer: Jay Falice; Archival Footage Research Assistant: Bianca Walker; Filmed with Panavision® Cameras and Lenses; Boat Charter: Delta Discovery Tours; Captain: Richie Blink / Archival Footage: Owens Home Movie Archive; Kinolibrary Film Collection; Historic Films Archive; Internet Archive; Southside Movie Project; Pond 5; Chicago Film Archives; Shutterstock / Special Thanks: Prospect New Orleans; Wandering Cameras, LLC

Ada M. Patterson

the hammeress in a state of disgrace, 2024
Acid dye and india ink on pongee silk
102 ⅜ × 55 ⅛ in.

the hammeress in a state of disgrace, 2024
Acid dye on pongee silk
102 ⅜ × 55 ⅛ in.

the hammeress in a state of disgrace, 2024
Acid dye, india ink, and acrylic on pongee silk
102 ⅜ × 55 ⅛ in.

the hammeress in a state of disgrace, 2024
Acid dye on pongee silk
102 ⅜ × 55 ⅛ in.

the hammeress in a state of disgrace, 2024
Acid dye on pongee silk
102 ⅜ × 55 ⅛ in.

the hammeress in a state of disgrace, 2024
Digital video, sound
6:23 min.

All works courtesy of the artist and Copperfield, London
Support for this project was provided by the Dutch Culture USA program by the Consulate General of the Netherlands in New York
Commissioned by Prospect.6

Brooke Pickett

How To Make Drinkable Water Out Of Air, 2024
Oil on canvas
60 × 84 in.

A Perpetual Search For The Perfect Place, 2024
Oil on canvas
72 × 96 in.

A Powerful Transmitter, 2024
Oil on canvas
60 × 84 in.

Retrofitted, 2024
Oil on canvas
60 × 84 in.

Structural Solutions, 2024
Oil on canvas
72 × 96 in.

Survival Soup, 2024
Oil on canvas
72 × 96 in.

What To Eat, What To Drink, What To Leave For Poison, 2024
Oil on canvas
72 × 96 in.

All works courtesy of the artist
Major support for this project was provided by The Helis Foundation. Additional support was provided by the Eugenie and Joseph Jones Family Foundation, the Selley Foundation Fund, the Ella West Freeman Foundation, and the Keller Family Foundation
Commissioned by Prospect.6

Marcel Pinas

AFAKA BUKU, 2024
Corten steel
Fifty-six sculptures: dimensions variable

Courtesy of the artist
Commissioned by Prospect.6

Stephanie Syjuco

Phantom Visions (The Lacustrine Village of St. Malo), 2024
Wheat pasted digital print on paper
Dimensions variable

Courtesy of the artist
Support for this project was provided by the National Endowment for the Arts
Commissioned by Prospect.6

Dewey Tafoya

Metl, 2024
Serigraph on amate paper, gold leaf, vegetable-tanned cowhide, waxed thread, metal eyelets, steel scroll box, and adobe tiles
192 × 48 in.

Milli, 2024
Serigraph on amate paper, gold leaf, vegetable-tanned cowhide, waxed thread, metal eyelets, steel scroll box, and adobe tiles
192 × 48 in.

Tlalli, 2024
Serigraph on amate paper, gold leaf, vegetable-tanned cowhide, waxed thread, metal eyelets, steel scroll box, and adobe tiles
192 × 48 in.

All works courtesy of the artist
This project was made possible through major funding from the Mellon Foundation
Commissioned by Prospect.6

Ashley Teamer

Claiborne at the Epoch, 2024
Inkjet prints, thread, canvas, acrylic felt, velcro, and zippers
70 × 94 in.

Courtesy of the artist
Major support for this project was provided by The Helis Foundation. Additional support was provided by the Eugenie and Joseph Jones Family Foundation, the Selley Foundation Fund, the Ella West Freeman Foundation, and the Keller Family Foundation
Commissioned by Prospect.6

Claiborne: The Next Millennia, 2024
Inkjet prints, thread, canvas, acrylic felt, and velcro
70 × 66 in.

Courtesy of the artist
Major support for this project was provided by The Helis Foundation. Additional support was provided by the Eugenie and Joseph Jones Family Foundation, the Selley Foundation Fund, the Ella West Freeman Foundation, and the Keller Family Foundation
Commissioned by Prospect.6

Tambourine Cypress, 2024
Enamel and powder coat on steel, brass, cymbals, and wind chimes
Approx. 186 × 148 × 110 in.

This sculpture was co-commissioned by Prospect New Orleans for Prospect.6: *The Future Is Present, The Harbinger Is Home* and Arts New Orleans for the City of New Orleans Percent for Art Program. Additional support for the commission was provided by the Eugenie and Joseph Jones Family Foundation, the Selley Foundation Fund, the Ella West Freeman Foundation, and the Keller Family Foundation

Clarissa Tossin

Future Geography: Cassiopeia A Supernova, 2024
Used Amazon.com delivery boxes, archival inkjet print on photo paper with lamination, and wood
61 ½ × 56 × 1 ½ in.

Courtesy of the artist
Commissioned by Prospect.6

Future Geography: The Five Galaxies of Stephan's Quintet, 2022
Used Amazon.com delivery boxes, archival inkjet print on photo paper with lamination, and wood
66 × 82 ½ × 1 ½ in.

Courtesy of the artist and Commonwealth and Council, Los Angeles
Commissioned by the Frye Art Museum for the exhibition *Clarissa Tossin: to take root among the stars*, October 7, 2023 – January 7, 2024

Future Geography: Rho Ophiuchi Cloud Complex, 2023
Used Amazon.com delivery boxes, archival inkjet print on photo paper with lamination, and wood
57 ¼ × 64 ¾ × 1 ½ in.

Courtesy of the artist and Commonwealth and Council, Los Angeles

Future Geography: Tarantula Nebula, 2024
Used Amazon.com delivery boxes, archival inkjet print on photo paper with lamination, and wood
45 ¾ × 75 × 1 ½ in.

Courtesy of the artist
Commissioned by Prospect.6

We are stardust, 2024
Dye-sublimation print on chiffon
Eighty-six flags: dimensions variable

Courtesy of the artist
Commissioned by Prospect.6

Arlette Quỳnh-Anh Trần

The Curator Ghost, 2024
Single-channel video, color, sound
17:49 min.

Courtesy of the artist
Commissioned by Prospect.6

Tuan Mami

Can This Plant Invade The Land?, 2022
Black-and-white video, silent
10:10 min.

Courtesy of the artist

Endless Home, 2024
Ten speakers, ten 'Nón Lá' (Vietnamese traditional hats), ten interviews
Durations vary
Dimensions variable

Courtesy of the artist
Commissioned by Prospect.6

Myth East Mist, 2015
Video, color, sound
16:16 min.

Courtesy of the artist

'Ngàn Dặm' THOUSAND MILES, 2024
Video, color, sound
11:51 min.

Courtesy of the artist
Commissioned by Prospect.6

Seeding the Future, 2024
Table, collected Vietnamese seeds, clay, and wall drawing with clay
Dimensions variable

Courtesy of the artist
Made in collaboration with VIET (Vietnamese Initiatives in Economic Training) Community Resource Center
Commissioned by Prospect.6

A Silent Process, 2023–2024
Three-channel video installation, color, sound
Duration varies
Videography by Tuan Mami and Chen Kuan Yu; Stage Design by Joyce Ho

Courtesy of the artist

Survival Plant, 2023
Video, color, sound
21:10 min.

Courtesy of the artist

Didier William

Gesture to Home, 2024
Acrylic on panel, ink, and carving on sculpting epoxy
Dimensions variable

Courtesy of the artist
Support for this project was provided by the Ed Bradley Family Foundation
Commissioned by Prospect.6

Amanda Williams

In Her Rich Deposits of (Blue), 2024
Carver Innovation Blue Casein Paint
Dimensions variable

Courtesy of the artist
This project was made possible through major funding from the Mellon Foundation. Additional support was provided by the Joyce Foundation and the Graham Foundation
Commissioned by Prospect.6

Yee I-Lann

Tepo Aniya Nombor Na (Mat with a Number), 2020
Bajau Sama Dilaut pandanus weave with commercial chemical dye
144 × 168 in.
Weaving by Sanah Belasani, Kinnuhong Gundasali, Noraidah Jabarah (Kak Budi), Roziah Binti Jalalid, Darwisa Binti Omar, Adik Enidah, Dela Binti Annerati, Adik Asima, Dayang Binti Tularan, Tasya Binti Tularan, Adik Alisya, and Erna Binti Tekki

Courtesy of the artist and Silverlens, Manila & New York
Support for this project was provided by the National Endowment for the Arts

Exhibition Venues

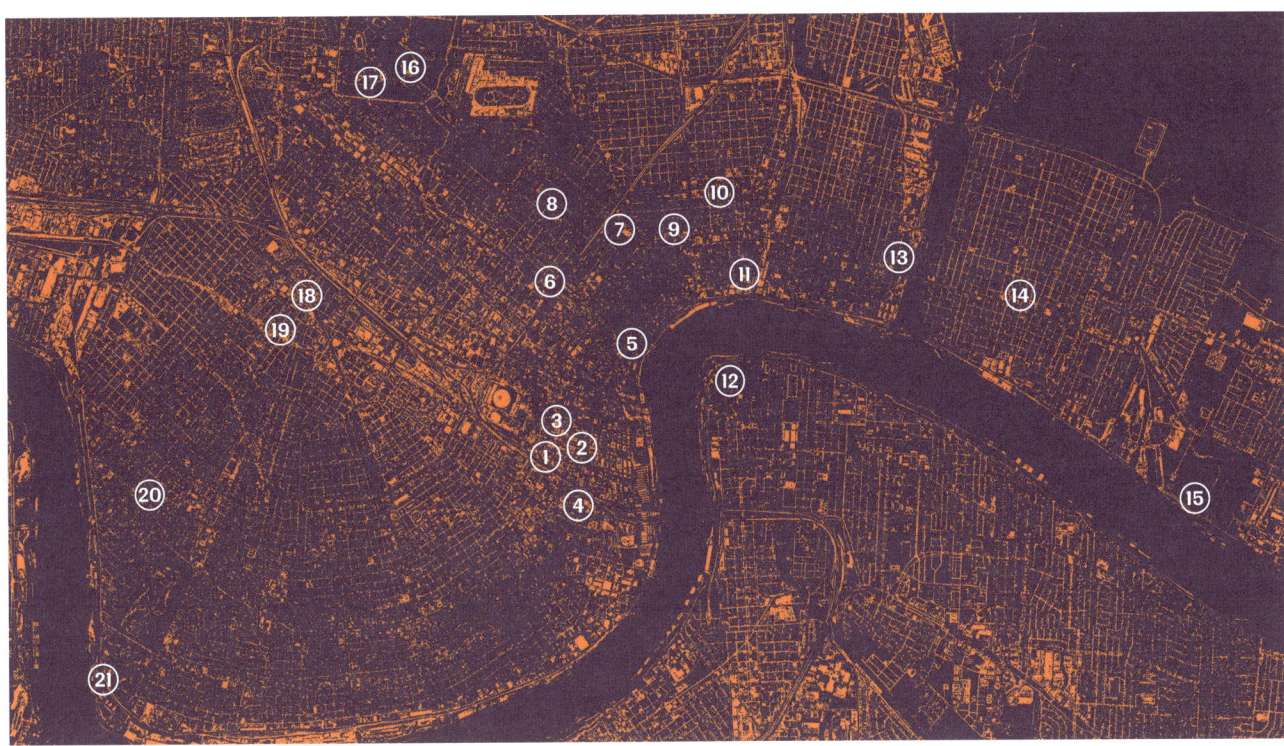

1   Ogden Museum of Southern Art
⊙ 925 Camp Street
   New Orleans, LA 70130
▷ Downtown/CBD

Ewan Atkinson
Thomas Deaton
L. Kasimu Harris
Joan Jonas
Brian Jungen
Tessa Mars
Ada M. Patterson
Brooke Pickett
Ashley Teamer

Located in the vibrant Warehouse Arts District of downtown New Orleans, Louisiana, Ogden Museum of Southern Art holds the largest and most comprehensive collection of Southern art and is recognized for its original exhibitions, public events and educational programs that examine the development of visual art alongside Southern traditions of music, literature, and culinary heritage to provide a comprehensive story of the South. Established in 1999, and in Stephen Goldring Hall at 925 Camp Street since 2003, Ogden Museum welcomes almost 85,000 visitors annually, and attracts diverse audiences through its broad range of programming including exhibitions, lectures, film screenings, and concerts, which are all part of its mission to broaden the knowledge, understanding, interpretation and appreciation of the visual arts and culture of the American South.

2   Contemporary Arts Center, New Orleans (CAC)
⊙ 900 Camp Street
   New Orleans, LA 70130
▷ Downtown/CBD

Shannon Alonzo
Eddie Rodolfo Aparicio
Andrea Carlson
Hannah Chalew
Myrlande Constant
Christopher Cozier
Christian Việt Đinh
Jeannette Ehlers
Abdi Farah
Cathy Lu
Meleko Mokgosi
Ruth Owens
Stephanie Syjuco
Yee I-Lann

The Contemporary Arts Center, New Orleans is a touchstone for Contemporary Art in New Orleans and the Gulf South, enhancing connections between artists and communities and providing a forum for ideas and the exploration of a just society through artistic creation, public engagement, and institutional practice.

3   Harmony Circle
⊙ Harmony Circle
   New Orleans, LA 70130
▷ Downtown/CBD

Raúl de Nieves

Formerly known as Lee Circle, the roundabout that connects New Orleans's Central Business District and the Lower Garden District was originally named Tivoli Circle and consecrated as a park in 1807. The original name derives from the legendary beauty of the centuries-old gardens in Lazio, Italy, and is usually associated with public garden parks in Europe. In 1884, a monument was erected to Confederate General Robert E. Lee by the Robert E. Lee Monumental Association and the location's name was changed to Lee Circle.

In 2017, Mayor Mitch Landrieu ordered the removal of the bronze statue of Lee from the sixty foot tall pedestal along with three other Confederate monuments across the city. New Orleans's city council voted to give the circle two names in 2022. The circle itself retains the historic name, Tivoli Circle, while the grassy park area within was renamed Harmony Circle.

4   Hancock Whitney Welcome Center at Merchant House
⊙ 1150 Magazine Street
   New Orleans, LA 70130
▷ Downtown/CBD

Ronald Cyrille aka B.Bird

The Hancock Whitney Welcome Center at Merchant House served as a hub for Prospect.6: *The Future Is Present, The Harbinger Is Home*, the sixth iteration of the city-wide art exhibition Prospect New Orleans. The Center also featured a shop for Prospect.6 exhibition guides and other P.6 merchandise.

5 The Historic New Orleans Collection (HNOC)
⊙ 520 Royal Street
   New Orleans, LA 70130
▷ French Quarter

Didier William

The Historic New Orleans Collection (HNOC) is a museum, research center, and publisher dedicated to the stewardship of the history and culture of New Orleans and the Gulf South.

Founded in 1966 through the estates of General L. Kemper Williams and Mrs. Leila Moore Williams, HNOC has helped local residents and visiting tourists better understand the multicultural history of the region through thought-provoking exhibitions; original books, periodicals, and articles; and its public research center. In addition, it offers a robust programming schedule and an extensive array of educational resources for teachers and students of all levels.

6 Lemann Park & Playground
⊙ 628 N Claiborne Avenue
   New Orleans, LA 70112
▷ Tremé

Ashley Teamer

The 2017 Parks Build Community initiative transformed a vacant parcel of land, located on the historic Lafitte Greenway, into a vibrant public gathering space and playground now known as Lemann Park.

7 New Orleans African American Museum (NOAAM)
⊙ 1418 Governor Nicholls Street
   New Orleans, LA 70116
▷ Tremé

Abigail DeVille
Joiri Minaya
Amanda Williams

The New Orleans African American Museum is located in the Tremé section of New Orleans, a neighborhood that was home to the nation's largest, most prosperous and politically progressive community of Black people by the mid-1850s. In the eighteenth century, the land was occupied by the Morand Plantation and brickyard, which was later acquired by hat maker and real estate developer Claude Tremé. In 1810, Tremé sold the land to the city of New Orleans, and it became home to many free persons of color. Today, NOAAM preserves the history and elevates the art, culture, and contributions of African Americans in New Orleans and the African diaspora through exhibitions and community engagement.

8 Alone Time Gallery
⊙ 2338 Barracks Street
   New Orleans, LA 70119
▷ Tremé

Arturo Kameya

Founded by Sheila Santamaria, Alone Time Gallery is an artist-run space for people to express themselves and have a good time.

9 Sweet Lorraine's Jazz Club
⊙ 1931 Saint Claude Avenue
   New Orleans, LA 70116
▷ 7th Ward

L. Kasimu Harris

A true community cornerstone, Sweet Lorraine's Jazz Club, owned by Paul Sylvester, has been offering live music and entertainment just outside the French Quarter for over thirty years. Since the 1940s, for three generations Paul Sylvester's family has owned an assortment of restaurants and clubs around the 7th ward including Melvina's & Lorraine's Garden of Joy, Sylvester's Seafood & Restaurant, The Circle Bar, Lorraine's Lounge, and Lorraine's Dugout which is the current location of Sweet Lorraine's.

Sweet Lorraine's is Sylvester's love letter to jazz culture and to his mother Lorraine. Since the club's rechristening and opening in September 1999, Sweet Lorraine's has hosted musicians from the local, national, and international jazz scene. It has also been the clubhouse of the social aid and pleasure club, the Black Men of Labor.

10 UNO St. Claude Gallery
⊙ 2429 Saint Claude Avenue
   New Orleans, LA 70117
▷ 8th Ward

Deborah Jack

The University of New Orleans, School of the Arts Gallery on St. Claude is a singular aspect of the university among other institutions of higher education in the city; UNO is the only local university to maintain an off-campus art gallery. Situated in the St. Claude Arts District, it is in a unique position of community outreach to its neighborhood, as well as other institutions and organizations in the fields of the arts. In this light, it is an asset to the university, in its mission to advance shared knowledge and add to our region's culture and economy.

As a nonprofit academic resource, the gallery culturally enriches the metropolitan area with presentations of contemporary visual arts. It shows research, experimentation, and individual expression in an academic environment. It represents the visual arts at UNO to the city and to its peer institutions.

11 New Orleans Center for Creative Arts (NOCCA) and Press Street Railroad Yards
⊙ Corner of Royal Street
   and Homer Plessy Way
   New Orleans, LA 70117
▷ Marigny

Abigail DeVille
Stephanie Syjuco

Founded in 1973, New Orleans Center for Creative Arts is a regional, pre-professional arts training center that offers students intensive instruction in culinary arts, dance, media arts: filmmaking & audio production, music (classical, jazz, vocal), theatre arts (drama, musical theatre, theatre design), visual arts, and creative writing, while demanding simultaneous academic excellence.

NOCCA's campus sits on the site where, on June 7, 1892, a 30-year-old African American man named Homer Plessy attempted to board a segregated train car at Press and Royal Streets in New Orleans. Louisiana's Separate Car Act, passed in 1890, required that rail passengers be segregated. A group of New Orleanians called the Comite' des Citoyens had selected Plessy to build a case to challenge the law, but the US Supreme Court upheld Louisiana's segregation law. Plessy v. Ferguson ultimately became known as the "separate but equal" law that was overturned in 1954 with Brown v. Board of Education.

12 Algiers Point
⊙ 200 Patterson Street
   New Orleans, LA 70114
▷ Algiers Point

Abigail DeVille
Jeffrey Meris

First settled by the French in 1719 and annexed by the city of New Orleans in 1870, Algiers Point is the second oldest neighborhood in New Orleans. The land was initially settled as the Company Plantation, named for the private enterprise (Company of the West, later Indies) that was granted a commercial monopoly to develop Louisiana. For the following century this land functioned chiefly as a commodity plantation and as a jail compound for enslaved Africans, who were either sold or forced to work locally. During the nineteenth century the neighborhood and its shipping and railroad industry rapidly developed. In 1895 a fire destroyed most structures on Algiers Point. Most of the neighborhood's signature late-Victorian architecture was built in 1896.

Algiers Point is located across the Mississippi River from the French Quarter. Take a short ferry ride or the Crescent City Connection bridge to discover the neighborhood's historic architecture and stroll the Jazz Walk of Fame.

13 Music Box Village
⊙ 4557 N Rampart Street
New Orleans, LA 70117
▷ Upper 9th Ward

Abigail DeVille
Stephanie Syjuco

The Music Box Village is New Orleans Airlift's ongoing experiment in "musical architecture". With over sixteen "musical houses"to date, the outdoor sonic sculpture garden is both an interactive art-site and a performance platform for one-of-a-kind concerts, artist residencies, and interdisciplinary works.

14 5523 Saint Claude Avenue
⊙ 5523 Saint Claude Avenue
New Orleans, LA 70117
▷ Lower 9th Ward

Stephanie Syjuco

Once a Family Dollar, 5523 Saint Claude has also been home to a free store and event space for artists, community organizers, and performers run by the Greater New Orleans Caring Collective.

15 Ford Motor Plant
⊙ 7200 N Peters Street
Arabi, LA 70032
▷ Arabi

Zalika Azim
Teresa Baker
Mel Chin
Jeannette Ehlers
rafa esparza
Blas Isasi
Eisa Jocson
Maia Ruth Lee
Kelley-Ann Lindo
Karyn Olivier
Venuri Perera
Dewey Tafoya

In the early twentieth century, Henry Ford built assembly plants and factories throughout the US. Just east of New Orleans, Arabi provided an ideal location to export cars to Central and South America and offered easy access to railroad lines and the Mississippi River. Assembly operations began in Arabi in 1923. At peak production, as many as 1,000 workers turned out 300 cars per day until 1933. The plant has served at different intervals as a parts and distribution center for American and Japanese cars, and as a storage facility for the US Army, coffee and twine shipments, and most recently, the film industry.

16 New Orleans Museum of Art (NOMA) Sydney and Walda Besthoff Sculpture Garden Sculpture Pavilion
⊙ I Collins Diboll Circle
New Orleans, LA 70124
▷ Mid-City

Tuấn Andrew Nguyễn

The Sydney and Walda Besthoff Sculpture Garden occupies approximately eleven acres in City Park adjacent to the New Orleans Museum of Art. Atypical of most sculpture gardens, this garden is located within a mature existing landscape of pines, magnolias, and live oaks surrounding two lagoons. The garden design creates outdoor viewing spaces within this picturesque landscape. Originally conceived in 2003, the Sculpture Garden doubled in size in 2019 and has grown to include more than 90 sculptures and a sculpture pavilion.

17 The Peristyle at City Park
⊙ 42 Dreyfous Drive
New Orleans, LA 70124
▷ Mid-City

Nadia Huggins

In 1907, architect Paul Andry created this neo-classical pavilion with a colonnade as a venue to dance en plein air. Today, the Peristyle overlooks the picturesque Bayou Metairie and is one of the most popular venues in City Park.

18 Xavier University of Louisiana Art Gallery
⊙ I Drexel Drive
New Orleans, LA 70125
▷ Gert Town

Tuan Mami

Xavier University of Louisiana's Art Collections and Gallery's primary mission is to increase the knowledge and understanding of our diverse global contemporary culture through the micro-lens of the vast visual histories and cosmologies of the descendant communities of Louisiana. The Art Collections and Gallery believes in the power of art to change communities. It facilitates this transformation through the organization and production of exhibitions, publications, educational materials, conferences, lectures, workshops and other public programs, with a particular emphasis on the study, presentation, preservation and promotion of art produced by Louisiana-based artists and artists of African descent throughout the world.

19 Xavier University of Louisiana Art Village
⊙ 3500 Pine Street
New Orleans, LA 70125
▷ Gert Town

Stephanie Syjuco
Amanda Williams

The Art Village is home to Xavier University of Louisiana's Department of Art and Performance Studies. The Department fosters a dynamic learning environment where students can realize their creative potential. Students develop skills in both traditional and contemporary artistic practices through a blend of studio work, seminars, and theory. Majors and minors gain valuable experience in visual art, culture, and communication.

20 Newcomb Art Museum of Tulane University
⊙ Woldenberg Art Center
6823 Saint Charles Avenue
New Orleans, LA 70118
▷ Uptown

Bethany Collins
Clarissa Tossin
Arlette Quỳnh-Anh Trần

The Newcomb Art Museum of Tulane University builds on the Newcomb College legacy of education, social enterprise, and artistic experience. Presenting inspiring exhibitions and programs that engage communities both on and off campus, the Museum fosters the creative exchange of ideas and cross-disciplinary collaborations around innovative art and design. The Museum preserves and advances scholarship on the Newcomb and Tulane art collections.

21 The Batture
⊙ 25 Walnut Street
New Orleans, LA 70118
▷ Uptown

Andrea Carlson
Christopher Cozier
Marcel Pinas

In New Orleans, the Batture refers to the alluvial land between the low-tide of the Mississippi and the levee. The word "batture" comes from the French word "to beat," referring to the land "beaten" by the river. As the Mississippi River moves on its way to the Gulf of Mexico, it leaves behind deposits of land which, over time, form the batture.

In the 1800s, the Bisso family from Genoa, Italy, began five generations of maritime operations on the Batture at the foot of Walnut Street. Currently a heavy industrial yard between Walnut and Lowerline Street, this space is slated to be revitalized as a ten-acre park. This new oasis will center around a sprawling lawn and food and drink options from local chefs.

Contributor Biographies

SUSAN BRENNAN CO-ARTISTIC DIRECTORS

Miranda Lash

is the Ellen Bruss Chief Curator at the Museum of Contemporary Art Denver. Lash's recent museum exhibitions include *Suki Seokyeong Kang: Mountain—Hour—Face* (2025), co-organized with Leilani Lynch; *Cowboy* (2023), co-organized with Nora Burnett Abrams; the traveling midcareer survey *Tomashi Jackson: Across the Universe* (2023); and *Clarissa Tossin: Falling from Earth* (2022). In 2016 Lash and Trevor Schoonmaker co-organized the acclaimed group exhibition *Southern Accent: Seeking the American South in Contemporary Art*. In 2014 Lash organized the traveling retrospective *Mel Chin: Rematch*. From 2008 to 2014, Lash was the founding curator of modern and contemporary art at the New Orleans Museum of Art. She currently serves on the board of the Joan Mitchell Foundation and was a 2022 fellow with the Center for Curatorial Leadership.

Ebony G. Patterson

is an artist with an expansive practice that addresses visibility and invisibility, through explorations of class, race, gender, youth culture, pageantry and acts of violence in the context of "postcolonial" spaces. With the strong sensibility of a painter, Patterson works across multiple media including tapestry, photography, video, sculpture, drawing, and installation. Patterson has taught at the University of Virginia, Edna Manley College School of Visual and Performing Arts, University of Kentucky, and was a visiting professor at the School of the Art Institute of Chicago. Her work is in the public collections of Los Angeles County Museum of Art, Nasher Museum at Duke University, National Gallery of Jamaica, Pérez Art Museum Miami, Studio Museum in Harlem, the Whitney Museum of American Art, among others. In 2021 Patterson was included in both the Liverpool and Athens Biennials. She lives and works in Chicago, IL and Kingston, Jamaica and is co-represented by Monique Meloche Gallery, and Hales New York/London. Patterson is the recipient of the 2023 David C. Driskell Prize and is a 2024 MacArthur Fellow.

CATALOGUE ESSAYISTS AND POETS

Antawan I. Byrd

is Assistant Professor in art history at Northwestern University, Evanston, and Associate Curator of Photography and Media at the Art Institute of Chicago. His recent curatorial projects include shows on the work of Kader Attia (2017), Sanlé Sory (2018), the Medu Art Ensemble (2019), and Mimi Cherono Ng'ok (2021). Byrd was a curator for the Lagos Biennial of Contemporary Art (2019), and the Bamako Encounters, Biennial of African Photography (2015). From 2009–2011, he was a Fulbright fellow and Curatorial Assistant at the Center for Contemporary Art, Lagos. Byrd is currently co-curating a survey exhibition on Pan-African art and culture opening in December 2024 at the Art Institute.

Lora Ann Chaisson

is the Principal Chief of the United Houma Nation, and the Southeast Regional Alternate Vice President on the National Congress of American Indians Executive Committee. She is a founding member of the Workforce Grantmaking in Native Nations & Communities Committee. In addition, Chief Chaisson serves on the executive boards of the American Indian Alaska Native Tourism Association, the United States Department of Labor Native American Employment and Training Council, the Inter-Tribal Council of LA / Institute for Indian Development and StrongHearts. She is an alumnus of the American Indian Opportunity Ambassador Program and is Vice-President of Tribal Solutions Group.

Dr. Joshua Lewis

is a systems ecologist and geographer based at Tulane University in New Orleans. His research is focused on the ecological and political dimensions of infrastructure planning, water management, and climate adaptation along urbanized coastlines. Previously he has worked at the Stockholm Resilience Centre, KTH Swedish Royal Institute of Technology, and African Centre for Cities at the University of Cape Town. The overall aim of his research and civic participation is to support, grow, and strengthen democratic decision-making to address environmental and social dilemmas facing coastal communities.

Ada Limón

is the author of six books of poetry, including *The Carrying*, which won the National Book Critics Circle Award for Poetry. Her most recent book of poetry, *The Hurting Kind*, was shortlisted for the Griffin Poetry Prize. She is the 24th Poet Laureate of the United States, the recipient of a MacArthur Fellowship, and a *TIME* magazine woman of the year. As the Poet Laureate, her signature project is called *You Are Here* and focuses on how poetry can help connect us to the natural world. Her first books for children include *In Praise of Mystery* and *And, Too, the Fox*.

Kei Miller

is the author of eleven books that range across genres—fiction, nonfiction, and poetry. He is interested both in the movement between genres and between creative writing and literary scholarship. In 2014 he won the Forward Prize for Poetry for *The Cartographer Tries to Map a Way to Zion*, his novel *Augustown* won the Bocas Prize for Caribbean Literature, and his collection of essays, *Things I Have Withheld* was shortlisted for the Baillie Gifford Prize. He has also written several essays of literary scholarship in the field of Caribbean literature. Miller joined the English faculty at the University of Miami in 2021. He previously taught in the UK at the Universities of Exeter, London, and Glasgow. Miller has an MA in Creative Writing from Manchester Metropolitan University and a PhD in English literature from the University of Glasgow.

Karisma Price

is a native New Orleanian, and is an assistant professor of English at Tulane University. A poet and screenwriter, she is the author of *I'm Always So Serious* (Sarabande Books, 2023) which was a *New York Times* Editors' Choice Pick. Her work has appeared in publications including *Poetry*, *Indiana Review*, *Academy of American Poets Poem-A-Day Series*, and elsewhere. She is a Cave Canem Fellow, was awarded the 2020 J. Howard and Barbara M. J. Wood Prize from the Poetry Foundation and is the 2023 winner of the Stanley Kunitz Memorial Prize from the *American Poetry Review*. She holds an MFA in poetry from New York University.

Quintron

has been inventing electronic gadgets and creating genre-defying noise, soundscape, and house rocking dance music in New Orleans for over twenty years, much of it in collaboration with artist / puppeteer Panacea Theriac aka Miss Pussycat. He is a Grammy-nominated songwriter with dozens of full-length albums, as well as a frequent collaborator with a wide swath of the American musical landscape, including The Oblivians, Steve Riley and the Mamou Playboys, and New Orleans RnB legend Ernie K-Doe. Quintron continues to live and work in New Orleans, Louisiana, as well as touring, teaching, and lecturing in this world and beyond.

Maurice Carlos Ruffin

is the author of national bestseller, *The American Daughters*, as well as *The Ones Who Don't Say They Love You*, a One Book One New Orleans selection, which was longlisted for the Story Prize. His debut, *We Cast a Shadow*, was a finalist for the PEN/Faulkner Award, the Dayton Literary Peace Prize, and the PEN America Open Book Prize. All three books were *New York Times* Editor's Choice selections. Ruffin is the winner of the Iowa Review Award in fiction and the Louisiana Writer Award. Ruffin is an associate professor of creative writing at Louisiana State University.

CATALOGUE CONTRIBUTORS

Emily Alesandrini

is an independent curator, art historian, and writer working in New Orleans and New York. Her research concerns contemporary representations of race and gender with a particular focus on issues of opacity, ornament, and the diasporic body in art by women and artists of color. Alesandrini has contributed to exhibitions and publications at the Studio Museum in Harlem, the Contemporary Arts Center in New Orleans, the Ford Foundation Gallery, and the Elizabeth Foundation for the Arts. She earned her BA at Smith College and is a doctoral candidate in art history at Bryn Mawr College.

Grace Aneiza Ali

is a Guyanese-born curator and assistant professor in the Department of Art and Art History at Florida State University and an Andrew W. Mellon Foundation Fellow at the Huntington Museum in Los Angeles. As a curator-scholar of contemporary art of the Global South, her curatorial practice examines the nexus of art and migration. Her book, *Liminal Spaces: Migration and Women of the Guyanese Diaspora* explores the art and migration narratives of women of Guyanese heritage. Ali serves as Editor-in-Chief of the College Art Associations' *Art Journal Open* and on the International Board of Advisors for *British Art Studies*.

Dr. Jordan Amirkhani

is curator and head of research and project development at Rivers Institute for Contemporary Art & Thought in New Orleans. Amirkhani has written scholarship and essays on the work of various contemporary artists, and her work has been featured in national and international publications, including: *The Paris Review Daily*, *Art in America*, *Mousse*, *Baltimore Arts*, *Boston Art Review*, *X-Tra*, and *Burnaway. org*. Her emphasis on contextualizing contemporary art and artists working in the American South garnered her a prestigious Creative Capital/The Andy Warhol Foundation "Short-Form" Writing Grant in 2017 and three nominations for the Rabkin Prize in Arts Journalism in 2017, 2018, and 2019.

Adrian Anagnost

is associate professor of art history and core faculty of the Stone Center for Latin American Studies at Tulane University. Anagnost's writings, on contemporary art, landscape, and the persistence of colonial spatiality in modern architecture and urbanism of Brazil and the US, have appeared in *Design Issues*, *Modernism/modernity*, *Konsthistorisk tidskrift*, *revue d'art Canadienne*, and *Journal of Global South Studies*. Anagnost was co-leader of a 2021–2022 Mellon Sawyer Seminar, which explored approaches to art, memory work, and activism surrounding the continued spatial legacies of slavery and colonialism across the Gulf South, Latin America, Canada, and the Caribbean.

Jovante Anderson

is a scholar and community organizer whose work focuses on queer and trans aesthetics and politics in the Caribbean. He is a PhD candidate at the University of Miami in the department of English and his work has been supported by grants and fellowships from the American Ethnological Society, the Center for Global Black Studies, the Nomadic Archivist Project, and the Carter G. Woodson Institute, where he is completing his dissertation on the cultural and political histories of pornography in Jamaica. Anderson was the first co-recipient of the Poet Laureate of Jamaica Young Writers' Prize for Poetry in 2018.

Camille Gallogly Bacon

is a Chicago-based writer and the co-editor-in-chief of *Jupiter Magazine*. She is cultivating a "sweet Black writing life" as informed by the words of poet Nikky Finney and the infinite wisdom of the Black feminist tradition more broadly. Her practice is invested in illuminating the wayward ingenuity of the Black creative spirit and excavating how aesthetics can catalyze a collective reorientation towards relation, connection, and intimacy and away from apathy and amnesia.

Laura Blereau

is a Louisiana native curator and writer. Her work explores art and technology, feminism, and social history. Based at the Newcomb Art Museum of Tulane University since 2017, she has curated exhibitions including *Legacy Traces: Recent Additions to the Collection* (2024), *Core Memory: Encoded* (2022), and Brandan 'BMike' Odums: *Not Supposed 2-BE Here* (2020); and co-organized *Unthinkable Imagination: A Creative Response to the Juvenile Justice Crisis* (2023) and *per(Sister): Incarcerated Women of Louisiana* (2019). Blereau previously served as curator at the Hilliard Art Museum in Lafayette, and as a director of the Bitforms Gallery in New York.

Erica N. Cardwell

is a writer, critic, and educator based in Toronto. She is the recipient of a 2021 Andy Warhol Foundation Arts Writers Grant and a New York State Council for the Arts Support for Artists Grant. Her writing has appeared in *ARTS. BLACK*, *Art in America*, *frieze*, *BOMB*, *The Believer*, *The Brooklyn Rail*, *C Magazine*, *Kenyon Review*, and other publications. She is assistant professor of creative writing at the University of Toronto Scarborough. Her book *Wrong Is Not My Name: Notes on (Black) Art* was published by the Feminist Press in March 2024.

Re'al Christian

is a writer and editor based in Queens, NY. Her work has appeared in *BOMB* Magazine, *The Brooklyn Rail*, *Art in America*, *Artforum*, and *Art Papers*, where she is a Contributing Editor. She has written texts for catalogues and anthologies including *And ever an edge* (Studio Museum in Harlem 2024), *Track Changes: A Handbook for Art Criticism* (Paper Monument 2023), *Howardena Pindell* (Garth Greenan and Dieu Donné 2022), and *On the Town: A Performa Compendium* (Gregory R. Miller & Co. 2021), among others. She received her MA in art history from Hunter College and her bachelor's degree from New York University, where she double majored in art history and Media, Culture, and Communication.

Kim Córdova

is a Mexican American art writer. Her work has appeared in *The New York Times*, *ArtForum*, *e-flux*, *ArtReview*, *deAppel*, *frieze*, *SFMOMA Open Space*, and *Momus* where she was the Mexico City Contributing Editor. Her work has been recognized by the Andy Warhol Foundation Arts Writer Grant and has been shortlisted for the International Award for Art Criticism.

Caroline Cox

is a Louisiana native and the curatorial fellow and editorial assistant for Prospect.6. Prior to joining Prospect, they/she held curatorial positions at the Whitney Museum of American Art, the Smithsonian American Art Museum, and the New Orleans Museum of Art. She has a BA in art history and Economics from the University of Notre Dame. Their honors senior thesis explored race, landscape, and cultural memory in the work of Dawoud Bey and Kevin Beasley.

Mira Dayal

is an artist, writer, editor, and educator based in New York. Her studio work is often site-specific and involves subtle, laborious applications of materials; critical reflections on changing technologies; and formal explorations of the limits of language. Dayal recently edited, with Josephine Heston, *Track Changes: A Handbook for Art Criticism*, published by Paper Monument with significant support from Critical Minded. She was previously ideas editor at *Art in America* and an associate editor and regular contributor at *Artforum*. Dayal is currently on faculty at Barnard College and the School of Visual Arts.

Marissa Del Toro

is assistant director of exhibitions and programs at NXTHVN in New Haven, CT. Since 2021, Del Toro has also worked with Museums Moving Forward, a data-driven initiative to support greater equity and accountability in art museum workplaces. Previously, she served as 2021–2022 curatorial fellow at NXTHVN and as the 2018–2020 Diversifying Art Museum Leadership Initiative (DAMLI) Curatorial Fellow at Phoenix Art Museum. She holds her MA in art history from the University of Texas at San Antonio, and is originally from Southern California, where she received her BA in art history from the University of California, Riverside.

Ben Depp

is an artist based in New Orleans. In 2014, he began creating aerial photographs using a powered paraglider, which allows for hours of exploration, a low flight path, and a time-intensive search for surprising compositions. Depp has been exploring and photographing South Louisiana's coastal landscapes for ten years. His work is part of the permanent collections at the Ogden Museum of Southern Art and the Historic New Orleans Collection. His photographs are featured in Joshua Lewis's essay, pages 190-196. To see more of his work, visit www.bendepp.com.

Daisy Desrosiers

is the director and chief curator of Gund Gallery at Kenyon College since 2021. She was previously the inaugural director of artist programs at the Lunder Institute for American Art at the Colby College Museum of Art. Recent projects include the exhibitions *No Justice Without Love* at The Ford Foundation gallery in NYC; *Christine Sun Kim: Oh Me Oh My* in collaboration with Remai Modern, The Tang, and CAG; Beverly Buchanan's The Idea Was to Capture Something Closely Related to a Feeling and *Ming Smith: Jazz Requiem-Notations in Blue*. She was also one of the inaugural co-curators of the first MOCA Toronto Triennale, GTA21, in 2021 and on the jury of the Canadian Pavilion for the 60th International Art Exhibition-La Biennale di Venezia 2024, awarded to artist Kapwani Kiwanga in 2024.

Kale Bantigue Fajardo
is an associate professor of American Studies and Asian American Studies at the University of Minnesota, Twin Cities. He is the author of *Filipino Crosscurrents: Oceanographies of Seafaring, Masculinities, and Globalization* (2011) and co-editor of *Q&A: Voices from Queer Asian North America* (2021). His research, writing, and art practices engage with histories of Filipinx masculinities, travel and migration, place-making, and photography in the diaspora; as well as issues related to water, oceans, rivers, bays, etc. He is currently working on a book titled, *Another Archipelago: Filipinx Migrant Masculinities and Visual Cultures—from St. Malo, Louisiana to Portland, Oregon.*

Kaitlin Garcia-Maestas
is the curator and director of exhibitions at Socrates Sculpture Park in Queens, New York and co-curator of Desert × 2025. Born and raised in New Mexico, her curatorial practice challenges the role of colonial narratives in shaping our understanding of land, place, and identity. For over a decade, she has dedicated herself to advocating for and realizing large-scale, site-specific installations by historically underrepresented and early career artists. Formerly, Garcia-Maestas was associate curator of visual arts at the Momentary, the contemporary satellite space of Crystal Bridges Museum of American Art, where she developed a robust exhibition program focused on site-specific, architectural interventions, including new commissions by Martine Gutierrez, Matthew Barney, Xaviera Simmons, Nicholas Galanin, Andrea Carlson, and Tavares Strachan. She previously held curatorial positions at the Denver Art Museum and Biennial of the Americas.

Kendyll Gross
serves as the assistant curator for the Newcomb Art Museum. She holds a BA from Emory University and an MA in art history from The University of Texas at Austin. She previously served as the curator of public programs for the Art Galleries at Black Studies (AGBS) at The University of Texas. Her most recent exhibition, *Victory Workers* (2024), foregrounds twentieth century African American artists who depict Black labor. In 2021, she curated *The way back home with AGBS*, which featured works by Austin-based artist Ariel René Jackson.

Marcela Guerrero
is the DeMartini Family Curator at the Whitney Museum of American Art, New York. Most recently, she curated *no existe un mundo poshuracán: Puerto Rican Art in the Wake of Hurricane Maria*, and *Martine Gutierrez: Supremacy,* at the Whitney, and she was also part of the curatorial team that organized *Vida Americana: Mexican Muralists Remake American Art, 1925-1945* in 2020. Guerrero's writing has appeared in several exhibition catalogues and in art journals such as *caa.reviews*, *ArtNexus*, *Caribbean Intransit: The Arts Journal, Gulf*

Coast: A Journal of Literature and Fine Arts, and *Diálogo.* Born and raised in Puerto Rico, Guerrero holds a PhD in art history from the University of Wisconsin, Madison.

Jasmin Hernandez
is a lifelong New Yorker and the Black Latina founder of the award-winning Gallery Gurls. She's been published in *ELLE*, *Harper's Bazaar*, PopSugar, Refinery29, *Somos*, Bustle, *SEEN*, among others, and is the debut author of *WE ARE HERE* (Abrams, 2021).

Dakota Hoska (Oglála Lakȟóta Nation, Pine Ridge, Wounded Knee)
is the associate curator of Native Arts and NAGPRA coordinator at the Denver Art Museum (since 2019). She also served as a cratorial research assistant for the exhibition *Hearts of Our People* at the Minneapolis Institute of Art (2015-2019). Hoska holds an MA in art history (2019) and a BFA in drawing and painting (2012). She currently serves on multiple national advisory councils including the CCNMWA. Hoska frequently writes about and presents on issues related to curating Native North American art collections. Her latest essay can be found in the exhibition catalog *Jeremy Frey: Woven* (2024).

Erica Moiah James
is an art historian and curator teaching in the Department of Art and art history at the University of Miami. Before arriving in Miami, she was the founding director and chief curator of the National Art Gallery of the Bahamas and an assistant professor of art history and African American Studies at Yale University. Her research centers on Indigenous, modern, and contemporary art of the Caribbean, Americas, and the African diaspora. Her forthcoming book is entitled *After Caliban: Caribbean Art in the Global Imaginary* (Duke University Press).

Nicholas Laughlin
is a writer, editor, and literary curator born and based in Trinidad and Tobago. He is festival and programme director of the literary NGO the Bocas Lit Fest; former editor of the magazines *Caribbean Beat* and *The Caribbean Review of Books*; and co-director of Alice Yard, a contemporary art collective based in Port of Spain. He has published two books of poems, most recently *Enemy Luck* (2019), and written numerous essays and articles on Caribbean literature and contemporary art.

Eileen Jeng Lynch
is the Bronx Museum's Director of Curatorial Programs who stewards the museum's curatorial initiatives and exhibition schedule with an eye toward expanding its presence in the Bronx and beyond. Jeng Lynch made her curatorial debut with *Abigail DeVille: Bronx Heavens*, and a continuation of that survey *In the Fullness of Time* traveled to the Bowdoin College Museum of Art. Jeng Lynch also organized *Bronx Calling: The Sixth AIM Biennial*. Previously, Jeng Lynch was the senior curator of visual arts at Wave Hill and has held positions at RxArt, Sperone Westwater, and the Art Institute of Chicago. As the founder of Neumeraki, Jeng Lynch has launched national and global community-based projects.

Dessane Lopez Cassell
is a New York-based editor, writer, and curator. She focuses on film and visual art, and their intersections, with a particular interest in race, gender, myths of paradise, and voices from the African and Caribbean diasporas. Cassell's writing has been published in various magazines, journals, and books, including the *Los Angeles Times*, the Criterion Collection, Hyperallergic, *Film Comment*, MUBI, and *Seen journal*.

Leilani Lynch
is the associate curator at the Museum of Contemporary Art Denver. Lynch has organized numerous museum exhibitions, including *gala porras-kim: A hand in nature* (2024); Steven Yazzie: *Meandered* (2024); Ken Gun Min: *The Lost Paradise* (2024); and Anna Tsouhlarakis: *Indigenous Absurdities* (2023). From 2015–2022, Lynch held several curatorial posts at The Bass, Miami Beach. There, she curated exhibitions with artists including Jamilah Sabur (2022), Cara Despain (2022), Naama Tsabar (2021), Karen Rifas (2018), Aaron Curry (2018), Mika Rottenberg (2017) in addition to co-organizing exhibitions by Adrián Villar Rojas (2022), Haegue Yang (2019), and Paola Pivi (2018).

Laurel V. McLaughlin, PhD,
is a curator, art historian, writer, and educator whose work explores research-based sculpture, installation, new media, and social practice. Her work has been published in *Art Papers*, *BOMB Magazine*, *The Brooklyn Rail*, *C Magazine*, *Performance Research*, *women & performance*, *ASAP/Journal*, and she co-edited *Tania El Khoury's Live Art: Collaborative Knowledge Production* with Carrie Robbins (Amherst College Press, 2024). McLaughlin recently co-convened the symposium Magical Thinking at MASS MoCA with manuel arturo abreu, and is undertaking research for *How do you throw a brick through a window...* as a 2022 Andy Warhol Curatorial Research Fellow.

C.C. McKee
is Assistant Professor of History of Art at Bryn Mawr College and a current Mads Øvlisen Postdoctoral Fellow at the University of Copenhagen. Their research focuses on the intersections of art, colonialism, and natural science in the modern Atlantic World (c. 1750-1950) with an emphasis on the Caribbean. McKee also maintains an active curatorial practice (with past projects in Chicago, Philadelphia, Miami, and Port-au-Prince), writes art criticism, and researches the exploration of colonialism and slavery's injurious ecological "afterlives" in contemporary Caribbean and African Diasporic art. Their writing has appeared (or will appear) in *Art Journal*, *liquid blackness*, *CASVA Seminar Papers*, Bloomsbury's *33 1/3 series*, *ArtForum*, and Hyperallergic.

Larissa Nez (Diné)
is of the Mud People and born for the Mountain Cove People. Her maternal grandfather is of the Red Running into the Water People and her paternal grandfather is of the Big Water People. She is currently a PhD student in the Department of Ethnic Studies at the University of California,

Berkeley. Centering critical Indigenous theory, decolonial theory, and the Black Radical Tradition, her research explores the relationship between Blackness and Indigeneity, as political projects and social analytics. Her research shows how Black and Indigenous people are imagining and building worlds and futures that are dialectically and intimately connected to the past and present, land/water/sky and body, and the material and spiritual.

Tausif Noor
is a critic, curator, and PhD student in global modern art at the University of California, Berkeley. His criticism and essays have appeared in *Artforum*, *The New York Times*, *The New Yorker*, and the *New York Review of Books*, among other venues, as well as in various artist catalogues and monographs. He is a recipient of a 2023 Grace Dudley Prize for Arts Writing from the Robert B. Silver Foundation, as well as a 2023 Andy Warhol Foundation/Creative Capital Arts Writers Grant for Short Form Writing.

Sadaf Padder
is a Brooklyn-based independent curator, writer, and community organizer who is focused on excavating under-recognized contemporary art movements and histories related to the South Asian and Caribbean diaspora. She has curated exhibitions across the country focusing on themes of social justice, futurism, radical liberation movements, climate change, and neo-mythology to weave connections between various communities. Padder is a Create Change alumna with the Laundromat Project, a featured curator with Artsy, as well as a 2022–23 Emily J. Hall Tremaine Fellow via Hyperallergic. She is also a board member of the Vera List Center as well as a co-director of Grown in Haiti, a reforestation organization located in the mountains of Jacmel.

Jerry Philogene
is Associate Professor and Director of the Black Studies Program at Middlebury College. Prior to Middlebury, she was Associate Professor in the American Studies Department at Dickinson College, where she specialized in interdisciplinary American cultural history, art history, and visual arts of the Caribbean and the African diaspora with an emphasis on the Francophone Caribbean. Her publications have appeared in peer-reviewed journals and exhibition catalogues. Dr. Philogene is also an independent curator. In 2023, she co-organized with Dr. Katherine Smith *Myrlande Constant: The Work of Radiance*, an exhibition on the contemporary textile works of Haitian artist Myrlande Constant, Fowler Museum, UCLA, 2023. Dr. Philogene is the recipient of a 2020 Andy Warhol Foundation Arts Writers Grant for her book manuscript *The Socially Dead and Improbable Citizen: Visualizing Haitian Humanity and Visual Aesthetics*. She is also writing a monograph on Haitian modernist artist, Luce Turnier.

Dr. W. Brian Piper
is the Freeman Family Curator of Photographs, Prints, and Drawings at the New Orleans Museum of Art (NOMA). At NOMA his curatorial credits include *Called to the Camera: Black American Studio Photographers* (2022), *Picture Man: Portraits by Polo Silk* (2022), *Debbie Fleming Caffery: In Light of Everything* (2023), *Changing Course: Reflections on New Orleans Histories* (2018), and *Show and Tell: A Brief History of Photography and Text* (2024). Piper holds a PhD in American Studies from the College of William and Mary and has written widely on a variety of photographic subjects.

Risa Puleo
is an independent curator based in Chicago whose work bridges methods of institutional critique with decolonial and abolitionist practices. Puleo was most recently part of a team of curators organizing the 2023 Counterpublics Triennial in St. Louis. Her contribution negotiated the ethical terrain of presenting public art in a city entangled in histories of dispossession and police surveillance.

Sherae Rimpsey
is an artist and writer. She has exhibited her work in the US and internationally. She is a featured artist along with Clifford Owens on Kamau Amu Patton's *Second Mind / Alto Age,* a limited edition artwork and recording commissioned by the Pulitzer Arts Foundation, in conjunction with their exhibition *Terry Adkins: Resounding*. Rimpsey has a BFA in Technology & Integrated Media with an emphasis in Visual Culture from the Cleveland Institute of Art and an MFA in writing from the School of the Art Institute of Chicago. Her first full-length book of poetry neon neon is out now.

Seph Rodney, PhD
is a former senior critic and opinions editor for Hyperallergic and is now a regular contributor to *The New York Times*. He has also written on art for CNN, NBC, *Art in America*, *American Craft Magazine*, and several other publications. In 2020 he won the Rabkin Arts Journalism prize and in 2022 won the Andy Warhol Foundation Arts Writers Grant. He is also a curator of contemporary art and a co-curator of *Get in the Game*, the largest exhibition that SFMOMA has undertaken, which opened October 2024.

Alex Santana
is a writer, editor, and curator with an interest in conceptual art, political intervention, and public participation. Currently based in New York but originally from Newark, NJ, she has held positions at the Smithsonian American Art Museum, the Joan Mitchell Center, Mana Contemporary, and Alexander Gray Associates. She has curated exhibitions at Smack Mellon, the Latinx Project at NYU, the Ely Center of Contemporary Art, and Knockdown Center. Her interviews and essays have been published by Hyperallergic, *Intervenxions*, *CUE Art Foundation*, *Terremoto*, *The Brooklyn Rail*, *Precog Magazine*, NXTHVN, and Artsy.

Delphine Sims
is an assistant curator in the Department of Photography at the San Francisco Museum of Modern Art. She recently completed her PhD in the History of Art Department at UC Berkeley. Delphine has held positions at several museums including: predoctoral fellowships at the Center for Advanced Study in the Visual Arts within the National Gallery of Art and the Metropolitan Museum of Art, and curatorial roles within the Berkeley Art Museum and Pacific Film Archive and the Santa Barbara Museum of Art. In addition to exhibition catalogs, her writing can be found in *Aperture*, *MATTE Magazine*, and *The Believer*.

TK Smith
is a curator, writer, and cultural historian. Currently, he is a doctoral candidate in the History of American Civilization program at the University of Delaware. He has written for *Art in America*, *The Brooklyn Rail*, and *Art Papers*, where he is a contributing editor. In 2021, he was the inaugural writer-in-residence at the Vashon Artist Residency. In 2022, he was a recipient of an Andy Warhol Arts Writers Grant. Smith was Monument Lab's 2022–2023 writer-in-residence. Most recently, Smith completed a curatorial residency at Yinka Shonibare's G.A.S. Residency in Lagos, Nigeria.

Bradley Sumrall
is a writer and curator based in the Historic Faubourg Tremé of New Orleans, Louisiana. He is currently Curator of the Collection for the Ogden Museum of Southern Art, where he is responsible for building, researching and interpreting the nation's most comprehensive collection of the art of the American South. He has written extensively on the art and culture of the South, and has served as curator for over eighty museum exhibitions. His exhibitions have been reviewed in *Art in America*, *Artforum*, *Hyperallergic*, *Terremoto*, *Forbes*, and *Art&Antiques*, among other online and print publications.

Lê Thuận Uyên
is a curator based in Hanoi. She is currently the artistic director of The Outpost—a Hanoi-based organization dedicated to the collection, presentation of and audience generation for contemporary art in Vietnam. Her practice investigates formal articulations that are rooted in the social context and aesthetic traditions of Vietnam. Uyên is also a keen advocate for integrating art experiences into the universal educational system, as well as building capacity for the Vietnamese art landscape.

Diya Vij
is the curator at Creative Time and is committed to critically investigating the evolving role of public art in politics and civic life. Over the past decade, she has held programming, curatorial, and communications positions at major New York City institutions. At Creative Time, she commissions and stewards large-scale public artworks, initiates public programs, and helps guide the curatorial direction of the organization. She currently serves on the boards of the Laundromat Project and the Poetry Project and is the co-chair of the board of A Blade of Grass. She was a co-curator of the Counterpublic Triennial 2023 in St. Louis, MO.

Ian Wallace
is an art historian and curator based in New York. He received his PhD from the CUNY Graduate Center in 2021. He is currently associate curator at Amant. His writing

has appeared in *BOMB*, *Art in America*, *The Brooklyn Rail*, *Whitehot Magazine*, and on artforum.com, among others. He has contributed to exhibitions at the Fondazione Prada, Venice; MoMA, New York; the Museum of Jurassic Technology, Los Angeles; and the Städtische Galerie im Lenbachhaus, Munich, among other institutions. In 2022, he was assistant to the curator of the 59th Venice Biennale, *The Milk of Dreams*.

Terence Washington
is a writer and independent curator based in Philadelphia. He has worked for the National Gallery of Art, NXTHVN, and the Museum of Fine Arts, Boston, and has written essays on artworks by Kevin Beasley, Sherman Fleming, Zora J. Murff, among others.

Ivy G. Wilson
has written on contemporary art and the Global South, including recent essays on the Propeller Group and Enrique Chagoya. As a cultural critic, he has given numerous gallery talks as well as presentations at some of the most notable art institutions in North America, including the Museum of Contemporary Art (Chicago), the Art Gallery of Ontario (Toronto), and Guggenheim (New York). He is currently writing a series of essays on "The Global Aesthetics of Minor Diasporas."

PROSPECT.6 EXECUTIVE DIRECTOR'S COUNCIL

L. Kasimu Harris
is a New Orleans-based artist whose practice deposits a number of different strategic and conceptual devices in order to push narratives. He strives to tell stories of underrepresented communities in New Orleans and beyond. Harris has shown in numerous group exhibitions in the US and internationally and has had eight solo photography exhibitions. He earned a BBA in Entrepreneurship from Middle Tennessee State University in 2004 and an MA in Journalism from the University of Mississippi in 2008. Harris's writing and photographs were featured in "A Shot Before Last Call: Capturing New Orleans's Vanishing Black Bars" in *The New York Times*.

Kristina Kay Robinson
is a poet, writer, and visual artist born and raised in New Orleans, Louisiana. Her written, visual, and curatorial practice centers and interrogates the modern and ancient connections between world communities. Robinson's work both at home and abroad focuses on the impact of globalization, militarism, and surveillance on society and their intersections with contemporary art and pop culture. Her writing has appeared in *Art in America*, *Guernica*, *The Baffler*, *The Nation*, *The Massachusetts Review*, and *Elle* among other outlets. Robinson is a 2019 recipient of the Rabkin Prize for Visual Arts Journalism. Currently she serves as the New Orleans editor at large for the Atlanta based magazine *Burnaway*.

Marta Rodriguez Maleck
is a transdisciplinary artist, researcher, builder, storyteller, and witness. Their

practice celebrates that which is often stigmatized through thought-provoking dialogue. Their frank approach and dark humor is leveraged to address intersections of sexuality, race, gender, and culture as it relates to acceptability and shamelessness. They received a MFA from the University of Pennsylvania and a BFA from the Rhode Island School of Design. Their work has been exhibited and screened internationally, featured in *The Guardian* and the Criterion Channel, and most recently at EFA Project Space in New York. You can catch episodes of their podcast *Reports from New Orleans*, which features New Orleans artists on Montez Press Radio in New York.

PROSPECT.6 CURATORIAL ADVISORY COMMITTEE

Ron Bechet
was born in New Orleans and lives in the Gentilly neighborhood. He began his college career with an athletic scholarship at Mississippi State University but returned to New Orleans to study art at the University of New Orleans where he earned his BA. He later earned an MFA in painting from Yale University. His work is inspired by observations of the consequences of forces of nature and time on place and the human experience, as well as the cultural practices of the African diaspora and New Orleans African American culture and ritual. He has worked on several community-based projects in collaboration with other artists and community members. He is professor of art at Xavier University of Louisiana where he has been teaching for more than twenty years.

Zoe Butt
is a curator and writer, nurturing critical thinking and historically conscious artistic communities, fostering dialogue among cultures of the globalizing souths. Possessing an extensive exhibition, publishing, and public-speaking history globally, in 2022 she founded 'in-tangible institute,' seeking a robust ecology for locally responsive curatorial talent in Southeast Asia. Zoe holds a PhD by Published Works, Center for Research and Education in Art and Media, University of Westminster, London. She has been published by Hatje Cantz; JRP-Ringier; Routledge; Sternberg Press, among others and is a MoMA International Curatorial Fellow, NYC; member of Asia Society's 'Asia 21' initiative, NYC; and member of Asian Art Council, Solomon R. Guggenheim Museum, NYC.

Raphael Fonseca
is a curator of modern and contemporary Latin American art at the Denver Art Museum. He is the chief curator of the 14th Mercosur Biennial, Porto Alegre, Brazil, 2024. Besides that, he curated the 22nd SESC_Videobrasil Biennial (Brazil, 2023), along with Renée Akitelek Mboya and Solange Farkas, and worked as a curator at the Contemporary Art Museum of Niterói (Brazil, 2016–2020). Among his projects, he collaborated as a curator with Haus der Kunst (Germany), ICA Singapore, O sage Art Foundation (Hong Kong), Bienalsur (Argentina), Framer Framed (Netherlands), and CIAJG (Guimarães, Portugal).

Tumelo Mosaka
is a Johannesburg born and New York based independent curator. He is the Mellon Arts Project Director for the African American and Diaspora Studies at Columbia University. Mosaka has worked within and outside museums exploring global transnational artistic practices especially from Africa, the Caribbean, and North America. He has curated numerous exhibitions both locally and internationally exploring the history and memory of Black representation across the globe.

Krista Thompson
is an art historian and Professor of art history at Northwestern University. Her writings and curatorial projects focus on modern and contemporary art and visual culture of the Africa diaspora and the Caribbean. She is the author of *An Eye for the Tropics* (2006), *Developing Blackness* (The National Art Gallery of The Bahamas, 2008), and *Shine: The Visual Economy of Light in African Diasporic Aesthetic Practice* (2015). She has received grants and fellowships from the Dedalus Foundation, the Andy Warhol Foundation, and the J. Paul Getty Foundation, and was awarded the David C. Driskell Prize from the High Museum of Art in 2009. In 2023, Thompson was elected to the American Academy of Arts and Sciences.

Dyani White Hawk (Sičáŋǧu Lakota)
is a multimedia artist and independent curator based in Minneapolis. Through painting, beadwork, installation, performance, and curation her practice challenges the lack of representation of Native arts, people, and voices in our national consciousness while highlighting the truth and necessity of intersectionality and relatedness across life. White Hawk has received numerous awards, including an Arts and Letters Award in Art (2021), McKnight Visual Artist Fellowship (2021 and 2014), United States Artists Fellowship in Visual Art (2019), and the Joan Mitchell Foundation Painters and Sculptors Grant (2014), among others. She was featured in the 2022 Whitney Biennial and had a recent solo exhibition at the Museum of Contemporary Art Denver and Kemper Museum of Contemporary Art.

Artistic Directors' Acknowledgments

In creating Prospect.6: *The Future Is Present, The Harbinger Is Home* we sought to honor New Orleans and situate this city within a global discourse. To conceptualize this project, we drew from our respective professional and personal communities, bringing to P.6 our learnings from those who have over the years shaped our thinking, our values, and our commitments to the field. The development of this project was a love letter to the artists' practice and the ways that artists challenge us to see the future. The execution of this project was possible because a small group of highly committed and talented individuals put forward an extraordinary effort in completing this exhibition and realizing its many dreams. The memory of our labors together lives on this publication. We remain forever grateful.

We begin by giving a tremendous thanks to the 51 artists of P.6 for embarking on this journey with us. Thank you for your trust in us, and for your commitment to sharing your best and most forward-facing work. Thank you for stretching us and teaching us along the way. We are humbled and in awe of your vision.

We owe sincere thanks to our Executive Director, Nick Stillman, for his unwavering support of our vision and his commitment to our process. Thank you, Nick, for your belief in us, we are truly grateful to have built this with you. Our sincere thanks to Prospect's Board President and Chairperson, Christopher J. Alfieri, our position's sponsor, Susan Brennan, and to Prospect's board for their advice and support throughout this process.

P.6 builds upon the foundation left behind by its previous iterations. We are grateful to Prospect's founder, Dan Cameron, for envisioning this ambitious platform. We thank Dan and Prospect's previous Artistic Directors: Franklin Sirmans, Trevor Schoonmaker, Naima Keith, and Diana Nawi, for their good counsel and camaraderie along the way.

The staff of P.6 was managed with care, commitment, and thoughtfulness by Director of Curatorial Affairs, Andrew Rebatta. The installation of P.6 coalesced thanks to the ingenuity, knowledge, and networks of Exhibitions Manager, LB Barfield. Curatorial Fellow and Editorial Assistant, Caroline Cox, brought an extraordinary level of dedication and a discerning eye for details to all aspects of our production. P.6 benefited greatly from the experience, effectiveness, and good humor of our Registrar, Linda Stubbs. Operations & Visitor Services Manager, Erin Foster, courageously oversaw countless aspects of our visitor experience, gala, and facilities' needs and brought Prospect's signage to a new level of visibility. Manager of Storytelling and Communications, Tarah Douglas, excelled at crafting the public-facing aspects of our communications, website, and social media in ways that were both sensitive and inspiring. Programming Director, Denise Frazier, assembled a powerful slate of public programs that reflect her warmth and love for the city's creatives. Programs & Audience Engagement Manager, Kalea Cook, brought forward valued community connections and engagement throughout P.6's planning and run. Our installations were supported by an impressive team of Exhibition Coordinators: Devin Balara,

Michelle Belfield, and Benny Brown; and Head Preparator, Sam Hollier. We also wish to acknowledge Stephen Montalvo, for his excellent management of P.6's audiovisual needs, Elizabeth Smith, for her eloquent label texts, and Nicole Bunis for her expert label and vinyl text production.

For the first time in Prospect's history, P.6 produced two publications to document the triennial: an affordable, portable guidebook available at the exhibition's opening and this robust publication with installation photography, which we are proud to produce with Monacelli, an imprint of Phaidon. This ambitious level of scholarship is possible thanks to our incredible Publications Manager and Editor, Ana Clara Silva. Thank you, Ana Clara, for your flawless organization and commitment to producing this layered and beautiful documentation of our work. We thank Consulting Editor, Rob Goyanes, for his insightful reviews of our texts. We thank Chris Wu, Eric Price, Emily Chin-Longobardi, and the team of Wkshps for their design not only of this book, but also for the impactful graphic identity of the entire triennial. Many thanks also to Erik Kiesewetter of Constance for the elegant design of the P.6 map.

We envisioned this publication as a global convening of artists, authors, and experts from their respective fields. We thank our essayists: Antawan I. Byrd, Lora Ann Chaisson, Joshua A. Lewis, Quintron, and Maurice Carlos Ruffin for their keen and creative insights into the future of New Orleans and Prospect. We are grateful to Ada Limón, Kei Miller, and Karisma Price for their rich and profound poems, which we have gratefully used to complement the ethos of our project. We thank our entry writers for their deep engagement with the artists' practices. We appreciate their openness and adaptability, particularly as many of them drafted brilliant texts about artworks as the works themselves were being created.

The development of the P.6 artist list owes much to our team of Curatorial Advisors: Ron Bechet, Zoe Butt, Raphael Fonseca, Tumelo Mosaka, and Dyani White Hawk, each of whom drew from their respective geographic expertise and beyond. We thank our advisors for their generosity in sharing not only artists recommendations, but also meaningful context around artists' practice. As our New Orleans-based advisor, Ron also shared an abundance of knowledge regarding New Orleans's history and institutions, often working alongside us and our artists, which was essential to the project's success.

We are fortunate that an abridged but substantial portion of P.6 will travel on to the Museum of Contemporary Art Denver during the summer of 2025. We sincerely thank the staff and board of MCA Denver for their support throughout the development of this project. We are deeply grateful to Nora Burnett Abrams, former Director of MCA Denver and current Director of the Institute of Contemporary Art, Boston for her unflagging encouragement since the earliest stages of our engagement as Co-Artistic Directors. Many thanks to MCA's exhibition's team: Associate Curator, Leilani Lynch; Exhibitions and Registration Coordinator, Rebecca Gates; and Exhibitions Manager, Anderson Heagy, for their expertise around the presentation of P.6 in Denver.

FROM EBONY

To my first love and home, my mother Thelma Verona Ferguson, who taught me to draw people and walked hand in hand with me on this long journey. For her to witness me first as an artist in Prospect.3 and now as a Co-Artistic Director is an incredible gift. To Oscar Zepheniah Patterson, my father who taught me how to draw birds, gone but always present in my dimples, I love you. To Petrona Morrison, thanks for being a constant mentor and friend. To Savannah Jubic, my incredible studio manager and assistant who held so much together for me as we took this journey. To my Aunt Asha Thomas and Aunt Dian Samuels, thanks for taking care of me on this journey. To my Band of Sisters and friends who caught me in the most trying time of my short life, you know of parallel struggles on this journey, I love you. Monique Meloche Gallery and Hales Gallery New York and London and to colleagues who would offer advice along the journey, thanks for your continued belief and support and the constant watering of this tree. To the artists, thanks for trusting me with your time, your space, and your vulnerability. What we do is hard, what we do is not often understood. But we do it first because for us there is no other way and we do it because we believe in possibilities. My gratitude to you is neverending. To our small but MIGHTY Prospect.6 Staff, none of this lift would be possible without you. We are so blessed and fortunate not just to have you by our side—but you said yes to us! It means that you too believed in the endeavor. It has been my honor to bare and bear witness to you. Bonded forever, Mimi and Bonny.

FROM MIRANDA

My deepest thanks goes to the artistic community of New Orleans. I was a young curator beginning to establish my voice when I arrived in New Orleans in 2008. In so many ways, this community raised me professionally. Thank you for your patience and for welcoming me into the magic that is this city. Thank you to the Joan Mitchell Foundation, for supporting many P.6 artists through residencies at the Joan Mitchell Center and for having me serve on your board these past five years. It has been an honor. Thank you to the love of my life and my rock, Jim Mulvihill and to our beloved, amazing boys, Francis and Joseph Mulvihill. Thank you to my mother, Sara Velasco, for your consistent support and care along every step of my journey. Thank you to my father, Michael Lash, for instilling in me a sense of wonder and curiosity about the world. To my siblings Cristina and John Lash, and my familia in California and New Mexico: Your love is my harbor and my wellspring of confidence. A special thanks to the most supportive mother and father-in-law I could have ever asked for, my Louisiana family Jan and Jack Mulvihill. Many thanks to Jami Attenberg for being an inspiring friend and supporter in ideating about New Orleans. I also wish to honor my mentor Bill Fagaly (1938–2021) for his pivotal role in sustaining Prospect and for modeling how to approach curation with adventurousness and joy. To Ebony: I never tire of calling you my gift. Thank you for being my partner through this incredible journey.

Miranda Lash and Ebony G. Patterson
Susan Brennan Co-Artistic Directors

Acknowledgments

Alex Abalos
Zarouhie Abdalian
Adam Abdalla
Nora Burnett Abrams
Dr. Rosanne Adderley
Akron Art Museum
Saniya Alderson
Lisa Alexis
Alexander Gray
    Associates, New York
Alice Yard
American Machinery
    Movers
Jordan Amirkhani
Andrea Andersson
William Andrews
Jackie Anyanwu
Ida Aronson
Jami Attenberg
Nic Brierre Aziz
Dr. Mia Bagneris
Beth Bahls
Devin Balara
Ellen Balkin
Porscha Banker
Larry Barabino
Davon Barbour
Bruce "Sunpie" Barnes
Madeline Barnes
kai lumumba barrow
Batture Engineers
Ron Bechet
Michelle Belfield
Tabbie Benanti
Etelvina Benjamin
Dan Bingler
Willie Birch
The Black School
Christa Blatchford
Sesthasak Boonchai
Kyle Brown
Tap Bui
Bunmi The Artisté
Dartanya Croff
Sarah Bishop
Laura Blereau
Violet Bordin
Hunter Braithwaite
Rachel Breunlin
Benny Brown
Colin Brown
Nicole Bunis
Paul Calder
Keith Calhoun
Dan Cameron
Tony Campbell
Mayor LaToya Cantrell
Nathan Cassiani
Choke Hole
Ben Clark
The Clark Collection
Daniel Clifton
Steve Cohen
Anne Collins Smith
Commonwealth and
    Council, Los Angeles
Company, New York
Jeremy Cooker
Copperfield, London
Bryon S. Cornelison
Margot Coutour
Cultural Counsel

Maya Curtis
Lisa D'Amour
Sakinah Davis
de boer, Los Angeles &
    Antwerp
Mitch de Rubira
Kyle DeCoste
Frederick "Wood"
    Delahoussaye
Denali Art Solutions
Terry DeRoche
Dan Desmond
Morgan Dillon
Downtown Development
    District
Rosa and Seth Dunlap
Cameron Eaton
Edna Karr High School
Dean Brian Edwards
Brett Egan
Ian Epps
B Everfield
Matt Farah
Jonathan Ferrara
DiQuan Forcell
Fort Gansevoort,
    New York
Kelsey Foster
Keith Fox
François Ghebaly,
    Los Angeles &
    New York
Thomas Friel
frieze
Daniele Gair
Olivia Gallo
Betsie Gambel
Antonio Garza
Cynthia Garza
Mamie Gasperecz
Jennifer Ghabrial
Jillian Gibson
Steve Gilliland
Gladstone Gallery,
    New York
Henry Gordon
Dr. Tammy Greer
GRIMM, Amsterdam,
    London, New York
Melissa Guion
Dale Gunnoe
Bruce Hamilton
Gia Hamilton
Justin Hamilton
Daniel Hammer
Evan Hammond
Nancy Hampton
Daniel Levon Harding
Cherice Harrison-Nelson
Elizabeth Hefler
Leah Hennessy
Carolina Hernández
Christopher Herrera
Dr. Yuri Herrera
Camille Hill-Prewitt
Patton Hindle
Lauryn Hinton
Cô Hoa
Doanh Hoàng
Sam Hollier
Sarah House
Michael Howard

Klaas Hubner
Phil Hull
Hull Designs
David Hurlbert
Nicole Hutchison
Independent Curators
    International
Jack Shainman Gallery,
    New York
Ben Jacobson
James Cohan, New York
Willo Jean-Baptiste
Trécha Gay Jheneall
Dr. Yu Jiang
Joan Mitchell Center
Hannah Joffray
Kela Johnson
Dr. T.R. Johnson
Lexus Jordan
Sarahbelle Juneau
Chú Kang
Naima Keith
Will Kiel
Erik Kiesewetter
Terence King
MaPó Kinnord
Monika Kozicz
Samantha Eroche Kreiger
Julie LaCour
Kevin LaJoie
Phượng Lê
Veronique Le Melle
Dani Leal
Antarah Leilani
Morris Less
Arthur Lewis
Jebney Lewis
Renee Longdon
Ngô Lụa
Alegra Lumpkin
Shana M. griffin
Steven Ma
Amy Mackie
Jenna Mae
Kevin Mah
Dalton Major
Dontré Major
Alexis Marceaux
Alex Marks
Delfeayo Marsalis and
    the Uptown Jazz
    Orchestra
Don Marshall
E Marshall
Mayor's Office of Cultural
    Economy
Chandra McCormick
Valerie McGinley
Kesha McKey
Anna Mecugni
Mahala Miller
Saiya Miller
Cameron Mitchell-Ware
Lưu Mo'
Stephen Montalvo
Tim Morales
Claire Mullholem
Dru Murphy
Museum of Contemporary
    Art Denver
Daisy Nam
Jeanne Nathan

Diana Nawi
Jason Neville
New Orleans & Company
New Orleans Tourism
    and Cultural Fund
Amy Newell
Melissa Newell
Carolina Nitsch
Alexis Nguyễn McCloud
Cyndi Nguyễn
Cynthia Nguyễn
Diễm Nguyễn
Hảo Nguyễn
Khai Nguyễn
Linda Nguyễn
Ashley O'Neill
Ozone 504
PATRON Gallery,
    Chicago
Martha Pearson
Derik Penny
Ken Pickering
Sierra Polisar
Maurita Poole
Porter Art Services
CCH Pounder
Renaud Proch
Dom Prout
Quintron
Anna Raginskaya
Richard Read
Aaron Ready
Darryl Reeves
Shaun Richards
Aaron Richmond-Havel
Risk Strategies
The Rivers Institute
Colin Roberson
Rachel Roberts
Veronica Roberts
Marta Rodriguez Maleck
Aimee Rogan
Ama Rogan
Arthur Roger
Mark Romig
Lisa Rotondo-McCord
Ylva Rouse
Elizabeth Rouselle
Sam Ruchti
Matt Russell
Elise Ryan
RZI Lighting
Sheila Santamaria
Valesca Santos
Heidi Schmalbach
Trevor Schoonmaker
Kelly Schulz
Robyn Dunn Schwarz
Emily Sebastian
Paul Shaw
Joe Shores
Matthew Showman
Silverlens, Manila &
    New York
V. Joy Simmons
Sharlene Sinegal
    DeCuir
Franklin Sirmans
Reid Smarts
Nathan Smith
Tiffany Smith
Aimee Solomon

Sông Community
    Development
    Corporation
Kenneth Spears
Sam Springston
Stone Center for Latin
    American Studies
Flannery Strain
Maddie Stratton
Linda Stubbs
A Studio in the Woods
Studio Reciprocity
Cô Sự
Bradley Sumrall
Paul Sylvester
Bob Tannen
Tanya Bonakdar Gallery,
    New York &
    Los Angeles
Krista Thompson
Cô Thuý
Tina Kim Gallery,
    New York
Sidney Torres
José Torres Tama
Panacea Theriac
Stephanie Travers
Jonathan Traviesa
Michel Varisco
VEGGI Farmers
    Cooperative
The Verbena Group
Monique Verdin
Vietnamese Initiatives in
    Economic Training
    (VIET)
VietNola50
Phoebe Vlassis
Kim Lan Vũ
Jason Waggenspack
Nari Ward
Whatever Works
Emma Whisler
Hancock Whitney
Jason Wiese
Emily Wilkerson
David Williams
Maici Williams
Michael Williams
Schuyler Williams
Ariel Wilson
Matthew Wilson
Jane Winslow
Sarah Woodward
Mere Younger
Zach Smith Consulting

Prospect New Orleans

Funders and Supporters

Saints

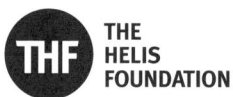 THE HELIS FOUNDATION

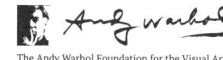 Mellon Foundation

Angels

OPEN SOCIETY FOUNDATIONS

LAMBENT FOUNDATION

Ford Foundation

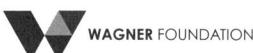 The Andy Warhol Foundation for the Visual Arts

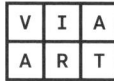 WAGNER FOUNDATION

The Gore Family Foundation

The Stephen Reily Family Fund

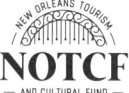 NATIONAL ENDOWMENT for the ARTS arts.gov

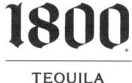 HANCOCK WHITNEY

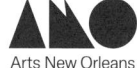 VIA ART

Bloomberg Philanthropies

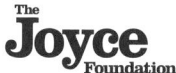 PAN AMERICAN LIFE INSURANCE GROUP

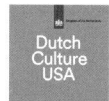 NEW ORLEANS TOURISM NOTCF AND CULTURAL FUND

1800 TEQUILA

art production fund

Eugenie & Joseph Jones Family Foundation

ANO Arts New Orleans

The Joyce Foundation

Dutch Culture USA

Ed Bradley Family Foundation

Major supporters

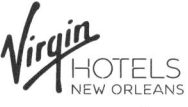 Virgin HOTELS NEW ORLEANS

The Selley Foundation

The Keller Family Foundation

The Norman & Emmy Lou Illges Foundation

Graham Foundation

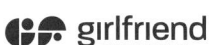 girlfriend DONOR ADVISED FUND

Walda Besthoff

Ella West Freeman Foundation

TERRA FOUNDATION FOR AMERICAN ART

K: Danish Arts Foundation

de boer ANTWERP & LOS ANGELES

The New Orleans Recreation & Culture Fund

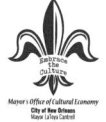 Embrace the Culture Mayor's Office of Cultural Economy City of New Orleans

LEHMANN MAUPIN

Teiger Foundation

SOHO HOUSE

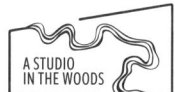 A STUDIO IN THE WOODS

NCJ≷ National Council of Jewish Women Greater New Orleans Section

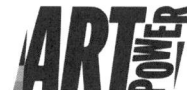 ART POWER!

JOAN MITCHELL FOUNDATION

Media partners

Cultural Counsel
New Orleans & Co

Glasstire
WWNO

frieze

Hotel partners

The Columns
Hotel Henrietta
Hotel Saint Vincent
Le Pavillon Hotel
Maison Metier
   The Unbound
   Collection by the Hyatt

The Mary Beth Hotel and Gallery
The Old No. 77 Hotel
NOPSI Hotel New Orleans
OMNI Royal Orleans
   OMNI Riverfront Hotel
Peter & Paul
The Chloe

The Celestine
The Roosevelt New Orleans
   A Waldorf Astoria Hotel
The Windsor Court

Reproduction Credits

All artworks are reproduced courtesy of the artist unless otherwise noted. The following applies to images and words for which additional acknowledgment is due.

pp. 1, 21, 23, 27, 43–50, 56–59, 64–66, 68–70, 75–82, 91–92, 95, 114–115, 117 (bottom), 118–119; 122–125, 128, 134–135, 137–139, 146–148, 152–153, 155–162, 166, 168–170, 174–175, 177, 182–183, 186, 197, 204, 206–207, 209 (bottom), 210–211, 213, 218–221, 223–227, 234–237, 248–253, 255 (bottom), 291–292, 296–297. Photos: Alex Marks; pp. 2–3,17, 24, 34–37, 40, 51–55, 71–74, 83–84, 86–89, 140–143, 171, 173, 178–179, 199 (middle right), 203, 205, 214–215, 217 (bottom), 228–233, 245, 246, 255 (top), 256–257, 259, 238–239. Photos: Jonathan Traviesa; pp. 4–5, 149 (bottom), 150: Photos: Bernie Ng; p. 19: Courtesy of Miranda Lash; pp. 30 (top), 98 (top and bottom right), 99–100, 198, 199 (top, middle left, bottom left), 200 (bottom): Photos: Lauryn Hinton; p. 33: Copyright Ada Limón, 2023. All rights reserved. The reproduction of this poem may in no way be used for financial gain.; pp. 38–39, 117 (top), 120–121: Courtesy of the artist and Commonwealth and Council. Photo: Jeffrey Johnston; pp. 60–61, 63, 240–243: Courtesy of Newcomb Art Museum of Tulane University. Photo: Jeffery Johnston; pp. 96–97, Benry Fauna; p. 98 (bottom left): Courtesy of Newcomb Art Museum of Tulane University, Photo: Ashley Lorraine; pp. 126–127, 129, Photos: Andrew Williamson; p. 149 (top): Photo: Jörg Baumann; pp. 151, 294–295: Courtesy of Gladstone Gallery New York; pp. 163–165: Courtesy of the artist and Tina Kim Gallery, Photo: Hyunjung Rhee; pp. 191–195: Photos: Ben Depp; p. 200 (top). Photo: Annie Flanagan; p. 201 Video: Gian Smith; p. 202: Courtesy of Allison Glenn; p. 264: Courtesy of Xavier University of Louisiana, Archives & Special Collections; p. 265: Courtesy of Emily Alesandrini

ADDITIONAL IMAGE CAPTIONS

p. 1: Arturo Kameya, *Whatever comes first*, 2024; pp. 2–3: Blas Isasi, *1,001,532 CE*, 2023–2024; pp. 4–5: Eisa Jocson and Venuri Perera, *Magic Maids*, 2024. Performance documentation, Esplanade—Theatres on the Bay, Singapore; p. 6: Stephanie Syjuco, *Phantom Visions (The Lacustrine Village of St. Malo)*, 2024 (detail); p. 95: Mel Chin, *Pool of Light*, 2024–2025 (detail); pp. 96–97: *King & Blue: The Vanishing Black Bars & Lounges Experience*, organized by L. Kasimu Harris featuring Delfeayo Marsalis and the Uptown Jazz Orchestra. Sweet Lorraine's Jazz Club, November 2, 2024; p. 98: *Tambourine Cypher Part I*, artist talk and performance. Tulane University, Freeman Auditorium, November 3, 2024. Top, L to R: Dr. Kyle DeCoste, Gladney, Ashley Teamer, Rosalie Washington, and Aaron Washington; p. 99: Chokhole (top) and Edna Karr High School Marching Band (bottom) perform in *Love Burst*, an activation for the unveiling of Raúl de Nieves's *The Sacred Heart of Hours and the Trees of Yesterdays, Today, and Tomorrow*, 2024. Harmony Circle, October 31, 2024; p. 100: Chokhole performs in *Love Burst*, an activation for the unveiling of Raúl de Nieves's *The Sacred Heart of Hours and the Trees of Yesterdays, Today, and Tomorrow*, 2024. Harmony Circle, October 31, 2024; p. 197: Thomas Deaton, *Last Megalopolis*, 2024 (detail); p. 198: *Quintron's Weather Warlock*. The End of the World, New Orleans, November 3, 2024; p. 199: *Seeding the Future*, performance by Tuan Mami. Xavier University of Louisiana Art Gallery, November 1, 2024. Top, L to R: participant, Lan Vu, Mrs. Sự, Diễm Nguyen, Doanh Hoang. Middle left, L to R: Doanh Hoang, Tuan Mami, Thúy Kang; p. 200: *Quietly Amongst the Disquiet*, film and performance by Tuấn Andrew Nguyễn in collaboration with Thảo Nguyễn and Marion Hoàng Ngọc Hill. Patrick F. Taylor Library, Ogden Museum of Southern Art, November 2, 2024; p. 201: *Magic Maids*, 2024 (video stills). Performance documentation, New Marigny Theatre, New Orleans, Louisiana, November 1, 2024; p. 202: Bethany Collins, *Civil Dusk*, 2024. Performance documentation, Marigny Opera House, New Orleans, Louisiana, November 2, 2024; p. 291: Raúl de Nieves, *The Trees of Tomorrow (Strength)*, 2024 (detail); pp. 292–293: Jeannette Ehlers, *Hoist and the Unseen: Journeys Through Tempests in Times of Hunger*, 2024 (detail); pp. 294–295: Joan Jonas, *stream or river, flight or pattern III (Journey)*, 2016/2017 (video still); p. 296–297: Amanda Williams, *In Her Rich Deposits of (Blue)*, 2024 (detail). New Orleans African American Museum (NOAAM)

Published on the occasion of the exhibition
Prospect.6: *The Future Is Present,
The Harbinger Is Home*

Presented throughout the City of
New Orleans, November 2, 2024–
February 2, 2025

The related exhibition *Selections from
Prospect.6: The Future Is Present, The
Harbinger Is Home* was presented at the
Museum of Contemporary Art Denver
May 23–August 24, 2025

Published in the United States in 2025 by

Monacelli
A Phaidon Company
111 Broadway
New York, New York 10006
phaidon.com/monacelli

Phaidon SARL
55, rue Traversière
75012 Paris

In association with

Prospect New Orleans
P.O. Box 58800
New Orleans, LA 70158
prospectneworleans.org

ISBN 9781580936750

Library of Congress Number 2025931517

Susan Brennan Co-Artistic Directors
Miranda Lash
Ebony G. Patterson

Editor
Ana Clara Silva

Consulting Editor
Rob Goyanes

Editorial Assistant
Caroline Cox

Design
Chris Wu with Emily Chin-Longobardi,
Wkshps

Printed in Canada

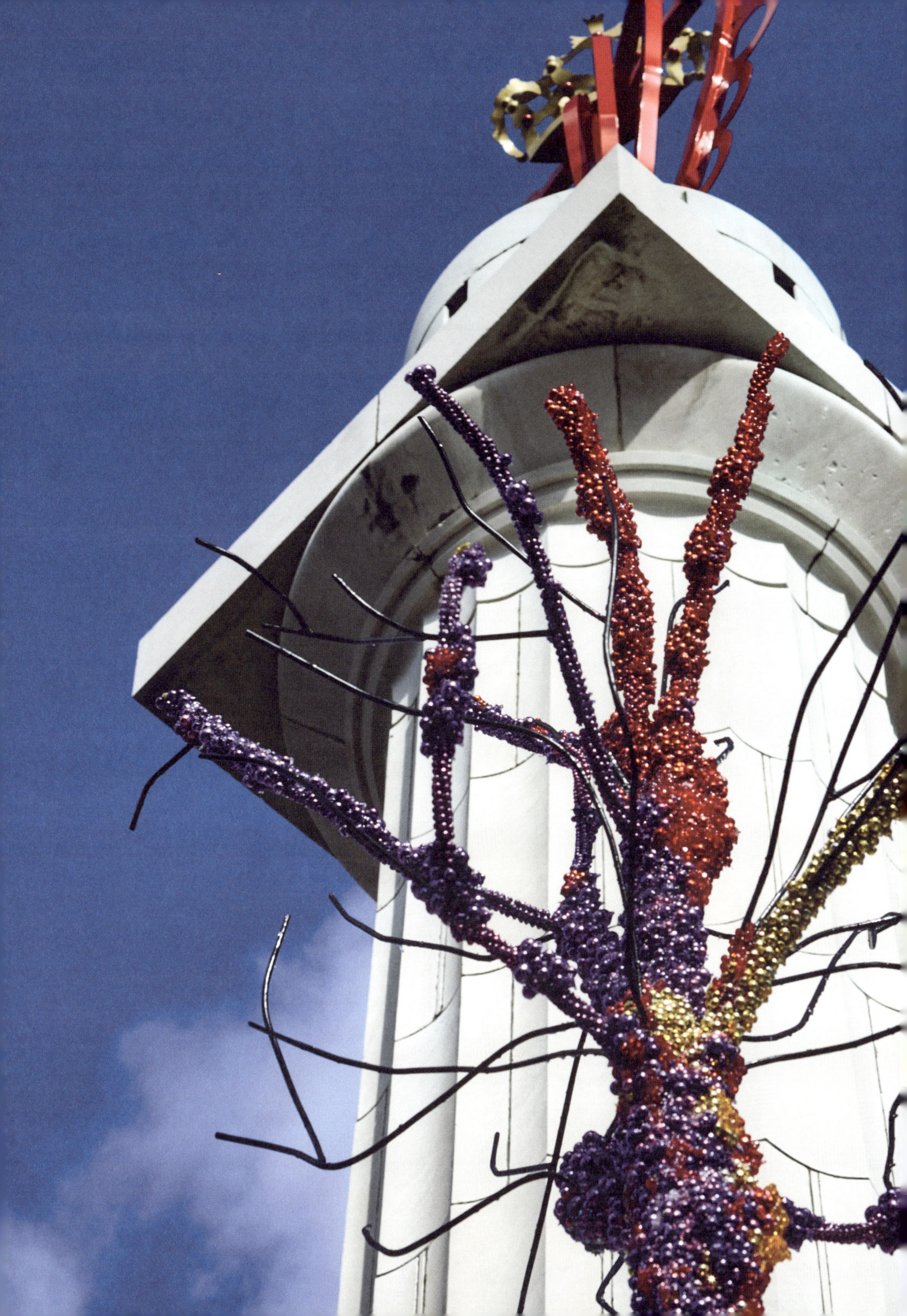

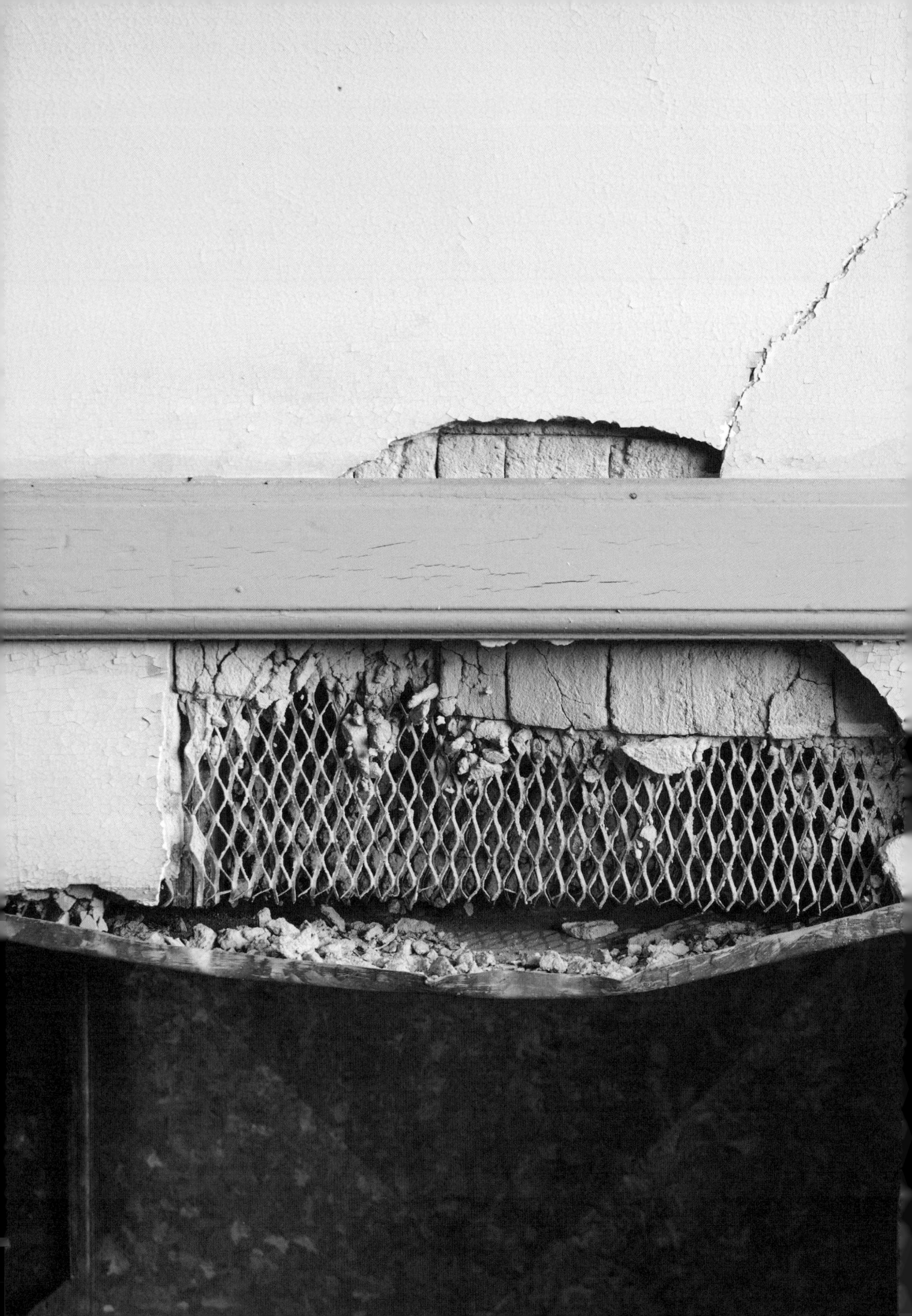

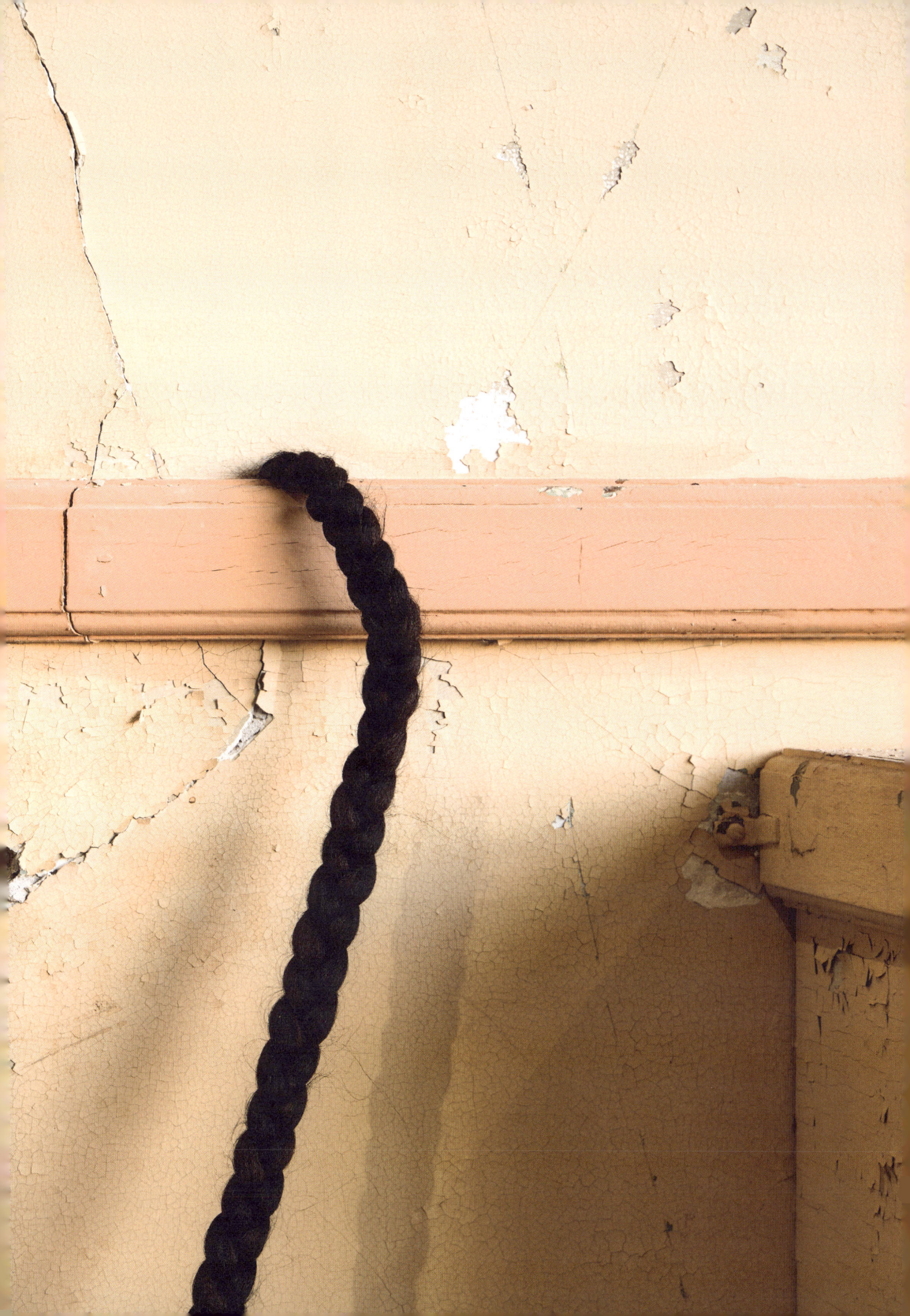

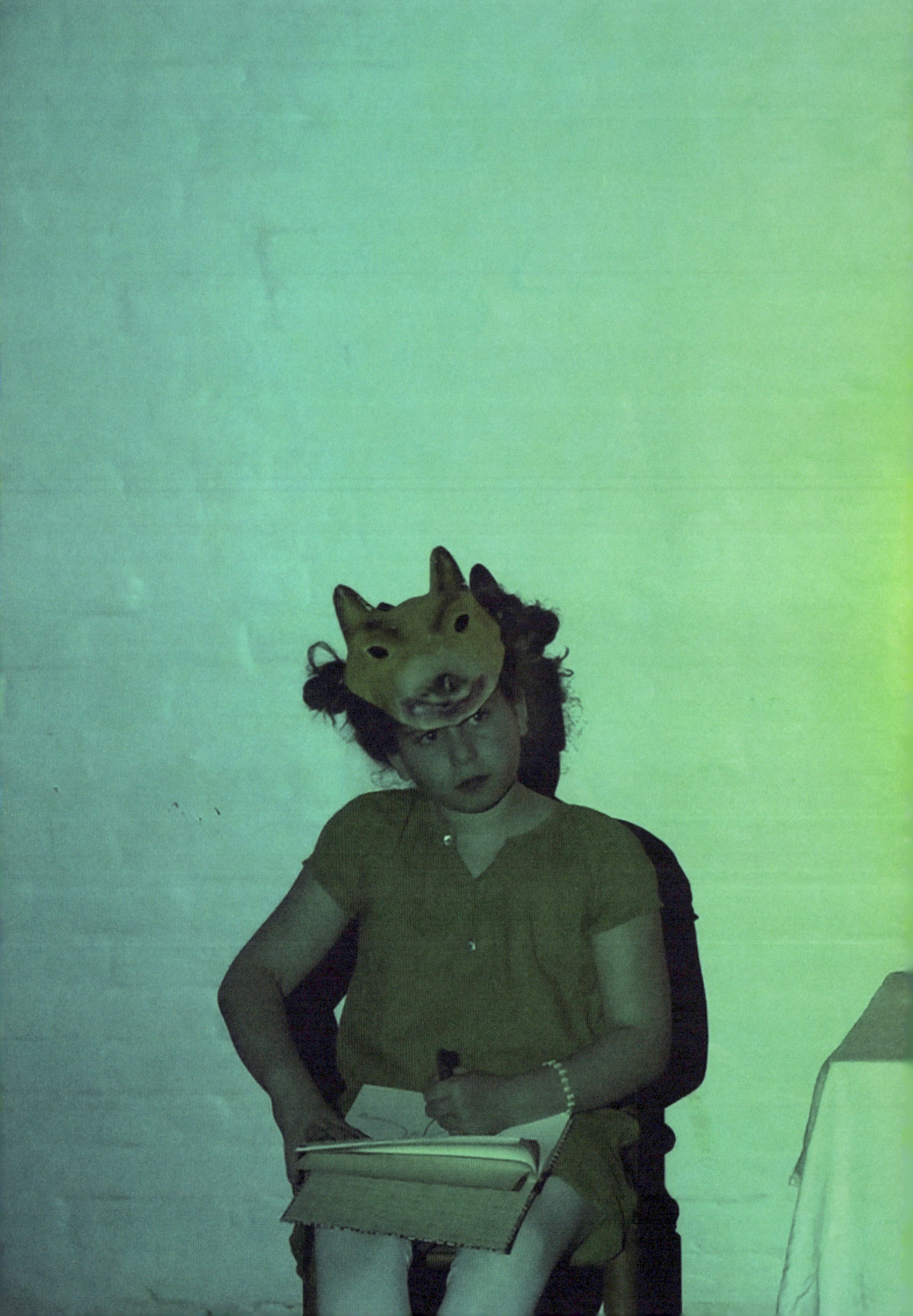

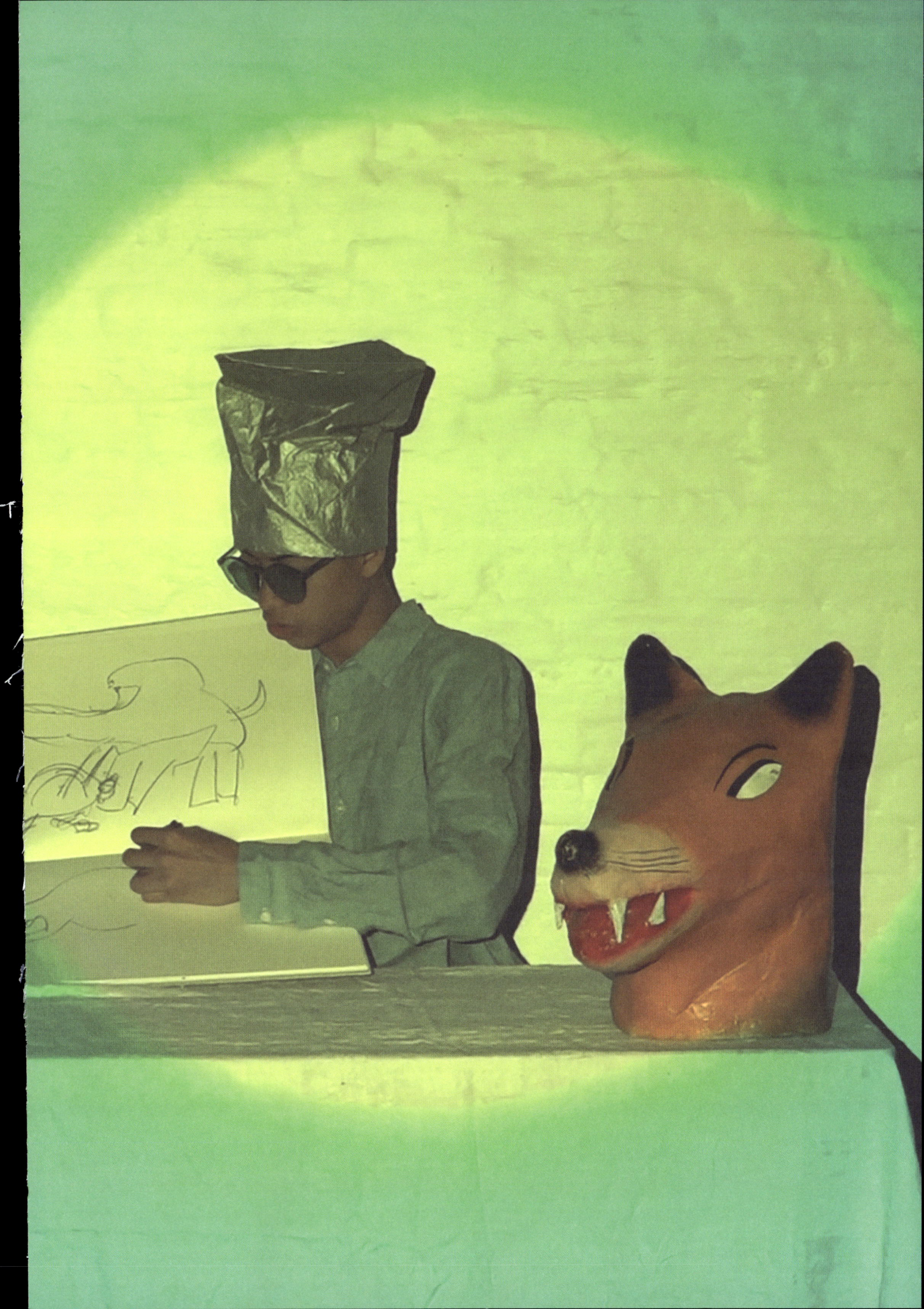

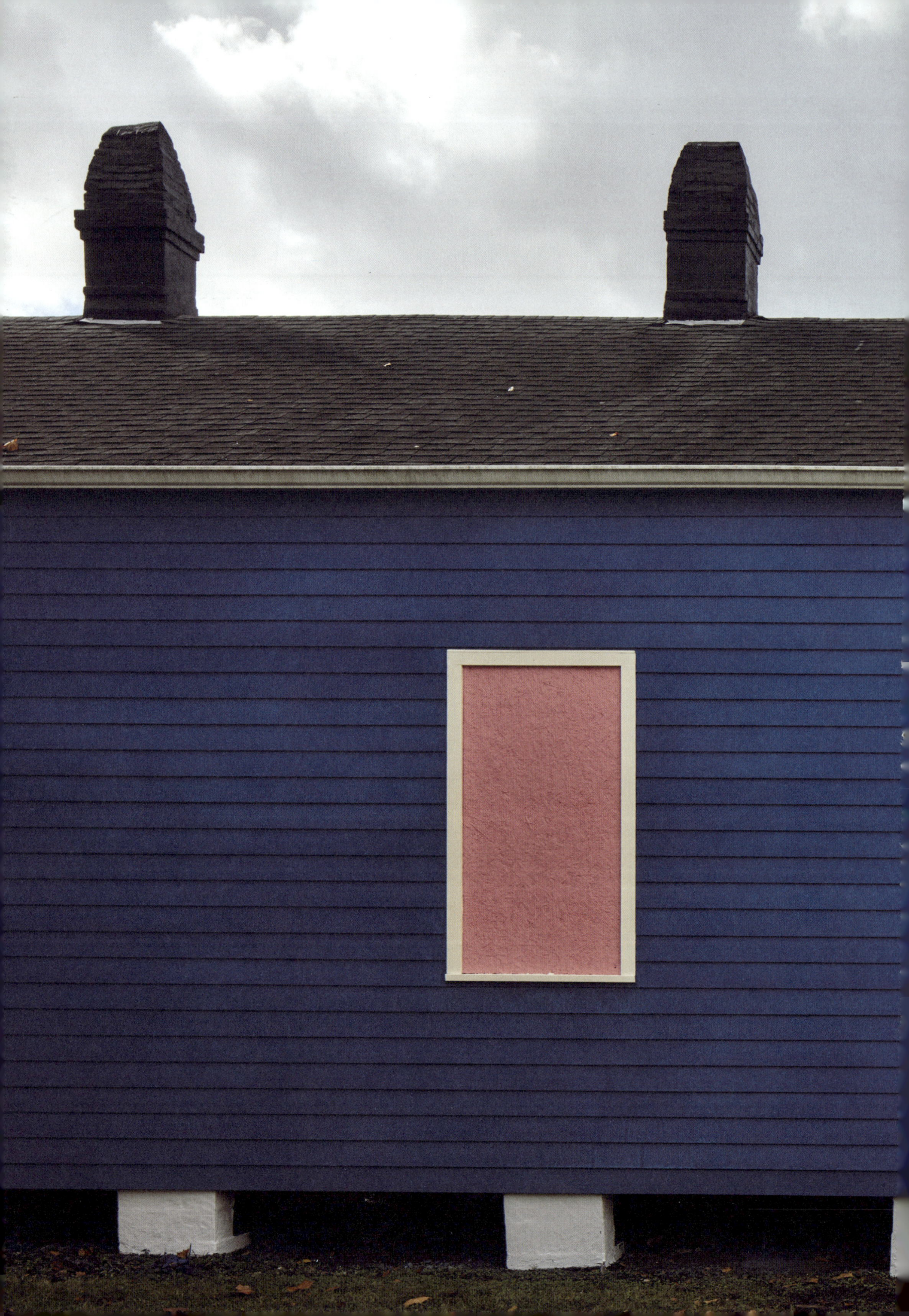